INTERNET GOVERNANCE:

CREATING OPPORTUNITIES FOR ALL

The Fourth Internet Governance Forum

Sharm el Sheikh, Egypt

15-18 November 2009

Edited by William J. Drake

Copyright © 2010 United Nations

Published by The United Nations Department of Economic and Social Affairs.

One United Nations Plaza New York, NY 10017

United Nations Publication
Sales No. E.10.II.A.15
ISBN 978-92-1-104612-0

Table of Contents

IV. Preliminary Events

V. Proceedings

Managing Critical Internet Resources

Security, Openness and Privacy

Diversity and Access

Internet Governance in the Light of WSIS Principles

Taking Stock and the Way Forward: On the Desirability of the Continuation of the Forum

VI. Appendices

Message by Sha Zukang
United Nations Under-Secretary-General for Economic and Social Affairs

Since its inaugural meeting in 2006, the Internet Governance Forum has brought together representatives from the United Nations, national governments, the private sector, civil society, and NGOs to discuss public policy issues related to Internet governance.

In the last four years, the Forum has matured and evolved. The annual meetings, held in Athens in 2006, Rio de Janeiro in 2007, Hyderabad in 2008 and Sharm El Sheikh in 2009, have engaged thousands of stakeholders from around the world. The Forum has shown itself to be a place where all stakeholders can share opinions and work toward a common understanding of issues and challenges in Internet governance.

The theme of the fourth meeting in Sharm El Sheikh was "Internet Governance: Creating Opportunities for All". The meeting was attended by stakeholders from some 100 countries and covered public policy issues such as openness, privacy and security, access and diversity, and management of critical Internet resources. The meeting also provided an opportunity for consultations among Forum participants on the desirability of the continuation of the Forum beyond its five-year mandate.

This publication contains the proceedings from the 2009 meeting in Sharm El Sheikh. It also includes views expressed by participants on the future of the Forum including their suggestions for its improvement should its five-year mandate be extended by the General Assembly in the fall of 2010. It is a valuable record for those interested in following the evolution of international dialogue on Internet governance issues.

As information and communication technology evolves and extends in reach, global policy discussions on future Internet development play an ever greater role. They can help ensure that the Internet's potential to advance economic and social development is maximized. Indeed, there are countless ways that Internet can advance peace, democracy, freedom of speech and rule of law, as well as improve the lives of the poor and the vulnerable in our societies. It is a communications medium, an educational tool, and a business necessity that must be made accessible to all people, regardless of their circumstances. International cooperation and coordination will be critical to achieve this objective.

I. Introductions

The Third IGF Book

Markus Kummer

This book documents the proceedings of the fourth meeting of the Internet Governance Forum (IGF), held in Sharm el Sheikh from 15-18 November 2009. It is the third publication in a series. Documenting the IGF proceedings, in accordance with its mandate as set out in the Tunis Agenda on the Information Society. Two books on the IGF have previously been published, the first one covered the meetings held in Athens, Greece, in 2006 and in Rio de Janeiro, Brazil, in 2007 and the second one the meeting held in Hyderabad, India, in 2008.

This publication contains excerpts from the transcripts of all the main sessions as well as reports of the workshops and other events held at the Sharm el Sheikh meeting. More than 100 workshops, best practice forums, dynamic coalition meetings and open forums were scheduled around the broad themes of the main sessions and the overall mandate of the IGF. The full transcripts of all the main sessions and all the reports can be accessed on the IGF Web site in full.

Five years after Tunis, the IGF has found its place in the constellation of international institutions dealing with Internet related public policy issues. While there was some scepticism to begin with, there is now a broad recognition that there is a complementarity of functions between the IGF and international organizations and institutions dealing with Internet related policy issues. While at first sight there might be some apparent overlap in terms of substance, there is no such overlap in terms of functions, as the IGF is not a decision-making body. It is more like an incubator for ideas and policy initiatives that will be brought to maturity elsewhere. The IGF serves as a platform for dialogue that can prepare decisions that are taken by organizations and institutions that have the ability to do so. The IGF mandate as stipulated by Tunis Agenda for the Information Society is to provide a platform for multistakeholder dialogue on public policy issues pertaining to the Internet and also to limit its abuses. It is here to stimulate debate and discussion. The IGF's methodology is based on the exchange of information and the sharing of good practices. The IGF is not here to make decisions, but decision-makers attend the IGF meeting and go back to their respective institutions where they may take decisions taking into account the discussions held at the IGF meeting. In addition, the approach taken within the IGF is always to look at an issue from multiple angles and by all stakeholder groups, whereas most of the existing institutions have a more narrow focus and examine issues through one specialized group of experts.

The IGF started as an experiment. However, through the four meetings held across different continents, the IGF has found a way of bringing together all stakeholder groups, governments, the private sector, civil society, international and intergovernmental organizations as well as the academic and technical communities. The IGF succeeded in facilitating a dialogue between bodies dealing with different cross–cutting international public policies regarding the Internet and discussing the issues that do not fall within the scope of any existing body.

Much progress has been made from Athens in 2006 to Sharm el Sheikh, allowing generalizations and issue segmentation to closer linkages between the main themes. Over time, it became apparent that some themes were closely linked and had to be discussed in tandem. Discussing security without addressing the Internet's openness and Issues related to freedom of expression would not give the full picture. The same convergence emerged with issues of access and diversity.

The agenda of the Sharm El Sheikh meeting touched on a broad range of public policy issues related to the Internet, in line with the definition of Internet governance as set out in the Tunis Agenda. A strong theme in all the events was the role of children and young people in creating the information and knowledge society. In this context, the meeting also discussed new issues related to the continued growth of social networks, and the ensuing governance issues that are emerging, in particular, the need for new approaches regarding privacy and data protection, rules applicable to user-generated content and copyrighted material, and issues of freedom of expression and illegal content.

One key agenda item was the possible extension of the IGF mandate beyond the original lifespan of five years. This was based on the Tunis Agenda which, in Paragraph 76, requests the Secretary-General "to examine the desirability of the continuation of the Forum, in formal consultation with Forum participants, within five years of its creation, and to make recommendations to the UN Membership in this regard". This consultation took place at the Sharm El Sheikh meeting. It was initiated by an online process and an open consultations in Geneva. This publication contains excerpts of the Sharm El Sheikh consultations. Again, readers are encouraged to visit the IGF Web site, which contains all contributions made during the preparatory process and all statements that were delivered ait the Sharm El Sheikh meeting, both verbatim in written form as well as in videos. Many speakers emphasized the usefulness of the IGF as a platform for dialogue, free from the pressures of negotiations. They praised its ability to reform itself on a continuing basis, based on the comments made by stakeholders in the open preparatory process for the annual meeting. In this way, the IGF was seen to be a flexible model that could adapt to changing circumstances. Furthermore, the spreading of the IGF model to regional and national IGF type processes was mentioned as a witness for the validity of the IGF concept.

The 2009 meeting saw an increase in the number of participants from developing countries, in particular from Africa. Participants from Africa represented 32 %, from Asia 17 % and from Latin America and the Caribbean 5% of the total. Participants from Western Europe made up approximately 27 % of participants, Eastern Europe represented 5% and participants from North America made up 12% of the total. The gender balance was further improved. Whereas in 2008 13.6% of all participants were women, in 2009 this figure increased to 29 %, close to the 30% target set by the United Nations Development Fund for Women for sufficient participation of women.

This book also includes chapters with some historical context which assess how dialogue on the IGF's main themes evolved over the first four years and the extent to which there has been progress in terms of collective learning and consensus building. The authors, mostly from an academic background, analyze how the respective theme has been discussed in the main sessions from Athens through Sharm el Sheikh and evaluate the level of progress attained over the course of these four meetings in terms of promoting collective learning and mutual understanding among stakeholders. The views expressed are those of their individual authors and do not necessarily reflect the views or positions of the United Nations itself or any of its organs or agencies. However, it is my hope that they contribute to the collective discourse on Internet governance.

My thanks go to all those stakeholders who are so committed to the IGF process. Without their dedication and enthusiasm the IGF would not be what it is: a collective endeavour to foster a better understanding of how the Internet works. My thanks go also to Under-Secretary-General Sha Zukang and his staff in the United Nations Department of Economic and Social Affairs for their ongoing support of the IGF process in general and their assistance in producing this publication, in particular to Haiyan Qian, Marie Oveissi, and Elvira Doyle; the publications team led by Valentina Kalk, and designer Marko Srdanovic; also to Chengetai Masango here with me at the IGF Secretariat and all the interns and fellows who have helped with various aspects of the project, in particular to Barrack Otieno and to Kyle Shulman. Of course, this publication would not have been possible without the dedicated work of our editor, William J. Drake.

The Fourth IGF Meeting

Nitin Desai

The fourth edition of the IGF held at Sharm al Sheikh was judged to be a success by most observers and participants. The excellent organisation of the conference facilities and logistics by the Egyptian hosts, the work done by the MAG in organising the main sessions, the commitment and effort of the workshop organisers and, most of all, the enthusiasm of the participants, particularly the many young people who livened up proceedings, helped to make this a most memorable event.

Every IGF builds on the modalities developed at earlier IGFs and this was true for the Sharm al Sheikh meeting also. The new structure for the main sessions gave more time for interaction and participation by the attendees. This evolution is understandable as many of the participants are now veterans and are familiar with the issues. They do not need to be educated or advised by expert panels. This growing familiarity has also made it much easier to handle the dialogue on issues that were considered contentious and that remain so to this day.

The IGF has also evolved in the way in which the workshops connect with the main discussion. They now play a major role in feeding ideas into the main panel discussion. They provide the community that participates in the IGF an active role as organisers and not just as passive attendees. In a very real sense the IGF is a cooperative endeavour of a diverse group of stakeholders who have learnt not just to talk to one another but also to work with one another.

All of this is valuable. But it is worth keeping in mind that the IGF cannot fulfil its role in Internet governance if it becomes just a gathering place for old friends. Every IGF involves not just veterans from earlier IGFs but also new participants. The fact that the IGFs have been held in different regions adds to this capacity to provide a space for new comers, particularly the young ones. By doing so it not only helps to democratize internet governance but also plays a certain educative role as new participants come away from the meeting with some exposure to the experience of other countries, corporations, NGOs and internet managers. This educative dimension was particularly evident at the Sharm al Sheikh meeting.

Sharm al Sheikh also saw a major dialogue on the functioning of the IGF. The outcome of this is reflected in this book. And the dialogue continues as the member states of the UN consider the future of the IGF beyond its current five-year term. The other stakeholders who participate in the IGF also have to consider whether it has splayed a useful role in Internet governance. But in answering this question it is worth bearing in mind the concept of Internet governance that guided the deliberations of the Tunis phase of the WSIS that decided to set up the IGF.

The Tunis agenda defined Internet governance as *"the development and application by governments, the private sector and civil society, in their respective roles, of shared principles, norms, rules, decision-making procedures, and programmes that shape the evolution and use of the Internet."(Paragraph 34, Tunis Agenda).* Given this definition the questions that we need to ask are whether the IGF has

- Helped in the evolution of principles, norms and rules (e.g. on child pornography) for the internet
- Influenced the decision making procedures in the institutions that have operational responsibility for internet management (e.g. ICANN)
- Catalysed programmes that could further the effective use of the net (e.g. multilingualism and IPV6)

The Tunis agenda also had some more specific substantive concerns about these matters and they are captured in the goals set for Internet governance in the agenda: *"The international management of the Internet should be multilateral, transparent and democratic, with the full involvement of governments, the private sector, civil society and international organizations. It should ensure an equitable distribution of resources, facilitate access for all and ensure a stable and secure functioning of the Internet, taking into account multilingualism."* (Paragraph 29, Tunis Agenda)

The most overarching goal set by the Tunis summit is in the first sentence above. But it would be too much to expect that the IGF, an open dialogue forum for all stakeholders with no decision-making capacity, is the answer to the goal of a management system for the Internet multilateral, transparent and democratic system, with full stakeholder involvement. That remains work in progress.

The IGF was an attempt to provide a space where the stakeholders mentioned in the Tunis goal were brought together on a platform where they were equal in their role in the dialogue. In this sense it is part of the effort to meet the goal set by the member states of the UN at Tunis. The question however is whether the IGF has been able to make a difference in the knowledge, attitudes and perceptions that guide the decisions taken by all stakeholders, including those in charge of managing the global internet, each in their respective area of responsibility.

The Tunis agenda also mentions goals about the distribution of resources, about access, stability and security, multilingualism and this has determined the way in which the IGF main sessions were structured. Has the IGF played some role in furthering these goals

- Through voluntary partnerships,
- Through a better exchange of knowledge about good practices, or
- Through an influence on the decisions made by those who control the management of the Internet?

The answers to the questions posed above will vary from "Yes" to "Maybe" to "No". They will also vary between and amongst stakeholders. The challenge now is to ensure that all the voices that were heard in Sharm al

Sheikh with their answers to these and other questions about the impact and functioning of the IGF will continue to resonate in the corridors of power. This book, which captures the full flavour of these discussions, will surely help to ensure that they do.

Editor's Introduction

William J. Drake

This is the third volume of IGF proceedings to be published by the United Nations. Like the IGF itself, the books have enjoyed the flexibility to experiment with different approaches in fulfilling their mandate. The first volume in the series, *Internet Governance Forum (IGF): The First Two Years* (edited by Avri Doria and Wolfgang Kleinwächter) included, inter alia, background papers offering stakeholder perspectives; IGF Secretariat materials on the preparatory process; edited transcripts of the main sessions at the 2006 Athens and 2007 Rio de Janeiro meetings; and, *en bloc*, the organizer-submitted reports of the workshops and related events held at the two meetings. The second volume in the series, *Internet for All: Proceedings of the Third Internet Governance Forum, Hyderabad, India 3-6 2008* (edited by Don MacLean) followed a different model. It eschewed background papers, sharply reduced the coverage of the preparatory process, and grouped together the transcripts of the main sessions and the workshop and related reports according to theme. Both models worked well and had different advantages in terms of making the meeting records accessible and putting them in context.

This volume continues the experimentation and embodies both continuity with and change from its predecessors. As in the previous volumes, the transcripts of the main sessions have been substantially edited to enhance their readability. Long interventions have been compressed; ungrammatical formulations have been corrected; and off-topic, redundant, or other bits of commentary that are not needed to convey a speaker's position on the issue at hand have been eliminated. The latter includes expressions of thanks and related comments, although these have been retained where particularly appropriate. The net result of this editing was a 45% reduction in the length of the record that nevertheless preserved almost all the interventions in the main sessions. The complete transcripts, as well as the complete texts of other materials extracted herein, remain available on the IGF website.

Also retained from the previous volumes is the practice of identifying the interventions by audience members in the main sessions as being "from the floor". But whenever the excellent transcribers were able to capture the names of the people making the comments, these identifications have been inserted into the text.

The reports on the workshops, best practice forums, open forums and dynamic coalition meetings have been included largely as submitted and in full. The principal editing performed involved harmonizing the formatting of names and event titles; deleting redundant or outdated passages retained from the initial proposals that listed actors in the field, web site addresses, and topics that would be cover; and changing the abundant and stylistically variable listings of points to either uniform bullet points or regular text, as appropriate. The lengths and narrative styles of the reports vary rather widely; it might be desirable for future reports to be prepared in accordance with a standardizing template.

As in the second volume, the organizer-submitted reports of the workshops and related events have been grouped thematically with the edited transcripts of the main sessions. Hence, the transcripts and reports, which together constitute the bulk of the book, are presented under the titles of the four thematic main sessions: Managing Critical Internet Resources; Security, Openness and Privacy; Diversity and Access; and Internet Governance in the Light of WSIS Principles. Also herein are the edited transcripts of the other sessions held in the main hall, including the preliminary events (the Orientation Session, and Regional Perspectives); the Opening Ceremony and Opening Session; the Closing Ceremony; and the Emerging Issues session, which in the 2009 meeting was focused on the impact of social networks.

Included as well are the edited transcripts of two novel events on the Sharm el Sheikh program. The first was the Taking Stock and the Way Forward session, which this year was a UN consultation focused on the desirability of the continuation of the forum. The consultation was chaired by Mr. Sha Zukang, the United Nations Under-Secretary-General for Economic and Social Affairs.[1] Forty seven attendees representing all stakeholder groups were invited to make brief statements on whether the IGF should be continued beyond the five year mandate given to it in the Tunis Agenda for the Information Society. The views expressed were almost uniformly positive. Also included are extracts from written statements that were not delivered orally at Sharm el Sheikh; as with the main session transcripts, the complete statements can be consulted on the IGF website.

The second event was an honorary session on, Preparing the Young Generations in the Digital Age: A Shared Responsibility. This was organized by the host country and featured a keynote address by H.E Ms. Suzanne Mubarak, the First Lady of Egypt and the President and Founder of the Suzanne Mubarak Women's International Peace Movement. The edited transcript of this event is included in an appendix. In addition, the appendix contains extracts of remarks by the Chairman and the Executive Coordinator at the Open Consultation in Geneva on 9 February 2010 on the feedback received regarding the Sharm el Sheikh meeting.

In addition to the above materials, this year's volume contains the full text of the Chairman's Summary of the meeting. It provides concise summaries of the sessions, as well as the prepared closing remarks of H.E. Dr. Tarek Kamel, the Egyptian Minister of Communications and Information Technology. And unlike the previous volumes, the book does not include information from the preparatory process, all of which is readily available on the IGF website.

The biggest change in this year's volume concerns the background papers. As it was being prepared, the IGF was nearing the end of its mandate from

---

[1] In fact, the consultation was initiated prior to the meeting in an online process that included a questionnaire prepared by the IGF secretariat. A synthesis paper reflecting all the commentaries received is available in all UN languages on the IGF website.

the Tunis Agenda, and a United Nations decision on the forum's possible continuation was pending. As such, the time seemed right to reflect on the IGF's contributions to our collective understanding of the issues, institutions and interests that comprise the Internet governance landscape. To do this, rather than assemble a large set of brief stakeholder perspective papers as per the first volume, this year's edition offers a smaller set of more detailed research-oriented papers. While the authors mostly work in academic settings and were thus amenable to this type of endeavor, they also have varied connections to the stakeholder communities involved and are veteran participants in the IGF process.

Each of the first five papers takes up one of the themes that have been discussed repeatedly in the IGF main sessions: openness, diversity, access, security, and critical Internet resources. The authors were asked to read through the transcripts and then briefly a) describe how the dialogues from Athens through Sharm el Sheikh have addressed their respective topics; b) assess the progress, if any, that could be detected in terms of clarifying the issues, promoting mutual understanding, and identifying options for action; and c) offer some recommendations on how the topics could best be taken forward in future IGF meetings.

The sixth chapter addresses the cross-cutting theme of development and, given the comparatively diffuse treatment of the topic to date, concentrates more on the forward-looking task of offering recommendations. Finally, the seventh and eighth chapters shift the focus to the IGF's procedural innovations; they explore the dynamics of multistakeholder participation, and the utility of a forum focused on dialogue rather than decision-making, respectively. It is hoped that in the aggregate, these papers present a useful synoptic overview of some of the IGF's main concerns and dynamics during its first four years.

Editing an IGF book is a somewhat unwieldy undertaking. The materials involved are voluminous in quantity and in a variety of formats and styles that must be converted and harmonized for publication. For their excellent assistance with these tasks, the editor would like to thank Barrack Otieno and especially Kyle Shulman of the IGF Secretariat. He also would like to thank Markus Kummer for inviting him to take on this project, and for accepting his proposal of the background papers section; and the staff at United Nations Department of Economic and Social Affairs for their support.

II. Background Papers

Critical Internet Resources:

Coping with the Elephant in the Room

Jeanette Hofmann

The management of critical Internet resources was a central topic throughout the World Summit on the Information Society (WSIS) process and also played a prominent role in the creation of the IGF. Seemingly irreconcilable disagreements over how to govern the Internet formed the starting point for the IGF, and some protagonists believe that progress on this matter should be the benchmark for assessing its achievements. Civil society proposed a new multi-stakeholder forum as a procedural compromise. If governments were unable to reach consensus by means of formal negotiation, a less restricted, declaration-driven space may offer a more constructive framework to overcome the political deadlock. Now that the five-year term of the IGF reaches its end, it is worth reflecting on how the IGF approached the issue of critical Internet resources and which role it may play in the further development of Internet governance.

The first section of this paper considers the topics discussed under the heading of critical Internet resources at the plenary sessions of the IGF: the Internet address space and the pending transition to IPv6; the future of the Internet Corporation for Assigned Names and Numbers (ICANN) after the end of the Joint Project Agreement (JPA); enhanced cooperation, the second Internet governance related outcome of WSIS; and new Top Level Domains (TLDs) and Internationalized Domain Names (IDNs). The second session discusses the changes in the IGF's approach to critical Internet resources: What, if anything, has been achieved since the inception of the multi-stakeholder forum? The final section offers some thoughts on the specific contribution of the IGF to the development of Internet governance arrangements. It comes to the conclusion that one of the important yet undervalued achievements of the IGF lies in the creation of a shared frame of reference that enables meaningful debates across stakeholders and political cultures.

Three out of four IGF meetings devoted a main session to the management of critical Internet resources. In Rio, the scope and definition of critical Internet resources played a central role. From the perspective of developing countries, electricity may well constitute a critical Internet resource. Other participants cautioned against overly broad definitions and recommended that the IGF should focus on issues requiring global coordination. While the workshops have offered a mixture of global and local aspects, the main sessions have indeed centred on problems of global or transnational coordination.

A common and typical element of all subjects discussed at the IGF concerns the uncharted territory in the management of critical Internet resources. In a global space without a formal constitution and established procedures, changes in the governance arrangements or the introduction of new resources require experimentation. There are no well-tried models and methods on how to transition to a new address space under conditions of self-regulation. Likewise, there are no good examples of how to govern such a rapidly changing and expanding resource in a consensual, integrative manner. Hence, each new task in the area of critical Internet resources turns out to be pioneering work with uncertain outcomes. The debates at the IGF should be read in this spirit.

IPv4 and IPv6: Two Protocols Running in Parallel for Our Lifetime?

The addressing system of the Internet is facing the most important change since its inception in 1983. Experts expect the pool of unallocated addresses to dry out in the very near future. Although IPv6, a new and much larger address space has been available for about ten years, Internet service and content providers so far have not deployed the protocol to a significant extent. The slow uptake of IPv6 poses a serious problem because the two protocols defining the address space, IPv4 and IPv6, are incompatible; they speak different languages, as it were. This means that organizations and end users will have to use IPv4 and IPv6 addresses in parallel until all devices connected to the Internet have migrated to the new standard or are at least able to communicate in both languages. Consequently, the demand for IPv4 will keep growing even after all available IPv4 addresses have been allocated. The IGF has addressed the issues related to the transition from the various perspectives of equipment vendors, network operators, Regional Internet Registries (RIRs) and governments.

One of the first questions that may come to mind concerns responsibility: Who is actually in charge of the transition from IPv4 to IPv6? For the actors involved in Internet address management, the migration process is a shared responsibility. There is no single organization that coordinates this process on a global level. As a RIR representative explained at the meeting in Sharm El-Sheikh, "We have a great number of people who do need to move forward at the same time".[2]

The transition affects almost every product that "speaks IP", and IPv4 is indeed deeply embedded in the Internet's infrastructure. Moreover, it touches upon a lot of commercial investment in an economic environment of fierce competition: The equipment vendors need to update their products, the network operators need to update all component of the transport infrastructure, each application and website on the Internet needs to understand the new protocol, and so do the various generations of equipment on commercial and private premises. Because the Internet protocol affects so many elements of digital communication, the transition proves to be a painful process that may take much longer than originally expected. One expert predicted that both protocols, IPv4 and IPv6, will run in parallel for "at least our lifetime!"

The RIRs support the transition process through training activities in all of the five world regions. In a growing number of countries---Japan, India and

---

[2] www.intgovforum.org/cms/2009-igf-sharm-el-sheikh.

Egypt were examples mentioned in the main sessions---governments play an active role in encouraging more collaboration within the private sector concerned. While the Internet industry welcomes such initiatives, their effects so far have not been overwhelming. Some observers therefore have suggested that governments should assume a more encouraging role and, for example, create monetary incentives for the adoption of IPv6.

At the time of the IGF meeting in Sharm El-Sheikh in 2009, IPv6 deployment amounted to a mere "fraction of one percent" of all Internet traffic. This raises the question as to why the uptake of IPv6 is so slow and what are the obstacles that prevent vendors and operators from offering IPv6. At the Hyderabad meeting, network operators described the problems that impede a smoother transition to IPv6. From their perspective, the central issue is the lack of customer demand for IPv6. Deployment of IPv6 will not bring any new features; on the contrary, if implemented successfully, it will be completely invisible to end-users. Some observers conclude from this that customer demand will not be a driver of the migration until the shortage of address space becomes noticeably "painful" and starts hampering the growth of the Internet.

A related problem concerns the costs of the transition, which cannot easily be passed on to customers. One participant described the resulting business dilemma: "IPv6 brings three new features: address space, address space, address space"---features not easily sold as added value to customers. Financial constraints may slow down the adoption process to the operators' regular upgrade cycles where IPv6 will compete against other priorities that are backed up by customer demand. In many cases, developing countries are facing even tighter budgets for the migration process. At the Sharm El-Sheikh meeting, a participant explained the situation in Pakistan: "It took us nearly two decades to deploy an IPv4 infrastructure. And then the next thing we know...that address space is going to be out soon, and with IPv6 coming in, we have that same issue again of building that new infrastructure".

As a RIR representative summed up the situation around the time of the Sharm El-Sheikh meeting, "in fact, IPv6 isn't necessary on today's Internet. But it's going to be very necessary in two years' time." So, will the invisible hand of the market still be able to handle the transition process without major hiccups along the way? Notwithstanding the good economic reasons working against early deployment of IPv6, the Internet industry regards the market as the most effective mechanism available for coordinating all the players involved in the transition.

In light of the slow uptake of IPv6, the main session at the IGF meeting in Hyderabad also raised the issue of IPv4 address scarcity. One the proposals on the table to mitigate the shortage of IPv4 address space concerns the creation of a market for excess address space. Over the last decade, the RIRs have treated Internet addresses as a public good that cannot be traded. Should this policy be changed so that organizations can sell underutilized address space and thereby enable a more efficient use of the four billion IPv4 addresses? As it turned out, no reliable data exist on the actually utilization rates of IPv4 and, thus, on the potential size of such a second hand market for

Internet addresses. Large parts of the address space may not appear in the routing tables of the Internet because they are used in private networks.

While some address policy experts recommend a trading system as a means to mitigate the risks associated with the depletion of the address pool, others caution that the share of unused address space available for sale might be too small to make much of a difference to the upcoming bottleneck. Irrespective of such trading provisions, the RIRs reported in Sharm El-Sheikh on new policies concerning the last blocks of unallocated IPv4 address space. The regional communities designed specific allocation rules for the last "slash eight" address block (approx. 16 Million addresses) in each region to ensure that new businesses will have access to IPv4 addresses for many years to come.

Against the background of the problems surrounding IPv4, in Sharm El-Sheikh the ITU raised the possibility of an intergovernmental registry to supplement the regional allocation structures for IPv6. While the ITU regards such a public registry as a way to ensure that their member states, particularly developing countries, have access to the new address space, other participants emphasized their trust in the existing regional allocation structures.

Enhanced Cooperation: A Living Concept in a Changing Context

As a concept, "enhanced cooperation" goes back to the final phase of the negotiations of the Tunis Agenda (TA). This may explain why the language of the paragraphs 69, 70 and 71, which describe this outcome of WSIS, seems particularly vague and open to manifold interpretations. The authors of the respective paragraphs drew a link between a consensual need for enhanced cooperation and "international public policy principles pertaining to the Internet" (§ 69) but the nature of this link remains unclear. A main session at the IGF meeting in Hyderabad aimed to flesh out the possible understandings of this new concept and to discuss the actions taken by the UN to support the process towards enhanced cooperation.

In light of the TA's request to provide annual performance reports on enhanced cooperation, a representative of United Nations Department of Economic and Social Affairs (UNDESA) summarized the responses given by nine organizations on their actions[3]. According to the UNDESA, the organizations concerned understand the concept to mean the "facilitating and contributing to multi-stakeholder dialogue" as well as "formal or informal cooperative arrangements" reflecting the multi-stakeholder approach. The nine organizations engage in multi-stakeholder activities for reasons of information sharing and consensus-building. Tasked with taking stock of these Internet related actions, UNDESA notes a lack of "practical guidance as

---

[3] The organizations that are regarded as relevant for the process towards enhanced cooperation are: Council of Europe, ITU, ICANN, ISOC, NRO, OECD, UNESCO, WIPO, W3C.

to what makes up an enhanced level of cooperation or what makes cooperation truly enhanced".[4]

Government representatives at the main session in Hyderabad highlighted different aspects of enhanced cooperation. For some, the key element consists in "governments on equal footing". Consequently, the crucial question is to what *extent* the "present arrangements for Internet governance do enable governments, on equal footing, to develop public policy principles" pertaining to the management of critical Internet resources. The participation of governments in ICANN through arrangements such as the Governmental Advisory Committee (GAC) is considered as not conducive to enhanced cooperation because the GAC has an advisory role in contrast to the US government's supervisory role.

For other governments, the central point of enhanced cooperation is what it does not imply: enhanced cooperation, according to this interpretation, neither affects the mandate of existing international organizations nor envisages the creation of new formal structures. Enhanced cooperation should be understood as a *process* enabling governments, international organizations and other stakeholders, *in the future*, to develop "globally applicable principles on public policy issues".

A participant from civil society portrayed "enhanced cooperation" as a means to "do global public policy in a legitimate and participative manner" to shape the Internet towards the objectives defined by WSIS. He interpreted enhanced cooperation as the process which aims to fill the gap between the vision of a "people-centred, inclusive and development-oriented Information society" as described in the Geneva Declaration of Principles and "actual public policy making".

This public policy-driven interpretation contrasts with the eyewitness' account of the negotiation process. From the negotiator's perspective, enhanced cooperation constitutes a compromise. Although the majority of governments agreed that Internet governance should be improved, governments held different views on how such improvements should be achieved. While some governments aimed to enhance and re-distribute public authority in Internet governance through new policy structures, others insisted on an evolutionary approach within the existing organization framework. The "creative ambiguity" inherent in enhanced cooperation, which reflects the overall commitment to change but does not detail specific paths towards this goal, was a prerequisite of agreement to the Tunis Agenda.

Whereas enhanced cooperation and the IGF initially looked like different processes after WSIS, the latter appears now as one form of enhanced cooperation. As one of the participants at the main session put it, enhanced cooperation should be understood as a "living concept", not only because existing governance arrangements are not perfect but also because their context keeps changing.

---

[4] All quotes from the transcript, "Arrangements for Internet Governance, Global and National/Regional", www.intgovforum.org/cms/hyderabad_prog/AfIGGN.html.

Post-JPA and the Internationalization of ICANN

In September 2009, the JPA, one of the two contracts between the US government and ICANN, was replaced by a new arrangement, the Affirmation of Commitments (AoC). The main session on managing critical Internet resources in Sharm El-Sheikh discussed the meaning of this change and the ways in which it may affect the internationalization of ICANN.

From the perspective of ICANN, the AoC adds several new elements to the management of critical Internet resources. The central change is that ICANN has to commit itself to act as a responsible organization "in the global public interest". The AoC recognizes ICANN's organizational independence and introduces four periodic review processes to assess if ICANN meets its commitments. Furthermore, ICANN will analyze and publish the positive and negative effects of its decisions to explain how its policy decisions are reached. It is also worth mentioning that, unlike the JPA, the AoC does not include an expiration date; it is intended to be a long-term agreement.

Many speakers at the IGF acknowledged the AoC as a major step towards the internationalization of Internet governance. At the same time, however, several observers predicted that, as a consequence of the new agreement, "not so much will change in the business that ICANN does". A number of participants pointed out that the Internet Assigned Numbers Authority (IANA) contract, which covers among other things administrative functions related to the root zone file and the address space, represents the "bigger step" towards the internationalization of ICANN. Another protagonist reminded the audience that the US Government remains "the sole global authority" that approves all delegations and re-delegations of TLDs and that most likely the authority for signing the root will also lie with the US Government. Along the same lines, a government representative questioned the independence ICANN has gained through the AoC.

The IANA contract, the second contract between the US government and ICANN, ends in September 2010. Should the responsibility for the IANA functions also be delegated to ICANN, as one speaker suggested? Although the audience welcomed the prospect of a further internationalization of the management of critical Internet resources, it did not agree on an adequate organizational arrangement for the IANA functions. Whereas some speakers firmly believed that intergovernmental organizations would provide a suitable home, others argued that civil society should not longer look to governments but rather build organizational structures by itself: "We should look more to create structures that accrue trust on themselves".

Some participants welcomed the AoC, particularly the newly introduced review mechanisms, as an opportunity to "engage ourselves and help out with this new and more open model". In the same vein, another actor characterized the new review panels as a "step towards a real form of global accountability to a global public". Nevertheless, there are challenges, as another speaker cautioned, and these challenges are about the implementation and the methods of these new processes. Self-reviews by ICANN, other participants agreed, are not "a substitute for accountability".

While the AoC means progress to many observers, it leaves several questions unanswered. One of the gaps highlighted in the main session at the meeting in Sharm El-Sheikh concerns the IANA contract and the political implications of DNSSEC: "As if the root zone management has nothing to do with the whole issue", as a participant put it. Other gaps highlighted by a critic concern a more explicit "commitment of ICANN towards freedom of expression, association, and the right to privacy".

Modifications of the DNS: DNSSEC, IDNs and New TLDs

Around the time of the IGF meeting in Sharm El-Sheikh, the technical community was planning to modify the domain name system in four different ways. A first change concerns the introduction of IDNs, that is domain names containing characters with non-Latin scripts. ICANN has developed a fast track process to enable the creation of new country code TLDs (ccTLDs) for countries with languages based such scripts. The second modification relates to DNSSEC, a set of extensions designed to prevent specific types of attacks by authenticating the origin of DNS data. DNSSEC is scheduled to be added to the root in summer 2010. A third change pertains to the long-awaited delegation of new generic TLDs. The fourth change involves adding IPv6 addresses to the name servers in the root. The so-called glue records enable TLD servers to respond to queries from hosts with IPv6 addresses. The main session on critical Internet resources in Sharm El-Sheikh addressed the first three of these modifications.

Given that the DNS has not been subject to substantial changes for a long time, the technical community conducted studies to understand the potential impact of these modifications on the performance of the Internet. A central outcome of the "root scaling study" is that stress for the DNS might result from the rate rather than the extent of changes. As one of the authors of that study explained, "The root system...can accept lots of changes, and over time it is possible to change all of it, if we have to. But it takes time." Members of the audience inquired about the policy implications of this recommendation: Will the signing of the root result in further deferrals of new TLDs? The root scaling study suggests that the root should be signed before new TLDs are added because DNSSEC will enlarge the size of the root.

Participants involved in applications for IDN ccTLDs expect the new ccTLDs to significantly trigger local content and multilingual applications. Yet, one expert added a note of caution. Even if IDN ccTLDs are introduced very soon, it will take some time until all relevant Internet applications are able to understand the new language scripts. This includes also email, which may take a year to implement.

The introduction of IDN ccTLDs may also raise regulatory issues. These concern, for example, the relationship between incumbent operators and the new, non-Latin ccTLD. In Japan, a complex selection process has been set in motion to determine which organization and which policies should govern the new non-Latin name space. The option of having two different ccTLDs proves to be a domestic challenge as a participant of the Japanese policy process explained. Another observer warned against using the introduction of

IDN ccTLDs as an opportunity to withdraw recognition of existing ccTLDs: "One would encourage every government and society to be respectful of their ccTLDs in this transition."

While optimists expect the deployment of IPv6, DNSSEC and new TLDs to be an equal playing field for all countries and stakeholders, including those in the global south, other participants expressed concerns over high application fees for new gTLDs. The costs of the application process may exclude applicants with less financial resources. Claims to geographic names which were mentioned in Sharm El-Sheikh only in passing, may become a regulatory issue to be discussed at future IGFs.

In sum, the participants of the main sessions on critical Internet resources have approached the various subjects in a rather pragmatic way. Compared to the antagonistic atmosphere throughout WSIS, matters of principle have lost some of their traction. The focus of the debate has shifted from the role of governments and intergovernmental processes to concrete regulatory issues relating to critical Internet resources. The changing agenda probably reflects the different composition of the multi-stakeholder audience, which includes not only a higher number of civil society and private sector participants but also many practitioners. Perhaps it also indicates a certain fatigue on issues that require a long-term approach.

Building Capacity and Breaking a Taboo: Achievements of the IGF

An objective assessment of the achievements of the IGF throughout its first years is of course not possible. Perceptions on the IGF's performance differ depending on one's own expectations, aims and experiences. The following observations draw on the transcripts of the main sessions on critical Internet resources and on personal impressions, including those gained as a member of the Multistakeholder Advisory Group (MAG).

It is no coincidence that this chapter's first section on the topics discussed at the IGF mainly relies on the meetings in Hyderabad and Sharm El-Sheikh. Only the third and the fourth meeting were able to address the management of critical Internet resources in a detailed and systematic manner. The first IGF meeting in Athens remained more or less silent on all controversial issues; it simply omitted critical Internet resources from the agenda. Although the MAG had tried hard to provide a balanced and diverse program, it could not agree to include critical Internet resources in the program. A significant number of MAG members feared that a main session on critical Internet resources would be used for pillorying ICANN.

The widely shared concern of merely reproducing lines of conflict in the well-known WSIS style also affected the public debate at the first IGF meeting. When a participant brought up the issue of political authority over the DNS root and address space, the panel did not respond. Instead, the moderator encouraged the panel and the audience to stay away from this topic: "...the thoughts that are unspoken in the room and maybe on the panel are that if we have learned anything from the last four years of these discussions, it's that the idea that Internet governance is a lot broader and a lot more than just that

8

one issue. And that we have all talked about that issue and we kind of recognize it is the gorilla in the room that's far away. But there's other issues that we want to talk about that we feel that are just as pressing, such as security, openness, access, and diversity. And it might be a sign of the health of the dialogue that we actually remain mute on this one topic but actually have a lot to say on the others."[5]

It is worth reflecting on these early episodes in such detail because they illustrate what a long way the IGF has come since its inception in 2006. Looking back, the first meetings of the multi-stakeholder advisory group were shaped by a pervasive sense of risk. The idea of an open multi-stakeholder dialogue, be it in the form of plenary sessions or self-organized workshops, was met with uncertainty and a vague desire for control: How could an open dialogue be organized in a constructive way? Which topics should be on the agenda? Should the number of workshops be restricted, and how would their outcomes relate to the IGF itself? Could self-organized workshops be defined as a supporting program independent of the actual IGF?

With the memories of the WSIS debates still fresh, the program of the first IGF aimed to avoid controversial issues altogether. At the time of the IGF meetings in 2006 and 2007, the management of critical Internet resources in general and the future of ICANN in particular came close to being a taboo. The same was true for the topic of "enhanced cooperation", which, according to some actors, should not be at all addressed at the IGF on the grounds that the Tunis Agenda defined it as a separate process completely independent of the IGF. Enhanced cooperation, in this view, would become an intergovernmental equivalent to the IGF.

In 2008, at the meeting in Hyderabad, the situation had changed. Multi-stakeholder dialogue and self-organized workshops were not longer regarded as dangerous. The MAG not only allocated two main sessions to the issues of management of critical Internet resources and enhanced cooperation, it also began experimenting with the meeting format. The second plenary session was designed as an open dialogue without any panels or speakers to channel the discussion. It was the goal of this new format to allow more time for public exchange and focus on the contributions from the audience. This new open format proved to be so successful that it was extended to other main sessions in the following years.

A closer look at the first open dialogue in Hyderabad reveals a surprising degree of diversity in terms of how the audience addressed the various topics. The discussion on the Internet address space focused, among other things, on the slow uptake of IPv6. It highlighted some of the problems that organizations of the Internet industry face in light of the pending transition. Thus, the "take away" of this part of the open dialogue was a perhaps more comprehensive understanding of the complexity as well as the financial constraints involved in the market-driven transition process.

---

[5] See, www.intgovforum.org/cms/IGF-Panel1-301006.txt. More commonly, IGF participants have referred to the "elephant in the room"---hence the title of this chapter.

9

The open debate on enhanced cooperation, on the other hand, illuminated the broad range of possible interpretations of this concept including the specific language of the Tunis Agenda supporting these diverging views. Particularly striking were the different perceptions of the respective paragraphs 69 to 71. While some emphasized the importance of "equal footing" as a benchmark for assessing Internet governance arrangements, others regard the *process* towards enhanced cooperation mentioned in paragraph 71 as the key to its correct interpretation. From an advocacy perspective, in turn, enhanced cooperation makes sense in the context of the WSIS vision of a people-centred and development oriented information society.

The strength of this first multi-stakeholder debate on enhanced cooperation was that it went beyond a mere exchange of opinions. It acknowledged the ambiguity of the term, presented the variety of meanings and, above all, managed to portray these meanings as equally legitimate. The notion of enhanced cooperation as a "living concept" brought up by one of the panellists testifies to this achievement. The mutual respect shown for conflicting views among the audience suggests a collective learning experience which allowed the participants to fully benefit from the diversity of political values and rationalities assembled at the meeting. While the discussion on the management of the Internet address space offered insights on the challenges of a self-governed industry, the debate on enhanced cooperation enlightened the audience on the scope of valid interpretations. One of the moderators summarized this discursive accomplishment by speculating on the future role of the IGF in this field: "So perhaps there is a role for the IGF in this context. As a non-threatening environment for discussion, where we don't have to make decisions, we can talk, share practical experiences from different perspectives, and as we heard this morning, move to the point, perhaps, where we can listening to each other, moving from a disconnected series of statements to a shared conversation, no longer comfortably numb, perhaps, but invigorated by a true exchange of views."[6]

Although the IGF has not led to a convergence of expectations and views, it has created a communicative space which in itself leaves an imprint on further debates on the management of critical Internet resources. A first indicator of such changes can be seen in the fact that fundamental matters such as the legitimacy of the current political oversight arrangements have ceased to overshadow all other relevant aspects of Internet governance. While still regarded as important, Internet governance arrangements are now discussed in more specific ways, thereby better reflecting the perspective of those actors who negotiate and implement regulatory rules. From a regulatory perspective, however, Internet governance arrangements present themselves in a variety of ways. Political oversight over the DNS differs from that over the address space. As the example of the Internet address space demonstrates, no single actor has proved to be powerful enough to organize the transition from IPv4 to IPv6. Furthermore, political concepts such enhanced cooperation or the AoC are assuming new meanings when put to

---

[6] www.intgovforum.org/cms/hyderabad_prog/OD_CIR.html.

practice. A pragmatic debate of the management of critical Internet resources is able to take notice and acknowledge such changes.

To some extent, the increasing emphasis on policy questions reflects the particular structure and composition of the IGF. While WSIS was essentially an intergovernmental process with additional multi-stakeholder provisions, the IGF is, as one of the speakers at the stock taking session in Sharm El-Sheikh characterized it, a "hybrid of U.N. intergovernmental and nongovernmental protocol and practice where individuals and institutions concerned with Internet governance and development gather". This hybrid creates a space "where all stakeholders feel comfortable, to the extent they can contribute meaningfully and openly in discussion, debate, and collaborative planning with other stakeholders."[7] As a result of this unique space, more attention is given to the operational but also the civil liberty dimension of Internet governance.

The most important merit of the IGF so far might actually lie in the area of capacity building. Thanks to the IGF, a greater number of people today have a more comprehensive picture of the management of critical Internet resources, including the various interests and conflicting visions surrounding this field. At the stock taking session in Sharm El-Sheikh, one of the speakers expressed this in the following way: "I don't deny that for national or international bureaucrat accustomed to the rigidities of forms and format, it can appear irritatingly messy. But we are prepared to take a bit of mess in exchange for the extraordinary capacity building potential that this forum offers". The specific charm of capacity building in the context of the IGF is that it works both ways. All information providers are at the same time information recipients.

A closer integration of the various rationalities and goals shaping Internet governance has been achieved and the actors involved may have a better sense of the interplay but also the inconsistencies between criteria of global legitimacy, practical requirements of the policy processes, and the logics of the market. Interestingly, the multi-stakeholder dialogue also undermines the traditional distinction between technical and public policy issues in Internet governance that still shaped the thinking reflected in the Tunis Agenda. Discussing policy implications of technical decisions has become a common practice at the IGF.

Thanks to the pragmatic focus of the discussions, the participants have developed a level of confidence and ownership in the process that enable public exchange even on controversial or complex aspects of the management of critical Internet resources. Considering how strong the original concerns were against putting the management of critical Internet resources, and thus ICANN, once again at centre stage, this is no small achievement. The big animal in the room, be it a gorilla or an elephant, has disappeared. At least for the time being.

---

[7] www.intgovforum.org/cms/2009-igf-sharm-el-sheikh.

Lessons Learned: The Strength of Intangible Outcomes

WSIS was the first public international process that addressed the management of critical Internet resources from an intergovernmental perspective. Moreover, it was the first time that ICANN itself became an item on the international agenda. With hindsight, WSIS will probably be regarded as a turning point in the development of Internet governance. Even if the endless controversies seemed counterproductive more often than not, WSIS set an irreversible process in motion that has profoundly transformed the political landscape of Internet governance. Two points are worth stressing in this context.

First, WSIS made it clear that ICANN is accountable not only to one government and the relevant Internet industry but to a much broader global community of stakeholders. Second, WSIS expressed an, albeit vague, need for a general normative framework, the so-called globally applicable public policy principles, arching over the regulatory and operative matters of Internet governance. In the long run, the performance of policy making and the legitimacy of political oversight structures could be assessed against such a consensual framework. The WSIS documents specify a few basic principles that may help pave the way towards such ambitious visions. Considering the status quo of the debate on enhanced cooperation, however, the development of a consensual set of public policy principles for Internet governance still seems a long way.

The unilateral oversight arrangement in Internet governance formed a key issue throughout WSIS and for some it remains the raison d'être of the IGF. At the moment, however, a full internationalization of critical Internet resource management can at best be conceived as a long-term process. As a minimum, steps towards internationalization would require broad political consensus on the type of the intended arrangement that would replace unilateral oversight, including its scope, goals and underlying norms. Throughout its first term, the IGF has largely managed to remove the taboo surrounding ICANN and the management of critical Internet resources after WSIS. Five years after WSIS, international public debates on Internet governance can take place without getting bogged down in ideological deadlocks. In view of the likely renewal of the IGF's mandate, one may ask what lessons can be learned from the present achievements or, to be more precise, how can the IGF use its specific strengths to support the goal of a legitimate management of critical Internet resources as outlined in the WSIS documents.

At the formal consultation held by the UNDESA at the meeting in Sharm El-Sheikh, a considerable number of speakers emphasized the IGF's "significant impacts on Internet governance", which are, as one participant conceded, "not easy to measure, but still very real".[8] Lacking formal decision-making authority, the IGF can only produce soft outputs in the form of collective learning, networking or influencing more powerful third parties. The relevance of soft and hard-to-measure results is not undisputed though. Can the IGF really be a "catalyst for change", as one speaker portrayed the forum,

---

[8] The transcripts of the stock taking consultation held by UNDESA can be found at, www.intgovforum.org/cms/2009-igf-sharm-el-sheikh.

merely by providing a space for exchange of experience and opinion? Sceptics suspect that the ostentatious appreciation of the IGF's soft outputs is a mere pretext to fend off attempts to create a formal international decision making authority. However, the discursive achievements of the IGF deserve to be taken seriously.

The multi-stakeholder and trans-disciplinary perspective of the IGF fosters a dialogue among actors who normally operate in more or less separate worlds. Conversations between different stakeholders groups which evolve almost naturally at IGF meetings used to be rare and rather complicated to organize. Even in the Internet world where organizational boundaries are often informal, professional boundaries may prove to be pretty tight. Multi-stakeholder interaction across professional boundaries is a necessary precondition for developing a common understanding of the issues in Internet governance. An important, yet somewhat undervalued achievement of the IGF consists in shared frames of reference which build conceptual bridges between stakeholders, regions and political cultures. Some evidence for such processes of "semantic world ordering" can be found in the emerging terms of art such as 'critical Internet resources', 'multi-stakeholder approach' or even 'enhanced cooperation', which are gradually acquiring stable sets of meanings. While the development of collective frames of reference do not necessarily mean consensus, they indicate progress in debates on policy principles and goals. As one speaker at the UNDESA consultation in Sharm El-Sheikh observed, "we have become more receptive to each other's perspectives and concerns. As participants have adapted to this open environment, we have seen rhetoric reduced." Put differently, the IGF helps developing a common ground around the policy issues related to Internet governance it addresses; a common ground which allows people with diverse backgrounds and competences at the very least to agree on what they still disagree upon.

Shared understandings of the problems at hand not only facilitate political debate, they are also an essential element of public and private regulation. Policies governing the allocation of Internet addresses, the introduction of new TLDs or accountability provisions for ICANN draw their rationales from general accounts of the issues they aim to tackle. Problem statements of the pending address shortage, desirable competition in Internet's the name space or the need to hold ICANN accountable imply observations, values, concerns and expectations. Such perceptions don't originate from single actors; they are the result of public reflections or "joint authorship". A growing number of people, organizations and events contribute to the evolving semantic framework underlying Internet governance, and the IGF, including its recent regional offshoots, has arguably become the most important open platform for its review and continuous transformation. Due to its transnational scope and its links to other international organizations, the IGF's multi-stakeholder dialogue contributes to the emerging transnational public sphere in the field of Internet governance. This is also reflected in the fact that some of the policy principles shaped throughout WSIS and the IGF are migrating to other organizations both on the national and international level. In the case of ICANN, for example, they have been adopted as building blocks for the recently created accountability framework.

The present strength of the IGF lies in this specific type of discursive capacity building at the interface of intergovernmental organizations, civil society advocacy and private self-regulation. While the patronage of the U.N. lends authority and structure to the IGF, the multi-stakeholder approach has managed to override many of the constraining provisions typical of U.N processes. In particular, this concerns privileges of participation and speaking rights. The unique combination of institutional anchoring in the U.N. and experimental multi-stakeholder arrangement turns the IGF into a laboratory of transnational coordination that seems to work precisely because it does not draw on formal decision-making but the legitimacy of the institution. It is no secret that the efficacy of regulatory norms generally depends to a considerable degree on their acceptance by the people concerned. This is particularly true for transnational regulation where enforcement capacities are weak and compliance is uncertain. Internet governance arrangements thus depend on the consent of the governed and the question is if and how the IGF can be used to enhance such consensus-building processes.

Conclusion

Throughout its first five years, the development of the IGF was largely driven by the expectations and the feedback and of its attendees. Each annual meeting has experimented with new communication formats in order to get the most out of a multi-stakeholder dialogue aiming to increase the capacity for collective deliberation in the Habermasian spirit of an "ideal speech situation". The future role – and legitimacy – of the IGF will depend on its ability to reconcile the diverse expectations that have emerged in light of the present experiences. This concern in particular growing calls for outcomes: How can insights gained at IGF meetings are made more durable? Can agreements reached in open discussions be recorded in forms that would allow other organizations to benefit from them? And finally, should the IGF set itself tasks and design communication formats that explicitly target consensual outcomes? Considering its tradition of trial and error, the IGF should not shrink back from experimenting with new ways of organizing debates and documenting them. The regional IGFs may have already taken the lead in this context and should be able to demonstrate how to best respond to the quest for outcomes.

However the IGF will deal with the call for more tangible outcomes, its future role, and political weight, will likely be that of a soft normative authority rather than a formally constituted body passing judgments. Its strength lies in creating a global public sphere for Internet governance rather than in setting rules. The IGF is also good at linking principal concerns to practical experiences; a well-suited basis for sounding out scenarios of internationalization.

Openness:

Protecting Internet Freedoms

Olga Cavalli

The Internet has from its early days been an open platform for communication and knowledge sharing. This openness has been the key factor in it success. But in recent years, it has become one of the main points of contention in the global debate about Internet governance. The World Summit of Information Society (WSIS), especially in its second Phase in Tunis (2005), pushed the issue up the agendas of governments, the private sector, civil society, and the technical community worldwide. This chapter assesses how the openness of the Internet has been addressed during the four meetings of the Internet Governance Forum (IGF) from 2006 through 2009, and the shifting terms of the debate over time. The dialogue in the IGF has covered freedom of expression, privacy, cyber security, interoperability, intellectual property and free content. As security is addressed elsewhere in the book, this chapter will concentrate in particular on the relationships between openness and freedom of expression, the free flow of information and intellectual property.

Since the creation of the TCP/IP protocol and the establishment of its early institutional structures, the Internet has grown and consolidated to become the major communication platform as we know it today. It is an essential tool allowing societies to produce, find and share any kind of information from any place in the world that is connected, and it is the basis of what is called "The Information Society." The centrality of the Internet as a medium allowing the open exchange of knowledge, ideas, opinions, and information was stated in the outcomes documents of the WSIS. Paragraph 4 of the Geneva Declaration of Principles establishes that:

> We reaffirm, as an essential foundation of the Information Society, and as outlined in Article 19 of the Universal Declaration of Human Rights, that everyone has the right to freedom of opinion and expression; that this right includes freedom to hold opinions without interference and to seek, receive and impart information and ideas through any media and regardless of frontiers. Communication is a fundamental social process, a basic human need and the foundation of all social organization. It is central to the Information Society. Everyone, everywhere should have the opportunity to participate and no one should be excluded from the benefits the Information Society offers.[9]

Two years later, in 2005 during the Second Phase of the WSIS, all stakeholders including more than 170 national delegations as well as civil society, private sector and academic representatives, agreed to the Tunis Agenda of the

---

[1] The declaration is available at www.itu.int/wsis/docs/geneva/official/dop.html.

Information Society. In paragraph 42, the agenda makes reference to the freedom of expression and dissemination of knowledge.

> We reaffirm our commitment to the freedom to seek, receive, impart and use information, in particular, for the creation, accumulation and dissemination of knowledge. We affirm that measures undertaken to ensure Internet stability and security, to fight cybercrime and to counter spam, must protect and respect the provisions for privacy and freedom of expression as contained in the relevant parts of the Universal Declaration of Human Rights and the Geneva Declaration of Principles.[10]

The principle of "free flow" of information was constructed from Article 19 of the 1948 Universal Declaration of Human Rights (UDHR): "Everyone has the right to freedom of opinion and expression; this right includes freedom to hold opinions without interference and to seek; receive and impart information and ideas through any media and regardless of the frontiers." Nevertheless, the significance and implementation of the free-flow principle has been contested by governmental and nongovernmental stakeholders. Factors like competing interests, the complexity of the issues, and variations in national legal systems and traditions can make it difficult to reach broad agreement on either restrictive or permissive interpretations.[11]

Openness as a main theme in the IGF brings to the debate the challenges to the freedom of expression in the light of privacy rights, security and stability of the Internet and intellectual property rights. Openness in Internet governance is important to all stakeholders and it should be acknowledged as one of the integral attributes of the Internet that merits protection at all levels.[12] The treatment of openness in the four meetings of the IGF will be reviewed and we will also analyze how the debates may have influenced relevant regulations in light of events that have brought them to the attention of the media and national policymakers.

As indicated in its mandate, the IGF has met four times in different continents; this process also included preparatory meetings, where openness was always mentioned as a relevant issue. All stakeholders emphasized its importance as one of the key founding principles and characteristics of the Internet. The open nature of the Internet was seen as part of its uniqueness and its importance as a tool for advancing human development, as the

---

[2] Available at, www.itu.int/wsis/docs2/tunis/off/6rev1.html.

[3] See, William J. Drake, "The Distributed Architecture of Network Global Governance", in, *Governing Global Electronic Networks: International Perspectives on Policy and Power*, William J. Drake and Ernest J. Wilson III, eds. (Cambridge, MA: MIT Press, 2008), pp. 47-48.

[4] See Christian, Moeller, "Openness as a Prerequisite for Freedom of the Media", in, *Internet Governance in a Global, Multistakeholder Environment*, Wolfgang Kleinwächter, ed. (Berlin: Marketing Für Deutschland GmbH, 2007), p. 76.

Internet should help to ensure a fairer distribution of scientific knowledge among countries.

Athens: Human Rights, Freedom of Expression and Networks

The dialogue during the first IGF meeting in Athens showed that open networks, freedom of expression and free flow of information, ideas, and knowledge were major concerns for all participants.[13] Different views were expressed relating to the fear of online censorship given the new empowerment that Internet brings to the users. The role of major corporations in using their technological power, faced with the demands by some governments for the blocking of content, captured most of the dialogue's attention. Also the role of the Internet Service Providers (ISPs) was reviewed as they are in key intermediary positions, particularly in countries with restrictive laws on information and communication. Also of interest were the tensions strict intellectual property rights and access to knowledge, the balance between the rights of the consumer and the content producer, and threats to human rights. From a different perspective, another key element of openness that was discussed involved keeping the infrastructure free and open. Interoperable networks with low or reasonable access costs were seen as key tools that allow users to exchange content and knowledge.

Questions about the responsibility of network operators and level of regulations were present in the debate. Regulations differ from country to country and, in general, the Internet has been much less regulated than the traditional broadcast and print media. This fact brought to the discussion the relevance of security and network management strategies. The technology that allows parents to control and filter what their children can see similar to what is utilized by operators to manage their networks and to enable free flow of information. It was noted during the discussion that network operators management approaches can directly impact the flow of information, and it was suggested that measures should be taken to ensure that that free flow of information is maintained. The fact that network operators decide if voice over IP traffic can pass through an exchange point or not, and at what speed with what quality of service, was pointed to as something that could harm the free flow of information if it is not properly regulated or reviewed.

Whether and how to revise copyright laws in the context of Internet was also mentioned. Working within the constraints of strengthened copyright rules could push against sharing. The Internet was described as a new global library, in principle available to all and especially important for developing countries and distant locations with scarce access to public libraries and universities. In these cases, Internet could be an opportunity where, for example, all scientific research that is publicly funded can be made freely available, but in order to allow this, new alternatives to copyright may need to be established. Copyright was mentioned as a relatively new invention in human history and in this sense the possibility of explaining to governments

---

[5] IGF Athens transcripts available at, www.intgovforum.org/cms/athensmeeting.

the importance of promoting the interests of users in freedom of expression and access to information was mentioned.

Rio: Collaborative Culture, Information, and Scientific Knowledge

The dialogue that started in Athens continued in the second meeting of the IGF in Rio. This time the focus broadened to include the collaborative production of culture, information, and scientific knowledge, along with similar concerns raised the first year about liability of Internet service providers and the liability of online service providers.[14]

It was pointed out that freedom of expression and free flow of information, as stated in Article 19 of the UDHR, the Geneva Declaration of Principles and the Tunis Agenda should be considered relevant elements of local regulations and further international cooperation.

Interoperability limitations were described as a major barrier to an open Internet in developing countries, and openness was emphasized as a key factor for innovation as it lowers barriers for new competition in the markets. The Budapest Open Access Initiative was brought out as one example of a document that allows scholars and institutions worldwide to make scientific knowledge available, in contrast to intellectual property restrictions that make information access exclusive and proprietary. Achieving the right balance between these two issues was seen as a big challenge.

Search engines were mentioned as key elements in reaching information. The degree to which they are transparent was considered an openness issue, as they should neither exclude, filter, and unduly preference particular sources of information. The search engines' claims to be neutral and impartial was discussed.

There was a debate on to the level of regulation or self-regulation that is needed, and a general sense that a mixed solution may be a good way to face this challenge. This could include both soft and hard law instruments. It was mentioned that debates in the World Intellectual Property Organization (WIPO), such as on the development agenda, and in the UN Educational, Scientific and Cultural Organization (UNESCO) should be considered and that legislation should be adapted to the new world of cyberspace.

In its economic dimension, the debate went through different regulations related to intellectual property, software and licensing regimes. There was discussion of open standards as elements to promote innovation and development of value added services and products in countries that need to enhance their economies and industries.

Openness brought into the debate questions related to access, diversity, and security. Privacy rights, the right to information, and the fight against criminality could end up promoting regulations that may go against the free

---

[6] IGF Rio transcripts available at, www.intgovforum.org/cms/secondmeeting.

circulation of information and contents. As the Internet was considered a well-adapted space for pluralism and cultural diversity, it was expressed that openness should be preserved and enhanced. The maintenance of an open Internet, as it was originally envisioned, should be an essential requisite for any law or regulation related to it.

Hyderabad: Security, Privacy and Openness

The even broader scope of the dialogue held in Hyderabad included not only the openness perspective but also privacy and security. Although all these three concepts are related, the following paragraphs summarize the most relevant ideas expressed about openness.[15] Freedom, as one of the main features of the Internet, was mentioned as a desired characteristic to be kept, but at the same time, finding the right balance between national security and privacy was considered important as but difficult.

There was discussion about the treatment of the free flow of information in the outcomes of the Organization for Economic Cooperation and Development (OECD) Ministerial meeting that was held in Korea in 2008. During the OECD meeting, participants agreed on the relevance of information flow, Internet technology and innovation to economic growth, while recognizing that there are risks associated with the use of these technologies and the need to address them in an appropriate fashion, including the concept of accountability: obligation flows with information. It was recognized that there is a tension on how much monitoring is needed and the difficulties of finding the right balance between openness and this needed monitoring. There was also discussion of the International Telecommunication Union (ITU) meeting held in South Africa, the World Telecommunication Standardization Assembly. The Global Network Initiative was considered of great importance as well.

Users become their own publishers creating blogs or having their profiles in a social network, and at the same time they are using services from an ISP as a communication channel for interacting with many other users who are also posting and creating content. This content may cross borders, and if the countries involve insist that there should be common cross-border rules then the data flow might never happen, as there are few possibilities that similar legislative regimes could replicate from one country to another.

Sharm el Sheik: Openness, Social Media, and Web 2.0

At the fourth IGF, the increasingly important question of privacy was assessed in relation to Web 2.0, social networking and cloud computing.[16]

---

[7] IGF Hyderabad transcripts available at, www.intgovforum.org/cms/2008-igf-hyderabad.

[8] IGF Sharm El Sheik transcripts available at, www.intgovforum.org/cms/2009-igf-sharm-el-sheikh.

There should be ways to look at privacy, security and trust as mutually beneficial and enhancing as opposed to trading them off against each other.

In relation with social media, it was mentioned that there are internal rules developed by large networks in the form of the terms of use. The way in which those terms are used and their complementarity with the protection of privacy and openness is also an issue that should be considered and discussed. People use the Internet trusting that this is a viable media for them to exchange their views, to have their dreams, to realize these dreams, and through their work, cultural exchange, to understand other cultures. This trust should not be undermined by criminal activities or other threats. In this sense, education and openness were mentioned as key elements to achieve such a trust.

Freedom of expression was mentioned as a collective right, like communication. In this view, it is the right of peoples to express their cultures, their traditions, their languages and to reproduce these without any limitation or censorship. Also access to information of public acts and activities was indicated as relevant to transparency.

It is important that states do not generate limitations or obstacles to that free access to information or free expression. The state should have the responsibility to regulate efforts to make effective the exercise of human rights. The only limitations acceptable in terms of freedom of expression or access to information should be those that protect other human rights and those that protect a higher interest or a higher value than the one they are limiting.

The Search for Rules

The framers of the Internet did not design their network with visions of mainstream dominance. Instead, the very unexpectedness of its success was a critical ingredient. The Internet was able to develop quietly and organically for years before it became widely known, remaining outside the notice of those who would have insisted on more cautious structures had they only suspected how ubiquitous it would become.[17]

Today the cost of copying digital content is very low and exchanging it over the Internet is easy. This fact, produced by the usage of computers and digitalization of all contents, brings new policy challenges but also opens the door to new business models for accessing digital content. Some new business models could prevent unauthorized content usage without unduly restricting the free flow of information. During the OECD Ministerial Meeting held in Seoul, these issues were discussed and it was indicated that many new business models are emerging around the provision of content, and that this area is evolving rapidly.[18] Some new media player web sites provide users

---

[9] Jonathan Zittrain, *The Future of the Internet and How to Stop It* (New Haven: Yale University Press, 2008), p. 7.

[10] See, OECD Ministerial Meeting 2008, available at, www.oecd.org/dataoecd/62/27/40780975.pdf.

with a wide variety of videos, music, radio channels and online games of authorized downloadable content. Users can stream media or listen to music without the fear of breaking any rule against unauthorized use.

Some new intellectual property rules may result in barriers against the free flow of information. There are new regulations that intend to punish those who download music and content illegally. During 2009, the so-called HADOPI[19] Law in France, approved the establishment of state agency to track and punish illegal downloader's, whose Internet access accounts would be shut down for up to a year. But the French Constitutional Council ruled that "access to public communication services on line" was a human right, and that only a judge could cut off an individual's Internet access.

The Anti-Counterfeiting Trade Agreement (ACTA) is also one example of these rules. Its scope is broad and it includes also copyright infringement using the Internet. This plurilateral agreement intends to create standards for intellectual property rights enforcement through a new international legal framework. ACTA would also require that existing ISPs no longer host free software that can access copyrighted media; this would substantially affect many sites that offer free software or host software projects. Countries may join ACTA on a voluntary basis and it would create its own governing body. Many voices were raised against ACTA negotiations not being opened to the public, as critics charged they should be conducted in a more inclusive way with civil society and developing countries representatives.

Recently representatives of many developing countries agreed on the need for an interoperability framework to help advance the Millennium Development Goals (MDGs). A multistakeholder event named "Global Governance meeting on interoperability frameworks 2010", held in Rio de Janeiro debated how to bring ICT into the MDG agenda, given the impact of the global economic crisis on countries capacities to achieve its development objectives. A Government Interoperability Framework was pointed to as a relevant factor to ensure that the use of ICT is focused directly to development. This is an important need especially for the developing world, and it is reflected in the Latin American and Caribbean Plan of Action eLAC 2010. eLAC proposes to promote the interoperability of standards-based e-government systems in Latin America and the Caribbean in order to ensure that the option of inter connecting services within a single jurisdiction or across different jurisdictions remains open, as stated in its Goal 38:

> Promote the interoperability of standards-based e-government systems in Latin America and the Caribbean and continue with the development of a regional interoperability platform and standards for e-government services in order to ensure that the option of interconnecting services within a single jurisdiction or across different jurisdictions remains open, taking into account recommendations relating to work in this area such as The White Book on e-government Interoperability.

---

[11] HADOPI stands for Haute autorité pour la diffusion des œuvres et la protection des droits sur Internet.

The fact that eLAC effort is multistakeholder adds value to it, as several private companies are developing products and giving services that are not always totally compatible with existing platforms. This is especially problematic in developing countries where the price of buying and updating ICT infrastructure is in general higher than in the developed world.

Taking a look from the service provider's perspective and its relation with the user, it is important to remember that the Internet was built as an open architecture network, allowing its growth without a central control. The fact that operators are technically able to use network traffic management tools to treat packets differently has raised public concerns that the open architecture guiding the Internet's development might be in jeopardy. In 2008, the FCC concluded that an ISP was discriminating against certain P2P applications using packet inspection techniques, "regardless of the amount of congestion of the network," as stated by FCC Chairman Kevin Martin.[20] But after an appeal filed, the Court allowed in April 2010 the Internet service companies to block or slow specific web sites.

ISPs argue that using these traffic control tools, they allow them to manage a balanced distribution of bandwidth among all users. As the world is not equally cabled and broadband access is a scarce resource in developing countries (especially in rural areas), this argument may be true. In some developing areas, national and international backbone capacity is extremely expensive and it should be used in a very efficient and equal manner among ISPs' customers.

People store great amount of data somewhere in the network, and this cloud of services is every day more powerful in space and speed, offering different type of services for free or at a very low price. At the same time many states are trying to control this flow of information, and this is a big challenge to the freedom of expression.

There may be reasons raised by states for filtering or blocking content, and these actions are supported by private actors. Internet censorship and surveillance violate what is called the end-to-end principle of network design and therefore risk the future growth of the network and the innovation that might derive from it. The end-to-end principle stands for the proposition that the "intelligence" in the network should not be placed in the middle of the network, but rather at the end-points. By imposing control in the middle of the network rather than at the user level, the censors are stymieing the further growth of the network.[21]

---

[12] "Statement of Chairman Kevin J. Martin Re: Formal Complaint of Free Press and Public Knowledge Against Comcast Corporation for Secretly Degrading Peer-to-Peer Applications", Broadband Industry Practices, File No. EB-08-IH-1518, WC Docket No. 07-52, Federal Communications Commission, April 22, 2008, Available at http://hraunfoss.fcc.gov/edocs_public/attachmatch/FCC-08-183A2.pdf.

[13] For a discussion see, Ronald Deibert, John Palfrey, Rafal Rohozinski, and Jonathan Zittrain, eds., *Access Denied: The Practice and Policy of Global Internet Filtering* (Cambridge MA: MIT Press, 2008).

Some kinds of content such as references of a certain culture or religion may be upsetting for some governments. This fact has caused several censorship events to social networks and content sharing web pages during 2010. If content is not considered appropriate by someone, this should not be a reason for limiting access on the whole web platform. The problem that some web sites like Google, YouTube, Orkut or Facebook are facing is that in occasions some content that is illegal in one country is not illegal in another. They also claim that it is extremely complicated to supervise all the content that users upload into these platforms. For this reason Facebook may consider making this type of content inaccessible to users in the country.

Orkut, a very popular social network in Brazil owned and operated by Google, received a complaint from users saying that some content was offensive for them, this resulted in a request from the local court for a daily payment while the pages remained hosted in the social networking platform. Google claimed that the company did not have technical possibilities to monitor every page on Orkut, but this was not a valid explanation for the court.

Balance is needed and also difficult to find, if there are restrictions to an open Internet the limits should be narrow and clearly stated, if there are national security reasons, they should be defined. The problem seems to be the definition of these barriers to openness and the distortion that they may have if used inadequately.

Conclusion

Regulations play an important role in shaping services and defining the functioning of the Internet. All parties need to be heard and considered. Finding a right balance seems to be difficult to achieve and this is why dialogue and exchange of information in a multistakeholder environment is the only way to move forward and try to find practical ideas and solutions to the diverse problems brought by the open structure of the Internet, the content exchange and the freedom of expression.

The recent changes made to the Intellectual Property Law in Chile are a good example of how regulations can be modified to address some concerns of the society.[22] It incorporates the concept of "fair use" that allows a limited use of some sources of information without requesting a specific authorization from their authors. This usage is limited to some activities like book reviews, journalist investigations or academic purposes. This concept is already present in the United States legal framework and this change in the Chilean law is the first one made in Latin America. Fair use of copyrighted material and other limitations and exceptions are important for the Internet economy. For example, one force driving the expansion of the Internet as a tool for commerce and education is the user's ability to locate useful information with widely available search engines. These search engines are based on the fair use concept to show the results of each query.

Another regional example worth mentioning is that the European Commission recently announced its five-year "Digital Agenda" plan for telecommunications and IT in Europe, which includes a commitment to open standards and interoperability through an improved ICT standard setting framework, and the creation of a single market for the European Union cultural content and innovations.

Using open standards, working towards a more flexible legal framework related to copyright, committing to interoperable networks and creating platforms to share cultural content are relevant steps towards a more balanced model for a digital information-based economy. This can only be achieved through an open dialogue space where governments, civil societies, users, academics and business representatives can exchange ideas on an equal footing, finding innovative ideas and synergies among them. And this is exactly what the IGF was meant for, a global, open, multistakeholder dialogue where all actors can interact; openness is the fundamental element of the Internet and as it is for the IGF.

New challenges will arise in the Internet era and in the digital economy as new services are constantly being developed. There will be new platforms and new ways of interaction between users, in relation to content, their work, their universities, and their families. The overwhelming amount of data that we are all producing, needs to be stored, cared, managed, secured, copied and protected. There are no clear rules in relation with this data stored in "the cloud", where does it belong to and under which legislation it will fall. Governments must protect this information and at the same time they must protect the right to communicate; the gap between security and censorship can be a thin one. Every community has the right to protect its culture as it is reflected in digital content on the Internet, but this protection should not prevent others from communicating using the same technology platform.

All the information and the innovation that is generated today by the Internet would not exist if the concept of openness were not present from the very beginning and if it were not preserved until today. Perhaps the big challenge is not only to find the right balance between regulation and free flow of information, but more important, to avoid any regime that would inhibit the ability of the users to communicate, of the technology providers to continue enabling access, of the service providers to offer new services and of the academics to investigate and achieve innovation. And the IGF is the space for this debate.

Diversity:

Achieving an Internet that is Really for All

Hong Xue

The Internet is an inherently diversified arena. Diversity is to the Internet as biodiversity is to the nature. In the Internet Governance Forum (IGF), diverse stakeholder groups discuss diverse issues from diverse viewpoints, but everyone shares a common belief in communication, understanding and construction. Diversity also is a principle that has been supported by the World Summit on Information Society (WSIS). For example, the Geneva 2003 Declaration of Principles stress cultural diversity, linguistic diversity in the generation of local content, and media diversity.[23] Similarly, the 2005 Plan of Action and Tunisia Agenda for the Information Society[24] state that cultural identity, cultural and linguistic diversity, traditions and religions should be respected; and that the creation, dissemination and preservation of content in diverse languages and formats, and people's access to knowledge and information and diversity of choice, should be promoted. Finally, diversity also can be viewed as important to the United Nation's Millennium Development Goals (MDGs) on promotion of equality, education and sustainable development.[25]

Diversity was identified as one of the broad themes of the inaugural IGF in Athens. At each annual meeting since then it has been discussed as one of main session topics. Irrespective of other evolutions in the meeting agendas, diversity has been preserved as a key topic for multi-stakeholder policy dialogue.

The IGF discussions have generally focused on four topics: contents accessed and created in international or local languages, application tools for Internet usage, internationalized domain names (IDNs), and people with disabilities. Discussions on these topics also have extended into topical areas addressed elsewhere in the IGF agendas, such as technical standards and policies on education and copyright.

---

[1] "Geneva Declaration of Principles", WSIS-03/GENEVA/DOC/0004 (12 December 2003), at www.itu.int/wsis/docs/geneva/official/dop.html, and "WSIS Plan of Action", WSIS-03/GENEVA/DOC/5-E (12 December 2003), available at, www.itu.int/wsis/docs/geneva/official/poa.html.

[2] "Tunisia Agenda for the Information Society", WSIS-05/TUNIS/DOC/6(Rev. 1)-E (18 November 2005), at, www.itu.int/wsis/docs2/tunis/off/6rev1.html.

[3] "MDG Action Points: Addendum to the Background Note by the Secretary General on Committing to Action: Achieving the Millennium Development Goals", available at, www.un.org/millenniumgoals/2008highlevel/pdf/addendum.pdf.

Athens

At the IGF in Athens, the main session on diversity featured, apart from the Chairman and the Moderator, ten panellists from governments, intergovernmental organizations (IGOs), private sector, and civil society, including academia. Although the views of the panellists varied, there was consensus that diversity is integral to the Internet, and about plurality, richness, and being local to reflect the whole spectrum of human endeavours. Diversity also was seen as being about marginalized or disadvantaged groups like women, youth, people with disabilities and indigenous peoples, and closely linked to access and participation.

Primary among the issues discussed by the panellists and the other participants were issues of language, literacy, and disability. The promotion of multilingualism was underscored as an important issue of diversity. Linguistic divides, like digital divides, hinder people's abilities to access, create and disseminate knowledge and information. Concerns were expressed that minority and indigenous languages were disadvantaged on the Internet for knowledge production and access, both at national and international level. The participants emphasized the importance of preserving cultural heritage and indigenous knowledge. It was pointed out that language policies supporting diversity should not be limited to written languages, but also should cover oral cultures with or without writing system. The participants advocated enabling people to create contents and access the Internet in local languages by overcoming technological and policy barriers.

With respect to technological barriers, various technical solutions were identified. These included using broadcasting or audiovisual materials for multilingual communications, or developing localized software (browsers, search engines, operating system, etc.) to facilitate access and the creation of local content. IDNs were identified as a key nexus of technology and policy issues. The introduction of native scripts in the domain name system would enable non-Latin script users to access and navigate the Internet. In addition, it was important to advance language communities' involvement in decision-making about code-points and the maintenance of stability and security of the Internet.

Laws and policy may also pose barriers to diversity. It was mentioned that the translation of international content into local language was important to bring all the people online. Copyright and other restriction in the cultural arena, such as bilateral trade agreements, could increase the costs of translation and limit the use of translated contents. It was also suggested that cultural policy be developed to support multilingual content that may not be commercially viable.

The lack of literacy was identified a big challenge to diversity. Illiterate people are completely voiceless on the Internet and can hardly create and share knowledge. To address the problem, it was important to review education policies that prioritize dominant languages and international contents and to enable the people who can only communicate in local (spoken or written) language to access and use the Internet.

People with disability are stakeholders in Internet governance, and facilitating their use of the Internet should be a priority. It was suggested that technologies and policies be adopted to facilitate disabled peoples' participation in the development process.

Finally the Discussion referred to the Universal Declaration on Cultural Diversity adopted at the United Nations Educational, Scientific and Cultural Organization (UNESCO), and suggested the establishment of multi-stakeholder programs involving relevant international institutions, e.g. UNESCO, the International Telecommunication Union (ITU), and the Internet Corporation for Assigned Names and Numbers (ICANN). And apart from the main sessions, there were parallel workshops focusing on diversity. Of note was that at the workshop, Towards a Multilingual Global Internet: Avoiding the Risk of Fragmentation, which was organized by UNESCO, ICANN and National Telecommunication Regulatory Authority of Egypt, one speaker suggested set up a global fund for IDNs.

Rio de Janeiro

At the IGF in Rio de Janeiro, diversity was again a main session topic. Apart from the Chairman and the Moderator there were eight panellists and four discussants, three of which had been on the panel in Athens. Not many of the workshops held in parallel to the main sessions submitted reports, and of those that did, none were primarily concerned diversity.

At the main session, each panellist's presentation was much longer than those given in Athens. Speakers reemphasized that diversity must be multi-dimensional and inclusive of all the people, especially disadvantaged ones, such as immigrants or African children. Language, culture, and media diversity, education in local languages, the creation of local contents and enabling people with disabilities were consistently addressed. It was mentioned that diversity was an important tool to empower people and help change society.

With respect to new or more deeply probed topics, a couple of technology and policy issues arose. It was mentioned that open and non-proprietary standards were important to the compatibility of and innovation in devices and software. Some speakers argued that adherence to standards, especially accessibility standards, may be an alternative way to promote diversity. Free and open source software was addressed as an important element to generate local contents, translate international contents and support people with disabilities. IDNs were again an intensively discussed issue, but more people noted their limit role in creating local contents and offered caveats about new risks of phishing and other security problems. It was also mentioned that IDNs would need to cooperate with application technologies, such as emails or electronic address books, to be really useful.

The proliferation of strict intellectual property norms concerned the panel. The need to balance intellectual property protection and spread of knowledge was mentioned. It was proposed to set up a group to find a solution to releasing copyrighted materials for local language use and enabling disabled people. There was also discussion on supporting the measurement of diversity by developing tools and criteria. It was suggested that the ITU, UNESCO and other international organizations responsible for WSIS follow-up should coordinate work on the issues that had been identified.

Hyderabad

The IGF in Hyderabad reformed the meeting format by combining the relevant themes into one super main session followed by open dialogues. Hence, for the main session on, "Reaching the Next Billion", there were two sub-sessions, "Realizing a Multilingual Internet" and "Access: Reaching the Next Billions", which addressed diversity and access, respectively.

In the sub-session on, "Realizing a Multilingual Internet", apart from the Chairman and the Moderator, there were six panellists from governments, technical community, civil society and the private sector. A couple of new case studies on enabling diversity were presented, and there was special attention paid to development challenges in India, the host country. The issues that were primarily discussed, such as the localization and availability of contents and tools, and IDNs, were largely not new, particularly to the audience who had been following the IGF from Athens. However, the discussion was not short of new elements and flashes of genius ideas. For example, it was mentioned that online communication is increasingly occurring in media rather than in written forms, and that the multilingual Internet was spreading to the mobile network. In addition, rather than a text-based mobile Internet, there would be a breakthrough to a voice-based Internet.

It was discussed that there were no common framework and terminologies to address multilingualism and multiculturalism. It was suggested that certain standard or a shared models be created for the adoption of scripts and languages online to prevent the risk of having only scripts depicted online and not having languages, especially oral languages. It was considered that the IGF might move the discussion forward on this in particular.

The newly introduced open dialogue following the two sub-sessions proved more communicative and interactive than the panel discussion. The dialogue sought to identify the linkages between diversity and access, and provided the opportunity for more participants (including remote participants) to join the live discussion. However, the new approach may have been more successful in form than in substance, as the discussion seemed to do more to refresh peoples' memories than to inspire new ideas. It was argued that multilingualism is more than written languages and extends to access and the creation of content. For the analysis of diversity in the social, political, or economic arenas, geography, culture, language and the script used to represent the content should be considered.

Remote participation technology, despite problems of slow speed and intermittent transmission, attracted participants from around the world and significantly enriched the dialogue.

There were 61 workshops held parallel to the main sessions, five of which were on diversity. Among the pertinent workshops that submitted reports, the Linguistic Diversity Dynamic Coalition's session was important. The Coalition adopted a set of detailed recommendations for the facilitation of language diversity, such as writing a training manual in several languages informing the general public about the stakes related to the presence of languages in the cyberspace, and brought the recommendations forward to the IGF as a whole.

Sharm El Sheikh

At the fourth IGF, access and diversity formed one main session that was split into two sections. The section of diversity involved seven panellists from international organizations, the private sector, civil society, and the technical community, plus the Chair and the Moderator. The discussion focused on diversity in language and access by persons with disabilities.

With respect to language diversity, the participants addressed character coding, necessary application technology, IDNs and the generation of local contents, with a focus on Arabic language and scripts. Egypt, the host country, encouraged ICANN to accelerate its process on multi-lingualization and to make it a priority in order to ensure the continued coherence of the Internet.

What was new and somewhat inspiring to the audience was that ICANN green-lighted the fast-track IDN country-code Top-Level Domains (ccTLDs) process after almost 10 years of technology and policy development on IDNs. Without prejudice to the ISO 3166 standard and other string requirements, ICANN approved non-Latin character ccTLDs through compressed and simplified policy development procedure in order to address the pressing needs of the countries and territories that use languages based on scripts other than Latin. An IDN ccTLD string must constitute a meaningful representation of the corresponding country or territory name. It was announced that Egypt's country-code domain name registry filed the first application for a non-Latin script ccTLD.

With respect to people with disabilities, the discussion was informative and insightful. The UN Convention for People with Disabilities and the MDGs were cited to emphasize the rights of persons with disabilities to access and express themselves on the Internet. In addition, the Dynamic Coalition on Accessibility and Disability made a statement to address the need of the people with disability. At the Chair's request, the participants endorsed the message by acclamation.

Among more than 100 workshops parallel to the main sessions, a few were on diversity. The Workshop of Promoting Cultural Diversity through Cultural Heritage in Cyber Space discussed the important role played by world digital libraries in preserving cultural heritage. The Workshop of Global Internet Access for Persons with Disabilities addressed the access challenges for persons with disabilities, including the UN Convention for Persons with

Disabilities and the specific measures that can be taken in order to implement accessibility.

The remote participation facility was significantly improved in Sharm El Sheikh. The entire meeting was webcast, with video streaming provided from the main session room and audio streaming provided from all workshop meeting rooms. All main sessions had simultaneous interpretation in all UN languages. The online platform allowed for remote participants to interact with the meeting. Unfortunately remote participation may not have reached its full potential in some workshops due to unpreparedness of the organizers or moderators. In some circumstances, questions and comments made via online platforms were not responded to equally with those raised physically in the conference room.

Assessment of Progress

The four-year old IGF is only an infant, but the discussion on diversity has become gradually mature and forms the basis of future development. The progress that has been made should be recognized.

Multi-Stakeholder Participation

The IGF discussions on diversity followed the WSIS principles and the recommendations of the Tunis Agenda that the international management of the Internet should be multilateral, transparent and democratic, with the full involvement of governments, the private sector, civil society and international organizations.[26] In the four IGF meetings, all stakeholder groups were able to share their opinions on an equal footing. The discussion on IDNs, local contents and digital media demonstrated that multi-lingualization of the Internet is an integral part of a multilateral, transparent and democratic process involving all stakeholders.

Multistakeholderism makes the IGF a unique global forum to bring UNESCO, ICANN, private sector, technical community and civil society together. Through multi-stakeholder discussion, each stakeholder group can see its strengths and limits more clearly than before. UNESCO has the history and mission to promote culture diversity, and adopted the Universal Declaration on Cultural Diversity in 2001 and Convention on the Protection and Promotion of the Diversity of Cultural Expressions in 2005, but it is relatively new to the cyberspace. Involvement in the IGF discussion enabled UNESCO to expand its ambit to the Internet and engage more stakeholders in international cultural diversity programs. ICANN plays a significant role in the Internet governance by managing the Internet domain name system, but its technology and policy development was rarely scrutinized in a wider global context. The IGF provided such a unique opportunity to place ICANN's IDN program under the spotlight of the global diversity dialogue and to enable the other stakeholders that had not been involved in the ICANN process to make comments and contributions. The technical

---

[4] See the Recommendations of the Tunis Agenda in regards to Internet Governance, paragraphs 29 and 53.

community was inspired to engage in out-of-the-box thinking on technology for diversity and to take social economic impact into account. Civil society acquired the global audience for debates and deliberations on diversity policy. It is hoped that, through the IGF diversity discussion, all the stakeholder groups become more aware of the necessity of strengthening cooperation with each other for the further development and deployment of technical standards and policies on the Internet.

Capacity Building

The IGF discussion on diversity provided the opportunity for minority or indigenous groups, disabled people or other disadvantaged groups to build capacity for global participation by accessing new information and knowledge, presenting their independent views, and joining cross-stakeholder debates. It is inspiring to see that people who were unfortunately disfranchised in other forums were able to be united and form a dynamic coalitions at the IGF to advance their agendas even when the IGF was not in session. The Dynamic Coalition on Accessibility and Disability and the Dynamic Coalition for Linguistic Diversity are two prominent examples. The former aims to facilitate interaction between relevant bodies, and ensure that ICT accessibility is included in the key debates around Internet governance in order to build a future where all sectors of the global community have equal access to the Information Society. The latter encourages civil society, the private sector, research institutions and NGOs, as well as governments and organizations to adopt and implement measures enhancing equitable multilingualism.

Enriching and Deepening Understanding

The IGF discussion enriched and deepened the multi-stakeholders' understanding on key issues of diversity. Since the first IGF, the dialogue has covered a widening range of topics, such as access to information, the creation of content in local language, IDNs, improving and reviewing literacy, and enabling people with disabilities. Through mutually-inspired cross-stakeholder group discussion, new dimensions were presented to enrich people's understanding. For example, IDNs were identified as an important issue for diversity from the beginning, but their limitations were revealed through deepened discussion. Notwithstanding their importance for content access and location, IDNs cannot substitute for content creation, nor can they achieve their full potential until the needed standards and application technologies are deployed. Similarly, the linkage between diversity and access was gradually clarified through discussion. Consequently, in the two most recent IGF meetings, diversity and access were merged into one main session.

Looking Forward

Although it is important to recognize the progress that has been made in the IGF diversity discussions, their imperfections should not be overlooked. A Chinese adage says, "enlightened by looking at both side while benighted by heeding only one side". For the purpose of improvement or amendment, it is necessary to look at the "other side". The following comments are intended as constructive criticism for the betterment of the IGF.

"Renewing" the Discussion

While new information and case studies were presented, since the key issues on diversity were identified at the inaugural IGF, there has not been enough new thought, vision, or perspective over the past three years. The IGF discussion on diversity should stimulate new thinking and move the discussion forward. It is important to take stock and build on the previous discussions, but not to repeat them. Compared with the other main themes, the diversity discussion has been less dynamic and inspirational. For example, in the thematic session of Managing Critical Internet Resources in Sharm El Sheikh, another dimension of diversity acknowledged in WSIS principles—diversity of choice—was raised. It was mentioned that the Internet should remain open to new approaches, so long as they don't result in fragmentation. The handle system that had been used by the publishing industry for 10 years could offer an alternative to the DNS system used presently for the Internet. In addition, the discussion on IDNs went deep into the diversity considerations of IDN management, which was timely for ICANN's fast-track IDN ccTLDs and new gTLD programs.[27] The session on diversity was comparatively static after four years, partially because there were many old faces or insiders invited to present every year. Some people have been invited to present on the panel two or three times now. New people and fresh ideas should be introduced.

More Concrete Outputs

The IGF provides not only an open forum for discussion, but also a venue for all stakeholders to collaborate on developing public policy for the Internet. The Tunis Agenda says the IGF should identify emerging issues, bring them to the attention of the relevant bodies and the general public, and, where appropriate, make recommendations. Although the increased comfort with the multi-stakeholder model is a kind of output, there have not been more tangible deliverables. The IGF had not provided concrete advice or recommendations to the relevant intergovernmental bodies and other entities on the diversity issue. At the other international fora dealing with diversity, the influence of the IGF may hardly be felt.

On the other hand, the deliverable outputs were not presented to the relevant international or national policy bodies and the general public. All through the four IGFs there were some brilliant statements or proposals raised, such as the statement made by Dynamic Coalition on Accessibility and Disability at Sharm El Sheikh, the suggestion to develop cultural policies in support of multilingual contents that are not commercially viable in Athens, and the proposal to set up a group to find solutions to releasing copyrighted materials for local language use and for enabling disabled people in Rio de Janeiro. Although the IGF has no intention to become a decision-making forum, the

---

[5] It was mentioned that new gTLDs and regional TLDs reflecting African values, culture and history could be managed by people from the relevant countries and regions. On the other hand, some speakers noted the importance of introducing competition in the selection of the registry to run the new IDN TLDs.

consensus reached through the IGF dialogues could indeed be helpful to decision-making at the other fora.

In addition, the IGF could produce and offer useful capacity-building outputs, such as off-line/online training and toolkits aiming at greater awareness and better understanding of diversity issues to facilitate national and international public policy making.

Better Organization

The IGF has grown into large-scale global meetings. Every time there has been thousands of participants. But although the meeting format has been improved to allow more communications between the panellists and audience and more effective remote participation, the discussions could be more responsive and interactive among the panel and the audience. If the moderators could intervene appropriately in a timely manner, each issue and question would be responded to and panellists would not talk to themselves.

If the IGF were equipped with more resources and staffing, its meeting preparation could be more professional. It has been suggested that those so-called preparatory or organizing meetings well before the pertinent main sessions should be open to the relevant stakeholder groups, rather than excluding the organizations that had been involved in developing the themes, topics and programs from the beginning.

With respect to the program, there should be more panellists presenting from the users' prospective on the diversity panels. The IGF has emphasized the importance of fully engaging those whose primary interest is the use of the Internet, and has stated that its discussions are relevant to the users' interests and concerns.

Conclusion

The IGF is a unique place to discuss diversity issue. As a multilingual, multicultural and multi-stakeholder global dialogue forum, its diversity is self-evident. Multistakeholderism allows all groups to present their diverse opinions in the same forum. Many of the diversity issues addressed are not being discussed effectively anywhere else. Segments of the issues were being discussed elsewhere, but their totalities. Most importantly, there has never been a global forum to accommodate all aspects of the diversity discussion, from indigenous cultural heritage to IDNs, from international law to national policy, from the facilitation of people with disability to the generation of Internet contents in local language. At the IGF, all these seemingly unrelated topics were discussed together by various stakeholder groups. Despite the difficulties and challenges, the IGF discussion on diversity is significant to the development of global Internet governance. It is hoped that the IGF will move the discussion forward to enhance cooperation between stakeholder groups and influence the development of public policies for the Internet.

Access:

The First and Final Frontier

Willie Currie and Anriette Esterhuysen

From the outset of the World Summit on the Information Society (WSIS) process, expanding access to the Internet was identified as a fundamental challenge to achieving an inclusive information society. For developing countries it was the primary rationale for getting involved in the WSIS process in the first place. The Geneva Declaration states that "Universal, ubiquitous, equitable and affordable access to information and communication technology (ICT) infrastructure and services, constitutes one of the challenges of the Information Society and should be an objective of all stakeholders involved in building it."[28] It is therefore not surprising that the Tunis Agenda for the Information Society includes access in the mandate of the Internet Governance Forum (IGF). Paragraph 72 e) requires the IGF "to advise all stakeholders in proposing ways and means to accelerate the availability and affordability of the Internet in the developing world."

One of the questions that has been posed over the last five years is how effectively the IGF has played this role. If one looks at the transcripts and summaries of the main sessions on access at the IGF over the last four years, it is evident that a great deal of advice has been exchanged by stakeholders from governments, the private sector, civil society and international organizations. Yet, it is difficult to establish its impact. As a space that exists primarily for policy dialogue on Internet governance, the IGF has no mechanism to negotiate uptake of advice by stakeholders. Nevertheless the main sessions and open dialogues on access provide a rich vein of thoughtful debate, statements and arguments about the best way "to accelerate the availability and affordability of the Internet in the developing world." They are also interesting in that they reflect difference in perspective, e.g. between civil society and business, and demonstrate, over time, a trend towards greater consensus.

Over the four years of the dialogue on access at the IGF, the discussion shifted from a focus on specific challenges and solutions, such as international interconnection costs and Internet exchange points (IXPs), to more general and structural factors such as policy and regulation and their role in ensuring that markets are both enabled, and effectively regulated. A key cross-cutting thread was the importance of competition in driving down the cost of access and of open access models to increase access to the Internet through enabling innovation, and localised solutions. The tension between whether access will be addressed most effectively by 'the market' alone, or by public sector-led

---

[28] Paragraph 21, Section B2 of the Declaration of Principles, "Building the Information Society: A Global Challenge in the New Millennium", 12 December 2003, available at, www.itu.int/wsis/docs/geneva/official/dop.html.

initiatives largely dissolved over time as consensus emerged that a multiplicity of interventions and roles are needed.

Yet it also emerged that policy reform does not always lead to increased access, usually because of a backdrop of poor governance. Like other development challenges such as health, education, and food security, addressing Internet access has economic and political dimensions.

This assessment of how the IGF has addressed access draws on the invaluable transcripts[29] of the main sessions provided by the secretariat and lets stakeholders do the talking. It captures the voices of participants in their own words to demonstrate the diversity of positions that have been debated over the four years of IGF access sessions. Following this sampling of viewpoints and voices on access, we reflect on what progress has been achieved in terms of clarifying issues, promoting understanding, and identifying options for meeting the challenge of 'access for all' to the Internet. We conclude by suggesting an approach for taking the issue forward.

Athens

Ulysse Gosset, a broadcaster from France 24 Television, opened the main session on access in Athens by noting that "when we talk about broadband, the digital divide is enormous, it's an abyss. Sixty percent of Americans and Europeans have access to broadband and only forty percent in Asia. And 0.1 percent of Africans have access. So there is a genuine lack of equality in access."

The access session took forward the WSIS debate on International Internet Connectivity (IIC) that was the focus of paragraph 50 of the Tunis Agenda, which acknowledged that "there are concerns, particularly among developing countries, that the charges for international Internet connectivity should be better balanced to enhance access." The debate on the issue began when Juan Fernandez, from the informatics and communications industry in Cuba, stated that, "the main obstacles to access to the Internet are hunger, lack of education, discrimination and exclusion. So those who are ill, those who are hungry, those who are illiterate, and those who are excluded from everything also would be excluded from new technologies and from the Internet." He went on to say that "once the underdeveloped countries have undertaken this tremendous effort and sacrifice to create the minimum conditions for them to be able to connect up to the Internet, then they find themselves confronted with a situation where they have to pay for the connection up to the Internet at the same level as the developed countries....And these poor countries seem to be financing the Internet by this system." This point was taken further by Kishik Park, chairman of ITU-T Study Group 3 and head of the IPv6 Forum in South Korea, who said that "...several years ago, some international interconnection rate was set...about five billion US dollars developed countries paid to developing countries. But at that time mostly we were using some accounting rate system. ..What happened these days? Now, about three

---

[29] The Internet Governance Forum website carries the transcripts of the main sessions on access, www.intgovforum.org/cms.

billion US dollars every year, developing countries are paying to developed countries."

These viewpoints were challenged by Sam Paltridge, communications analyst in the division of information, computer and communications policy of the OECD, who said that, "if you look at the most recent data, it shows out-payments increasing to a number of countries, and to Africa as a whole. And I believe that this is probably because of the growth of mobile communications in Africa...there was never actually a strong relationship between telecommunication development and the amount of settlements that were paid. There is a much stronger relationship for development with reform to telecommunication markets." Craig Silliman, deputy general counsel of Verizon Business, took the point further to say that regarding the cost of international interconnecting links...the Internet is a network of networks, which means when you are buying interconnectivity on a global basis, you have a choice of literally dozens of providers in a market that is intensely competitive. We have seen prices drop in this market by over 90% over the last couple of years."

The second issue that received attention was the question of the value of Internet Exchange Points (IXPs) for keeping Internet traffic within a developing country to cut down on the cost of international transit through developed countries. Mouhamet Diop, secretary general of ISOC Senegal, gave the example of Senegal where Somitel, a subsidiary of France Telecom provides Internet access to more than four other countries using SAT3. "All these countries pay for access to the Internet through local transit in France. So all this is going out of Africa for a service that remains in Africa." The solution to this problem is for developing countries to set up IXPs and Bill Woodcock, research director at Packet Clearing House, gave the example of Indonesia where "APGI, the Indonesian ISP Association has got an exchange point going in Jakarta. They have 110 Internet providers interconnected there. It's one of the largest exchange points outside of the five or six largest developed countries."

The question of the relationship between the market and the government with respect to access came under focus. Milton Mueller, a professor at the Syracuse University School of Information Studies and a partner in the Internet Governance Project, made the point that "we're basically talking about universal service, about the classic division between the dynamism of the market to get you about 80% of the construction of the infrastructure, and that there is always a role for governments and subsidies and redistribution for filling out anywhere from 2% to the final 20%, depending on what kind of country and what kind of economy you're dealing with."

Vincent Waiswa Bagiire, director of the Collaboration on International ICT Policy for East and Southern Africa, gave the example of the East African Submarine Cable System (EASSy) in which the World Bank was willing to provide funding to a private sector consortium provided they undertook to allow open access to the cable to bring down costs and not establish a monopoly, as was the case on the west coast of Africa with the SAT3 cable and the high costs of access associated with monopoly provision. Parminder Jeet Singh, executive director of IT for Change in Bangalore, argued that "at the international level, we think the default ICT policy globally has been set to a private sector default...We want to bring back the balance between the public and the private in ICT policy, because that's a very important issue for development and the proper role of public investment and public regulation has to be established."

Bill Woodcock said that the most important issue confronting access to the Internet is the monopolization of the local loop...And I would really like to see the local loop, the right of way opened up to access by those who would put in new fiber networks." Milton Mueller challenged this point saying that "you can't regulate a loop if there is no loop. For many parts of the world, the question is not how we regulate the local loop. It's how do we build a local loop. And frequently you can build obstacles to the creation of infrastructure if you focus on exporting western models which presume a monopoly, universally covered infrastructure and you are trying to regulate access to it to allow other competitors to enter, then you have a completely different problem when there is no local loop and you have to build one."

A number of speakers emphasized that access was not just about infrastructure but also about the capacity to use it. Hugo Lueders, secretary general of the European e-Skills Certification Consortium, said "there is a world beyond the cable...there are real issues of formal and informal education" and gave the example of the Athens e-skills declaration of 2002. Georg Greve, president of the Free Software Foundation Europe, made the link between freedom, openness and access and argued that it was important to have "the freedom to adapt your software to your local cultural context, through your language, that you can change it so that the users in your country can actually use it. Free software is defined by the four freedoms: unlimited use for any purpose, the freedom to study, to modify and to distribute."

Rio de Janeiro

Helio Costa, minister of communications in Brazil, introduced the access session in Rio de Janeiro by posing the question of "who may be the next billion people to be connected to the Internet? How do they differ from those who are already connected?"

Mike Jensen, independent Internet and telecom consultant, identified the goal as "affordable universal broadband – affordable for the next billion, the bottom of the pyramid, and universal in terms of complete coverage across the world or across every nation." He highlighted five things to be done to achieve this goal:

- More competition and innovation in the Internet and telecom sector;
- Much more backbone fiber, national and international;
- More effort to build demand, especially by national governments to build useful local applications;
- Improved availability of electric power;
- Better indicators for measuring progress.

Valerie D'Costa, program director of infoDev, reflected on three points to be considered in connecting the next billion. She said "we should think about what the user interface device should be and particularly the promise of mobile and wireless technology. She argued that "one of the learning points about better serving the next billion users is to listen better to what they need. A lot of discussion centers around how to get broadband connectivity to the under-served But less attention is paid to what those villages will use a one megabit line for". She said that we need "to expand the evidence base showing the causal link between ICTs and development, between technology and development, between the Internet and development." Sylvia Cadena, project coordinator of a Latin American community wireless initiative, presented a perspective of people working in the field of community wireless networks and argued that in addition to applied research into wireless technologies and better attempts to integrate community wireless networks into regulatory processes, that reforms were needed in four areas to enable a wireless network to serve a rural community – certification, regional integration, a change in attitude to rural communities to stop treating them as the exception to the norm, and making services with greater demand in rural areas like voice, messaging and emergency communication for disaster a right.

Anita Gurumurthy, executive director of IT for Change, argued that it was important "to see ICTs not just as commercial or business infrastructure but also as development infrastructure, where the public interest is clearly separated from the rest, just as it is in the case of public health or public education. Basic access calls for the essential role of the state in creating that comprehensive ecosystem which makes access meaningful...It is the nature and manner of use of technology by communities that needs to determine infrastructure policies and frameworks of governance. So far the business use of technology has monopolized policy frameworks...We need to think of the 6.6 billion people in the world and not just the next billion."

Jacquelyn Ruff, vice president of International Public Policy and Regulatory Affairs at Verizon, posed the question of "what is it in terms of a policy, legal, and regulatory framework that will help draw capital to the areas, especially in the developing world, that need it in order to get to the next billion? The factors to consider include is there a transparent and stable regulatory environment; respect for the rule of law; openness to foreign investment; a commitment to encouraging competition; good licensing and spectrum allocation procedures, a flexibility for innovative services, such as Voice over IP and finally an environment that enables local developers to create attractive and useful content?"

Radhika Lal, policy adviser on ICT for Poverty Reduction, UNDP, argued that "we don't just look at all the sort of blockages on the supply side, but we need to bring the consumer, the citizen back in. What is the role of the state in terms of looking at the demand side? Countries like Estonia where access to the Internet is a right has meant very high rates of penetration and dynamic business growth. So these things don't need to be antithetical. It's possible to have a very strong empowerment and rights-based framework and yet create the conditions for very strong private sector development."

Hyderabad

Kiran Karnik, founder-director of ISRO's Development and Education Communicational Unit, opened the access main session by remarking that "nothing could be more important than to discuss in this IGF the ways and means by which we can increase that access and move not just to the next billion, but the next billions." Shri S.K.Gupta, adviser to the Telecom Regulatory Authority of India, said that "we need to understand who are these next billions? They are a sizable but less affluent population spread mainly in rural and semi-rural areas, economically not strong, young, with aspiring futures, maybe having limited exposure to Internet or computer or ICT applications. The next billion will demand access networks with enhanced capabilities and widespread applications and services of perceived utility, supportive regulatory and policy frameworks, and collaborations across industry to support different applications, like e-commerce, e-governance, e-education and e-health."

Peter Hellmonds, head of corporate social responsibility, Nokia Siemens Networks, made three points: "first, for there to be increased access, we need a sufficient supply and an effective demand. And a functioning market that is competitive is very essential as competition drives down prices, it increases choice and it expands access. Second, simply building networks alone is not sufficient as there are other factors affecting demand, such as the awareness of people, their incentives, their motivation and their capabilities. Third, next to the increased coverage of networks and capacity building, the ability of applications that need to be adapted to the needs of the end users including in rural areas is key to improving the development outcomes."

Alison Gillwald, director of Research ICT Africa, noted that "the evidence of policy failure in increasing access to the Internet in Africa was often as a result of poor institutional arrangements and poor governance. If there are any lessons for Internet governance from telecom reform, it's that you simply can't graft reform onto existing governance systems. They have to be owned and developed organically. The failures of market reform in telecommunications and the resulting high prices they have produced are because the reform model has neither become a market model nor remained a strong public utility but remained somewhere in between. With the emphasis on markets and competition, one asks, if the evidence is so strong that competition policies produce results, why has it not been done? If it creates demand and brings down prices, why hasn't it been done? And that's really a political challenge, it's not an economic challenge, that one has to look towards governance systems and how one might reform those. It's not that markets are not working in Africa but we don't have working markets because they are not fully competitive."

Brian Longwe, director of the African Internet Service Provider's Association, gave the example of the money transfer system called M-PESA that Kenyan mobile operator, Safaricom, introduced which has reached four million subscribers in two years. Part of M-PESA's success was because "financial and communications regulators in Kenya decided not to subject M-PESA through treating their services as a bank but chose to perceive M-PESA as a non-bank payment service. Regulators can either promote innovation, access and development or hinder it."

Anriette Esterhuysen, executive director of the Association for Progressive Communications, raised the issue of the social impacts of access: "when we talk about access and filling the access gap, are we talking about creating more consumers of telephony and Internet services or are we also talking about creating citizens, creating empowerment, entrepreneurs, researchers? The Internet is not populated by passive users who wait for other people to generate useful content. What has been responsible for the explosion in Internet usage and social networking platforms and multimedia is users creating content that is relevant to themselves and those they associate with."

Sharm el Sheikh

Hopeton Dunn, director of the Caribbean Program, Telecommunications Policy and Technical Management, University of the West Indies, introduced the main session on access at Sharm El Sheikh by remarking that, "when we speak about access, we are speaking not only about the physical ability to connect to a network, but about a great range of additional means by which access is to be attained such as financial access, the ability of people to afford the content, to afford the connectivity. We are talking about the essential activity of literacy to access, including information literacy, all the cognitive skills associated with being able to use the network. We are talking about access to relevant content, to institutional support, including political access and a voice. We are talking about linguistic access and access by the disabled."

Ben Akoh, program manager of the Open Society Institute of West Africa, argued that "spectrum is the lifeblood of infrastructure, of telecommunications, of access eventually". He said "we must begin to see spectrum and its management as a major component of access by reclaiming unused spectrum space, effectively leveraging the benefits of digital dividends arising from digital migration and specific advocacy and policy recommendations need to be made about how this is handled...Access to spectrum should be couched under the themes of access to information and freedom of expression."

Pierre Dandjinou, CEO of Strategic Consulting Group in Senegal and Benin, motivated for a switch in the connectivity paradigm to address mobile broadband in Africa. African countries need to work out the best market structure for mobile broadband, the best use of spectrum for mobile broadband as well as the role of governments and regulators to make it happen. In addition high taxation on mobile services should stop and an effective strategy to produce reliable power supply developed.

Mohamed El Nawary, vice president of Telecom Egypt, highlighted the significance of submarine cable infrastructure to the Middle East and Africa and the importance of a diversity of cables and routes across the Mediterranean. He noted that, "much of the world's IP transit is happening here which raises the issue of cost and the need to review IP transit versus IP

40

peering. With enough traffic happening in this region, we wonder if very soon this will become an important enough network access point for the rest of the world to consider peering with us and hence reduce our cost of Internet access."

Ernest Ndukwe, CEO of the Nigeria Communications Commission, argued that "for many developing countries, the last mile or last meter access to the Internet has to be wireless and it is important that last meter access is developed side by side with national and regional backbone infrastructure to ensure affordable bandwidth costs, interconnection, interlinking and peering. I recently launched a campaign for what I termed fiber without borders. Africa today needs optic fiber highways crisscrossing the continent. There is no doubt that if this happens, this will help aggregate African data traffic, reduce costs of access, increase regional transit footprints, encourage regional peering, facilitate development of local content and enhance the contribution of Africa to the knowledge resource on the Internet."

Ermanno Pietrosemoli, president of EsLaRed in Venezuela, examined the use of low cost solutions for connectivity in developing countries. He said that for rural areas WiFi solutions can be easily modified to provide connectivity to rural villages even at long distances as compared to more expensive WiMax and cellular solutions. He said that "in the quest to see how big a distance could be reached, we made an experiment in April 2006 where we were able to take advantage of a clear line of sight between a mountain that is 4,300 meters high and a hill that is 125 meters and we were able to span a distance of 280 kilometers with just normal off-the-shelf WiFi gear and external antennas."

Rohan Samarajiva, chair and CEO, LIRNEasia, drew attention to "two experiences that we have had in the last 10 to 15 years. The extraordinary success is mobile telephony. Because we licensed a large number of companies in certain countries, we now have a situation, for example, in India where we are connecting 15 million people a month. We have a situation where affordability is now becoming not a problem. In India, in Bangladesh, in Pakistan, a mobile phone is extraordinarily affordable. The prices, the ARPU (the average revenues per user) are below $5 and the companies are making profits and investments. What we need to do is to develop government policies that will leverage this model to the broadband arena. When it comes to universal service, which is the abject failure, there is no country that I know of where this has worked well. We have $4billion unspent in Brazil. We have $4billion unspent in India. So the model will be served by reducing taxes and by freeing up frequencies, by focusing on the business approach of a budget telecom network model and the government action that can support it rather than pure government action alone."

Assessment of Progress

The access debate at the first IGF in Athens paid considerable attention to international interconnection costs and IXPs as issues that affects the affordability of the Internet. While the two poles of the debate around Internet interconnection costs were explored, there was no resolution of the issue and it is interesting that it did not surface much in the access sessions of the following three years. Does this suggest that the topic does not really have 'legs' and is an issue that can be parked as unresolved but not resolvable? Perhaps.

A key observation from the second IGF meeting in Rio de Janeiro was the semblance of convergence of opinion and recommendations on how the availability, accessibility, and affordability of the Internet can be improved upon in the developing world. Three main areas in which opinions were seen to converge were identified: first, there appeared to be agreement that the competitive market model has been effective in increasing access in developing countries. There were therefore calls for policy coherence in the telecom sectors of developing nations – specifically "for the principles of competition to be consistently and evenly applied to all areas of the telecom sector".

Second, there was recognition of the applicability of collaborative models, with an emphasis on the roles of the public sector and communities, for providing access in areas where traditional market models seem to have failed. Such areas include rural and other under-served areas where the participation of diverse network operators and providers – including municipal government authorities, co-operatives, and community operators has contributed to increasing access. There were therefore calls for the review of policy and regulation, and the establishment of incentives to facilitate increased participation by this cadre of operators.

Third, there continues to be conviction and consensus on the potential of ICTs as tools for development – particularly at the level of rural and local access. ICTs can be used in increasing accessibility to healthcare and education; they can help in decreasing vulnerabilities and improving citizen engagement with governments and their institutions. There was a therefore a call for the promotion and adoption of a multi-sectoral approach in achieving universal, affordable and equitable access. Specifically mentioned was the integration of ICT regulation and policy with local development strategies, as well as the exploitation of complementarities between different types of development infrastructure (for example transport networks, water pipes/canals, power/electrification, communication etc.).[30]

The access debate in the third IGF at Hyderabad picked up on some of the issues raised in Rio, namely, that if most people think that competition has resulted in lower costs of communication why has this not been uniformly the case, especially in Africa? The answer seemed to be that the competition dimension of communications reform often ran into problems of governance in developing countries. There was insufficient political commitment to competition by developing country governments, and "it's not that markets are not working in Africa but we don't have working markets because they are not fully competitive", Alison Gillwald argued. This suggests that where there is failure of the policy to extend affordable access to the Internet, the problem may lie at the doors of governments that do not implement

---

[30] Abiodun Jagun, "Building Consensus on Internet Access at the IGF," APC, May 2008, at, www.apc.org/en/system/files/APCIssuePaper_200805_IGF_EN.pdf.

communications reform effectively to increase access for citizens and reduce the cost of communications for consumers.

The access session at the fourth IGF in Sharm El Sheikh was notable for the emphasis placed on the importance of mobile as the path to broadband access to the Internet in developing countries and the need to allocate spectrum effectively to do so. This was coupled with two innovative interventions: the notion of fiber across borders in Africa and the budget telecom network model developed in South Asia.

Over the four years of main sessions and open policy dialogues on access, the issue of Internet access has been explored from the last mile or meter through national backbone networks to international fibre optic cables. Suggestions have been made on reducing costs by implementing IXPs to keep local traffic local, and the question of international interconnection costs has been debated back and forth. Stakeholders have emphasized that it's not just about the supply of the cable, a matter of physical infrastructure but also about building the capacity to use the networks and to develop local content in local languages to build demand. And it has become clear that mobile broadband is the way forward in developing countries, based on increasing competition and reducing costs for low-income users and allocating spectrum to increase mobile broadband use. In this process, national and international broadband networks operating on open access principles become ever more important to enhance fibre across borders. The question of power supply becomes integral and with it multi-sectoral approaches to exploiting complementarities between different types of development infrastructure like transport networks, water pipes/canals, power/electrification, and fibre cable networks. Linked to this, and not sufficiently explored at the IGF, is the importance of using renewable energy resources when expanding infrastructure.

Taking the Issues Forward

The dialogues on access to the Internet at the IGF discussed here started during an Internet and telecoms boom (2006) and continued into a period of global financial crisis (2009). It is interesting to see that many of the points made by stakeholders in the debates are to do with the proper role of the public and private sectors with respect to increasing universal affordable access. While the value of competition as a spur to access was acknowledged, the role of governments with respect to development and governance was also emphasized. A key point coming through the debates was that the role of governments and of the market doesn't need to be at odds. "It's possible to have a very strong empowerment and rights-based framework and yet create the conditions for very strong private sector development," in Radhika Lal's words. This fits with the lessons of the financial crisis---that regulation matters, that markets need clear and simple rules and the interplay between governments and markets is crucial.

The way forward on access to the Internet is to explore this dynamic further and the IGF dialogues should continue to expose new thinking and positions to support the achievement of universal affordable broadband as a right of citizens of developing countries in the near future---to push beyond the final frontier where there is Internet for all. Strengthening the development agenda in the IGF can make it a valuable forum for exploring how issues that are of concern in developed countries, such as network neutrality, can impact on access in the developing world where it is often not discussed.

The IGF would do well by focusing on different forms of access, e.g. public access and the role of public institutions in providing access. It could place greater emphasis on approaching access from the perspective of social and economic, cultural and civil and political rights. One pitfall that the IGF should avoid at all costs is to make the assumption that equitable access is no longer a priority. This is refuted by the evidence of a growing broadband divide, and of access gaps remaining even in countries with extensive infrastructure. As more and more social, economic and political transactions and relationships take place, at least in part, on the Internet, the importance of access will increase.

Conclusion

The IGF has been an extremely valuable space for broad-based discussion of access. That the impact of this discussion is hard to measure does not detract from its value. Dialogue, and the diversity of discussion enabled by the IGF format (workshops that drill down into specific areas and main sessions which provide a broad overview of a theme) contributed to building understanding on key issues, such as the role of policy and regulation, of market failure, and of the potential for local initiatives and innovative business models.

But there were also gaps. The lack of competition in international fibre and satellite connectivity has not really been addressed. Nor has the impact of vertical integration in the mobile industry. There is an assumption that 'any' access is better than 'no access at all'; an assumption that should be examined much more carefully. Ongoing and new exclusions based on age, gender, ability, and class should also receive more attention. As stated above, a 'rights-based' approach to access has not been given much consideration. Many participants, including from governments, appear to feel threatened by the language of 'rights'. They should view it as an opportunity for strengthening a public interest approach to Internet governance. Now that a country like Finland has made broadband access a 'right' more government will hopefully be open to this approach.

Probably the primary weakness has been not so much in the discussion itself, as in the limited participation of developing counties. Unless people from those parts of the world where access is still limited and very expensive join the debate, the potential of this forum to inform, connect, and inspire will not be sufficiently realised. Regional IGFs are filling this gap, but they often lack the participation of people who are not yet connected.

While there is more emphasis on a development agenda in the IGF, growing this process will not be easy, and ultimately it has to be led by developing country participants and take place at regional and global IGFs. It should also include those communities within the developed world who still lack access. We need the voices of the people who still experience the consequences of not having sufficient and affordable access inside the IGF to make sure the topic remains alive and the dialogue relevant.

Security:

The Key to Trust and Growth of the Internet

Alejandro Pisanty

The subject of Internet security has been scrutinized throughout the World Summit on the Information Society (WSIS) process (2002-2005) and subsequently in the Internet Governance Forum (IGF). In the IGF, Security was selected---along with Access, Openness, and Diversity---as one of the four main themes for discussion; a fifth, Critical Internet Resources, was added subsequently.

Security is a concern for many people and organizations involved in and around the Internet – in its operation, usage, service delivery, and standards-setting environments. The Internet Engineering Task Force (IETF) has long had the norm that every Request for Comments (RFC) must contain pertinent security considerations for the standard to which it refers.

A related concern is trust: a lack of security can undermine trust on the Internet and make people refrain from using it actively in order to reap the benefits of the Information Society. This is one of the reasons that WSIS paid so much attention to security.

Security was in the minds of the creators of the Internet. The basic design was that the network itself would be mostly open, and security mechanisms would use the efficiency of the network to protect the information through appropriate cryptography, which was already available.

As the Internet expanded, especially after the invention of the World Wide Web, millions of people with little or no computer experience became Internet users. Numerous mechanisms to abuse, circumvent, or social-engineer the security mechanisms appeared as well. Also, as more and more forms of human conduct were translated to the Internet, malicious behaviour was adapted and many forms of fraud and other crimes were taken into the networks.

Security has been treated with attention in the IGF. Every meeting of the IGF has had one main session dedicated to security, either on its own or in combination with other themes like privacy and openness. The Multistakeholder Advisory Group (MAG) of the IGF has taken great care in calling together qualified speakers from many different functional communities and geographies for these sessions. Furthermore, a large number of workshops on security and related issues have taken place.

In the following, a summary is presented for the main session discussions on security at each of the IGF meetings from 2006 to 2009, complemented by elements from the workshops. The Hyderabad session of 2008 is given a slightly different treatment because it had already absorbed two years of development of the IGF, so it showed some effects of the previous years' discussions, and also two years have passed since the session and therefore we can begin to identify its impact. This is followed by a brief analysis of the dialogues in the IGF, as well as some recommendations for the future treatment of security in the IGF.

Athens

The discussions about security in Athens were exploratory in many senses. This was the first IGF meeting, so although speakers were experienced in their fields and many had already met, the discussion context was new. The combination of speakers and the purpose of the meeting were equally novel.

The session covered a large number of subjects; many were dealt with in some depth while others were barely mentioned, due mostly to time constraints. The relationships between these subjects are complex and therefore the discussions touched upon many different issues.

This free flow of conversation allowed many unplanned topics to emerge. Several security issues were first treated in the IGF in this session, including stakeholders' roles and the problems they face. Other problems discussed were definitions and status of Internet security, cooperation, and the relationships between security and other aspects of the Internet and the Information Society. A more detailed breakdown follows:

A lively discussion took place. One speaker described his view of the main factors of Internet security that need attention, which are availability of the network, integrity of transmissions over the network and confidentiality of communications, especially in the face of intelligent adversaries trying to break these three features. Another speaker added that a key issue for security is that violations are now made for financial gain, and no longer for technical prestige. A third speaker noted that many measures intended to increase security are taken at the expense of privacy.

A workshop before the main session discussed the security-privacy nexus and its relationship with identity online. In this view, security and privacy protection have to be built together, since privacy is essential for individual freedom in a free and open society. A panellist mentioned that not only actions of criminal individuals should be considered; he also stressed "threats from the state, from states which use information technology to settle accounts [and...] criminal action by governments."

Several speakers argued in favour of a proactive instead of reactive approach to Internet security; for looking into the future threat landscape. The need to consider continuity of operations as a priority was stressed. Some participants also emphasized both the need and the difficulty of reconciling legal frameworks among countries, a task with which the European Union has had intensive experience.

In contrast, another speaker espoused moving away from the plethora of problems and looking instead at the positive side. In his view, while not denying the problems, there are more successes than failures in Internet security, as proven by the fact that extensive transactions, including e-commerce, take place on the Internet. He said that security is not only a question of technology; a holistic approach is needed, in which people are included and considered, since people themselves are often the weakest links and the cause of security breaches.

Looking at responses to security threats, others spoke about the work of Computer Emergency Response Teams (CERTs) and cooperation among them as part of the framing of the subject. Yet another speaker stated that international cooperation among governments alone may first worsen some problems before producing improvements, because this form of cooperation could overrule other collaborations that already take place.

Reports made in the meeting showed that at the time there was a transition in response depth and promptness of some countries' CERTs and ISPs, with fast improvement in tracing and stopping spam and phishing as well as virus spread. This was achieved by intensifying purposeful cooperation, mostly among business, academic and technical stakeholders.

The discussion took up the question whether governments should establish policies and procedures with respect to the responsibilities of providers, the software industry, and all other players in the field. Among the responses, two contrasting viewpoints were offered. One was that users should (almost forcibly, as in the case of "Internet drivers' licenses") receive basic training about security. The other was that the open nature of the Internet would make it very difficult to impose education on all users.

A round of discussion centred on the roles that governments can take in order to foster or improve Internet security. Options discussed included responsibility for critical infrastructures; legislation on behaviours which should be criminalized; coordinating security measures among sectors including business, academia, and civil society; and undertaking regional cooperation. Further, the European Union's Cybercrime Convention and threats from and against the state were mentioned.

All speakers agree that Internet security can only be approached by the cooperation among stakeholders, both in their own countries and across borders. Some stated that high levels of cooperation are already taking place, within countries and internationally. What may be lacking is cooperation across sectors, i.e. governments, the technology community, the legal profession and legislatures, regulatory experts, businesses, and others.

A further insight on cooperation in Internet security was provided by one speaker: the forms of cooperation prevalent between network providers, specifically telephony providers and carriers, who own and control their networks, do not map easily to the Internet. The Internet demands cooperation far beyond what has been practiced among traditional network operators. In addition, cooperation with and among developing countries has to include creating security awareness among decision-makers, as well as capacity building.

It was suggested that a top-down approach to introducing secure conduct for all stakeholders will take too long and probably not succeed in the end. A bottom-up approach including a code of conduct must be tried. This approach was further enriched with a call to share best practices and technical arrangements, such as the ones used in Canada at the time of the meeting to fight botnets and spam.

Other examples of cooperation among WSIS stakeholders cited include the OECD anti-spam toolkit, described as a starter set for policies; the Anti-Phishing Working Group (APWG), and the Mail Anti-Abuse Working Group (MAAWG). Both working groups are based on cooperation among many sectors, among which are CERTs, service providers, software companies, and in some cases law-enforcement authorities. The success of the APWG and the MAAWG arises from their lightweight, multistakeholder, problem-oriented memberships and missions, and the focused cooperation among their members.

Throughout the session, speakers and participants showed some of the known problems in Internet security and the ways in which they are being addressed. While this was not a technical or a training session, the depth of the problems and the combination of power and limitations of some solutions were described.

An important component of many solutions to security problems is the development of public-key cryptography and the accompanying credentials and certificates. These are used for providing electronic signatures and proof of identity in order to increase the security of some systems. Speakers stated that the development and implementation of these and other solutions are best left to the technical, academic and private sectors, whereas laws and policies are the responsibilities of governments. Mulstistakeholder cooperation enhances effective solutions.

Contributions from speakers through remote participation brought up a fresh variety of issues such as electronic identification and authentication as well as the effect of open standards on Internet security. Resonating with the open standards or at least an "open approach", there followed statements that openness contributes greatly to Internet security whereas "security by obscurity" does not. This links to the "Openness" and "Diversity" themes of the IGF.

Interoperability and diversity provide both challenges and improvements to Internet security. The technical nature of these issues is addressed in technical standards-development organizations (SDOs). A productive discussion of these issues in the IGF, therefore, can concentrate on general ideas which could feed the technical and democratic processes of the standard-setting communities.

A closing round touched on the value of the session and of the IGF itself. The wide range of views was found to be exciting; it is agreed the added value of the IGF is in bringing together parties that don't usually get together. The knowledge obtained during the discussions in the IGF can then be taken to other areas where decision-making bodies actually meet. The emerging view, picked up by the Chairman of the session, is that the wide range of subjects raised can feed into adaptable systems to find solutions. Bringing together all stakeholders can help each of them do his or her job more effectively.

Rio de Janeiro

The security discussions in Rio de Janeiro picked up various themes from the Athens meeting, with some repetition as well as progress in identifying problems and questions more sharply. The panel opened by stating that clear thought about security requires defining the object to be secured.

The speakers discussed both individuals' and organizations' security, as well as problems that arise from the perspective of national security. The notion of security about which the IGF speaks remains very open. The discussions can be grouped together in roughly the same format as in Athens.

Concepts of security expressed during the meeting included:

- "Security as control of the future", adjusted by views of what is being secured (an individual's information, a country's assets) and the openness and creativity, therefore unpredictability, of the Internet
- Trust and confidence in commercial transactions
- Reliability
- Resiliency of networks
- National security, with implications for Internet-mediated attacks on vital infrastructures of countries
- Security of the "end point", computers and devices connected to the network
- Security of the network
- Security of users or citizens against fraud and crime
- Security of users or citizens to protect their privacy
- Security as an obligation of the state

Cooperation for security was recurring theme in the discussions, as already observed in Athens. Speakers stated that there is a need for stronger cooperation among governments and for supporting it with the work of international organizations. It must be built on successful, fruitful cooperation among stakeholders in the technical and operational communities of the Internet, business and civil-society organizations, etc.

Cooperation is needed for building up the capacity of developing countries to deal with security issues. Examples of already existing cooperation, such as among CERTs, were shown, with emphasis on the varied nature of the participating organizations (technical, academic, business and governmental). This cooperation may extend into education. Education is required in order to promote a security-oriented mindset among software developers to diminish software vulnerabilities which are part of the security problem.

Several speakers expressed the need for cooperation to support capacity-building in the judiciary power. Another speaker, underlining the needs for security of information at the national level, put forward a view expressing a perceived need to establish "international organisms that do not exist right now but should exist" as well as international agreements.

This set of issues was present again in Rio de Janeiro. It appeared mostly in examples (notably, the contributions of CERTs) and was reflected in the discussions about cooperation and the relationship with other issues. Speakers in Rio went less into detail about the solutions to specific problems than they did in Athens. Policy-making was the principal focus.

The issues discussed or mentioned in relationship with Internet security were, among others, the possible mandate of international organizations to regulate the Internet (strongly opposed by private-sector speakers), free or open-source software, sales of private data in black or open markets, civil liberties, and compliance and the risk of overregulation. At the end of the session, speakers converged in recognizing again the necessity of a multistakeholder approach to the problems of Internet security. In the words of the Chair of the main session, "the dynamic nature of the Internet requires agile tools and the constant updating of methods, as well as intense cooperation and the adoption of preventive steps, without losing sight of each country, each culture, each nation."

Hyderabad

The meeting of the IGF in Hyderabad had the main discussions on security divided in two panels: "Dimensions of Cyber-security and Cyber-crime" and "Fostering Security, Privacy, and Openness". They were followed by an "Open Dialogue on Promoting Cyber-security and Trust". The summary presented here covers all three sessions.

In Hyderabad, the discussions on security began to include emerging topics like online social networking and other sources of user-generated content. The contributions were varied and diverse. Many continued trends and subjects from Athens and Rio de Janeiro. For brevity, they are grouped in a slightly different way.

An opening speaker stated that there begins to be an agreement on the definitions of cybercrime and the related categories of cyberterrorism and cyberthreats. He said further that traditional crime has moved online, by using cyberspace for known crimes of the real world. As examples he mentioned money laundering, sexual exploitation of children, gambling, intellectual property and identity theft, extortion, threats, illegal drugs, and prostitution. He also said that new crimes like phishing continue to appear.

Other risks to consider are threats to countries' critical infrastructure (electrical power lines, water distribution systems, transportation, etc.) and cyberterrorism. In all cases, investigating threats and responding to crimes is complex because of challenges like geographical distance and cross-border operation. More cooperation is needed with developing countries to avoid the appearance of "cyber-havens", similar to those existing for money laundering.

In the first meetings of the IGF, in Athens and Rio de Janeiro, the word "cybersecurity" was used only a dozen or so times, compared with several hundred for "security". In those meetings, it was introduced only by the International Telecommunications Union (ITU) and a few speakers, mostly in reference to the ITU's presentations. It appeared somewhat more often in Hyderabad with a variety of meanings.

Speakers described many instances of cooperation between stakeholders for Internet security. One panellist described new institutional models of response to address cyber-threats and forensic issues. As in Athens and in Rio de Janeiro, many speakers mentioned CERTs and Computer Security Incident Response Teams (CSIRTs, an extension of the CERT concept) and the collaboration among technical, business, civil-society and government stakeholders. This collaboration is increasing.

One of the co-chairs of the Open Dialogue recognized the need to tailor solutions to the problems and circumstances. There is no "one size fits all" solution, he said. According to one speaker, not only the concept of cyber-security (understood most generally) but even the concept of "data as an asset" is missing in developing countries. The digital divide is a challenge for capacity building on Internet security.

User-generated content and online social networking services increase the challenges of security as users expose personal information that can be used to hurt them or their organizations. A better understanding of this problem is based in turn on understanding privacy. In developing countries, he noted, laws for privacy protection are incipient and often not observed. According to the same speaker, sometimes people may be ready to relinquish some privacy for the sake of protection against threats.

One of the co-chairs summarized the session as follows: there is an emerging consensus that the nexus of cybercrime, cybersecurity, privacy and openness is a joint responsibility of all stakeholders. In the words of one speaker, all stakeholders should work together in synergy. The IGF provides a space "for developing deeper understanding of the different viewpoints, the different perspectives", and brings forward the balance between rights and responsibilities and the importance of education.

A co-chair of the open dialogue relayed the impossibility of summarizing the rich debate that took place in the session. He called to "move from discourse to action". For this purpose, he pointed to the issue of child protection against sexual abuse and pornography. He said it has been "debated at length and [...] the discussion has matured enough to create a common environment where all relevant stakeholders could build trust and work together."

Sharm el Sheikh

In the Sharm el Sheikh meeting of the IGF, security discussions continued to evolve. Thanks to the presence of various experts, some concepts were made more clear-cut. Other speakers extended the discussion to further areas concerned with security, such as personal life and gender perspectives. They also increased the attention given to the effects of user-generated content.

Discussions of national security perspectives almost vanished. The main session was titled "Security, Openness, and Privacy", which clearly picks up from the conclusions of the meetings in Hyderabad. This session was opened with the question whether security, openness, and privacy are opposed, or whether there are ways in which they can enhance each other. Some participants added the considerations of trust and accountability. According to one speaker, accountability can increase security if, for example, companies are held liable for the security of their software products, or operators are made responsible for the security of their networks. If this happens, trust also grows. The ways in which accountability can be achieved remain open.

One of the panellists connected privacy to consent and to exploitation and abuse in private spaces. She applied a gender and a feminist analysis to this problem by explaining online risks specific to women in unequal societies, such as gender-specific exploitation and abuse, and the equally specific need for protecting the privacy of women and other disadvantaged sectors of society.

Another panellist stated that today there is virtually no limit to the amount of information that can be recorded. There is also almost no limit to the scope of analysis that can be performed on that information, nor to the time that the information can be stored and recovered. The information is not owned by those who produce it but in many cases, due to contractual consent, by those who store it. Each of us produces a "data shadow" which becomes larger each day. This "data shadow" is beyond the individual's control due to the commoditization of ever-cheaper technology and services.

"Online social networking sites" are of increasing importance. They are based on an exchange in which the user provides personal information and the sites sell access to focused publicity based on the user-provided information. Individuals' and organizations' security may be threatened by misuse of the recorded information in unpredictable ways, particularly in the long term.

The problems in social networking are complex because information can also be used by malicious parties against the users of the social sites. These are problems of conduct and not of technology; in a related session this author stated that "Social media don't kill, rape, or traffic with images of child abuse. People do."

Many speakers in the session and workshops insisted that problems arising from human conduct must be addressed as such, not as problems of technology, and dealt with by means of education and legal measures.

For one of the speakers, the important balance to be achieved now is not security versus privacy, because these two must come together, but instead liberty versus control. Liberty includes access to information and freedom of expression. Several speakers and participants stated that governments should not put laws in place to limit these freedoms, but to guarantee them.

Therefore security considerations, in turn, should not be used as an excuse for filtering or censorship.

Finally, another speaker insisted repeatedly that all security and privacy analyses must be made with a human-rights perspective. Cybersecurity as national security was mentioned only once by a speaker and was never the centre of discussions or analysis.

In his statements at the close of the IGF meeting of 2009 in Sharm el Sheikh, Mr. Sha Zukang, Under-Secretary-General of the United Nations Organization, stated the following overview regarding issues related to security:

"Consensus has been building that cybercrime, cybersecurity, privacy and openness were the joint responsibility of all stakeholders, and the UN General Assembly was considering the issue of cybersecurity in its current session. Issues of access and diversity remain central to the IGF; the Internet offers unprecedented opportunities for countries and people in all corners of the world but the conversion of that potential into reality requires that the Internet be managed for the benefit of humanity as a whole."

Concerning the emerging theme of social media, Under-Secretary-General Sha said the real issue was whether, on balance, the variety of content available on the Internet through social media was ushering in a better-informed society, and felt this was a perspective worth further discussion.

The final messages of the meeting reiterated the importance of multistakeholder cooperation, the impressive speed of change in the Internet security landscape, and the consequent rapid creation of new issues.

Assessment

The discussions about security in the IGF have drawn together participants from varied geographic, institutional, professional, and stakeholder backgrounds. Deep technical expertise has been brought together with experience in policy formulation and execution, and with principled advocacy. These discussions have not converged on a single definition of Internet security or on a single concept as a central concern for the IGF.

A mapping between the subjects discussed in the IGF and those of interest outside the IGF shows that the IGF condenses the highest level of aggregation of the subjects globally. There is little room for in-depth discussions of technical, legal, legislative, international relations, political economy, and many other aspects of the global debate. Further, there is a time lag of approximately two years between the time a subject enters the mainstream of more than one community of interest, and the time it enters the IGF.

There is a similar time lag in the reverse direction. It takes approximately two years, at least, from the moment a participant first meets a subject in the IGF to the time IGF-gained perspectives begin to show in the specialist communities.

Some subjects that have been mentioned in the IGF have been moved elsewhere. National security and threats to national critical infrastructures have been discussed in the IGF; however, the publicly known discussions about "cybertreaties", definitions of hostile conduct in cyberspace, etc. take place elsewhere. The parties in those discussions clearly do not entrust them to the IGF environment. As of this writing, there are first signs of agreements to deal with these matters among a group of countries around the UN General Assembly.

The positive feature of interactions in the IGF is that all participants are given the opportunity to listen to and interact with parties they usually don't meet, particularly those outside their national environment or the communities of interest in which they usually act. With the knowledge and relationships gained, they can continue to collaborate with the people and organizations they met in the IGF.

The nature, level of aggregation, and time lag between IGF and non-IGF spaces have made it very difficult for participants to propose general agreements in the IGF that all participants can support as recommendations or other "concrete outcomes".

As Under-Secretary-General Sha indicated in his speech about the continuation of the IGF, early in 2010, cybersecurity may become a subject of discussion in the UN General Assembly, where it would be debated by governments alone. The WSIS framework requires the discussions in the General Assembly to be broadly and deeply informed by the knowledge and principles supported by all stakeholders and to absorb the lessons of the IGF.

WSIS outcome documents prescribe a framework for a people-centred Information Society, and for the participation of all stakeholders in Internet governance. Following that framework, even in the General Assembly, will be essential for managing the most important Internet security risks and their discussion in the IGF.

Recommendations

The IGF can contribute to the global debate of the security aspects of Internet governance and should continue if it fulfils a set of conditions:

- Technical expertise continues to be available in the MAG and in the IGF meetings
- All stakeholders meet on an equal footing
- All participants recognize that the greatest value of the IGF is the frank and open exchange of knowledge and informed opinion among stakeholders
- Nothing reduces the opportunity for frank and open exchange, as would happen with the discussions of agreed outcomes, recommendations, or negotiated text
- Capacity building and development take centre stage to fulfil the WSIS mission of creating a people-centred Information Society

Conclusion

Security debates show that the IGF is an agora and a crossroads. It is a place to discuss, with pride in full citizenship among equals, to push the limits of in-depth, mutual understanding and civic commitment for the common good. It is colourful, varied and multicultural, due to the diversity of participants in geography, experience, and roles in society.

The IGF flattens hierarchies, opens ears and minds, and gives something to everyone who is open enough to take it. It is not an appropriate venue to make far-reaching decisions, since these require clear definitions and complex structures.

The IGF has yet to agree to a precise definition of its objectives in Internet security. Every time it comes close the target moves; this will continue to happen because of the speed of change of the Internet. The IGF will function better without hanging on to a given definition; instead, it will be able to adapt its contents and participation by keeping the definition and list of security problems open and updated.

For decisions such as recommendations or the declaration of consensus, the IGF would need structures and measures to ensure representation, equity, accountability, appeal, reversal and redress of decisions. However, these structures and the discussions to create "agreed text" would stifle the productive debates that now take place.

The handling of issues on Internet security shows the benefits of the opposite: intense discussions take place, knowledge is brought in, and the participants take their new knowledge, understanding and relationships to the spaces where decisions can be effectively made. These decisions concern technology, technical standards, operational rules, best practices, legislation, law enforcement, judicial practice, legislative harmonization, international agreements, and so on. The organizations that make those decisions are effective if they are oriented to the solution of specific problems, bring together the right mix of stakeholders, and have adequate and efficient decision-making structures.

The IGF functions better as a crossroads than as a destination. And, if the Forum is good enough to allow the free flow of ideas and expertise, it embodies ideas in flux, respect and good use for knowledge, an open spirit of collaboration, and the general concern that the Internet is for everyone.

IG4D:

Toward a Development Agenda for Internet Governance

William J. Drake

Development has occupied an unusual space in the Internet Governance Forum (IGF). On the one hand, the Tunis Agenda for the Information Society that was adopted by the second World Summit on the Information Society (WSIS) in November 2005 contains provisions declaring development to be central to Internet governance and to the mandate of the IGF. Moreover, developing country governments and other stakeholders made it clear during both the WSIS negotiations and the IGF launch process that they were expecting the IGF to focus on development, and that this figured in their support for its creation. These expectations also were reflected in various statements made at the first IGF in Athens in 2006 and the second IGF in Rio de Janeiro in 2007, both of which were held under the overarching theme of "Internet Governance for Development".

On the other hand, despite all the invocations of its importance, development was not designated a distinct topic in its own right that would receive focused and intensive treatment in the IGF. Security, openness, diversity and access (SODA) were selected as the themes of the Athens main sessions, and critical Internet resources (CIR) became a main session theme beginning in Rio. Like the closely connected matter of capacity building, development was positioned as a horizontally cross-cutting concern that should be addressed along the way in the SODA and CIR sessions. In conceptual terms this framing seemed sensible enough to many participants, since development considerations do arise across the other thematic areas. But in practical terms, this model, which has been retained since Athens, has meant that serious attention to Internet governance for development (IG4D) generally has been crowded out in the dialogues on the selected themes, each of which entails a wide range of other pressing issues.

Accordingly, the approach taken here is necessarily a bit different from that of the background papers in this volume on the SODA and CIR themes. Since there has been much less discussion of development to look back on and assess before making recommendations, the paper largely concentrates on outlining an option for future activity. The proposal elaborated in the following pages is that with an appropriate measure of recognition and support, interested parties could evolve a "development agenda" that would give more meaning and political impetus to the often-professed conviction that Internet governance should be conducted in a manner that promotes development.

The paper is organized as follows. The first section briefly highlights the ways in which development has been addressed in the IGF to date, and underscores in particular the comparatively limited attention that has been devoted in this context to the roles of global governance mechanisms.

Against this backdrop, the second section takes note of efforts in other international arenas to devise development agendas for global governance in order to tease out pontential lessons for an initiative on Internet governance. The third section then lists some possible foundational elements of a development agenda, while the fourth schematically outlines some steps that could be taken to carry such an agenda forward in the IGF.

IG4D in the IGF

In general, the IGF main sessions have concentrated more on Internet issues than on Internet governance institutions. Most of the discussion has been devoted to raising awareness about selected issues, considering the challenges they pose, and identifying broad priorities for future action---i.e., to initial agenda setting. In contrast, much less time has been devoted to drilling down into the details of the governance systems that have been or could be designed to address those issues. The CIR sessions offer some limited exceptions, but usually there has not been focused debate on the development and application, especially at the global level, of shared principles, norms, rules, decision-making procedures, and programmes that shape the evolution and use of the Internet. Undoubtedly, this approach has promoted fluid and dynamic conversations that were less politically sensitive than what might have ensued from plunging into the dissection of particular governance mechanisms. But while it increased key stakeholders' comfort levels and support for the IGF in the wake of the difficult WSIS debates, the approach often has given the discussions a rather institutionally ungrounded flavour.

This dynamic has been particularly evident with respect to IG4D because it has been positioned as a dimension of the other themes rather than as a theme for debate in its own right. A close examination of the main session transcripts from Athens through Sharm el Sheikh underscores the general point, but also reveals some variation across cases. For example, in the security sessions there has been much discussion of problems like the spread of malware, cybercrime, and child pornography, and of the importance of privacy, trust, reliability/resiliency, critical infrastructure protection, and capacity building. Along the way, participants have taken note of the important work being done inter alia by the Internet Engineering Task Force (IETF), the Anti-Phishing Working Group (APWG), the Mail Anti-Abuse Working Group (MAAWG), the Computer Emergency Response Teams (CERTs), the Council of Europe (COE), the Internet Corporation for Assigned Names and Numbers (ICANN), the International Telecommunication Union (ITU), the Organization for Economic Cooperation and Development (OECD), and the Internet service providers (ISPs). But there has been rather little discussion of the substantive content and effectiveness of the governance regimes and programs they have devised to manage the problems under consideration, and even less of how well these address the particular challenges faced by developing countries.

Similarly, in the openness sessions there has been dialogue on issues like freedom of expression and censorship, intellectual property rights and access to knowledge, and interoperability and open standards. But there has been much less commentary on the substance of the relevant human rights and international telecommunication instruments, industry self-regulatory practices, standards development processes, World Intellectual Property Organization (WIPO) arrangements, and so on, or of their implications for development. With the partial exception of internationalized domain names (IDNs), on which ICANN's role has been discussed, much the same could be said of the sessions on diversity. None of this is to suggest that the sessions have not been useful and informative; rather, it is simply to note that the development dimensions of specific governance systems, particularly those at the global level, generally was not a major item that each endeavoured to address.

IG4D concerns have been flagged a bit more often in the other main sessions. On access, the discussions of international interconnection charges have not gone into the details of traffic management and the contractual relations between service providers, but developing countries' concerns were raised, and the construction of Internet Exchange Points (IXPs) was promoted as a key part of the solution. Also raised in some sessions was the importance of enabling telecommunications policy environments at the national level, e.g. of independent regulators, competition, effective spectrum management, flexibility on the licensing of independent ISPs, and competitively neutral universal service funds. However, relevant global governance frameworks, like the General Agreement on Trade in Services (GATS) of the World Trade Organization (WTO), and their implications for developing countries again were not debated.

Unquestionably, the most institutionally focused debates have pertained to CIR. This is not surprising, since it would be difficult to discuss IPv4 and IPv6, IDNs, generic and country code Top Level Domains (TLDs) or ICANN's relationship to the US Government without devoting some time to the relevant policies and practices of ICANN and the Regional Internet Registries (RIRs). Even so, attention to the specific ways in which the global collective management of these issues does or does not impact development per se was eclipsed by other, more politically-oriented discussions.

Arguably, the most frequent references to IG4D have been made in two settings. One was the experimental main session on "Internet Governance in Light of the WSIS Principles" that was held at Sharm el Sheikh. Half of the session was devoted to the implementation of the development-related provisions in the WSIS principles on Internet governance. While most of this open dialogue again focused more on issues than on the institutional frameworks devised for them, it did seem to help strengthen the conviction among many participants that the IGF should endeavour to address development more directly in future meetings.

Based on their written descriptions and reports, the other setting has been some of the workshops and related events organized during the first four IGFs. The linkages between institutions and development appear to have been considered to varying degrees in certain open forums and dynamic coalition meetings, and in workshops on such topics as ccTLD management, IXPs and traffic exchange, multilingualism and IDNs, sustainable development, national initiatives on access and security in developing countries, and capacity building. In addition, beginning at the Rio de Janeiro meeting, the present author has organized a series of annual workshops on the notion of a development agenda for global IG4D. But while there have been some opportunities for their organizers to report back in main sessions, these workshops and other events did not notably increase the visibility of development on the IGF's overall agenda.

The situation now appears to be changing somewhat. At Sharm el Sheikh and at the 2010 open consultation and open planning meetings in Geneva, a growing number of voices were raised in support of increased attention to development. In consequence, it was decided that there will be a main session on IG4D in Vilnius, and a multistakeholder group was formed to organize the event. Hopefully the session will subsequently be seen as a worthy addition to the IGF program that should be repeated at future meetings. But even if that happens, one three-hour session per year would not by itself make the focused consideration of IG4D a central element of the IGF's identity and mission. What would needed is a broader initiative on the part of interested stakeholders in which such main sessions serve as a foundation and focal point.

This initiative could be organized under the rubric of a development agenda. As has been demonstrated by experience in other international policy arenas, adopting an "agenda" framing connotes commitment to an integrated set of activities that are to be kept in play and systematically taken up over time. This can help raise the visibility of the efforts involved, mobilize participation and support, and encourage the collective monitoring and assessment of progress on objectives. On what sort of model could such an agenda be constructed, and what might it entail in substantive and operational terms? These questions are taken up in the next sections of the paper.

Development Agendas: Concepts and Experiences

As a starting point, it is useful to briefly consider a few previous experiences in the multilateral system with development agendas, and their potential lessons for an initiative on Internet governance. Doing so quickly makes clear that there is no single model to follow, and that what may be appropriate in a given context may not be desirable in another. This is important to keep in mind due to the unique properties and highly distributed nature of the Internet governance environment.

A particularly prominent model worth considering is that of the United Nations Development Agenda. In his preface to a UN report on the matter, former Under-Secretary-General for Economic and Social Affairs José Antonio Ocampo refers to the objectives set by various UN conferences and summits and explains:

> This comprehensive set of development goals, of which the MDGs are an integral part, has come to be called the United Nations Development Agenda. It serves as the internationally shared framework for development---for action at the global, regional, and country levels. The Agenda encompasses inter-linked issues ranging

from poverty reduction, gender equality, social integration, health, population, employment and education to human rights, the environment, sustainable development, finance and governance. It includes as well systemic issues, such as the differential impact of globalization, inequalities among and within countries, and greater participation of developing countries in global economic governance. And it also addresses the question of inter-linkages between development and conflict.

Two elements have permeated the content and character of the Agenda since its inception. First is a fundamental concern with equity and for equality of all persons, as human beings and as citizens...the second essential element: partnership. The conference process has engaged all the key stakeholders: governments, United Nations system organizations, other intergovernmental and non-governmental organizations, civil society, and the private sector.[31]

So the development agenda being pursued here comprises efforts at the global, regional, and national levels to achieve progress in a broad range of issue-areas, and it is informed by a guiding concern with social justice and based on multistakeholder engagement. All these elements are necessary in an overarching framework for UN development activities. But in the particular context of an Internet governance effort, some of them might present significant challenges.

For example, consider the matter of goals. Everyone can agree on the importance of, say, reducing poverty and unemployment, and on how to measure progress on these scores. In contrast, in the Internet governance arena there may be universal agreement on broad objectives like promoting security, openness, diversity and access, but the discussions in the IGF and the WSIS before it suggest that the interpretation and implementation of these terms could give rise to significant disagreements. Moreover, the precise meaning of the term, IG4D awaits serious analysis, deliberation and consensus building at the international level. Of course, there is already a good deal of agreement among some parties about what kinds of policies and processes are best suited to the development of the Internet and to Internet-enabled development (which linked but distinct concepts). But as is evidenced by their positions and practices, other parties have rather different views. For that matter, many IGF participants' perspectives may vary significantly with respect to the meaning of the root term, "development".[32]

---

[31] United Nations Department of Economic and Social Affairs, *The United Nations Development Agenda: Development for All*. New York: United Nations, 2007, Sales No. E.07.1.17, p. iii, at, www.un.org/en/development/devagenda/UNDA1.pdf.

[32] It would not be helpful here to wade into the troubled waters of development analysis and argue that a IG4D agenda should embrace a particular perspective. That said, a suitable conception would need to at least take into account the people-centred definition offered by the Nobel Laureate, Amartya Sen: "Development consists of the removal of various types of unfreedoms that leave people with little choice and little opportunity of exercising their reasoned agency...[It involves the promotion of] crucial instrumental freedoms, including economic opportunities, political freedoms, social facilities, transparency guarantees, and protective security." *Development as Freedom* (Oxford: Oxford University Press, 1999), p. xii.

In light of the nascent state of the IG4D dialogue and the wider differences of view in this policy space, it might be foolhardy to begin a development agenda initiative by trying to reach firm agreements on substantive objectives regarding the many issues involved. A better approach at the outset would be to define the agenda in more neutral and procedural terms, i.e. as a sustained effort to simply "connect the dots" between Internet governance and development and ask how the former impacts the latter, as seen through the lenses of different analytical/political perspectives.

Another challenge in applying the UN model to Internet governance concerns levels of social organization and action. Internet governance may take different forms at different levels---e.g. national, regional, plurilateral, global. In principle, a truly holistic and comprehensive development agenda would need to address governmental and nongovernmental arrangements at each. Could a process rooted in the IGF realistically expect to take up and foster productive dialogue, analysis and action across all of these? There are significant grounds for scepticism that this could work well, at least in the initial phase. Hence, although many observers would argue that the most pressing IG4D issues involve national policies and practices, I would suggest bracketing such items, i.e. keeping them in mind but not making them a principal focus of analysis and debate at the outset. [33]

For at least four reasons, it seems better for a development agenda effort to begin by exploring global IG4D issues and institutions. First, national-level policies and activities for Internet-enabled development are already being discussed in a variety of other international settings. In contrast, the possible links between development and the range of global Internet governance mechanisms are not being addressed elsewhere in a coherent and focused manner. Second, this approach could help to address the concerns and promote the engagement of those developing country governments and other stakeholders who believe that more attention should be devoted in the IGF to global public policy and institutions.

Third, at the national level, discussions of governance issues often get mixed together with other "Internet for development" questions like the technology's application to address social, economic, and political challenges, as well as with the broader, parallel discussions of information and communication technology for development (ICT4D). Disentangling and drilling down on the governance dimensions often has been difficult in the IGF, and it would be even more so if people become drawn to applications issues, as often happens with ICT4D. Fourth, any serious probing into the full range of development-related national actions would probably lead to discussions of particular countries' policies, which could prove to be even more sensitive and problematic in the IGF context than discussing the procedures and outputs of global institutions. So while in the long-term a broader orientation would be worth pursuing, at the outset it would be good to stick to the already dauntingly large and diverse landscape of global governance mechanisms. However, one exception may be necessary: it

---

[33] In a similar vein, this discussion brackets the point that development is a generic concept of concern to all countries regardless of national income and related measures. The point is taken, but the concern of this paper is with development in the developing countries.

would be useful to consider how national-level institutional and related factors affect developing countries' participation in global arrangements; we will return to this point later.

In considering development agendas focusing on global governance mechanisms, the multilateral system offers two other models from which lessons can be learned. One is the WTO's Doha Development Agenda. This was sketched out in the 2001 Ministerial Declaration that launched the current, on again/off again Doha Round of multilateral trade negotiations.[34] The declaration nominally proposes to make development promotion the overarching objective of the negotiations. In particular, it commits governments to take into account the different stages of development and concerns of countries in the global South when negotiating international rules of the game and national schedules of commitments.

The WTO framework provides two main mechanisms for development promotion. The first is increased and more effectively coordinated technical assistance and capacity building to enhance developing countries' ability to participate in and conform to the international trade system. The second is special and differential (S&D) treatment. This may entail, for example, lower levels of obligation to conform to international regime disciplines; more time and flexibility in adjusting to such disciplines; and asymmetric concessions in the reduction of tariff and non-tariff barriers to trade. S&D treatment generally is a "best endeavour" rather than a mandatory and precise commitment, and a pre-round proposal by a group of developing countries to change that was rejected. Moreover, developing countries and development proponents maintain that the industrialized countries have yet to adequately undertake this best endeavour effort in the torturous Doha Round. But disagreements over the extent of implementation do not negate the fact that the principle's recognition provides a useful tool for analysis and advocacy.

The WTO approach does not put on the table the reform of the international regimes for trade in goods, services, and trade-related intellectual property. Nor has it has not been a game changer in terms of the fundamental bargaining dynamics and offers made in the current round. Nevertheless, it institutionalized a normative baseline against which governments and other stakeholders can undertake principled evaluations of the negotiation's conformity with development objectives, and at least holds out the possibility of support and flexibility for developing countries.

A different and more consequential model is embodied in the WIPO Development Agenda. After it was proposed by Argentina and Brazil in 2004, a coalition of developing countries collaborated with civil society organizations and academics in an effort to bring a new balance to the global intellectual property regime. Instead of viewing intellectual property protection as an end in itself, the goal was to recast it as a means to promote development and related global public interest objectives. The initiative has been the subject of substantial controversy and difficult negotiations over the years, but the bargaining, proposals, counterproposals, concessions and so on

---

[34] The declaration and related materials are available at, www.wto.org/english/tratop_e/dda_e/dda_e.htm.

along the way need not be recounted here. Suffice it to say that in September 2007, the WIPO General Assembly formally adopted the agenda, and that it is now in the implementation stage. The agenda comprises 45 recommendations grouped into six clusters.[35] In relation to the focus of this paper, among the more notable of these are:

- technical assistance shall be development-oriented, demand-driven and transparent, taking into account the priorities and special needs of developing countries, especially the Least Developed Countries (LDCs)
- increased funding is required for capacity building, which is to be mainstreamed into all relevant operations
- technical assistance staff and consultants shall be neutral with respect to national policy choices
- particular emphasis shall be given to the needs of small and medium-sized enterprises (SMEs) and institutions dealing with scientific research and cultural industries
- developing countries shall be assisted, inter alia, in dealing with anti-competitive practices, promoting development-oriented intellectual property cultures and national laws, and accessing information and expertise from WIPO and diverse other sources
- the negotiation of international rules of the game shall be participatory and member-driven, and take into account the interests of all member states and the viewpoints of other stakeholders, including civil society; and shall take into account different levels of national development, and the balance between costs and benefits to all members
- global instruments are to consider the preservation of the public domain, entail flexibilities of interest to developing countries, and facilitate access to knowledge and technology by developing countries
- there shall be expanded efforts to bridge the global digital divide in accordance with the WSIS outcomes, and to promote discussions on intellectual property-related aspects of ICT and its role in economic and cultural development
- there shall be an annual progress reviews and an mechanism for the evaluation of all development-related activities using specific indicators and benchmarks, where appropriate
- new studies are to be undertaken assessing the economic, social and cultural impact of the use of intellectual property systems
- WIPO shall enhance its cooperation with other UN agencies and organizations, and ensure the wide participation of civil society in its relevant activities

Even this partial list of the recommendations makes it clear that WIPO's is a holistic, multidimensional development agenda. From a procedural standpoint, it establishes that development promotion should be a key criterion in the ongoing monitoring and evaluation of policy processes and outputs, and erects standing mechanisms to that end. Procedural institutionalization of this sort establishes processes through which interests can be mobilized, ideas can be fleshed out, and policy proposals can be defended more effectively over time. Of course, as with the Millennium

---

[35] See, www.wipo.int/ipdevelopment/en/agenda/recommendations.html and the related materials on the WIPO web site.

Development Goals or the WSIS targets, establishing criteria and monitoring progress do not by themselves catalyze real change. But such steps do establish a collective framework for the aggregation and sharing of information and some important normative guidelines, and as such they may motivate some actors to consider whether and how they might tweak their approaches to enhance the attention given to development.

From a substantive standpoint, to the extent that WIPO's agenda ultimately impacts its rules and programs that are applicable to the networked environment, it will be affecting a piece of the global Internet governance landscape. Whether similar recommendations would be worth considering in relation to other global arrangements pertinent to IG4D is a question that merits consideration. Certainly, one can imagine arenas in which some of the individual elements of both the WTO and WIPO agendas could be relevant, such as strengthening and systematizing capacity building initiatives to make them more development-oriented; taking into account the particular needs of SMEs and community-based non-profit institutions; and offering special treatment in cases where full and immediate compliance with rules is not feasible, or where resources are required of or allocated to stakeholders, particularly governments or nongovernmental actors from LDCs. Equally, there are arenas in which they might not be relevant; for many Internet governance issues, preferences or slower or lighter implementation of commitments, as per S&D treatment, would not be helpful concepts. Different types of collective action problems require different types of solutions, and the challenge in global IG4D would be to identify the functionally sound and politically viable options for each, as necessary.

Whatever the relevance of any individual provisions might be, it is clear that the neither the WTO or WIPO models could simply be transposed as a whole into global Internet governance. These models were devised for centralized intergovernmental organizations that have significant budgetary and staff resources, deal with single functional issue-areas, and host the negotiation of binding international treaties and national commitments. In contrast, Internet governance is marked by a highly distributed and heterogeneous institutional architecture, a much wider diversity of issues and interests, and a rather variable geometry of political alignments and divisions across topics. And the only institutionalized process (as opposed to institution) that has the sort of mandate needed to host such a cross-cutting effort is the IGF, which has no members, few resources, and no capacity to facilitate negotiations or urge participants toward anything other than voluntary, consensus-based action.

These considerations mean that an IGF-based agenda would need to a consensual affair based on shared interests and participatory design. It could consist of a holistic program of monitoring, analysis and action intended to mainstream development considerations into decision-making across global Internet governance mechanisms. In the first instance, it could be fundamentally informational in nature, and concentrate on surfacing, aggregating, assessing, and making accessible knowledge and information. Where conditions allow, it might also entail promoting voluntary norms in order to encourage entities with decision-making roles to enhance the development-sensitivity of their procedures and outputs. Whether participants within those entities might ever choose to go further that this, e.g.

by negotiating a different blend of policy outputs, necessarily would be an internal matter to be decided therein, rather than in the IGF discussions.

Substantive Focus

On what, substantively, might such a development agenda focus? Broadly speaking, global Internet governance mechanisms are created in three ways: the negotiation or collaborative design in intergovernmental, private sector, or multistakeholder settings of shared principles, norms, rules, decision-making procedures and programs; the coordinated convergence of independent practices, as when powerful states or firms that have the ability to shape a global policy space mutually adjust their policies and practices along the same lines; and the unilateral imposition of order by powerful states or firms. Of these, probably only negotiated shared frameworks would have any hope of attracting a consensual effort in the IGF context, at least at the outset. It would make sense to begin with this comparatively "low hanging fruit;" more sensitive or complex issues could be taken up later on if a sufficient degree of cooperation and trust has been established.

Negotiated frameworks can be mapped according to a number of typologies. But for simplicity's sake, we can differentiate between those that focus primarily on the logical and physical infrastructure of the Internet, and those that focus primarily on the Internet's use for information, communication and commerce (IC&C). Of course, some issues and frameworks spill across this boundary line, but usually one arena is more in the foreground of the institutional mission than the other.

Some governance mechanisms have a direct and significant impact on the Internet and its usage, while others have a relatively indirect and light effect. With regard to Internet infrastructures, the most important mechanisms at present would be those pertaining to the root server system, domain names, IP addresses, technical standards and protocols, and network security/cybercrime. Of less direct and configurative consequence would be governance mechanisms pertaining to the broader ICT landscape, e.g. the networks, services and resources upon which the Internet often relies and with which it will increasingly interact in the context of digital convergence. These include, inter alia, the international regimes for telecommunications regulation and standardization, radio frequency spectrum management, and trade in telecommunications services. While these are typically regarded as being outside the realm of global Internet governance, they are nevertheless important ordering mechanisms that help shape the topography within which the Internet is embedded.

With regard to IC&C, the most important global governance mechanisms at present would be those pertaining to intellectual property, trade in information-based services, information security/cybercrime, and some aspects of global electronic commerce and of content regulation and cross-border information flow. Examples of mechanisms of less direct and configurative consequence, or geographical reach, would be, e.g., those on personal privacy, consumer protection, competition policy, spam, and linguistic and cultural diversity. The various capacity building initiatives and development assistance programs cut across the infrastructure/IC&C divide and usually have an indirect effect on the Internet per se but are important nevertheless.

Presumably, it would make sense to begin by focusing on those governance arrangements that have the most direct and significant impact on the Internet and its usage. The challenge would be to assess the institutional procedures and substantive policy outputs associated with these mechanisms and to specify their current or potential relevance to development. In each case, one could attempt to identify "what works" for development, at least in the sense of reflecting good or best practices, and which may pose difficulties and hence merit adjustments. More concretely, a development agenda could be organized around three issue-sets:

Capacity Building and Development Assistance

Capacity building clearly should be a one of the main foci of any development agenda. The dialogues over the years in WSIS, IGF, ICANN and elsewhere have made it clear that is a priority that is widely embraced by all stakeholders and is most welcomed by governments and non-states actors in developing countries. At the same time though, there has sometimes been a tendency to almost idealize capacity building as a panacea. Such arguments may be seen by some as implying that capacity is a substitute for politics, as if training people will resolve (or perhaps push to the side) all the problems on which stakeholders have been divided. For example, prior to the launch of the IGF, the then chair of the G77 and China, Pakistani Ambassador Masood Khan wrote to the IGF chair stating in part,

> You inquired about the content of the development agenda of the IGF. I would like to refer once more to Paragraph 65 of the Tunis agenda which clearly underlines the need to maximize the participation of developing countries in decision regarding internet governance in a manner that "should reflect their interests". This paragraph needs to be operationalized through the IGF. It must also be noted that this paragraph is not limited to capacity building issues. It casts the net wider to highlight the systemic perspective of development oriented Internet Governance. G-77 and China would like to mention this because we noticed that many interventions yesterday adopted a reductionist approach to the development aspects of internet governance limiting it to capacity building. The issue is more complex and has been addressed in a number of paragraphs in the Tunis Agenda including paragraph 49 which reaffirms commitment on the part of international community, "to turning the digital divide into digital opportunity" by ensuring harmonious and equitable development for all and addressing issues like international interconnection costs, technology/know-how transfer, multilingualism and providing the users with choice of different software models including open source, free and proprietary software.[36]

---

[36] "Statement by H.E. Mr. Masood Khan, Ambassador and Permanent Representative of the Islamic Republic of Pakistan, on Behalf of the Group of 77 and China at the Consultations on the Establishment of the IGF", Geneva, 17 February 2006, pp. 1-2, at, www.intgovforum.org/contributions/IGF%20Statement%20by%20PR.pdf.

In a similar vein, at the Tunis WSIS in November 2005, members of the civil society Internet Governance Caucus made several interventions questioning suggestions that the proposed IGF focus largely on capacity building. And at the at the Athens IGF in 2006, former ITU Secretary-General Yoshio Utsumi rejected the notion that, "with just more capacity building...developing countries will come around to a certain enlightened point of view. We have heard this often, and it borders on arrogance."[37]

Hence, work undertaken on capacity building would need to be sensitive to its proper place in a larger constellation of efforts to link governance and development. It also would need to recognize that capacity building initiative vary widely in many dimensions. To note just two: some are designed to provide general background in the field, while others drill down into particular issue-sets and even focus on building technical or legal skills. And while many focus on helping development countries to participate effectively in governance mechanisms as they are, others are more geared toward empowering developing country actors to identify and promote their own interests irrespective of how these conform with the existing policy frameworks. It would be useful for a development agenda to take into account these and other sources of variation and thereby help developing country stakeholders to identify which offerings from which organizations provide which kinds of support so that the most informed choices possible can be made.

An obvious way to do this would be to aggregate information about the range of offerings available from international organizations, national governments and their development agencies, the business and technical communities, civil society and academia. Such information could be presented in a standardized manner that would allow easier comparisons and contrasts between the options, as well as the exchange of best practices among the entities providing such services. The point would be to surface and systematize the information in ways that makes it more accessible and usable, and then to promote dialogue and analysis on that basis.

By extension, the same sort of exercise could be undertaken with respect to larger and more institutionalized development/technical assistance programs. During WSIS Phase II there was an effort to take stock of the programs offering financial and related aid for ICT4D. The vehicle for this endeavour was a single consultant's report that was not discussed in an open manner by the full range of stakeholders involved and did not yield much follow-on activity. A different and more open process, geared toward specifically Internet-related technical assistance, could be imagined.

Finally, the approach suggested here could be extended by making the connections between capacity building and development programs, on the one hand, and the on-the-ground needs of developing country governmental and nongovernmental stakeholders, on the other. As noted previously, trying to consider all aspects of national policy making with respect to Internet governance could prove politically difficult, uncomfortably delve into the

---

[37] See the transcript at, www.intgovforum.org/cms/IGF-OpeningSession-301006.txt.

details of particular countries' experiences, or get mixed up with ICT4D-style applications issues. But a more focused assessment of how developing countries organize themselves to participate in global processes, and the capacity and related constrains they encounter, could be useful in matching programs and needs. Instructive in this regard is the 2002 report from the Panos Institute, *Louder Voices*. For example, based on interviews with developing country participants in such bodies as the ITU, WTO, and ICANN, the report concluded that, "some fellowship programmes result in 'the wrong people attending meetings for the wrong reasons.'"[38] Assessing how the national-level interface with global processes is currently organized and could be enhanced would seem a useful component of a development agenda initiative.

Institutional/Procedural Issues

A second set of activities could involve assessing and exchanging information on how the processes followed in global governance may affect developing country participation. The heterogeneous array of institutions and collaborations involved often employ different procedures and embody distinctive organizational cultures in accordance with their particular histories. These factors can impact the level and quality of participation in a variety of ways, e.g. pro or con, formally or informally, and directly or indirectly.

With regard to intergovernmental organizations, one trend of note has been for non-universal bodies, including regional organizations like the European Union or plurilateral organizations like the OECD and the G-8, to adopt policies which, due to the scope of influence of the governments involved, end up becoming de facto global rules. The inability of non-members to participate in the design of such policies may raise questions from a development standpoint. Universal multilateral bodies can pose other challenges. Developing country governments, particularly the LDCs, may find it difficult to send representatives with the requisite specialized expertise to multiple, lengthy and sometimes simultaneous negotiations and expert meetings scheduled throughout the year. This is especially problematic for the dozens of countries that have small and understaffed permanent UN missions, or no missions at all, in Geneva where the greatest concentration of multilateral activity on global ICT and Internet issues occurs.

In addition, intergovernmental organizations vary in the extent to which they invite the engagement of nongovernmental actors, including those from developing countries. Some organizations effectively limit the participation of particular stakeholder groupings to selected informational events and

---

[38] Don MacLean, David Souter, James Deane, and Sarah Lilley, *Louder Voices: Strengthening Developing Country Participation in International ICT Decision-Making* (London: Panos Institute, 2002), p. 28. Report available at www.panos.org.uk/images/books/Louder%20Voices.pdf. For an updated assessment of these issues see, David Souter, "'*Louder Voices*' and the International Debate on Developing Country Participation in ICT Decision Making", in, *Governing Global Electronic Networks: International Perspectives on Policy and Power*, William J. Drake and Ernest Wilson IIIrd, eds. (Cambridge, MA: The MIT Press, 2008).

hallway encounters on the margins of regular meetings. And even when there are no formal barriers at the door, there can be constraints on the extent and effectiveness of participation, e.g. rules concerning speaking rights and recognition, seating arrangements, access to documentation, roles in preparatory processes and expert meetings, and so on.

Nongovernmental organizations and processes native to the Internet environment present different challenges. Some industry bodies that take important policy decisions operate on a pay to play basis, or simply do not allow participation by non-member entities, whether governments, individual entrepreneurs, technical community representatives, or civil society. For their part, the formally open multistakeholder processes may entail informal barriers to full participation. Some have rather conflictual organizational cultures in which one must prove oneself through a history of quality contributions in order to be taken seriously. Challenging peer-to-peer dialogues can present difficulties for people accustomed to enjoying a certain status and respect based on their positions and home organizations, or who have different cultural and linguistic backgrounds. Often, face-to-face meetings are simply moments in long-running and complex processes that have evolved in multiple online and offline settings. This can make it difficult for a "newbie" of any sort, and especially one from a different background, to just jump in and figure everything out. Moreover, meetings that are held around the world, often off main travel routes, in order to promote outreach in different regions may pose significant funding and logistical challenges for some stakeholders. And of course, inadequate multilingualism and translation facilities are a perennial problem in many Internet-native collaborations. Finally, even if all these informal barriers can be negotiated, developing country participants may well find that development considerations are simply not a part of the conversations being had and cannot be interjected easily.

It often is difficult for organizations and participants accustomed to one way of doing things to change their modus operandi in order to facilitate the meaningful engagement of new actors. This is especially so if they are not clear on how doing so would benefit the work they are doing. But change is not impossible. For example, in light of the multistakeholder dialogues on Internet governance in the WSIS and IGF, the OECD took the decision in 2008 to open its Internet-related work to the participation of the technical community and civil society, both of which have become seriously involved and are making significant contributions. In parallel, organizations like ICANN also have taken steps to broaden participation by actors from developing countries. There is clearly more to be done though, in both intergovernmental and nongovernmental settings.

A neutral, non-decision making, multistakeholder setting like the IGF could provide a good setting in which to consider these issues. The aggregation and sharing of information, experiences and best practices concerning whether and how developing countries participate and development considerations are addressed might encourage entities to undertake some internal self-assessment and to consider the viability of tweaking their procedures. For example, they might consider the terms and conditions of information dissemination and participation; ways to reduce newcomers' sense of information overload, and related intellectual barriers to entry, e.g. by preparing customized background materials; establishing development-oriented focal points in the staff, or sherpas or a buddy system for meetings; holding special sessions in their meeting programs focusing on development-related issues; enhancing remote participation opportunities; having solid mechanisms for evaluations and feedback from participants who are experiencing challenges; expanding formal outreach and capacity building efforts and inter-institutional partnerships; or even mainstreaming developmental implications as a factor in evaluating policy options, where applicable.

Policy Outputs

Finally, a third focus could be on the substantive policy outputs of global Internet governance mechanisms. It is not necessary for present purposes to attempt to map out in detail the specific issues associated with particular key institutions that would merit consideration; indeed, it would be premature to do so. Deciding which topics and possible connections to explore would necessarily be the subject of debate and collaboration among the interested parties in the IGF. That said, to make the possibility less abstract, it might be worth simply mentioning a few illustrative examples.

With regard to the governance of CIR, there are a number of issues that could merit assessment. For example, how do current policies and contracts pertaining to the gTLD registry, registrar, and related services markets affect individuals, organizations, and communities from developing countries, whether as users or as potential market entrants? How might the approaches currently being devised for new gTLDs---on such issues as pricing, vertical integration, geographic names, IDNs, and content-related issues like "morality and public order" objections to proposed strings---impact development trajectories? What about the authority relations and management of ccTLD delegation and re-delegation processes, the WHOIS framework, the Uniform Dispute Resolution System, or IPV4 exhaustion and the allocation of/transition to IPV6? And of course, there are the issues pertaining to ICANN's legal form, location, and relationship to the US government. These items generally have been discussed in political terms with respect to the internationalization of authority, but are there also any specific concerns from a developmental standpoint? Whatever the answer may be, it might be helpful to the global dialogue to clarify the matter.

Other infrastructural issues may be worth exploring. The question of international interconnection has come up in the WSIS and IGF discussions, but there has not been a focused and empirically informed discussion that drills down into the changing economic organization of global interconnection and traffic management. This has been taken up in some intergovernmental settings, but without the sort of broad-based participation that could yield balanced and widely supported assessments.

Some technical standardization processes may pose challenges beyond the sort of procedural difficulties in participation that were mentioned above. For example, intellectual property limitations are being built into the increasingly diverse array of network equipment, customer devices, services and applications associated with Internet access. Developing country entrepreneurs and firms may thus find themselves at a disadvantage when seeking market entry, and the costs to developing country users may inhibit the Internet's expansion and application in business and other domains.

The heterogeneous realm of network and information security governance could raise other concerns. Arrangements that globalize particular definitions of cybercrime or methods of addressing it, whether intergovernmental or self-regulatory, may pose challenges to local legal systems, capacities, and social orders. They may also be insufficiently attentive to developing country's greater levels of vulnerability and sensitivity to spam, malware, network attacks and the like. And the key roles played by nongovernmental actors may put developing countries at a disadvantage insofar as their stakeholders are often less well resourced and equipped to collaborate or negotiate with Northern counterparts.

With regard to the governance of IC&C, the establishment of increasingly strict rules and enforcement mechanisms for intellectual property may have numerous implications for development that merit consideration in a multistakeholder setting dedicated to the Internet. The same could be true with respect to trade in content-based services, e-commerce mechanisms that have been designed primarily by and for the industrialized countries, and so on. The developmental consequences of weak or minilateral global governance mechanisms pertaining to personal privacy, consumer protection, competition policy, spam, linguistic and cultural diversity, and so on might merit consideration as well.

Again, these are just a few examples of the kinds of items participants might decide to flesh out and consider. For effect, examples were mentioned where there might arguably be problems to be addressed. If the IGF process revealed that in at least some of these cases there is room for a better fit between governance outputs and development, this could help to stimulate and support problem-solving discussions within the relevant decision making bodies and among other concerned actors, such as development agencies or the research community. Alternatively, it might be that upon examination, it becomes clear that there is no "there there" and all the policies currently being pursued are entirely beneficial or neutral with respect to development. In this happy event, the focus going forward could be on learning lessons from these successes and identifying practices worth replicating. Moreover, working through to such conclusions could have the salutary effect of dispelling misunderstandings and contention around the issues in question so that collective energies can be directed to items where there is consensus that more work is needed, be it institutional procedures, capacity building, national governance frameworks, or something else. Either way, at least asking the questions and having an open, global, multistakeholder dialogue arguably would strengthen the social foundations of the Internet more effectively than declaring issues to be out of bounds and leaving sources of dissatisfaction or unease to fester and manifest in other ways.

For at least three reasons, such an effort would not be duplicative of work being undertaken elsewhere. First, the discussions on these issues in the relevant decision making bodies usually do not position developmental impacts as key criteria for evaluation. Second, many of the organizations involved do not have the sort of open, global, multistakeholder participation that characterizes the IGF, so the ways that problems and possible solutions are framed therein is correspondingly different and may ultimately elicit less broad-based support. Moreover, those bodies which do allow such participation may attract partially or wholly different set of actors. And third, as the only global collaborative process that is not limited by a specialized mandate, the IGF is uniquely positioned to facilitate holistic assessments that draw unconstrained linkages between issues, probe multidimensional problems, identify orphaned issues and gaps in the governance architecture, and make intelligible the whole terrain. Even if they are being managed in other organizations, setting issues in such a holistic framework for multistakeholder dialogue could broaden and deepen collective learning and provide value-added feedback into those bodies, as the IGF has already done.

Going Forward

The IGF is uniquely suited to provide an umbrella or setting for the activity suggested here. Its mandate in the Tunis Agenda specifically envisages cross-cutting dialogues and holistic assessments regarding global governance mechanisms and developing country concerns in these provisions:

> b) Facilitate discourse between bodies dealing with different cross-cutting international public policies regarding the Internet and discuss issues that do not fall within the scope of any existing body;
> c) Interface with appropriate inter-governmental organisations and other institutions on matters under their purview;
> d) Facilitate the exchange of information and best practices...
> f) Strengthen and enhance the engagement of stakeholders in existing and/or future Internet Governance mechanisms, particularly those from developing countries;
> g) identify emerging issues, bring them to the attention of the relevant bodies and the general public, and, where appropriate, make recommendations;
> h) Contribute to capacity-building for Internet Governance in developing countries, drawing fully on local sources of knowledge and expertise;
> i) Promote and assess, on an ongoing basis, the embodiment of WSIS principles in Internet Governance processes...[39]

But how could such an effort be put in place? It is not possible to spell out a complete and acceptable plan of action in the abstract. Any truly viable proposal would have to be the product of dialogue and collaboration among a range of interested parties who would be willing to undertake the efforts required. Nevertheless, to facilitate discussion we can at least sketch out a few possible elements:

---

[39] World Summit on the Information Society, "Tunis Agenda for the Information Society," WSIS-05/TUNIS/DOC/6(Rev.1)-E, November 15, p. 11, available at www.itu.int/wsis/docs2/tunis/off/6rev1.doc.

Institutionalize a Development Day as a regular feature of the IGF program. Devote one day of the four-day meetings to exploring development-related themes. The third day might be optimal, as the main session(s) on IG4D could then be informed by the prior SODA and CIR discussions and delve more deeply into their main implications for development. Perhaps one session could be on capacity building, procedural, and participation issues, while the other would be on the policy outputs of global governance arrangements. Alternatively, one of the three hour blocks could be devoted to something other than another large plenary dialogue; there are a number of interactive meeting formats to choose from in revisioning the allocated time, e.g. regional, stakeholder, or interest-based break-out meetings and report-backs on an agreed set of issues...

Designate a special track of workshops focused on IG4D. The Multistakeholder Advisory Group (MAG) and/or open planning meetings could indicate suggested topical foci that would feed into the main sessions, it being understood that strong proposals on these themes would enjoy special consideration, and that a representative of each event chosen would be invited to participate in a linked main session.

Encourage organizers of open forums, best practice forums, and dynamic coalitions to build in development components, as appropriate. The organizers and participants in these events could devote some portion of their time to explaining how they approach development concerns, and could provide short written materials on the same.

Establish a multistakeholder group to assess and share information on the issue-areas outlined above. It would be impossible to conduct serious analysis and have intensively focused debates solely within the existing framework of annual main sessions and workshops. This is true for other issue-areas as well; it could be desirable for the IGF to also serve as a convening unbrella framework under which communities of expertise and practice organize to work on selected issues in accordance with annual, renewable mandates. IG4D could serve as the test case for such a model.

Some innovative design would be necessary to get this right. On the one hand, the traditional UN working group format could be too bureaucratic, politicized, and wedded to formal outputs to be appropriate. On the other hand, the IGF's existing alternative, the dynamic coalitions, for a variety of reasons generally have enjoyed rather limited government participation and mixed success. A model would be needed that combines the strengths of the Working Group on Internet Governance (WGIG)---e.g. balanced multistakeholder participation and expertise, open peer-to-peer dialogue, consensus-based conclusions---with the flexibility and openness of a "birds of a feather" meeting.

Most of the group's work through the year could be conducted online. For internal communication it could use modern collaborative tools (social networks, Google Docs, etc) that were not available at time of the WGIG. In parallel, an open interface for document sharing and public engagement would be required. Points of consensus and well specified disagreement in the group's deliberations could be brought into the relevant main sessions for broader discussion. These could be in the form of "messages" from the group which do not require subsequent plenary-level adoption; this model has been employed effectively in the European Dialogue on Internet Governance.

Provide analytical and logistical support. Some of the early arguments made during the WSIS process for a new multistakeholder institution suggested that it should have both a cross-cutting, holistic mandate, and a staff with the resources and capacity to monitor developments across the Internet governance landscape, aggregate and present information in an accessible form, conduct research, prepare background materials for meetings, and so on.[40] While budgetary constraints impose significant limitations, a small, expert research staff would be essential for this and any other focused initiatives, and such in-house assets could be complemented by external collaborations. An open secretariat that enjoys good relations with the various stakeholder communities and nearby international organizations possessing specialized ICT policy expertise could presumably develop a web of supportive relationships and generate materials reflecting the full range of perspectives involved.

Provide high-level political endorsement of a development work program. If the decision is taken to continue the IGF beyond its initial mandate, the renewal could helpfully entail recognizing IG4D as a (not the) major focus of work that merits support. In this context, steps also could be taken to encourage greater participation by governments and other stakeholders from the developing world.

Conclusion

The approach outlined here is a still evolving concept that probably raises more questions than it answers. A broad dialogue involving all segments of the IGF community would be required to arrive at a formulation that could really work. But in the meanwhile, it is hoped that this paper contributes to thinking about the prospect of mainstreaming development considerations in the IGF and in global Internet governance processes.

---

[40] For example, the civil society declaration to the Geneva summit in December 2003 called for the establishment of a multi-stakeholder "observatory committee" that would track and map the most pressing developments in governance decision-making, and assess and solicit stakeholder input on their conformity with the stated objectives of the WSIS agenda. Similarly, the Internet Governance Caucus and some of its individual members variously argued for an IGF that would be able to undertake, inter alia, the systematic monitoring of trends; the comparative, cross-sectoral analysis of governance mechanisms, with an eye toward lessons learned and best practices that could inform individual and collective institutional improvements; and the assessment of horizontal issues applicable to all arrangements, e.g. the promotion of transparency and inclusive participation. Some of this thinking was carried forward into the WGIG Report and ultimately into the Tunis Agenda's mandate. For an example, see, William J. Drake, "Reframing Internet Governance Discourse: Fifteen Baseline Propositions," in, *Internet Governance: A Grand Collaboration*, Don MacLean, ed. (New York: United Nations Information and Communication Technology Taskforce, 2004). Performance of these functions would require some research and logistical capacity, and a stream of activity that goes beyond an annual meeting and the preparation thereof.

Multistakeholderism and the IGF:

Laboratory, Clearinghouse, Watchdog

Wolfgang Kleinwächter

The UN Secretary General's report on the IGF from May 2010 uses 57 times in eleven pages the words "multistakeholder", "stakeholders", or "government, private sector, civil society and technical community"---the main actors in Internet governance.[41] The repetition of the "multistakeholder" terminology is not a big surprise, but it is a remarkable indication that the controversial concept of "multistakholderism" that emerged in the World Summit on the Information Society (WSIS) is now a more or less accepted guiding principle of global Internet governance.

In general terms, multistakeholderism means the inclusion of a broad range of governmental and non-governmental stakeholders into the development and implementation of policies, in particular the parties who are directly affected by or concerned with a specific issue. The understanding of "multistakeholderism" in Internet governance was developing bottom up in a political process as an alternative to the conflicting proposals for "private sector leadership" or "governmental leadership" in the WSIS process. However, from a theoretical point of view, the multistakeholder Internet governance policy concept is not yet defined. So far there is only little academic analysis and a broad range of ad hoc opinions and weak theories about what multistakeholderism is or should be.

Nevertheless the concept is seen as an innovative mechanism for policy development and decision-making---first of all on the global level---that could eventually produce results which are not reachable anymore with the traditional political and diplomatic instruments of the 20th century. The complexity of today's global issues calls for a "new thinking" and a "new 21st century diplomacy" which goes beyond the traditional understanding of international relations as intergovernmental relations with the sovereign nation-state at the top of the decision making hierarchy. The Internet and borderless cyberspace---where now nearly two billion people around the world can interactively communicate anytime, anywhere on anything in text, voice, audio, photo or video regardless of frontiers---challenges the traditional understanding of national sovereignty over a geographical territory with fixed borders.

When the UN General Assembly launched the WSIS process by adopting UN resolution 56/183 in December 2001, the word "stakeholder" was not common language in the UN context. UN documents normally refer to

---

[1] "Continuation of the Internet Governance Forum: Note of the UN Secretary General", ECOSOC, May 2010, available at, http://unpan1.un.org/intradoc/groups/public/documents/un-dpadm/unpan039074.pdf.

"member states" or "governments" if they describe rights, duties and responsibilities of actors in a certain field. However, when the UN community discussed the feasibility of convening the WSIS, the UN member states acknowledged that the issues were so complex that it would make sense to extend the number of participants beyond national governments and to invite also the private sector, civil society and the technical community. Paragraph 3 of UN Resolution 56/183 recommended, "that the preparations for the Summit take place through an open-ended intergovernmental preparatory committee, which would define the agenda of the Summit, finalize both the draft declaration and the draft plan of action, and decide on the modalities of the participation of other stakeholders in the Summit".[42]

NGOs in the UN

The idea to include non-governmental actors into a policy development process under the UN umbrella within a World Summit produced a number of complicated procedural questions. The whole first preparatory meeting (PrepCom1) for WSIS I in Geneva, in June 2002, was occupied by the discussion what the role of the non-governmental stakeholders should and could be.[43] The problem was not totally new for the United Nations. The UN itself has a long tradition to collaborate with a broad range of non-governmental organizations (NGOs), mainly via the Economic and Social Council (ECOSOC).[44] Furthermore, the UN Educational, Scientific and Cultural Organization (UNESCO), one of the key partners in the WSIS process, had a long tradition to work together with non-governmental organizations in related fields like education, media, communication, culture and science.[45] And the International Telecommunication Union (ITU), another leading partner in the WSIS process, changed its constitution at its Plenipotentiary Conference in Kyoto in 1994 to allow private sector members (mainly telecom operators and IT manufacturers) to join the organization.[46]

But neither in ECOSOC nor in UNESCO or in the ITU do non-governmental actors have negotiating or voting rights. The role of NGOs or private sector members is mainly to give input into a policy development process that is

---

[2] UN Resolution 56/183, December, 21, 2001, available at, www.itu.int/wsis/docs/background/resolutions/56_183_unga_2002.pdf.

[3] See, Wolfgang Kleinwächter, "Multistakeholderism, Civil Society and Global Diplomacy: The Case of the World Summit on the Information Society," in, *Governing Global Electronic Networks: International Perspectives on Policy and Power*, William J. Drake and Ernest J. Wilson III, eds. (Cambridge, MA: MIT Press, 2008).

[4] Currently more than 3200 NGOs have a so-called "consultative status" with ECOSOC. http://esango.un.org/paperless/Web?page=static&content=about.

[5] UNESCO has official relations with 335 NGOs; see, "UNESCO and NGOs," resources available at http://portal.unesco.org/en/ev.php-URL_ID=32906&URL_DO=DO_TOPIC&URL_SECTION=201.html.

[6] The ITU has 565 private sector members and 153 "Associates." See the list available at, http://www.itu.int/members/index.html.

managed and led by the governments of the member states. They are the lower (and powerless) part of a hierarchy, with the governments on top.

From Hierarchies to Networks

The WSIS process started with this traditional system of subordination. But as soon as the Internet became the subject of the negotiations, the "hierarchical approach" was challenged. The developers, providers and users of Internet services---the private sector, civil society and the academic and technical community---proposed an alternative policy development process which was based on a more "network approach".

In the first preparatory phase (July 2002 until December 2003) when WSIS discussed media and telecommunication policies, there was just "summit business as usual". NGOs like the Word Press Freedom Committee (WPFC), the International Association of Publishers, the International Federation of Journalists (IFJ), the International Association for Media and Communication Research (IAMCR) and others wanted to have a say on issues like the human right of freedom expression. Private sector companies, coordinated by the International Chamber of Commerce (ICC), wanted to have a say in policies like financing the bridging of the digital divide. This was not so different from discussions during UNESCO General Conferences and ITU Plenipotentiary Conferences, where NGOs and private sector members are lobbying governments and have a chance to say something in the beginning of plenary sessions, but do not have voting rights in the final negotiations which take place in governmental working groups.

This changed when Internet governance was introduced into WSIS. It started at the end of PrepCom2 (February 2003) and peaked for the first time during the Inter-Sessional meeting in Paris (July 2003). Originally Internet governance was not on the list of pressing issues under the WSIS mandate. WSIS was primarily aimed at the development of policies and actions to bridge the digital divide. In the regional preparatory conferences in Asia, Europe, Africa and Latin America, Internet governance was just a minor point. Only the last of the series of five Ministerial Conferences---for West-Asia in Beirut in early February 2003---raised the issue of Internet governance in more detail and "woke the dog".[47] When the WSIS stakeholders reconvened for PrepCom2 in February 2003 in Geneva, "Internet governance" moved quickly into the centre of the political debate. As a result governments decided to set up a special sub-working group to deal with it.

---

[7] The report of the West Asian Regional Conference for WSIS ("Beirut Declaration"), February, 5, 2003, stated, inter alia: "The responsibility for root directories and domain names should rest with a suitable international organization and should take multilingualism into consideration. Countries' top-level-domain-names and Internet Protocol (IP) address assignment should be the sovereign right of countries. The sovereignty of each nation should be protected and respected. Internet governance should be multilateral, democratic and transparent and should take into account the needs of the public and private sectors as well as those of the civil society." See, www.itu.int/wsis/documents/listing-all.asp?lang=en&c_event=rc l wa&c_type=all.

Governmental vs. Private Sector Leadership

The sub-working group started during the Inter-Sessional PrepCom in July 2003 in Paris and was immediately confronted also with procedural questions. During the first meeting of the group that took place in form of a night session in the basement of UNESCOs headquarter in Paris, nobody controlled who was in the room. As a result, the discussion started as a multistakeholder dialogue. Governments raised public policy issues related to the Internet and experts from the private sector, civil society and the technical community added their special expertise with regard to the technical, economic and social dimensions of Internet governance.

Although some governments questioned whether the presence of non-governmental stakeholders in the room would be in line with the procedural rules of the summit, the dynamics of the discussion sidelined quickly these objections. The majority of the governments realized that they do miss the specific technical expertise which is needed to understand how the Internet works and how the critical Internet resources are managed and coordinated. This additional expertise and input was seen as a very welcomed and a needed contribution for an enhanced understanding of the Internet challenges. But later, the experts were excluded, and even the CEO of ICANN was kicked out of the room during PrepCom3++ (December 2003) when the final negotiations started.

The Internet is indeed different from media or telecommunication, where UNESCO and ITU member states have long experience. While media and telecommunication was developed first in the national context and within a national legal framework, the Internet emerged in the 1970s and 1980s from the very beginning as a global borderless network of networks in the shadow of national and international regulation. The Internet was never a "law free zone" but no country adopted specific laws for the Internet similar to the traditional press, broadcasting or telecommunication laws.

Even the delegation of country code Top Level Domains (ccTLDs) became not the subject of national policy discussions or intergovernmental negotiations, as was the case with country codes for the telephone system. The domain name system (DNS) followed a procedure based on policies developed by the developers, providers and users of the Internet services themselves and fixed in so-called "Request for Comments" (RFCs), drafted and adopted by the Internet Engineering Task Force (IETF). No national government and no national parliament was involved when Jon Postel, one of the fathers of the global DNS, introduced the 243 ccTLDs and started to delegate it, very often by a handshake, to trusted managers in the respective countries.

The private sector policies for the management of root servers and the allocation for domain names and IP addresses proved to be stable, secure and robust long before WSIS started to discover these issues as relevant for global public policy making. But after the Paris Inter-Sessional meeting, a political debate started about the introducing a new political mechanism overseen by governments. The debate escalated soon around the question whether the management of these critical Internet resources (CIRs) should remain in the hands of the private sector, notably within ICANN, IETF and the RIRs, or should be moved to an intergovernmental mechanism, probably the ITU.

While the US government was clearly outspoken in favour of a continuation with the functioning system under private sector leadership, the Chinese government argued that private sector leadership was good for one million Internet users but probably not good enough for one billion. The majority of the non-governmental groups were more in favour of a continuation of the existing mechanisms. Vint Cerf, one of the fathers of the Internet and during this time Chair of the ICANN Board captured the thinking when he said that in considering changes, the first thing is "to do no harm". And he added, "If it isn't broken, don't fix it". Furthermore there was confusion about what Internet governance means. While some understood it as the management of CIRs only, others had a much broader understanding and subsumed under the term shared Internet global rule systems for e-commerce cybercrime, the protection of privacy, intellectual property and so on.

WSIS I and the Creation of WGIG

WSIS I did not produce any common position on Internet governance. The only agreement which was reached was to postpone a final decision and to ask UN Secretary General Kofi Annan to set up a Working Group on Internet Governance (WGIG) with a mandate to define what Internet governance is; to identify public policy issues which come along with Internet governance; and to recommend to governments what to do before the convening of the second summit, scheduled for Tunis, November 2005. However, the "agreement on the disagreement" included two important elements that had long-term effects. Article 49 of the WSIS Geneva Declaration of Principles, which established the WGIG, stated, inter alia: "The management of the Internet encompasses both technical and public policy issues and should involve all stakeholders and relevant intergovernmental and international organizations."[48]

Article 49 implies two main conclusions: First, it is impossible to separate the technical from the political issues with regard to Internet governance, which means that organizations dealing with the various aspects of Internet governance and touching either political or technical issues have to work together and enhance their communication, coordination and collaboration. And second, to be workable, stable and robust solutions there is a need to involve all relevant governmental and non-governmental stakeholders, operating on the various layers of the Internet.

In other words, Article 49, without anticipating a special model for Internet Governance, proposed a multistakeholder framework. Consequently, when Kofi Annan established the WGIG, he did it not in the traditional way by inviting governments as members and non-governmental experts as observers, but rather followed the WSIS recommendation and composed the

---

[8] Geneva Declaration of Principles, December, 12, 2003, available at, www.itu.int/dms_pub/itu-s/md/03/wsis/doc/S03-WSIS-DOC-0004!!PDF-E.pdf.

"Group of 40" by choosing 20 governmental and 20 non-governmental representatives as WGIG members, with equal rights.

At the eve of the first WGIG meeting, Kofi Annan outlined his expectation for the outcome of WGIG during the Global Governance Forum in New York (March 2004):

> "The issues are numerous and complex. Even the definition of what we mean by Internet governance is a subject of debate. But the world has a common interest in ensuring the security and the dependability of this new medium. Equally important, we need to develop inclusive and participatory models of governance. The medium must be made accessible and responsive to the needs of all the world's people...in managing, promoting and protecting [the internet's] presence in our lives, we need to be no less creative than those who invented it. Clearly, there is a need for governance, but that does not necessarily mean that it has to be done in the traditional way, for something that is so very different."[49]

This multistakeholder nature of the WGIG---based on flexible rules of procedure which gave all members of the group the same rights in speaking and drafting---produced indeed a new culture of interaction. The debate became less an ideological battle how to succeed with the own position and more a collective search to find common answers to new emerging global challenges. It was bottom-up and not top-down, it was not "tit-for-tat" but rather looking for a rough consensus.[50]

The collaborative multistakeholder spirit allowed the production of concrete results. Of particular importance was the carefully formulated definition of Internet governance: "Internet governance is the development and application by Governments, the private sector and civil society, in their respective roles, of shared principles, norms, rules, decision-making procedures, and programmes that shape the evolution and use of the Internet."[51] This definition rejects the concept of one stakeholder leadership in Internet governance as some governments suggested during WSIS I. Instead, the WGIG definition proposes an inclusive and participatory concept which gives all stakeholders a place by referring to their "respective roles". It links them together in a network of shared rights, duties and responsibilities. This definition allows a high degree of flexibility in its implementation and rejects the concept of "one Internet governance model fits all Internet governance challenges". It allows a rather dynamic use of different governance models

---

[9] Kofi Annan, "Internet Governance Issues are Numerous and Complex", New York, 25 March 2004, at www.unicttaskforce.org/perl/showdoc.pl?id=1333.

[10] For discussions, see, Don MacLean, "A Brief History of WGIG," and William J. Drake, "Conclusion: Why the WGIG Process Mattered", in, *Reforming Internet Governance: Perspectives from the UN Working Group on Internet Governance*, William J. Drake, ed. (New York: United Nations Information and Communication Technologies Taskforce, 2005).

[11] "Report of the Working Group on Internet Governance", Geneva, July 2005, at, www.wgig.org/docs/WGIGREPORT.pdf.

for different Internet governance issues. Based on this definition, the governance model in the fight against cybercrime can look different than the governance model for the allocation of domain names.

WGIG: Forum Function and Oversight Function

In the final stage of the WGIG, two other issues moved into the centre of the debate: the "forum function" and the "oversight function". Both issues were linked to the question how stakeholders should be involved into global policy development (forum function) and decision-making (oversight function). Naturally WGIG members from the governments prioritized the "oversight function". In contrast, WGIG members from the private sector rejected the introduction of a new governmental oversight body but were also indifferent with regard to the creation of a "forum", which some of them disqualified as a new costly "talking shop". But the WGIG members from the civil society and the academic and technical community gave the "forum function" the highest priority.

The argument of the civil society in favour of a Forum was that the creation of a discussion space for multistakeholder dialogue could be a useful next step in a bottom up global policy development process towards new "inclusive and participatory models of governance", as was called for by Kofi Annan. Such a forum could improve the knowledge of all stakeholders and enhance the interaction among them with the aim to create a climate of better understanding of the many new emerging issues. This would enable the existing intergovernmental and nongovernmental institutions to take decisions of a higher quality within the frameworks of their respective mandates.[52]

The discussion of the "forum function" within the WGIG produced a rough consensus but the "oversight function" remained controversial, not only between governmental and non-governmental stakeholders but also among the governments themselves. One group wanted to have a heavy "UN Internet Organization (UNINO), another group was more in favour of a lightweight "Intergovernmental Internet Council" overseeing the existing private Internet governance mechanisms. And others argued in favour of the existing ICANN model where governments are included as a stakeholder in

---

[12] The idea to create such a discussion space originally in the form of a "Multistakeholder Observatory Council" was proposed for the first time in a statement of the Civil Society Internet Governance Caucus (IGC) at the WSIS Inter-Sessional Meeting in Paris, July, 16, 2003. Such a council, "could serve as a meeting point for improved coordination, consultation and communication on ICT issues. Such a "Council" should be composed of representatives of governments, private industry and civil society. It could promote the exchange of information, experiences and best practices on issues from privacy to free speech on the Internet, from Ipv6 to ENUM. Listening to the experiences of others is a cheap investment and could become a source of inspiration for innovative policy in the 21st Century. See: www.itu.int/wsis/docs/pcip/plenary/internet_governance_group.pdf.

its own rights via the Governmental Advisory Committee (GAC) but called for an end of the unilateral oversight of the US government over ICANN.

WSIS II and the Launch of the IGF

The WGIG Report became the blueprint for the final negotiations in the second Summit. WSIS II, held in November 2005, adopted in its "Tunis Agenda for the Information Society" the WGIG's definition and the recommendation for a new IGF but could not agree on a new oversight model. The compromise in the "oversight controversy" was to launch an open process of "enhanced cooperation" among governments and also among governments and non-governmental institutions with the option to develop and introduce at a later stage a "new cooperation model", as proposed by the European Union.

The IGF and the process of enhanced cooperation are not formally interlinked. The Tunis Agenda gave the IGF a rather clear mandate but a life span for only five years, with the option for renewal. The process of enhanced cooperation was vague defined and did not include a timetable. The interpretation of "enhanced cooperation" differed widely and reached from an understanding, that at the end of the process there will be a new centralized intergovernmental body to the expectation that such a process will enhance the communication, coordination and collaboration among existing governmental and non-governmental institutions and lead to a more decentralized multilayer multiplayer mechanism with distributed decisions making and oversight procedures.

However based on the accepted definition of Internet governance, there was a clear understanding that both the IGF and the process of enhanced cooperation have to include all stakeholders in "their respective roles". It was also a more or less common understanding that both processes, regardless of their separate mandates, are informally interlinked. Nevertheless the open question remained what in detail the "respective role" of the main stakeholder groups could and should be with regard both to the forum and the oversight function.

IGF: Kick Start in Athens 2006

Before the first IGF there was a lot of uncertainty. Will the IGF become a useless "talking shop", just "another annual Internet conference"? Will it lead to a new intergovernmental body? There was no model of how to organize such a forum which was convened by the UN Secretary General but was not a traditional UN conference and included all stakeholders. Also how to prepare the forum was not clear, although the Tunis mandate of the IGF was a helpful guideline. The Internet community indeed entered unchartered territory. Key milestones before the start of the first IGF in Athens were the establishment of a small and light weight executive secretariat in Geneva, the formation of a Multistakeholder Advisory Group" (MAG) and the nomination of its Chair. This Secretariat/MAG/Chair model copied the successful WGIG structure. Also the procedures for the MAG and its interactions with the broader public was copied from the WGIG. This removed a lot of traditional formalities of UN conferences and allowed flexible and open communication among the stakeholders.

A significant indication of this new approach was the simple fact that during the first IGF in Athens in October 2006, there were no nameplates on the tables in the main conference hall for governments or observers, as it is normally the case in a UN conference. This small element of removing formal barriers demonstrated the differences. The IGF positioned itself from the very first day as a space for a more informal multistakeholder dialogue and not as diplomatic negotiation place.

But more important than the formalities was the substance. To get started, the MAG preferred to begin with important but less controversial issues like Access, Openness, Security and Diversity. As the following IGFs proved, it was a wise decision not to start with the most controversial issue like the management of CIRs. This allowed the Athens IGF to put a more constructive multistakeholder dialogue into the centre of the debate while not by ignoring conflicts, but by avoiding a heated ideological debate.

Athens was not without controversies. But the way, for instance, the controversies around freedom of expression in the Internet in the Openness main session was discussed, where governments, private sector and civil society representatives expressed rather different ideas, was very encouraging and demonstrated that even very controversial positions, policies and practices can become the subject of a civilized debate if the stakeholders respect each other in their respective roles.[53]

To demonstrate and accept such a respect was easier in the environment of the IGF than it is in a diplomatic conference, which is aimed to adopt recommendations with commitments. With other words, the absence of the pressure at the end of the meeting to agree on a disagreement "opened the mouth" and allowed the development of a new open discussion culture. The "listening to the argument of others" became as important as the presentation of the own position.

A New Discussion Culture

This new discussion culture allowed the MAG in the preparation of the 2nd IGF to broaden its approach and to accept, among others, the proposal to add CIR as a fifth key issue to the IGF agenda. At the Rio IGF, CIR was discussed as openly as was the controversy over freedom of expression in Athens. The various stakeholders had a chance to hear something critical from other groups that they normally do not meet in their day-to-day operations. And they had a chance to justify their policies and to learn about their weaknesses and deficiencies without being "punished" at the end of a meeting by a "Declaration".

---

[13] See, *Internet Governance Forum (IGF): The First Two Years*, Avri Doria and Wolfgang Kleinwächter, eds. (Paris/Geneva: ITU/UNESCO, 2008), p. 124.

Step by step the acceptance of the multistakeholder dialogue grew. The fact that the key decision makers from the various stakeholder groups---from ITU, UNESCO, ICANN and IETF to Google, Yahoo, Cisco, Skype and Microsoft, from Parliamentarians and governmental representatives, including Prime Ministers and ministers from the world leading Internet countries like the US, EU, China, Egypt, Brazil, India and others to NGOs like APC, ISOC, Article 19 and the Free Software Foundation---left their "silos", came to the IGF meeting, entered into the dialogue with friends and opponents from other parts of the world and other stakeholder groups and came back to the next meeting, produced soon a value on its own which was quickly recognized by the majority of the participants.

The informal nature of the IGF is a great benefit which allows also experiments with new forms of discussion and an unorthodox approach to critical and controversial issues, as mentioned above with regard to CIR. And it allows a permanent critical re-evaluation and permanent change and improvement. A good example is how ICANN changed its position with regard to the IGF. In the beginning ICANN was rather sceptical and feared that a discussion of CIR in the IGF could lead to an un-needed politization of the management of technical key resources and to the development of a governmental controlled oversight mechanism. But the practical experiences spoke a different language. Yes, ICANN´s policies on root server management, iDNs or new gTLDs were critically reviewed in IGF workshops and main sessions. But the critical dialogue turned into constructive debates where all sides enhanced their knowledge, learned from the arguments of "the other side", and got a chance to adjust their own approaches in the light of open and frank discussions. ICANN understood quickly that the IGF is a useful space to do both outreach and to learn. And for those parts of the Internet community that do not go to ICANN meetings, it became a good opportunity to get additional information and to test the willingness of ICANN to react to justified criticism by the broader Internet community.

There is no formal linkage between the IGF discussions and ICANN decisions. But the policies ICANN has developed in the last years with regard to IDNs, DNSSEC, and new gTLDs would have been probably taken in a different way without the IGF debates. Also governments learned via the IGF that it makes no sense to reduce the CIR debate to the question of whether a new intergovernmental body is needed or not. And even the decision by the US government, to end its Joint Project Agreement (JPA) and to enter into an Affirmation of Commitments was probably also influenced by the IGF.

Regional and National IGFs

Another remarkable effect of the global IGF is that the model is being copied both at the regional and national level. Regional IGFs are now organized on an annual basis in East and West Africa, in North America, in Latin America, in Asian and in Europe. National IGFs are taken place now in more than 30 countries, including Russia, Germany, Brazil, Hong Kong, France, Denmark and the UK. All these regional and national IGFs copy more or less the multistakeholder dialogue model from the global IGF by linking it to the specific challenges in their regions or countries. These regional and national

IGFs have a double function: They are used to transfer the knowledge and experiences from the global IGF into the regional and national context. And they prepare the national and regional Internet community for the participation in the next global IGF. The interesting observation here is that the majority of these regional and national IGFs emerged bottom as a multistakeholder project.

A good example is the case of the IGF from Germany. After the first IGF in Athens there was a debate about a German IGF. For formalistic reasons the Ministry of Economics of the German federal government took the lead but what it organized was not really a multistakeholder dialogue, but more a classical bilateral consultation with private sector and civil society. This created some frustration among the local Internet Community in Germany. Groups like the German Trade Union ver.di, ISOC Germany, the German Association for the Internet Economy (eco), the German ccTLD Registry DENIC, ICANN recognized At Large Structures and the German Association of the United Nations took the idea of an IGF-Germany in their own hands and stimulated a real multistakeholder dialogue. This concept was rather successful. During the recent IGF-Germany in June 2010, the dialogue between governmental and non-governmental stakeholders reached a new level. Three ministers from the federal and the regional government and five members of the German Parliament, the Bundestag, participated in the meeting with more than 100 participants and prepared the German Internet community for the fifth IGF in Vilnius. The top-down approach turned into a network approach and the public authorities were pulled into an innovative process which worked both ways: Improved understanding and more knowledge on all sides.

A similar example is the emergence of the "European Dialogue on Internet Governance" (EURODIG), which has been held in Strasbourg 2008, Geneva in 2009, and Madrid in 2010. Originally the European Parliament wanted to organize an IGF-Europe. But it was too slow and too bureaucratic. The dynamics of the process, again driven by a small multistakeholder core team which included inter alia, the Council of Europe, the European Broadcasting Union, the European Regional At Large Organization, various European ISOC Chapters, EURO-ISPA, the ICC, and representatives of the government of France, Finland and Switzerland pushed for an EURODIG and succeeded. The 3rd EURODIG in April 2010 in Madrid saw more than 400 participants from all stakeholder groups. The meeting was hosted by Telefonica under the Spanish EU Presidency. The 4th EURIDIG will take place in June 2011 in Beograd in Serbia.

Civil Society as a New Stakeholder in Intergovernmental Organizations

It is also interesting to note that the multistakeholder model has been seen as an attractive new approach for policy development by other intergovernmental organizations. The Organization for Economic Development (OECD) adopted at its Ministerial Conference in Seoul in July 2008 a resolution that paved the way for the creation of a special civil society advisory group within the OECD (CISSAC). The CISSAC has now like other sub-bodies of the OECD, representing business, trade unions and the technical community, a number of rights and responsibilities, which include also the right to comment on governmental drafts.

Also the ITU was originally inspired by the IGF. At its Plenipotentiary Conference in Antalya in 2006, just after the end of the first IGF, it formed a special working group to explore how civil society could be included into the work of the ITU. The problem here was that the ITU invited only member states to join the working group. Consequently this governmental committee did not recommend the inclusion of civil society into the policy architecture of the ITU. When ITU Secretary General Hamadoun Touré addressed the ICANN meeting in Cairo in October 2008, he argued that the IGF is a "waste of time". Nevertheless he came both to Hyderabad and Sharm el Sheikh, although this did not change the ITU's approach to multistakeholderism. When the ITU organized its 4th World Telecommunication Policy Forum (WTPF) in Lisbon in April 2009, individual representatives of the civil society got only an exceptional permission to participate in the forum as silent onlookers and had no right to speak.

The IGF: Strengths, Weaknesses, Opportunities, Threats (SWOT)

With all the achievements and failures, the IGF is still in its childhood years. The parents see already the "talent" of the baby, but it is needs to learn a lot until it is mature enough to take its place in the broader system of international politics. During the consultations on the feasibility of the continuation of the IGF a lot of arguments were put forward pointing to the strengths and weaknesses of the IGF and discussing the opportunities and threads.

The most important strength of the IGF is obviously that it offers a space for high-level open, free and unlimited discussion in an informal way among various stakeholders on all relevant issue. There is no other place in the world where actual and emerging issues around Internet polices can be discussed as in the IGF. Other global gatherings of Internet experts have a much more limited scope and do not outreach to such a broad and high quality group of people representing constituencies that normally sit in their individual institutional silos to manage their respective day to day operation. It is the cross-institutional, cross–disciplinary, cross-constituency nature of the IGF and the high level of its participants that makes it attractive to everybody. Furthermore it has a great teaching, educational and capacity building dimension. People come to learn, exchange best practice experiences and enrich their knowledge, which enables them to qualify and improve their activities at home when working for policy development, economic initiatives and technological innovations. The "network building capacity" of the IGF, the individual and institutional contacts enabled through the IGF are also a very important part of the process.

The lack of a clear output from the meetings is seen on the other hand as one of the IGF weaknesses. At the end of the annual IGF results from the forum cannot be presented in facts and figures. There are no final recommendations, no agreement among governments, no concrete commitments from stakeholders. However this weakness is seen by a large part of the community as a strength. The argument is that the absence of the pressure to agree on something at the end of the meeting has liberated the debate and has to be seen as an enabler for processes that emerge very often indirectly as the result of the IGF in other places. It is true that the IGF makes no decisions, but it attracts those who do make decisions and equips them with better knowledge to do so. Another weakness, mentioned by many groups is the informal mechanisms for the preparation of the annual meetings, including the procedures for the composition of the MAG, the financial support for the Executive Secretariat and its weak and voluntary reporting back mechanisms.

One of the biggest opportunities of the IGF is to stimulate informal and formal arrangements for sustainable Internet governance solutions, to function as a laboratory, a clearinghouse and a watchdog. The IGP has the "power of inspiration". If sustainable results in Internet governance become more visible and it can be proven that the multistakeholder dialogue of the IGF has contributed to certain achievements, the IGF will be more seen much more also as a source of inspiration for other fields of global policies as climate change, environment, energy and the Millennium Development Goals.

One threat for the IGF is that the five year old baby is killed in the cradle. Governmental or non-governmental groups who had too high expectation what the IGF should deliver could turn their dissatisfaction into opposition campaigns and a policy blockade. Another risk is that the IGF is captured by groups of stakeholders and misused to push for single political or economic interests. Furthermore there is a risk that the needed enhancement of the formal procedures can lead to a bureaucratization that could fire back and remove the dynamics of the processes.

Summarizing the SWOT analyses, it can be said that the IGF cannot be replace by another meeting or an intergovernmental process because it is unique. The IGF does not and is not intended to substitute other meetings or processes where Internet issues are discussed. Within five years the IGF has positioned itself as a corner stone and an indispensable link within the architecture of interlinked Internet events and processes.

Towards a More Inclusive and Participatory Model of Governance

The IGF is a learning process. A lot of improvements can be achieved. Proposals how to overcome weaknesses of the IGF could include, inter alia:

First, the introduction of innovative forms of visible output results which avoids the need to enter into negotiation processes on diplomatic language for adoption by the IGF participants but which goes beyond today's chairs conclusion, the publication of the proceedings in an UN book and the archiving of the transcripts, audio and video streams. One option, which is used for instance in some national and regional IGFs, is the sending out "Messages". These would be to "Whom it concerned"; they would not represent a negotiated and agreed text, but rather reflect two or three key points from the discussion in a workshop. Such "short messages" (could be labelled and numbered as "IGF SMS") could be formulated by an appointed neutral rapporteur after each workshop. There would be no need to have a "drafting committee" because the messages from the main sessions and workshop would be generated bottom up just by compiling the feedback from the various meeting rooms, probably coordinated by the Executive Secretariat which could appoint, in agreement with the MAG, a "Special IGF SMS Coordinator". An IGF short message would have no legal status as an UN recommendation has, but would be a "source of inspiration" where the "binding power" comes from the strengths of the idea and the quality of the argument.

Second, the composition of the MAG could be improved by introducing a new system for nomination. A 50 member MAG could include 20 governmental representatives and 10 each from private sector, civil society and the technical and academic community. While governments would nominate their own candidates, the candidates from the non-governmental stakeholder groups could be selected by a neutral Nomination Committee (NomCom). To populate leading bodies via a NomCom is in the Internet world a common and successful practice. ICANN's NomCom selects half of the ICANN Board Members. ISOC and IETF have their own NomComs to select directors. To combine the NomCom procedure with a governmental selection process would strengthen the legitimacy of the MAG and enrich the concept of multistakeholderism by further formalizing procedures.

Third, the UN and the IGF stakeholders could encourage more conceptual work with the aim to get more clarification about the potential, the opportunities and risks of the multistakeholder model in the development of Internet governance policies. The concept, as it was underlined above, is still vague defined and partly misunderstood. The IGF could, inter alia, start a publication series on related issues. It could commission a study on multistakeholderism and Internet governance in cooperation with the "Global Internet Governance Academic Network" (GIGANET), which emerged itself as the result of a discussion among WGIG members from the academic community in 2006 and has now an annual academic symposium on the eve of each IGF. Another option would be to launch a commission with the mandate to explore the multistakeholder model for further Internet governance arrangements, as the UN has done with regard to the role of NGOs and civil society in the UN policy process in 2004 via the "Cardozo Commission".

It seems that the multistakeholder concept is in particular useful on the global level where no single authority has a central decision making capacity and where the existing intergovernmental mechanisms have reached the limit of their capacity to find quick, flexible and sustainable solutions to new emerging issues of a global nature. However the multistakeholder policy mechanism is not a substitute for the traditional intergovernmental system of international relations, but adds a new layer to global policy making and is aimed to improve the quality of decisions which has to be made by authorized institutions.

If it comes to this decision-making, the question of legitimacy moves into the centre of the debate. Democratic elections on a national level are seen as a primary source of legitimacy in the present system of international relations.

However there are also other sources of legitimacy rooted in recognized knowledge and expertise, market acceptance or grass root foundation. It is correct that intergovernmental organizations like UNESCO and ITU get their legitimacy from its member states and their (elected) governments. But also non-governmental organizations like ICANN or IETF have their own legitimacy to take decisions. Here the legitimacy comes from the constituencies they represent which have the recognized knowledge and expertise, the market acceptance or the grass root linkage. And as interest conflicts among legitimate governments within intergovernmental organizations are a rather natural thing, so are conflicts also among governments and non-governmental global groups who have a legitimacy to act on behalf of their constituencies. This should not be seen as a barrier for reaching solutions but needs probably enhanced negotiation procedures. In a more philosophical sense, conflicts are always driving forces for development as long as they are worked out on the basis of well-recognized principles.[54]

Conclusion

The IGF offers such an ideal meeting point for various groups with different interests to come together and to figure out how their conflicts can be settled and turned into processes that lead to sustainable solutions of Internet problems of a common nature. This brings indirectly six additional functions to the IGF which are not yet described so clearly in its mandate but could play a greater role in the mid-term perspective: The observatory function, the school function the laboratory function, the clearinghouse function, the scout function and the watchdog function.

With regard to the observatory function, the IGF is an ideal place to "observe" the broad range of Internet developments, globally and locally. It could be the place where all information about new Internet applications and problems, national and international Internet policies and other Internet related facts and figures can be collected and made available to the broader Internet community.

With regard to the school function the IGF is a space where people can come to learn and to get all the knowledge they need to understand Internet governance. It is like a "global school" where participants learn from each other and can listen to high-level experts. It is interesting to note that the GIGANET has decided to have its annual symposium always at the eve of the IGF. And also the emerging Schools of Internet Governance, which will soon have four branches in Europe, Africa, South America and Asia, are linked closely to the IGF.

With regard to the laboratory function the IGF is a unique place to test and figure out what works and what not in Internet governance. The workshops create platforms where good and bad examples can be discussed, and where stakeholders can learn from each other and get the needed inspiration to translate the global experiences into national and local policies.

---

[54] It is worth noting that in the Articles of Incorporation of ICANN from October 1998 there is a clear reference to international law. See, www.icann.org.

With regard to the clearinghouse function, the dialogue among various governmental and non-governmental organizations and institutions can clear the air with regard who has to do what. It could lead to a more enhanced and developed division of labour where institution can spin a web of interactions, which also can be formalized in informal MoUs, Statement of Intent or Affirmation of Commitments to avoid heavy legal negotiations which need formal judicial processes like the ratification of conventions by national parliaments.

With regard to the scout function the IGF is a great place to look into latest Internet developments and to find out what may be the next issues. It is a place where the future can be explored, and it can be also an early warning system that helps to identify emerging problems social, political or economic problems.

The watchdog function works because stakeholders have an opportunity to raise their critical points. If a government or an Internet user has concerns about ICANN, IETF, ITU or UNESCO, or with policies executed by national governments and global Internet companies, the IGF is a good place to raise the issue and to enter into a dialogue to get the point recognized.

Whether the IGF can be turned into such an observatory, a school, a laboratory, a clearinghouse, a scout or a watchdog remains to be seen. But the chances are good that in five years from now, when the IGF becomes a "teenager", it will have not only found its place in the global diplomacy architecture of the 21st century, but that it has also a growing number of followers from other areas of global policy who try to benefit from the experiences the IGF has produced in its pioneering work.

Towards an Internet Governance Network:

Why the Format of the IGF is One of its Major Outcomes

Bertrand de La Chapelle

Since its first annual event in 2006 in Athens, the Internet Governance Forum (IGF) has generated its share of interrogations from people more familiar with traditional inter-governmental negotiations who are sometimes baffled by its working methods. "The IGF? What outcomes does it produce in the end? Does it have any concrete impact on the development of international public policy? Is this more than a glorified talking shop?"

The IGF may lack glamour in our media-driven era: no ambitious-sounding final declaration to bring back to capitals as testimony of days of hard drafting work; no major photo-op of world leaders shaking hands in front of lavish banners. Still, out of the spotlight and in its own quiet way, the IGF is triggering a deep transformation in the way global policy issues are addressed in our interconnected world.

What if the main outcome of the IGF was the way it functions? And its main contribution the growing trust and understanding fostered among its diverse participants, their mutual acceptance of their respective value(s)? What if it was, at its own pace, building the foundations of a method, a multi-stakeholder interaction protocol allowing governments, civil society and the business sector to collaboratively design globally applicable public policy principles? If this is the case, the main result of the IGF is actually its format and it is worth taking the necessary time to continuously improve it.

In developing its working methods, the IGF has been like a boat sailing out of the harbour, avoiding dangerous reefs on both sides: either too much formality or too much informality. Maintaining a delicate balance between competing objectives of flexibility and efficiency was the recipe adopted so far. It must remain a key feature in the future evolution of the IGF.

This chapter has two objectives. First, it is a modest attempt to memorialize the lessons of the first five years of this innovative experiment: how, under the legitimizing convening power of the United Nations Secretary General, the principles of open participation and self-organization produced an innovative format whose key characteristics deserve to be preserved in the future. Second, looking forward, we'll try to identify the major issues that the IGF must address if, as expected and hoped, its mandate is extended for another period of five years: in terms of organizational improvements, of more tangible outcomes and last but not least, of its contribution to the emergence of an Internet Governance Network.

The First Five Years (2006-2010): the Birth of an Innovative Format

The creation of the IGF was a last minute compromise during the Tunis phase of the World Summit on the Information Society (WSIS), an exit route to avoid the contentious issue of Internet governance blocking a final agreement. The idea had been largely shaped by the Working Group on Internet Governance (WGIG) established by the first phase of the Summit, and the UN Secretary General was requested to be the convener of this "new forum for public policy dialogue" that was supposed to work in a "multi-stakeholder, transparent, multilateral and democratic manner."

The WSIS, arguably for the first time in UN history, affirmed the principle of multi-stakeholder governance. But what did it mean? What were supposed to be the "respective roles" of the different stakeholders? How was this forum supposed to function?

The Tunis Agenda (Para 72) gave the IGF a relatively broad mandate but scant precise indications regarding the expected modalities of its operation. As a result, the UN Secretary General designated his special advisor for Internet Governance, Nitin Desai, with the help of Markus Kummer, the Swiss diplomat who had acted as Executive Secretary for the WGIG, to initiate the process and identify a way forward.

Building on the positive experience of the creation and operation of the WGIG, a method was chosen that, from the onset, put the IGF on a course that was very different from traditional UN procedures and approaches. A first consultation meeting in Geneva in early 2006, open to all interested participants, discussed the possible modalities and explored various options. On the basis of extensive consultations, three major principles emerged to guide the organization of the first IGF: openness, self-organization and a flexible relationship with the United Nations. The first five years of the Forum have confirmed the validity of these principles and are mostly responsible for the success of this experiment.

Openness

Openness to All Actors. In a radical departure from traditional intergovernmental processes, the IGF has from the onset been open to all willing stakeholders, even individuals, without a formal accreditation process. The preparation of each annual IGF is done in large part through three "Open Consultations" held in Geneva.

The invitation to the first IGF by UN Secretary General Kofi Annan was issued to WSIS accredited entities but also to: "institutions and persons with proven expertise and experience in matters related to Internet governance." In other words, the traditional criterion of representation was replaced by a criterion of relevance to the topics at hand. This formulation has been maintained since then. The first founding principle of the IGF is therefore the right for any entity or individual to participate in an appropriate manner.

Contrary to what some had feared, this did not lead to overwhelming attendance and in the five following years the number of participants has increased without making the IGF unmanageable either in terms of numbers or in terms of the behaviour of the participants. This was the first successful bet.

Equal Footing. The second bold decision was to place all participants on an equal footing. No nameplates, reserved seats, speaking orders or other distinctions between actors, in spite of their considerable diversity of geographical origin, field of activity or even rank. Implicitly, this meant that the determining criteria in their interaction would be their capacity to fruitfully contribute to discussions: in other terms, their competence rather than who they were supposed to represent.

No doubt that this initially surprised many participants and even made some ill at ease. However, in spite of the limitations of the WSIS process, regular individual interactions had already taken place between the different categories of actors in the course of the four years of the Summit. The fact that many participants in the first IGF actually knew each other from the WSIS process certainly helped everybody accept this equal footing rule: some form of mutual recognition of competence had already taken place between governments and other actors. Without this previous experience, no doubt that the equal footing format could not have been put in place.

In the five following years, as interpersonal relationships and growing understanding developed among repeat participants, this fundamental principle was maintained, while the format of the main sessions evolved towards more direct exchanges.

Since the very first IGF, space has been reserved for stakeholders to organize workshops on topics of their choice, and an online open call for proposals is launched each spring by the Secretariat. Workshops must ideally be organized on a multi-stakeholder basis or at least have presenters from the different groups in order to guarantee full representation of the diversity of viewpoints. The number of proposals has grown significantly, requiring incentives to encourage proponents to merge in order to reduce the overall number, but the diversity of topics and the bottom-up agenda setting that this procedure allows guarantees that the agenda is not rigidly set and can adapt to a rapidly changing environment.

The IGF is fully open and takes place each year in a different region. Nevertheless, many interested actors cannot participate directly, due to financial and time limitations. This is particularly true for developing countries. In the course of its first five years, significant efforts have therefore been undertaken to develop remote participation, in particular through live webcasting and the creation of local hubs where people assemble. Full recording of the sessions and workshops are now available in video or audio format on the UN web site. And in a major innovation for the UN environment, the main sessions are also fully transcribed in real-time, providing invaluable archives for the future and extreme transparency of deliberations.

Self-Organization

If openness is the first founding principle of the IGF, self-organization by the stakeholders themselves is clearly the second, allowing a bottom-up agenda setting and an evolving format. Building on the open consultations and workshop proposals, a Multi-stakeholder Advisory Group (MAG) has progressively defined the general structure of the annual event, the format of the main sessions and the main thematic pillars. A methodological stocktaking session at the beginning of each year is also an opportunity to provide input and refine the working methods for the next event in an iterative manner.

The Multi-stakeholder Advisory Group (MAG). Perhaps the most significant innovation of the IGF process, the MAG is composed of about 40 people drawn from the diverse stakeholder groups. The UN SG, taking into account proposals by the stakeholders themselves, formally nominates them. An annual rotation of about a third of the members has become the practice. Nitin Desai, UN SG representative for Internet Governance, has chaired the MAG since its creation.

Acting as a sort of program committee, the MAG is the *de facto* embodiment of the "bureau" mentioned in article 78 of the Tunis Agenda and is a clear affirmation of the multi-stakeholder nature of the IGF, by allowing all stakeholder groups to interact directly. The choice of this unique format was a conscious departure from the pure governmental bureaus used in UN processes or even the transitional formula adopted during the WSIS with the three distinct structures for governments, business and civil society. The first five years have firmly demonstrated the value of a single multi-stakeholder group instead of a traditional bureau.

Devoted to methodology rather than content, the role of the MAG is to assist the UN Secretary General in the preparation of the annual event. It has however been instrumental in defining the general structure of the meeting and its main themes.

The Main Sessions: From Panels to "Open Dialogues." Beyond the principles of open access and equal footing, organizers of the first IGF had little indications regarding the types of interactions expected. It was therefore decided to structure the initial program around a few main sessions, taking the form of expert panels on general topics, chaired by representatives from the host country. This allowed a balanced representation of the different categories of actors on the panels, on the basis of recognized competences. Two additional sessions, respectively called "Emerging Issues" and "Taking Stock", and short opening and closing ceremonies, completed the program. Initially moderated by professional journalists, the panels however allowed little interaction with the room and were sparsely attended, as participants were more attracted by the more interactive workshops.

In the course of the following editions, as participants became more familiar with one another and comfortable with unscripted interventions from the floor, panels have been progressively replaced by so-called "open dialogues." Moderated now by members of the community instead of journalists, these three-hour sessions without introductory presentations allow free but structured debates among all participants, in an increasingly direct manner, building on the discussions held in the workshops. Simultaneously, the agenda itself progressively dealt with more contentious issues.

Three Thematic Pillars. Negotiations on Internet governance were difficult during the WSIS and the creation of the IGF was in large part a compromise to continue these discussions. A repetition of previous inconclusive debates would have burdened the IGF from the onset and possibly threatened the open format it was supposed to experiment with. The initial main panel topics chosen were very general and non-controversial: Security, Openness, Diversity and Access, rapidly nicknamed the SODA Agenda.

However, in parallel with the evolution towards more interaction, a re-clustering of the main session themes progressively converged towards three major pillars, that have been maintained in the last three IGFs: 1) Access and Diversity; 2) Security, Privacy and Openness; and 3) Critical Internet Resources. Grouping Security, Privacy and Openness was a major signal: it highlighted that these three important objectives are not necessarily antagonistic and can, on the contrary, reinforce one another. The introduction of the theme of Critical Internet Resources was a neutral way to address, inter alia, the most sensitive topic of the WSIS: the management of the Domain Name System, including the role of ICANN and the United States government. Likewise, it is expected that the theme of Access and Diversity, initially focused on the regulatory frameworks enabling or limiting connectivity, will progressively cover access to content and the very sensitive issues of filtering, blocking and censorship. A fourth main session, with a different topic defined each year through the MAG, provides additional flexibility in the Agenda-setting.

Nothing guarantees that these three thematic pillars will remain unchanged in the future. But they provide a minimum framework ensuring that all sensitive issues can be addressed in the open dialogues.

Annual Stocktaking. Each year in February, the first open consultations in Geneva are devoted to taking stock of the previous IGF and identifying possible modifications in the IGF format and working methods. This short feedback loop, in the absence of too formalized rules of procedure, has been critical in the early years to smoothly evolve the process, allow experimentations and introduce pragmatic changes.

In 2009, in the context of the debate on the "desirability of the continuation" of the IGF after its initial period of five years, an extensive online consultation on possible further improvements identified several avenues to be discussed below.

A Flexible Relationship with the United Nations

At the same time it endeavoured to avoid rigid rules of procedure to allow an open and inclusive interaction among all potential stakeholders, the IGF has successfully leveraged the legitimacy provided by its various links to the United Nations.

The UN Secretary-General as Convener. The Tunis Agenda formally entrusts the UN SG with the responsibility to convene the IGF. His personal representative for Internet Governance, acting as Chair of the MAG, has played a critical role in spearheading the first formative years, largely building upon his past experience as Under-Secretary General for Social and Economic Affairs and organizer of the Johannesburg Summit.

This arms-length arrangement offers enough legitimacy to encourage governments to participate in confidence while providing the necessary flexibility to introduce very original open rules of engagement.

A Meeting on UN Territory. As a consequence of the convening role of the UN SG, the IGF meetings take place on UN territory, as the raising of the UN flag at the beginning of each meeting and the responsibility of UN Security illustrate. This has required the signing of a host country agreement that sometimes proved difficult to finalize, but it guarantees independence of the IGF dialogue from potentially varying host country political agendas.

UN rules of engagement requiring participants to refrain from naming and shaming individual countries or entities, however unpleasant for advocacy groups, have also contributed to the capacity to freely address any topic.

A Lightweight Secretariat Based in Geneva. The day-to-day preparation of the annual event, the conduct of the open consultations and MAG meetings and the management of the IGF Web site have been under the responsibility of a small Secretariat led by Markus Kummer, the Swiss diplomat who played a similar role for the WGIG. Working initially with extremely limited human resources, it has leveraged internships and part-time contracts in a very thrifty manner, forming a very cohesive and efficient team whose neutrality has been regularly praised by participants all over the world.

Although it is nominally attached to the Department for Economic and Social Affairs (DESA) in New York, this Secretariat is based in Geneva in the "Palais des Nations." This helps organize open consultations with limited visa constraints and provides a location in a centrally located time zone, making the Secretariat more easily accessible from all world regions. This also encourages participation in the consultations of local government missions following Geneva-based international organizations, some of which are dealing with topics directly related to the IGF.

A Trust Fund for Multistakeholder Financing. Multi-stakeholder financing is important for the credibility of a multi-stakeholder process. But the UN framework has proved useful again via the establishment of a dedicated Trust Fund, to which a diversity of actors contributes. The level of resources for the Secretariat certainly deserves to increase further, as well as the diversity of sources, but the mechanism ensures a degree of autonomy to the process and a clear identification of costs.

Moreover, this creates an accountability feedback loop: should the IGF cease to provide participants with sufficient value, there is no doubt that funding would dwindle, unlike some international processes that continue by sheer habit and inertia long after they have outlasted their utility. It is important to note in addition that the funding of the annual event is mostly borne by the host country. The fact that, in its first five years, the IGF has found governments in all regions willing to support this expense is a direct testimony to the interest that this experiment has triggered.

Designation of the MAG. Here again, a delicate balance has been reached through: 1) a bottom-up nomination of candidates by the stakeholder groups themselves (according to their own procedures), and 2) their formal selection by the UN Secretary General. On the basis of submissions, the Secretariat prepares a proposed slate that is sent to DESA for final approval by the UN SG. This ad hoc procedure, nicknamed the "Black Box" approach, was essential to kick-start the whole process and largely built – again – upon the precedent of the WGIG. It may however lack in transparency what it achieved in efficiency and may need to be revisited.

Looking Forward: Refining and Spreading the Method

The Tunis Agenda, in its paragraph 76, "asked the UN Secretary General to examine the desirability of the continuation of the Forum, in formal consultation with Forum participants, within five years of its creation and to make recommendations to the UN membership in this regard." Accordingly, during the 2009 IGF in Sharm el Sheikh, a dedicated consultation chaired by UN Under-Secretary General Sha Zukang, allowed forum participants to present their views on that topic. The outcome was overwhelmingly in favour of a continuation but the final decision will naturally rest upon the UN General Assembly in 2010.

On this occasion, a broad consensus also emerged in favour of further improvements to the IGF working methods, should the Forum be continued for another period of five years. This does not need to be interpreted as requiring a change in its already broad mandate or the abandonment of the principles highlighted above: they have largely contributed to its recognition and should be preserved. The purpose is rather to stay in line with the spirit of continuous self-improvement and adaptive modus operandi that has characterized the IGF so far, and to identify ways and means for the IGF to fully fulfil its mandate and deliver more tangible benefits to its participants and the world.

Several complementary efforts will provide a framework for such a discussion. In particular: the methodological stock-taking traditionally organized in February will happen this year in November, as the IGF in Vilnius will take place earlier, in September; and the ECOSOC in July is expected to request the Chair of the Commission on Science and Technology for Development (CSTD) to initiate a multi-stakeholder working group to examine improvements to the IGF working methods.

To provide input into both discussions, the second part of this paper will therefore highlight some of the questions that deserve to be addressed. Without any attempt at being exhaustive, it will focus on: organizational matters, the production of more tangible outcomes and the development of an Internet Governance Network.

Organizational Improvements

MAG Composition, Formation and Role. The multi-stakeholder MAG has been a key tool for the development and organization of the IGF, facilitating compromise and the peaceful introduction in the Agenda of the most sensitive issues, acting as a light steering group for the process. But its current composition, designation modalities and mission were accepted mostly because they make all participants "equally unhappy": each stakeholder group considers its own representation insufficient and accepts the "black box" nomination process only because its candidates are selected.

The exact extent of the MAG role is also a subject of debate: some actors want to give it more decision-making power, like a traditional bureau, while others are reluctant to do so given its multi-stakeholder nature. Finally, the actual engagement of its members varies greatly and some would like to condition membership to effective participation.

This is not surprising. There is a major underlying question here: How to constitute a limited group in a multi-stakeholder environment that would be sufficiently recognized as representative of the diverse viewpoints and by the various actors to be imbued with some decision-making capacity? This touches upon deep issues of legitimacy, transparency and accountability. In this respect, the IGF acts as a laboratory to address very difficult challenges that all multi-stakeholder efforts are currently facing.

In discussing the MAG's evolution, some important features can be kept in mind:

- Partial rotation (1/3 each year) allows institutional memory and fresh blood
- Presence of the successive host countries (at least 3 of them) ensures transmission of experience
- Even relatively quiet participants also play a role by monitoring discussions, hence ensuring a broad level of consensus
- Geographic, gender and stakeholder balance is easier to achieve when members themselves have a diversity of personal experiences
- Formal selection by the UN SG confers legitimacy but stakeholders want more direct influence on the selection of their representatives

In that context, some key questions could be:

- How to ensure rotation without eliminating key contributing actors? And how to ensure their participation without creating permanent seats for some?

- How to establish a more direct way for non-governmental actors to designate "their" members, without creating artificial "constituencies" and silo effects?
- In what domains – if any – could/should the MAG be given more decision-making power?
- Should the MAG choose/elect its own Chair?
- Could regional IGFs play a role in the composition of the MAG?

Articulation between Workshops and Main Sessions. This is a recurring topic of discussion and significant progress has already been accomplished: the format of main sessions has evolved, the three main pillars have emerged and workshops are supposed to produce reports. But more can be done. Workshops allow in-depth analysis of the various dimensions of an issue. Main sessions, on the other hand, should aim for synthesis. They help measure actual progress in the understanding and identify the next steps. Strengthening this iterative cycle of analysis and synthesis is critical: it is the very engine that can transform constructive dialogue into action.

The larger question is: How to progressively bring actors with divergent viewpoints towards better understanding and the definition of common objectives? Some issues to explore in this respect could be:

- How to encourage/force proponents addressing the same topic to combine efforts, in order to reduce the overall number of workshops?
- How to aggregate the results of related workshops to feed them into main sessions? Could intermediary wrap-up sessions be introduced?
- How to document progress in the understanding of issues?
- How to associate more closely the organizers of workshops with the preparation of the corresponding main sessions?

Broadening and Deepening Participation. A natural tension exists between the desire to engage a growing number of actors and the need to keep the meetings manageable in terms of number of participants. Moreover, the number of attendees should not measure the success of the IGF but rather the quality of their interaction. Of particular importance in this respect is to ensure the participation of actors from developing countries. This objective is explicitly mentioned in the IGF mandate and inclusiveness is a key principle of the IGF.

The general question, how to simultaneously broaden and deepen participation in the IGF, could be addressed in two complementary ways: through the development of remote participation and through funding to help needing actors attend the physical meetings. Key questions in this respect could be:

- How to further develop remote hubs and ensure that they provide full participation capacity beyond mere remote attendance?
- How to generate additional financing to facilitate participation from developing countries? In a decentralized or centralized way?
- How to establish fair criteria for selecting beneficiaries of such funding?

More Tangible Outcomes

Open dialogue in the IGF has been possible in large part because the meeting produces no negotiated documents. This critical feature is coherent with the designation of the IGF as a "forum for policy dialogue" and its "non-binding" nature. But several actors underscore the provision in the IGF mandate indicating that it can produce recommendations, at least on emerging issues, and would like it to produce more visible outcomes. Others fear that any collective drafting exercise would destroy the free and open interaction format and bring back the tedious negotiation sessions that characterized the WSIS process.

The IGF already produces considerable amounts of written material, including the real-time transcripts, the workshop reports submitted by the organizers and a Chairman summary of discussions after each annual meeting. An edited version of the transcripts, highlighting the main arguments, now serves as de facto proceedings. But these documents are more adapted for reference (they will represent a treasure trove for future scholars studying the process) than for actual policy-making. More concise or structured products would be welcome. A few possible paths to explore are listed below as food for thought in this respect.

Decision-shaping versus Decision-making. This key distinction is a discreet but important outcome of the first five years of the IGF. The now famous Tunis definition of Internet governance can be summarized as, the multi-stakeholder elaboration and application of shared regimes that shape the evolution and use of the Internet. Before any such governance regime can be drafted, preliminary agreement among interested stakeholders is required on the nature of the issue, the stated objectives and the methodology to achieve them. The IGF is the place to do this.

The IGF is not a decision-making body. It however contributes to shaping the decisions that will be made in various other spaces and facilitates communication between them to ensure coherence. In this regard, it is more a process than an event. Documenting how it already has impacted discussions in other organizations will be more important than trying to develop a decision-making capacity that could put it in competition with the very structures it can help. As the saying goes: "everybody wants coordination but nobody wants to be coordinated." Maintaining the IGF role as decision-shaping space is the best way to prevent discussions on its hierarchical positioning vis-à-vis other processes and avoid unnecessary duplication.

Defining Issues in Terms of Common Concern. In Internet governance matters, the WSIS has demonstrated that beyond superficial agreement on general principles, various actors have very different perspectives, apparently incompatible. However, as a famous advertisement said: a different point of view often comes from a different observation point. Actors determine their positions according to their specific interests but are not necessarily aware of all the dimensions of a given issue, let alone the perspective of the other actors. Like the five blind men and the elephant in the eponymous story, each of them only possesses a valid but partial understanding.

The multi-stakeholder format of the IGF allows all categories of actors to share their own vision of a topic without the pressure of negotiating documents. The result is a common picture of all dimensions of the issue, a necessary prerequisite to designing any policy. In many cases, a positive outcome of these discussions is to formulate a contentious issue in more neutral terms that present it as a common concern or interest rather than rigid advocacy positions.

An example would be to reformulate the intense debate around Net Neutrality as, Principles for Network Traffic Management. Another example for the future IGFs could be reframing the hotly contentious topic of "unilateral control of critical internet resources" as, Guaranteeing the Integrity of the Root Zone File. Such formulations help synchronize discussions in other forums and facilitate interaction and identification of common goals between actors. Reframing contentious issues in terms of common concerns or interest would constitute very concrete outcomes of the IGF.

Calling for Inputs. The IGF is only a part in a larger Internet governance ecosystem. A broad range of institutions already addresses on a daily basis the issues on its agenda. They produce considerable written resources that are insufficiently known by IGF participants or are too detailed to be examined directly in the short time frame of the IGF. They could be invited to prepare short and synthetic issue papers, potentially along a simple template, to document their activities and perspectives on a specific topic. Preparation or collation of such background material could be a prerequisite for workshop organizers and serve as input into sessions.

Likewise, workshop organizers could be requested to identify on the spot a few key points of agreement among their participants. This concise on-site reporting would be fed into the main sessions. Finally, national and regional IGFs could identify "key messages" to be carried forward to the global event, providing valuable input in the discussions. The European Dialogue on Internet Governance (EuroDIG) has for instance already explored this approach with a certain success.

Recommendations. The term "recommendation" has been misleading the discussions on possible IGF outcomes. Its similarity with the terminology widely used in intergovernmental processes evokes images of painfully negotiated resolutions. However, recommendations can have a more informal nature, particularly if they relate to process and simply encourage relevant actors to deal with a particular topic. The annual Chairman's summary can easily reflect an emerging consensus regarding the next desirable steps in the treatment of a particular concern, including encouraging the formation of a corresponding thematic network (see infra).

Of particular importance is the role the IGF can play in raising awareness on an emerging issue. Its flexible agenda setting allows quick reactivity: policy issues related to social media and cloud computing have for instance very rapidly been brought to the attention of a much broader audience, giving added impetus and visibility to existing discussions, or even triggering new cooperative activities.

Finally, and even if the notion of recommendations "of the IGF" of "by the IGF" as a whole still raises ongoing concerns, forum participants seem willing to explore the concept of "recommendations presented AT the IGF." Prepared by inter-sessional processes or agreed among a limited group of actors during a dedicated workshop, such documents would clearly identify the signatories to avoid confusion. They could, inter alia, highlight a specific area of concern, propose a formulation or encourage a specific course of action. Fully in line with the self-organizing nature of the IGF, they would require no explicit endorsement by all participants but the IGF would help initiators raise awareness and garner support for the approach.

Increased Visibility. A wealth of information is already available on the IGF web site. However, it is still primarily presented according to the needs and interests of actors participating in the preparation of the event (MAG members, workshop organizers) rather than the participants themselves, let alone the general public.

Pending availability of additional financial or in-kind support, functionalities of the site could be developed to allow more structured access to the existing substantive information: workshop reports, speakers biographies, background documents, videos, active entities, related events, etc...

Towards an Internet Governance Network

Providing an annual "watering hole" for the main actors interested in Internet Governance, the IGF has been independently replicated at national and regional levels, has triggered the creation of so-called Dynamic Coalitions and inserted itself in a complex web of existing institutions. These developments point towards the emergence of an Internet Governance Network, united by the growing adoption of the multi-stakeholder interaction rules developed in the IGF, like the Internet and the World Wide Web are united by the TCP/IP and HTTP/HTML protocols.

The Network of IGFs. The IGF was initiated as a single annual event. However, less than three years after its creation, its innovative format and fundamental principles have rapidly been replicated, with minor variations, at national and regional levels. Regional initiatives have emerged in Europe (EuroDIG), in East and West Africa, in Latin America, in the Caribbean and in Asia. National IGFs are now taking place in more than 25 countries, including the United States, Russia, Brazil, and several European Union members.

Governments, academics, business actors or NGOs, depending on the local situation, may have launched these initiatives, but all endorse the principles of openness and self-organization. This spontaneous replication shows no sign of abating and is the most potent demonstration of the value of the multi-stakeholder approach and the structuring role of the IGF as a laboratory to define new protocol(s) of interaction.

In many ways, the development of this network of independent initiatives mirrors the initial stages of the Internet or the World Wide Web. Individual groups of actors or entities, by spontaneously adopting the multi-stakeholder interaction protocol for their own purposes become, ipso facto, part of the larger community sharing the same methods. Each new addition to the network reinforces its value for existing participants, creating a positive feedback loop that accelerates adoption.

As upcoming discussions address the improved working methods for the IGF, it will be important to make sure that new modalities maintain a similar potential for autonomous replication.

From Dynamic Coalitions to Thematic Networks. Dynamic Coalitions (DCs) was a term coined as early as the first IGF to designate the grouping of various actors interested in the same topic. Expected to be fully multi-stakeholder and to work between annual IGF meetings, they were the closest attempt to establishing formal working groups. Several have been created in the course of the first five years and were granted specific slots at IGF events to present the results of their activities.

Unfortunately, this notion has revealed itself to be too ambiguous. Many DCs have conducted little effective activity and, apart from rare cases, the limited participation of governments and businesses in the active ones has oriented their work towards more traditional civil society advocacy. This situation, however, can be potentially remediated in two complementary directions.

On the one hand, the most advocacy-oriented DCs can evolve into "like-minded groups" trying to develop specific recommendations to be presented at the IGF (see above). Retaining multi-stakeholder participation would remain critical for their credibility, but they would only need to recruit governments and businesses sharing their approach, instead of an artificial open door policy that prevents progress.

On the other hand, if the IGF manages to reframe contentious topics into issues of common concern or interest, as suggested above, new "Thematic Networks" could be initiated by willing facilitators to organize inter-sessional work on these topics. With a clearly neutral orientation (as opposed to advocacy), they could in particular foster the organization of specific multi-stakeholder events or "Thematic IGFs" that would later feed into the global IGF. Without exclusivity, existing international organizations could play a facilitation role according to their respective domains of competence.

Connecting Processes and Institutions. The IGF is part of a larger governance ecosystem and one of its major missions is to facilitate the circulation of information between organizations dealing with cross-cutting issues. By offering a neutral facilitation space, the IGF enables all institutions dealing with Internet governance to present their activities in dedicated "Open Forum" sessions. This helps disseminate information and allows them to attract new stakeholders in their work.

But it also helps evaluate how much these institutions have endorsed the multi-stakeholder approach in their own activities. As a result, peer pressure and emulation naturally introduce a feedback loop that spreads best practices. Tellingly, specialized UN Agencies and other international or regional organizations have begun to play roles in the convening or facilitation of regional or thematic IGFs, and the practice of multi-stakeholder workshops and study groups is organically spreading among them.

This implements in a non-coercive manner the provisions of Article 72i of the Tunis Agenda that request the IGF to "promote and assess, on an ongoing basis, the embodiment of WSIS principles in Internet governance processes."

The IGF and its replicas act as informal communication clearinghouses between institutions and this role will expand if they begin to produce specific input documents or synthesis for the IGF. In this emerging governance network, every entity is a node that receives inputs from organizations and actors it is connected with, processes these inputs according to its own internal procedures, and disseminates the results to other nodes.

This peer-to-peer approach is markedly different from the hierarchical relationships that characterize traditional international processes and too often leads to intense turf battles between institutions about their respective domains of competence. Should the IGF become able to produce informal recommendations regarding common challenges and objectives, it would help break the silos that too often prevent effective collaboration between institutions and catalyze joint efforts to address urgent problems.

Conclusion

As participants gather in Vilnius for the last meeting of the first mandate and look back at what has been accomplished, those who took part in the WSIS cannot but measure the difference in tone and engagement of the different actors. If the IGF, in the first years of its young existence, has accomplished anything, it is the demonstration that a truly open multi-stakeholder policy dialogue is possible, with all actors on an equal footing, deciding by themselves, in a collaborative manner, their modalities of interaction and the agenda they intend to address.

The demonstration was powerful enough to have triggered in the last two years the emergence of numerous national and regional initiatives in all regions of the world, using similar methods to foster regular dialogue among all stakeholders. This is no small feat in such a short period of time. The principles and pragmatic approach that allowed this format to emerge deserve to be preserved as we discuss the continuation of this innovative experiment and possible improvements to its working methods. The next five years, should the mandate of the IGF be renewed, are not about what needs to be corrected but how to move further down this path. The IGF does not need to be fixed, but perfected.

History has produced its share of ambitious declarations filed as soon as they were signed, because they were merely cover-ups for persistent distrust. In the growingly interconnected and interdependent world of the Digital Age, only agreements based on true mutual understanding have a chance to be respected. Only regimes elaborated with the participation of all stakeholders will have a chance to be implemented. This was the main message of the WSIS. A legitimate desire for rapid and concrete outcomes should therefore not lead back into well-trodden paths: traditional intergovernmental negotiations are not an option for Internet governance. Continuing to collectively build this multi-stakeholder "Internet Governance Protocol" is, even if the pace initially appears slow. And the IGF is more than ever the main laboratory to do it.

The emergence of an Internet Governance Network is a proof of the success of this approach. Helping it to develop should be a major objective for the coming years. In a time when new international tensions seem to be erupting on a daily basis, any tiny oasis of trust building is sufficiently rare to deserve notice and care. It is the shared responsibility of all stakeholders to nurture it and help it grow in a balanced manner during their ongoing discussions.

III. The Chairman's Summary

Chairman's Summary

Fourth Meeting of the Internet Governance Forum (IGF)

Sharm El Sheikh, Egypt, 15-18 November 2009

The fourth meeting of the Internet Governance Forum was held in Sharm El Sheikh, on 15-18 November 2009. It focused on the overall theme of 'Internet Governance – Creating Opportunities for All'.

With more than 1800 participants from 112 countries the Sharm meeting had the biggest attendance so far. 96 governments were represented. 122 media representatives were accredited.

Each of the main sessions was organized in a manner specific to the issue under discussion. While the discussions on some issues were organized as panel discussions, others were organized as moderated open discussions and some in a mixed format with both panels and discussions.

Parallel to the main sessions, more than 100 workshops, best practice forums, dynamic coalition meetings and open forums were scheduled around the broad themes of the main sessions and the overall mandate of the IGF.

The IGF programme and meetings were prepared through a series of open, multistakeholder consultations held throughout 2009, a process that also designed the IGF's interactive and participatory structure.

The entire meeting was Webcast, with video streaming provided from the main session room and audio streaming provided from all workshop meeting rooms. The proceedings of the main sessions were transcribed and displayed in the main session hall in real-time and streamed to the Web. The text transcripts of the main sessions, the video and audio records of all workshops and other meetings were made available through the IGF Web site. This set up allowed for remote participants to interact with the meeting. All main sessions had simultaneous interpretation in all UN languages.

Opening Ceremony and Opening Session

In his opening address to the meeting, Mr. Sha Zukang, Under-Secretary-General for Economic and Social Affairs, expressed his gratitude to the Government and people of the Arab Republic of Egypt for their warm welcome and generous hospitality. The Under-Secretary-General noted that as we progressed in bridging the digital divide and building the foundation for the emerging information and knowledge society, the way in which we would deal with the Internet became increasingly important. The theme of the fourth meeting of the Forum "Internet Governance: Creating Opportunities for All" was therefore most timely and appropriate. It allowed the meeting to re-examine and to reflect on the main themes of the IGF – access, diversity, openness, security and privacy and critical Internet resources. He also stressed that though the digital divide was wide – with Africa and Arab States lagging behind Europe, Asia and the Americas – gains were being made. Mr. Sha described the IGF as fostering dialogue by giving voice to a wide range of views and bringing together diverse cultures. The IGF worked through voluntary cooperation, not legal compulsion. IGF participants came to the Forum to discuss, to exchange information and to share best practices with each other. While the IGF did not have decision-making abilities, it informed and inspired those who did.

The Under-Secretary-General drew attention to a critical decision that needed to be taken about the future of the IGF. He reminded the meeting that the Tunis Agenda specifically called on the Secretary-General "to examine the desirability of the continuation of the Forum, in formal consultation with Forum participants, within five years of its creation, and to make recommendations to the UN membership in this regard". He encouraged all participants to contribute fully to the consultations. He requested that people who found the Forum valuable say so and tell him in what ways they found it valuable. To explain how it could be improved, and to explain how the IGF had fulfilled its purpose. He requested participants to be open and honest with one another, as was the IGF custom. Based on the consultations, he would report back to the Secretary-General, who would then make his recommendations in his annual report to the General Assembly, next year, on WSIS follow-up and implementation.

In concluding his address, Mr. Sha invited H.E. Mr. Tarek Kamel, Minister of Communications and Information Technology of Egypt to assume the chairmanship of the conference.

Mr. Kamel recalled that since its earliest days, the success of the Internet had been based on collaboration. As the network had grown to connect all continents and countries, the spirit of collaboration had remained a touchstone that had been captured and embodied in the IGF. The IGF had proved over four years that it was not just another isolated parallel process, but that it had managed to bring on board all the relevant stakeholders and key players. Further, he noted that the crucial development role of the Internet should be recognized globally, and the global community should ensure that barriers to participation by developing countries should be removed. With opportunities there were rights and also responsibilities, and in tomorrow's cyberspace the IGF should address important issues such as cross-border security, youth experience, multilingual content, and enhanced broadband capacity in developing countries, among others.

The Prime Minister of Egypt, Mr. Ahmed Nazif, drew attention to how important the Internet and ICTs had become. During the recent economic crisis, growth of the ICT sector in Egypt continued at double-digit rates, and had been a key driver of the economy. Only through open and consistent dialogue could the true potential of the Internet as a tool for growth and herald of economic and political freedoms be maximized. The Prime Minister saw in the continuation of the IGF a real priority. The IGF had provided a valuable space for continuous education on the prospects of the Internet and the global cyberspace and it was a precious learning tool for the young generations. The strength of the IGF was its all-inclusive, all-comprehensive nature.

The Secretary-General of the International Telecommunication Union (ITU), Mr. Hamadoun Touré, said that it was a major milestone for the meeting to take stock and look ahead to the future of the IGF and its continued role, looking at enhanced cooperation and at which areas of the IGF mandate needed to be further examined. As the organization that organized the World Summit on the Information Society from which the multi-stakeholder model of the IGF emerged, the ITU had been an active participant in and supporter of the IGF. The IGF was a unique forum where all stakeholders could share opinions on an equal footing. The Forum was a place where progress could be made on certain topics, and matured topics introduced into other more formal processes, arrangements and organizations for further consideration. Among other things, Mr. Touré drew attention to the ITU's framework on cyber security. He also asked participants to look at the bigger picture in the context of the Millennium Development Goals (MDGs) and the objective to meet their targets by 2015. The IGF would be a clear part of that process.

In his keynote address, Sir Tim Berners-Lee, creator of the World Wide Web and Director of World Wide Web Consortium (W3C) emphasized the importance of a single Web that could be shared and used by all. He noted the importance of the Web to enhance the lives of people with disabilities. He said the W3C championed open standards that were royalty free so they could be openly shared. He also announced the launch of the World Wide Web Foundation, an international, non-profit organization that would strive to advance the Web as a medium that empowered people.

In a second keynote address, Mr. Jerry Yang, Co-Founder and Chief Yahoo!, saw the power of the Internet in its ability to connect communities. The network's impact had created social and economic opportunities from healthcare to education and fostered a next generation of entrepreneurs.

During the opening session, the following speakers, representing all stakeholder groups, addressed the meeting:

- H. E. Mr. Moritz Leuenberger, Federal Councillor, Head of the Department of the Environment, Transport, Energy and Communication, Switzerland; and H. E. Mr. Jozsef Györkös, State Secretary, Ministry of Higher Education, Science and Technology, Slovenia (Joint Statement representing the Chair of the Council of Europe Committee of Ministers);
- Ms. Lisa Horner, Global Partners and Associates;
- H. E. Ms. Åsa Torstensson, Minister for Enterprise, Energy and Communications, Sweden, representing the EU Presidency;
- H. E. Ms. Viviane Reding, European Commissioner for ICT and Media;
- H. E. Mr. Pedro Sebastião Teta, Vice Minister, Information and Communications Technology, Angola;
- H. E. Mr. Augusto Gadelha, Vice Minister, Science & Technology, Brazil;

- Ambassador Philip Verveer, Coordinator, International Communications and Information Policy, Department of State, United States;
- H. E. Ms. Nathalie Kosciusko-Morizet, Secretary of State for Prospective and the Development of the Digital Economy, France;
- Ms. Lynn St. Amour, President & CEO, Internet Society (ISOC);
- Mr. Abdul Waheed Khan, Assistant Director-General for Communication and Information, UNESCO;
- Mr. Subramanian Ramadorai, Vice-Chairman of Tata Consultancy Services Ltd, Chairman, ICC-BASIS;
- Mr. Rod Beckstrom, President and CEO, Internet Corporation for Assigned Names and Numbers (ICANN);
- Mr. Jean Rozwadowski, Secretary General, International Chamber of Commerce (ICC);
- Mr. Nitin Desai, Special Adviser to the Secretary-General for Internet Governance.

All speakers emphasized the importance of the Internet as an enabler for economic growth and social development. The IGF was appreciated for its open multistakeholder model, with examples of new national and regional IGF initiatives illustrating the spread of the multistakeholder ideal and its value in policy discussion.

A common thread through all the speeches was the endorsement of the IGF as a platform for fostering dialogue. Eleven speakers specifically supported an extension of the IGF mandate. The speakers also emphasized the importance they attached to the IGF, stressing that it had proven to be useful and noted that the IGF should continue to meet beyond the 2010 meeting in Vilnius.

Main Thematic Sessions

The second and third days of the meeting were designed around four main themes, two for each day:

- Managing Critical Internet Resources;
- Security, Openness and Privacy;
- Access and Diversity;
- Internet Governance in the Light of WSIS Principles.

The sessions on Managing Critical Internet resources and Internet Governance in the Light of WSIS principles were held in the form of open discussions without panellists in order to promote greater participation by all stakeholders to inform and provide their perspectives. A chair and moderators managed both sessions, with resource persons called on from the audience. The session on Security, Openness and Privacy was introduced by a panel of expert practitioners who set the stage and brought out options, and were followed by comment and discussion from the floor. The session on Access and Diversity also used a panel of expert practitioners, and then was split into two sections to draw in the outcomes of related workshops on Diversity and Access respectively.

Managing Critical Internet Resources

Chair:

Mr. Nitin Desai, Special Adviser to the Secretary-General for Internet Governance.

Moderators:

Mr. Chris Disspain, Chief Executive Officer, .AU Registry; Chair, Council of Country-Code Names Supporting Organization (ccNSO)

Ms. Jeanette Hofmann, Senior Researcher, London School of Economics and Political Science (LSE)/Social Science Research Center Berlin

The session was held in the form of an open discussion and focused on four main topics:

- Transition from IPv4 to IPv6;
- The importance of new TLDs and IDNs for development;
- The Affirmation of Commitments and the IANA contract and recent developments in the relationship between ICANN and the U.S. government;
- Enhanced cooperation generally and the internationalization of critical Internet resource management.

The Chair, introduced the session and noted that many of the issues were discussed at the IGF in Hyderabad in 2008, and asked that remarks focus very sharply on what had happened over the past year.

The moderators introduced Mr. Paul Wilson, Director General of the Asia Pacific Network Information Center (APNIC) as resource person for the discussion on transition from IPv4 to IPv6.

Mr. Wilson described how IPv6 addresses were being deployed, the role of different stakeholders, and noted that ISPs had provided trial and production services. A lot of IPv6 equipment, devices, and applications were also available. Governments in particular had paid more attention to IPv6, and many had led deployment initiatives.

IPv6 had been deployed in what was known as a dual stack implementation, where both IPv4 and IPv6 were run at the same time. In the future, IPv4 would remain, even when IPv6 was dominant, and network translation systems would allow both systems to work. It was important not to think of the transition as a single event like Y2K, but rather as a process of deployment. He added that there was a perception that the transition was slow, or that it could be faster. But, for business the transition had been a choice and would happen when it was justified. The Internet's success was based on competition; ISPs would deploy IPv6 resources when customers needed them.

Many speakers emphasized the importance of training and awareness raising. The Government of Egypt informed the meeting of a national IPv6 Taskforce that looked at ways to accelerate the transition. A speaker from the ITU noted that the ITU Council established a working group to help members with the transition, particularly to support developing countries.

Introducing the second topic, TLDs and IDNs for development, Mr. Patrik Fältström, Cisco Systems Inc., noted that we had entered a period of great change for key resources of the Internet. In 2010, DNSSEC would be introduced and the root would be signed by many TLDs. IPv6 addresses for DNS services, new TLDs, in ASCII and IDN, and IDN ccTLDs, under a program that ICANN launched just a few hours before the session began, would be added to the root. These changes would place stress on the root system. He suggested that the rate of change would have greater impact than the changes themselves.

Mr. Bob Kahn, one of the founding fathers of the Internet, reminded the meeting to remain open to diversity of choice. As an example, he described an identification system used by the publishing industry, the 'handle system'. It was secure and had been working for 10 years. He indicated that it could offer an alternative to the DNS system used today for the Internet. He emphasized that we should remain open to new approaches, so long as the Internet would not fragment.

A number of speakers, while recognizing the importance of all these changes, emphasized the importance of ensuring the security and stability of the Internet. Others noted that it would take time for important applications, such as email, to work and to accept these new identifiers. It would take time even with the fast track on new IDN ccTLDs. A speaker noted the importance of introducing competition in the selection of the registry to run the new IDN registry, and that the selection process should be open and transparent. These represented new national level Internet governance issues shared by the community. This session was particularly timely, as it coincided with the opening of applications for new IDN ccTLDs as a result of the fast track process. Both the governments of Egypt and Russia announced that they would file applications as soon as it was possible to do so.

A ccTLD operator from Africa said there was a need to support ccTLD technical operations and management in developing countries. He also expressed concern that as new gTLDs and regional TLDs were introduced, the rich culture of Africa would need to be protected, so that the values, culture and history the identifiers might seek to represent could be managed by people from those countries and regions.

The third issue, the Affirmation of Commitments (AoC), which replaced the Joint Project Agreement (JPA) between the United States Government and ICANN, was introduced by ICANN's CEO and President, Mr. Rod Beckstrom. He reviewed the AoC and its 11 key paragraphs. The AoC provided a commitment to the public interest model and to the enhanced role of all governments in the ICANN Government Advisory Committee (GAC). The AoC established four review teams that would examine ICANN's performance.

Speakers from all stakeholder groups welcomed the AoC as a positive development. One speaker noted the AoC took direction from the WSIS Tunis Agenda, another welcomed the AoC as a step towards greater internationalization, and hoped for more and made the remark that the more international and inclusive ICANN should strive to be "WE CAN."

Looking forward, many suggested after the AoC, the next step should be to address the IANA contract between the United States Government and ICANN. Some recommended that an international body should be selected to takeover the IANA contract, others suggested that the IGF should debate the issue, a recommendation that was greeted with strong support.

The final item was enhanced cooperation, introduced by Ms. Haiyan Qian, Director of the Division for Public Administration and Development Management (DPADM) in the United Nations Department for Economic and Social Affairs. Ms. Qian reported on enhanced cooperation and the process within the UN. She informed the meeting that the UN General Assembly adopted another resolution asking the Secretary-General to submit a report on the process of enhanced cooperation and Internet public policy, including the work of relevant organizations. The report had been submitted to the Economic and Social Council (ECOSOC), but the matter had been deferred for review until 2010 in New York. Ms. Qian said major points of the report were the continuation of inclusive multistakeholder dialogue, and that the IGF should be utilized for that dialogue. A number of participants noted different interpretations of what was meant by "enhanced cooperation" in the Tunis Agenda, and that this had caused confusion and difficulty in making progress.

One speaker noted that during WSIS there was no agreement on one interpretation of enhanced cooperation, but it provided room for interpretation. Some were able to interpret enhanced cooperation as improved dialogue between governments, or dialogue between governments and other stakeholders that did not exist before. Or, some argued for one centralized process of enhanced cooperation, and others for multiple processes to improve public policy related to Internet governance. Discussions made clear that progress had been made with regard to all of these different interpretations.

Others noted that in ICANN many steps had been taken to improve the operation of the GAC, and this could be taken as progress in enhanced cooperation. Others asked for more openness and multistakeholder participation in intergovernmental organizations.

In closing the session, Mr. Kamel noted that regarding the fast track for new IDN ccTLDs, it was important to ensure that IDNs could be utilized by users. This would take investment to ensure that applications and content were ready. The AoC was an excellent step forward, it provided accountability and independence, but more was needed. There should be greater involvement of the global community in all aspects of the system, and it would be legitimate to ask the United States to open and revisit the discussion of the IANA contract, and it should start soon.

114

The Session Chair summarized the discussion, noting that with the transition from IPv4 to IPv6 there was a two-year window with much work ahead. He noted that while participants welcomed the AoC, there would be much more work to do to implement the AoC. Beginning discussions about the IANA contract could be an opportunity to carry this process forward. He said enhanced cooperation was in part about reducing conflict, and that had been achieved in the IGF and elsewhere.

Security, Openness and Privacy

Co-chairs:

H. E. Ms. Jasna Matic, Minister of Telecommunications and Information Society, Serbia;

Mr. Sherif Hashem, Vice Executive President, Information Technology Industry Development Agency, Egypt.

Moderator:

Mr. Marc Rotenberg, Executive Director, Electronic Privacy Information Center (EPIC).

Panellists:

- Mr. Joseph H. Alhadeff, Vice President for Global Public Policy and Chief Privacy Officer, Oracle Corporation;
- Ms. Cristine Hoepers, Senior Security Analyst and General Manager, CERT.br;
- Ms. Namita Malhotra, Researcher, Alternative Law Forum, Bangalore;
- Mr. Bruce Schneier, Chief Security Technology Officer, British Telecom;
- Mr. Alexander Seger, Head of Economic Crime Division, Directorate General of Human Rights and Legal Affairs, Council of Europe;
- Mr. Frank La Rue, UN Special Rapporteur for Freedom of Opinion and Expression.

Ms. Matic opened the session by indicating that these topics had been an issue for as long as the Internet had been in existence. They had become much more important recently, given the billions of people using the Internet each day. Security, openness and privacy were interlinked and the key question was to find the right balance among access to knowledge, the freedom of expression, and intellectual property rights. She also discussed the increasing importance of privacy in the light of the new social network phenomenon and reminded participants that children were the easiest targets since they were at the same time the most vulnerable and most trusting group and the earliest adopters of new technology.

Mr. Hashem spoke of the challenges in trying to find the right balance for society and made reference to the Egyptian experience in this regard. He emphasized the need for partnership between government, private sector, NGOs, education, academic institutions, research and development. This was important, because the issues and risks would change over time, with emergent technologies and new societal ways of using technology, and it was only by working within a partnership that the challenges would be met.

Among the points mentioned was that privacy was key to personal autonomy. However, it was often used as a way of simply protecting the privileged. Various laws had been misused and in that context, laws on pornography were mentioned as having been used to limit women's ability to participate in the public sphere. A panellist noted that not only freedom of expression and privacy should be considered rights, security was also an important right.

The discussion evolved around the relationship between privacy and security and it was mentioned that perhaps a real trade-off would need to focus on liberty versus control. The importance of the equitable distribution of access was also mentioned, as well as the importance of accessing different points of view.

Addressing the challenges facing the future of the Internet today, various issues were mentioned, such as the problem of establishing a culture of trust, the separation of valid security countermeasures from those that would be established in order to collect data for control and suppression. Another challenge mentioned involved contextual integrity in data aggregation, and the role of powerful corporate and national entities in the use and abuse of data. The biggest challenge faced was balancing the interests of the powerful with the interests of the world's peoples, creating a person-focused Internet that would ensure the confidentiality, integrity and availability of computer data and systems, and the protection of personal data within a global environment.

Another challenge concerned the issue that rights were currently protected by the constitutional nation state, yet people lived in a borderless global network. This meant there would need to be a human rights perspective beyond technological development and commercial developments. The interaction of all these elements was from a human rights policy and perspective, which would guarantee that the focus would be on human beings and their benefit.

Another challenge involved the absolute openness of the Internet and the concern that this openness could be used to create more leverage for the already powerful ones and not to empower communities and to let them voice their concerns.

In the discussion on cybercrime, it was mentioned that in trying to protect people some were trying to control everything: to gather more data, and to get information about everything that was done online. It was mentioned that this would not help, because no one would be able to go through that information quickly enough to respond to and fight cybercrime.

The discussion on social networks showed that there were limits to what should be traded in terms of fundamental rights. It was also mentioned that it would be problematic to give rights the same economic status as services and things. Privacy was discussed as a fundamental and inalienable human right and not a commodity; human rights were therefore not something that could be bartered.

In discussing privacy and the protection of personal data, one of the ways forward mentioned was to think about contextual integrity of information; that information given away for a certain purpose could not be used for anything else. Part of this would involve looking at whether consent was an important legal tool, in the context of privacy.

The discussion also touched on anonymity. Eliminating anonymity on the Internet would be very hard, as would designing an Internet architecture that did not permit anonymity. It was also commented that anonymity, as a fundamental property of the Internet, was a social good, a political good, and an economic good.

It was recommended that in terms of achieving the appropriate balance between security, openness and privacy, people should use their buying power to convince vendors to improve the security of their products, and should fund research more broadly. The Council of Europe's Convention on Cybercrime was also mentioned as part of the solution on how to deal with security.

In their concluding remarks, both chairs reiterated the importance of trust when the subject of security, privacy, openness was considered. Education and openness were key to achieve such a trust, and trust was a result of education and of involving all stakeholders in the community.

Access and Diversity

The session was split into two parts, and drew on outcomes of related workshops, which had been held earlier in the Forum.

Diversity

Chair:

Mr. Talal Abu-Ghazaleh, Chairman, Talal Abu-Ghazaleh Organization.

Moderator:

Mr. Jonathan Charles, Presenter, BBC World News.

Panellists:

- Mr. Gerry Ellis, Accessibility and Usability consultant, Feel The BenefIT;
- Mr. Shadi Abou Zahra, Activity Lead, WAI International Program Office, W3C;
- Ms. Cynthia Waddell, Executive Director, International Center for Disability Resources on the Internet (ICDRI);
- Ms. Andrea Saks, Convener of the joint coordination activity on accessibility and human factors, Coordinator, Dynamic Coalition on Accessibility and Disability;
- Mr. Abdul Waheed Khan, Assistant Director-General for Communication and Information, UNESCO;
- Mr. Abdulaziz Al-Zoman, SaudiNIC (.sa);
- Mr. Dwayne Bailey, Research Director, ANLoc (African Network for Localisation).

The moderator noted access and diversity could be considered as two sides of the same coin; they were issues that affected hundreds of millions of people not yet involved in the Internet conversation, and of concern for the Forum in particular was diversity in language and diversity concerning disability.

The Chair objected to the narrow focus of diversity on language and disability, and recommended that the IGF and the Global Alliance on ICT for Development (GAID), as 'two children of WSIS', produce a list of issues pertaining to diversity and ICT. Education, infrastructure, open platforms and open source technologies should be included in discussions about access and diversity. Further, in his role as a businessman, he called on businesses worldwide to be more active in these issues.

One panellist showed how he navigated Web pages and used email using screen-reading technologies, in a demonstration of the accessibility challenges people with visual disabilities face using the Internet. A key point of his demonstration was that accessibility versus inaccessibility had no impact on aesthetics or functionality of a Web site for the regular user.

A speaker drew attention to the fact that one tenth of the world's population had disabilities and that two billion people were impacted by the challenges of disability. They were found in every social and demographic group. The UN Convention for People with Disabilities included stipulations that provided rights of accessibility on the Internet. If the principles of the convention were properly followed, the needs of people with disabilities would be largely addressed. One such principle was that of Universal Design, which called for the design of products, environments, programmes and services in a way that addressed the needs of people with disabilities and included assistive devices where needed.

During the question and answer session, a participant noted that accessibility was not just about the ability of disabled people to access information, but was also about their ability to express themselves freely. It was pointed out that the Millennium Development Goals (MDGs) did not include disability as a priority.

The panel presented a message, prepared by the Dynamic Coalition on Accessibility and Disability, addressing the needs of people with disabilities. It raised awareness for the obligations deriving from the UN Convention and the tools available to make the Internet and the Web accessible for people with disabilities. At the Chairman's request, the participants endorsed the message by acclamation.

The second part of the session addressed multilingualism. The first speaker noted that language could be a barrier. He spoke briefly in Hindi, a language spoken by many at the Forum, but not interpreted as an official UN language and therefore not understood by all participants. He asked the question whether agricultural information could be shared with farmers, if it was not in their language?

It was asserted that a majority of the world's languages were declining in use and faced extinction. The Internet was proposed as a way to help preserve indigenous languages, culture and knowledge digitally. A project to establish Arab domain names was discussed with emphasis on the successes, but also the unique challenges posed by establishing non-Latin script online, not just in the characters and technical concerns, but in the direction they were typed, for example right to left rather than the more common left to right.

The point was made that 2000 languages were spoken by one billion people in Africa. 200 of those languages were spoken by more than 500,000 people and 15 African languages were spoken by more than 10 million people. However, these languages were almost not present in a significant way in the information age. A number of interventions noted that the inability to access information online in a locally understood language could be life-threatening.

A key point was made that IDNs were not the only issue concerned with multilingualism and ICTs. A number of interventions also stressed that many diversity issues could be addressed by technology, now or in the near future.

In concluding the session, the chairman asked participants to join him in commending the Egyptian efforts towards the development of a knowledge society and in encouraging ICANN to accelerate its process on multilingualization and to make it a priority in order to ensure the continued coherence of the Internet.

Access

Chair:

Mr. Amr Badawi, Executive President, National Telecommunications Authority Regulation (NTRA), Egypt.

Moderator:

Mr. Hopeton Dunn, Director, Caribbean Programme in Telecommunications Policy and Technology Management (TPM), Mona School of Business, University of the West Indies, Mona, Jamaica.

Panellists:

- Mr. Ben Akoh, ICT Programme Manager, Open Society Initiative for West Africa;
- Mr. Pierre Dandjinou, CEO, Strategic Consulting Group;
- Mr. Mohamed El Nawawy, Vice Chairman Telecom Egypt;
- Mr. Ernest Ndukwe, Chief Executive Officer and Executive Vice Chairman, Nigerian Communications Commission;
- Mr. Ermanno Pietrosemoli, President, EsLaRed.

The chairman stated that access included financial access, the relevance of literacy to access, political access which gave voice to linguistic access, and access by the disabled. Desirable access to the Internet was further defined as being connected to the Internet at the right speed, linked to the right content at the right time and place. Issues concerned with infrastructure were now secondary, because advances had been made, specifically with mobile phones and Internet penetration in many parts of the world.

The main issues where progress was most needed were characterized as policy, regulation and rights. Speakers noted that regional and national backbones should be strengthened as well as security issues connected with new services and higher bandwidth and availability needed to be addressed. One speaker noted serious policy and regulatory bottlenecks in many developing countries and regions. True access would not be achieved without appropriate regulatory regimes being put in place.

Many agreed that progress had been made regarding infrastructure, notably that submarine fibre cable systems had been built and provided increased bandwidth and higher quality connectivity. However, it was noted that landlocked countries still struggled to access coastal Internet cables, and that broadband access was still limited and costs were still high.

Spectrum and its management was indentified as a major and a fundamental component of access. A speaker suggested spectrum should be used more effectively, for example reclaiming unused spectrum space. Also, new technology that used spectrum more effectively should be adopted in the developing world, not just developed markets.

Speakers proposed ways to effectively provide access for rural areas, and wi-fi solutions were named in particular, as they were easily modified to provide connectivity to meet local needs. Taking advantage of geography and special antennae, a test project that was able to span a distance of 240 km with normal wi-fi connections was described as a promising solution.

A participant proposed developing government policies that would leverage and extend mobile technologies into the Internet sector in Africa and Latin America. This model had proven to work in South Asia.

In conclusion, the Chairman noted that the access panel sought to provide ideas and food for thought about affordable access, notably regarding better spectrum management. He suggested there was an opportunity to provide broadband at reduced cost if governments managed spectrum more efficiently, for example, utilizing empty TV channels in areas where TV was not much used. Especially for rural areas, universal service funds could be a means to reduce the cost of accessing the network. He recalled that new submarine cables had provided much cheaper international bandwidth to all developing countries, and those savings should be passed on to end users. Lower costs for consumers would accelerate growth, and he encouraged operators to do that.

Internet Governance in the Light of the WSIS Principles

Chair:

Mr. Ahmed El-Sherbini, Deputy to the Minister for International Cooperation, Director of the National Telecommunications Institute, Egypt

Moderators:

Ambassador Jānis Kārkliņš, Ambassador of Latvia to France and Permanent Representative to UNESCO

Ms. Anriette Esterhuysen, Executive Director, Association for Progressive Communications (APC)

Mr. Bill Graham, Global Strategic Engagement, the Internet Society (ISOC).

The chair began by recalling that the IGF was created as a product of the WSIS, and that the IGF was mandated by the Tunis Agenda to promote and assess on an ongoing basis the embodiment of the WSIS principles in the Internet governance process. The session was therefore intended to exercise that right and to determine whether the WSIS principles had been taken into consideration in the governance of the Internet.

The session was divided into two main segments. The first section concentrated on principles, which were adopted in Geneva and Tunis, and particularly on paragraph 29. The second part was devoted to a debate on how Internet governance influenced the evolution of inclusive, non-discriminatory, development oriented Information Society and made reference to paragraph 31 of the Tunis Agenda.

In the first part, several of the major Internet governance institutions indicated that even before WSIS, there had been a commitment to what eventually became the WSIS principles. This was taken as an indication that the WSIS principles had not arisen suddenly out of a few months' meetings in

Geneva but, in fact, had been a developing trend in the world towards more transparent and more democratic multistakeholder processes. The convening of the IGF and the processes it had followed were part of an ongoing evolution, as the WSIS before it was part of an ongoing evolution, an evolution that had not been completed.

Many specific examples were given of work that was being done that clearly responded directly to the WSIS principles. One example was the multistakeholder work that had been done by the Council of Europe, the Association for Progressive Communications and the United Nations Economic Commission for Europe on the development of a trilateral initiative to launch a code of good practice on information, participation, and transparency in Internet governance.

Another example was given by the Organisation for Economic Co-operation and Development (OECD) of the process it went through when it brought the technical community and civil society into its structure as advisory committees.

There were also many indications given of areas where work would need to be done in the future, for example in the area of multilingualism. Some institutions also identified problems that various stakeholders still had with full participation of all stakeholders.

The discussion looked at ways in which the IGF could become more inclusive to participants from the developing world. There was no doubt that the developing world had made progress in many cases due to increased multistakeholder participation and more open processes, with examples being given of improvements in Argentina and Pakistan.

There were comments on the importance of the WSIS statement about respective roles of the different stakeholders. Participation was not a simple thing and there were different levels of participation by different stakeholders that were required at different stages in the process, moving from discussion through to a decision.

In general, business held the view that they had increased their outreach and credited that, to some extent, to WSIS. Civil society and technical organizations indicated that they too had become increasingly engaged with other stakeholders in a multilateral and transparent fashion. More examples of the influence of WSIS principles were given by civil society and the technical community than were given by governments, although it was made clear that some governments had made an effort to adapt to multistakeholder processes.

During the discussion of people-centred and inclusive development in the second section of the session, it was pointed out that three years of workshops had gone on before there was a main session on this topic. It was explained that these workshops had gone a long way in clarifying the concept of Internet governance for development and the specific things that should be focused on in going forward. Several times in the discussion, the point was made that there needed to be more main sessions on the WSIS principles and that Internet governance for people-centred development should become a main theme, rather than being an overarching theme, as it had been for the first four years.

Some speakers saw a need for benchmarks of a people-centred development, and a few examples were given such as, human rights and the degree of participation by developing country government in the IGF, both international and regional/national. Suggestions of ways to draw in developing countries included capacity-building for government officials in national governments. It was also brought out that participation in these open mechanisms and concentration on development was not a simple thing, but was complicated and time consuming. There were questions about whether it could be simplified to make it more accessible and easier, particularly for government officials, to participate.

A final point discussed in the session involved the consideration of economic realities, specifically some of the economic factors that have worked against the ability of developing nations to participate.

In concluding, the chair brought out two main points for emphasis. The first point was that a serious and sincere effort had been made by many to adhere to the WSIS principles in the Internet governance ecosystem. He also noted that there was still a lot of work that needed to be done to get everybody on board and to adhere to the all WSIS principles. The second point was there was a need for more serious engagement of the developing countries in the IGF activities.

The chair made a call on governments from developing countries to get more involved in the IGF activities, to make use of this forum, to get their voice heard, and to get their opinions on the issues related to Internet debated. He also called on the IGF secretariat to devise means and ways to motivate the governments of developing countries to get more involved in the IGF.

Host Country Honorary Session: Preparing the Young Generations in the Digital Age: A Shared Responsibility

The First Lady of Egypt, H.E. Ms. Suzanne Mubarak, President and Founder of the Suzanne Mubarak Women's International Peace Movement, addressed Forum participants in a special session. Her address focused on youth empowerment and the safety of children and young people on the Internet.

The First Lady was introduced by the Chairman, Mr. Tarek Kamel and she was thanked for her address by Under-Secretary-General Sha Zukang.

An international panel commented on the issues raised by the First Lady.

The signing of a number of MoUs between the Suzanne Mubarak Women's International Peace Movement and several business entities and NGOs concluded the Honorary Session.

A more detailed report is made as a Special Annex to this Chairman's Summary.

Taking Stock and Looking Forward – on the desirability of the continuation of the Forum.

Chair:

Mr. Sha Zukang, Under-Secretary-General for Economic and Social Affairs

The session was held in two parts, one part before and the other after lunch. The focus of this session was on whether or not the mandate of the IGF should be extended beyond the provisional lifespan of five years, as stipulated by paragraph 76 of the Tunis Agenda, which requested the Secretary-General to hold "formal consultations with Forum participants" on the "desirability of the continuation of the Forum".

These consultations were initiated by an online process, starting with a questionnaire prepared by the IGF secretariat. A synthesis paper reflecting all commentaries received was made available in all UN languages as an input into this session.

Mr. Sha, in his introductory remarks, recalled that this question had been a common thread throughout the meeting. There were powerful statements for an extension of the mandate at the opening session, starting with the Prime Minister of Egypt, but also other Ministers and representatives of the other stakeholder groups who spoke out in favour of a renewal of the mandate. Similar views were echoed in the other sessions, when panellists and chairmen noted the usefulness of the IGF in promoting a common understanding of issues.

Compared to the other Main Sessions, the consultation was held in a more traditional setting, with 47 speakers, representing all stakeholder groups, delivering a short statement on this subject from the rostrum. In addition, nine statements of participants who were not given a speaking slot due to time constraints were posted on the IGF Web site as part of the official record of the formal consultation.

The first two speakers were the two men also known as the 'Fathers of the Internet', Mr. Bob Kahn and Mr. Vint Cerf (through a video statement). The two co-inventors of the TCP/IP both valued the IGF as a neutral space for dialogue and supported the extension of its mandate. The IGF was an ideal setting in which to raise many issues ranging from abuses of the Internet to cooperation and could be used for making the Internet a better, safer, and more effective place in which to conduct global affairs.

Many speakers emphasized the usefulness of the IGF as a platform for dialogue, free from the pressures of negotiations. The spreading of the IGF model to regional and national IGF type processes was mentioned as a witness for the validity of the IGF concept.

H.E. Mr. Samuel Poghisio, Minister for Information and Communication of Kenya, expressing his support to an extension of the IGF mandate, made an offer to host the 2011 meeting.

45 speakers and nine written statements supported a continuation of the Forum.

A majority of speakers and written submissions supported an extension of the mandate as it is, that is, to continue the IGF as a multi-stakeholder platform that brings people together to discuss issues, exchange information and share best practices, but not to make decisions, nor to have highly visible outputs.

The other speakers, while supporting a continuation of the IGF along similar lines to its current form, called for some change, ranging from small operational improvements to major changes in its functioning, such as adding provisions that would allow it to produce outputs, recommendations and decisions on a multistakeholder consensus basis, or to finance the IGF through the regular UN budget.

Among the suggested areas for improvement were the following:

- International public policy issues;
- Capacity-building;
- Participation by developing countries;
- Transparency;
- Communications;
- Remote participation;
- Creating a data base for best practices;
- Visibility for outcomes.

Most of those who supported the continuation of the forum would like to do so for at least another five-year term.

Two speakers, while welcoming the success of the IGF and not opposing an extension, said it had not met expectations as regards 'enhanced cooperation' in the area of Internet governance. They also linked the IGF to unilateral control of critical Internet resource, an issue that needed to be addressed in the future.

Egypt, the host country, supported the continuation of the forum, while stressing at the same time the need to review its modalities of work, to increase institutional and financial capacity of its secretariat. Egypt supported maintaining its dynamic nature and multistakeholder approach under the UN umbrella, which gave it legitimacy.

The Chairman concluded the meeting by stating that he would now report back to the Secretary-General on the discussions held in Sharm El Sheikh. The Secretary-General would then make his recommendations to the UN Membership, as requested by the Tunis Agenda.

Emerging Issues - Impact of Social Networks:

Co-chairs:

H.E. Mr. Samuel Poghisio, Minister for Information and Communication, Kenya

Mr. Tarek El-Sadany, Senior Adviser to the Minister for Technology Policies, Ministry of Communications and Information technology, Arab Republic of Egypt

Moderator:

Mr. Simon Davies, Founder and Director of Privacy International

Panellists:

- Mr. Sergio Suiama, Prosecutor for the State of São Paulo, Brazil;
- Mr. Sunil Abraham, Director of Policy, Centre for Internet and Society;
- Ms. Rachel O'Connell, Chief Security Officer, BEBO;
- Ms. Grace Bomu, Manager, Actor and Policy advocate, Kenya-Heartstrings Kenya and Fanartics Theatre Company;
- Ms. Rebecca MacKinnon, Open Society Institute fellow, Global Network Initiative co-founder.

The session focused on the development of social media and explored whether these developments required the modification of traditional policy approaches, in particular regarding privacy and data protection, rules applicable to user-generated content and copyrighted material, as well as freedom of expression and illegal content.

The growth of social networking in Brazil, a country with 68 million Internet users, was given as an example of some of the problems that could arise. Most of the popular sites in that country were those offered by companies based in the United States. Legal problems experienced by Brazilian users of online social networking sites had lead to US companies, with small branches based in Brazil, being sued for liability in Brazil. A proactive response by some companies had led to criminal activities being reduced, primarily in the arena of child abuse images. The main issues raised by these cases were questions of whether the local arm of an online company was responsible individually or whether it was the whole transnational entity; the capacity to enforce national laws on crimes committed on social networking services; the feasibility of ensuring minimum levels of social accountability and transparency. The panellist finally emphasized the importance of foreign companies in complying with local laws, in order for the successful Brazilian case to be replicated in other countries.

One panellist raised nine emerging issues regarding social media Web sites and categorized them under a wide spectrum; intellectual property rights, morality laundering, the hegemony of the connected; and the hegemony of text. Morality laundering was claimed to be used to impose a morality regime by owners of Web sites. It was noted that the online industry worldwide conducted a lot of filtering at the back end, and there were linkages to governments and law enforcement. When asked if the automation of enforcement should exist, the panellist agreed, however more transparency should exist first.

Another panellist identified trends that were counteracting and limiting the impact of social networks. These included liabilities imposed by certain governments on social networking services, which were seen as limiting the reach of international networking sites. The owners of social networking services also sometimes imposed restrictions, often in response to spam, or conditions in terms of service defined by the owner's bias, which did not apply to the geography and culture of the user. The speaker was leading a global initiative that would try to create global solutions that were both flexible and tailored to individual situations. The terms of use of many social media and services were described as being complex, and users were not always clear of their rights and responsibilities, therefore literacy training was proposed as being necessary.

The impact of social networking tools was analyzed with regard to marketing activities of performers and producers of artistic work in Kenya. The theatre company the panellist works for targeted actors that came from slums and ghettos. The emergence of social networking had transformed how they sold their plays and developed their concepts. The panellist described how actors and fans (via Facebook) were said to have a major influence on the way in which their plays and scripts were developed. There was also an issue of fan participation and contribution causing abuse, excessive traffic, and the difficult issue of how to manage and to address speech that was controversial or abusive, which was sometimes directed from competitors using anonymous names. The tools of social networking had opened up new horizons and promoted freedom of expression, however at times also highlighted the problem of balancing between traditional cultural boundaries, in what might be viewed as abusive content, and what can be referred to as artistic expression.

One panellist reminded the floor about the power of social networks in citizen empowerment, and making governments and other institutions more accountable to individuals. Concerns over how to deal with liability issues, and content regulation by governments were raised. This highlighted the dilemma of social networking sites which had to choose whether to regulate content due to government pressure, or not to provide their service in those countries. Civil liberties of users would be infringed in both cases.

A speaker from the floor informed Forum participants that a dynamic coalition on social media and legal issues had been formed during the Sharm meeting. Issues such as the right of anonymity, deletion of personal information, child-generated content, among others would be considered by the coalition. Policy issues associated with cloud computing were indentified as critical new concerns that should be considered by the Forum in the future.

Closing Session

Several speakers, representing all stakeholder groups, addressed the closing session. They acknowledged that the issues of access and diversity remained central to the IGF. As the next billion people was coming online, new challenges and opportunities would emerge. The importance of what the Internet offered was unprecedented in terms of opportunities for mankind to promote economic development, social inclusion, expression of culture, and ideas in the rich array of languages. Common to all the speeches was the recognition that Internet governance needed to be based on multistakeholder cooperation. As one speaker pointed out, the lack of multi-stakeholder involvement in the past had often led to ill-informed decision-making.

Mr. Sha Zukang, Under-Secretary-General for Economic and Social Affairs, in his concluding remarks stressed the centrality of the principle of inclusiveness and the need for continued discussions on public policy issues related to the Internet. He recalled that he would present a report to the Secretary-General on the consultation on the desirability of the continuation of the Forum, as mandated by the Tunis Agenda. The Secretary-General would then communicate his recommendations to the UN Membership.

All other speakers expressed their support for an extension of the mandate and emphasized the value of the IGF as a platform for multistakeholder dialogue.

The speakers included the following stakeholder representatives:

* Ms. Anja Kovacs, Fellow, Centre for Internet and Society;
* Mr. Raúl Echeberría, CEO of LACNIC and Chair of the Board of the Internet Society (ISOC);
* Mr. Herbert Heitmann, Chief Communications Officer, Global Communications, SAP; Chair, EBITT Commission, ICC;
* Mr. Aurimas Matulis, Director, Information Society Development Committee, Lithuania.

The representative of Lithuania, extended an invitation to all participants to attend the Fifth IGF Meeting in Vilnius on 14-17 September 2010.

In his concluding address, the Chairman of the Fourth IGF Meeting, Mr. Tarek Kamel, called for further steps towards enhancing international involvement in the management of critical Internet resources. With regard to the IGF mandate, he noted that the unprecedented participation in this year's meeting showed the need for further deliberations and for the IGF to continue. The Chairman saw a wide consensus on the need for the extension of the IGF mandate, with the legitimacy provided by the United Nations umbrella as well as the dynamic nature of the event, which had been very clear in Sharm El Sheikh and needed to continue. He was confident that this message, representing the views of all stakeholders, would be conveyed to the Secretary-General.

Closing Remarks

H.E. Dr. Tarek Kamel
Minister of Communications and Information Technology
Egypt, 18 November 2009

Respectful audience, ladies and gentlemen,

I would like to start by thanking the U.N. team and the IGF Secretariat for co-organizing this successful event in Egypt. Special thanks are due to Mr. Sha Zukang, United Nations Under-Secretary-General for Economic & Social Affairs, Mr. Nitin Desai, and the whole U.N. team that worked behind the scenes in contributing to the success of this event. But also, special thanks to the IGF Secretariat, led by Mr. Kummer, and his staff as well as the interpreters and the scribes.

I want to thank the local team from Egypt at the Ministry of Communication and Information Technology, the technical team, the organizational team, as well as all the support staff. Special thanks are due, as Chairman Desai has mentioned, to the team led by Dr. Hoda Baraka, the Deputy Minister, Nermine El Saadany, Christine Arida, Manal Ismail, and Nevine Tewfik and their supporters.

I also want to thank the chairs of the various sessions and the sponsors of our events, the Telecommunication Regulatory Authority, Telecom Egypt, ITIDA, as well as the private sector sponsors. Special thanks are also due to the high level participation of Egypt's First Lady Mrs. Mubarak, as well as Prime Minister Nazif, and also special thanks are due to the very lively participation and thoughtful deliberations from all over the world that were really remarkable and unprecedented.

This huge participation showed the need for further deliberations for the IGF to continue. As Mr. Sha has mentioned, we have had participants that exceeded 1800, representing governments, civil society, and private sector, throughout the event more than 200 remote participants from all corners of the world were following up what we are doing, and 27,000 viewers from 116 countries have watched the live on demand webcast using streaming. Egypt's technical team, led by Raafat Hindy, has immediately responded to the request of the forum participants during the CIR session and has established on the spot an IPv6 networking in the congress centre. I want to give them special thanks for what they have been doing, not only on the IPv6 level, but also for the support of the whole Congress.

The participation at this event has really shown us the need for cross-border cooperation on the main themes of the IGF that were well selected by the Multistakeholder Advisory Group. Child safety has evolved as one of the emerging issues. And Egypt has shown its leadership with the participation and initiatives of Mrs. Mubarak. We think this needs to be broadened on a geographical level in the future.

Access, ladies and gentlemen, should remain on the IGF discussion table, because African countries and other developing countries still have issues of affordability and other major barriers to broadband connectivity. We need to come up with innovative solutions and business models for remote access in deprived areas.

The importance of multilingualism was very much highlighted. We still need to work more together on enriching local content. We welcome ICANN's decision for starting the fast-track process and choosing the Sharm El Sheikh IGF to announce this major step. This shows that we are on the right track.

We acknowledge the U.S. administration for signing the Affirmation of Commitments with ICANN, but we still need further steps for more international involvement in the management of critical Internet resources through revisiting the IANA contract as it has been mentioned. I sense consensus among our participants for my call, the other day, upon the U.S. administration to start an early dialogue in 2010 on the IANA contract before its expiration in October 2011. There are workable solutions that need to be explored for a more constructive dialogue on the issue, and this will add increasing maturity to the already maturing process of the IGF. This step will add a lot of positive spirit to the improving overall spirit that we have already been witnessing here in Sharm El Sheikh. And I fully share the vision of chairman Nitin Desai that we have been witnessing a very positive spirit, even between some constituencies that we thought are more or less competitive and confrontational.

My thanks to all the stakeholders for the spirit of cooperation and a special thanks to the ITU for their understanding of the IGF issues and especially the opening remarks of Secretary-General Dr. Hamadoun Touré. There has been a very positive spirit from other decision-making bodies to work on implementing the outcomes of the mature discussions within the IGF process. We think this is a step forward.

The global IGF requires more localization, and there is a rising need for the regional IGFs to become part of the process in the future, and we will also need more funding mechanisms, for stronger regional participation, especially from the developing countries. We have seen a positive contribution from the youth within the last couple of days. I urge the IGF MAG advisory group to increase youth participation and have for them a separate panel in order to engage them early enough in the process.

In my view, I could almost see a wide consensus on the need of the continuation of the IGF process with the legitimacy provided by the U.N. umbrella as well as continuing the dynamic nature of the event, which is very clear that it needs to continue. I see this well reflected in the Chair's report that was just printed and distributed. And I am confident that Mr. Sha will convey this message to the Secretary-General of the U.N.

Lastly, I wish Lithuania, our next host, all the success in preparing this event. I wish you, distinguished participants, a safe trip back home, and the conference is adjourned.

Thank you.

Annex: Host Country Honorary Session

Preparing the Young Generations in the Digital Age:

A Shared Responsibility

The First Lady of Egypt, H.E. Ms. Suzanne Mubarak, President and Founder of the Suzanne Mubarak Women's International Peace Movement, addressed Forum participants in a special session. Her address focused on youth empowerment, and the safety of children and young people on the Internet.

The First Lady was introduced by the Chairman, H.E. Mr. Tarek Kamel. Mr. Kamel informed the meeting that Ms. Mubarak had been one of the very early voices worldwide to support the empowerment of end-user views on the Internet. The First Lady had also long supported initiatives to address the challenges associated with child online safety.

Ms. Mubarak, in her opening remarks, noted how timely the themes of the 2009 IGF were. She praised the Forum for enriching the debate on Internet governance, and for having brought vital social dimensions to the heart of discussions. The IGF had integrated central topics and ideas such as digital citizenship, media literacy, culture creation, and youth empowerment, to explore how the Internet could be used to benefit all people. She commended the Forum on the choice of the overall title of the event: 'Creating Opportunities for All'. She noted how the theme shared important interdependencies with other human development goals, such as health for all, education for all, and food security for all, a topic she had addressed at the FAO a few days before. The theme also raised questions about the current status of our socioeconomic development, and about our ability to achieve the Millennium Development Goals by 2015. Ms. Mubarak illustrated how the IGF could be used to help ensure that these goals were achieved.

Ms. Mubarak noted Egypt's population was more than 80 million people and continued to grow. The country had struggled to bridge the divides that hindered capacity for how the Internet could be used, and how human development goals could be advanced by the Internet. Egypt had worked hard to reduce access and language barriers to modern technologies, and had made ICTs more affordable and useable. The increased use of ICTs had a profound effect on society, and had brought many changes. The Suzanne Mubarak Women's International Peace Movement had launched the Cyber Peace Initiative to capitalize on the powerful medium. The Cyber Peace Initiative promoted young people as leaders, and sought to create a global forum of peace, using the Internet.

Egypt had succeeded in reaching out and had engaged parents, educators, and especially youth, along with members of government, law enforcement, the judiciary, the private sector, and the civil society in a serious dialogue on Internet safety. Practical steps had been taken to protect and expand children's rights. The Cyber Peace Initiative had formed Internet safety focus groups, bringing together young people and their parents. They had brought attention to the need to bridge the digital divide between generations.

Ms. Mubarak highlighted that technical dimensions of the Internet such as information leakage and regulatory models for privacy, or ethical dimension of the Internet such as the control of one's own data and respect for privacy, could not be considered without taking into account the impact on children and young people as the direct beneficiaries. In addressing all these problems, she remarked that she was proud of the achievements of the Cyber Peace Initiative regionally and internationally. Further, she noted the creation of new initiatives such as World Wide Web Foundation, launched by Sir Tim Berners-Lee at the opening session of the IGF, the 2CENTRE Cybercrime Training Initiative and the teens' Internet safety camps.

The First Lady reminded the Forum that the Internet would continue to be a reflection of the global reality we lived in. As the divisions between transparency and privacy were erased, as the walls between the physical and virtual reality faded away, we would continue to feel reverberations of those challenges on the net through more discrimination, more violence, more instability. And it was for this reason that we should work harder to ensure that the focus of Internet governance became more people-centred, and that the Internet became a catalyst for human development. In closing, she outlined her vision of the Internet of tomorrow which held the real promise that we would be able to look at our computer or mobile screens and see a world where people lived in dignity, security and peace.

Under-Secretary-General Sha Zukang thanked Ms. Mubarak for sharing such an important message. He noted that the future of the Information Society would be led by today's children and young people, and that, fundamentally, sustainable development was about meeting the need of the present without compromising the ability of future generations to meet their own needs. He said the Information Society had to be made safe for children and young people, and that this could be achieved, as Ms. Mubarak suggested, by education and shared knowledge. He said the First Lady had provided much food for thought for the session that was to follow on new social media and collaboration tools. Mr. Sha presented a small gift on behalf of the IGF to Ms. Mubarak as a token of thanks for her important contribution to the Forum.

Ms. Hoda Baraka, First Deputy to the Minister of Communications and Information Technology of the Arab Republic of Egypt, moderated an international panel that commented on the issues raised by the First Lady.

The panel consisted of the following personalities:

- Mr. Robert Pepper, Vice President Global Technology Policy, Cisco;
- Ambassador David Gross, former U.S. Coordinator for International Communications and Information Policy, Department of State, United States;
- Mr. Jovan Kurbalija, Founding Director of DiploFoundation;
- Ms. Marilyn Cade, President, ICT Strategies, mCADE llc.;
- Mr. John Carr, Secretary of the Children's Charities Coalition on Internet Safety.

Ms. Baraka introduced the panel with a statement that the empowerment of youth had already been evidenced at the IGF by the youth involved in logistics, many workshops and in other roles at the forum.

The panel talked about current trends and concurred on the importance of involving youth and young people in discussions on Internet governance. Young people were leading the Internet revolution. It was noted that over 1.5 billion people were using the Internet and that the Internet was moving to broadband and as a result there was an exponential increase in traffic worldwide, driven by video. A unique characteristic of video was that it allowed communication in natural culture, fostering participation and cultural diversity. Video was a socio-economic driver for youth; the promotion and enablement of video content was therefore desirable. As the Internet spread, and content and services became more sophisticated, programmes such as the Cyberpeace Initiative would become more important. The Internet could be leveraged to produce opportunities for young people as well as challenges. It was suggested that the long-term way to deal with Internet safety and security problems as related to children was by parental involvement and oversight, and by the teaching of values.

One panellist noted that the IGF had served as a bridge between various players in the rapidly changing digital world, between the players he referred to as "digital natives", that is users who grew up with the Internet, and the "digital migrants", the generation of users that adopted the use of the Internet later in life. The DiploFoundation was given as an example for the process of online learning.

The "culture of the IGF" had helped bridge the interests and concerns of the old and new users of the Internet in their respective online experiences. Young people often did not distinguish between the online and offline worlds. Young peoples' skills and leadership in a lot of areas online meant that the traditional roles of adults and young people were in many ways reversed in our digital world.

Speaking about the need to protect children on the Internet, a panellist referred to a survey of governments conducted by the ITU in the field of child protection and child safety on the Internet. Over 80% responded that exposure to illegal and harmful content as well as bullying were their priority issues. The panellist held the view that not enough was being done and not fast enough by the Internet industry to protect children.

In the final part of the Honorary Session, Ms. Mubarak witnessed the signing four partnership agreements on behalf of the Cyber Peace Initiative with key organizations and multinational corporations and presented three certificates of recognition to young people and organizations that excelled in serving the young generations through ICTs.

The partnership agreements were with the following institutions:
- Family Online Safety Institute, FOSI;
- IBM Corporation;
- The 2CENTRE project with Microsoft, one of the founding partners of the Cyber peace Initiative;

- Oracle Corporation.

Certificates of recognition were presented to:
- Net Aman, in recognition of their role in disseminating the safety message throughout Egypt;
- DiploFoundation, for their role in knowledge generation and special teaching methodology;
- The United Nations Global Alliance for ICT and Development (UN-GAID) Committee of e-leaders for their special effort to engage young people in the field of ICT for development.

Annex

Internet Governance – Setting the Scene

Orientation Session

Co-moderators:

Ms. Nermine El Saadany, Director, International Relations Division, Ministry of Communications and Information Technology, Egypt

Mr. Markus Kummer, Executive Coordinator, IGF Secretariat

Panellists:

- Mr. N. Ravi Shanker, Joint Secretary, Department of Information Technology, Ministry of Information Technology, Government of India
- Ms. Marilyn Cade, President, ICT Strategies, mCADE llc
- Mr. Rafik Dammak, Masters research student, Graduate School of Interdisciplinary Information Studies, University of Tokyo
- Mr. Lee Hibbard, Media and Information Society Division / Directorate General of Human Rights and Legal Affairs, Council of Europe (CoE)
- Mr. Jovan Kurbalija, Director, DiploFoundation
- Mr. Alexander Ntoko, Head of ITU Corporate Strategy Division, ITU
- Ms. Virginia Paque, Program Coordinator, Internet Governance Capacity Building, DiploFoundation and co-coordinator of the Internet Governance Caucus (via video link-up)
- Mr. Nii Qaynor, Chairman and Chief Executive Officer, Network Computer Systems; President, Internet Society of Ghana

The session was introduced by Mr. Kummer who said the intention of the session was to help newcomers and other participants understand the IGF and to find their way around the programme.

He invited Ms. Divina Frau-Meigs to commemorate Mr. Francis Muguet, who had passed away unexpectedly on 4 October 2009. Mr. Muguet had been a keen and significant participant in the World Summit on the Information Society and the Internet Governance Forum. Ms. Frau-Meigs noted that his contributions were many, important, and that he would be missed. The meeting observed a minute's silence to honour his memory.

Introducing the IGF, Mr. Kummer remarked that the IGF had been convened as a platform for multistakeholder dialogue. Different from other UN processes, in the IGF all stakeholders were in the room as equals, and while the IGF did not have "the power to take decisions", it had "the power to put issues on the agenda of international cooperation".

Ms. Nermine El Saadany, the co-moderator of the session, welcomed the participants to Sharm El Sheikh, the city of peace, and introduced the panellists. All speakers then stressed the importance of the multistakeholder model of the IGF and its role as a forum for dialogue as being essential and unique. One speaker noted that as the IGF matured, it should strive to feed into more formal processes organized by IGOs and other entities, and also that the IGF should be considered within the broader perspective of WSIS.

A number of panellists noted the importance of the IGF to development, and that this reflected the success of the theme of the 2008 IGF, "Internet for All". The 2008 meeting had been able to help stimulate Internet governance related discussions and activities in many countries. The meeting in Sharm should ensure the development agenda was further brought to the forefront of discussions.

Panellists also emphasized the importance of capacity building, and that many organizations were now conducting training and education related to Internet policy issues. One speaker noted that the digital divide in Africa was as deep as ever, however, the cross-cutting themes of development and capacity building combined with the non-binding nature of discussions in the IGF had made it easier for developing country stakeholders to participate more fully in discussions. Regional and national IGF processes were noted as a new phenomenon that were helping to spread the development agenda, but more needed to be done.

Panellists from different stakeholder groups and regions described new partnerships and working relationships that had been enabled by the IGF process. It was also noted that the "'footprint' of Internet governance had increased enormously over the four years of the IGF. As the Internet had become more central to people's lives answers, practical questions such as the need to protect children online, issues raised by social networks, and the need to include consideration of human rights in the Internet governance context were important.

The moderators provided a walkthrough of the programme, and noted the visit of Ms. Suzanne Mubarak, First Lady of Egypt, who would give a special keynote presentation and lead an honorary session on "Preparing the Young Generation in the Digital Age, a Shared Responsibility."

More than 100 events would be held outside the main sessions, all were self-organizing and were based on the principle of multistakeholder cooperation. Through this methodology, real partnerships had emerged. Like the Internet itself, the value of the IGF was at the edges. A highlight of the programme was identified as a session focusing on persons with disabilities. The moderator reminded the Forum that according to UN statistics about 10% of the world's population were people with disabilities. There were UN conventions in place on disabilities, there were both obligations that addressed the issues and tools available, and the session would be aimed at raising awareness.

One speaker joined the Forum virtually from her home in Venezuela and emphasized the importance of remote access. The meeting would connect 11 remote hubs around the world and potentially many hundreds of people. Remote access could help overcome temporal, travel and financial constraints, it allowed people to contribute and made the IGF more inclusive.

Regional Perspectives

Moderators:

Ms. Christine Arida, Director of Telecom Planning and Services, National Telecom Regulatory Authority, Egypt

Mr. Markus Kummer, Executive Coordinator, IGF Secretariat

Panellists:

- Mr. Carlos Afonso, Planning Director, Rits (Information Network for the Third Sector), Rio de Janeiro, Brazil
- Ms. Alice Munyua, Member of the Board of Directors, Communications Commission of Kenya (CCK), Vice Chair, Kenya Network Information Centre (KENIC)
- Mr. Thomas Schneider, Information society coordinator, International Affairs Department, Swiss Federal Office of Communication (OFCOM)
- Mr. Ayman El-Sherbiny, Information Technology Officer, ICT Division, ESCWA, Lebanon
- Mr. Issah Yahaya, Head, Policy Planning, Monitoring & Evaluation/Telecoms, Ministry of Communications, Ghana

The session panellists were introduced by Ms. Christine Arida. They and brought together different regional experiences as they had emerged from various regional and national meetings, discussed how their different priorities were linked, and identified the commonalities and differences of each region.

Speakers presenting on the East African and European IGFs noted that they were not held as preparatory meetings for the global IGF, but had independent value, designed to identify local needs and priorities and to seek local solutions. Both noted there was a need for discussion to continue at a global level, but the regional initiatives could and would continue independently of the global discussions. This was noted as an interesting development, one speaker from the floor observed that the inspiration behind the IGF was global but the impact had now become local.

Each regional IGF had a different structure. The Caribbean IGF held its fifth annual meeting in August, noting it had existed longer than the global meeting. The Arab IGF team was also not formed specifically to contribute to the global IGF, but had been working independently, particularly on issues of domain names and multilingualism. The priority of the Arab region had shifted in the past years from those of language toward those of access. Access was noted as a priority by all the regional contributors, with problems of high prices as well as availability of broadband infrastructure common to all. Access to content and the creation of local content, and quality of service were also a theme mentioned by multiple presenters. Both the Latin American and East African speakers mentioned harmonization of national regulations and policy on access as priority issues.

The East Africa IGF involved five East African countries, Burundi, Kenya, Rwanda, Tanzania, Uganda, with observers from Sudan and Somalia. It was described as a three-stage process that began with a national online discussion for a period of about one to two weeks, moderated by national animators. From the online discussions, face-to-face national IGF meetings were organized for all the stakeholders to validate the online work, and consensus was built on national IG issues. The regional IGF brought together the national initiatives and provided an opportunity for national issues to be debated and discussed at the regional level. The presenter informed the Forum that an outcome of the East Africa-IGF was a decision by the government of Kenya to offer to host the global IGF in 2011.

The presenter from Europe emphasized the outreach to and inclusion of participants from Eastern and South-eastern Europe, and the increased and very active participation of youth as important developments. Cybercrime and cybersecurity were noted as key issues by all participants, the Arab and East Africa region described the creation of CERTs/CSIRTs at the national and regional levels as priorities that should be implemented. The Latin America and Caribbean regional meeting stressed the importance of privacy and remarked on the need for legal and regulatory harmonization generally within and among countries. Further, concern should be focused on the user and their rights, and that particular attention should be paid to social networks, cloud computing and e-government services. The European meeting – known as European Dialogue on Internet Governance (EuroDIG) also noted questions of privacy, as well as the reliability of the Internet.

All panellists described how their respective meetings discussed critical Internet resources, focusing on the joint project agreement (JPA) between the U.S. Government and ICANN. The meetings in West and East Africa and the Arab region noted the importance of ccTLDs and that they operated in a stable and secure manner. A representative of the African Union Commission introduced a regional African discussion that had been held in Sharm shortly before the IGF began, and also noted agreement that ccTLDs should be managed at local level and domestically have the needed skills and experience to manage their critical resources. He also noted Africa needed more national, regional and international peering points so that the cost of Internet traffic could be reduced and sustainable development ensured.

Each meeting had produced reports of their respective events, the presenter from Europe described how they had created a notion of 'messages' as an outcome. The document, 'Messages from Geneva' was not a negotiated document, but from each session a message of outcomes and recommendations, if appropriate, had been written, and everyone participating was free to say if they agreed or disagreed with the message.

Presenters from the floor informed the Forum about national IGF initiatives that had taken place in Spain, which would host EuroDIG 2010, and IGF USA, which developed a national perspective on the global IGF issues. The meeting in the US also included a youth panel, and discussed issues that were central to the IGF meeting in Sharm el Sheikh.

IV. Preliminary Events

Orientation Session

15 November 2009

Moderators:

Ms. Nermine El Saadany
Director, International Relations Division, Ministry of Communications and Information Technology, Egypt

Mr. Markus Kummer
Executive Coordinator, IGF Secretariat

Panellists:

Mr. N. Ravi Shanker,
Joint Secretary, Department of Information Technology, Ministry of Information Technology, Government of India

Ms. Marilyn Cade
President, ICT Strategies, mCADE llc

Mr. Rafik Dammak
Masters research student, Graduate School of Interdisciplinary Information Studies, University of Tokyo

Mr. Lee Hibbard
Media and Information Society Division / Directorate General of Human Rights and Legal Affairs, Council of Europe (CoE)

Mr. Jovan Kurbalija
Director, Diplo Foundation

Mr. Alexander Ntoko
Head of ITU Corporate Strategy Division, ITU

Ms. Virginia Paque
Program Coordinator, Internet Governance Capacity Building, Diplo Foundation; and Co-coordinator, the Internet Governance Caucus

Mr. Nii Qaynor
Chairman and Chief Executive Officer, Network Computer Systems; President, Internet Society of Ghana

Extracts from the Transcript of Proceedings

MARKUS KUMMER:

I will begin by saying a few words on the IGF, what it is and what it is not. The IGF is a child of the World Summit on the Information Society. It was decided in Tunis back in 2005 to give a mandate to the Secretary-General of the United Nations to convene a multistakeholder platform for dialogue on the issues related to Internet governance. The important word in this context is "multistakeholder;" the IGF is unlike a traditional U.N. meeting, which is essentially intergovernmental. Here it is a meeting where all stakeholders, governments, private sector, civil society, the technical community, international and intergovernmental organizations sit down as equals in the room to discuss matters related to Internet governance. And Internet governance is based on the definition agreed on in Tunis that relates to policy issues with regard to the development and deployment of the Internet.

This year in Sharm El Sheikh is the fourth meeting of the IGF, following Athens in 2006, Rio in 2007, and Hyderabad in 2008. Our main axis of discussion has been along five main themes: access, diversity, openness, security, and critical Internet resources. In Hyderabad we began to look at the interrelationship between these themes. The program is developed in a distributed, bottom-up way. The main group in this regard is the Multistakeholder Advisory Group, which advises the Secretary-General in convening the meeting. And we have, throughout the year, open calls for contributions, as well as planning meetings that are open to all stakeholders, and rolling documents that push the agenda forward.

The nature of the IGF is that it's not to replace any existing organizations or to take decisions. But the IGF can shape decisions that are taken in other organizations. It has not the power of redistribution, but it may have the power of recognition. It can recognize issues. It can put them on the agenda of international cooperation. And the new phenomenon in this regard, and we look at it in the latter part of the session, is the spread of national and regional IGF-type processes.

An important part of this year's meeting will be the review session. The IGF was originally given a mandate of five years with a clause to review it and to take stock. And based on this report, the Secretary-General will then make recommendations to the U.N. membership on whether or not to continue the mandate. I will ask now my co-moderator to introduce the panellists, and they will then tell us what they have gotten out of the IGF so far.

NERMINE EL SAADANY:

Let me first, on behalf of the Egyptian government, welcome you all in Sharm El Sheikh, the City of Peace. This session today will help in explaining what the IGF is---the process and the agenda---and to highlight some of the key aspects that we're going to live together the following four days. I will now take advantage of being both the moderator and the host country representative start by sharing our views. By hosting the IGF this year, Egypt wants to emphasize the responsibilities that both developing and developed countries are equally sharing. Bringing the forum to the African and Arab region for the first time signals that this forum and the question of its continuation could not be completed without adding the opinions of the developing countries and tackling their needs. The IGF is the only place that paved the way for the involvement of all stakeholders in the process and established a healthy and productive dialogue between all parties. This dialogue surely helps in creating a common background with regard to the different themes and issues. Hosting the IGF enabled the Egyptian community to get more engaged in the discussions related to the forum and stimulated national and regional awareness of Internet governance issues. The Egyptian government has been investing a lot in mobilizing and coordinating the community to ensure a successful event.

N. RAVI SHANKER:

The theme of the current IGF is well articulated: Internet opportunities for all. And the development agenda is certainly getting more focus, which is laudable. This moves us beyond the fourfold ideas that emerged at Athens of access, diversity, openness and security, and the new theme that evolved in Rio, management of critical Internet resources. While the IGF is a non-outcome oriented event, we learned a lot of lessons from hosting it that helped us to stimulate activity in the ICT and Internet sector. We have launched the national knowledge network, which is basically democratizing education and bridges a huge digital divide gap in the arena. We also felt that as a nation the development agenda needs to be put into focus, and have tried to take to all the rural areas common service centres or info kiosks. Telemedicine and e-learning will be important focal areas of development.

MR. NITIN DESAI:

One of the very important aspects that has been considered in IGF is capacity building. In Egypt, in our endeavour to prepare for this IGF, we have been building the capacities of a group of experts to enrich awareness about Internet governance issues. In collaboration with DiploFoundation, the Egyptian task force of IGF organized a series of workshops for the Egyptian community to introduce them to the themes of the IGF so that we can all come here well prepared and can integrate into the discussions.

JOVAN KURBALIJA:

When I was asked to reflect on capacity building, I thought of using the visual association or metaphor of a compass, because we usually need a compass to see where we are. So I will use two type of compasses. One is to navigate the evolution of capacity building in the IGF context, and the other one is to navigate our next four days at the IGF in Sharm. The IGF's capacity building is a good example of what can be achieved if you work in a bit longer time span. In four years, the IGF has achieved a lot in inclusive participation. It was one of the highlights of the last IGF in India, and our Egyptian hosts have made additional step forward. Now, let me illustrate this revolution in capacity building with a story. Back in 2005 I was one of the members of the Working Group on Internet Governance, and a one meeting I asked the other members if they could explain to their friends and relatives what they were doing. Very few could do it. I wasn't among them. The IGF was a new topic. There were many acronyms. Many friends were telling me, "Jovan, you are dealing with computers. Could you come to my home to fix my printer?" Today they ask me if Internet governance could help to control what their children are accessing on the Web, or the privacy status of their Face Book accounts. In four years' time, there has been enormous evolution in general understanding about Internet governance, so there are more questions. Many of the answers must be provided on the national level, but at international level the place where they are discussed and sometimes provided is the IGF.

Another major change over the last four years has been that international organizations, including ITU, UNESCO, and the World Bank, have trained many people in Internet governance issues, including infrastructure and multilingualism. ICANN has also trained huge number of people, and the Internet Society is one of the most prominent players in capacity building, especially on the national level. There have also been more specific targeted capacity-building programs, including summer schools organized in various regions. My organization does capacity-building involving training, research, and policy immersion. An increasing number of universities worldwide are introducing Internet governance in postgraduate studies and undergraduate curriculum of their programs. The IGF has galvanized those developments, and has become the natural host of capacity building.

The second compass should help us navigate the next four days. The IGF is a great learning experience, providing context for the exchange of knowledge and acquiring of new skills. I'm sure that each participant in this room, and more than 1,500 people, will have their unique stories about experiences at the IGF. For many, it will be the first exposure to Internet governance, while others have been in this process for a long time and the IGF will help them to fine-tune their knowledge. Others are involved in specialized area such as privacy or data protection, and IGF will help them to make links with other fields, to move beyond their policy silos, to see what has been done in other areas. How to navigate this richness of the program over the next four days? The compass will direct us to workshops and panels where you can listen to the leading experts, and it will point to the Internet Governance Village where you will be able to meet people, chat and learn by osmosis. Probably an "intellectual knowledge bazaar" will describe what will be happening in the village. The third direction our compass will point us, especially if you are a digital migrant as I am, is to visit the digital dive booth at the youth corner where digital natives, young people will help you to understand their role and the new challenges of the governance. The fourth and the last direction that at least my IGF compass will point to is the debating club, where you can sharpen your arguments and listen to young people arguing on the key issues. So take out your IGF compass, open your radars, and be prepared to enjoy and learn.

RAFIK DAMMAK:

My first experience was at the IGF in Rio de Janeiro as a kind of youth representative, with other fellows, presenting what we had done in an online roundtable, and voicing our vision for youth in Internet governance. Our main participation was in the Emerging Issues session, and it energized us to continue the experience at the following IGF meeting. So we organized a first workshop focusing on youth issues, and the work was done by a team of volunteers from the old online roundtable, and new people. This year we will organize again a workshop with only young panellists, with partners like the DiploFoundation, Cyber Peace Initiative, and the Net-Aman from Egypt.

ALEXANDER NTOKO:

A process was launched in 2003 when world leaders thought that it was important to see how we could accelerate the achievement of the Millennium Development Goals using ICTs. It was the first time that we had all four stakeholder groups, governments, civil society, international organizations, and business, functioning on an equal footing. We like to say in the ITU that WSIS was probably the first forum where civil society was not demonstrating outside, because they were inside, on the same footing as everybody else. And we think that this is a unique opportunity because it creates this environment where people can discuss on an equal level and share ideas that can be fed into more formal processes. They are trying to arrive at some common understanding or a shared vision of the solutions to the problems. But thee ideas which have matured to a certain extent need to be followed up on through formal arrangements and mechanisms. The ITU is an intergovernmental treaty organization with 191 member states. The IGF gives us an opportunity to get some ideas and see how they can mature and be fed into our own development and global standards processes. We meet people that we normally would not meet in our own organization, so IGF is an experience that is unique. The IGF needs to be seen within the broader picture of WSIS and the agreements that were undertaken by world leaders in Geneva and in Tunis.

MARILYN CADE:

There are three words that make up the title of IGF. Governance does not mean government, it means governance. And without going into great detail, there was an extensive discussion over a six-month period in a multistakeholder environment that defined "governance" very broadly, to include the acts and responsibility of each individual person and each individual sector. I see "multistakeholder" within the IGF as something that we have built and must continue to build. It means that each of you are an expert, but in a different way than you are an expert in another intergovernmental organization or in a national organization. "Multistakeholder" here comes with the modifying phrase, "interacting on an equal footing," so here each of us individually is entrusted with respecting the perspectives and the role of each other person and each other sector. Civil society and NGOs, the business community, the technical community, the governments with more than one ministry involved, and the intergovernmental organizations are all contributing to this unique environment. When I interact in other intergovernmental organizations and in national organizations, I also find varieties of multistakeholder behaviour or interactions. But "multistakeholderism" within the IGF is different and very reliant upon active participation. So here you do not just listen, but rather actively participate and raise questions and get to know the different stakeholders and their perspectives. That means when you come to the IGF, it's a lot more work. You don't just come to attend a workshop session; you actually have the opportunity to build a workshop. And one of the real contributions that I've seen throughout the four years of the IGF is that the planning and organizing of each of the sessions is also multistakeholder. The opportunity we have is to keep reaching out and making sure that participants understand the uniqueness of multistakeholderism here.

NII QUAYNOR:

The IGF deserves appreciation for getting African issues close to the global community, which has been very helpful for us. The technical community started a journey about ten years ago from Cape Town, and we ended up going through ten different countries and arrived in Egypt just this past May, and we thank the government of Egypt for its support and commitment throughout our entire journey over the past decade. The cross-cutting themes of multistakeholderism and capacity-building create a great learning environment for Africans, and since it is "nonbinding" the sensitivities are a little lower, which really helps us. Nitin Desai has often said that IGF brings together people who would not ordinarily meet, and that has been of benefit for us. The multistakeholder process is something that we should all try to take back home, in the sense that whatever organization we are in, we should make an effort to hear what the other sides are concerned about and make sure that the relevant groups that deal with any given issue are within the community. For example, if you are discussing infrastructure-related issues, you'd better make sure that the technical community is well represented, so that the discussion can be rooted in some reality.

The best thing for a participant to do to get the most out of it is a bit of immersion. There is so much going on, and you might say that the workshops become even more important than the main sessions. And that means that you have to immerse yourself in the community and really chase all the issues that seem exciting and interesting for you. Of course access remains a major concern for Africa and the developing world, and we'd like things to be much more affordable and readily available, and we'd like to encourage the necessary investments to make that realistic. Other issues facing the African community include diversity, security, and capacity building. The multistakeholder process makes it possible for us to make some progress on these.

LEE HIBBARD:

I come from an intergovernmental setting, a pan-European space with 47 members talking about human rights, the role of law, and democracy. From the first IGF, my perspective started to change, and my colleagues and I quickly realized the importance of multistakeholder dialogue. Talking among only one stakeholder group isn't enough when you're dealing with things like the Internet rights and freedoms, it is important to talk to businesses and civil society. An analogy I'd make is between 20th anniversary of the fall of the Berlin Wall and an event we took part in last week in Berlin with Google called "breaking borders." In many respects, the IGF too is about breaking borders by simply bringing people together to talk. Intergovernmental

145

decision-making is one thing, but face-to-face discussion with youth, with persons with disabilities, with many stakeholder groups, is invaluable. We have to use that dialogue to make better Internet governance policies, whether standards, guidelines, or whatever. Without the IGF, I don't think that the Council of Europe would have been able to be as reactive in developing tools and guidelines on human rights as it has been. And if the IGF wasn't there, we might not have produced certain texts at all, such as a standard on the public service value of the Internet.

The Council of Europe is now working not only with Europeans, but with many other actors in the IGF and outside, which is wonderful. At this meeting we have 21 people from the Council, we're organizing or co-organizing with other actors seven different events, and we are involved in panellist roles in at least 13 other events organized by other stakeholders. The IGF has allowed us to encourage signatures and ratifications of certain international treaties, it's helped us to cooperate outside of Europe, and it's helped to put human rights on the map with regard to Internet governance. That's very important. We're working more with the private sector than ever before, thanks to the IGF, and back home, even in very formal settings where there's lots of protocol like ministerial conferences, we're applying the multistakeholder principle. So for the first time at the end of May in Reykjavik, we had ministers sitting around tables, and many had associated youth delegations, and we had civil society and private sector actors talking together with ministers. That was quite an achievement. And the IGF allows the Council of Europe to test ideas and work in progress, so we're developing different fields of work, whether it's to do with new media, or cross-border Internet traffic and what that means from a human rights perspective. And when things are completed, it helps us to share them with all of you. So overall there's lots of value for us here at the IGF.

MARKUS KUMMER:

The second part of this panel will look at the program in a more down-to-earth way. First of all, thanks to our hosts for producing a printed program, it is very helpful. Just a word of caution, the deadline for the printed program was roughly a month ago and there have been some changes since, so please also check the most current version on our Web site. It has been mentioned that the main sessions are the backbone of the IGF, but I often say the IGF is like the Internet itself: The value added is at the edges, and there's much value added in the workshops. We have more than 100 events in parallel outside these main sessions. They're all self-organized under the steering of the Multistakeholder Advisory Group. We force the organizers to embody the multistakeholder principle in their events; for a workshop to be accepted, it needs to have multistakeholder participation. And through this cooperation, real partnerships have emerged.

You will see in the program that we have colour-coded the different workshops, with each colour corresponding to one of the main themes. So if you are particularly interested in security or diversity, you can pick your workshops on that basis. Looking at the main sessions, we have various formats this year. We have had some panels this morning. This afternoon, the opening ceremony will be more formal. There will be a sequence of distinguished speakers. Tomorrow morning, we will have a session on critical Internet resources. That will be open moderated debate without any panel.

One session I would like to highlight is that on diversity. We have a dynamic coalition on accessibility for people with disabilities that worked very hard on presenting this topic. According to U.N. statistics, about 10% of the world's population is made up of people with disabilities. There are U.N. conventions in place on these disabilities, with obligations, and there are also tools available. So this is a session aimed at raising awareness, and the people organizing this have prepared a message to come out from Sharm El Sheikh. Another session I would like to highlight is on Taking Stock and Looking Forward, where we will talk about the mandate of the IGF. We opened registration for this session on our Web site, but we discovered that the interest is so great that we have too many speakers. So we encouraged speakers to gather together in the various stakeholder groups so that one statement is on behalf not just of a single individual but of one important group, or a group of institutions within that group. We will have to limit the statements to about ten from each stakeholder group, and the speaking time to three minutes. Finally, there is one special event, the host country honorary session. Please, Nermine.

NERMINE EL SAADANY:

We feel very honoured to have for the first time in the history of the IGF the high-level participation of the First Lady of Egypt, Mrs. Suzanne Mubarak. Mrs. Suzanne Mubarak has been very active since her early career in many areas, and one of those areas is the helping people with disabilities and special needs. Another issue that is very close to her heart is protecting children in cyberspace. We are going to have her in an honorary session titled "preparing the young generation in the digital age, a shared responsibility."

MARKUS KUMMER:

We are very honoured to have your First Lady with us. I am given to understand that the remote participation is now ready, so Ginger you have the floor.

VIRGINIA PAQUE:

I am very fortunate to have this opportunity to speak with you today from Maracay, Venezuela. I join other remote participants, hubs, and presenters in thanking the IGF host, the Secretariat, and community for making this possible. Some of us are used to immediate connections and efficient tools, and we forget sometimes that remote participation is a complex process. To be here with you today in a session that starts at 3:30 in the morning took a bit of planning, a constant source electricity, and hence good weather, too. The planning in Sharm El Sheikh was much more complicated, as teams worked to set up a system capable of connecting 11 remote hubs around the world and possibly hundreds of individual remote participants. It is well worthwhile as remote participation overcomes financial, temporal, and travel constraints, allows a more global impact, and enhances the IGF's concrete progress towards diminishing the digital divide through improved participation and inclusion. There are not many discussion forums in the world that can point to such success.

I am part of the DiploFoundation team that has worked on the "IGF: Identifying the Impact" report, which I hope you have all seen by now. This is our first review of the subject, which we hope to study more thoroughly during the next year. Trying to identify the impact of the IGF has turned out to be far more complex than expected. The IGF is a discussion forum. It's a conference. It's a meeting of minds and ideas. It is words. How can we measure the impact of words? Even with the wide range of information available in an Internet search, I found very little guidance on how to identify the impact of discussion. Often it is measured in terms of cost/benefit, or of environmental impact. The most relevant report I found was an article suggesting that the presence of discussion can generate outcomes that are perceived as more equitable and fair in some circumstances. That suggests a baseline for assessing the probable impacts of proposals to integrate deliberation into political decision-making.

Almost without exception, the interview participants in the impact study seemed to assume that the IGF should and will continue. They were committed to improving a process that they are invested in. A strong majority of them were involved in taking home, sharing, and spreading, multiplying the impact of the IGF in their local communities. To collect words and ideas, and to take them home and put them to work. We must plan for that and do it on purpose, not just let it happen. How long did we plan for this meeting? More than a year. This is a continuous process, not a four-day process. We post mailing list messages, go to IGF open consultations, and plan workshops all to create an impact during these four days. We now must plan to maximize this impact by using the required reporting from workshop panels to publicize the results of the workshops at the regional, national, and especially local levels. This is not the responsibility of the IGF Secretariat.

MARKUS KUMMER:

This meeting will deploy a special effort to bring in young people. Gender, we realize is an area where we do need a constant effort. I can only encourage you, madam and others who want to promote the role of women within the IGF and within Internet governance, to go to the meeting of the Dynamic Coalition on Gender, and I would very welcome if a strong message comes out of that. Would you like a last few words?

NERMINE EL SAADANY:

I would just notify the distinguished delegates that there is a youth camp that started two days ago, and that tomorrow there will be a workshop run by youth from 11 years to 17 years old. So it will be interesting if we can participate in this and encourage them and listen to their needs and issues.

MARKUS KUMMER:

Finally, I would like to highlight that we have two papers posted on our Web site as input into the discussions. One of them has been translated in all U.N. languages, and it summarizes all contributions we received on the stock-taking process with regard to the IGF mandate. The other paper relates to the substantive agenda. The translations are being done by the U.N. in Nairobi and we have not received all the languages yet but should in the course of the week; in the meanwhile the English paper is available now.

Regional Perspectives

15 November 2009

Moderators:

Ms. Christina Arida
Director of Telecom Planning and Services, National Telecom Regulatory Authority, Egypt

Mr. Markus Kummer
Executive Coordinator, IGF Secretariat

Panellists:

Mr. Carlos Afonso
Planning Director, Rits (Information Network for the Third Sector), Rio de Janeiro, Brazil

Ms. Alice Munyua
Member of the Board of Directors, Communications Commission of Kenya (CCK), Vice Chair, Kenya Network Information Centre (KENIC-Kenya's ccTLD manager)

Mr. Thomas Schneider
Information society coordinator, International Affairs Department, Swiss Federal Office of Communication (OFCOM)

Mr. Ayman El-Sherbiny
Information Technology Officer, ICT Division, ESCWA, Lebanon

Mr. Issah Yahaya
Head, Policy Planning, Monitoring & Evaluation/Telecoms, Ministry of Communications, Ghana

Extracts from the Transcript of Proceedings

CHRISTINE ARIDA:

On this panel we would like our analysts to give their perspectives on the priorities for their regions and how those link to the global dialogue. We want to make this panel as interactive as possible and to hear from the floor, from other regional meetings, and from also maybe national meetings. So I will start to with Mr. Carlos Afonso giving us a perspective from the Latin American region.

CARLOS AFONSO:

The second Latin American/Caribbean preparatory meeting of the IGF was organized by the APC, the Nupef Institute, the Information Network for the Third Sector, and the Latin American/Caribbean Network Information Center, the LACNIC. It was supported by CGI.br from Brazil, the National Research Network, APC, ISOC, and ICANN, among others. It was an interesting meeting, held in August for three days. I will present quickly a summary of findings and outcomes based on the individual reports from the sessions. Session one was about access. Among the challenges discussed were universalization of the infrastructure, including end-user access tools; and building capacities to empower as many users as possible and stimulate them to learn about the technologies and their potential to improve the quality of lives. Also discussed was affordable connectivity; in most of the region, there are few backbone providers per country, frequently just one. Where there is more than one national backbone, the deployment of Internet exchange points is necessary. In countries like Brazil, these IXPs are non-profit services which do not add to the cost of bandwidth, and to the contrary, help reduce costs by optimizing national or in-country regional traffic. Broadband ought to be universalized, using an optimal combination of fibre and digital radio as well as regulatory and public-policy incentives.

Another issue was the harmonization of regulatory practices. This is especially important for the Caribbean, where there are many small countries with divergent regulatory practices, which makes it difficult to set a public policy for developing infrastructure and attracting private investment. A related point is appropriate legislation to assist in planning investments and combining market competition with adequate regulation to ensure universalization. The market by itself will not guarantee universalization, while significant restrictions to private initiative or the replacement of state operators by private monopolies might preclude innovation. Governments need to develop strategic planning in the deployment of these technologies. International connectivity costs was another point. These impact directly the price of access for the final user, and most countries do not have the leverage to negotiate better terms of trading international bandwidth. In the Caribbean, for instance, not all countries have access to submarine cables. Local content, it's recognized that extending access to all requires incentive to develop local content for all. National strategies for producing appropriate local content, which add value to the access and connectivity policies, are needed. In this sense, the Internet is also an effective medium for social inclusion in citizens' participation in democratic processes, allowing for significant improvements in transparency, in efficacy, in government. Finally, access to communicate and exchange information is the basis for realizing the right to communicate, a fundamental right for every citizen.

The second session was on privacy. The main issue to emerge was the need for legal and regulatory harmonization generally within and among countries. Also discussed were the need to create structures to protect privacy; the importance of training stakeholders on privacy, especially lawyers, judges, policymakers, civil society advocates and the individual user; privacy issues concerning social networks, cloud computing, and e-government; and the situation of workers. Users need information about the implications of what they are doing in social networks, in simple language. And the privacy difficulties related to jurisdiction, where data is stored in another country, and issues involving multinational companies.

Session three was on critical resources and focused on the governance of the DNS, IP addresses and the root system. There was consensus that these resources need to be unique and globally coordinated and the challenge in this regard are, on the one hand, to legitimate coordination, and on the other, to identify the best global practices to manage these resources. Statements were made on the importance of the Anycast system, the positive contributions of IXP initiatives, Internet exchange points, agreement that the regional management of I.P. addresses has been satisfactory, and the protracted process of creating new gTLDs. IDN zone stability was regarded as essential, and the deployment of DNSSEC constituted an extremely important step in the direction of DNS stability. Session four on openness and security stressed the balance between legal and enforcement needs on the one hand and freedom of expression on the other hand. Session five was on multilingualism and accessibility and set the theme in context of the Internet as a tool for human development. It was noted that universal access funds are still not used in many countries in the region and should be effectively and urgently disbursed. Finally, we had a dialogue on openness, including free expression, access to knowledge and information, and open infrastructure, opportunities, standards, software, and governance.

CHRISTINE ARIDA:

Okay, thank you, Carlos. The reports will be shared on the Web site, so you will be able to download and read them there. Next is Mr. Thomas Schneider to talk about the European IGF, EuroDIG.

THOMAS SCHNEIDER:

The objective of the European Dialogue on Internet Governance, or EuroDIG, was to establish a platform for discussion among all European stakeholders. To exchange views and best practices and raise awareness about Internet governance issues. Europe is a very diverse region and you have at least five opinions on any one issue, normally, so establishing common ground was another objective. As was feeding the European view into the global discussion. Unlike the global IGF, it was a real bottom-up initiative launched by a group of people sitting at a table in an ICANN meeting in Paris in 2008. The structure is very light. There is no chair. There is no Multistakeholder Advisory Group. It's just an open network where everybody can join and work with us in a consensus-based process. We have very limited resources, of course. The network started with five people and it's now an organization and it's growing and growing. And we have more or less all the relevant institutions and stakeholders present in the EuroDIG structure.

We had the first EuroDIG in 2008, organized by the Council of Europe in their facilities in Strasbourg. This year's meeting was co-organized by the Swiss Federal Office of Communication and the European Broadcasting Union with the support of the Council of Europe, and was held at the EBU headquarters in Geneva. We had comparatively few panels and so-called experts on the podium, so many sessions were just one moderator guiding an interactive discussion with the room. We had a session with members of the European Parliament of the European Union, the parliament of the Council of Europe, and national parliaments including non-EU member states. It was interesting to get feedback from people that had been elected to take care of the needs of the people, what they cared about and so on. We also had quite a number of youth representatives that took active part in the discussion and were not shy about telling us if something we discussed was absolutely unimportant or outdated according to their views. And that also added to the very interesting and lively debate. And we made efforts to include the countries from central and eastern, south eastern Europe that normally have the least means to participate in Internet governance discussions and mechanisms. We ran a students program for these regions and invited the ten best students to participate in the discussion.

There are a few things that we have done differently that could useful to discuss with the global IGF and with other regions. We have "outcomes" in the sense that we created a document that you can see on the Web site, eurodig.org, called "Messages from Geneva." It is not a negotiated document, but rather the organizers of the sessions were responsible for listing the key issues and common ground identified. And everybody is free to say, "I disagree with this view" or "I agree with this view."

In terms of content, our workshops and plenary sessions considered topics like end-user access to and choice in services, privacy, the reliability of the Internet, cyber crime, and media literacy. We also had a session on how we imagine the Internet of 2020 and what the challenges could be. We had a session on access to content online, and the question of should you regulate or not new media like social networking sites. Then we had a discussion of the post-JPA era, 15 days before the publication of the Affirmation of Commitment, so we had some ideas but didn't know for sure what was going to come. And there was the last session discussion on the future of EuroDIG and the creation of a European IGF, and the main common ground was that our societies are based on fundamental freedoms, human rights and the rule of law, and these should be valid on the Internet as they are in the real world. There was common ground that the Internet has become an infrastructure of public interest, and has therefore a public value which people should be aware of, and that stability and security is crucial because we all rely on it more and more in our daily lives. Access too is crucial, to services, content, diversity, and media education.

The last point is that the EuroDIG should be seen as the European IGF, and that we would try to put it on a more sustainable basis. The Council of Europe offered Secretariat support for future EuroDIG meetings, which was welcomed, so we are now discussing future meetings. Spain will host the EuroDIG in 2010, and it will continue after that in countries like Serbia and others.

CHRISTINA ARIDA:

Thank you. Let me turn to our next panellist, Ms. Alice Munyua, who will be reporting on the East African IGF.

ALICE MUNYUA:

The first East African IGF was held in 2008 and the second in 2009, both in Nairobi. It has been convened mainly by Kenya, but the other countries have been involved since the outset---Uganda, Tanzania, Rwanda, and Burundi, and in 2009 we had the pleasure of inviting Sudan and Somalia to participate officially as well. All the stakeholders have been involved and very actively participating and contributing to the process, and the new entrant this year was our parliamentarians. We had an IGF parliamentarian session that was hosted by the Kenyan National Assembly and its speaker, and we had parliamentarians from the four other East African countries too. That process developed a resolution to work collaboratively to develop policies on broadband access, cyber security and cyber crime, and other issues.

There was some consensus on cybercrime and cyber security. With broadband now in the region challenges are going to be experienced from fraud to cyberstalking to spamming, and participants requested governments to come up with a policy at the international level and to develop national and regional CERTs in collaboration with international organizations that are working on this. There was also consensus on access, a major issue in our region. Yes, there is broadband at the eastern coast but the costs have not come down at the user level. There was a lot of concern about local content that is relevant and in the languages of our region as well. We also felt that there was a need to look at mobile content solutions by all stakeholders. Critical Internet resources were identified as a theme at the regional level, and our main concern was strengthening our ccTLDs. For some of them, it's an issue of redelegation, but mainly its about engaging in ICANN's process, ensuring DNSSEC, ensuring the security and stability of the Internet, and the new generic top-level domains.

Consumer issues and consumer protection was also quite a big issue, including promoting awareness. Also addressed were topics like quality of service and policy and regulation, and that's where we feel that the global IGF can be of immense assistance through all the discussions and the debate. So, again, what was presented to the parliamentarians or the policymakers was focused on coming up with a regional policy and a framework for collaboration. We feel, like the Europeans, that the East African IGF and the national IGFs will continue, but we need a model to integrate organizations and communities into global policymaking processes. The consensus of the forum, which was captured in a communiqué, was to pursue the NKRUMAH agenda. NKRUMAH, the initials of the vice president of Ghana, a staunch pan-Africanist, had "N" representing network development; the "K" representing knowledge; the "R" for regional priorities; the "U" representing Ubuntu, meaning people, and Umoja, togetherness; the "M" for multistakeholder and good management; the "A" representing assembly and ambassadors; and the "H" representing high-level engagement on processes and policies. We very strongly support the continuation of the global Internet Governance Forum, and Kenya officially made its intention to host the 2011 IGF, if the mandate is extended. The next East African IGF is going to be held in Uganda, hosted by the Ugandan government and other stakeholders.

CHRISTINA ARIDA:

Thank you, Alice. Let me introduce Mr. Issah Yahaya, who will discuss the West African IGF.

ISSAH YAHAYA:

The West African IGF was held on the 14th to 16th October 2009. It was organized by AfriNIC and the Minister of Communications on behalf of the government of Ghana. The theme was "Promoting the Multistakeholder Model for Further Internet Development in Africa." Participants came from the academic community, civil society, government, the private sector, and the technical community. The objectives of the forum included identifying of obstacles that impede the growth of the Internet; identifying ways to accomplish related tasks more effectively and efficiently; staying informed of industry trends and understanding the resources required; and developing relationships with other organizations that are also tasked with common goals. The opening challenge as read out by the minister in his address was that good Internet governance is critical for sustainable development. The imperative for West Africa is to embrace the spirit behind the IGF, which is based on multistakeholder approach and addresses critical issues. Other challenges were the need to strengthen the Internet industry and build a multistakeholder model. Affordable access should continue to be the priority in order to improve Internet usage as a tool and enabler of socioeconomic development. Affordable access starts from optimizing traffic flow paths and inter-networking by encouraging local interconnection via the setup of exchange points and production of local content.

The global IGF has been a successful initiative that has helped to create an open environment. Hence, there was support for the renewal of the IGF mandate after the first five years. And there was a desire to organize a West African Internet Governance Committee on the stakeholder model for the West African IGF. So in the communiqué, the West African stakeholders urged active participation in the IGF in Sharm El Sheikh, and increased participation in ICANN especially, with governments in the GAC. And work to broaden popular awareness of IGF issues in general, and West African priorities in particular, as well as building Internet resource management with continental partners, such as FOSSFA, OSIWA, and ECOWAS. And finally, further engagement of Internet governance experts from AfriNIC, AfNOG, AfREN, and AfriSPA in the region's policymaking processes.

CHRISTINA ARIDA:

Thank you. The African momentum is something to be proud of. Let me call on Dr. Ibaa Ouieshak to give us a perspective from the Arab region.

IBAA OUIESHAK:

The most important thing to know is that the Arab team has not been formed specifically for the purpose of the IGF. This team was working on issues before the IGF process was created. Initially it was working on domain names

155

and multilingualism issues, which became a focus in the IGF, so the Arab region from day one was in full accordance with the IGF. Yesterday there was a meeting of the team to which we invited people from our region, international organizations like ITU and ESCWA, who contributed substantively. The priority was given again to multilingualism, mainly due to the extraordinary evolution these days with IDNs. ICANN will very soon be inviting applications for IDN ccTLDs. Everyone was very enthusiastic about this, but also stressed that this is only the beginning. Now that we can have IDNs in the root zone of the Internet, it's up to us to continue working on this and on filling the standardization gap, and the gaps on the application levels, in order to bring to the end user a fully usable and secure and stable system. And then we moved to infrastructure. Migration to IP Version 6 was discussed and we noticed that there needs to be a regional plan given the expected depletion of the IP version 4 address space within the next three or four years. Hopefully a plan will be finalized and go into action before the depletion of the space. We need to insist to the RIRs that they take into consideration the situation of countries that are developing and did not have the chance to get as much address space as their friends from the developed countries. Appropriate measures should be taken to not reproduce the same situation even with potentially undepletable IP Version 6. On cybersecurity, there is a strong need to have a consistent policy to coordinate national actions at the regional level. We should draw inspiration from already existing initiatives of the ITU, and also need to develop national CERTs. There is a momentum in the Arab world regarding creating CERTs but we need more and to push them to coordinate with each other. There was also a contribution from our colleagues in ESCWA, the U.N. agency responsible for western Asia. They did a very good study on Internet governance issues that will be introduced within this forum.

I join our colleagues in Latin America in saying that access remains a very critical issue due to the cost of interconnection fees. The pricing model applied now means that the one who connects pays everything. It's not balanced, like telephony, by exchanging traffic and having settlements. One side pays it all, even if there is parasite traffic coming from the other side like spam or attacks. We pay for this, and the others send us spam; there is a big need to change this, because it affects the price that the end user pays. And no national policy can help, so there is need for regional and international coordination. And the last point, which was also mentioned, is the right of access to all information available on the Internet by everyone, with no discrimination against people coming from a certain region or a certain country. As you can see, the priorities of the Arab region are in line with things that are discussed at the IGF. For us, multilingualism remains a particularly high priority because it constitutes a barrier for the users in our region.

MARKUS KUMMER:

Just a very few words as a reaction. I think they all underlined one of the findings of WSIS: international coordination does not work if there is no coordination at the regional and the national level. I was also struck by the various regional meetings. They may have started as preparatory meetings for the global IGF, but increasingly they are a value in themselves so there's a need to continue irrespective of what happens at the global level. I think this is an interesting development. Who would like the floor?

FROM THE FLOOR:

I co-coordinate the Spanish IGF. Our national forum was launched in December 2008, and we have a very active platform that is truly multistakeholder. Madrid also will be hosting EuroDIG 2010 with full support from the Spanish IGF advisory group. The forum will be taking place at the end of May, at the same time that Spain holds the European Union presidency. Advisory group members act in their personal capacities but they are expected to provide links to their respective groups of interest. They are members of the government, the private sector such as Telefonica, Google Spain, et cetera, and civil society, the technical community, academic community, ISOC, Internet users, et cetera. You are all invited to join us in Madrid, 2010.

FROM THE FLOOR:

My name is Esam Abulkhirat. I am representing the African Union Commission. We had a workshop on Internet governance on the 13th of November here in Egypt that was jointly organized with the Ministry of Communication and Information Technology. The workshop participants considered ccTLDs to be national critical resources for the development of the knowledge economy and stressed that their management must be done by national stakeholders and conducted professionally. Other priorities included promoting localization of Internet development using different languages and the development of local content; promoting awareness and end-user education through various forms of media, including TV; encouraging stakeholders to collaborate through public/private partnerships; installing a common infrastructure at a level of standard that considers security, openness, and privacy of all African people, women and youth; developing African model laws or legal reference frameworks on cybersecurity that consider the specificity and values of the African countries, in line with international initiatives; dealing with cybercrime, cyber security, privacy and openness as a mutual responsibility of all stakeholders; and raising awareness and training people to handle Internet security problems. We also suggested improving the IGF's functioning so that it is more pragmatic, while maintaining the multistakeholder approach; and encouraging regional IGFs in Africa to address the African agenda and to increase participation in the global IGF.

I also want to mention that the heads of states and governments of the African Union are meeting twice a year, and they decided to dedicate the next common meeting in January 2010 to ICT in Africa, the challenges and prospects for development. Sub-themes will be an enabling environment, ICT infrastructure development, Africa and the economics of the Internet, capacity building, research, and development. Also, in the last two weeks in Johannesburg, the ministers of Africa met in extraordinary session and recommended some points relevant to our forum here. The African Union Commission and the U.N. Economic Commission for Africa would jointly develop a convention on cyber-legislation, based on the continent's needs, which adheres to the legal and regularity requirements on electric transactions, cybersecurity, and personal data protection. It was recommended that the member states of the African Union adopt this convention by 2012. They also recommended that critical resources like ccTLDs be managed domestically with the needed skills. And to put in place arrangements at peer with other continents to reduce the cost of communication and connections; build strong and efficient public-policy partnerships for economic and sustainable growth; ensure feasible and implementable action plans; and establish dot Africa as a continental top-level domain for use by organizations and individuals, with guidance from African Internet agencies.

FROM THE FLOOR:

I wanted to stress something that was raised earlier by Alice---that for our IGF in East Africa, the inspiration is international but the impact is local. We have been able to isolate and highlight issues that are purely regional, to link to international issues, and to establish linkages with stakeholders at the local level and the national level. We have been able to move the debate from the technical level to the parliament, which has a very critical role to play to ensure that they pass legislation that is going to support, enhance the usage and safeguard the Internet. Finally, the East African IGF is now self-sustaining and will continue as a driver of Internet governance in the region. We are particularly proud that our parliament is now part of that process.

FROM THE FLOOR:

I am Lambert Van Nistelrooij, a member of the European Parliament. It's very important that we show in our regions our commitment to the development of the Internet. We just finalized a comprehensive legal framework in the European Union that strengthens the position of the citizens. It's important to have this broad basis and to find solutions that are tailor-made to parts of the world. For the future of the IGF, this is a very important thing.

MARKUS KUMMER:

Parliamentarians have been increasingly active in the IGF and have emerged as a new stakeholder groups, and we welcome this very much.

FROM THE FLOOR:

My name is Marilyn Cade and I am one of the co-organizers of the IGF U.S.A. We had a very multistakeholder organizing group, and we held a one-day session that focused on the themes of the global IGF and on developing a national perspective with a global view. We have to deepen the awareness and understanding within the United States about what Internet governance is. We concluded our meeting with a version of the session that will take place here, on examining the advisability about the continuation of the forum. And we did have a youth panel and incorporated youth into all of the sessions. We will file a report, Markus, with more details.

FROM THE FLOOR:

I am Catherine Trautmann from the European Parliament. The next year will be very important for the European Union. For the first time, the European Parliament will be a co-decider of the roadmap for broadband, which is a step forward. Next year will be also a period of investment in fibre and deployment of satellites, so the infrastructure will be very strong and broad. We have decided to recognize that the Internet is a main way to exercise fundamental freedoms and rights. This is a way forward also for the end users, with the progress of the rights for consumers, and the right to be recognized as a citizen on the Internet. We are very much in favour of continuing the global IGF exercise because we think it inspires the work we do as a legislature and our agenda on public policies. We are glad to be here.

FROM THE FLOOR:

My name is Deidre Williams, and I come from Sir Arthur Lewis Community College in St. Lucia in the West Indies. The Caribbean had its fifth IGF, at the end of August. The interesting move was from a purely technical interest towards an interest in the part that human beings have to play in what is happening online. In terms of what we need in the Caribbean, the Caribbean Telecommunication Union is part of Caricom. Their interest up to now has been largely technical. The governments in the Caribbean appear to me to be not very interested, at least not in the English Caribbean. We need as much feedback and publicity as we can get to galvanize our governments to take part.

MARKUS KUMMER:

I would like to thank you very much, and would also ask you to join me in giving a hand to our panellists.

V. Proceedings

Opening Ceremony

15 November 2009

Speakers:

Mr. Sha Zukang
United Nations Under-Secretary-General for Economic & Social Affairs

H. E. Mr. Tarek Kamel
Minister of Communications and Information Technology, Egypt

H. E. Mr. Ahmed Nazif
Prime Minister, Egypt

Mr. Hamadoun Touré
Secretary General, International Telecommunication Union (ITU)

Special Keynote Addresses:

Sir Tim Berners-Lee
Father of the World Wide Web, Director of World Wide Web Consortium (W3C), United Kingdom

Mr. Jerry Yang
Co-Founder and Chief Yahoo, Yahoo – USA

Extracts from the Transcript of Proceedings

MR. SHA ZUKANG:

Excellency Mr. Prime Minister, Excellency ministers, my colleague Nitin Desai, excellencies, ladies and gentlemen, I'm delighted to be here with you in Sharm El Sheikh for the 4th meeting of the Internet Governance Forum. I would like to thank the government and the people of the Arab Republic of Egypt for their warm welcome and generous hospitality. We are gathered here at the IGF to address important public policy issues related to the governance of the Internet. It is clear that we share a common understanding as we progress in bridging the digital gap and building the foundation for our emerging formation and knowledgeable society. The way we deal with the Internet will become increasingly important. Therefore, the overarching theme for our meeting, "Internet Governance - Creating Opportunities for All," is timely and appropriate. It will allow us to re-examine and reflect upon the main theme of the IGF---access, diversity, openness, security, and critical Internet resources. Since the time this powerful tool for development was first introduced to the world by the United States, which has continued to lead the world in innovations in information and communication technology (ICT) and Internet applications, the Internet has brought profound changes. Even in

161

the last five years during the time of IGF, the Internet has continued to evolve every single day, and at a very fast pace. The number of people going online has surpassed 1 1/2 billion, a quarter of the world's population. Fixed broadband subscribers more than tripled from 150 million in 2004 to an estimated 500 million by the end of 2009, according to the International Telecommunication Union (ITU). There are now 4.6 billion mobile cellular subscribers around the world, some 600 million of them being broadband subscribers. Though the digital divide is wide, with African and Arab states lagging behind Europe, Asia, and the Americas, gains are being made. In 2005, more than 50% of the people in developed regions were using the Internet, compared to 9% in developing regions, and only 1% in least developed countries. By the year 2009, the number of people connecting in developing countries had expanded by an impressive 475 million to 17.5%, and by 4 million to 1.5%, while Internet penetration in developed regions increased to 64%.

Against this backdrop of rapidly changing Internet demographics, there are questions about how best to manage critical resources, expand access, and fully integrate all the world's languages. These issues and other aspects of the Internet governance must be addressed for the sake of development, especially in light of 2015 target of achieving the Millennium Development Goals. The IGF brings together diverse cultures: the nongovernmental Internet community with its tradition of informal bottom-up decision-making, the dynamism and inventive spirit of the private sector, the networked world of advocacy groups that make up civil society, and the politically sensitive world of governments and intergovernmental organizations. The IGF works through voluntary cooperation, not legal compulsion. IGF participants come here to discuss, to exchange information, and to share best practices with each other. While the IGF may not have decision-making abilities, it informs, and it inspires those who do. It can identify challenges and issues of concern, issues that may need to be tackled through formal processes. The IGF thus provides a neutral space where all actors have a chance to express their views, be heard, and create a momentum for mobilizing decisions and actions.

In this dialogue, the voice of the developing countries must be heard. Good and democratic Internet governance is a means of achieving development for all. I invite each of you, regardless of country, role, or status, to express your views, to make yourselves heard, and understood, and to understand the views of others in the spirit of inclusion and open debate.

This brings me to a critical decision that we will have to make about the future of IGF. The World Summit on the Information Society recognized that the Internet needed new ways of addressing governance issues. Heads of state and government gathered in Tunisia in 2005 and carefully considered some of the founding principles of the Internet. They decided to ask the Secretary-General of the United Nations to convene a new multistakeholder platform to discuss public policy issues, what we now know as the IGF. At its inception, the IGF was given provisional life span of five years. The Tunisia agenda specifically called on the Secretary-General, "to examine the desirability of the continuation of the forum in formal consultations with forum participants within five years of its creation, and to make recommendations to the U.N. membership in this regard." These important consultations will be held at this meeting in Sharm El Sheikh later this week. I encourage you to participate fully in these meetings and to share your views. If you believe the forum is valuable, I would encourage you to say so, and tell us in what ways. If you believe it can be improved, I would encourage you to say that too, and to tell us how. If you believe that IGF has fulfilled its purpose, I would encourage you to speak out against extension of the mandate and tell us why. I invite all of you to create a checklist against the IGF mandate as set out in the Tunis Agenda for the Information Society and to tell us precisely to what extent has the forum addressed its mandate successfully, partially successfully, or unsuccessfully.

The last, but not least, question is whether we should continue to discuss enhanced cooperation as a part of the forum. Should we instead enhance our cooperation on other platforms, and if so, which? Let us be open and honest with one another, as is the IGF custom. Based on the consultations, I will report back to the Secretary-General of the United Nations. He will then make his recommendations in his annual report to the General Assembly next year on WSIS follow-up and implementation. In closing, let me reiterate that the Internet is a powerful tool. It will assist us to reach the Millennium Development Goals and improve the lives of millions of people by 2015. With its overarching development perspective and cross-cutting priority of capacity building, the IGF fully complements one of the United Nations' central mandates: To promote higher standard of living, full employment, and conditions of economic progress and development. We in the United Nations Department of Economic and Social Affairs (UNDESA) will be listening very carefully and humbly to what you have to say over the next few days.

According to the IGF practice, the host country has the chairmanship of the forum. Thus, let's endorse this tradition with acclamation. Now, I have the honour to hand over the chairmanship to His Excellency, Dr. Tarek Kamel, the minister of communications and IT of Arab Republic of Egypt.

H.E. MR. TAREK KAMEL:

Your Excellency Dr. Ahmed Nazif, prime minister of Egypt, Your Excellency, Mr. Sha Zukang, U.N. Under-Secretary-General for Economic and Social Affairs, honourable ministers and delegates, respectful audience, ladies and gentlemen, it gives me great honour that I stand here today addressing your distinguished gathering for the 2009 meeting of the IGF in Sharm El Sheikh. Allow me to start by welcoming you to Egypt and specifically to Sharm El Sheikh, the City of Peace, which has witnessed many historic meetings of world leaders. Today, I am proud that Sharm El Sheikh is witnessing, again, the opening of yet another historic meeting, a meeting of Internet governance world leaders and pioneers. As I look around this hall, I feel especially excited to be welcoming from all corners of the world fellow ministers, heads of international organizations, private sector leaders, civil society activists, as well as professors and parliamentarians. A special welcome is also due to Egypt's prime minister, Dr. Ahmed Nazif, who has honoured us with his presence here today.

I'm also extremely excited to see so many old friends and familiar faces from the Internet experts community who have long contributed to the development of the Internet worldwide. Their achievements during those earlier phases are not confined to technology and innovation, but they go far beyond that to Internet public policies on which we have put the first bricks in place many years ago. Today, I look back to those times. I feel proud to be coming from that community of experts with whom I shared very special memories. I still remember the first workshop that the Internet Society (ISOC) organized in Palo Alto during INET 1992 with Vint Cerf, Larry Landweber, and George Sadowsky from the U.S. They had invited us young pioneers and entrepreneurs from the developing countries to work in introducing connectivity to our countries. I do still remember the early African birds of a feather meetings at the INET conference in Cotonou with Nii Quaynor, from Ghana, Pierre Dandjinou from Benin, Lamia Chafei and Kamel Saadaoui from Tunis, as well as many other African friends. They all worked to establish the necessary Internet infrastructure and the AfriNIC that today satisfies the needs of Africa for registering IP addresses. I still remember activating the first digital link across the Mediterranean, and my frequent visits to Dr. Nazif's office, when both of us were in our previous capacities, asking him for financial and political support for my new endeavour to introduce Egypt to connectivity with 64K around the Mediterranean. I equally recall receiving an e-mail from Lynn St. Amour approving the first ISOC chapter in the region in Egypt at IDSC/RITSEC. This all has happened with collaborative efforts of many supporters like Dr. Hisham El Sherif, Dr. Adeeb, Ms. Azza Torky, and Ms. Nashwa, and later of another generation with Mostafa, Christine, Manal, Baher, Nawawy, Azhary, Bichara and many other friends. They all contributed heavily to the development of the Internet in this country and in the region.

I feel proud about these memories, but I feel even more proud to stand here hosting and chairing the IGF this year, and to be witnessing how Internet public policy has evolved. It has extended from discussion within a small group of experts to a multistakeholder process among a wide range of professionals representing various sectors and fields. Indeed, the IGF has proved over four years that it is not an isolated parallel process but rather has managed to bring on board all the relevant stakeholders and key players.

The Internet in Egypt also has evolved from being led by a group of pioneers in the early '90s to an overall national agenda only a couple of years later. Facing the same challenges as in other parts of the world, Egypt encountered the changing dynamics produced by the evolution of IP technologies. The whole communication model has been changing from a legacy structure led by PTTs to a new and innovative user-centred model involving new policies, business models, and service delivery frameworks. Empowered by the political support of President Mubarak since 1996, the Internet community in Egypt has managed to achieve a breakthrough through a deregulated framework for service provision with strong private sector involvement. The political support also has meant that Egypt enjoys as free and open an Internet platform as in many developed countries in the world. This has encouraged continuous investment in infrastructure and enabled us to enjoy double-digit growth in the Internet and the ICT sector. It wasn't very long before we realized that this deregulated framework is not only suitable for the

Internet but that it could be applied in other disciplines as well as in other services. Hence, in 1999, with the formation of the Ministry of Communication and Information Technology, the development of a complete strategy for the ICT sector began: to build an Information Society in Egypt and position the country as a regional communication hub. Today, after ten years, it is no surprise that Egypt has managed to make its ICT sector competitive within the region and beyond. It is also no surprise that this sector is significantly contributing to national efforts to raise productivity in other sectors.

Innovations in broadcasting and streaming technology, as well as the evolution of user-generated content, are transforming the Internet into a platform where we communicate, work, learn, and be entertained. Hence, the crucial developmental role of the Internet is now more than ever well recognized globally. This is especially true in developing regions where the next billions of users are expected to emerge, especially using mobile Internet facilities and service. The Internet is thus becoming for developing countries a space of opportunities that should be handled with due attention. The Internet community should actively engage and make effort to remove any barriers to those emerging markets. It is also vital to ensure that the unique structure of the Internet is preserved, maintained, and built upon. The IGF has laid a strong foundation for the policy dialogue needed to address those challenges. The agendas of Athens, Rio, and Hyderabad were carefully selected to include the various aspects of Internet governance. With this year's IGF under the overall theme of creating opportunities for all, I believe the ground is set for our deliberations.

I am also sure that you all share with me the belief that with opportunities and rights come responsibilities. We are here to address our responsibilities towards today's and tomorrow's cyberspace. It is our responsibility within IGF to dig into the current mechanisms and propose creative models to address policy challenges like cybersecurity; youth, empowerment, and online child safety; multilingual content, multilingual domain names and search engines; broadband access in developing countries; the implications of social networks, which are changing the way our younger generation thinks and interacts; and privacy, with the evolution of Internet mobility using smart phones and other technologies. The IGF should continue to provide a venue where such new policy issues are surfaced, voiced freely and discussed constructively. The IGF community should equally continue to work together and be as creative as our pioneers of the early Internet phases were.

This year's IGF is an important one, as recently there have been a number of milestones related to the heated worldwide discussion on global Internet governance. The Internet Corporation for Assigned Names and Numbers (ICANN) has made a significant move towards improving its accountability by signing the new Affirmation of Commitments with the U.S. administration. This development recognizes the success of ICANN's multistakeholder model, and marks the start of a new era for ICANN and the global community. However, the worldwide Internet community still looks forward to further international involvement in managing critical Internet resources by revisiting the current IANA contract, without affecting the robustness of the global Internet. Equally important is the new decision to launch multilingual domain names in Arabic, Chinese, Korean and other languages, and I am glad, Mr. Prime Minister, that Egypt will make use of the fast-track process starting tomorrow morning by applying for the first country top-level domain, dot masra in Arabic, to be one of the first Arabic and multilingual country top-level domains. This will offer new avenues for innovation, investment, and growth, and hence we can truly say that the Internet speaks Arabic.

It is a great moment for us, and I am happy that this takes place here in Sharm El Sheikh as a recognition of our work with relevant constituencies worldwide over the last three years. Ladies and gentlemen, having witnessed how this process has developed, and where we stand today, one can fairly say in spite of the existence of some gaps, that the IGF has definitely proved to be an excellent venue to integrate the views of the different stakeholder groups. Looking at its future, we think the IGF should be allowed to maintain its innovative multistakeholder approach. It should continue to act as a venue for policy dialogue with more focus in the future on localized needs of the emerging regions of Africa, Latin America and Asia. The IGF should build upon the momentum while broadening participation and linking national and regional policy dialogues to the global.

In conclusion, through the IGF process, all of us are together shaping the civilization of our modern age. From within Egypt, the land of civilization, we are adding here another brick this week. And while I'm sure that many people have been working around the clock to make this meeting a success, I believe special thanks should be extended to Mr. Sha Zukang and the whole U.N. team, to chairman Nitin Desai, Mr. Markus Kummer, and all members of the IGF Multistakeholder Advisory Group for their continuous effort in preparing for the forum. And I would also like to thank our local team in Egypt, especially Hoda and Nermine, who put an outstanding effort to make this meeting a real success. And our sincere gratitude goes to you, Mr. Prime Minister, for taking the time to share with us your valuable thoughts. Allow me to present to you, on behalf of the participants, a small gift as a token of appreciation and to you, ladies and gentlemen, I wish you a very fruitful meeting and hope you will enjoy our stay in our beloved country.

H.E. MR. AHMED NAZIF:

Distinguished guests, ladies and gentlemen, I am pleased to welcome you all in Egypt. Sharm El Sheikh is a symbol for peace and proof of how peace can be translated into development and progress. It is four years since the creation of the forum as one of the important outcomes of the World Summit on the Information Society held in Geneva and Tunisia. Looking back, we can see the progress that has been realized and the tremendous potential and opportunities in sight. Today, we meet at an important moment where cautious optimism prevails that the world is getting out of the devastating recession cycle. For ICT, such a moment carries great opportunities, as this sector is ready to resume its growth globally. The ICT sector will have a chance to serve as a catalyst to support a robust exit from the recession for all other sectors of the world economy. And it should also enable us to take measures to avoid the recurrence of the processes that led to the previous crisis.

166

Egypt has succeeded in dealing with the world financial and then economic crisis with the least possible negative impact. Our bold and ambitious economic report program since 2004 has helped us in achieving unprecedented rates of growth in the three years before the world financial crisis. This enabled our economy to face the strong impact of the crisis, which was clear in sectors connected with the outside world, such as tourism, the Suez Canal and trade. We maintained growth during the crisis at the rate of 4.7%. In addition, our banking reform program minimized the impact of the world financial crisis. It is important to note that a substantial component of our banking reform program aimed at capacity building and increased utilization of ICT in the operation, governance, and regulation of our banks. It is also worth noting that the ICT sector in Egypt kept its growth curve during the year of the crisis at a double-digit rate. This is a clear indication about the rich potentials it entails.

I would like to share with you some insight about the successful experience of Egypt in building its ICT sector as a base for the knowledge society in the last decade. Our approach was based on three pillars. The first was to create an appropriate institutional framework. That was realized by the establishment of the Ministry of Communications and Information Technology, with a mandate to build and implement an ambitious plan of action for the future of ICT in Egypt. This was followed by the creation of several subsidiary institutions to support the ministry, such as the National Telecommunications Regulatory Authority and the Information Technology Industry Development Authority. One of the important tasks of the ministry was to achieve adhesion to international agreements that enhance our global participation in ICT developments, and to guarantee intellectual property rights. The second pillar aimed at laying the foundation for a strong domestic ICT industry. Our task was to stimulate the development of a competitive ICT environment in Egypt, with the participation of domestic and foreign private sector operators. Our indicators in these regards are reassuring. The sector has attracted over 8 billion U.S. dollars of investment over the last four years, and has contributed positively to public proceeds and to our job creation programs. Mobile users have jumped to 54 million subscribers in Egypt with a penetration rate of 70%. We are still adding 1 million new subscribers each month, one of the highest growth rates in the world. Internet penetration also rose to almost 20% with over 15 million users in 2009, turning the Internet into a real tool of empowerment and enabling the dissemination of different sorts of e-applications among our citizens. We achieved 750 million U.S. dollars of export proceeds from the ICT sector. Our goal is to reach $1 billion next year, and exceed $2 billion of exports by 2013.

The third pillar was to promote initiatives that help in the dissemination of ICT technology benefits in our society. We are happy that ICT has contributed directly to the well-being of our population by increasing their access to basic e-government services. We are using the technology to support the reform of our social and health care programs by issuing family smart cards. We embarked on a new Egyptian education initiative that has been recognized worldwide by UNESCO in 2008 for its unique model of governance that includes public-private partnerships in infrastructure development and an integrated reform program for schools. The e-content industry in Egypt is also serving the needs of millions of Arabic speaking cyberspace users. Egypt's role in reaffirming cultural diversity as a core value of Internet governance through the dispensing of Arabic content is both influential and effective. One of our numerous projects in this area is the "Memory of the Arab World," a specialized Web portal to collect heritage materials, including oral histories from all around our region. The challenges we face for the future are the challenges of growth, and the country's ability to breed highly qualified ICT professionals and experts according to global market needs and standards. Equally challenging is the development of innovation and entrepreneurship. Our efforts here are directed towards expanding and facilitating research and innovation through several means, including the establishment of research centres of excellence, and technology incubators linked to ICT businesses.

I trust that the distinguished community of experts present here today will be following a similar path at the international level, as the strength of the IGF lies in its all-inclusive nature. Only through an open and consistent dialogue can we maximize the true potentials of the Internet as a tool for growth and a herald of economic and political freedoms. Your forum is a valuable space for continuous education on the prospects of the Internet and global cyberspace. I'm sure that the knowledge you generate will be used as precious learning tools for the young generations, and I see the continuation of this forum as a real priority. Through the process of regular evaluations, I am confident that we will be able to expand and administer the global cyberspace in forums that mirror our aspirations for freedom of access, usage, and expression on one side, and equality of opportunity in education and research allocation on the other side. Finally, I hope that this round of the IGF will be a leap into a more prolific and assertive dialogue, and that Sharm El Sheikh will offer you the atmosphere required to bring out the best this dignified congregation of minds has to offer.

MR. HAMADOUN TOURE:

Your Excellency Prime Minister Dr. Nazif, Excellency Ambassador Sha Zukang, and Ministers, Ambassadors, leaders of industry, CEO of ICANN, I also recognize in this room the presence of Dr. Tim Berners-Lee and Dr. Bob Kahn, two of the fathers of the Internet as we know it today. This is a major milestone in the IGF process that will include both taking stock and looking ahead. Taking into account the experience acquired during the last three IGF meetings, framing the decisions which will be taken concerning the future of IGF, looking at the best ways of serving the needs of the global community and engaging strongly in the process of enhanced cooperation. And seeing which aspects of the IGF mandate still need to be thoroughly considered so we can collectively share the same sense of accomplishment.

The IGF was an outcome of the World Summit on the Information Society, organized by the ITU, which was the most wide-ranging, comprehensive and inclusive debate ever held on the future of the Information Society. For the first time governments, the private sector, civil society, and international organizations worked together hand in hand. At the close of that summit in Tunis in November 2005, we agreed on the importance of strengthened cooperation among all stakeholders. ITU continues to believe in the spirit of the agreement made at Tunis, and has been an active participant in the IGF process. We have a delegation of 14 ITU officials organizing or co-organizing 11 events. Over the past four years we have been implementing both the letter and the spirit of our WSIS commitment in areas as diverse as accessibility and climate change, and cybersecurity, and we have redoubled our efforts over the past 12 months. In today's world, ICTs are part of the solution, not part of the problem. They are playing a key role in addressing the financial crisis. It is no coincidence that many of the world's stimulus packages include ambitious broadband infrastructure initiatives. These will help us to bridge the emerging broadband divide, and they will help us to meet the Millennium Development Goals. This can only happen when the right regulatory environment is in place, an environment that favours content generation. In Beirut earlier this week, in our most successful global symposium for regulators to date, the ITU worked together with over 750 CEOs and policymakers from around the world to discuss these issues. ICTs will also play a crucial role in helping us address climate change issues, and the ITU is lobbying hard ahead of the Copenhagen conference next month for this to be widely recognized.

The ITU is also playing a lead role in coordinating global cybersecurity efforts. I launched the Global Cybersecurity Agenda (GCA) in 2007, which is now in its operational phase with a physical home in Malaysia at the headquarters of the International Multilateral Partnership Against Cyber Threats (IMPACT). Within the GCA, we also launched the child online protection initiative this year, and this is now in its operational phase as well, with guidelines available for all stakeholders. Distinguished colleagues, the IGF is a unique forum where all stakeholder can share their opinions on an equal footing. In the spirit of paragraph 72 of the Tunis Agenda, IGF is a place where we can make progress on certain topics, and introduce mature topics into other more formal processes and organizations for further consideration. We welcome the new Affirmation of Commitments as the opportunity to increase ICANN's accountability and to enhance cooperation among all stakeholder groups in the management of Internet critical resources. I take this opportunity to congratulate my friend, Rod Beckstrom, on his election as CEO of ICANN, and I wish him success in his new function.

ICANN is recognized as a central authority on Internet names and addresses. ITU is the recognized organization for communication infrastructure that also supports the Internet. We have to look at ways to eliminate frictions between our different organizations and between all stakeholders during the IGF process. We have to work together. I would like us to remember to look at the big picture and what we are trying to achieve; WSIS set forth goals and principles and asked us to meet tangible targets by 2015. The IGF is a clear part of that process. And as we take stock and look ahead this week, I would like us to work out how we can best meet the WSIS targets and the Millennium Development Goals and make the access, use, creation and sharing of information a basic human right. This is when we can safely say we have come from the Information Society and have entered the knowledge society that we are dreaming of.

SIR TIM BERNERS-LEE:

Back in 1989 there was no World Wide Web, but we had all the pieces. Using the very strong structure of the Internet, which had been built beforehand, I proposed the language HTML that produced the Web. It's worth remembering that the thing that made the Web work was universality. The core value that it is one universal space. Two Webs doesn't work, it has to be one Web. It has to be one Web for all kinds of information, no matter what hardware you have, no matter where you buy your computer from or what sort of device you have. Back then, the World Wide Web did not speak Arabic. But when XML was created, it was designed to use Unicode, so then the Internet could speak Arabic. So the universality of the Web includes its internationalization. That means not just different characters, not just whether or not your letters go across this way or across that way or down that way. It means how different cultures in the world need to be able to use the World Wide Web.

In 1994, we formed the World Wide Web consortium, W3C. In W3C we have all kinds of people coming together to decide on the future of the Web protocols. It was sponsored by industry with, unlike most standard bodies at the time, a large technical staff to help things move rapidly. But it was not just industry. Also governments, individuals, academics, all coming to the table in what we now call a multistakeholder group, to produce standards. Working closely with the Internet Engineering Task Force, we put the http process through. But many other areas have branched out since then, and there are a lot of recommendations that have been produced. In 1997, we realized we needed to specially recognize the potential of the Web for people with disabilities. The Web could, in fact, be easier for people with disabilities because you could put up alternative forms of the same material and link them together. So the Web Accessibility Initiative was started back in 1997. After that, we also had an internationalization group, and both accessibility and internationalization cut across all the work the W3C has done.

To keep it one Web we had a consortium that did open, royalty-free standards. At a certain point, the consortium fell into a trap and technology was almost abandoned completely because a member of a working group had hidden the fact that they were going to announce that they wanted to charge royalties. So the consortium worked out a royalty-free policy, which was very important. As time went on though, standards didn't seem to be enough. The Web is very large, and has 10 to the power 11 Web pages---that's 10 with 11 zeros, about the same number as there are nerve cells in the brain. So we realized that we needed to study the brain. We don't really understand the Web's complexity, and some of the people that we knew that were doing really exciting work didn't have a community in which to share and publish it, so we started talking about Web science. So three years ago, we started a research initiative that has now become the Web science trust in order to get academics to think about this. And when we had to think about the objective we thought, "Okay, well, Web science surely should be that the Web should serve humanity to its utmost."

But for that we needed more than science. The people who were working on the standards and on the science were early adopters, but we needed to think about the other 80% of the world at the time who were not using the Web at all. And so we realized that we also need to think about society in general, and about people who are less privileged, who may be in disconnected rural areas, or in poor urban areas. So our conclusion was that we should create a World Wide Web Foundation to think about these things, and in the time-honoured method of sending a message over the Internet, it is my pleasure today, ladies and gentlemen, to officially launch the World Wide Web Foundation here at the IGF. We are very lucky to have gotten support from the Knight Foundation, which has given us the bootstrap grounds to built it on. We need to bring in funds and produce programs. The main thing that everybody involved will be doing is learning about what's needed, about all the things that are happening now. We will have a Web Foundation workshop tomorrow for people who would like more information. Now when we look at the Web, we don't see it anymore as connected computers or as connected Web pages; if you want to understand why somebody follows or makes a link, you're looking at people. So we look at the Web now as humanity connected by technology, and we want it to empower people. I hope that together we can work together and achieve great things.

MR. JERRY YANG:

I want to offer a reflection on the profound impact the Internet has already had, and on the importance of connecting more people, especially those in developing and emerging countries. And just as importantly, on ensuring that we deliver meaningful experiences and content to this next global wave of Internet consumers. My partner David Filo and I started Yahoo! almost 15 years ago, in 1994, as a hobby. The first name we called it was Jerry and Dave's Guide to the World Wide Web, and I'm glad we didn't keep that name. Pretty soon we realized that when people used it to find what they were looking for they were so happy they called out, "Yahoo!" and we put an exclamation behind our name and off we went. When we started, there were fewer than 10 million globally on the Internet. That's less than one-third of one percent of the world population back then. The Internet backbone traffic at that time amounted to 17 terabytes per month. Back then, people talked about online bulletin boards, and the mobile Internet was unheard of. But there was a sense among those in technology and engineering circles that this was the beginning of something huge. We had a passion to create a community of knowledge and information and to connect local communities to the people of the world. We understood from pioneers like Tim and Vint Cerf that there was a tremendous amount of social value to the Web, and we had an opportunity to make big and positive impacts in people's lives. Back then, the Internet was built on the same foundations and ideals as today: Openness, freedom of expression, universal access, global participation, and the power of information.

So where are we now? In 2009 there are more than 1.6 billion people on the Internet, about 25% of the world's population. The Internet's backbone traffic has exceeded 8 million terabytes a month, about a 500,000-fold increase since 15 years ago. Today there are more than 200 million Web sites, 90,000 new sites being created each day, and on Yahoo! we have over 600 million people visiting us every month and 8 billion minutes spent from those visitors. There are 300 million Yahoo! e-mail users, sending 100 billion messages a month, and 11 million people on our Yahoo! instant messaging sending 81 billion messages each month. And 120 million people in what we call Yahoo! Groups, communicating across 10 million different groups of activity from local schools and sports to diseases and support groups.

What's astonishing is not just those numbers, but the impact the Internet has had on so many people around the world. From socioeconomic opportunities to providing better health care and educating the next generation of students and entrepreneurs. The Internet today is about the intersection of the world and my world, friends, family, community, social network, and work. Like no other medium, the Internet has shown tremendous ability to mobilize people for the good. A few years ago, Hurricane Katrina devastated the southern coastline of the United States. People around the world wanted to find ways to help and Yahoo! was able to use our Web site to raise over $57 million from 400,000 people in two weeks. The first $42 million came within the first 48 hours. And just recently, Yahoo! in the Philippines used Flickr, Yahoo!'s online photo sharing site to create a database of missing people from the Typhoon Ketsana. This database helped families find friends and family members who went missing in this disaster. In Yahoo! Groups we see 10 million different groups that are serving different needs. One of them is called the Development Cafe, which offers job postings and knowledge sharing free of cost that is particularly welcomed by the members from emerging economies. This successful group has been included in a global poverty network hosted by the UNDP. These are just a few examples and there are countless from other Yahoo! services and other Web services in general.

So the question is: What's next? We're still missing three out of every four people that walk this planet online. We need to close this gap and get the next billion people online and then the next billion after that. We also must ask: Who are the next billion? Half of the next billion users are expected to come from emerging markets and developing countries. Many will also come from aging populations in both the established and emerging markets, and from those with accessibility challenges. These will very important audiences. Let me just focus on the large underserved audience, those citizens living in emerging markets. Today, there are approximately 325 million Internet users in what we call the emerging markets, and that number is expected to grow 19% annually through 2012. Many will come from less affluent populations in semi-rural areas, relatively poor, young, and enthusiastic, with a great capacity to learn. Many will need and want more content in their native languages, and still others won't just be bound by languages and barriers, but have other challenges such as reading, literacy, etc. There are three aspects we have to focus on: access to the Internet, content and user experiences, and our responsible engagement in those markets.

First, there are plenty of brilliant minds in this room working on access. We need to increase access, whether its broadband, mobile, Wi-Fi, or Wi-Max to bring the Internet within reach of more people. Historically we've seen that when broadband penetration reaches around the 20% mark, where Egypt is, we see a tipping point and a rapid acceleration in Internet adoption. And there's another benefit. According to the 2009 World Bank report, for every 10 percentage point increase there is a corresponding increase in economic growth of 1.3 percentage points. This is an area where government and private industry can partner. Private investments can help build infrastructure, but also must see a market opportunity. Clear and consistent government regulation can also help encourage private investment. Bringing down the cost of access is critical. Disposable income is minimal in emerging economies, so providing low-cost service or free Internet at cafes can help bring more people online.

Just as important is the content and the user experience. We are sometimes consumed by assigning numbers to our goals while losing sight of why we set them in the first place. The Internet isn't just about getting as many people online as possible, but making sure that once they do they have something to gain, something meaningful to experience. We must provide relevant, local content. We need to offer communication tools that enable people to connect their community and the larger world. And with the right tools, the Internet can provide online commerce opportunities to help to lift people out of poverty. An encouraging move recently is the ICANN decision to establish non-English language domain names. This is an important step in keeping the Internet even more global. Internet growth and innovation is enhanced through international participation, and this program has the potential to help bring more people online that don't use Roman characters in their lives. At Yahoo!, we're dedicated to localization, by being global but acting locally, we strive to bring consumers a more in depth, relevant, and positive Internet experience. We were the first to launch Web sites in many international markets. Currently we operate in over 40 different countries, in 25 different languages. As many of you may be aware, we also recently acquired Maktoob, the largest Arabic language Internet site. According to the World Bank, there are more than 320 million Arabic speakers in the world, but less than 1% of all online content is in Arabic. The partnership aims to strengthen and support Arabic content on the Internet, adopting current products to the Arabic language, while also working with local developers to create new and compelling products. So for example, Yahoo! Mail and Messenger are among the leading communication tools in the world and will be made available in Arabic for the first time next year. Yahoo! also offers user-generated community applications such as Yahoo! Groups and Yahoo! Answers in multiple languages, including in Arabic soon.

As we develop content for the next billion Internet users, ensuring that we are providing applications and content that work well on mobile platforms is also essential. The vast majority of people in emerging markets will first experience the Internet on a mobile device. This mobile first generation is completely different than those who grew up with personal computers. There's 4.5 times more mobile users than the average PC users in those developing countries. For example, in India, it's up to 8 times. So we need to go beyond just addressing the distribution of smart phones. Inexpensive mobile devices have gained significant traction in less developed towns across Africa and Asia, and those are also portals to the Internet and vast amounts of information and opportunity. I'd like to talk briefly about how important it is to also engage in all these different markets in a responsible way. We recognize the political, social, and economic environments in markets around the world are deeply complex, a complexity that is mirrored in the online world. This presents challenges for any company, especially one in our industry. As an Internet pioneer in these emerging markets, we've gained important insights and experience and we're committed to responsible global engagement. This means being sensitive to local laws, customs, and norms while protecting and promoting the rights of our users. We believe our engagement in emerging markets can be a positive force by increasing access to information, a key IGF theme, as well as by supporting a thriving marketplace and exchange of ideas by bridging local, regional and international communities with innovative communications tools. Our belief in being responsible is why Yahoo! is a co-founding member of the Global Network Initiative or GNI, a multiyear effort involving an international group of information and communications companies, civil society organizations, academics, investors, and others. The members of GNI commit to protecting freedom of expression and privacy, partnering with others to ensure collective governance and accountability in promoting the GNI and its objectives throughout the world.

All the things I've just discussed -- access, local content, communication and responsible engagement -- are connected, interrelated, and necessary to get the next billion people online and thriving. We all need to be sure that we're educating the next generation of online consumers, whether young or old, about Internet usage and about keeping their kids safe online. This is an exciting time for our industry and for the global expansion of the Internet. The Internet can positively transform lives, societies, and economies. It can connect local communities to a much larger world. We have the opportunity to welcome another billion more people to the Internet, and with that opportunity, we also have enormous responsibility to ensure the Internet is ready for this eager group of future online explorers, entrepreneurs, scientists, educators and leaders. We need to make sure that what they have at their fingertips will enable them to prosper and that collectively, we will also benefit. And we can make this happen. I would encourage further development of an Internet based on openness, freedom of expression, privacy, universal access, global participation. I encourage more collaboration between but and private sectors to ensure we can tackle the most challenges collectively. I encourage the development of more local and relevant content. In business, we know the demand is already there, and we will play our part to meet those needs. I encourage Internet users to continue to create local language content. I encourage governments to create rules that allow users to create that content to flourish. In closing, I am certain that this dedicated group of citizens from around the world here at the IGF can think and work collaboratively to create an environment that welcomes the next billion people to a vibrant and global Internet. Thank you again to the IGF for giving me the great privilege to speak with you and thanks to all of you for your commitment to help to shape the Internet in a positive way for the people of the world.

Opening Session

15 November 2009

Speakers:

H. E. Federal Councillor Moritz Leuenberger
Head of the Department of the Environment, Transport, Energy and Communication, Switzerland

H. E. Mr. József Györkös
State Secretary, Ministry of Higher Education, Science and Technology, Slovenia
(Joint Statement representing the Slovenian/Swiss Chair of the Council of Europe. Committee of Ministers)

Ms. Lisa Horner
Global Partners tld, UK

H. E. Ms. Åsa Torstensson
Minister for Enterprise, Energy and Communications, Sweden. Representing the EU Presidency

H. E. Ms. Viviane Reding
European Commissioner for ICT and Media

H. E. Mr. Pedro Sebastiao Teta
Vice Minister, Information and Communications Technology, Angola

H. E. Mr. Augusto Gadelha
Vice Minister of Science & Technology, Brazil

Ambassador Philip Verveer
United States Coordinator, International Communications and Information Policy, United States Department of State

H. E. Ms. Nathalie Kosciusko-Morizet
Secretary of State for Prospective and the Development of the Digital Economy, France

Ms. Lynn St. Amour
President & CEO, Internet Society (ISOC)

Abdul Waheed Khan
Assistant Director-General for Communication and Information, UNESCO

Mr. Subramanian Ramadorai
Vice-Chairman of Tata Consultancy Services Ltd, TATA, Chairman, ICC-BASIS, India

Mr. Rod Beckstrom
President and CEO, Internet Corporation for Assigned Names and Numbers
(ICANN)

Mr. Jean Rozwadowski
Secretary General, International Chamber of Commerce (ICC)

Nitin Desai
Special Adviser to the Secretary-General on Internet Governance

Extracts from the Transcript of Proceedings

H.E. FED. COUN. MORITZ LEUENBERGER:

Thank you for giving Switzerland the possibility to speak in the name of the
Council of Europe, the presidency of which is changing this week from
Slovenia to Switzerland.

Freedom goes hand in hand with responsibility. We heard good examples of
Internet usage from the head of Yahoo!, but there are also people who misuse
the Internet for criminal purposes, such as terrorism, pedophilia or hacking
attacks on states, businesses, or individuals. This minority is a danger to the
freedom of others. Freedom should only be restricted to where this is
necessary to protect the freedom of others. And that is why the Council of
Europe has drafted nonbinding recommendations and binding conventions.

The Council of Europe strongly supports the multistakeholder approach of
the Internet Governance Forum (IGF). The Internet must not be misused as an
instrument in the struggle for power, neither by economic forces nor by
political regimes. And this also means creating platforms that enable all
stakeholders to freely exchange their views and experience without any
pressure to negotiate. The IGF is such a platform.

DR. JÓZSEF GYÖRKÖS:

The Internet is a space of enormous opportunity and freedom. That said, it
must be also place of responsibility. The Council of Europe fully supports the
IGF process as a space which promotes transparency and participation. We
believe in a multistakeholder approach to dialogue and the development of
Internet policy and in a rights-based approach. The 47 governments of the
Council of Europe agree on the public service value of the Internet, which is
an essential tool for everyday activities and must be accessible, affordable,
secure, reliable, ongoing. The Internet constitutes a pervasive social and
public space which should have an ethical dimension, and should foster
justice, dignity and respect for the human being based on respect for human
rights and fundamental freedoms, democracy, and rule of law. Our collective
responses can be found in conventions on cybercrime, data protection,
protection of children against exploitation and abuse, prevention of terrorism.
A new convention on counterfeiting of medical products will also be opened
for signature very soon. The Council of Europe's human rights guidelines for

European Internet service providers and for European online game providers are notable examples of responses that have been worked out with the private sector.

MS. LISA HORNER:

Multistakeholder participation is arguably more important in the Internet governance sphere than in other policy areas. The Internet is central to everyday lives and activities, business and commerce, and increasingly government services and communication. That's why freedom of expression is a foundational right, essential for the realization of other fundamental social goods such as development, association and peace. The key challenge for Internet governance is to mediate between different users and uses, ensuring that everyone's needs and interests are met whilst at the same time protecting and expanding our fundamental human rights. We need to make sure that the characteristics and tools that we value the Internet for are preserved and expanded. We need to support and expand the Internet as a tool for empowerment and human development. The public interest must not be eroded. Multistakeholder collaboration based on shared values and guided by common principles is the only way that we can ensure this.

We need to ensure that all relevant stakeholders are at the table, including, to name just two examples, some of the major businesses that are notably absent, and Internet users themselves, particularly from poorer countries of the world. The IGF's dynamic coalitions are one space where constructive engagement could yield really positive results. But the coalitions need better participation from all of us. I urge everyone to engage in these spaces, especially in the freedom of expression online and the Internet rights and principles coalitions that are working to preserve the public interest dimensions of the Internet and to protect human rights.

H.E. MS. ÅSA TORSTENSSON:

The four IGF meetings prove that all the stakeholders support and defend the underlying values of the IGF and of the World Summit of the Information Society (WSIS), in particular, the right of freedom of opinion and expression. These are global concerns that must be addressed in a global forum. The E.U. firmly believes that the IGF should continue beyond its first five-year period, which expires at the end of the next year. It is necessary to retain a forum that does not make binding decisions that could require long periods of consultation and negotiations. It is exactly this lack of negotiated binding outcomes that makes the IGF such an indispensable and flexible tool for policymakers around the globe.

The Internet cannot be controlled or governed by any one actor. This is part of its success. The European Union wants the Internet to be a global network that is open, resilient, and accessible to all. Respect for human rights and the rule of law are of fundamental importance. Citizens should be able to communicate freely and securely with everyone, regardless of national borders. As long as users respect the right of freedom of others, we must ensure that they all have the same right and ability to contribute to the evolution of the Internet. Restrictions or limitations to the freedom of expression must be in accordance with international human rights law.

The private sector should continue to be responsible for the day-to-day coordination of the Internet's global system of unique identifiers. ICANN has proven effective in ensuring that the domain name system has kept pace with the rapid growth of the Internet over the last ten years. That is quite an achievement for one organization, and we should all contribute to ICANN's further development. This is why we welcomed the Affirmation of Commitments as an opportunity to transfer oversight of ICANN to the entire global community. This can be done through a framework of reviews and recommendations in which all stakeholders participate, but requires that there is transparency and accountability.

H.E. MS. VIVIANE REDING:

Since Athens 2006, the IGF has continued to show its value, and the consistently high number of participants demonstrates that there is a real need for such a forum. It is a unique forum, where we can engage in open, nonbinding, multistakeholder dialogue. I am aware that some criticize precisely this recipe for success, but I will ask them: How else can we build together a global response to the global challenges raised by the Internet? Where else can any Internet player from anywhere in the world come and express his views? Where else could we have such open, enriching debate?

The IGF succeeds because it deals exactly with these questions. For example, the European Commission has been working since 1999 to make the Internet a safer place for children. Our safer Internet program supports awareness-raising activities toward children, parents, teachers, and it is run by local bodies across Europe, under the umbrella of the Insafe network. The safer Internet day, on the 11th of February every year, is now shared by more than 60 nations worldwide. And much of this has been agreed upon during the discussions between stakeholders in the IGF.

The IGF also succeeds because of the participation of governments and public administrations. Governments must play a role in the public policy Internet issues, where the general public interest must be protected. The billions of Internet users who are not with us today expect their governments to protect and promote their interests. If users want to keep an open and neutral Internet, they must actively encourage their governments to protect it, and governments must respond as positively as the European Union has done this month with the first-ever legislation protecting the access rights of Internet users. With its emphasis on the local as well as on the global, with its depth and its range of issues, with its diverse audiences, we need IGF. Before the next meeting in Vilnius there will be discussion on whether the IGF should continue beyond 2010. For me, for the European Union, the answer is very easy. The IGF must continue, and I invite all of you to support it.

H.E. MR. PEDRO SEBASTIAO TETA:

The IGF is acknowledged as a promoter of progress and access to Internet in Africa. That is why we pay a great deal of attention to the IGF and we support its continuation using perhaps new models. We welcome the active participation, which is promoted by this forum, on behalf of member states, business, civil society, the youth, women, et cetera. I'm convinced of its success and its contribution to the development of the Internet in Africa, since when we decide something together we arrive at better decisions and we also make the Internet more democratic.

H.E. MR. AUGUSTO GADELHA:

We had the privilege to be the second organizer of the IGF, in Rio de Janeiro, Brazil. We have witnessed through the three first IGFs that it has matured and we could have discussions with more objectivity. The IGF has contributed very much to the global awareness of important issues, and we believe IGF has to continue. When it comes to the possibility of renewal of the mandate by the United Nations, are one must bear in mind that the IGF is neither a self-contained process nor a decision-making body. Its efficiencies cannot be measured on the quality of its outcomes alone. The IGF is, rather, a facilitating process for the implementation of all of the WSIS action lines regarding Internet governance. Despite all the progress since Tunis, the diagnosis that led to the creation of the IGF remains valid.

AMB. PHILIP VERVEER:

The Internet is the largest and most successful cooperative arrangement in history. It achieved incredible scale with unprecedented speed, and it is constantly growing and evolving. While the Internet, in that sense, is exceptional, it's also emblematic of an important contemporary development, the growing importance of multinational, nongovernmental organizations. Given the Internet's origins and history as a cooperative venture among stakeholders of every description, the creation of an institutional framework for the constructive and open exchange of ideas has proven extremely useful. That the IGF has fulfilled its mandate in extremis is evidenced by the large gathering of hyper-accomplished individuals in this room. The United States enthusiastically joins our friends in the European Union and Brazil in indicating our view that the IGF ought to be extended well into the future.

H.E. MS. NATHALIE KOSCIUSKO-MORIZET:

If we have an idea that can be described by a photo or word, it is something that can be forgotten over time. And we have the right to move on to other things, to change what we said at one point, making sure that this is not held against you later on. This notion is being brought into question by the infallible memory of the Internet. So there must be a right to forget, to make sure that something that we wanted to share at one point but later on wanted to take back remains personal. This is not a theoretical question. In the United States, 35% of employment recruiters say that they eliminated candidates because of words or photos on the Internet they judged inappropriate. So I'm underscoring this as an example of what the IGF's contribution could be, because it brings together all of the actors, not on a negotiating platform. It enables us to develop a mentality in order to come up with something that can be translated into reality and provide guarantees for data and users. And that is why I invite all of those who want to do so amongst us to create a group on this issue within the IGF. Additionally, I suggest that in June 2010, we, in France, hold a multi-actor meeting on this topic in order to give further thought to this right to forget information or word in Europe.

MS. LYNN ST. AMOUR:

The IGF has emerged as an important meeting place for those interested in the value, the potential, and the future of the Internet. It is a forum we can come together to forge relationships, explore ideas, and share our inspirations when we return home and resume our work. That is why we strongly support continuing the IGF.

This year's Nobel Prize in Economics went to Eleanor Ostrom for her work on common pool resources. Her work shows that better outcomes are achieved for a common pool when several factors exist, including the presence of a community with a strong social network and shared norms, and with community-based rules and procedures. An element of her work particularly relevant to the IGF's role was to demonstrate how important it is for stakeholders in a common pool to know and interact with each other. The IGF is an opportunity to expand these social networks and strengthen norms.

The Internet works precisely because all organizations work together collaboratively, respecting individual roles, and in the public interest. We call this the Internet model of development, and we calm the diverse environment of stakeholder the Internet ecosystem. Although conceived four decades ago, that model continues to foster a vibrant environment of innovation and creativity. What better proof could we want of its importance? In the best tradition of the Internet model, the IGF provides a forum for new voices to participate in a dialogue, to talk openly about challenges and to discuss how to address them. It is the Internet Society's hope that those governments and institutions that have not yet embraced the open and inclusive model will experience the value and the benefits this model can bring not only for the stakeholders but for mankind.

MR. ABDUL WAHEED KHAN:

UNESCO has consistently underscored that Internet governance mechanisms should be based on the principles of openness, freedom of expression, diversity, and interoperability. And throughout the process, UNESCO has stressed that the multistakeholder approach is the most effective modality to address global Internet policy issues. The offers an opportunity to address an enlarged policy agenda, embracing these principles and creating conditions for the Internet to provide opportunities for all. Internet governance must be part and parcel of a global governance that is founded on universal ethics.

The Internet must be linguistically diverse so that all language groups can harness its unique potential. We welcome ICANN's fast-track plan for the introduction of country code IDNs, and I am pleased to announce that we will shortly sign a partnership agreement with ICANN and other many stakeholders to contribute to their full development. The empowering role of the Internet in fostering free expression is still too frequently cut across the world. The IGF offers a unique platform to highlight the need for an open, unrestricted flow of ideas on the Internet.

MR. SUBRAMANIAN RAMADORAI:

In India we are seeing that when policies and regulation support the ability of companies to compete, innovation and entrepreneurship thrive. Perhaps some of these issues could be considered as you deliberate over the next few days. It is forums such as the IGF that enable the voice of all stakeholders across the world to be heard. The IGF is critical because it is that special place where we all come together to share, learn, and listen. Governments, businesses, civil society, technical experts, academics, international and intergovernmental organizations and individual users, we all have roles to play in this development.

The IGF has catalyzed increased communication between different stakeholders in India. The same is true of many other regions and countries. One of the reasons business supports the IGF is because it is a unique opportunity for exchange, building relationships, and understanding each other better. That is why business is here to participate in this IGF, and to support its continuity. As we engage, let us keep in mind the 4A's that will play a key role: access, affordability, and appropriateness of applications. Let us remember the millions of poor around the world waiting hopefully on the sidelines, to whom we all have a responsibility.

MR. ROD BECKSTROM:

I would like to thank you, the IGF community, for what you have done. You have delivered some very clear messages over the last three years, and you've been heard. You urged ICANN to become more global, and On October 1st we signed an Affirmation of Commitments with the United States Department of Commerce that makes us more accountable and transparent to the world. We also thank you for advocating IDNs. Last month, after years of work by many parties, we were able to commit to formally launch IDNs for country codes, with a formal application process starting tomorrow, November 16th. As Minister Kamel said, the Internet now speaks Arabic. But while there are advances, we also know that we have further to go. Many of you have noted that there are only generic top level domains in Latin characters such as dot com, dot net or dot org. They're not yet available in IDNs. And many parties around the world have suggested that this is an issue of equity and it should be addressed with the opening of gTLDs under the IDN scheme.

Within this ecosystem, how exactly does ICANN fit in? ICANN has four functions. We facilitate and are involved in the management of Internet names, addresses, the domain name system that links those two, and publishing standards of Internet protocols and parameters. We do none of them alone. We do everything together with our partners in the ecosystem, because the Internet is this masterful collaboration platform where so many partners come together. We thank you for having advanced these efforts, for having advanced our organization, and we hope that you'll not only live but go through significant evolutions in the coming years.

MR. JEAN ROZWADOWSKI:

With a network of local representations in over 120 countries, the ICC is the world organization working on behalf of businesses everywhere to promote cross-border trade and investment. As the voice of global business, the ICC is very aligned with the open dialogue mode and raison d'etre of IGF. ICC's BASIS initiative recognizes the value of working with all stakeholders to build smart, sound Internet policies that allow us to play our parts effectively. We strongly support the continuation of the IGF in its current format with all of us participating on an equal footing.

The implications of IGF discussions to date have been far-reaching. Because we do not meet here to negotiate, community leaders can participate in frank and open discussions that have ultimately led to more informed policy and decision-making within their respective communities and organizations. There is no existing alternative to the IGF. Without it, many of us would have no occasion to exchange views and experiences. Appreciation of the needs of others would be greatly undermined. The IGF spurs cooperative efforts and reduces duplication. It also links people, topics, and other forums and processes. Over the last four years, we have seen rhetoric give way to substantive discussions. We have witnessed many of the ideas generated and best practices exchanged at the forum applied in practice at national and regional level. In turn, the involvement of local sources of knowledge and expertise in Internet governance issues has been strengthened by the emergence of IGF-related initiatives. So we are proud to have strong representation here.

MR. NITIN DESAI:

I'm here more as the chairman of the multistakeholder advisory group (MAG), which has to organize this meeting, so my remarks will be more on process than on the substance. In the IGF, the process is the product, which is something we should keep in mind. The work for this meeting is done by all of the members of ithe MAG, and it's not just the fact that they participate in the three meetings we have through the year, planning the agenda and the structure of this meeting. It's also the amount of unpaid work that they do as moderators, as facilitators for workshops, as resource persons, as people who are available for any emergency.

The uniqueness of the IGF is not just the format of the meeting itself. It is also special in the way in which this meeting is organized. It's not organized by a classical U.N. Secretariat working away in some remote office, but rather by the stakeholders themselves. Not just in the workshops, which they organize almost entirely on their own, but even the main meeting.

Another innovation of the IGF is its transparency, the fact that every MAG meeting has an open consultation attached to it. So everything that gets done is known to all stakeholders in good time, and they have the full opportunity to be able to shape the agenda, the structure of the meeting.

The IGF has been shaped by the ways Internet processes operate. First, respect for all points of view---when you have a request for proposals on technical standards, you have to respect all points of view that come up. Second, it must be a dialogue of good faith. You cannot dismiss something that somebody says simply because of who that person is. No ad hominem arguments, you have to treat each position on its merits. You may disagree with it, but disagree on the substance, not because of who said it or where it came from. And I could go further and say a dialogue of good faith is one in which you enter willing to be converted, not just to convert the other person.

Third, keep an open door. Anybody who has something to contribute is free to come in and join the meeting, just as with Internet standardization. These are very important principles in a multistakeholder environment. There is a natural way of deciding who comes if it is purely an intergovernmental meeting. There is no natural way of deciding who comes if it is a multistakeholder meeting. You have to keep the door open and say that anybody who has a concern or an issue is most welcome to walk in and join in this meeting.

What is unique about the IGF is the way it has tried to bring in stakeholders who normally would not meet each other. Many of you meet separately in your own fora to discuss the issues that we discuss here. I'm sure businesses have their own groups for that. I'm sure the Internet community does, so do NGOs and so do governments. What is unique about the IGF is all four groups are being brought together here to build bridges and listen to each other's point of view. That is crucial.

This requires a little adjustment because the professional cultures of the groups who are here differ. The diplomatic culture of governments when they meet in international fora is different from the culture of nongovernmental organizations, activist organizations when they meet. And that is different from the dialogues of the Internet technical community when it meets, and that again is different from the way in which businesses will talk with one another in their fora. So when we get together, a little adjustment of culture is required. And one of the things that I take joy in is that over these four years, this adjustment has taken place. People have learned to adjust to the differences of culture which people bring to the table here.

I would really stress the importance of bridge building. If you are building bridges, you don't start by yelling at the person on the other shore, you must learn to talk peacefully with the person. So I stress that this is a forum about ideas and principles, not judging individuals or finger pointing. Over the next three days when you have your vigorous dialogues and differences of opinion, when you start losing your temper, just ask yourself, how important is this issue from the perspective of the millions who are the future users of the Internet. That's the thought that I leave you with.

Managing Critical Internet Resources:

Report of the Main Session

16 November 2009

Chair:

Mr. Nitin Desai
Special Adviser to the Secretary-General on Internet Governance and
Chairman of the Multistakeholder Advisory Group

Moderators:

Mr. Chris Disspain
Chief Executive Officer, .AU Registry; Chair, Council of Country-Code
Names Supporting Organization (ccNSO)

Ms. Jeanette Hofmann
Senior Researcher, London School of Economics and Political Science
(LSE)/Social Science Research Center Berlin

Extracts from the Transcript of Proceedings

NITIN DESAI:

Let me welcome to you the first thematic substantive session of the fourth
Internet Governance Forum. The theme of this session is critical Internet
resources. The Multistakeholder Advisory Group (MAG) has suggested a
four-part agenda. The first is the transition from IPv4 to IPv6. The second is
the importance of new TLDs and IDNs for development. The third is the
Affirmation of Commitments, the recent development in the relationship
between ICANN and the U.S. government. The Affirmation of Commitments
and the IANA contract. And the fourth is enhanced cooperation generally
and the internationalization of critical Internet resource management.

This is a very wide-ranging agenda, and to the extent possible we should try
and stick to the sequencing. Quite a few people will wish to participate more
than once since we will be going sequentially from topic to topic, so I would
request they keep their remarks short. I realize you may have some complex
argument to present, but if it is a very long position that you wish to
elaborate, I could request the Secretariat to see whether a written submission
can be put on the Web site. But let us try to keep this as a conversation to the
extent we can. These are topics that we have discussed in the past. In
particular, we discussed them in Hyderabad. So I hope that your remarks will
also focus attention very sharply on what has happened over the past year,
which we need to discuss here in this forum in Sharm El Sheikh.

We do not have a panel. All of you are experts on this, so there is no need for us to have a panel. What we do have to ensure the flow of dialogue and to identify people for speaking are two facilitators, both of them members of the MAG. One is Chris Disspain, and the other is Jeanette Hofmann. Both of them are members of the MAG, and they will orchestrate this debate and invite people to join in the conversation.

JEANETTE HOFMANN:

Our first topic is IPv4-IPv6, the transition and the problems that are still in the way. And we have asked Paul Wilson from APNIC to give us a brief overview about what has happened since we discussed this topic last year.

FROM THE FLOOR:

Jeanette mentioned to me this morning that she thought the fascinating thing about this IPv6 transition is that everyone and no one is responsible for it. That is very true. There is no one who is responsible for the entire IPv6 transition. But, in fact, the same thing does go for many things that happen on the Internet. This is why the Internet is referred to as an ecosystem, not as an enterprise or a machine. But in the case of the v6 transition, there are quite well-known roles for a whole group of actors and stakeholders. The stakeholders themselves know what they need to do. What's a little bit new about this process is that we have got a great number of people who do need to move forward at the same time. It's not that they need to be strictly coordinated and dance terribly well together, but we do need to move forward towards this same goal, and that it is already happening. We have, over the last year, IPv6 addresses being allocated in increasing and substantial numbers all around the world. We have ISPs actively planning and deploying and providing trial and production services for IPv6. We have IPv6 in the operating systems, which are sitting on our desks and on our laptops. We have IPv6 in a lot of the infrastructure equipment that is operating on the Internet. We have got IPv6 being brought in, introduced to many parts of the DNS and being supported by registries and registrars. We have IPv6 in software applications, in many major applications that we use. We also have governments taking active interest in IPv6.

There are a couple of areas that are moving a little slower. We're not all carrying IPv6-capable smartphones and PDAs in our pockets. We might not all be using or in a position to use the IPv6 in our cable and DSL connections at home. But these things are coming. We have seen IPv6 appearing in the Internet, on the routing system, and now, over 2,000 of about 30,000 autonomous systems which are in the routing system. And we see an increase in the IPv6 traffic on the Internet. The reality is this has only just started, so only a fraction of 1% of Internet traffic is IPv6. So it's a slow start, but the good news is that this is actually growing at an exponential rate. The transition is something that is going to go on for some time. It's not an event. It's not like Y2K, although that's an analogy we hear. It's a process that will be under way for a decade or more. That is not a new realization, it is exactly as the transition has been discussed and planned over the last ten years.

Where v6 is being deployed and we have existing networks, clients, infrastructure, and services, v6 is joining in a dual-stack transition. Dual stack means you have got v4 and v6 both running on a particular device or network. The trick will be in a couple of years' time when we have rapidly reduced or greatly reduced number of IPv4 addresses to distribute, because new network are going to need to be deployed with IPv6. IPv4 in limited numbers will still be available, essentially private addresses. But in both those cases, a technique called network address translation is needed to allow us to reach from an IPv6 connection through to an IPv4 service or server. And this is where we hear that network address translation will not suddenly disappear with IPv6. As servers and services transition from v4 to v6, we're going to have a gradual shift over to v6, and your v6 connections will then magically access those services using IPv6. The transition is something that will happen behind the scenes and very gradually over, as I say, the next ten years. In that time, IPv4 is going to continue to work.

There's a perception that this transition somehow should be faster. And it's sometimes said that the Internet has been unable, in some way, to transition to IPv6. It's actually not the case. It's a question of choice on the part of those who are in the position to transition to IPv6. It's a choice that we will, at some point in future, transition when we're ready, when it's justified. The fact is the Internet -- its success is based in the fact that it is a highly competitive environment. Business has to think very hard these days about where to put resources, about what will give better service and value to customers and win market share. And so far, there have been other priorities. So this is actually an informed, intelligent business decision. The fact is, IPv6 isn't necessary on today's Internet, but it's going to be very necessary in two years' time, and two years is a critical period for business planning. We are seeing a lot of movement in indicators---addresses, routes, and traffic on the Internet. We are also seeing a lot in surveys of intentions and plans on the part of ISPs.

JEANETTE HOFMANN:

Deployment of IPv6 is still under 1%. So Paul if I ask you what has happened since last year, we have to say not that much. But you said the transition will take place when it's justified. If I understand correctly, we will run out of IPv4 addresses, unallocated IPv4 addresses, in two or three years. So is transition not justified for at least five or six years?

FROM THE FLOOR:

Planning for the transition is justified and necessary now because in two years' time, an ISP that needs new addresses to build a new network is likely to get IPv6 rather than IPv4. And that's where a two-year planning horizon is really quite realistic. On the question of numbers, the Internet is full of very big numbers and a fraction of 1% of anything on the Internet can still be quite substantial. And over the next two years, we do expect there to be a really rapid increase in deployment.

FROM THE FLOOR:

Hello. My name is Jonne Soininen from Nokia Siemens Networks. The things that are happening are not always visible to the outsider, but there has been a lot happening during the last year. A lot more talk, a lot more interest, a lot of operation. Vendors are getting even more prepared than they were before. And even parties that haven't been very active or haven't known about this are becoming aware of the IPv4 depletion issue and are preparing. I also would like to comment on something Paul said earlier on: many of the smart phones that we provide do already support IPv6. They don't get much use at the moment as the operators haven't launched the services widely yet, but we are prepared and you can use them as soon as these services come online.

FROM THE FLOOR:

I am Naoko Amino, working for the Ministry of Communication, Japan. I would like to talk about the steps we are taking on IPv4 exhaustion. This year we are holding a working group to reveal the methods of promotion of the IPv6 migration among ISPs to general users, business users and so on. And we are holding a working group to study the Internet of Things using IPv6. We need more IPv6 engineers, and we believe government should support their training, so we have educational programs for them establishing IPv6 test beds. We would appreciate it if we can collaborate with many countries. We also have in cooperation with the Japanese Internet and telecommunications industries a Task Force on IPv4 Address Exhaustion. We would like to continue sharing information and cooperating with many countries to take the action to overcome IPv4 address exhaustion.

FROM THE FLOOR:

(Paul Wilson) The RIRs along with many collaborators have been involved with the technical training of Internet operators for many years and IPv6 has been a priority for several years now. The correct and efficient operation of Internet networks, particularly in developing countries, is something that absolutely relies on human resource development, which is crucial with IPv6. So we're spending a lot of time on technical training as well as the broader outreach and information.

FROM THE FLOOR:

I'm Sami Al Basheer, the director of the development bureau of the ITU, the International Telecommunication Union. Of course this is a process and it will take some time. The ITU Council took a decision to form a group to work on this, to help our members, especially the developing countries, in terms of capacity-building and know-how and so on. The developing countries are concerned not to be left out in this, like what happened at the start of the Internet when they had to wait a long time. International organizations, the business communities, and civil society will all have to work together to make this transition happen as soon as possible and on an equal footing around the world. I just want to emphasize, as our Secretary-General did yesterday, that the ITU -- and when we say the ITU, we mean our members, the telecommunication administrations -- are open to work with everybody on an equal footing to make this transition happen in the manner we do with all Internet governance issues.

FROM THE FLOOR:

I'm Izumi Aizu. Just to follow up my government colleague from Japan, I'm the member of the task force for the IPv4 depletion, as well as the government organizing study group. A simple question about to Paul, when you prepare the dual stack, meaning v4 an v6, you cannot really have it unless you have the v4 already. So that may accelerate the consumption--- if I'm wrong, please correct me. On the penetration or the deployment of IPv6 in Japan, it used to be higher than others, and now we see a little bit saturation. We did a survey last year of ISPs and only eight are deploying IPv6 connectivity service. 20 are planning, and 80 have no plan yet. And this growing sort of attitude of "wait and see," we don't know exactly why this is happening. It's very difficult to send a clear message because there's no economic demand and return in a short range.

FROM THE FLOOR:

I'm Raul Echeberria from LACNIC, the regional Internet registry for Latin America and the Caribbean. And I agree with the colleague from Nokia that many things are happening but probably are not very visible. One of the things that is happening is that the number of people that is trained on IPv6 is really big. In our region, LACNIC has trained this year more than a thousand people in hands-on activities. It's not just to explain what is IPv6, but to train the people in how to develop and deploy IPv6 in their networks. And it is having also an impact on the number of IP addresses that is being allocated. But the difference is that the people that receive the addresses now are starting to work immediately on deploying IPv6 in their networks. Also, most of the IXPs in Latin America are running IPv6. 75% of the Latin American ccTLDs are accessible by IPv6 by primary or secondary servers at this moment. Haiti is the poorest country in region and they have an IXP that connects a hundred percent of the ISPs in the country. What that means is that all the local traffic remain in the country, and they run IPv6. So while I understand that people say that developing countries are concerned about this, regions like mine are getting progress on this field, so I'm very optimistic.

FROM THE FLOOR:

I am Zicai Tang and I'm part of the Chinese delegation. I'd like to thank the Egyptian government and the Secretariat of the IGF for their warm hospitality and arrangements. On the issue of IPv6 present, we're fully aware of the importance of IPv6. As of September of this year, the number of mobile Internet users in China has reached 192 million, an increase of 62.7%. We predict the continuous rapid development of mobile Internet worldwide with the comparable rapid development of demand for IPv6 addresses strengthening international cooperation, and coordinated development of IPv6 is now a consensus in the international community. We hope that all countries will strengthen their exchange and cooperation in the application of IPv6 to the industry and networks.

FROM THE FLOOR:

I'm Rod Beckstrom, the President and CEO of ICANN. This is a really important conversation. There's a lot of confusion about how Internet addresses and allocations work, and I want to address it because ICANN is the central authority on Internet address allocations. It allocates those through the Regional Internet Registries (RIRs) that distribute them to ISPs and other parties. There's some misconceptions that are very fundamental that need to be addressed. Or, rather, let us put the truth on the table. There is no difference in how emerging countries have been treated historically in IPv4 allocations and other countries. The addresses were available to parties when they needed them. The constraint is to use IPv4, you have to have the hardware and software -- you have to have the network routers and switches -- you have to install your networks, and need the addresses, and when parties did in emerging countries, like all other countries, those addresses were allocated through the RIRs and ISPs. If anyone in this room has a single example of a corporation or a NGO or a government not receiving an address allocation, please let me know. With respect to IPv6, let us be clear: There are trillions of trillions of addresses available. Literally trillions of trillions. There's plenty of addresses. Addresses are not a constraint in IPv6. It's the hardware, the software, the upgrades to the network systems that take a lot of time and money. So that's what we're talking about. The addresses are absolutely available. Every country's treated equally. And I really appreciate the fact that Secretary-General Touré of the ITU recognized yesterday that ICANN's role as the central authority on names and addresses, because that will also enable us to work more productively with all partners in the ecosystem including the ITU, whom we respect and value. But I want to make it clear: IPv6 addresses are available. The constraint is upgrading networks. Paul Wilson, maybe you can speak to how you can allocate IPv6 addresses when people are ready for them?

FROM THE FLOOR:

The IPv4 and IPv6 addresses are being allocated by all of the RIRs now, according to policies that are determined by the regional Internet communities, at an increasing rate. We are allocating to ISPs in 150 countries. There are more than 2,000 autonomous systems which are separate networks appearing in the Internet routing tables. The amount of IPv6 address space that is available is absolutely astronomical. 300 trillion, trillion, trillion addresses, if you like. An analogy is, if the address space of IPv4 were represented by a golf ball, then IPv6 would be approaching the size of the sun. When we hear that the addresses are being allocated rapidly wherever they're needed, it's natural to ask how many there are left, but there are literally trillions and trillions of addresses left. We could take the highest density of Internet utilization or penetration in any part of the world, multiply that level of penetration across the entire planet by another factor of thousands and we would still not have scratched the surface.

FROM THE FLOOR:

I'm Tom Will Sanford from a trade body in the U.K. Paul in his opening remarks said that no one's in charge, and he's quite right. But I do think there needs to be one or more bodies in charge of marketing the concept. If I talk about the Internet in the U.K. with the general business confederation, the issue is below their radar. It's not in our top hundred issues. I think there is a distinct need for some marketing push. Not implementation and not telling people what to do, but persuading.

FROM THE FLOOR:

I'm Fouad Bajwa from Pakistan. In my country, the biggest problem that we face, although the capacity building has started, is what's going to happen with the equipment, the infrastructure that's required? It took us nearly two decades to deploy IPv4 infrastructure, and then the next thing we know the address space is going to be out soon. With IPv6 we have the same issue of again building new infrastructure and it's going to require capacity building, it's going to require new equipment. There's no second-hand equipment for IPv6 going to be available. And there's the requirement to have more information of how economically IPv6 is going to benefit a developing country.

FROM THE FLOOR:

My name is Christine Arida and I'm from the National Telecom Regulatory Authority of Egypt. We have in Egypt an IPv6 task force that's been looking into how to enable a faster transition to IPv6. There are economic challenges when the ISPs are newly investing in infrastructure and then they realize some of it is not IPv6 enabled, or they don't have IPv6 options. So they have to make an additional investment, and it's a financial burden so they have to see the benefit of that. Governments can help. Egypt's NRN network which is government funded was asked to be IPv6 enabled, so this gives the backbone builders the chance to put investments into IPv6 and it makes it easier. Now, with respect to capacity building, we've had a very good experience. I don't know if someone from AfriNIC is here but they've been active. We've had all through Africa so many IPv6 training sessions, two of them already in Cairo were very beneficial, and so RIRs are helping very well.

JEANETTE HOFMANN:

So do you think that one potential role of governments would be to hand out subsidies to companies that have financial problems with the transition?

FROM THE FLOOR:

Not in that sense, but when you're forward looking on national network building, you can put the IPv6 component in there to make it easier for the investment to come.

FROM THE FLOOR:

I'm Milton Mueller at Syracuse University and part of the Internet Governance Project. The dialogue is getting mixed up here. We're talking about two issues that are related but not the same. One of them is the problem of migrating to a new technical standard, which is always difficult, particularly when the old standard is so deeply embedded and the new one is not backwards-compatible. The other is the issue of address scarcity. Now, obviously address scarcity is a factor in motivating the migration, but it's clearly not a sufficient factor until you reach a crisis point. I would like to point out that the dialogue about address scarcity is embedded in an institutional rivalry between the ITU and ICANN, and for those of you who are not part of that rivalry, I just want to make it clear to you, that beneath the surface of many of these conversations, this rivalry is going on. I think it needs to be acknowledged. I think the dialogue about address scarcity policy needs to be extracted from this rivalry so that we can have an intelligent and honest discussion of what is the best way to ration or allocate IP addresses without getting stuck in a debate about whether you're for or against ICANN or the ITU. So when Paul talks about the vast size of the IPv6 address space, he is correct, but he also knows that the units or the chunks of IP address space that would be given out routinely are also extremely large and there will be vast amounts of so-called waste or unused addresses. So we do have to worry about how many addresses we're giving out, and to think about potential scarcity. We do have to think about overly liberal allocations in the early stages, and developing countries are correct to be worried about that. This does not necessarily mean that the RIRs are doing something wrong. In fact, I think they've been very attuned to this problem. It doesn't necessarily mean that the ITU should take over addressing or that ICANN is the sole central authority for addressing. It's simply a fact that scarcity could exist and we have to worry about how we allocate IPv6 addresses.

JEANETTE HOFMANN:

Two questions arise from that. First, how will IPv6 addresses allocated, will it be different in any way from IPv4 address allocation? Second, RIRs are now preparing for the depletion of the pool of unallocated IPv4 addresses, so what will happen when we run out? How will we deal with the problem that there is still a high demand? Perhaps somebody from the RIRs could speak up on this issue.

FROM THE FLOOR:

Thanks, Paul Wilson. I mentioned earlier the processes which are underway in each of the regions in guiding and refining the address management system and the policies under which we operate, and that system is very much one of balancing efficiency and responsibility, so Milton's reference to the large blocks of IPv6 address space is quite true. The blocks of address space which are being allocated are astronomical, in comparison with what is available through IPv4, and that is a conscious decision on the part of the community to ensure that there are no barriers to IPv6 adoption, that there is an efficient routing system and aggregation within the system that will prevent ISPs from having to come back regularly to the RIRs. But what I said as well still stands in terms of the supply of addresses available. One of the major topics of conversation in all of the regional address policy processes has been the fate of the remaining IPv4 address supply. There is, at the moment, no rationing of IPv4 addresses. The projections that we have for the next two years assume an ongoing rapid rate of deployment of IPv4 addresses. However, each of the RIRs has policies in place for the last portion of address space that they will receive to ensure that there is an ongoing supply of small blocks sufficient, as Izumi mentioned before, to support a dual stack transition for many years to come. And those blocks would be available for existing and new ISPs that could come along for years during the ongoing transition to v6.

FROM THE FLOOR:

Thank you. My name is Viv Padayatchy. I'm the chairman of AfriNIC, the regional registry responsible for IP address allocation in Africa. AfriNIC has a support program for running technical training for network engineers for the uptake of IPv6 technology. We also provide training on IP address allocation for both IPv4 and IPv6. If any of you in the African region here need some support, whether it's technical or whether it's just informational regarding IPv6 allocation or training, please get in touch with me or we have several board members who are present here. We also have our chief technical officer, who is present at this IGF meeting.

FROM THE FLOOR:

I'm Olivier Crepin-Leblond, an ISOC ambassador. Is it possible right now to get connected via IPv6 to the Internet from the main session room here?

FROM THE FLOOR:

Raul Echeberria from LACNIC again., To Olivier's question, this is something that we usually do in all the RIRs IETF meetings. Two responses to things said before. One is that the RIRs have stayed out of any controversy between ICANN and ITU, which doesn't affect the allocation system. The other is that I agree with Milton regarding the management of the resource, while this is a huge number of IPv6 addresses we have to take care because anything could happen in the future that could demand more addresses.

FROM THE FLOOR:

Patrick Fältström with Cisco. You will probably see some IPv6 on this network shortly.

FROM THE FLOOR:

I'm Willie Currie from the Association for Progressive Communications. I was interested to hear Paul Wilson talk of an ecosystem, and I think it would be quite useful to explore this concept further. Is it self-regulating, and more than the play between regulation and deregulation? This has characterized the governance debate over the last 20, 30 years. If it is more than a matter of regulation and deregulation, if it is some combination of regulation and deregulation, then should there not be some consideration of public options in regard to nudging ISPs towards faster adoption of IPv6? How do the various components, public, private, fit into that? I am thinking that in a way, the analogy is the economic crisis, where it became apparent that before the crisis there was limited coordination between the central banks around the world. After the crisis, they realized they needed to coordinate more effectively. If one looks at climate change and say we shouldn't worry because an ecosystem is self-regulating, then maybe it will precipitate a disaster.

FROM THE FLOOR:

Rob Beckstrom, I wanted to take on the question of how can the nudging be done. I had some interesting conversations with Vint Cerf and others in Washington recently because Vint cares a lot about IPv6 and is worried it won't happen. And I said it's a network effects problem. Until everyone else does it, you don't have a lot of advantage being a first mover unless you are building a whole new network. Many of you might have heard of "Cash for Clunkers," a program in America where you can trade in old gas-guzzling cars and get new small cars and money. So the idea I came up with was doing network cash for clunkers, which is if your routers and switches are so old they can't support IPv6, let the government have an incentive structure to trade those in and upgrade to IPv6. In the case of cars, they are equipment, whereas with IPv6 it's more about software and the configuration. Each country could consider national programs to incentivize the adoption of IPv6 with DNSSEC, so there's a security benefit as well. And those programs could be in the form of tax credits, or they could be in the form of accelerated depreciation on the assets, which is similar to a tax credit. Or they could be in the form of subsidies or other development grants. But there's many different formats that can be used, if the countries of the world could look at using stimulus funds to upgrade network infrastructure to move to IPv6 and DNSSEC, it would be really great. And by the way, this is a case where the ITU can help out because it has relationships with the ISPs and the telecom providers for that physical layer of upgrade. ICANN's little role in this is the network addresses that we allocate to the RIRs. Again, there are enough addresses for everybody. If anyone in the room has heard of anyone who couldn't get an IPv6 address, please raise your hand. Okay. I don't see any hands. So there are enough addresses, trillions and trillions. But we have to get the infrastructure upgraded so let's all partner. You know someone who didn't get an IPv6 address?

FROM THE FLOOR:

I'm Sureswaran Ramadass, Professor and the Director of the National Advanced IPv6 Centre of Excellence at Universiti Sains, Malaysia. Actually, Rod, my concern's different. Since there are so many IPv6 addresses, why can't we have additional organizations giving them out?

(Beckstrom) But you got what you wanted, so what's the issue?

(Ramadass) Exactly, what's the issue? Why can't we have additional organizations giving them out?

(Beckstrom) Someone who knows how the router system and BGP works can probably help me. The reality is you want the addresses allocated in a fashion that makes some sense because the border gateway protocol assignments are important. Anyway, there's routing implications. Do you have a problem with the RIRs? Is that what you are saying?

(Ramadass) No. I am saying there should be an alternative for someone to seek.

(Beckstrom) Why? If you get what you need, why do you need something else?

(Ramadass) Not in the way I want it.

(Beckstrom) What way are you not getting it?

(Ramadass) I'd like multiple organizations to choose from. That would be good.

(Beckstrom) We have five RIRs. Go wherever you want in the world.

(Ramadass) I can't go to the other RIR, can I? Can I? Can you answer that? Can I go to AfriNIC?

JEANETTE HOFMANN:

I think the first thing we should notice is ICANN suggested the ITU as one potential forum to discuss the future role of governments in the transition process. If that isn't good news, I don't know what good news is.

FROM THE FLOOR:

(Beckstrom) Let me make clear. What you are saying is, even though you are getting what you want, you want a different political body. You have a political issue. You do not have a functional issue.

(Ramadass) I want an option to be able to choose between A or B to apply for IPv6 addresses.

(Beckstrom) Why? Give me a business reason. Not a political reason, a business reason.

(Ramadass) Okay. It's called non-monopoly. It's called why we also decided that there should be many telecommunication companies. Why ISPs shouldn't be just one in a country, but many. That same reason is why there shouldn't just be one RIR giving out IPv6 addresses.

(Beckstrom) It doesn't make any sense. You are getting it for free.

(Ramadass) I am not getting it for free. That's the whole point. I am paying for it.

NITIN DESAI:

We need to wrap this up. This conversation can continue a little later.

FROM THE FLOOR:

My name is Nii Quaynor. I'm from Ghana. I am an operator. I am very, very happy with the way the number systems work. I am extremely pleased with the opportunity Africa has to participate in making its own policies regarding address assignments for its operators. We like the fact that it's an open process, and we can all participate collectively in a multistakeholder environment to achieve that. And we believe that any form of change that takes that opportunity away from Africa is not in the interest of Africa or in the interest of developing countries. We would like to all participate together to make policies which are localized, that benefit all of us in the development of a single Internet, not multiple Internet.

FROM THE FLOOR:

The ITU was mentioned many times. I want to make sure that we don't misunderstand this. There is no intention in the ITU to do what the ICANN does. It's very clear. What we are saying is that we don't want the ICANN to do what is the mandate of the ITU. You see?

CHRIS DISSPAIN:

It's the same thing.

FROM THE FLOOR:

I repeat if it's not clear. There is no intention in the ITU administrations --and we are not talking here about any Secretariat position in this, it's membership driven---we have no intention to do the business of the ICANN.

JEANETTE HOFMANN:

Thank you.

[applause]

FROM THE FLOOR:

What everybody is talking about within the ITU and for around the world is we don't want ICANN to do what is the mandate of the ITU of policy-making, public-policy issues and so on.

CHRIS DISSPAIN:

Jeanette and I agreed that we would try to make sure this session didn't just become about ICANN. So we have done really well so far. And we are moving on now to new IDNs and new gTLDs. Because the introduction of IDNs and new gTLDs has an effect on the root of the Internet, we are going to talk about the root scaling study and what should happen with that. Just before I pass you over to Patrik Fältström, who is going to do the introduction on this, there is a piece of news. I have been asked by the Egyptian and Russian governments to tell you that as of today they have both put in applications for IDN ccTLD. Apparently there was some kind of competition going on, and I don't know who got in first, but I do know that Manal was in the office until 2:00 this morning to make sure that Egypt's application got in on time. So I think you deserve a round of applause for that.

[applause]

So on that note, I will pass you over to Patrick who is going to do the introduction.

FROM THE FLOOR:

Let's start by looking at what kind of changes have been made and are happening at the moment. The first one is the addition of internationalized ccTLDs. From a technical standpoint, it's not much more than adding a couple of new TLDs, but for the users it has big impact. And for the various protocols that use domain names, it has a big impact. So the size of the root zone will increase. There will be some new registries added. There will be some more policies added to the global system. And that of course creates some stress. The second change that is happening is that we are going to add DNSSEC to the root zone. There are some ccTLDs and other TLDs that are working on using DNSSEC. My country, Sweden, was the first one that signed our zone a couple of years ago. But more countries will follow, and the signing of the root zone that is currently scheduled to happen during the first half of 2010 will create some issues. The size of the responses will be larger. There will be more stress on the root system itself. There are some key management issues. We need to know how we are going to handle the request for key management from the top-level domains, et cetera. So DNSSEC's addition will require changes in various places, specifically for the people that also want to verify those signatures on the DNS responses.

The third thing is that we are adding IPv6 addresses for the DNS servers, something that is called glue records in the DNS. This is also something that creates changes. The DNS servers can no longer only use IPv4, but also IPv6, when they are issuing queries. The root servers needs to respond to IPv6 queries. The TLD servers need to be able to respond. And clients need to know whether they are going to use IPv4 or IPv6. The last thing is the addition of international gTLDs and other top-level domains. And the question there is whether we are going to add one, three, or three million of them. These changes make myself and many of the others a little bit nervous. We have not changed the DNS much in the last couple of years, and then suddenly we are going to make four changes within like six months. Of course, coming from a technical environment, we know that when we say something is going to happen within six months, it normally takes ten years, but it is still a very short time period.

Because of this, there have been a couple of reports written. I was myself part of writing one regarding root scaling, the implications of root scaling for the

196

stability of the DNS system. And the conclusions from those reports is that the number of root zone TLDs that are added doesn't have so much impact. It is the rate at which the TLDs are added which is the problem. The root system can accept lots of changes, and over time it is possible to change all of it, if we have to. But it takes time. Let me give you a couple of examples. When a top-level domain wants to change something in the root system, it could be anything from changing the e-mail address of a contact to changing the IP address of one of its name servers, they contact IANA. IANA is authenticating the request to make sure it is really the requesting party that has sent in the request. The change is implemented, and then published in either the WHOIS servers or in the root zone itself. So there are several steps there from provisioning to publication. And those changes, regardless of where they are, might impact the amount of staff and human resources needed, the name servers, hardware, routers, switches, and finally budget processes of the organizations that are paying for this. Because even the root system is something that is run by multiple organizations, each one having its own business case, and if they have to change lots of things that they are doing, that takes some time. So the rate of change has much more impact than the actual changes themselves.

The last thing I wanted to talk about is IDN issues and the developing countries. The developing countries actually have it much easier than the rest of us, because they don't have so many old things to change or replace. They can immediately jump into a system where they use IPv6 in internationalized domain names. Myself, it has been very, very difficult just being able to handle the few characters we use in Swedish, which are only three. Being able to do a presentation that I held yesterday morning where I tried to include some Arabic in my PowerPoint slides, that was not easy. So all of us have to work together because we share the responsibility to ensure that the Domain Name System continues to be stable. And we have to be careful with the changes we are making and add them in a cautious and careful way because we don't want to break the DNS.

CHRIS DISSPAIN:

So news is coming in thick and fast. We have an application for an IDN ccTLD also this morning from Saudi Arabia. So congratulations to Saudi Arabia.

[applause]

FROM THE FLOOR:

My name is Alejandro Pisanty. I am from the Internet Society and the National University of Mexico. The introduction of IDN ccTLDs provides an important opportunity to recognize the management of ccTLDs that is continuously evolving at present. Many ccTLD managers have started in research organizations, in small community organizations, and have done an heroic job in expanding the Internet in their own countries for many years. The IDN ccTLD should not be used to cut off this recognition by starting a new officially mandated ccTLD registration. One could encourage every government and society to be respectful of their ccTLD in this transition. My nightmare scenario is that a policy-making body which is not well informed or is captured by some interests could create and mandate registrations and do things that do work very well but seem to work, like only doing business with organizations that are registered in the new IDN ccTLD and, therefore, stabbing in the back a community operator who has been working heroically.

FROM THE FLOOR:

Hello, Milton Mueller again. I wanted to talk about the impact of the root scaling study on the new gTLD process. ICANN's fundamental function is to make policy regarding which new TLDs are available. And many people have been very disappointed that for after ten years, it has still not implemented an ongoing process for the addition of new TLDs. Starting in 2006, it seemed to solve that problem with a very extensive policy-making process to add new top-level domains. And now the root scaling study comes along and some people have interpreted it to mean that the new TLD process should be deferred because of the impact on the root zone administration and provisioning. I would like to point out that the real issue here is that somebody has made a decision that the root zone will be signed in July of 2010. And I have to ask, where did this decision come from? I can tell you it did not come from an ICANN or an IGF process. It did not come from any bottom-up process. It came from negotiations among the United States government, VeriSign, and, secondarily, ICANN. And the process of root signing that is being imposed in this way is really sort of an arbitrary constraint that's been thrown into the middle of the new TLD process. ICANN created a lot of expectations that there would be an ongoing new TLD process, and then all of a sudden this interruption came from nowhere saying that there's going to be a root signing at a fixed day and this makes it possibly impossible to proceed with these new TLD plans.

FROM THE FLOOR:

Chuck Gomes from VeriSign. I have a question for Milton, because I don't see the signing of the root as a constraint in introducing new gTLDs, or other TLDs for that matter. It will be done in July. What's the constraint?

CHRIS DISSPAIN:

I'm sure Milton will respond, but it might be at least in part that the root scaling report suggests you should do DNSSEC first.

FROM THE FLOOR:

(Mueller) Yes. The suggestion by some people is it is impossible to both have new TLDs and the DNSSEC happening at roughly the same time.

(Gomes) That's exactly my point, Milton. The report did say that if you have to make a decision, DNSSEC should be done first. Well, it's naturally going to happen first because there will not be any new gTLDs introduced before July. So what's the constraint? That condition will be met, as I understand it.

(Mueller) So you are saying that the new TLDs will be deferred for another year.

(Gomes) That's a totally different question, with different parameters. But what I am saying is, the plan right now is for the roots, all 13, to be on board with DNSSEC, signing the root by July. That will not cause any delay with regard to new gTLDs. There may be other factors that do, but I don't believe that does.

FROM THE FLOOR:

Patrik Fältström again. Let me emphasize what Chuck just said. What we found was that it is the rate of the changes to the root zone that is the issue here. When we add DNSSEC, that might multiply the size of the root zone by a factor of four. Because of that, it's better to add DNSSEC first while the zone is small instead of first increasing the size of the zone and then adding DNSSEC, because the multiplication effect of the change of the actual number of bytes of the size of the root zone will be four times larger if we do DNSSEC after. Of course, it's up to anyone to read our report and other reports and draw their conclusions.

JEANETTE HOFMANN:

From a technical point of view, how long would that delay the introduction of new gTLDs?

FROM THE FLOOR:

(Fältström) It's not a technical issue. It has to do with human resources, budgets, et cetera. What we suggest in our report---and other reports say different things---is that we need to have better communication and an early warning system that can say, okay, we add one thing, we look at how the change is adopted. Then we can calculate when we can take the next step. So we take one step at a time. It's very hard to extrapolate far into the future.

FROM THE FLOOR:

I'm Bob Kahn from the Corporation for National Research Initiatives. This is a helpful dialogue and I hope it continues. However, it is important to point out that this is a discussion in a context of a much larger set of diverse possibilities that we're going to have to deal with in the future, and I wanted to make a plea for everyone in this room to remain open to diversity of choice, going forward. The Internet is not a stable, locked-in system that has only one approach to doing things. It's going to change in the future. The networks will change, the technology will change. Maybe even every aspect of it will change as we go forward, and this is healthy. But I don't think we need to think about locking into one particular approach and we certainly don't want to go down a path that will cause the Internet to fragment.

Part of the discussion about IPv4 and v6 is to assume that we have some kind of continuity going forward. I think the roles that ICANN and the DNS are playing will continue to be important. But we will have a set of possibilities going on in parallel. One has to do with how we develop process. The IGF is a way of having good discussions about process. ICANN implements process. Many organizations implement process. And the other part of it is authentication. Whether we're authenticating systems, whether they're authenticating content, whether we're involving individuals or actual systems and those can be separated as well. So my whole motivation here was to essentially not take on existing processes, but to give us some independent ideas.

For example, publishers worldwide have adopted an approach using unique identifiers that they call DOIs. It's based on something called the Handle System. And this is literally a parallel to ICANN, working completely in parallel with it. And it works extremely well. It has multiple agents, it's got the equivalent of an unlimited number of equivalents to domain names, and it's been fully secure for ten years. The choice of the DNS was made back in 1984, and it was intended basically to simplify things, so people didn't have to remember IP addresses. It was not to lock in any particular method. In fact, my plea has been to remain open. If people have better ideas than DNS, let's move to them. You can give everything in a network an identifier. People have tended to focus on content for the most part, but we've worked with places like Cisco to demonstrate that you can identify a router with an ID and a router can be a mobile program that can move from place to place. If you give a mobile device a unique identifier, then it can resolve to the protocol it's willing to use, and I think devices in the future will have multiple protocols, so they'll be able to work on multiple systems. So my plea is to remain open to these new approaches, even though this discussion is about one particular approach.

FROM THE FLOOR:

My name is Andrei Kolesnikov. I'm representing Russia, the ccTLD dot ru, and I'd like to say that we applied for the fast-track process exactly at the time it was opened, so we are kind of competitors with our host in Egypt. These new things are making equal all the stakeholders around the world. We are all in the same boat doing a new thing, which is very exciting. I'd like to thank ICANN and the international Internet community for making the fast-track procedure real. It was relatively fast, okay? Even though some people called the fast track not very fast. But, you know, in the scale of Internet life, it's really fast. And also I should mention that ICANN did a good job assigning a random number so nobody knows who was the first, who was the second to apply. And also, work on the internationalization of the address space has just been begun because it will take a few years until the different applications understand the charter even though they will use different languages. So one example is e-mail from the IDN domains. It's not an easy one, my estimation is one year, at least, for this one. So again, thanks everybody.

FROM THE FLOOR:

Thank you so much. My name is Maria Häll, and I work for the Swedish government and also represent the Swedish E.U. presidency. We are very concerned about the stability and security of the Internet from both a public policy and multistakeholder perspective. We hope that you're going to take into account, no matter what decisions are taken with the DNSSEC signing, IDN introduction and gTLDs, that all these decisions need to take into account the concerns that were raised by Patrick.

FROM THE FLOOR:

My name is Izumi Aizu. I'd like to congratulate Egypt and Russia for applying for the fast track, and ICANN for allowing us to do so. In Japan, we deferred applying, although the existing registry manager, the JPRS, and any others who want to are welcome to. That was the conclusion of the almost one-year policy process with the public comment, and many meetings involving not only the domain name industry but also the ISPs, businesses, consumer bodies and others, and we concluded with a consensus to have this process. So now we are working on how to set up the selection process on level playing field. We need better choices for consumers, diversity, but we also need to keep one single global Internet. We are facing a challenge because we have two different ccTLDs. If the existing operator wins, then there will be one operator, but maybe two different policies. The government's telecommunications council is tasked to do the oversight, and like Alex said, we should respect all the pioneering work of the existing ccTLDs, yet there are calls to open up like Bob Kahn said, to see more diversity in a manner that keeps the unity or the global one Internet, but still expand furthermore of the greater choices. So our task is very difficult, even in Japan.

FROM THE FLOOR:

My name is Khaled Fouda. I work for the General Secretariat for the League of Arab States, and in response to decisions and resolutions by the Arab Telecommunications and Information Technology Council of Ministers, we have been working for quite a while now to apply for new top-level domains with the assistance of other regional and international organizations. We intend to apply for the dot Arab top level domain and its equivalent string in Arabic, dot arabie, and actually though our string is unique and well identified all over the world, we have two concerns. One is that new gTLDs might be delayed for quite a while and we want to move forward with this issue. Another is that new commercial and non-commercial TLDs might be treated similarly, and we don't believe that we should be treated like a commercial entity who is applying for a gTLD to financially benefit. So we heard that there might be a new approach to maybe geographic top-level domains and we want to know how can we go into that track or maybe can we apply for ccTLDs through the fast track.

CHRIS DISSPAIN:

That's a very interesting question. There's a lot of discussion going on within ICANN and its Government Advisory Committee (GAC) about what the position of geographic names should be, be they country or regional names. Anyone who is involved in that would encourage people like you and the people that you work with to get involved in that debate. Rod Beckstrom, you want to say something?

FROM THE FLOOR:

Yes. The policies for domain names and addresses are developed through a bottom-up process in ICANN involving the multistakeholder community. Chris is the chair of the Country Code Name Supporting Organization, which is the global body where those policies are developed for country codes. Avri Doria, who is here, is the chairperson of the Generic Names Supporting Organization. These are very subtle and sophisticated issues because other commercial interests that have a gTLD want to be treated similarly with new gTLDs whether they're under an international domain name or they're using the traditional Latin characters. Please come to the ICANN meetings. There are multiple standards bodies involved in the Internet. ICANN's role concerns names, addresses, the domain name system, and publishing the protocols and parameters that IETF develops. IETF, of course, is the standards group, or the technical group that developed IPv4, IPv6. They also developed DNS. HTML was developed by the W3C, which is a terrific organization. There's also OSI and of course ITU is a very important standards body in telecommunications. So none of us has a monopoly on standards.

JEANETTE HOFMANN:

Does that mean it's still an open question whether commercial gTLDs will be treated differently than non-commercial gTLDs?

ROD BECKSTROM:

The new gTLD process hasn't opened up yet. We have just reached agreement with the Universal Postal Union on dot post but that's been in process from the 2006 round. The new gTLD process is proposing that there be similar treatment between the two. There's some differentiation, but fundamentally similar. The real issue here is contractual. ccTLDs, or country code top-level domains such as dot eg and the new one that Egypt is applying for, have no contractual relationship with ICANN, usually. There's a working relationship. There may be an exchange of letters. In some cases, there's a framework that's signed. It's not the same ironclad contract that we have, for example, with VeriSign or that we have with the operators of dot info, et cetera. So we have contracts with generic top-level domain operators, but ccTLDs we don't because of the sensitivity of sovereignty issues. Obviously, people around the world would like to say, "Well, give can us the new IDN gTLDs with no contracts, we want to go do what we want to do," but that is not accepted by the community of all the stakeholders because there's issues of equities that are involved. So the issues are not finally settled. These IDNs are fast tracked. Fast track goes around the policy development process in some sense. At the same time fast track is happening, so Egypt can have their Arabic country code, the policymaking group is working on the long-term policies for the international domain names ccTLDs.

CHRIS DISSPAIN:

So those of you that may not yet be involved in the glorious policy development process, it's probably time that you were. There are all sorts of questions that need to be answered. I wonder how some people would feel about new gTLDs that might be brand names like dot ibm, or if say a cigarette company decided that they would like to get a gTLD. So there are all sorts of areas and issues that need to be sorted out.

FROM THE FLOOR:

Manal Ismail from the National Telecommunication Authority of Egypt, and I also represent Egypt at the GAC meetings. I wanted to congratulate my colleagues from Russia and Saudi Arabia for submitting their applications, and of course you know more than I do the amount of effort that this has been, and how this worked in a really multistakeholder approach with the cooperation and coordination of the different supporting organizations in ICANN. I would like also to thank ICANN for all their listening and understanding, as all our recommendations were reflected in the final plans. It's also been a lot of cooperation between all the Arab countries on a regional level, on one hand, and also with other countries that use the same script on the other hand, so it's still more cooperation and we need more. This should trigger more local content, more applications, and tools to really have a multilingual Internet, because the IDNs only are the key.

FROM THE FLOOR:

Willie Currie, Association for Progressive Communications. I don't think Milton's question has really been answered: Who has the policy authority to make the decision on the signing of the root by July next year? It seems to be a combination of the U.S. government, VeriSign, and ICANN, but has ICANN had a policy process on this matter? It's unclear to me where, exactly, the policy authority is, if we want to see Internet governance as a rule-based system.

CHRIS DISSPAIN:

I offered the opportunity for people to address that. They've chosen not to. We'll take it out of the room and deal with it then.

FROM THE FLOOR:

Guru from IT for Change, India. I just heard Rod say that the difference between the commercial and the non-commercial gTLDs is not that much, and my question was: if a group of pharmaceutical companies wanted to create a dot medicine, or maybe even Glaxo wanted to do a dot Glaxo, they would have the resources and the capacity to apply for the gTLD. But if a group of civil society organizations want to create a dot public health or a dot civil society, the capacities that they have would be dramatically different from those of a large company.

CHRIS DISSPAIN:

He didn't say that there was not much difference between a commercial and a community gTLD, but rather that there's not a lot of difference in the process for creating a commercial or a non-commercial gTLD. And that it is still the subject of ongoing discussion.

FROM THE FLOOR:

My name is Sammy Buruchara. I'm the chairman of Kenya ccTLD KENIC. And my concern really is that we've been talking about the digital gap, and there is a need to support ccTLDs in developing countries, especially in Africa. We still have very few ccTLDs that are fully in operation, and my concern is that with the new gTLDs and geographic names there would be a danger of people's values and cultures being managed by entities from other regions simply because their countries or ccTLDs are not developed enough to apply for management of those names. Is there a provision to ensure that as they try to build their capacities, that those values and names will protected so that we do not have a scramble for names specific to a people or a region that end up being managed by people that are not representative of them.

CHRIS DISSPAIN:

We're going to call this particular bit of the session to a close and move on to the Affirmation of Commitments (AoC) and the IANA contract.

JEANETTE HOFMANN:

The AoC replaces the Joint Project Agreement (JPA) between ICANN and the U.S. government, and we've asked Rod Beckstrom to explain to us what it actually means.

FROM THE FLOOR:

Thank you for this opportunity, and for being the catalyst for the affirmation occurring in the first place. IGF has had a tremendous impact in your previous meetings by shaping the environment that led to the affirmation document. Namely, your concern that ICANN was too U.S.-based, and should become more of a truly international entity, which it clearly is with all the stakeholder groups that are involved. So let's talk about the affirmation.

The AoC has 11 paragraphs on four pages. It is publicly posted. Most people have focused on Paragraph 9 about reviews, but there's 10 other paragraphs. The first paragraph has some very significant words, this document constitutes an affirmation of commitments to institutionalize and memorialize the technical coordination of the Internet domain name and addressing system. So the document is institutionalizing and memorializing this relationship in coordinating the DNS. The second paragraph talks about how critical the DNS is to the global Internet, and its protection, and also supports the multistakeholder model. This is very significant. The U.S. government is making two commitments in here to ICANN and to the world: Committing to the multistakeholder model in writing; and committing that the public interest that ICANN must serve is global. Previously, if you'd looked at ICANN's incorporation, you could have argued, "Well, ICANN, because it's legally in the United States of America, legally the public interest concerns the citizens of that country," even though ICANN's always been focused globally. This makes it absolutely clear that ICANN's focus and public interest is global. It's in writing, it's very significant, and has been missed by most reviewers.

We move to the third paragraph. The third paragraph talks about how ICANN makes decisions. These decisions have to be made in the global public interest and they've got to be accountable and transparent. That's a big discussion all of us need to have, how do we continually become more accountable and more transparent? And also, that we should promote competition, consumer trust, and consumer choice in the DNS marketplace. Sometimes people ask, "Why is ICANN doing new gTLDs?" Paragraph 3 of the affirmation, subsection (c), "promote competition, consumer trust, and consumer choice in the DNS marketplace." Okay? That means as an entity, ICANN is committing to add more consumer choice. We're so delighted, and honoured, that Egypt is moving forward with your Arabic IDNs and pioneering the way in Arabic. That's one form of choice. New gTLDs. There's many forms of choice but we have to do it in the global public interest.

Paragraph 4 is where the Department of Commerce formally commits to a multistakeholder, private sector led model---including governments, NGOs, all groups---with bottom-up policy development for the benefit of global Internet users. And ICANN has to perform and publish analyses of the positive and negative effects of its decisions. This is a new requirement that we be more explicit in sharing how our decisions are reached. Paragraph 5, international domain names, basically states that both parties agree this has got to get done. Paragraph 6, the Department of Commerce affirms the U.S. commitment to ongoing participation in the GAC. The GAC is extremely important to ICANN. They have committed here, effectively in perpetuity. So the U.S. government is saying, "We will be involved in the GAC," it's not just a temporary working group, it's a long-term advisory committee. Paragraph 7, ICANN commits to adhere to transparent accounting and finance actions and fact-based policy development. What is fact-based policy development? We need to discuss that as a community. We need to decide what does that mean. And when we say the public interest, what does the global public interest mean? Is it just the value to Egypt of having a new Arabic country code extension? Is it purely economic? I think not. There's great social issues, cultural issues, the pride of people in their language. So we have to think about what all these terms mean.

On to paragraph 8. ICANN and the U.S. government are committing to a single interoperable Internet. That means the integrity of the DNS. That's a commitment. And this is a really powerful sentence here, ICANN is a private organization and nothing in this affirmation should be construed as control by any one entity. That's truly the U.S. government recognizing that ICANN is independent right there. And it's guided by you and other stakeholders that are involved in the processes. Very powerful. Then we get to paragraph 9. Four reviews are going to be done roughly every three and four years. The first is on transparency and accountability. The members of that are chosen by our chairman, Mr. Peter Dengate Thrush and Ambassador Janis Karklins, both in the room here. They will choose the members of the first review team quite soon. And then there's a lot of details on how those review teams will be constituted. The second review is on the stability, security, and resilience of the DNS system. Those will be run every three years and reported to the world and posted for public comment. The next review is on promoting competition, consumer trust, and choice. This is about adding more options in the DNS. The fourth review is about WHOIS. And ICANN is committing to reviewing its existing policy related to WHOIS, subject to applicable laws. Those are the applicable laws in every country and region of the world. The E.U. has very strong privacy protections. So recognition of the international nature of WHOIS and of the Internet and the policies. Also new is the formal commitment of global law enforcement and privacy groups in the WHOIS review. Both of those entities were never mentioned in previous documents relating to the formation of ICANN. So it's formally recognizing we need law enforcement involved, and we need to have the privacy groups involved.

On to ten. We commit to publishing the reviews openly to the world. And paragraph 11 has a really important comment that's often missed, which is that this agreement is intended to be longstanding. There is no end date to the Affirmation of Commitments. But either party can leave it at any time with 120 days notice. So this again is a great model of multistakeholder collaboration. This is a voluntary commitment by both parties, and it represents the spirit of the Internet in the same way that we work with the ccTLD operators on a voluntary basis. So that's the summary of the AoC. The other question was IANA. I have a very quick position, very simple. ICANN is a purpose-built organization to help run the DNS and names and addresses. IANA is a contract that was created by the U.S. government that continues until either September 30th of 2011 or October 1st and what the U.S. government does at that time is up to them and I have no comment. You should ask the U.S. government.

JEANETTE HOFMANN:

Thank you, Rod. I have one simple question before I open the floor. If the JPA had just been phased out, would it make any difference to the Internet?

FROM THE FLOOR:

Well, no. The Internet would keep going on. I think the beauty of the Affirmation of Commitments is it's basically saying, okay, you want to be more global? Be more global but you need to show you are a responsible citizen and you need to commit to how you are going to act in the global public interest. So I don't think it was essential, things could have moved on, but it was viewed as being beneficial to both parties.

FROM THE FLOOR:

On the issue of managing the critical Internet resources, this is a major issue of IGF, as it is stated in the Tunis Agenda, paragraph 72, subparagraph a). During the WSIS, parties reached an understanding on the definition of critical Internet resources which includes the management of DNS, IP addresses, and the root server system, of which the root zone file system is the most critical resource. Should there be a security glitch in the root domain name server, it could lead to the collapse and paralyze of the Internet worldwide. A certain change to the root zone file system could lead to the disappearance of the Internet of a given country from the global Internet map.

The report of the Working Group on Internet Governance set up during the Geneva phase of WSIS points out that the central issue regarding the management of root zone file system and root server system lies in the unilateral control by the government of one country, which was also a major reason for the establishment of IGF. The U.N. should continue its deliberations on this issue and seek solutions to this issue. We have also noted that the recent signing of the AoC by ICANN, which is a step forward towards establishing a new review mechanism in attracting wide participation of multistakeholders in the management of critical Internet resources. However, as was pointed out by some Ministers in their statements yesterday, the management and distribution of Internet domain names, IP addresses, and technical protocol parameters as well as the operation of the root domain server are all performed through the IANA function contract delegated to ICANN by the government of one country, which apparently enjoys rights that other countries do not enjoy. We should resolve this issue.

FROM THE FLOOR:

Willie Currie, Association for Progressive Communications. The AoC is a major important step forward in Internet governance, and it opens up the possibility of a range of actions to be taken in its wake. One of them is the transfer of the responsibility of the IANA contract to ICANN itself. There's no reason to wait until 2011 for this to take place. It goes to the issue of the integrity of ICANN as a rule-based decision-making body that it assume this responsibility as soon as possible. There are a number of reasons for saying this. The one is the debate we just had about the signing of the root. It seems that the authority for this lies with the U.S. government. And it's made very clear in its 2005 policy statement that it would not hand over control of the root zone file. That policy needs to be reviewed and is a missing element in the AoC. The other reason is that if one peruses the transcript of the ICM registry versus ICANN matter before the independent review panel, there seems to be a prima facie evidence that the U.S. government, through the Department of Commerce, was willing to use its control over the root as leverage in the .xxx decision. Namely, that if ICANN went ahead and approved .xxx, the U.S. government would refuse to enter that domain into the root. Now, this raises important freedom of expression issues. And the other gap in the AoC is that it does not include a commitment by ICANN towards freedom of expression, association, and the right to privacy. This is a gap. There was a very interesting session yesterday that said that this could be something that should be proposed as a bylaw change for ICANN. And I would certainly think that would be a useful thing to explore, particularly in the light of the new gTLD process.

FROM THE FLOOR:

Hi. Finally. I am Y.J. Park from Delft University of Technology. I am also one of the MAG members. First I would like welcome the U.S. government's willingness to move forward in terms of the internationalization of ICANN. However, despite some progress made in the AoC compared to the JPA, the AoC still confirms the special status of U.S. government as the sole global authority that approves all delegation and redelegation for the 251 ccTLDs and 21 gTLDs. According to the IDN fast-track process identified by ICANN, the U.S. government is about to exercise its power once again to approve IDN ccTLDs as the final authority. Such a practice of delegating sole power to a nation-state without global consensus is very unusual in the international community. As one of the academics who studies ccTLDs, my study found that the supervision of one nation makes it very difficult to have a more stable relationship between ICANN and ccTLDs. Therefore, taking advantage of this opportunity, I would like to urge that the next IANA contract should not repeat what the AoC did. Instead, the next IANA contract should identify an international body that will take over the current role of the U.S. government. Since the IANA contract is to expire in 2011, I would like to remind the IGF community here that we have only more than a year or so to identify the international body. Therefore, I would like to propose the IGF should start to encourage such discussion, who can replace the current supervisor that coordinates the global critical Internet infrastructure. As we all recognize in this room, ccTLDs and gTLDs, IDN ccTLDs, are critical Internet infrastructures for a nation-state. The global coordination of a critical infrastructure of a nation-state should not depend on another nation-state's approval. Lastly, I hope IGF can continue facilitate internationalization of ICANN.

FROM THE FLOOR:

Milton Mueller again. As a member of civil society, we welcome the U.S. government's step away from ICANN. The IANA contract would be a bigger step. I'm not sure I see the need to rush that and recognize that when many people call for internationalizing the IANA contract, they want to participate in the power of the U.S. government rather than eliminating that power. And I'm not sure that's always a good thing. Good that the global public interest is memorialized. It's very good that language about fact-based policy development and thorough and reasoned explanation is in there. We appreciate Rod's enthusiastic exegesis of the affirmation and particularly his explanation of what we hope will be a more balanced approach to WHOIS. The final and most important point I want to make is about accountability. We recognize that this is just a step towards clearing a path towards a real form of global accountability to a global public, and we view the U.S.' step away as a precondition to that. We do not think self-reviews by the ICANN community are a substitute for accountability. And we, the Internet Government Project, are releasing a new paper about this accountability issue and how we might go forward with it. That will be on our Web site at igp.org either today or tomorrow.

FROM THE FLOOR:

Yes, thank you so much. It's Maria Häll from the Swedish government and the Swedish E.U. presidency. The E.U. welcomes this new and more open working environment for ICANN with this AoC. We believe in the private sector-led, multistakeholder, bottom-up model for the technical coordination and day-to-day management of the DNS. We also welcome that the AoC highlights the role of governments and also the GAC. And also give more perspective on the public-policy issues. But of course there are challenges in the implementation of this AoC. And it's not only the review process that is very important. It's about a methodology and how this process is going to go on. It's all the other activities that are going to ensure transparency and accountability for ICANN. But this process also gives us more ability to engage ourselves. So that is actually something we need to think of, all of us, to engage ourselves and try to help out with this new and more open model.

FROM THE FLOOR:

Stefano Trumpy, representing Italy in the GAC. We concur with the statement of the European Union presidency. The AoC is a very relevant step forward for the internationalization of the management of DNS. And this is something that is going in the direction of the Tunis Agenda document produced in 2005. And the basic of this is that ICANN was sort of an institutional experiment. This bilateral declaration is recognizing this is the best model, I could say the unique model, to assure this service for the global community. And it is important also to note that yesterday, in the declaration of Mr. Touré, there was a recognition of this model. And this is a very important statement, of course. Now, ICANN has to demonstrate external accountability to the community of the Internet, and this will be a complex task.

FROM THE FLOOR:

Alejandro Pisanty, previously introduced, ISOC Mexico and UNAM. I have been a participant in the ICANN processes since the start and have been a member and vice-chairman of the board. I applaud the AoC as a very smart and forward-looking way of continuing the ICANN revolution and assuring that later, down the road, stuff like the IANA contracts can also be dealt in a more internationalized way. I would like to express an exception to the approach expressed by Ms. Park of looking for another international body to do the supervisory functions over the IANA contract, to substitute or complement the U.S. government functions. I think that particularly coming from academia and civil society, what we have to look for is not to have governments as proxies. It's an absurd contradiction sometimes that civil society organizations are looking for governments instead of building the organizations ourselves, as we have been doing with ICANN and with many other of the Internet governance bodies. We should look more to create structures that accrue trust on themselves, and that by circular architecture, become more reliable for every other party instead of calling for proxies for what we can do ourselves. I don't mean to exclude governments. But not as proxies being called for the creation of new bodies from civil society.

JEANETTE HOFMANN:

I still hope that they both sort of follow similar principles of creating legitimacy and that there won't be such a divide between private sector principles of running a global infrastructure and governmental principles.

FROM THE FLOOR:

This is Abdullah Al-Darrab from Saudi Arabia. I believe that everybody here would like to see ICANN more internationalized. Therefore, the affirmation is a step forward. However, as our ICT Minister mentioned several times, we would like to see ICANN become "WECANN." And here I would like to comment on a number of issues related to the affirmation. One is that as long as ICANN is working under the U.S. Californian law, then it is as independent as Motorola or Lucent. And we can say that if we apply this, Ericsson and Nokia and others are also independent. But this is, in my view, not the case. The second thing is a point that was raised many, many times during the WSIS process, and this is related to the management of the root zone. And I would like to make clear here that the point I want to mention should not be understood wrongly. Our relation with the U.S. government is excellent. It was excellent. It will continue to be excellent. So it should not be understood any other way. However, it is a principles issue that, per the WSIS, the management of critical resources is a point of international public policy that should not be done by a single government. And this point is not mentioned at all in the affirmation, as if the root zone management has nothing to do with the whole issue. So this is one of the things that needs to be resolved. There needs to be clear rules and regulations and processes on how to deal with the root zone. We had a case where a ccTLD of one of the Arab countries was taken out of the system. This isolated the country from the Internet for some time. I don't think anybody wants this to happen to him, so clear processes need to be done and agreed upon by all.

HERBERT HEITMANN:

I'm Herbert Heitmann and I am representing the ICC as the chairman of the Commission on E-Business, I.T. and Telecommunications. I want to say we very much welcome this development. I was extremely impressed when we met with Rod the first time how internationally he has set up his team. So I don't see any kind of concerns with the future direction. And I think it gives business a reliable future for the domain system, and we are very much supportive of this. You can always ask for more, but this is a good start.

CHRIS DISSPAIN:

Thank you very much indeed. We're going to move on to the final topic, which kind of dovetails into this, so we can still sort of talk about ICANN and the AoC, because the final topic for this morning is enhanced cooperation and the internationalization of management of the CIR. We're going to have a brief introduction from Ms. Haiyan Qian who will update us on the UN process concerning enhanced cooperation, and then we're going to throw it open for discussion on what does it mean, is enhanced cooperation simply governments improving its role and responsibility within ICANN, or is it other things as well. Is it, for example, the ITU improving its interface with civil society? But first an introduction from Ms. Qian.

FROM THE FLOOR:

Not long after the Hyderabad meeting the United Nations General Assembly adopted a resolution that requested the Secretary-General to submit a report on the process towards enhanced cooperation, and on public policy issues pertinent to the Internet. How this process can be pursued, based on the consultation of the relevant organizations, including international organizations. So Under-Secretary-General Mr. Sha Zukang of UNDESA invited ten relevant organizations to give their views and provide recommendations. And this report was compiled by us and submitted to the Economic and Social Council and will be taken up next year. Some of the key points are the following. Many of the organizations called for a continuation of the multistakeholder dialogue, which should be transparent, open, inclusive, and consultative before any decision is made. Some of them argued for using the IGF as a platform; for enhancing capacity building in the Internet-related issues, particularly for developing countries; and for more government participation and partnership with other stakeholders. There were cautions against creating any sort of intergovernmental body before evaluating the existing ones, and some believed that the existing intergovernmental bodies can play certain roles in dealing with public policies pertinent to the Internet.

FROM THE FLOOR:

My name is Peter Bruck. I'm the chairman of the World Summit Award and the chief researcher of the Research Studios Austria. The question of ICANN's independence has come up many times. My suggestion to those who consider that the solutions on the table are not appropriate is a structured mediation process to resolve it in the foreseeable future. It is important to take steps in that direction to come to a more creative and structured approach, instead of reiterating positions which will already well known and not very productive.

FROM THE FLOOR:

Peter Dengate Thrush, chairman of the ICANN board. I just wanted, in the spirit of sharing information, to make a correction to something that was said earlier about a ccTLD being removed from the root. There has never been an operating ccTLD removed from the root. Okay? There's a lot of myth and legend. I've checked this with the U.S. Department of Commerce, and with the IANA function. When I said "operating ccTLD," there was once a non-operating ccTLD for the outlying islands of the United States that had never been used and was taken out. But just to repeat: There has never been an operating ccTLD removed from the root.

FROM THE FLOOR:

My name is Maimouna Diop Diagne. I work for Senegal's government. I'm a member of the GAC. And I really welcome the AoC, and we are looking forward to its implementation, and we are also need to know how to improve participation of governments in the GAC, especially from developing countries. ICANN is private sector-driven now, and we are looking forward to having more GAC involvement but it will take time, so in the meanwhile my question is whether ICANN will work with the ITU.

FROM THE FLOOR:

I'm Abdullah Al-Darrab from Saudi Arabia. I have three quick points. The first one is a correction to the transcripts because I said that our ICT minister said several times that we would like to say ICANN to be "W-E-C-A-N-N" but not "weakened." The other thing, I thank the gentleman who tried to correct the information related to the deletion of the ccTLD. I would like to ask him if there are clear rules and regulations on when a ccTLD will be deleted, if that is very clearly agreed by countries. This is one thing. The third point is related to the enhanced cooperation. Being a person who participated in all the WSIS, I know as well as many people here in the hall the history behind the enhanced cooperation issue, and there was agreement to have two processes. One is enhanced cooperation to deal with international Internet-related public policy issues, for the governments to sit together. Of course with consultation of other stakeholders, but this is the main idea, and the WSIS mandated the U.N. Secretary-General to start this process in 2006. The other process is the IGF. So the enhanced cooperation process has not yet started, to our information. One step forward was taken by the ITU by creating a dedicated group for all governments to sit together and discuss international Internet public policy issues. We hope that this is a seed that will be really taken care of by the U.N. There are other small processes that need to be done by the individual organizations, but to support the main process to develop the international Internet-related public policy issues by the enhanced cooperation.

FROM THE FLOOR:

Parminder Jeet Singh from IT for Change. Part of what I was going to speak about was anticipated by the speaker who spoke just before me, but I have some further points. When I read the Tunis documents, I see that enhanced cooperation consists of two parts. And I have a feeling that the two parts of that process have been conflated into one. Getting reports from the relevant organizations is going on, but we are not able to go forward to create a process which addresses the primary purpose of enhanced cooperation, which was to create globally applicable public policy principles, which remains a very important need. I do not agree that we can go back to any process---ITU was suggested---or any other organizational system that was before the WSIS, because WSIS showed that the needs of Internet-related policy were different. The processes that are needed make them different, and I read in the Tunis Agenda that it speaks about a new process, and I wonder what is the timetable and what are the views on UNDESA starting this process at all. Another thing which caught my attention regarding development of public policy principles vis-à-vis IGF was a press note from Council of Europe. It says that they will use this event also to seek accession by other states to certain policy instruments that are being negotiated by certain countries. And I wondered whether this is the right method of developing public policies, when they get negotiated by a select group of countries and then you seek accession by different states to those treaties. This speaks to how important it is right now to globally get together in a democratic manner with the stakeholders and decide those principles.

FROM THE FLOOR:

My name is Janis Karklins. I'm a Latvian representative to and chair of the GAC. I had an honour and privilege to chair the preparatory committee of the WSIS second phase where these issues were discussed. I need to remind everyone that we could not reach full agreement and common understanding on one interpretation of "enhanced cooperation." The term allows many

212

interpretations and this is the beauty of multilateral negotiations, that we can agree on a term that allows interpretation. And I'm speaking in a very positive sense, because I think that we can interpret "enhanced cooperation" as enhanced cooperation among governments. We can interpret it as enhanced cooperation among other stakeholders and the governments, where this cooperation did not exist before. We can interpret it as a centralized process. We can interpret it as multiple processes in different places. We are on the way because all these advancements are taking place. The distinguished representative from Saudi Arabia mentioned one under the ITU Council's WSIS working group. This is a major step forward in ITU on the public policy issues related to the mandate of ITU, but the ITU does not have all mandates and there is, for instance, UNESCO, which has a mandate on multilingualism and multilingual content. I'm not aware if there have been any specific proposals to create special an intergovernmental task group in UNESCO, but this can be one of the options. I can tell you that in ICANN we have undertaken a lot of steps to improve the GAC's performance, and for me personally this is a step towards enhanced cooperation. This is how we, in governments represented in the GAC, interpret enhanced cooperation---to be more present, more productive, and more influential in the policy debates that take place in ICANN. I believe that these examples we will find reflected in the U.N. Secretary-General report that will be discussed in ECOSOC next year.

FROM THE FLOOR:

I'm Raul Echeberria. We discussed the meaning of "enhanced cooperation" last year and the year before. The explanation from Ambassador Karklins was very clear, but let me underscore what he said, we didn't have agreement on the meaning of the expression in Tunis. As we got the final agreement the night before the summit started, some level of ambiguity was needed. In the same the agreement, in the same paragraph, Paragraph 71, it says that the Secretary-General of the U.N. should start the process of enhancing cooperation and it also says that the relevant organizations should start the same process. So all of us have to work together in order to enhance cooperation, and this is what we have been doing. Nobody can say that we have not enhanced cooperation, we have made important progresses. It is enough and we can improve; some of us have called for more multistakeholder mechanisms, a more open mechanism in intergovernmental organizations like the ITU, for example, in which we would like to have more participation and to have more influence in discussions and decisions. Some organizations have made more progress in enhancing cooperation with other stakeholders than others have. At the regional level, really we can say that in Latin America, the cooperation between different actors, including governments, civil society, technical organizations, has been improved very much.

FROM THE FLOOR:

Alejandro Pisanty from ISOC Mexico and the National University of Mexico. It is time to move forward. It is time to stop discussing what "enhanced cooperation" means and to start to cooperate as best we can. IGF has beaten the ICANN-related issues to the very last drop. I don't see how IGF discussions can squeeze more out of it. ICANN participants have enough space now to move the issues there instead of using IGF to leverage outside space for ICANN. It is time to dispel the legend that the whole WSIS process was to create a separate, independent space to discuss and redo ICANN. It is time to use the ICANN experience of cooperation among multiple stakeholders, and there are many other forms of cooperation among multiple stakeholders that have appeared and been created during the IGF process. To apply this experience of cooperation and use it for dealing with really more substantive issues that concern users in developing countries, that concern the way to get access to deploy IPv6, to increase the security of the networks. It's time for all this multistakeholder experience to be applied elsewhere and to move IGF forward, to make IGF a promising venue for the following years, that will not only be about ICANN and the DNS.

FROM THE FLOOR:

How can we, within the framework of enhanced cooperation, enable all the stakeholders, including those in the developing countries, to participate in the process of transforming ICANN. Is IGF laying down any mechanism for the transformation to a new ICANN? Shall we come here after one year in the next IGF for the same declaration? Has IGF put in place a task force to define the functioning of the new ICANN?

FROM THE FLOOR:

My name is Bertrand De La Chapelle. I am the French special envoy for the Information Society and French representative in the GAC. I would like to continue on the line that Janis Karklins has mentioned, to highlight that we probably do not agree yet on what enhanced cooperation is, but there are a few things that have already progressed. The first thing is that enhanced cooperation is a goal. Paragraph 69 says enhanced cooperation in the future. It's because we don't know exactly how the interaction between the different categories of stakeholders will finally stabilize that we used this word in the WSIS. Enhanced cooperation is not only about ICANN. It's about public-policy setting. And this is much broader than the Domain Name System. It is a topic that we have to explore. Finally, the distinction that we have made in the WSIS documents between the goal of enhanced cooperation and the process towards enhanced cooperation is very operational here. And what we are focusing now is to encourage the different actors to discuss together their respective roles. And that means very concretely that each single organization that has a role, be it an intergovernmental organization or a non-intergovernmental organization, multistakeholder like ICANN, or even the IETF, or the RIRs, these organizations have to ask themselves, in our specific type of competence, what is the right balance between the different actors? And the IGF is a nice place for people to ask this question: How do we discuss the respective balance of the stakeholders according to each issue and each venue?

FROM THE FLOOR:

Ambassador Karklins was very clear on what happened in the WSIS, but his view is that the governments should probably have more say in the ICANN process. The ITU has always been open to the private sector, and this fact is not mentioned. We are the only intergovernmental organization of the U.N. in which the private sector works hand in hand with governments for the last 20 years or so. So it's not new. I know there are other stakeholders that still have to come into this international mechanism, like in the IGF. I think I agree with everybody who said that every stakeholder has a role. And we cannot sit here and assume that the different nations, the different governments, they don't know what they want, with their civil society, with their businesses, and with their government policies. So they go to the ITU sometimes and they go to the UNESCO in another capacity. But they all come to the IGF as stakeholders. What we have to do for the future is agree this great mechanism of the IGF should continue to be a forum for all of us to do our respective roles, whether it's in the ITU, in the UNESCO, in civil society organization, NGOs and so on, but we all come here and report and tell each other what we have done.

CHRIS DISSPAIN:

We are rapidly running out of time. The interpreters need to have their break and so do we. I think it's entirely appropriate that we should hear from Minister Kamel before we close and hear from our chair.

H.E. MR. TAREK KAMEL:

Thank you. Mr. Desai, ladies and gentlemen, I am very glad to see this very rich discussion happening here in Sharm El Sheikh in Egypt about the management of Internet resources. I wanted again to thank ICANN for opening up the window of the fast track for IDN multilingual domain name. And whether Egypt or Russia or whoever is the first to register, that is not the issue. The main issue, we need to promote that within our own countries as well. There is a level of effort that needs to be exerted in order to make sure that the awareness on a national level is happening. There are still a lot of effort that needs to be exerted and investment to be done in order to make sure that this is really reaching the grass-roots in our own countries.

Concerning the public-policy issue that has been debated, I think that Egypt thinks that the AoC with the U.S. government is definitely an excellent step forward, and provides ICANN with more accountability and independence. But we want to see more. And we want to see more worldwide Internet community involved in managing Internet resources, and specifically the revisiting of the IANA contract. It might be appropriate that we start here from Sharm El Sheikh, asking the U.S. government to open publicly a dialogue, maybe in 2010, about revisiting the IANA contract and how they think about this should be handled. There is an international community that is here well represented from government, civil society, and various organizations. And it's legitimate that we talk to Ambassador Philip Verveer who is representing the U.S. government here and the State Department about revisiting the IANA contract. We shouldn't wait until September or October 2011. I also agree with what Ambassador Janis and others, Alejandro Pisanty from Mexico, and Raul, have mentioned. Enhanced cooperation is not only the future of ICANN. Enhanced cooperation includes a lot of other issues that we will discuss the rest of the week. That would interest the developing world. There are issues relating to multilingual content, cybersecurity, outreach to larger segments of society, and connectivity. There are still some countries where penetration is low and where we need to exert more effort ---this goes for Africa, for Latin American, probably as well for Asia. So we shouldn't overlook that issue when we talk about the future of enhanced cooperation. The world is not yet equal when it comes to connectivity. But I am very happy with the discussions taking place here in Sharm El Sheikh and look forward to the rest of the week.

JEANETTE HOFMANN:

Before Nitin wraps up, I would like to thank you as a very constructive audience. I watched you. You were really listening to each other. That I found very impressive. Lots of you stayed in the room and didn't leave. So I think we have achieved quite a lot when we consider how we discuss these very issues during WSIS. We have become much more constructive, peaceful, and pragmatic. I think this is an achievement of the IGF.

NITIN DESAI:

Thank you very much to the two facilitators. I want to thank the Minister particularly for his remarks, which were so very helpful. I don't wish to take much time, but I would say my take-away from this on the first issue of IPv4-IPv6 is that we have a two-year window for the transition. That means we have our work cut out ahead of us when we review these situations next year in Lithuania. One of the very interesting suggestions that came up was the idea of some national program of incentives for the adoption of IPv6, and I think we could certainly think of that. We had a very interesting discussion on the new TLDs, the things that are happening on IDNs. I congratulate Egypt, Saudi Arabia, Russia, in being so early in positioning their new IDNs. We had a very interesting dialogue when Patrick raised the whole question of root scalability. As a layperson, the way I understood it was you can take as many drinks as you want but don't take them too fast. And if possible, take a meal, which is the DNSSEC, before you start drinking.

On the AoC, the general assessment, I think most people welcomed it as a forward step, but of course many people recognize that it is only a beginning. That many challenges have to be addressed. The way in which accountability will work is really a blank slate right now. It has to be spelled out. And I particularly welcome the suggestion made by the Minister that the IANA contract perhaps provides an opportunity for carrying this process of opening up one stage further. And I hope the message that goes from this IGF to the U.S. government could include this. On enhanced cooperation, I don't have much to say. The ambiguities that are there in the text came out once again. I only want to conclude by saying there's a mirror-image phrase: instead of saying "enhanced cooperation," we could say "reduce conflict." And one thing I will say is this; that our IGF process may not have secured enhanced cooperation, but it certainly has helped to reduce conflict. So on this happy note, let me conclude the session.

216

Managing Critical Internet Resources:

Reports of the Workshops and Other Events

WS 113.   Best Practices in ccTLD Policy and Operations

Report by: Bill Woodcock

Moderator: Ian Taylor, MP (Former Minister for Science and Technology [1994-97], current chair of the UK Conservative Party's Policy Task-force on Science, Technology, Engineering and Mathematics)

Panellists: Keisuke Kamimura (Senior research fellow and associate professor at the Center for Global Communications, International University of Japan); David Conrad (Vice President of Research and IANA Strategy at ICANN); Erick Iriarte Ahon (General Manager of LACTLD, a regional organization of ccTLDs in the Latin American region); Sabine Dolderer (CEO and member of the Executive Board of DENIC); Bill Woodcock (Research director of Packet Clearing House)

The workshop examined the governance and technical challenges facing the administrators and operators of the world's 252 national domain names. The workshop compared governance frameworks and policy models, discussed

217

accountability to the Internet community, and examined the procedures and technologies that make it possible for these national domains to thrive and support growing Internet economies within their regions. The high-level goal of the workshop was to map the roles and responsibilities of ccTLD administrators and communities and describe the elements of a model ccTLD policy and operational charter. Policy elements considered included the roles and responsibilities of respective stakeholders, the improvement of standards, procedures and management processes. Academic research on a measurement methodology for determining a ccTLD development index was discussed.

Keisuke Kamimura opened the session with comments on some of the findings of a research project, "Country Doman Governance", focusing on ccTLDs from a policy and technical perspective. The project aims to produce tools to improve the administration and governance of ccTLDs. Keisuke reported on statistical analysis his team had conducted, such as details of the total namespaces (second-level domains), prices, and actual use by classification. One finding was that out all namespaces, commercial and generic space is much in use, while others such as regional or more specific classified spaces are used to a much lesser extent. From a policy perspective, he noted a strong correlation between engagement in ICANN -- i.e. through participation the ccNSO and or GAC -- and pricing. He suggested ccTLDs should cooperate more fully with these ICANN related processes and look beyond their national boundaries to contributing to the global Internet processes.

David Conrad followed with a with a fifteen-minute presentation on the ccTLD change-request process, explaining in detail the procedural model that the IANA follows in accepting, authenticating, processing, and effectuating changes to the root-zone registry data associated with each of the Country Code Top Level Domains. David outlined seven steps IANA follows in the change process: acceptance, validation, confirmation, verification, authorization, implementation and completion. Describing each of the stages in the process, from the submission of a change request, which can be made by anyone globally, so allowing openness in submission of changes, to completion and entry in the root zone. All requests are validated, and further checks conducted to establish the authority and support for the request. Final steps are authorized by the U.S. Department of Commerce; with their role being to ensure ICANN has followed documents procedures. The changes are then implemented by VeriSign, which makes the changes and published the changes to the root servers. Each step can be fast or slow depending on the situation, with delays usually occurring in the confirmation stage when IANA corresponds with the ccTLD managers and other interested parties.

Erick Ahon then gave a twenty-minute LACTLD regional update, discussing and comparing regulatory and governance models used by the nations of the Latin American and Caribbean region, and presenting a variety of statistics and statistical analysis in support of his observations. Erick presented how the ccTLDs in the LAC region develop policies. He noted the basis for policy development was RFC1591. A key element of that document is that each ccTLD is responsible for the development of its own policy, while ensuring service to the local and global community. He continued to describe different policies adopted by ccTLDs in the region, including governance structures and the role of government and other stakeholders, as well as noting the influence of bilateral free trade policies of the United States.

Sabine Dolderer proceeded to give a twenty-minute presentation on the German experience with internationalized domain name deployment, including more than 500,000 domains with non-ASCII characters, a market that is still growing strongly. Sabine said Germany and DENIC had more than 5 years experience of policy development and implementation regarding INDs and there should be lessons in their experiences for the new IND process underway now. She also noted that these policies had been coordinated with .AT (Austria) and .CH (Switzerland), as it was essential for policies to be as consistent as possible across the German speaking community of ccTLDs. Problems encountered early on included involving registrars in the process, and IDN support by Internet applications such as email.

Bill Woodcock gave the last presentation, spending twenty minutes discussing operational best-practices in the anycast networks that provide Domain Name Service for most of the world's ccTLDs, and explaining how ccTLD registries can avail themselves of the service-provision networks built for this purpose. He noted DNS has become the primary application for anycast, although it can be used for the local distribution of most types of content where localizing traffic is important. Most ccTLDs are anycast at this time nearly all the root name instances are anycast servers. Anycast has become the predominant method of distributing DNS servers geographically. The main reasons for using anycast are latency reduction, load balancing, attack mitigation geographically and configuration simplicity. It provides redundancy and servers nearer to the users and an enhanced user experience, and protection against storms of attacks that are increasingly occurring on the net.

The session concluded with fifteen minutes spent on questions-and-answers, namely one regarding Internationalized Domain Names suggesting that they may introduce new problems particularly with cybersquatting, and one regarding language preservation. These were answered by Sabine and Keisuke who noted that extending the number of languages on the Internet was long overdue, and INDs would help more communication between peoples.

A question regarding ccTLD redelegation rules, particularly over the role of government and other stakeholders in administering the ccTLD and who should have control over the ccTLD was answered by David Conrad. David noted IANA follows policies provided in RFC1591, also re-clarified in document ICP1. IANA staff do not judge one application better than others when there is contention among requests for redelegation, instead it relies on input from the local Internet community to ensure that the body requesting the redelegation has the support of the local Internet community. He noted it can be a complicated process and one where there is some controversy that can cause delays to the process.

The session provided a broad overview of the operational and governance issues faced by the administrators of the world's Country Code Top Level Domains, and brought attendees up to date on the state of the art and best practices in the field. It gave participants pointers to additional sources of information, technologies, and communities-of-interest to support their ongoing and active participating in ccTLD management. We regard the session as a success, and look forward to conducting similar sessions at future IGF meetings.

WS 114. Need-based and Market-Based Internet Resource Allocation

Report by: Bill Woodcock

Moderator: Steve Ryan (Senior partner and head of the Government Strategies Practice Group in the law firm of McDermott Will & Emery)

Panellists: John Curran (President and CEO of ARIN); Paul Wilson (Director General of APNIC); Milton Mueller (Professor at the Syracuse University School of Information Studies and Delft University of Technology, Netherlands); Tom Vest (Consultant with the OECD Economics & Statistics Division, ICANN, and the RIPE NCC Science Group); Bill Woodcock (Research Director at Packet Clearing House)

The impending scarcity of IPv4 Internet addresses creates new challenges in address policy. Historically, Regional Internet Registries have relied on need-based resource allocation mechanisms, which have allowed the Internet to experience its unprecedented growth to date. But some economists have suggested that market-based allocation mechanisms can help manage the newly emerging scarcity. Each of the five registries is evaluating these questions, along with further complexity resulting from the matter of inter-regional transfer. This session presented a variety of perspectives, including participants from each of the five regions.

This workshop represented each of the major points of view in this critical discussion, and exposed the audience to all of the principal arguments under debate. The participants gave their contact information and welcomed all attendees to ask them further questions or follow up in greater detail on issues of interest throughout the remainder of the week, and in the future.

Steve Ryan began the session by outlining the issues and introducing the speakers. John Curran gave the first talk, explaining the system by which IPv4 and IPv6 addresses are currently allocated through the delegation hierarchy of the Internet Assigned Numbers Authority and the Regional Internet Registries; the community governance mechanism by which equitable access to resources is assured, and the regulatory principles that ensure conservation.

Paul Wilson continued, speaking on the issue of IPv4 address scarcity, and the mechanisms whereby unused addresses may be transferred to other parties who can justify a greater need. Milton Mueller went on to cast the scarcity of IPv4 addresses in a neoclassical economic framework, describing a range of possible future in which economic speculation might predominate over operational utilization of addresses, or an increasingly finely-granular transfer market might value individual use over the integrity of the routing system as a whole. Tom Vest spoke about the applicability and inapplicability of economic markets to IP addresses and other scarce public resources, and discussed the regulatory oversight required when market mechanisms are applied to public goods.

Bill Woodcock concluded by outlining the dangers of failure to uphold the balanced duties of access and conservation of both addresses and the routing tables which ensure Internet stability and functionality. He explained several of the fundamental incompatibilities between the very complex nature of IP addresses allocation and the insufficiently nuanced hammer of a monetized market, and described the disproportionately catastrophic effects such monetization would have on the developing world, exaggerating the digital divide.

This workshop successfully raised and addressed a critical issue of great topical importance, and provided a forum for all points of view on the topic.

WS 115. *The Role of Internet Exchange Points in Creating Internet Capacity and Bringing Autonomy to Developing Nations*

Report by: Bill Woodcock

Moderator: Bill Woodcock (Research Director at Packet Clearing House)

Panellists: Haitham El Nakhal (ICT Technical Affairs Advisor to the Egyptian Telecom Regulatory Authority and administrator of the Cairo Internet Exchange); Nishal Goburdhan (Chief Technology Officer at AfriNIC, and one of the founders of the Johannesburg IX); Roque Gagliano (Senior Project Engineer and Policy Manager at LACNIC, and past chair of NAPLA, the Latin American IX association); Michuki Mwangi (Senior Education Manager at ISOC, previously the founder of the Kenya Internet Exchange Point in Nairobi)

The workshop built upon the successful IXP Best Practices sessions at the 2007 and 2008 Internet Governance Forums. The main themes covered in this workshop were: how Internet bandwidth, the capacity to route Internet traffic, is produced within Internet exchange points, an overview of the distribution of Internet exchange points globally, and discussion of the role of Internet exchange points in making developing regions autonomous from the draining expense of international telecommunications carriage. The creation of an Internet exchange point is the single most economically-empowering decision that the Internet community within any region can make, and the one which will most secure their future as an independent and viable centre of local content and online community.

This workshop represented a global diversity of Internet exchange point perspectives, and brought light to numerous information sources and ongoing programs of public benefit. The participants gave their contact information and welcomed all attendees to ask them further questions or follow up in greater detail on issues of interest throughout the remainder of the week, and in the future.

Bill Woodcock began the session by introducing the speakers and the general concepts behind Internet traffic exchange and Internet Exchange Points in particular, and gave a brief update on the state of the world's exchanges in November, 2009. Specifically, there were 338 exchanges extant; the largest European exchanges were generating between half a terabit of bandwidth per second and two terabits of bandwidth per second; 88 countries have IXPs, while 159 do not yet; Europe had the highest annualized absolute growth over the course of the year, at 1.18Tb/sec, while Africa had the highest percentage growth, at 86%, up from 588Mb/sec in October of 2008 to nearly 1.1G in October of 2009; the Netherlands Antilles, Bulgaria, and Haiti all had new exchanges turned up in the past year, and Iceland, Bangladesh, Russia, and Uganda had the highest annualized percentage growth rates relative to the prior year. Still only 23% of Internet exchanges support IPv6.

Haitham El Nakhal then gave an update on the state of the Cairo IXP, detailing its history and participation, and explaining some of its notable operational and policy successes, particularly in mitigating the international fibber cuts that had proved so debilitating to many of Egypt's neighbours that lack IXPs. Nishal Goburdhan then gave an update on the state of the Johannesburg IXP, focusing on communicating the complex lessons learned by trial and error over the fifteen-year history of the exchange, and also discussing the causes of the failure of the Cape Town IXP, and how South Africa's ISPs are revitalizing it.

Roque Gagliano then gave an update on the state of Internet exchange points in Latin America and the Caribbean, focusing particularly on the fact that two of the world's three new IXPs in the last year were in the Caribbean, and how that was accomplished. He also detailed LACNIC and NAPLA's "Simon" project, which is quantifying the benefits of IXPs to traffic flow within the region. Michuki Mwangi concluded the session with an update on the state of IXPs in the African region. Specifically, there are 21 IXPs in 17 countries, including three in South Africa, and two each in Tanzania and Nigeria. In West Africa, only three countries, comprising only 20% of the region, have IXPs, and this is an area that particularly requires attention and development. East Africa, by contrast, is very fully-developed, with one or more IXPs in each country, and significant over-land fibber and microwave intra-regional connectivity, as well as ISPs peering at IXPs in multiple adjacent countries, the first step in developing multinational and regional networks.

The workshop built upon the successful IXP Best Practices sessions at the 2007 and 2008 Internet Governance Forums. Several themes were discussed that highlighted the role of Internet exchange points in making developing regions economically autonomous; how Internet exchange points foster the development of local content and culture; and how IXPs facilitate other critical infrastructure like the Domain Name System. We regard the session as a success, and look forward to conducting sessions on Internet Exchange Points and their benefits at future IGF meetings.

WS 120.   IPv6 Transition: Economic and Technical Considerations

Report by: Baher Esmat

Organizers: ICANN, NTRA, AfriNIC

Moderator: Sherif Guinena (National Telecom Regulatory Authority of Egypt)

Panellists: David Conrad (ICANN VP of Research and IANA Policies); Patrik Fältström (Consulting Engineer with Cisco System; Advisor to Swedish IT Minister); Gamal Hegazy (Solution Architect, Alcatel-Lucent); Mark Elkins (Posix Systems, SA; Board Member of AfriNIC)

Recent data showed that 12 /8s IPv4 blocks are being consumed every year, and as per potaroo.net, IANA would run out of IPv4 addresses in Sep 2011, while the RIRs would still have IPv6 blocks until Aug 2012. Speakers seemed to agree that IPv4 would continue to be there for a long time, in coexistence with IPv6. An analysis on the pros and cons of IPv6 in comparison to IPv4 showed that address space is the key advantage, while other features like mobility, QoS, and auto-configuration despite being theoretically good; many of them are still immature and have implementation problems in reality. The same analysis showed that IPv6 may not be better that IPv4 with regard to routing and security.

There was also the view that IPv4 exhaustion will result in more NATing, and that NAT in general breaks the end-to-end architecture of the Internet, which is not the case with IPv6. There was also the view that IPv4 addresses still exist (no real shortage), and a lot of services are being implemented and run using NAT, which seems to be working.

Technical/hands-on experience was shared. Acquiring IPv6 address space has been a straightforward process. AfriNIC have been promoting IPv6 and three years ago they used to give it for free. AfriNIC's goal was to raise awareness among community and encourage them to get ready so to minimize any risk of damage, and also to learn from mistakes made with IPv4 assignment. Deploying IPv6 is not difficult, it is rather another protocol running on the network, and it needs a bit of more knowledge. Some glitches with few services required digging for solutions, e.g. reverse DNS, double defining virtual hosts...etc.

A recent European Commission's research on IPv6 readiness showed that 92% of service providers surveyed do not have any IPv6 on their network, 17% of organizations use IPv6 in one sort or another, less than 30% of organizations are concerned about the problem, 70% do not see a business need, 57% indicated lack of user demand, and 75% indicated they want to be ahead of the game.

Speakers seemed to agree that IPv6 over the core network solutions is ready, but there is yet an issue with access particularly in cases where end-users CPEs do not support IPv6. Standardization for IPv6 consumer Internet could remove IPv4 dependencies on the long term. Some speakers were of the view that economically IPv4 is still cheaper than IPv6, so there is no incentive for service providers to move to IPv6. Some also raised the point in relation to lack of v6 services and applications (chicken and egg problem). Others believe that the cost of v6 transition is and should be part of the natural expansion of any network, and although there is yet a cost component, it is not substantial.

There was a view on transition strategies, that network and service providers as well as end users should take advantage of the lead time and consider an inventory of their hardware and software and check what components may need replacement or upgrade to be IPv6 enabled, and take this into account in their next phase of upgrades. Experiments are ongoing which consider the different network components and transition strategies.

Questions and comments from the floor were mainly about the cost involved in the transition to IPv6. It was indicated that the cost is not only the hardware and software costs which are not substantive, but also the costs involved in the reconfiguration. However; the panel seemed to agree that this coast is naturally embedded in the routine systems upgrades, but on the other hand this requires building human resources capacities capable of handling the v4/v6 transition. One comment was about statistics shared on readiness, noting that 15 years ago a lot of organizations did not realize they would need access to the Internet. There was an opinion that suggested developing a model transition strategy that developing Countries can consider while targeting transition to IPV6.

WS 204.   *The Governance Issues of Country Code Top Level Domains*

Report by: Y.J. Park

Organizers: Delft University of Technology, ITU

Panellists: Hans Klein (Georgia Tech, USA); Malcolm Johnson (ITU)

The following governance issues were addressed at the panel.

- Authority of ccTLDs and IDN ccTLD Fast Track
- Identity of Globalized ccTLDs
- Regional TLDs: .EU, .ASIA, and .ARAB
- ISO 3166-1 List as Bible of ccTLDs
  - Issue of Island ccTLDs
  - Geographical TLDs like .CAT
- The Role of USG as coordinator of the 252 ccTLDs in terms of delegation and re-delegation process
- Role of IANA under unclear procedural process Yuri Kargapolov (Ukraine) made a presentation on Ukraine government's experience of .UA re-delegation process since 2001. Country Code Top Level Domain of Ukraine .UA re-delegation is still being under negotiation with IANA/ICANN.
- Role of Government in terms of delegation and re-delegation Turkey made a presentation on how Government of Turkey plays a role for .TR after government passed legislation on .TR.

- Regional representation instead of national representation in the ICANN decision-making process
- Stable operation of ccTLDs Matthew (?) (AFNIC CEO) addressed the stability of ccTLD operation. (?)

Around 80 people attended ccTLD governance workshop. After panel's presentation, interactive discussion between the panel and attendees of the workshop continued. This workshop could identify the challenges of ccTLD governance issues as of 2009, which are still foreign to many stakeholders of IGF community. This workshop confirmed the lack of understanding of ccTLD issues especially political negotiation of TLD delegation and re-delegation matters in the IGF community.

WS 271. *Managing Internet Addresses: Global and Regional Viewpoint*

Report by: Adriana Rivero

Moderator: Vladimir Radunovic (Coordinator of the Internet Governance and Policy Educational and Training Programmes at Diplo Foundation)

Panellists: Haitham El-Nakhal (Egyptian Telecommunications Regulatory Authority); Germán Valdez (Communications Area Manager at APNIC); Heather Dryden (Senior Advisor on Internet governance at the Canadian Federal Ministry of Industry); Willie Currie (Manager of the Communications and Information Policy Program at Association for Progressive Communications); John Sweeting (Director of Network Engineering at Time Warner Cable, USA)

The aim of this workshop was to present detailed information about the functioning and main activities that the RIRs develop, including description and analysis of their processes (PDP, allocation process, criteria and evaluation of the requests), their involvement in the projects to foster the Information Society and their current challenges in the management of the Internet resources.

Haitham El-Nakhal presented "The Regional Internet Registry System." In his presentation he made a comprehensive description of the function and role of the RIRs in the management of the Internet addresses resources, including their structure, the bottom-up model, the Policy Development Processes, and how the policies (regional and global) are defined and reach consensus within each regional community with a multistakeholder participation. He also mentioned other roles performed by the RIRs beyond their registry function, such as education and training of their communities. Individual RIRs carry out activities that include training courses (DNS, Routing, IPv6, Security, etc) seminars, outreach activities, and statistical reporting, research and projects related to whois, RPKI, cyber security and encouraging the launching of IXPs, among others. In addition, RIRs conduct and fund research and development projects related to deployment of DNS root servers and ICT.

Germán Valdez's presentation on "Managing Internet Resources" intended to illustrate what is the core function of the RIRs, which is the distribution of the Internet resources. He explained the resource management before the establishment of the RIRs, and how it evolved into the RIR system under a bottom-up Policy Development Process. He described in detail how the analysis of resources request is done based on the principles of Conservation, Aggregation, and Registration and how the distribution of IP addresses is completed (from RIRs to customers and end users). He also presented the challenges that RIRs face in the near future with the depletion of the IPv4 addresses and how they are working informing and preparing the community and all interested parties to adapt to the new scenario.

Heather Dryden gave a government vision. She indicated that aspects related to RIRs of importance for Canada include:
- A good, efficient and uninterrupted functionality and operation of the Internet
- Welcomed the creation of a working group in ARIN, a place for governments to gather and to focus on some of the issues of particular interest to them, to influence appropriately and participate in the PDP of their region.
- Adoption of IPv6 is of great importance for the government – Canada is involved in the creation of an IPv6 Task Force and they are making recommendations to facilitate IPv6 adoption. The Canadian government is interested in the economic aspects of IPv6 adoption, and how they affect competition between ISPs. Concerned about Canadians continuing to have access to government services on line.
- She emphasized the importance of re-allocation of IPv4 addresses
- Made a note on WHOIS database and access for law enforcement

Willie Currie represented the civil society perspective.
- APC is particularly concerned over Internet rights i.e. rights of end-users (issues related to Internet governance and ICTs –
- He emphasized the critical role of the RIRs raising a question on the threats to the openness of their policy development process (PDP).
- Concerns over privacy aspects of WHOIS database and possible misuse for surveillance.
- Questioned the role of Internet Service Providers on protection of Intellectual
- Property rights and linkage with distribution IPs and identification of end-users
- Question on possibility that RIRs, through their PDP, and ASO introduce protection of freedom of expression and right to privacy into ICANN bylaws (which is not saying that they should become human rights enforcement bodies).

John Sweeting represented the private sector.
- Emphasized how the RIR system has supported his business interests during the 11 years he was involved in different companies obtaining resources from different RIRs.
- He highlighted the different roles of RIRs in different regions. They are all the same but, they are also different. Mission, vision and structure are unique to the requirements of the regions. The main advantage of the RIRs system is that they focus on the needs of the region and develop policies for that region by each particular region.

- He mentioned that this could be a disadvantage if you work with different RIRs since you need to know the policies on each particular region.
- Other notes about the RIRs: PDP works very well in each region, participation is open to anyone, enables sharing of experience among regions. Registration and accuracy of the WHOIS database is very important.

Germán Valdez commented the following on the question from Willie Currie about the WHOIS database: Within WHOIS database there is only information on a technical contact, for administrative and technical purposes about who is holding an IP address. There are different aspects of privacy - It is important to say that what data should be opened or not and what are the levels of protection published on the whois database is under discussion and is part of the PDP. Even law enforcement people can participate in the PDP with the technical Internet community. Comment from Remote Participant McTim to Willie Currie: "RIR do not route IP address blocks (except for those that they themselves use); RIR take no position on these subjects, they have a very limited role, they allocate and assign." German Valdez agreed with the comment from the remote participant.

Vladimir Radunovic posed a question to the panel about who is the community, how can one get involved in the community? Haitham El-Nakhal and German Valdez answered that everybody, every single person or entity can get involved and be part of the community and participate in the PDP (face to face meetings, mailing lists, policy discussions, remote participation, etc) Comment from Remote Participant McTim: "if civil society is really concerned about IP address WHOIS policies, they should get involved in making policy they live with." In response to Willie, he also stated: "Route aggregation has nothing to do with Intellectual Property Rights and surveillance".

Comment from Raimundo Beca, ICANN Board Member, speaking from his personal perspective. He stated that before the global policies IANA allocated with its own criteria, but the community had no opportunity to discuss on them. After the NRO creation, there are global policies that had made a very good contribution to the fairness distribution of IP addresses in the world. He mentioned the global policy about the allocation of the last 5 /8 to the RIRs which is based on a fair distribution, not on a need basis. He also raised a question to the panel about the global policy now under discussion for the re-allocation of IPv4 addresses. German Valdez highlighted the global cooperation of the Internet community reflected in the approval of the last 5 /8 allocations global policy. Haitham El-Nakhal also commented that the global policy of the last 5 /8 is a good example of cooperation between the 5 RIRs.

Heather Dryden comments on global policies: the important aspects are community's leadership and building up a collaborative model. John Sweeting: even though there are challenges in the future, the current RIR system has proven that it is able to deal with these challenges. The system is well prepared to deal with regional as well as global challenges. Willie Currie: Affirmation of Commitment (ICANN-DoC) should make it easier to civil society to get engaged in global policy. ICANN should thus be an accountable body. Other panellists have not discussed on global policy due to their direct involvement with RIR.

WS 273. A Methodological Proposal for Analyzing Governance of CIR Functions

Report by: David Satola

Organizers: Afilias, Alfa-Redi, the American Bar Association, the Council of Europe (CoE), Diplo Foundation, the Global Internet Policy Initiative (GIPI), ISOC Bulgaria, ISOC Pacific, The Oxford Internet Institute, and the World Bank

Moderator: David Satola (World Bank)

Panellists: Henry Judy (K&L Gates); Jan Malinowski (Council of Europe); Desiree Miloshevic (Afilias); Erick Iriarte (LACTLD); George Sadowsky (GIPI)

The Workshop considered a report on the most recent version of a paper setting forth an approach to analyzing the governance of Critical Internet Resource (CIR) functions from the standpoint of the legal corporate governance of ICANN. The paper was outlined in some detail by Mr. Judy, who was also one of the paper's principal authors. The workshop moderator, who was also one of the principal authors, then requested each of the remaining panellists to comment on the outline from their respective points of view. Questions and comments were then elicited from all in attendance.

In very general terms, the paper explores the connection between the corporate governance of ICANN and Internet Governance generally and presents the relevant provisions of ICANN's constituent instruments and their evolution as well as the functions performed by ICANN as evidence of this approach. In analyzing ICANN's functions, the paper presents ICANN's outsourcing and "in-sourcing" processes on an operational level, illustrates the process analysis to help establish its validity, and ties the functional analysis back to the constituent instruments. Finally, this paper examines the corporate governance implications of the recently adopted Affirmation of Commitments.

While the quality and usefulness of the paper was generally recognized, it was suggested that the authors consider adjusting it in a number of respects. The principal comments are set forth below:

- The paper did not make adequately clear that Internet governance generally and the governance of CIR functions in particular are a broader topic than an analysis of ICANN's functioning alone. In other words, the paper needed to more clearly recognize that many entities other than ICANN contribute to the overall governance of the Internet.
- Perhaps because the paper's primary approach was from the legal standpoint it might be read to suggest a certain fixity in ICANN's organizational arrangements. Although the paper noted that a capacity for flexibility was one of the advantages of ICANN current organizational arrangements, the tone of the paper might be read to suggest a sense of

caution about taking advantage of that inherent flexibility. It was noted that the dynamism and fluidity of the reality of the Internet may require an organizational adaptability.

- Mr. Malinowski suggested that the paper might be clearer on how, in its analysis, ICANN might adjust its governance structure and/or constituent instruments to emphasize human rights and what COE regards as the "public service responsibilities" of internet participants. The authors suggested how this might be done, but at the same time expressing no judgment as to the substantive nature of any particular adjustment. The workshop participants debated the legal basis, meaning, boundaries and desirability of any such adjustments.

- Mr. Iriarte noted that the legal analysis in the paper applied principally on the level of ICANN itself and from the standpoint of Anglo-American corporate and contract law. This was appropriate since ICANN was formed under that legal system and ICANN's contracts are enforceable by and against it under such law. Nevertheless, the reality on the ccTLD level is that tensions arise because the law of the applicable country may be based on a civil law or other legal system and because local governments may not view relationships with the ccTLD organizations as based in contract but as more subject to regulation in a manner that restricts or even abrogates contract rights.

- These comments stimulated a discussion on the general subject of disconnects among cultures, that is, because ICANN's corporate structure and certain key aspects of its operations are based on Anglo-American legal assumptions and because the paper necessarily deals with that reality, misunderstandings may arise not just as a matter of cultural differences but also because of differences in legal systems. The principal authors responded that they had considered these issues in their discussions among themselves during the drafting process and had briefly mentioned them in the introduction to the paper. They indicated that they would adjust the paper to reflect these issues more prominently but cautioned that it was not the aim of the paper to perform a cross-cultural analysis and that they were not equipped to do so in any case.

- It was noted that the paper explicitly assumed and stated an expectation that ICANN would continue for at least the intermediate term in its current organizational form, that is, as a not-for-profit, public benefit corporation chartered under California law. The question was raised whether the paper had considered or would consider performing the same type of analysis with regard to the alternative form that ICANN's President's Strategy Committee had put forward, namely, a private international corporation. The authors responded that they had actually begun to make such an analysis but, after getting into it, had concluded that it was a larger project than they had resources for and that they needed to make as their priority bringing the current project to a well-tested and documented conclusion. This might take a few months. They indicated that they would be open to the larger project under the right circumstances but not yet.

WS 287. *Adopting IPv6: What You Need To Know*

Report by: Chris Buckridge

Organizers: Number Resource Organization (NRO); Autonomica; International Telecommunications Union (ITU); Nominet

Panellists: Patrik Fältström (Cisco, Chair); Sureswaran Ramadass (NAv6, Chair); He Baohong (CATR of MIIT, China); Onur Bektaş (ULAKBİM, Turkey); Raúl Echeberría (LACNIC); Mark Elkins (Uniforum SA); Antonio M. Moreiras (Brazilian Network Information Center); Tom Wills Sandford (Intellect); Jonne Soininen (Nokia); Malcolm Johnson (ITU-T); Paul Wilson (APNIC); Salam Yamout (Cisco, Lebanon); Xiaoya Yang (ITU-TSB)

Below, the issues discussed by panellists and participants from the floor are arranged by theme rather than chronological order.

The Current IPv6 Deployment Situation

While IPv6 growth on the Internet is small, it is currently growing at an exponential rate. It is not necessary for all networks to deploy IPv6 immediately, but networks do need to be prepared for IPv6. For countries that have limited Internet penetration in IPv4 — for example, within Africa — it was suggested that networks could go straight to deploying IPv6 without worrying about the expense of legacy systems that more developed nations are grappling with. The ITU has recently conducted some studies into IPv6, which have showed a general lack of IPv6 readiness amongst ITU Member States. IPv6 progress happening in 2009 is less visible, however: it is now possible to build and operate IPv6 networks with less effort, so people are not making press releases about it any more when they deploy IPv6.

How IPv6 Addresses Are Distributed

The policies governing how IPv6 is distributed are developed and adapted over time in a bottom-up process by the Regional Internet Registry (RIR) communities. Refinements made through the policy cycle over time have made it easier to obtain IPv6 from the RIRs. One participant at the workshop confirmed that although their network had initially not met the AfriNIC criteria for an IPv6 allocation, the affected organisation had proposed policy changes, and the community had adopted a policy that helped smaller networks obtain IPv6. It was acknowledged that a very few IPv6 requests may have not met the criteria set by RIR communities; in the Asia Pacific region, however, under a new APNIC policy, anyone who qualifies for IPv4 automatically qualifies for IPv6.

Current Discussion About the Distribution Model

The ITU Secretariat and some of its Member States have expressed concerns about the uneven distribution of IPv6 allocated to date, and that due to a lack of human and/or financial resources, developing countries are under-represented in RIR processes. Some ITU Member States believe that the best way to safeguard equitable IPv6 distribution and secure assistance in deploying IPv6 is to move IPv6 address space management into the public sector. The ITU is launching a project to pursue the objectives laid out in WTSA Resolution 64, which encouraged the deployment of IPv6, but also instructed the ITU-T study groups to look at whether they could allocate and register addresses, and report to the Council 2009.

A study conducted by the National Advanced IPv6 Centre of Excellence (NAv6), Malaysia, has proposed maintaining the current ICANN/IANA/RIR structure, but expanding the RIR system to include an additional registry, empowered to delegate to a series of country registries. It was posited that local organizations could be better placed to ensure address conservation. The author of the study noted that the current RIR system provides fair distribution of IPv6 addresses, and that the proposed change will only work if address holders can still go to the existing RIRs for addresses.

There was discussion about how this form of alternative Internet Registry could affect the Internet. The proposal's author noted that under the RIR system, an organization operating in one particular region could only request resources from the RIR servicing that region. He commended APNIC on the job it had done to date, but suggested that once a network was denied an allocation by an RIR, there is currently no alternative source for addresses. A participant from the floor noted that the study treats IP addresses as a commercial resource, but that, IP addresses are a managed resource that they should not be subject to competition and must be managed to ensure the Internet's stability. Another participant noted that while collaboration between the RIRs and ITU was to be welcomed, competition in the distribution of IP addresses was not in the technical interest of the Internet. Another view was expressed that an end user cares only about quality of service, and having two Internet registry options will not automatically provide better choice or quality of service. Another participant from the floor noted that economists express scepticism about the private sector competing against the public sector. It was explained that the country-based registries in the proposal would not necessarily be publicly owned.

There was discussion about country registries within the current RIR structure. In the APNIC region, there are National Internet Registries (NIRs), but many organizations in those economies choose to request resources from APNIC directly. The RIPE NCC has discussed a country-based registry system in the past. The Russian and Middle East communities have discussed setting up separate registries but on both occasions this option was discounted, partially because setting up a separate registry risked limiting knowledge transfer with the global Internet community.

Supporting IPv6 Deployment

It was agreed that the biggest problem in deploying IPv6 is lack of knowledge. Governments play a vital role in promoting IPv6 to industry within their country and encouraging IPv6 deployment by requiring IPv6 compatibility where possible (similar to how some governments have supported digital TV rollout). The technical community also has a vital role in promoting IPv6 and educating network operators and business and government decision makers about the technical needs for IPv6. The IPv6

Forum has and continues to do a lot of work encouraging IPv6 deployment. At the workshop, it was acknowledged that there was some concern in developing regions about timely deployment of IPv6, but that this was to be contrasted with a note of optimism that the groundwork for IPv6 deployment was in place, including the human resources that the RIRs have helped to train. While the RIRs' core responsibility is the registration of Internet number resources, they also exist to serve the interests of their membership and communities. IPv6 adoption has become a priority for these communities, which has led to all five RIRs now being involved in promoting IPv6 adoption. The example of AfriNIC was given, where the goal is to deliver IPv6 training events in all countries in the AfriNIC service region by the end of 2010.

It was suggested that a more specific IPv6 campaign might be needed to correct a lack of awareness in the business community. This could include certain "tipping points", such as major services being made available only over IPv6, or an award presented at the IGF for the organisation that has done the most to promote IPv6. It was suggested that the RIRs could take responsibility for coordinating such a program. Those within the business community with an existing awareness of IPv6 are also working to encourage IPv6. ISOC presented an award to Google for their IPv6 adoption program at the recent IETF meeting.

Learning From Others: Specific Country Experiences of Deploying IPv6

China began the CNGI project to promote IPv6 in 2003. The first phase of the project is complete. Phase 2, which began in 2009, moves the focus from IPv6 on academic networks to IPv6 on industry networks. The project has funded development of the largest IPv6 network in the world. About one million students in China are already using this IPv6 network. The government has also funded large ISPs in China to encourage their IPv6 deployment and it is expected that the full commercial IPv6 network in China will be completed by 2020. China has found the requirements for transitioning from IPv4 to IPv6 in academic networks is quite different to transitioning in commercial networks. Change is required not only at the network layer, but the transition also requires changes to desktop applications that use the Internet. China is also investigating IPv6 security issues for the mobile Internet and pursuing further technical work to smooth the transition.

There has been an IPv6-capable National Academic Network (ULAKNET) in Turkey since 2003. The IPv6 Forum of Turkey was established in 2007. Nineteen Turkish ISPs now have IPv6 blocks from RIPE, but only two or three of those ISPs currently have visible IPv6 routes in the global routing table. The Turkish project to make the transition to IPv6 is funded by the government and began in February 2009. It will run for two years and consists of research into advanced IPv6 features, IPv6 security, and an IPv6-enabled honey pot. The project is also developing IPv6-enabled conferencing software. Turkey has a test network, IPv6-GO, which is being used to test IPv6 transition methods, IPv6-enabled applications, etc.

The Brazil National Internet Registry, register.br, first began making IPv6 allocations in December 2007. There has been a significant increase in the number of IPv6 allocations made to Brazilian networks since the beginning of 2008. During 2009, while Brazilian ISPs have not yet started giving IPv6 to their customers, they have been creating a test site for IPv6 or deploying their websites over IPv6. The Federal Government has launched an initiative that recommends IPv6 for the intragov.sp.gov.br network. In order to raise awareness, ipv6.br was launched in 2008. The website targets all stakeholders, from technical engineers to businesses. The European Union 6deploy project has been very helpful for Brazilian efforts to deploy IPv6. Nic.br produced IPv6 materials for ISP staff in Brazil under a Creative Commons license. It now uses these as part of capacity building workshops.

There are nine ISPs in Lebanon. These ISPs have been working with RIPE NCC and MENOG to spread awareness of IPv6. MENOG held a meeting in 2009 in Beirut that included a well-attended three-day workshop on IPv6. This meeting was the catalyst to begin IPv6 preparations in earnest. Since MENOG was held in Lebanon earlier in 2009, there have been five IPv6 blocks requested and delegated to Lebanese ISPs. The biggest IPv6 issues in Lebanon are business rather than technical concerns. Operators there still have questions about the business impact of operating two networks: IPv4 and IPv6.

It was generally agreed by all workshop participants that IPv6 deployment is the only option for future Internet growth and that all stakeholders, including the technical community, government, and business, need to work together to educate and encourage the community, particularly in developing areas, to prepare for IPv6 deployment. Looking long-term, IPv6 offers great opportunities: in the 1990s, there was an "IPv4 revolution", when the Internet blossomed and subsequently brought down prices for network access and networked devices. As IPv6 adoption spreads, enabling greater Internet penetration, there will be a similar effect.

WS 297. Introduction to Internet Operations

Report by: Kurt Erik Lindqvist

Panellists: Christian O'Flahert (ISOC); Michuki Mwangi, (ISOC, Africa, Kenya); Patrik Fältström (Cisco, advisor to the Swedish government); Jonne Soininen (Nokia Siemens Networks); German Valdez (APNIC); Kurt Erik Lindqvist (Netnod/Autonomica)

This workshop is designed to provide a basic understanding of the principles of Internet addressing, both numbering and naming. It will highlight how Internet naming and numbering differs from circuit switched telephony, for those with a regulatory background in telephony. It will provide a straightforward introduction to some of the fundamental technical concepts of Internet operations, presented by representatives of the Internet technical community. Presentations will focus on IP addressing, Internet routing and basic principles of the domain name system (DNS), and include details on the "why" as well as the "how". The workshop will conclude with a description of how traffic is routed across the Internet, including the difference between 'transit' and 'peering', and the role of Exchange Points (IXPs). This workshop is aimed at government representatives, regulators and others involved with Internet policy work. Participants do not need to have a technical background. With a more complete understanding of the concepts examined in this workshop, participants will be better equipped to fully engage in Internet governance discussions.

The workshop highlighted how the business models on the Internet have changed traditional telecom business models, what the enabling technologies where for these changes, and also explained some of the terminology used. The workshop also discussed the roles of governments in the current Internet names and numbering governance. Further we discussed how the current governance model uses bottom-up transparent processes in forming the number and naming policies. Last we got presentations on how Internet emerged in two regions, Africa and South America, and the experiences from forming the local governance structures and how operators and the community have cooperated and shared knowledge and experiences. We had some very interesting presentations on how the Internet, with new business models and bottom-up governance models have allowed for innovation and formation of new services.

WS 298.   *Transnationalization of Internet Governance: The Way Forward*

Report by: Ian Peter

Organizer: Internet Government Caucus

Moderator: Ian Peter, Internet Government Caucus

Panellists: Wolfgang Kleinwächter (Aarhus University); Janna Anderson (Imagining the Internet and Pew Internet, Internet research); Robert Kahn, (Internet co-Founder, Technical Community); Jeremy Malcom (Comsumer Association of Malaysia); Robert Pepper (Cisco Systems); Anja Kovacs (CIS India)

The Internet's present governance structures grew out of certain historical contexts, as well as some new socio-political realities around the Internet. In the context of rapid changes that the Internet has wrought, the key and emerging issues related to its governance could not have been anticipated by anyone. One thing however is clear by now; the Internet is not just a technical artefact, requiring technical governance with regard to keeping it running smoothly, but a key socio-political phenomenon requiring participative, inclusive and accountable political governance, which includes its transnationalization. It is important to analyze the needs of evolution and transnationalization of internet governance from various standpoints and the direction in which we might move from here.

The workshop briefly reviewed both existing structures and current gaps in Internet governance, then discussed the advantages and disadvantages of alternative models and present some institutional possibilities of what to do next. The workshop concluded that nothing is likely to remain static in this field. As the Internet grows and changes, so will its governance needs; the key question is whether its governance institutions maintain the flexibility to adopt to changing needs or whether new structures will be necessary to adjust to different circumstances.

WS 325. Understanding Internet Infrastructure:
           An Overview of Technology and Terminology

Report by: Bill Woodcock

Moderator: Bill Woodcock (Research Director of Packet Clearing House)

Panellists: Mark Tinka (Network Architect at Global Transit); Nishal Goburdhan (Chief Technology Officer at AfriNIC, and previously network architect at Internet Solutions); Christian O'Flaherty (Senior Education Manager at the Internet Society, and past manager at Global Crossing Latin America, LACNIC policy chair, and director of Argentina's national academic network); Art Reilly (Director, Strategic Technology Policy at Cisco Systems, and Cisco's principal representative to a variety of UN, ITU and WSIS-related activities on technology policy matters)

This workshop built upon very successful previous workshops at the 2007 and 2008 IGF meetings. The workshop provided an educational, factual backdrop to the policy debates which are the focus of the IGF. Many people in the civil society and intergovernmental spheres, whose interest in Internet governance is relatively recent, are potentially disadvantaged in fully participating in the policy debate by the abstruse technical terminology and concepts. This workshop served as a layperson's introduction to the topology of the Internet, providing definitions and explanations for key terms like transit, peering, hot-potato, exchange point, root and top-level domain name server, routing and forwarding, and the International Standards Organization's seven-layer protocol model. This background, provided at the very beginning of each year's sessions, gives participants the background to decode the arguments presented in other sessions through the remainder of the week.

The ninety-minute session began with an overview of the topics to be covered and brief introduction of the panellists and their backgrounds. Mark Tinka and Nishal Goburdhan presented a twenty minute walk-through of the Domain Name System, how domain names are constructed and secured, and how user-manipulated information like email addresses and web URLs are handled by the underlying mechanisms of the Internet. This was followed by a fifteen-minute explanation of the Internet Protocol version 4 and version 6 addressing schemes, routing mechanics, how the equitable distribution of infrastructural costs are guaranteed, and how these mechanisms differ from those of the twentieth-century telephony network. Art Reilly and Christian O'Flaherty then gave a fifteen-minute overview of the organizations of Internet governance, the roles, responsibilities, and method of public input to each, and how they all fit together to form a cohesive and comprehensive mechanism for guiding the productive, fair, and inclusive growth of a network which approximately doubles in size each year. Each of these presentations were accompanied by diagrammatic slides, containing definitions and additional information and references, which were made available to the participants and the public.

These presentations were followed by a twenty-minute Q&A session in which the panellists addressed participants' questions regarding the transition from Internet Protocol version 4 addresses to Internet Protocol version 6 addresses, routing diversity and the resiliency, the functional role of the Internet Assigned Numbers Authority and its relationship to ICANN and the United States Government, and a variety of other topics. As the inter-session break concluded, the Q&A session spilled over into the hallway and continued for most of another hour.

The session provided a quick but functional introduction to the key terms and concepts employed in Internet governance policy debates, and the technical reasons and causes which shape them. More importantly, it gave participants pointers to additional sources of information, and venues for active participation in the Internet governance process, as well as human introductions to individual experienced Internet engineering and governance participants who had agreed to provide mentoring and answer further questions through the week and beyond. We regard the session as a success, and look forward to conducting similar sessions at future IGF meetings, for as long as they may be desired.

OF 530.   ICANN Open Forum

Report by: Baher Esmat

Moderator: Chris Disspain (Chairman of Country Code Names Sponsoring Organization)

Panellists: Rod Beckstrom (President and CEO); Peter Dengate Thrush (Chairman of Board of ICANN); Janis Karklins (Chairman of Governmental Advisory Committee)

The forum intended to update participants on recent ICANN developments and in particular the Affirmation of Commitments (AOC) signed with the US government on September 30, 2009.

ICANN's Chairman of Board gave a brief description of ICANN, how it was established, and its mission. He also briefed participants on four recent developments in ICANN: 1) appointment of new CEO; 2) new gTLDs from the Generic Names Supporting Organization (GNSO) policy process to where we are today with overarching issues; 3) Internationalized Domain Names (IDN) ccTLD Fast Track process; 4) Affirmation of Commitments.

ICANN's President and CEO presented on ICANN and the Internet Ecosystem where he explained in a bit more detail the four primary activities of ICANN (names, numbers, root servers, protocol parameters), and how ICANN works with its partners in each activity. So he explained the interactions with Registries, Registrars, and Registrants in the domain name space, and with RIRs in the address space, and so on and so forth. He then talked about the AOC indicating that in addition to the review panels that are part of the AOC, there is also the ongoing work inside the organization that

ICANN management and their teams have started working on. So for example, looking at enhancing accountability and transparency, and impact it might have on each of the activities undertaken by ICANN. He finally stressed on the ICANN's mission of one world, one Internet, everyone connected.

The Chairman of the GAC noted that the AOC is not about the reviews, it is rather about perfecting the performance of ICANN's function. He also made a reference to the President Strategy Committee (PSC) that was setup to look into questions related to accountability and transparency. He went into describing each of the reviews in detail and gave his personal view as to the size of each review panel, which he thought would vary according to the area the panel is reviewing. He also referred to the work currently in progress with regard to terms of reference of the first review process and how things will develop from now until the ICANN Nairobi meeting in March 2010.

Comments and questions were primarily related to Affirmation of Commitments (AOC) and new gTLDs. There was recognition that AOC is mainly about perfection of the ICANN's core function. ICANN would welcome input from community regarding AOC review teams. All constituencies have to be represented in the review teams, and have to provide names for consideration for the different teams. It was stressed though that there has to be a balance between the size of the review team and its efficiency, and that the size would vary based on the area under review. There was also a suggestion of having the review team meetings broadcasted online so to allow for wider community participation. ICANN will continue to work with community on resolving issues pertaining to the introduction of new gTLDs.

ICANN's CEO concluded the session thanking the participants for their input and feedback during the session, and for their continuous engagement in the ICANN process which enriches ICANN and its work.

Security, Openness, and Privacy:

Report of the Main Session

16 November 2009

Chairs:

Ms. Jasna Matić
Minister of Telecommunications and Information Society, Serbia

Mr. Sherif Hashem
Vice Executive President of the Information Technology Industry
Development Agency (ITIDA), Egypt

Moderator:

Mr. Marc Rotenberg
Executive Director, Electronic Privacy Information Center (EPIC)

Panellists:

Mr. Joseph H. Alhadeff
Vice President for Global Public Policy and Chief Privacy Officer, Oracle
Corporation

Mr. Frank La Rue
UN Special Rapporteur for Freedom of Opinion and Expression

Ms. Cristine Hoepers
Senior Security Analyst and General Manager, CERT.br

Ms. Namita Malhotra
Researcher, Alternative Law Forum, Bangalore, India

Mr. Bruce Schneier
Chief Security Technology Officer, British Telecom

Mr. Alexander Seger
Head of Economic Crime Division, Directorate General of Human Rights and
Legal Affairs, Council of Europe

Extracts from the Transcript of Proceedings

MS. JASNA MATIC:

These topics have been at issue for a long time but have become much more
important now that billions of people interact with the Internet every day.

They are interlinked, and the challenge is to find the right balance between them. What I have been focusing on in Serbia is children's security, as they are the most vulnerable and trusting group and thus the easiest targets. At the same time, they are the early adopters of all the new technologies. So their privacy is a question that especially needs to be discussed. This is also closely linked to the new media literacy issue. A broad campaign needs to take place across the world in order for people to understand the privacy issues, what you should not disclose, and what can happen to you if you do. So I hope that after today's session we will be able to get closer to this balance.

SHERIF HASHEM:

In Egypt, we have tried to involve our key stakeholders to set up the right strategies for security and for openness and for privacy in drafting new cyber laws and in setting up a Computer Emergency Response Team (CERT). We also coordinate with the private sector, the Internet Service Providers (ISPs), to make sure that we have high-level professional training on security issues in various sectors, whether it be ICT, banking, finance, education, or others. The community could be at risk if we don't have the right resources and skills. We also partner with the NGOs, and we have the Cyber Peace Initiative that will be discussed on Wednesday, which has been training teachers and educating parents and students about the risks and threats to our kids. The First Lady had supported this initiative, and we will hear from her about this on Wednesday. Partnership with the law enforcement and legal system is also very important, and it's not just about regulations. So I leave you with these partnership thoughts, and I look forward to the reflections from the panellists.

MARC ROTENBERG:

We are proposing to cover a broad range of topics including respect for privacy and identity theft, Web 2.0 and social networking, cloud computing and illegal Web content, regulatory models and the open architecture of the Internet, net neutrality, and enabling frameworks for freedom. We have an excellent group of panellists to address these topics.

JOSEPH ALHADEFF:

As we look at a number of the technologies we're going to cover, we really are starting to describe a new ecosystem within which we spend large parts of our lives, whether it's the participative Web, whether it's the cloud computing aspects. I would assume right now, as we're speaking, there are people who are putting their own individual versions of what is being said by tweeting, blogging, and doing any of a number of other things. As has been mentioned we must understand how to balance and optimize because the issues are mutually beneficial and enhancing, as opposed to trading them off against each other. They are essential components of trust in the way people interrelate with each other, trust in the way a business transaction or commercial transaction may take place, trust in between citizen and government.

I want to mention a concept from the Organization for Economic Cooperation and Development (OECD) security guidelines, and that is that there is a role for everyone in this. So there is a role for the user, for the provider or the vendor, for the government, and these are changing. We have new types of services that are platforms and are not easily defined in the models that we use. We have new ways in which individuals are interacting with these services, becoming content creators, publishers, application developers. And we have to ask is the current legal construct related to the responsibility of actors suited to those people, or is that too much of a burden for individuals as opposed to commercial entities. When we look at how people work in the regulatory sphere and in terms of compliance, two terms come to the fore quite often, and they are accountability and transparency. We have to make sure that there is appropriate information to enable empowered decision-making by people who use services, and part of it is to ensure that in an accountability model you don't have overly constrained methods but rather flexibility in how to comply and ensure credibility. If trust is one of the new hallmarks of the medium, then privacy, security, and openness may become enablers of differentiation. And so one of the topics is privacy as a business advantage, capitalizing on the credibility of your systems in terms of accountability.

Part of this is the utility of fora like the IGF, where the conversation is enriched by a multistakeholder dialogue. These are the kinds of issues that really benefit from an interchange of ideas, not just presentations of ideas in a vacuum. The ability of people to understand privacy and security, the transparency related to that, accountability, are all related concepts. So we have to take a holistic approach, a multidisciplinary and multistakeholder approach to these issues. As we look at designing concepts, whether it's privacy by design or security by design, we are looking at a collaborative process in which you take into account the viewpoints of consumers or users, as well as the various disciplines within business and the cultural and regulatory contexts within which you operate.

CRISTINE HOEPERS:

I work with CERT.br, the Brazilian national CERT. What we see today is that we have people putting information on the Internet and not being aware of what that means, that the whole Internet can access the information. So one of the major issues today is to make people understand the risks. The technology is complex, it's difficult to remain secure, and the criminals are exploiting a lot of naive people who trust what people tell them. And the criminals are exploiting software weaknesses, so the design of the software is a problem. But the underlying problem is that we don't have universities preparing professionals that know the security implications. So we don't actually have people understanding what the problem is. It's very expensive to make secure software because people need to learn that from scratch. No one is preparing the engineers to make a project secured by design. So the companies need to come up with that solution.

One of the things that is really a problem is that people don't know what to do so they take countermeasures that were not needed. That can actually hinder our ability to implement really good countermeasures. When people ask for advice, we always say are you sure that you want to collect all that data? Are you sure that you need to implement this or that countermeasure?

So people are doing a lot of things but not necessarily getting more secure, and the situation is escalating. This is why it's really a policy issue, CERTs are doing the front line to keep up with the threats but we need to have more people thinking about how we are going to prepare the next generation of professionals to understand that you don't necessarily need to compromise privacy to be more secure.

NAMITA MALHOTRA:

I want to engage with the notions of privacy, openness, and security from a feminist perspective, and a perspective that takes on issues of sexuality as well. Privacy is a safe haven where people are able to control the terms under which they lead their lives. It is about personal autonomy, the desire to avoid being manipulated and dominated by others. This has to be understood in the context of community, culture, economic factors, et cetera. Feminists have always had a problem with the distinction between private and public because the notion of private has been part of the systematic oppression of women across the globe. And it is in private spaces that many people are marginalized and exploited, whether it's women as wives, children who are abused, or domestic workers who are exploited in homes. The private domain becomes the unregulated zone of life, where the reproductive, the domestic, the relational and familial dimensions are excluded from mainstream political and legal debate. Are there more useful concepts, such as maybe consent? In our current context, and especially from where I come from, the Indian context, and broadly speaking from an Asian context of a gendered world, of a heterosexual patriarchal world, it is often the body that can lead the same life publicly that is entitled to privacy; that legal and social regimes that often ensure privacy of those who could very well lead the same lives publicly, thus the grant of privacy rights is also an account of privilege and hierarchy.

It is important to talk about the Asian context and what's different and so complex about it. There are instances in the last two years where an IP address wrongly provided by an ISP has led to the arrest and imprisonment of a person. Also, several arrests have taken place of people who have posted on popular social networking sites such as Orkut and Facebook, which are becoming sites of surveillance for the state and local police as well. Issues of sexuality are also important, as two gay parties have been broken up, and in one instance the police was using the Internet to entrap four men into turning up at a public space. So until the moment of when the men turned up at the public space, both the policemen and the gay men on the Web site were doing the same thing, talking about fantasies, about desires. There are also examples of Web boards where a lot of political commentary takes place but a lot of surveillance happens there. This has translated into a climate of self-censorship, where people don't speak up either in mainstream media or in alternative spaces. The other aspect is that while privacy measures might be built into systems in the west, the ways in which they are implemented in Asia, including in cybercafés where a lot of people get access the Internet, are themselves regulated. The cafes have to hand over identities, retain data, and ensure that every computer in the space is facing outwards. So it shows how the state really does not have much regard for individual privacy. Another example is where online pornography that is provided through phone cameras or hidden cameras is put up voluntarily or without consent. But to address this issue, an anti-pornography law was put forward that didn't address privacy, but instead talks about how women should be attired in public and criminalizes movements and gestures that are provocative, including in traditional dances, as well as homosexuality. So a law that could have been used for protecting women against violence online or violations of their privacy is instead being used to limit their participation in the public sphere.

It is also said quite often that privacy means different things in the Asian context, and that it is maybe not a universal idea. The question to be asked is: what could be a universal idea? In a world with so many languages, it is probably hard to find some conceptual term on which even the people in this room could agree as having a specific meaning. It is also true that privacy, as such, has changed in its meaning. It used to mean something has been taken away and was seen as a deprivation or a lack, whereas in the modern world, the private sphere is usually enriched in the age of modern individualism. The ideas of family, of home, of leisure time, and all the various things that we call the private are very much a product of this particular time that we live in. So it may not be true across different cultures. Yet at the same time, that cannot be an excuse for how corporations deal with issues of privacy. It cannot be a way in which they can say that awareness has to be raised by the citizens themselves and not by the corporations, or that they have no responsibility with regard to privacy, because it is even more important that corporations have a greater liability in a society that is grappling with globalization, rapid changes in technology, modernity, and modern individualism that is different from the context in these countries before.

I would like to also talk about the peculiar idea of privacy in public. A lot of us put our own information out there but want certain aspects of privacy protected in the public sphere. That borrows the problem faced by homosexuals for the longest time: That your most private intimate acts had to be hidden from public scrutiny, but also had to take place in public spaces. So homosexuals of this world are probably better equipped to deal with issues around privacy and community than any others. But the Internet also twists the idea of privacy in public even further and makes it an interesting dilemma. The last point I wanted to make is that privacy is an account of privilege and hierarchy and that a body that does not fall within the narrow definition of normal is probably not a guarded privacy, whether it is because of divorce, abortion, homosexuality, promiscuity, or even being a victim of rape. A body that does not belong to the global knot may not be entitled to the same level of privacy because corporate entities do not recognize the rights at the same level. A body that is female is not entitled to the same level of privacy. A body that is not healthy is not entitled to the same level of privacy. Definitely not a body with AIDS or even swine flu. And these paradoxically are the bodies that have the greatest need to be able to control how and when information is made available to others. I would like to end with this quote, "Privacy is turned from exclusion based on self-regard into regard for another's fragile, mysterious autonomy."

BRUCE SCHNEIER:

We have to realize that we as a society are producing much more data than ever before, and that's not because of any malice or design. It's simply because computer mediated processes produce data. That's what they do. So as the phone system becomes computerized, more data is produced. As point of sale systems become computerized, more data is produced. As the registration system for this conference becomes computerized, more data is produced. So every time we go on the Web, whether we're using a social networking site or engaging in a purchase or simply surfing, data is produced. E-mail takes the place of voice conversations. It's more data. And this data has value. And we're living in a world where a lot of that data isn't owned by us. It's owned by phone companies or credit card companies or mediators or social networking sites. In cloud computing, more of our data will be given to somebody else for safekeeping. So a lot of this data that's about us, either as persons or businesses, is not under our direct control. And what can be done with that data is now less a function of what we want and more a function of local laws or agreements or terms of service. And what's also happening is that it becomes cheaper to store data of even marginal value than it is to throw it away. Data analysis becomes so cheap that data mining for marketing purposes becomes a reasonable thing to do. So we have a data shadow, we're leaving data about ourselves everywhere we go, with everything we do. So that's the first point.

The second trend I think is important is that I.T. is becoming a commodity. Users are now very sophisticated about the Internet and about computers. They're not technically sophisticated, they're socially sophisticated. They don't know how things work but they know what should work. They care less about details and more about results. I.T. is becoming infrastructure. We're seeing more and more sophisticated service offerings, rather than technical product offerings, more and more packaged solutions, so whether it's Gmail or Facebook or something else, these are just all ways people can interact with computers at a much higher social level. Moreover, I.T. is becoming a utility, something you need. You come to work, you expect a desk and a stapler and a phone and a computer. It's something that has to work. And all utilities, all infrastructure is outsourced. This is pushing the trend towards cloud computing and outsourced services. We can no longer directly affect the security, the privacy, the reliability of our data. We have to trust our providers. And whether you achieve that trust through audits, through contracts, through government regulation or another way, we need to get that trust, because without that none of this will function.

There's talk about security versus privacy, and how you balance them. That's a false dichotomy. When you think of a door lock or a tall fence, these are security measures that don't affect privacy. The real dichotomy here is liberty versus control. There are there are things we can do to foster each. People don't think about privacy unless it's brought front and centre by some event, or by losing it. It's not a normally a salient thing. Doesn't mean they don't care it, just means it's not salient. And markets tend not to be very good at dealing with non-salient features. Markets are good at things like price, which is always salient, or colour or the size of the thing you're buying. With non-salient features, the way you get them is through legislation. The government comes and sets things like building codes. None of us think the roof in this building is going to fall on us. But the building is strong because of local building codes. We need to enshrine privacy as a human right. Not something to be bartered away like other non-salient things, it has to be legislated so there's a floor.

ALEXANDER SEGER:

How can we ensure security while maintaining due process, freedom of expression, and privacy in a global environment where every country has different rules? Yes, data protection, privacy, and freedom of expression are fundamental rights, but security is also. Cybercrime and threats to cybersecurity are real threats. We talk about offenses against computer systems, offences through computer systems, or simply evidence on computer systems. We talk about crime for profit, identity-related crime, the terrorist use of ICTs, and so forth. With other types of crime, law enforcement and criminal justice institutions have the primary responsibility. With cybercrime, we have a role in the private sector---the financial sector, information security officers and companies, and so on. And we have to strengthen capacities in different countries to cope with cybercrime. We have the Budapest convention on cybercrime that is an important standard here. With regard to data protection and privacy, we do not have global standards. There was a very interesting meeting a few weeks ago of data protection commissioners in Madrid, and there is a potential to move towards global standards on data protection and privacy. Data protection and privacy are a fundamental right, we don't have to justify why we want to have it protected.

Data protection and privacy is also a condition for law enforcement. European law enforcement agencies don't exchange data with third countries if they don't have standards in place. Countries that offer off-shoring services, they need to be sure that standards are in place, otherwise, many countries will have difficulty to agree to have services and private data handled in by them. With regard to freedom of expression, due process, procedural safeguards, and other fundamental rights, it is very important to recall that the World Summit on the Information Society (WSIS) agreed to these values. We have to work towards Internet governance that is in full support of fundamental rights. In Europe, we have the case law of the European Court of Human Rights that is very important, and in the Convention on Cybercrime we have Article 15 on procedural safeguards. The Council of Europe also has developed guidelines on how law enforcement and Internet Service Providers (ISPs) can cooperate with each other in free respect of human rights. So there is a good ground to work towards globally common standards, regulations or codes that allow all of us to cooperate. And to the point that Joe and Bruce made, it is not a question of tradeoffs, security versus fundamental rights.

FRANK LA RUE:

I agree that security, openness and privacy are not in conflict with each other. But they have to be seen from the perspective of human rights policies and principles. They are also to be seen as a shared responsibility. I would like to begin with the question of openness. Freedom of expression is an individual right, but it is also a collective right, just as communication is. It is also the right of peoples to express not only ideas but their cultures, their traditions, and their languages, and to reproduce those without any limitation or censorship. This works in both directions, the freedom of access to information, and the freedom of expression. First of all, access to information on public issues is transparency. All public acts, activities, and policies, the documents or information, should be put to the service of the public. It is on behalf of the general interest that public officials act. There should be a mentality of absolute openness to all the media and all the forms of communication from the Internet, to the mass media, for public expression, to the artistic or cultural expressions of all peoples.

Which are the principles that we should apply as we exercise these human rights? Number one is the principle of equity and justice. Communication technology, instruments, and facilities should not be the privilege of the few, they should be made accessible to all. It is important that states do not generate different limitations or obstacles to that free access to information or free access to expression. The second principle is the question of plurality and diversity. There should be the possibility of accessing a variety of opinions and not the consolidation of one point of view. Openness means diversity and pluralism. The state has the responsibility to regulate to make effective the exercise of human rights. The only limitations acceptable in terms of freedom of expression or access to information are those that protect other human rights, that protect a higher interest or a higher value than the one they are limiting. And those should be very few and very qualified---the protection of children, for instance. Yes, there should be specific limitations by the state, but whether it be the protection of children or national security, or whether it be combating terrorism or combating organized crime, they should never be used as an excuse to create a mechanism filtering or of censorship. And countries can use different excuses---children, anti-terrorism, or even the protection of religions. That becomes a veiled form of censorship. We should not allow freedom of expression to permit hate language or incitement to hatred or discrimination or violence on the basis of racial differences, religious differences or linguistic differences, or gender or age or disability or any other difference. But it is important to limit this and not to fall into the trap of opening the censorship for all.

MARC ROTENBERG:

I would like to ask each one of you to say what you see as the single greatest challenge facing the future of the Internet today.

JOSEPH ALHADEFF:

I think the challenge is the concept of trust, and how to establish it, what's the language that you use in these new media in order to enable it. W are trying to figure out what is the first step, and that's one of the roles that the IGF helps to play, because the best way to start a dialogue is to understand the concerns of those people who are on the other side.

CRISTINE HOEPERS:

I think the challenge is to separate what is a valid security countermeasure from what is trying to pose as a security countermeasure just to restrict something or to collect data. And I think it will be very difficult for governments to deploy a lot of technologies that are supposed to be to make their citizens more secure. They have that intention, but they are not considering what are the side effects, or how that would affect privacy of the citizens. Trying to do something to make them more secure, they can make things even worse.

NAMITA MALHOTRA:

The challenge would be the role that powerful corporate entities have started to play in terms of data aggregation and how they use it or sell it. And what might be interesting would be to think about privacy as maybe layered in some ways, to think about the contextual integrity of information. There is information that you give to your doctor which you may or may not want your employer to know. So basically that I give information to some corporate entity and that it is protected within that domain.

BRUCE SCHNEIER:

When Marc first posed that I wrote down corporate interests, but in some cases it's government interests. Really the challenge is balancing the interests of the powerful with everybody else. Technology gives the powerful the edge to get more powerful. And depending on what country we are in or what the government is like, that's either the government or it's corporations doing things that are not in society's best interests.

ALEXANDER SEGER:

We have to talk about persons, about the identity of persons, about the security of persons, and about the rights of persons. And the issues there are how can we ensure the confidentiality, integrity and availability of computer data and systems?

FRANK LA RUE:

I think we have to have a human rights perspective beyond the technological development, the commercial developments.

SHERIF HASHEM:

I think the IGF should focus on inclusion and empowerment of society when we discuss issues relating to security, openness, and privacy. And this can be done only through partnership and openness.

JASNA MATIC:

This absolute openness has created a situation that is entirely new, and the biggest danger is how to use it not to create more leverage for the already powerful ones.

MARC ROTENBERG:

Well, this is interesting. We are gathered at a major international conference on the future of the greatest technological revolution of our era, and most of our panellists are primarily concerned about the rights of people. So watch out, technology. We are looking at you. Our audience now, you are invited to participate.

FROM THE FLOOR:

I'm Steve DelBianco. A few people stalked about privacy as a fundamental right for an individual. Are individuals allowed to negotiate away that fundamental right? Mr. Alhadeff said we should optimize, and the optimum configuration for my teenage sons is that they may want to give away some of their privacy rights, to let ads that are targeted to their interests show up on their applications, because they want to continue getting for free services like Facebook or Gmail or Twitter or Flickr. So should they be allowed to negotiate away what you are trying to establish as a fundamental right?

BRUCE SCHNEIER:

I think your son would probably sell his kidney, too, because the money would be sure worth it. There are limits to what should be traded in terms of fundamental rights. We have to be very careful about giving rights the same economic status as you do other things. So I think privacy should be a right and not a commodity.

JOSEPH ALHADEFF:

You have concepts of what's a right and what's control over certain types of information, and you have to start drawing fine lines around how you define these because we don't want other people making decisions for us. But on the other hand, there are populations where you may want certain protections like people who aren't familiar with the Internet, older.

REMOTE PARTICIPANT:

I am joining you from Brazil. Ms. Malhotra, you raised sexual and human rights, linking it with gender. How can we advance a more robust debate on freedom of expression, privacy, and sexuality?

NAMITA MALHOTRA:

One of the ways forward would be to think about the contextual integrity of information that you give for a certain purpose not being used for anything else. Also, consent or not giving your consent forms the bedrock of most sexual offenses, and the state criminalizes unnatural sexual acts between consensual adults, so look at whether consent is an important legal tool, whether it is more legally protected in other contexts than privacy.

CRISTINE HOEPERS:

CERT.br is not the police, so we don't actually investigate crimes, but we deal with people that are victims of cybercrimes. And there is a mix of the victims. They don't actually understand how that is perpetrated and the technology is making it very easy for the cybercriminals to pose as third parties, to insert and mix with the Web, and they even show fake pages to the victims who think they are doing the right transaction. There are a lot of people overreacting and that will not help either because no one will be able to go through all the information gathered. So it's a mix of having better software and technology and having people understand better.

FRANK LA RUE:

We cannot barter our human rights or even talk about stages, in terms of technology going first and human rights catching up later. It's the full exercise of all rights that will guarantee advancement at all levels, especially as a democratic society.

FROM THE FLOOR:

My name is Lisa Horner. It is refreshing to hear about the positive dimensions of freedom of expression and the ways in which the human rights framework actually specifies how we can balance between different social goods and rights, such as privacy, security, and expression. I think within the IGF, over the years, human rights have been presented in an increasingly negative way, focusing, for example, on how we have to have less expression and more security. In the first IGF, we had a whole session dedicated to openness and freedom of expression, but now we have a session on balancing different rights and freedom of expression isn't on the list. So what can we do to ensure that human lights standards are better included within everyday Internet policy-making, so that they are made the primary norms which underpin Internet governance processes? Is there a role for better coordination between the U.N. organizations that are involved in different elements of Internet governance, e.g. between the U.N. human rights organizations and the ITU, WIPO, et cetera?

FRANK LA RUE:

All the development has to be based on the human rights and this ultimately becomes the responsibility of the state. That's why I say that we don't have to see regulations in a negative way.

ALEXANDER SEGER:

One advantage in approaching this as cybercrime rather than information security or threats to cybersecurity is that the moment you talk about "crime" you talk about rule of law, conditions, safeguards, rules of procedure, et cetera. If we approach the issue as cybercrime, it will automatically take into account basic safeguards.

MARC ROTENBERG:

We have people who are following the conference on the Internet and sending in questions as well. This one is from Miguel Alcaine from El Salvador and he asks: Why haven't we discussed anonymity? We've talked a lot about privacy, but there is a difference between the right of privacy and the right of anonymity.

BRUCE SCHNEIER:

I think it's important that the Internet preserve anonymity, whether it's social or political or economic. It's fundamental for all these things. Actually eliminating anonymity on the Internet is very, very hard. You really cannot design an Internet architecture that doesn't permit anonymity. Just having something as simple as anonymous re-mailers, even in a perfectly identifiable system, brings back anonymity. So anonymity is a social good, a political good, an economic good, and it's a fundamental property of the Internet.

JOSEPH ALHADEFF:

Sometimes people talk about full identity or anonymity, and they don't talk about what's in the middle. And selective disclosure of identity as appropriate for the needs of the communication or transaction you're involved in is also part of the solution, because you don't need to actually disclose all elements for all transactions. There can be a selection of what is appropriate and you may even have pseudonymity for certain types of things, as opposed to anonymity, so I think we need to look at the broad panoply of tools that are available.

FROM THE FLOOR:

Vincenzo Vita from Italian Parliament. Where is the shadow limit between security and censorship? Like the connectivity suppliers are targeted by some draft legislation to introduce filtering argue that filtering is useless and even impossible.

FRANK LA RUE:

The limit between security and censorship is very difficult to establish, but it has to be established, and one of the ideas is that limitations do exist but have human rights criteria to them. They have to be established by law, by the judiciary, not by any administrative body, much less like it happens with Internet, applied by a private enterprise hired by the state to monitor, to screen. That's not acceptable. And it has to be applied in the protection of a higher good, to protect someone else's rights.

FROM THE FLOOR:

I'm Bertrand de La Chapelle. It's a pleasure to hear that privacy, openness and security are not contradictory, and anonymity or nondisclosure of names is a typical example where it can be a reinforcement of the security of the user. Social media are redefining some questions on privacy, freedom of expression, and even copyright, and if we dig deeper on the privacy notion, it's about somehow introducing a redefinition of what intimacy is. Intimacy was usually what you do in your home. Now we are exposing a lot of personal information voluntarily. So how do you manage online intimacy, those people you allow to see things about you and those who don't. The IGF allows us to sort out some sub-themes as an application of the general principles that we've adopted, and I hope that the some of the workshops will dig deeper and explore those elements. And when we talk about the governance of social media, there's the external governance, the international treaties, or the national laws, but there is also the laws that are developed internally by large networks in the form of the terms of use. The way those terms are being used and the fit with the protection of privacy and openness is also an issue that has to be discussed as those networks are transnational.

NAMITA MALHOTRA:

Being online is a lot about trust. There are different kinds privacy for private data give to the corporations, what you share with each other, and what someone does with your data. The idea is that you give out the information in different contexts and they should be used only within those contexts. It's actually quite endearing how humans are able to share so much information willingly, trusting the community, trusting society to not disclose or to use that information wisely. But unfortunately we do live in a world where the state picks up on certain aspects of what we put out there, or corporate entities, and it results in negative action such as arrests, harassment, censorship or banning.

JOSEPH ALHADEFF:

There's a lot of work going on related to use-based models because some information has gotten beyond the scope of notice and consent. I think more complex and difficult to deal with is the picture you take where the subject matter isn't the problem in question, it's something in the background. Where it's a third party that was caught in the background. And the question then becomes, you know, where is the responsibility to that person in the background who happens to be in a public place where you've taken a picture of someone you know? Both the photographer and the main subject are consensually posting this picture. And I don't know the answer to that one. The last thing I would say is that social media have also have a democratizing potential in the sense that the community itself has risen up against terms they don't like and has been the single most effective force to change them.

FROM THE FLOOR:

I'm Thomas Schneider and I have two remarks. The first one is with regard to this growth of so-called free services that you do not pay directly for through a fee, but you pay indirectly through by being profiled or other hidden costs. To what extent do you let users choose whether or not to use these services? Especially the ones that do not have the money, that do not really have a choice to choose services that are of a higher quality but they have to pay for. Is there a risk that we're getting into a two-class society, where the rich have the resources and the capacity and the education to protect themselves, and the poor that want to be part of the Information Society do not have the means to protect themselves? In the Council of Europe, some experts talk about outsourcing human rights from the responsibility of governments to private sector services, which creates a problem because the liability is not clear anymore. This is the first question. The second question is with regard to involving human rights experts in the structure of Internet governance. There was an answer by somebody that this should be done by the governments, they should defend the human rights of their citizens. In my experience in working in the ITU and in ICANN and in other bodies that deal with so-called technical questions, there are not that many human rights experts in governments' delegations because normally these are people that know about the technical aspects. The only thing that works is that stakeholders are involved and can exercise pressure on governments to make sure that a holistic picture of the society's interests is represented in these organizations.

BRUCE SCHNEIER:

The notion of cross-subsidies isn't new. I mean television is an old example of that. There's no way to charge for it directly so advertisers were brought in, and the customers of television were, in effect, the product that was being sold to advertisers. And that's no different from Google. So I don't think we can get away from cross-subsidies. And instead of it making a sort of a two-tier system of haves and have nots, I think you end up with a one-tier system like television. I mean, everybody uses Google, everybody watches television. Everybody in the United States has to buy cell phones with calling plans attached to them. I know it's different in other countries. So we can't get rid of them, but accountability and transparency can make that palatable to society.

FRANK LA RUE:

If you want a human rights focus, you want the authorities to learn about rights, and all states should have specialized people. You want corporations that develop the technology to have some of their staff specialized in the human rights perspective, but you also want the users and associations of users to be aware of their own rights and the exercise of their rights. I think you should bring in another actor, the specialized NGOs that are experts on the subject. There could be a dialogue that would guarantee this perspective.

FROM THE FLOOR:

My name is Zahid Jamal. Somebody mentioned the important role of international governmental organizations in the IGF. Does the existing Budapest convention, which is the only convention on cybercrime, have a role to play in bringing human rights, due process and safeguards into the structures of Internet governance?

ALEXANDER SEGER:

In the Council of Europe we developed the Budapest convention on cybercrime which proposes a proportionate and appropriate response. And I would appreciate if when implementing the convention, which I hope you all do, please take seriously Article 15 about conditions and safeguards. We have been working with countries on cybercrime legislation soon governments came back to us and said we have a problem from the community, in parliament, from our people. We have to find some safeguards there. And very soon we have started to then work with governments about data protection and privacy legislation. So it's built into the process.

FRANK LA RUE:

On what happens losing market share and defending human rights, there is no contradiction. You can never give in on human rights. I heard in some panel at this conference that first you develop the technology, you create the network in a new country, you bring up-to-date their possibilities of communication, and then slowly you bring up the issue of human rights and persuade them. It doesn't work that way. It works the other way around. First you have a human rights commitment. You strengthen democracy and democratic principles and then you bring up the technology. Otherwise, it will never work, and it is a self-defeating.

SHERIF HASHEM:

On the matter of setting up regulations, in Egypt we have involved the different stakeholders at the same table to discuss these issues because you cannot rely on really a cascaded process where you set up the regulation and try to convince the civil society to adopt it. You have to include them in the process. And that has worked beautifully in many of the laws like the child protection law that we passed last year or even the technologically-oriented legislation like the e-signature law and the telecom law. So if you involve society, the process will be longer, but you end up with something that is acceptable to almost all stakeholders.

FROM THE FLOOR:

I'm Jean-Marc Dinant. We have the false impression that the Internet is free, but there is a price to pay and the price is privacy. And marketing says, okay, thanks to us, the Internet is free. But marketing industry is paid by the companies. And who is paying the companies? The customers. So, in fact, the customer is paying twice. He's paying by giving up his privacy and paying a second time to get a higher price for the same product.

MARC ROTENBERG:

I think part of the may be the view that individuals face a choice only to keep information and thereby keep their privacy or disclose their information and thereby give up their privacy. The right way to understand it is whether their information will be disclosed, protected in law, used for an appropriate purpose, not exploited, and respected, which is a disclosure that occurs in the context of a legal framework, or whether their personal information is obtained and used for whatever purpose the business that obtains it chooses to use it for. It's this choice that is arising increasingly for the Internet.

FROM THE FLOOR:

I'm Stephen Lau from Hong Kong. When we talk about trust between government and its citizens, corporation and its employers and customers, nowadays it goes beyond that because once you put your personal data out on the net you can be sure it will be kept forever. It will be used, copied, forwarded, used inadvertently or otherwise by design, and you don't know which entity is doing it. And the sad thing is, the entity that uses your data may not even know that it is actually infringing or using your data. So the biggest challenge is to be aware of this danger. I was looking at the title of this conference, Internet governance, creating opportunities for all, and I thought it could read, Creating your data for all. So my challenge to the technologists, the pioneers, including of search engines like Google and other really brilliant algorithms is, is it possible to have personal data cast into oblivion and deleted by users.

MARC ROTENBERG:

This is an idea that is becoming popular, the ability to delete your history, if you choose to do that. In fact, arguably, the recent campaign involving the change in the Facebook terms of service was very much about that issue. Because as you know, many of the Facebook users objected to a change in the provisions which appeared to make it more difficult for people who chose to leave Facebook to be able to delete their account.

BRUCE SCHNEIER:

Technically, it's not possible to delete it. And you know that's true because you could have a copy of the data on a DVD in a file cabinet, and you just can't go in and erase that. It's non-erasable media, for heaven's sakes. But you can do it through legislation. If the issue is Facebook not deleting our data when we ask them to, all it takes is a law saying you have to do it, and then companies will follow. For a lot of these problems, there aren't technical answers, but there are legal answers. And that's really where we have to look when we move forward, with things like how our data is used, stored, bought and sold, and how long it's saved and how it's deleted.

JOSEPH ALHADEFF:

The problem is if it was posted, it may have been copied, it may have been downloaded, it may have been transferred and then the question is you may have deleted the source, but can you delete the tail after the source.

BRUCE SCHNEIER:

The answer is no.

FROM THE FLOOR:

I am Rikke Frank Jørgensen from the Danish Human Rights Institute. From a human rights perspective, how can we encourage or initiate a process to have a general comment on the right to privacy?

FRANK LA RUE:

The idea of getting a general comment from a human right committee establishing a standard is a great idea. As a matter of fact, the human rights committee is looking at a general comment or an update on their Article 19. But they didn't go as far as to look at the limitations in Article 20, I guess because they don't have agreement on that.

ALEXANDER SEGER:

We do have at the Council of Europe level, for our 47 member states, a treaty which dates back to 1981 on data protection. And it was recently decided by the Committee of Ministers of the Council of Europe that this treaty should be open to third countries. So here is a practical tool and existing instrument that any country that meets the same standards that are foreseen under that convention to join that treaty.

MARC ROTENBERG:

I should mention also that in Madrid there was a very important declaration by civil society groups on privacy issues that is available at the Web site of The Public Voice.

FROM THE FLOOR:

I'm Pavan Duggal. Five broad game changers are happening. Number one, there is a huge explosion in the adoption of smart communication devices. And that is happening more so in Asia-Pacific, India and China. Number two, there is a tremendous increase in the quantity and the quality of cybercrimes targeted against nations. The third, the emergence of the voice Web and the mobile Internet is suddenly changing the horizon. The fourth, cloud computing is bringing up new parameters. And finally, the fifth, social networking, including in the mobile space. Given these five broad game changers does the panel see some kind of paradigm shifts in how the issue of privacy is going to be viewed in the context of mobile platform and devices?

BRUCE SCHNEIER:

It used to be what I think of as a fortress computer centre, that if you wanted to be secure as a person or as an organization you would do it yourself. You could build your own walls. And what these trends indicate is that things are much more interdependent, that we're losing control of our data, we're losing control of our employees or even our notion of borders, with mobile computing and cloud computing and social networking. And, yes, criminals are getting much more sophisticated, and this points to the need for broad legislation, trust and accountability.

FROM THE FLOOR:

I'm Liesyl Franz and I'd like to talk a stab at answering the question Mr. Rotenberg posed about the challenges to the Internet. I would like to say that I fear a challenge to the Internet is the imposition of a regime or a set of regimes that would inhibit the ability of our technology providers to continue in the very business that enables the access, the services, and the innovation that so many people around the world are calling for. Some of these services that you have today and are relying on today would not have been created if there had been an environment that prohibited them. To address the various comments regarding corporate interests, companies do acutely recognize that it is in their interest to provide security, privacy, and dignity to their customers and users. I'm not saying that there aren't outliers, but it is important to recognize the efforts of technology providers to build security and privacy into their products and services. I think it's important to ensure an environment where industry, government, and civil society can engage in dialogue, both here at the IGF but also in our own jurisdictions. I do have a question: How do each of you, in each of your roles, engage with industry to help work together towards solutions?

ALEXANDER SEGER:

I think we need the cooperative approach. We cannot deal with cybercrime without working with the private sector. And we have, for the past years, have worked extensively with industry. We have been elaborating guidelines for cooperation between law enforcement and ISPs and have been quite successful in that. These guidelines are implemented in a number of countries. It is now accepted all over the world that law enforcement can receive and needs support from the private sector for training. At the same time we developed similar concepts for the training of judges. There is more of apprehension from the judicial side, they don't want to have direct private sector support because it could compromise their independence. So we also have found a way to establish possibilities for cooperation without compromising the independence of judges.

SHERIF HASHEM:

I mentioned earlier how in drafting legislation, we involved the private sector, and when discussing the final draft, we involved the NGOs and the industrial associations. Our CERT, which is established at our National Telecom Regulatory Authority has open links with all the key players---the ISPs, the GSM operators, even across different sectors. We fund the training of their professionals at the international level, have them get certified, so whether it is operational or the regulatory aspects, they are involved so they are not surprised by any move that we take. This happens in cooperation with civil society organizations that get us direct feedback from the customers.

JOSEPH ALHADEFF:

There's a broad range of consultation and facilitation already occurring, and the cybercrime treaty is a good example, where both civil society and business worked with governments on the terms in its formative stages. The encryption debate of a number of years back was another place where the dialogues were enjoined by all parties to a constructive and productive end. Fora like the OECD, where there is not just civil society, business and government, but also the technical community, is another important way of bridging these gaps. Does that mean that we agree all the time? Certainly not. But the dialogue has matured. I think that's true in the IGF too, where the dialogue has matured significantly since its early days, or even since the WSIS process.

FRANK LA RUE:

We have to make sure that in every country and at an international level, it is seen that way, that all governments actually seek this dialogue with civil society and with enterprises, and the other actors as well, because it can help the process of legislation and to draft international standards. It's generating this sense of trust amongst the different actors, which can actually enhance a stronger position, vis-à-vis those that are attacking privacy or using communications for criminal actions.

FROM THE FLOOR:
My name is Suliman Mustafa. I am from the Ministry of Telecommunication and Information, Sudan, and I am currently leading an Arab cybersecurity virtual group. I do agree with the speaker who says that openness and security and privacy are not in tension with each other, rather they're complementary. My comment is, how can we build something at a national level, then we can have on the regional level, and again worldwide level through IGF initiative so we can be able to face the cybercrime issue? In my opinion, the situation is really terrible.

FROM THE FLOOR:

My name is Cristos Velasco, Director-General of NACPEC.org and Ciberdelincuencia.org .Identity theft is both a consumer protection and a criminal issue under most countries' legislations, so I would like to know what you think about this issue and what are current European policies and American policies?.

MARC ROTENBERG:

It was recently reported in the United States that over 9 million Americans have been subject to this crime, which is about one out of every 30 people.

BRUCE SCHNEIER:

I don't like the term "identity theft." Your identity is the one thing about you that cannot be stolen. What this crime is, is fraud due to impersonation. It's not new. It's millennia old. What makes it new, what makes it different, is that it's automated and it's done remotely, and it is very profitable. And it's very international. We seem to be doing pretty well against it. It is very common, but if laws are set up right, it's relatively easy to clean up. The issue seems to be, is who is liable for the identity theft? If someone goes to my bank, impersonates me and steals money out of my account, I'm not involved, and if I'm liable for the loss, then there's no way for me to improve the bank's security. So as long as we build a legal system where the entity who is responsible for the risk is liable for the risk, then security naturally improves and you see that over the decades with credit cards or with check fraud. And when we have that, identity theft is mitigated down to reasonable levels of fraud that we accept in society. In areas where you have that mismatch, where the individual is liable for the fraud and the company is in a position to mitigate the fraud, there you have serious problems which can't be fixed, because the economic incentives just aren't aligned right.

JOSEPH ALHADEFF:

In situations like spam and identity theft you need more of a multipronged and collaborative approach. That doesn't mean that legislation wouldn't be part of it, but I don't think you fix it completely with legislation; it will involve education, outreach, cooperation, and maybe new technologies.

FROM THE FLOOR:

Bill Graham here, I'm actually channelling Michael Nelson at Georgetown University, who was having some problems with the remote site. He says, "I've found this panel to be a valuable and balanced discussion of a very complex set of topics, but like our moderator, I'd like more specifics. Much of my research and writing is about cloud computing and barriers to its adoption. I'm particularly concerned about policies designed to protect privacy or intellectual property rights being mis-applied in ways that could stymie development and use of new cloud services. How can we future-proof, copyright privacy laws so users can enjoy the potential of these new services while ensuring choice and transparency and accountability?"

MARC ROTENBERG:

We are running out of time so I'm going to ask our panellists to be very brief, just a sentence or two, please, in response to my question: Assuming you had a few minutes with your minister of communications to make a specific recommendation about the future of the Internet, something you would very much like to see your country do that you think should be a top priority, what specifically would you recommend?

CRISTINE HOEPERS:

The most important thing is education.

NAMITA MALHOTRA:

It depends on who you are, where you are, where you're located, whether or not this conversation is even possible. I don't think it will happen.

BRUCE SCHNEIER:

I think you should clean your own house, improve your own security. I think you should use your buying power to convince vendors to improve the security of their products, and I think you should fund research broadly and widely.

ALEXANDER SEGER:

I would recommend implementing the Convention on Cybercrime and data protection legislation in line with a treaty that is available at the Council of Europe.

FRANK LA RUE:

I would first try to convene a mechanism of consultation that draws all sectors in to build a consensus to draft a human rights-based policy. And I would suggest to establish a fund to subsidize access to communication by all those sectors that have not had access or any training.

SHERIF HASHEM:

When we talk about security, privacy, openness, it's about the trust. People use the Internet and they trust that this is a viable medium for them to exchange their views, to realize their dreams, and to understand other cultures. It's very important that this trust is not undermined by criminal activities or other threats. So education and openness are key to achieve such a trust. Trust is a result, not a concept that we start off with. And for education, we have to revise our message. Most people would agree that security is important, that privacy is important. But the problem is once this is agreed upon, managing the translation to how this affects business, how we share our private information so it doesn't undermine our security. When you talk about security within even a business environment, a CEO would be convinced that security is important. But how much budget is allocated there? It's critical, especially security experts. You are asking for a budget and the best result that you can show is that nothing happens. You are able to really avoid threats, but how you materialize this is very important. So again, the concept of education, involving all stakeholders in the community. We would like a coherent framework, a cooperative framework that involves all stakeholders so that people are not marginalized.

JASNA MATIC:

I don't think there's too much to say in conclusion. I think one thing is clear, however; that there's clear need for continuation of the Internet Governance Forum discussing this topic. The regulators, the legislators, the corporations, civil society, we all need to follow what's going on in order to be able to cope with it, and to be able to use this wonder of the Internet and not let the bad things prevail.

Security, Openness and Privacy:

Reports of the Workshops and Other Events

1. Security

BPF 68.   Developing Comprehensive Cybercrime Legislation

WS 72.   Children in the Web 2.0 World: The European Approach

WS 93.   The Global Partnership for Ensuring Online Child Protection
           and Safety: Effective Strategies and Specific Actions

WS 105.   Preserving Free Expression on the Internet and
           Protecting Children's Rights Online

WS 106.   The Mobile Internet in Developing Countries:
           Child Safety Dimensions

WS 151.   Cyber Security R&D: Developing a Vision and Road Map

WS 160.   Securing Cyberspace: Strategy for the Future

WS 206.   Domain Name Use: Theft, Threats and Solutions

BPF 210.   Child Online Safety on Developing Countries: Strategies for
           Moving Forward

WS 257.   The Privacy and Security Implications of Cloud Computing

WS 265.   Medicines on the Net: Risks and Benefits

WS 288.   Child Online Safety Indicators: Measuring the Un-measurable?

OF 531.   ITU Open Forum on Child Online Protection

OF 532.   ITU Open Forum on Cybersecurity

2. Openness and Privacy

WS 263.   Privacy, Openness, Online Advertising and Online Behavioural
           Targeting Advertising

WS 275.   Content Regulation, Surveillance and Sexuality Rights:
           Privacy, Agency and Security

WS 302.   Network Neutrality

WS 314.   Human Rights and Principles in Internet Governance:
           Practical Steps Forwards

WS 323.   Roundtable: Balancing the Need for Security and the Concern
          for Civil Liberties

WS 346.   Open Knowledge Environment in Bridging the Digital Divide for
          Innovative Research and Development

WS 361.   Open Standards: A Rights-Based Approach

OF 541.   Open Forum of the Council of Europe: Freedom of Expression
          and Access to Information in Online (Cross-border)
          Environments: International Cooperation in Connection
          with Critical Internet Resources

DC.   Freedom of Expression and Freedom of the Media on the Internet
          Dynamic Coalition Meeting

DC.   Internet Rights and Principles Dynamic Coalition Meeting

1. Security

BPF 68.   *Developing Comprehensive Cybercrime Legislation*

Report by: Alexander Seger

Organizer: The Council of Europe

*Moderator: Andrew McIntosh (Chair, Sub-Committee on the Media, and Rapporteur
on Media Freedom, Council of Europe Parliamentary Assembly [PACE], Strasbourg)*

*Panellists: Pavan Duggal (India); Ehab Elsonbaty (Egypt); Jayantha Fernando (Sri
Lanka); Marco Gercke (Germany); Cristina Schulman (Council of Europe)*

Comprehensive and consistent legislation is essential to help societies meet
the challenge of cybercrime and thus to enhance the security of and
confidence in information and communication technologies. Legal
frameworks should take into account the rights of users and the role of the
private sector on the one hand, and security concerns on the other. The
Convention on Cybercrime of the Council of Europe provides a global
guideline in this respect. More than 100 countries worldwide have
strengthened or are in the process of strengthening their cybercrime
legislation. The aim of the best practice forum is to share this experience and
encourage further action in other countries.

Through the Project on Cybercrime, the Council of Europe supports widely
the strengthening of comprehensive legislation on cybercrime, data protection
and protection of children against sexual exploitation and sexual abuse and to
promote relevant instruments globally. The aim of the project was to promote
broad implementation of the Convention on Cybercrime (CETS 185) and its
Protocol on Xenophobia and Racism (CETS 189), and to deliver specific
results in terms of legislation, criminal justice capacities and international

cooperation. The project relied on cooperation with a multitude of other stakeholders, be it national authorities, international organisations as well as the private sector and non-governmental initiatives.

The event underlined that comprehensive and consistent legislation is essential to help societies meet the challenge of cybercrime and thus to enhance the security of and confidence in information and communication technologies. Legal frameworks should take into account the rights of users and the role of the private sector on the one hand, and security concerns on the other. The Convention on Cybercrime of the Council of Europe provides a global guideline in this respect.

The workshop:

- Promoted globally harmonised legislation based on international standards, in particular the Council of Europe Convention on Cybercrime.

- Highlighted the substantial assistance provided by the Council of Europe within the Project on cybercrime to different countries to harmonise their criminal law provisions on cybercrime with those of other countries in order to facilitate international cooperation.

- The participants' questions underlined the complexity of the legislation on cybercrime and the need for assistance and international joint efforts

The Council of Europe Convention on Cybercrime is the only binding legal document in the world providing solutions for this issue. It is open for accession to every state and offers guidelines of conduct as well as legal basis for international co-operation to its Parties. It is designed to criminalise offences against the confidentiality, integrity and availability of computer data and systems, computer-related offences, content-related offences (i.e. child pornography, racism and xenophobia) and offences relating to infringement of copyright and associated rights in a consistent and harmonised manner.) In order to put a comprehensive legislative framework in place that is internationally harmonized and permits efficient international cooperation, countries should be encouraged to make use of the Council of Europe Convention on Cybercrime (CETS 185).

WS 72.   *Children in the Web 2.0 World: The European Approach*

Report by: Margareta Traung

Panellists: Ana Luisa Rotta (Spanish Safer Internet Centre); Katia Segers (EU Kids Online); Gry Hasselbalch (Safer Internet Centre, Denmark); Simon Grehan (Safer Internet Centre, Ireland); Dieter Carstensen (eNACSO); Rachel O'Connell (Chief Safety Officer of Bebo); Janice Richardson (Insafe Network)

Katia Segers presented the EU Kids Online project as a network of social science researchers from 22 Member States, coordinated by the London School of Economics. The project aims to find existing research on children's use of online technologies and existing policies on the issue, and to collect them in a database. The findings of the gathered research are compared in order to see the differences between the countries. The project also aims to identify gaps where more research is still needed. For example, there is more research available on access to Internet and use than there is on potential risks.

The follow-up project, EU Kids Online 2, therefore also includes in addition to the above actual research to be carried out via a questionnaire on the topics of online opportunities and risks. Some key trends that have been identified so far are:
- Children's use of internet continues to grow especially among younger children,
- The so called digital gap is closing,
- Accessing Internet from the home is becoming more common.

Rachel O'Connell presented the work that led to the signing of the "Social Networking Sites' Principles", where she helped to coordinate 18 social networking sites to develop good practice guidelines for social networking sites as regards privacy issues and protection of minors. She stressed the importance of self-regulation where industry and other stakeholders work together in order to mitigate risks, as well as parent's involvement and interest in their children's activities online.
She hailed the initiative of the establishment of the Principles as an extraordinary move by the Commission, which after a 9 months long drafting process lead to the signature of the guidelines on Safer Internet Day in February 2009.

The resulting 7 principles on how to implement safety on social networking sites shows that self regulation actually works well, as was already seen with the mobile phone agreement. The principles cover issues such as accessibility of information, the provision of user-friendly measures to report unwanted conduct, and recommendations on how to implement the Principles. During the drafting process it appeared that industry already did a lot, and had done a lot of things about safety but not in such a consolidated manner.

Each signatory of the Principles have made a self-declaration of which recommendations have been implemented on their social network sites. To ensure confidence in the Principles a review is being conducted in order to see if the measures that have been declared by the signatories have in fact been implemented.

Janice Richardson presented the Insafe network of awareness centres throughout Europe, coordinated by the European Schoolnet, which is a consortium of ministries of education from the Member States. In addition to carrying out awareness raising activities and campaigns towards children, young people, teachers, parents and other carers, the network also coordinates helplines, which have as their objective to be on the frontline to give advice not only to young people, but also to the Safer Internet Centres in order for them to know what are the issues they should focus on in their awareness campaigns. The Safer Internet Centres share information and best practices, build campaigns and assess the impact of their campaigns.

She also talked about the Youth panels, including the pan-European Youth Panel which got together at the Safer Internet Forum in October 2009 with 2 representatives from each Member State, which have been established in order to better understand what youth want and to let them have a say in the development of future awareness campaigns. Safer Internet Day, which is celebrated in February each year, is one of the biggest achievements of the Insafe network. Next Safer Internet Day will take place on 11 February 2010 with the slogan "Think before you post". It will be celebrated in an estimated 65 countries around the world.

Janice Richardson's presentation was followed by two case studies. The first one was from the Safer Internet Centre in Denmark, presented by Gry Hasselbalch. Denmark is digitally a highly advanced country in comparison with the rest of Europe with a very narrow digital gap which is decreasing. The Safer Internet Centre in Denmark has run campaigns particularly on privacy issues in cooperation with industry and social networking sites to make kids think about their privacy online.

The second case study was from Ireland, presented by Simon Grehan. In Ireland, the main task of the Safer Internet Centre is to facilitate the integration of ICT into the teaching in schools, by providing high quality tools, fact books and tips that teachers can use in class. The emergence of web 2.0 meant that teaching material had to be updated due to the fact that children became also producers of online material and not only consumers as previously was the case. They have also run awareness campaigns giving advice on how to report abusive behaviour, particularly on social networking sites. He also mentioned that the video clip that was produced by the Commission in consultation with Insafe for Safer Internet Day 2009 was broadcast over 1.000 times on Irish television.

After these two case studies, Dieter Carstensen presented eNACSO, the European NGO Alliance on Child Safety Online. The alliance is coordinated by Save the Children which is the world's largest child's rights organisation. He pointed out that there should be no difference in the rights for children between the online and the offline world, referring for example to the right of involvement, the right to be protected, the right to privacy, etc. He also talked about their involvement from the NGO perspective in the process leading up to the establishment of the Social Networking Sites' Principles.

After the presentations the floor was open for questions. A representative from the Telecoms regulator in Egypt asked about key indicators for measuring the impact of awareness campaigns, and how come underage children (i.e. children below the minimum age as established by social networking sites) have profiles on social networking sites. Janice Richardson suggested a number of ways to measure the impact of campaigns; by repeated surveys, by analysing the calls that the helplines receive, by analysing what is being reported to the social networking sites, etc. Regarding the second question she replied that the way to deal with underage children having profiles on social networking sites would be to set up dedicated social networking sites with positive content for smaller children where they are protected. Dieter Carstensen added that there are currently no technical tools to verify age. Privacy concerns must be dealt with and it is one of the most difficult problems right now.

A representative from the OECD wondered what made the Social Networking Sites' Principles initiative to be so successful. Dieter Carstensen replied that the success was due to the Commission being very focused on what they wanted to achieve, the NGOs involved were also keen to see the Principles happen, and the industry wanted to take their responsibility rather than taking the risk of being regulated.

A representative from the Human Rights department of the Swedish Ministry for Foreign Affairs asked about plans to bring the social networking sites principles to a global level, and if there was also any interaction with the Council of Europe as they are also concerned in these questions. Dieter Carstensen replied that even though the Principles was a European initiative, most of the signatories are huge global entities and therefore the principles are also more or less global, but he pointed out that they cannot be imposed on any non-EU member states. He also said that the principles are a working document that needs to be reviewed and improved and made stronger. Janice Richardson added that there is interaction in all related areas going on with the Council of Europe.

The moderator closed the workshop by concluding that:

- Shared responsibility and a multi-stakeholder approach are necessary. Not only parents are responsible for children's use of the internet, but also governments, industry etc have to work together to develop more effective awareness campaigns. In this respect Europe is doing well through the Safer Internet programme, where each Safer Internet Centre have advisory boards from different stakeholders, and ensure to listen to the voice of youth through youth panels.
- Self-regulation works well but must be followed up.

Results need to be disseminated and shared for best effect. it is necessary to measure the impact of the campaigns, as well as choosing the right topics to focus on.

WS 93. The Global Partnership for Ensuring Online Child Protection and Safety: Effective Strategies and Specific Actions

Report by: Anjan Bose

Panellists: Carmen Madrinan (ECPAT International); Mr. Anjan Bose (ECPAT International); John Carr (eNACSO); Cristina Schulman (CoE); David Miles (Family Online Safety Institute); Dorothy Attwood (AT&T); Ilias Chantzos (Symantec Corporation EMEA); Jean-Christophe Le Toquin (Microsoft EMEA); Liz Butterfield (Hector's World); Nevine Tewfik (Government/State: Cyberpeace initiative); Hala Tadros (Government/State: Cyberpeace initiative); Councilor Hatem Bagato (Head of Commissioner's Body, Egypt)

The panellists brought different perspectives, based on their work and experience, to bear on the issue of promoting safe and productive experiences on-line for children and youth, while addressing malicious, harmful or illegal behaviour on-line.

- Participants concurred that it is critical to mobilize various stakeholders, integrate diverse perspectives and address all the dimensions of the challenge in order to achieve results.
- More synergy is needed, with deeper understanding and cooperation between agencies.
- We need to reconcile freedom of access as well as responsibility.
- Industry has a responsibility to make the internet safer, but onus is on users as well.
- Stopping information does not solve the problem.
- We need to create an enabling platform, to embrace the technology and shape it in more creative ways. Input from the users, primarily from the youth is essential for the proper design and development of products that are used by them.
- We must create a culture of responsibility and digital citizenship, with rights and responsibilities online, just as in the off-line world.
- Strengthen national collaboration and coordination, institute legal measures, consistently advocate and raise awareness, enforce and monitor. In this regard recommendations from major international forums such as the world congress on sexual exploitation of children should be promoted and highlighted for states to ensure their implementation.
- Awareness of regional and cultural differences and consideration of social norms is imperative.
- We must look at the issue of empowerment and safety from the perspective of developing countries. They are focused on getting knowledge and catching up (deeper IT penetration). We need to find a balance between empowerment and safety.
- Education is important for users, parents, caregivers and educators. - Provide tools and resources to teach skills - Peer to peer methodology is effective - Empower older children to mentor the young - Learning needs to be cross-curricular and fun
- Provide clear legal basis in national legislations to investigate offences related to the sexual exploitation of children, including on Internet, and to hold offenders accountable.
- Efficient measures to be considered by all countries to prevent and combat sexual exploitation and sexual abuse of children, protect the rights of child victims and promote national and international co-operation.

Challenges:
- It is not so much a problem of money than a question of creating a culture of cooperation between people at national level. This can be done by bringing together all the key stakeholders who today are not used to discuss and coordinate their activities (NGOs, hotlines dealing with illegal content, industry and government, but also law enforcement, judges and prosecutors).
- Difficulties in implementing policies—no uniformity in approaches; those who monitor don't have child-friendly approaches; need better coordination between enforcers.
- Digital divide is widening between countries and between people.

- Children are not differentiating between off-line and on-line worlds.
- Addiction and psychological effects

Benefits:
- Benefits are multi-dimensional
- Economic development
- Cultural enrichment
- Potential of technology to make us more humane
- Sharing information between children can create a new sense of responsibility and engagement (example of an initiative on blood checks in the US)

Action Items:
- Reaffirm the need for national initiatives – experience and support from abroad can only help as much as there is a already rich debate in the country.
- Transfer knowledge and best practices
- Fellowship opportunities from developed countries to emerging knowledge societies, to form qualified cadres in internet safety
- Scholars from emerging knowledge societies to participate in international working groups when producing reports
- FOSI is developing a Global Resources Directory Portal (GRD)
- In order to put a comprehensive legislative framework in place that is internationally harmonized and permits efficient international cooperation, countries should be encouraged to make use of the relevant instruments developed by the Council of Europe - the Convention on the Protection of Children against Sexual Exploitation and Sexual Abuse (CETS 201) and the Convention on Cybercrime (CETS 185)
- The Council of Europe – through the Project on cybercrime – to continue supporting widely the strengthening of comprehensive legislation on cybercrime, data protection and protection of children against sexual exploitation and sexual abuse and to promote relevant instruments globally
- Call to add a clause to the Convention on the Rights of the Child (CRC) on on-line child protection
- Set standards
- Panellists continue to connect with each other and develop partnerships
- We must have political will and leadership

WS 105.   *Preserving Free Expression on the Internet and Protecting Children's Rights Online*

Report by: John Carr

Panellists: Dr. Alison Powell (Oxford Internet Institute); John Morris (Director, Center for Democracy and Technology); John Carr (European NGO Alliance for Child Safety Online); Bjorn-Erik Ludvigsen (CIRCAMP)

In much of the world, the internet is now an expected everywhere-always-on utility used for information gathering, communication and social networking.

Yet along with its incredible power to open access to knowledge, the same characteristics that make the internet so unique (its potential for openness, its facilitation of anonymity, and the proliferation of information and content across its platforms) create concerns that undesirable content is proliferating, and that children, in particular, are being exposed to specific risks (content, interactions) that are risky. This poses a conundrum: how to maintain the generative environment that inspires innovation and develops democracy, without increasing risk for the most vulnerable? How to design systems of governance that avoid unintended consequence?

Advocates of online child protection and freedom of expression share a deep-seated belief in the importance of protecting basic human rights. Yet these beliefs are often clouded by perceived (and real) opposition in the actual practice of law, policy, and regulation. This has restricted the policy options available for dealing with threats to both child safety and free speech online, and often resulted in these interests being portrayed as diametrically opposed.

Advocates on both sides of this debate first met in Oxford in October, 2009, to explore their different perspectives on these fundamental rights and to identify possible areas of agreement. By defining a new framework to discuss online child protection that rejects the current moral panics that have dominated the debate, and focuses instead on accurately defining risks in line with the evolving capacity of the child, participants were able to find much common ground. The most fruitful avenues came from calls for precision and transparency in policy responses that touch on these issues. Participants discussed how, by working together, both sides could advance their agendas and defend the rights of children while preventing child protection from being used as a strategic pretext for broader goals of censorship and repression.

As a follow up from this forum we conducted a roundtable workshop at the IGF in Sharm el Sheikh. We presented the major threads of the historic debate and then indicated ways that this debate can be expanded by mapping the common ground and continuing dissent between freedom of speech and child protection advocates. The workshop included an excellent discussion of the unintended consequences of poorly enacted legislation and poorly enacted technological regulation.

The ongoing importance of this topic was highlighted by the strong participation by a variety of stakeholders. As an exploratory or opening discussion between two sets of advocates who normally do not meet with each other, the value and importance of this workshop was widely recognized. It was agreed that ways should be found to continue the discussions. Perhaps at next year's IGF?

WS 106.   The Mobile Internet in Developing Countries:
           Child Safety Dimensions

Report by: John Carr

Moderator: Olivier Crépin-Leblond (ISOC England)

Panellists: Gitte Stald (Associate Professor, IT University of Copenhagen); Jonne
Soininen (Head of Internet Affairs, Nokia Siemens Networks); Rudi Vansnick
(Chair, ISOC Belgium); Anjan Bose (ICT Officer, ECPAT International); Ruben
Rodriguez (President, INHOPE, The International Association of Internet Hotlines)

It was noted that this session was the result of the merger of several
proposals, and that the title of the overall session had been changed. The
range of presentations reflected this. Whilst the first three speakers spoke
about the dangers of children accessing internet content, the last two speakers
concentrated their efforts on the use of new Internet technologies in the
context of sexual exploitation of children through the generation of
paedophile content, particularly in developing economies.

Gitte Stald: The mobile Internet takes the Internet to a new level of
portability. Use of the Mobile Internet is now increasing at a faster rate than
standard Internet connectivity using computers. In this field, technology in
developing countries is only two years behind technology in developed
countries.   Whilst most Internet access in the developed world takes place
using computers, the developing world is likely to access the Internet using
mobile devices. This is due to infrastructure reasons and cost, and means that
most children in the developing world will likely access the Internet through
a mobile device.

Jonne Soininen: Nokia has studied the Internet use on mobile phones and
over mobile networks for a long time. Obviously, Nokia has studied also
substantially how to keep children safe on-line, and what are the issues that
are faced by children and their parents when thinking about the Internet. The
issue of child safety online is no simple matter. This is trapped between
multiple gaps that complicate the matters. These are the generation gap,
technology gap, and different cultural gaps. As the parent-child relationship
should be based on trust, and only works well when trust exists, when the
trust deteriorates the whole normal upbringing is at risk. This is especially
noticeable in connection with the Internet. Parents may not have the ability to
help their children to understand the risks of the Internet. Despite the risks of
the Internet, there are many very positive new things coming from the
Internet that were not possible before. These can also help to deal with issues,
which could not be dealt properly before the ability to have digital options to
discuss issues that children feel they cannot discuss with their own parents.

Nokia has been studying different approaches to deal with the child safety
issues. With an issue as complex as child safety, it is clear that there is no
"silver bullet", and definitely technology solutions - in form of filtering or
other means - cannot answer the question alone. The complexities and the
different sides of the issue are just not possible to teach for a machine or
software to handle adequately. In addition, many of the technical solutions

can be circumvented. As the children are mostly more technically skilled than their parents, the parents may not even notice that the technical safeguards have been lifted. Thus, the parents cannot push the responsibility of being a parent onto any technology. Nokia believes that the right approach of keeping children safe is to educate the parents, and also the children about the capabilities of the devices and the right way of using the Internet. Practically, different actions have been taken ranging from making the consumers fully aware of the capabilities and the potential of Nokia devices, to contributing to activities that teach the children how to constructively use the Internet. A practical example of the later is the "Hiiripiiri" (www.hiiripiiri.fi) project, which has generated educational material provided to teachers to teach for young children to be used in ICT, media and online safety education. Nokia knows that building the needed trust is a challenging and difficult matter, where both the children and their parents have to learn. However, over time the trust will develop. Trust is like Rome, and it was not built in a day.

Rudi Vansnick: Many parents are clueless and many find it very difficult to effectively engage in their children's on-line activity. The current assumption that end users are responsible for security has been seen by many as inefficient and unrealistic. With ICT use now being more mobile supervision from parents/carers is harder. Also young children will not disclose if something goes wrong. Protecting children from accessing harmful or illegal content is only possible if parents are able to effectively use the appropriate technical solutions. The first step is good communication between children and their parents. In many cases we see that child victims are from social environments where knowledge and awareness of the dangers are non-existent. It seems as though getting tools and technical solutions to those parents is even more difficult than children accessing harmful and illegal content. Knowing this, it is very clear that other actions should be considered in order to make every parent, or any other person having the responsibility to protect children, aware of the possible danger while having access to the WWW. We may not consider having fulfilled that task by just putting banners, buttons and whatsoever information on a (web)page. The Safe Chat project for instance has proved children will try to avoid being controlled and will use the non-safe access to that chat room. Moreover, the offender will also try to get access to the Safe chat environment. Young children have a lifetime to use a particular brand and the reputation of those providing services is crucial not just to parents but to children who one day will grow and have children of their own. Companies have an opportunity to give parents more choice and see safety as a unique selling point. Parents will choose products that they see as safe.

Furthermore many service and mobile providers are global players and operate in less well developed areas where there is an absence of media literacy, and child protection standards, so it is especially important to recognise what help young children need in this context. This reflects the fact that this is very much a Corporate Social responsibility. There are a range of issues which need to be addressed:

3Cs: Contact, Content, Commercial agreements

3Gs: Gaming, Gambling, Girls

Schools have the possibility to install special software being some kind of electronic babysitting. Net nanny and Cyberpatrol are good samples. However no standard definition of usage has been done by government or by any official body. There is widespread support for some form of standardization for internet filtering tools among consumer organizations and other organizations involved in internet safety issues in Europe. Test results from internet content filter projects have shown considerable variation in the technical capability of the products and in the performance of other variables such as ease of use, security and over blocking. There are no standard test protocols or agreed processes for evaluating this software. Each test project has devised its own test method and evaluation system. According to stakeholders consulted, standardization would:

- Help consumers avoid the worst products more easily
- Help raise awareness of filters in countries where they are hardly used
- Help non-governmental organizations give advice to families about how best to use the internet safely
- Give consumers added confidence.

Anjan Bose: The mobile phone industry like other technical developments has to undergo research and development for development of their products. In practice, every bit of innovation is tried out for possible failures and design changes are made in advance to make the product successful. Similar approach should be taken for impact on the lives of children, particularly when they are a significant users of mobile devices worldwide. Applications developed for mobile phones should take care in advance about the possible child protection issues and in this regard, collaboration with specialized child protection agencies who are experienced on the issues that brings risk to children on-line, should be in place. Development of features and standards such as customized buttons on the mobile phones (that can be set by the service providers) for reporting easily to dedicated hotlines is one feature that can be easily added. Moreover, mobile service providers should have content filtering in place to make sure that already blacklisted sites (provided by the respective law enforcement of that country) are not accessible through the mobile phones.

What happens when the mobile phone is used for uploading illegal content? With travelling child sex offenders, who may exploit a child at a destination country may also record the scene of the offence, very conveniently on his/her mobile phone and then upload them to sites on-line with a few clicks. With the advent of 3G networks (even in less developed countries and developing countries in the East Asia Pacific for example) and emerging 4G mobile networks, that are going to provide broadband access through wireless, the implications on child protection is huge. Unless the users are registered for the service and the on-line transactions are logged, it will create an environment which perpetrators can take advantage of for exploiting children. Countries should have mechanisms in place, whereby an integrated system of reporting, take down of content and at the same time support and rehabilitation services for the victims should be in place. In many countries, reporting incidents directly to a national hotline through the cell phone has not yet been set up. With the growing popularity of the mobile Internet, it is essential that this channel should also be added for existing hotlines.

Clearly, what is illegal somewhere is sometimes legal elsewhere, so how do we tackle this? In some countries, there are no laws or definitions about child pornography and often this is misused, not only by producing images but also hosting content in such jurisdictions. Educating children and young people is of course of paramount importance to protect them from exploitation online. But every stakeholder in the society must play their part and assume responsibility to make sure that the framework for protection is in place. Mobile network providers can also come up with interesting and innovative ideas such as downloadable ring tones, animations etc. that alerts and creates awareness amongst young people, use SMS broadcast for promoting events on online safety, pass on useful safety tips and at the same time alert people against the criminal nature of the offences of sexual exploitation against children on-line and the seriousness of such crimes.

Ruben Rodriguez: Hotlines can be created to report illegal content, but in areas of the world where there is no legislation, what can a hotline do? Further progress is required worldwide to harmonize the legislation against child pornography in many countries. Industry is in a unique position to help the development in emerging countries, all countries are embracing electronic infrastructure development, why not lead in the efforts to harmonize legislation to safeguard the use of their services? Many models are already being implemented, these examples should be highlighted to emerging countries as best practices.

WS 151.   Cyber Security R&D: Developing a Vision and Road Map

Report by: Rajeshree Dutta Kumar

Organizer: Centre for Science, Development and Media Studies, (CSDMS)

Panellists: Tulika Pandey (Additional Director, Ministry of Communications & IT, Department of Information Technology, Government of India); Tracy Hackshaw (Internet Society Ambassador, Republic of Trinidad & Tobago); Sherif El Tokali (Assistant Resident Representative, Poverty Reduction, MDGs & Private Sector Team Leader, UNDP, Egypt)

The purpose of the Workshop was to primarily identify the research needs and opportunities associated with Cybersecurity, focusing especially discussion on those needs associated with supercomputing, user facilities, high-speed networks, laboratories, and other open collaborative science stakeholders. The Workshop sought to create a proactive and forward-looking approach to research and development in the Cybersecurity area from a rigorous analytical and technical basis that would stimulate new open science research directions and have a lasting impact on Cybersecurity.

Key Goals:
- Identify the research needs and opportunities associated with cybersecurity for science

- Gather future science cybersecurity priorities
- Develop a list of research and development priorities for Cybersecurity R&D
- Produce a report describing the results of the discussion, which will provide further impetus to the researchers and the studies in the field.

Ms Tulika Pandey opened the session by providing the platform for discussion. Ms. Pandey delved into the aspects of Cyber-security vis-à-vis security in the traditional environment. She also elaborated on the overlapping facets of Security, Information Security, Cyber Security and Network Security. Ms Pandey further elaborated on some of the security assumptions in IPv6 and urged network engineers and researchers to do an in-depth study of the IPv6 protocol for its security loopholes. She also listed some of the aspects possible security lapses that could occur in IPv6 deployment if the security requirements were not sensitively implemented.

While delving into the aspects of Cyber-security vis-à-vis security in the traditional environment she elaborated on the structural Planes and Layers of the Internet where the principles and policies of security whether technological or legal needed careful implementation. Emphasizing on the increasing critical need to develop new R&D Agenda for Cyber-security, she reasoned out the Why with the following observations on the recent Information and Communication exchange trends worldwide?

- Monitoring and control of various core infrastructure like electricity, water supply, and medical services are getting computerised, increasing their dependency on ICT
- The emerging information infrastructure differ radically in scale, connectivity and dependencies from traditional structures
- Communication systems are interconnected resulting in global inter-dependencies and vulnerabilities including threats to the national systems
- Protective measures require continual technological improvements and new approaches to minimize threats on ICT.

Tracy Hackshaw sought to tackle the issue from a non-technical perspective. He also sought to highlight the perhaps unique needs of Small Island Developing States (SIDS) where Cyber-security issues may have deeper and somewhat submerged dimensions, therefore requiring a multidisciplinary approach to R&D. Mr. Hackshaw's presentation argued, that in order to develop an effective global Cybersecurity R&D Agenda, the unique needs of SIDS needed to be factored in which include, inter alia:

- Social & economic dislocation
- Cultural Contestations
- Subjectivity of security
- High technological barriers

By referring to the case of Trinidad & Tobago, he suggested that the major research question for Cybersecurity first recognize that 'Technology WILL advance and along with it, the technological sophistication of Cybersecurity threats – this is certain'. With this recognition, we necessarily have to ask ourselves "How do we reconcile the fact the human behaviour is inherently unpredictable and irrational, despite the best social & economic theories to predict same?' Mr. Hackshaw's recommendations therefore were to develop a

Research Agenda, which engaged BOTH the qualitative and quantitative study of issues surrounding four (4) key dynamics:

Sherif El Tokali of the UNDP Country Office in Egypt presented a detailed examination of the current trends within the Cybersecurity R&D sphere and by linking the Egyptian experience with the wider international sphere also called for a multidimensional approach to counter Cybercrime. Sherif identified three (3) broad areas of Cybersecurity threats:

- Threats to individual users through viruses or identity theft, spam, spyware or pop-ups;
- Threats to businesses, governments or other organisations through exploitation of vulnerabilities in their data storage, industrial espionage, system downtime, etc. and;
- Threats to critical public infrastructures, including electronic communication networks, financial systems, emergency services, navigation systems, electrical power grids, air traffic control, and water control systems etc.

Opening the panel session with a call for a more localised approach to Cybersecurity, the discussions were actively ensued by representatives from countries like Mauritius, Mexico, Trinidad & Tobago and Egypt. The discussions moved to the peculiar issues in dealing with Cybercrime and Cybersecurity in their jurisdiction. Some of the core themes included:

- The need for international capacity building and knowledge sharing in the area of Cybercrime/Cybersecurity policies and legislation - reference was made to the toolkits and model laws produced by the ITU and Commonwealth Secretariat (for example);
- Knowledge sharing regarding practical solutions employed by the public and private sectors to combat Computer Misuse and Credit Card Fraud for example. The major or central outcome of the Workshop that emerged was the 'need to examine Cybercrime from a non-traditional viewpoint. Cybercrime and Cybersecurity are uniquely different from traditional crime and different approaches are required to not only protect, but also to develop proactive strategies to mitigate the potential risks.

WS 160.   *Securing Cyberspace: Strategy for the Future*

Report by: Ms. Liesyl Franz

Moderator: Ms. Liesyl Franz (TechAmerica)

Panellists: Mr. Dean Ceulic (ECO); Ms. Lesley Cowley (Nominet); Ms. Susan Daley (Symantec); Mr. Michel van Eeten (Delft University; Internet Governance Project); Mr. Roelof Meijer (SIDN); Rt. Hon. Alun Michael (Member, UK Parliament); Ms. Alice Munyua (Kenya Communications Commission); Mr. Wout de Natris (OPTA; London Action Plan); Dr. Khaled E. A. Ngem (IBM Egypt); Mr. Roland Perry (RIPE)

Securing cyberspace impacts civil society, the private sector, and governments. Users face numerous threats, e.g., crimes conducted over the Internet, compromised infrastructure, and malware. In many cases, resolution of cyber crime and security problems is achieved through national and transnational multi-stakeholder collaboration. Private sector actors and law enforcement actors often work together, recognizing the benefits of these lightweight and flexible cooperative arrangements to address cyber security and crime.

However, these efforts are not without challenges, including sharing information in trusted environments, insufficient cooperation mechanisms, and balancing privacy and free expression. Some governments also feel vulnerable and view the functioning of the Internet as a matter of national security that cannot be left to non-governmental bodies. Nationally, there are efforts to build Computer Security Incident Response Teams, identify leaders for cyber security, establish cyber security organizations and/or strategies, and improve the public-private partnership, while continuing to cooperate effectively internationally.

This workshop was intended to examine different initiatives dealing with cyber crime and cyber security issues, the alternative approaches they can take, and the different opportunities and challenges these approaches might present.
DNS and IP address registries, ISPs, software providers, legislative bodies, regulators and academia were represented, and shared their perspectives on efforts to address problems. While there are a range of domestic and transnational cooperative and collaborative multi-stakeholder efforts, numerous challenges remain including information sharing in trusted environments, insufficient cooperation mechanisms, unclear incentive structures, and achieving balance – or synergy – between security, privacy, and free expression.

Conclusions included:

Continued need for multi-stakeholder cooperation
- In a constantly changing online threat environment we cannot find solutions alone and will need to continue to learn to work together, learn from each other, exchange information and create best practices with industry, police and justice, ISPs, RIR and LIR, governments, enforcement agencies.

Transnational scope of the problem
- Collaboration is necessary and cannot be limited to a national level because of global dimension of internet. Bad actors are very often outside jurisdiction or treaties, move from one jurisdiction/country/domain to the next, or operate from "passive" jurisdictions. Collaboration enables preventive measures, sharing expertise, access to information.

Social dimensions (legal, economic) of the problem
- Addressing cyber security cannot not be just about technology. It cannot be solved simply by technological solutions, or solely by on organization/country – a transnational approach is needed that addresses people issues, effective policies/procedures, and role of technology (people, process, technology).

- There is a need for an appropriate and flexible legal and regulatory framework/environment that recognizes important role of collaboration/co-operation and can also adapt to changes in the threat landscape and recognize the shifting nature of cyber security/cyber space.
- Cyber security is a shared responsibility of all actors; each his own role in his own capacity. Self regulation does not mean no regulation, it means regulating oneself, assuming responsibility. As in the physical world, one cannot simply leave security to the authorities only.
- We appreciate the multi-stakeholder and self regulatory characteristic of the Internet which is in need of a wide cooperative approach which definitely must include all affected authorities. It's not always easy for legal authorities to sometimes leave the path of sovereignty, but it's the only way to go in the Internet.
- While continued and improved collaboration efforts are needed, IGP's Michel van Eeten suggested that none of the current efforts scale to level of current problems faced. Van Eeten also startled the group by suggesting that the efforts of formal law enforcement agencies in cyberspace were of limited relevance in creating a secure Internet. Instead of myopically focusing on making the Internet secure, he said there should be more efforts to find optimal levels of insecurity, with solutions taking into the account the benefit-cost incentives of each actor.

WS 206. Domain Name Use: Theft, Threats and Solutions

Report by: Ram Mohan

Moderator: Jim Galvin, Afilias (SSAC)

Panellists: Patrik Fältström (Cisco, Member of the SSAC); Pavan Duggal (Cybercrime Expert and Cyberlaws.net); Greg Rattray (ICANN and Member of the SSAC); Stefano Trumpy (IIT, Italy representative to ICANN's Government Advisory Committee and Member of the SSAC)

The loss or unauthorized modification of a domain name can have a lasting and material impact on the domain name owner and Internet user. Domain name owners may lose an established online identity and be exposed to extortion by name speculators. The loss of an active website and email can disrupt or severely impact the business and operations of the domain name owner, including (but not limited to) denial and theft of electronic mail services, unauthorized disclosure of information through phishing web sites and traffic inspection (eavesdropping), and damage to the domain name owner's reputation and brand through web site defacement.

The Security and Stability Advisory Committee (SSAC) advises the ICANN board and the community on matters relating to the security and integrity of the Internet's naming and address allocation systems. The Committee's membership draws from the commercial, not-for-profit, academic and law enforcement sectors, has broad geographic representation, and includes all segments of the Domain Name System (DNS) community. The Committee includes root server operators, generic and country code registry operators, registrars and address registries, and network security experts.

Patrik Fältström's primary point was that domain name hijacking is an economically interesting activity, i.e., where there is domain name hijacking there exist business cases for the bad behaviour. He described a number of ways with which a domain name could be hijacked. He pointed out that DNSSEC helps many of these cases and asserted that there are examples in Sweden where attacks were mitigated when the ISP was validating DNSSEC signatures. He closed by describing what can be done with a domain name when it has been hijacked, e.g., click-through advertising, stealing data, fraud, Trojan infections, and being added to a BOTNET.

Jim Galvin gave a detailed presentation of SAC040. The SSAC recommendations published in the report are as follows.

- Registrars are encouraged to offer stronger levels of protection against domain name registration service exploitation or misuse for customers who want or need them. Measures enumerated in this report can be offered as optional services to customers, individually or bundled.
- Registrars should expand existing FAQs and education programs to include security awareness. Registrars should make information concerning the measures they take to protect domain registration accounts more accessible to customers so that they can make informed decisions regarding protective measures when they choose a registrar.
- Registrars should consider the value of voluntarily having an independent security audit performed on their operations as a component of their security due diligence.
- ICANN and registrars should study whether registration services would generally improve and registrants would benefit from having an approved independent third party that will, at the request of a registrar, perform a security audit based on a prescribed set of security measures. ICANN would distinguish registrars that voluntarily satisfy the benchmarks of this security audit through a trusted security mark program that is implemented in a manner similar to the way that SSL certificate issuing authorities provide trust marks or seals for web site operators who satisfy that authority's security criteria.

Pavan Duggal described a contrived example of Meow, the cat that lives in the dirty corner of the street, creating a domain name. He used this to emphasize the deficiencies in the registration system today. He observed that a bad actor can conduct a lot of illegal activity without much fear of retribution by simply registering domain names. He identified four major problems with the system today.

- Inaccurate registration information is an international problem. The introduction of the UDRP was a watershed event in 1999. However, its usefulness is limited to protecting intellectual property interests. This problem is much broader than that.
- The privacy of Whois information needs to be considered. Whois information can be monetized. Consider the evolution taking place in social networks. How do we protect registrants, particularly when it is required by national legislation?
- Registrants need effective legal remedies when their domain name has been abused and the UDRP is not an appropriate remedy.

- IDNs add yet another dimension to the issues and challenges facing the use of domain names.

What we need is an international best practices for a legal structure to deal with domain name issues. ICANN can help in at least two specific ways. First, we need a security audit of registrars and registries. The system today is such that once you are a registry or registrar, you will always remain one. Second, the anti-fraud practices of registrars need to be improved.

Greg Rattray used the analogy that the Internet as a whole is an eco-system of which the DNS is just a part. There are a lot of complex interactions in the system. He focused on three main points.
- The DNS is vulnerable to being corrupted and thus leading users astray. We need to do more to prevent data corruption to protect users.
- The DNS has to be available. ICANN is focusing attention in the less technically aware regions of the world to make sure that TLDs in particular understand the technical threats and the remediation. They are working with ISOC to provide technical training and human capital building.
- The DNS is used to help BOTNETs grow and to command and control those BOTNETS - the DNS enables malicious activity. ICANN recognizes this as area in which they need to continue to work.

Stefano Trumpy summarized 5 key points for the closing.
- ICANN should participate in security activities. It derives most of revenue from the DNS and its related system so working to protect it and improve it is appropriate.
- We need DNSSEC as a tool to protect users. Adoption is accelerating and hopefully that will continue.
- ICANN should address the issue of Whois accuracy.
- ICANN should add ensuring security to its registrar contracts. We need registrars to increase sensitivity to security with registrants and to increase their cooperation during security events
- ICANN should provide best practices for ccTLDs and their registries, and create a campaign to get acceptance of them.

BPF 210. Child Online Safety on Developing Countries: Strategies for Moving Forward

Chair: *Antonio Alberto Valente Tavares (Presidente of NIC.br Board of Directors)*

Panellists: Cláudio Soares Lopes (General Attorney at Rio de Janeiro State); Andre Estevao Ubaldino Pereira (Prosecutor at Minas Gerais State and Brazilian Federal Senate Special Adviser); Carlos Eduardo Miguel Sobral (Chief of the Brazilian Federal Police Cybercrime Unit); Stenio Sousa Santos (Chief of the Brazilian Federal Police Child Sexual Abuse and Hate Crimes Unit); Izabela Piuzana Mucida (Federal police officer); Priscila Costa Schreiner (Coordinator of Cybercrime Unit at Federal Public Attorney Office in Sao Paulo); Rodrigo Nejm (Psychologist, SaferNet's awareness Director); Carlos Gregorio (II Justicia Senior Researcher, Argentine); Thiago Tavares Nunes de Oliveira (Founder and President of SaferNet Brazil)

The aim of this workshop was to examine the growth of child sexual abuse on the internet, evaluate the effectiveness of various measures now available to combat it, identify and discuss public policies, judicial cooperation and procedures in a multi-stakeholder approach and to consider what further steps need to be taken, particularly at an international level, within a developing-nation perspective.

Recommendations for Industry

In order to eradicate child pornography on the Internet, the industry must, as part of a joint effort of all responsible parties, commit to a minimum of:

- Notifying the corresponding authorities of any occurrences of child pornography detected in the profiles of users of online social networks, in order to enable the necessary investigations and actions.
- Preserving all data necessary for investigations for a minimum of six months or otherwise surrender such data to the corresponding officials, upon court authorizations.
- 1.3. Preserving the content published by users of social networks for an equal period of time, and surrender such content to the appropriate officials, upon court authorization.
- Fully complying with national laws regarding cybercrimes committed by citizens of the countries of Latin America and the Caribbean, or through Internet connections from these national jurisdictions.
- Changing customer service so that it can respond within a reasonable period of time to all claims made by email or conventional mail by individuals who have been victimized by false or offensive communities.
- Developing efficient filtering technology and implementing the involvement of human site administrators in order to prevent the publication of child pornography photographs and images in online social network services.
- Developing tools to enable hotlines to which children and adolescents can direct reports in order to allow the company's officers to analyze and remove any illegal content and inform the appropriate authorities about the inclusion in such contents of signs of child pornography, racism or other hate crimes, preserving all related evidence.
- Removing illegal content, whether by court order or upon the request of the relevant official authorities, while preserving the data necessary for identifying the authors of such content.
- Developing tools for communications with the relevant authorities in order to facilitate the management of reports, and the implementation of requests for the removal and preservation of data.
- Properly informing national users on the common crimes committed in online social networks (child pornography, hate crimes, and attacks upon reputation, among others).
- Developing educational campaigns on the law abiding and safe use of the Internet and on- line social networks.
- Financing the publication and distribution of flyers to children and adolescents in public schools containing information concerning the safe use of the Internet and social networks.

- Maintaining links in the sites of online social networks to sites for reporting problems or hotlines for the aid of children and adolescents.

Recommendations Regarding Public Policies

The need for the best interests of children to be the guiding principle for all measures adopted on this issue is to be borne in mind, specifically in the development of public policies intended to regulate online social networks. The implementation of the following public policies is recommended:

- Definition of response mechanisms for assisting the victims of abuse in the Information and Knowledge Society, particularly on the Internet or in online social networks. Likewise, information systems are to be created for providing assistance and quick support to children and adolescents concerned in any way about content on the Internet or in online social networks. For this purpose, it is possible to create mechanisms to aid online reporting, through toll free numbers, service centres, and so on.
- Definition of protocols to channel the illegal content that is reported.
- Creation of regional and international mechanisms for sharing information reported by private parties regarding these occurrences, in real time, in order to promptly generate protective policies and mechanisms. This is due to the type of problems involved in online social networks, which are often dispersed and not fully detected.
- Promotion of efforts to raise public awareness and to spread information through the press, the mass media, as well as through the social networks themselves, among others, all of which are effective means for promoting the responsible and safe use of tools of the Information and Knowledge Society.
- Promote the commitment and participation of public and private associations, as well as national networks of centres for accessing the Internet (if any), to ensure their participation in protection and in alert campaigns on the possibilities and risks involved in the Internet and online social networks.
- To promote specialized research in order to develop appropriate public policy. With regard to the online behaviour of children and adolescents, it is particularly recommended that research be conducted into the roles they play in the acquisition, production, storage and reproduction of illegal content, the protection measures they develop, the individual and collective motivations for such behaviours, as well as the actual dangers they face in the Information and Knowledge Society.

Recommendations for States and Education Institutions for Prevention and for Educating Children and Adolescents

Prevention is a priority —regardless of the policy, regulation or legal approach- in addressing through education the aspects identified as risks of the Information and Knowledge Society, specifically the Internet and digital social networks. This effort must include the active participation of children and adolescents themselves, as well as their elders and other individuals in charge of their care and teachers, and consideration of the best interests of children and adolescents as the basic principle. For this purpose, the following recommendations are to be considered:

- State and educational institutions must consider the role played by parents, or those responsible for the care of children and adolescents, in the education of the latter, including on the responsible and safe use of the Internet and online social networks. It is the duty of the State and educational institutions to provide information and to strengthen the capability of parents and responsible adults about the potential risk to which children and adolescents are exposed in digital environments.
- All measures involving the control of communications must respect the proportionality principle, and it must be determined that they are intended to protect and guarantee rights in a manner appropriate to this objective, and that no other measures exist for attaining the same results that would be less restrictive of such rights.

Children and adolescents must be clearly informed that the Internet is in no way a space free of rules, punishment or responsibility. They should be warned against believing that everything is allowed on the Internet, because each and every action will necessarily have consequences. They should be instructed in the responsible and safe use of the Internet and online social networks, specifically in regard to:

- Anonymous participation and the use of pseudonyms are both possible in online social networks. The process of education must reflect on the positive aspects of using pseudonyms as a means of protection, and the responsible use thereof, which includes not using them to deceive or confuse others regarding an actual identity, among other concerns. Children and adolescents must be alerted to the possibility of their being in communication or sharing information with someone in fact different from the individual they think they are in communication with. They must also be cautioned about the possibility of phishing allowed by anonymous participation and the use of pseudonyms.
- In the process of education it is necessary to emphasize, among other things, the respect for the personal affairs, privacy and reputation of others. It is important for children and adolescents to be aware that any data they reveal may end up endangering their rights and the rights of third parties.
- Children and adolescents must be informed that distributing content banned by local and regional laws (particularly child pornography), harassment (particularly sexual harassment), discrimination, the promotion of racial hate, defamation, and violence, among others are not legal on the Internet or in online social networks and are liable to legal punishment.
- The learning process must provide knowledge regarding the responsible and safe use by children and adolescents of privacy and safety policies and alerts included in access instruments and websites frequently used by children and adolescents, such as online social networks.
- Education policies expressed in language consistent with the age of children and adolescents must include an informational and developmental strategy to aid children and adolescents in managing the potential risks derived from the Information and Knowledge Society, specifically with regard to the use of the Internet and online social networks.

- Information must be provided about protection mechanisms and the civil, criminal and administrative liability for the violation of one's own rights or the rights of others on the net.
- Warnings must be made about the dangers of identity theft and impersonation that exist in online environments and that can lead to deceit.
- It is necessary to explain to children and adolescents in an easily understood manner the spirit of legislation concerning the protection of personal data and privacy so that they may grasp the importance of respect for the privacy of the personal information of each individual, themselves included.
- Education is necessary in regard to the uncertainty of the veracity of content and the validation of data sources. Children and adolescents must be trained and taught how to search for and be discerning about sources.

It is particularly recommended that a comprehensive and continuing education about the Information and Knowledge Society be developed, especially on the responsible and safe use of the Internet and online social networks and in particular by means of:
- Including, in all syllabuses at all educational levels, basic information on the significance of privacy and the protection of personal data and other aspects as mentioned in item three.
- Producing educational material, specifically, audio-visual material, web pages and interactive tools (such as online games) showing both the potential and risk involved. Such material must include information related to the mechanisms for the protection of rights. The nature of these topics and materials calls for the participation of and discussion by all parties involved in order to take into consideration local and cultural peculiarities.
- Teachers must be trained in how to enable the discussion and place the advantages and risks of social networks of the Information and Knowledge Society in due context, with the possible support of authorities responsible for the protection of personal data and any and all entities that work on that subject in different countries.
- The education authorities supported by authorities responsible for the protection of data (if any), the academic sector, civil society organizations, private sector entities, and (when necessary) with the aid of international cooperation must assist educators and support all work in the areas mentioned.

The appropriate authorities should establish guidelines by which schools and other educational programs can resolve incidents that arise in the usage of the Internet and online social networks by children and adolescents, using these incidents as an opportunity to educate but always bearing in mind the best interests of the children involved and without violating their rights or entitlements, in particular their right to education.

The next IGF in Vilnius should examine, within a developing nation perspective, what further steps need to be taken to implement these best practices recommendations to protect children on the Internet.

WS 257. The Privacy and Security Implications of Cloud Computing

Report by: Katitza Rodriguez and Graciela Selaimen

Moderator: Cristos Velasco (North American Consumer Project on Electronic Commerce)

Panellists: Pamela Harbour (Commissioner, US Federal Trade Commission); Joseph Alhadeff, (Vice President for Global Public Policy and Chief Privacy Officer, Oracle Corporation, Chair of BIAC's Information, Computer and Communication Committee, Vice Chair of ICC's Commission on E-Business, IT and Telecoms); Bruce Schneier (Chief Security Technology Officer of British Telecom); Alexander Seger (Head of the Economic Crime Division, Council of Europe); Hong Xue (Professor of Law and Director of the Institute for the Internet Policy & Law at Beijing Normal University); Michael Thatcher (Regional Technology Officer, MEA, Microsoft Corporation); Laurent Bernat (Principal Assistant within the Science, Technology and Industry Branch of the Organization for Economic Cooperation and Development); Simon Davies (Director, Privacy International); Jean-Marc Dinant (Expert Council of Europe, Researcher, Research Centre on IT and Law of the University of Namur)

Cloud Computing and its privacy and security implications are at the forefront of the news media debate around the world. However, only regulators from developed countries are discussing its privacy and security policy implications. In 2008-2009, the US Federal Trade Commission and The Ontario Privacy Commissioner discussed the matter. The Council of Europe raised the question of cloud computing, jurisdiction and international law enforcement at its Octopus conference in March 2009. The OECD discussed the subject during a workshop organized by the Committee for Information, Computer and Communications Policy (ICCP) in October 2009. Civil Society has advocated for strong data protection laws and heightened enforcement, while business interests dispute whether regulation is necessary and law enforcement agencies highlight the challenges for investigating cybercrime and securing electronic evidence when the data is stored in the cloud. Those services are being used all over the world. However, there is a lack of understanding of the issue and a lack of participation by stakeholders from developing countries in this debate.

Cloud Computing: your information on someone else's hard drives (Schneier)

Clouds: What's new is old is new, Mr. Joseph Alhadeff started his presentation by affirming that Cloud Computing is a concept that is very difficult to define. He offered some definitions and an overview of the taxonomy of cloud computing, and its evolution over the years. "Cloud computing is a model for enabling convenient, on-demand network access to a shared pool of configurable computing resources (e.g., networks, servers, storage, applications, and services) that can be rapidly provisioned and released with minimal management effort or service provider interaction." (NIST Definition v5).

Is cloud computing a new paradigm? Cloud computing is "an amalgam of existing technologies." "Some use models, coupled with scope of availability and ease of use is part of what is new (Alhadeff). Bruce Schneier started by posing a piercing assertion: cloud-computing means "your information on someone's else hard drives." "Cloud computing is all about outsourcing."

Benefits and Challenges

Cloud computing services help reduce capital expenditures; you can pay for what you use, release resources when not needed, turn your organization's fixed cost into a variable cost, and may improve security. (Alhadeff) There are several risks involved in cloud computing. If a company disappears: who will end up with my data? There are political risks because now our data is moving across international borders: where is my data, what sort of law exists, etc. (Schneier) Michael Thatcher, Microsoft's Regional Technology Officer for the Middle East and Africa, stressed that the challenges are the political and legal strategies, and models and practices necessary to handle the global databases.

Regulatory Framework

Users frequently pose standard questions such as "where is my information hosted?" and "who controls it?" Who has access? How is being used? Who is it being shared with? Who is looking out for my interests? The answers to these questions raise a reflection on "what are good security and privacy policies, practices and controls that should be put into practice in cloud computing?" (Alhadeff) All the choices involved in computing today are about trust. Trust your hardware, software, and operating system, your vendors. In this regard, reputation is essential, and companies have to compete for reputation, since it's based on reputation that users will make decisions. (Schneier) Thatcher posed another question: how do we actually handle the global data flows? What are the agreements that we abide by? Who is processing that personal data and who is actually controlling the processing of that data? Are you controller or a processor? Who is ultimately responsible for the protection of my data at the time that someone gets it?

Users are becoming publishers, content creators, and application developers: Is it appropriate to apply today's regulatory paradigms to those individuals when acting in that capacity? "When you think about the cloud, the cloud is the ultimate definition of an ecosystem. How is accountability established in the ecosystem? How do we map today's norms in a cloud - which is not a new set of technology or a new set of issues but perhaps a new application of those issues in the way that technology is deployed?" (Alhadeff).

Alexander Seger stressed the urgent need for effective law enforcement mechanisms to deal with issues of security and privacy in regards to data stored in the cloud. For him, it's necessary to develop international standards on law enforcement access to that data. There is also a need to establish globally trusted privacy and data protection standards, like Privacy Convention 108, which is open to any country to accede. In Seger's opinion, a cloud provider that cannot guarantee data protection and privacy standards as well as procedural safeguards will have a competitive disadvantage. There is a lack of awareness by the users in regards to what might possibly happen with one's data stored in the clouds, Pamela Harbour added. The possibilities of use of personal data for marketing purposes, for example, is one of the threats that users may not be aware of - in the Commissioners' opinion, the users still don't have enough information to make meaningful decisions. Ms. Harbour also stressed that cloud computing exacerbates potential security problems and claimed that in this context, responsibility and accountability must be more assured than ever. She explained that in the US, the FTC holds business accountable - including for actions of third parties, although ISPs frequently claim they have no direct responsibility for third parties. The Commissioner also reminded the audience that privacy and security form an important dimension of competition and stressed that adequate information for the users is essential.

Laurent Bernat presented a definition of cloud computing and listed some of its benefits and its facilitation to innovation. However, Bernat also offered a view of the issues raised by cloud computing, and, regarding those that are directly related to privacy and security, he showed how cloud computing magnifies cross-border privacy issues, especially stressing the fact that laws are inherently local, and the cloud is inherently global. Bernat also explained that part of the OECD work on this theme is dedicated to the reflection on how to turn security and privacy into a competitive advantage to the market rather than a showstopper. For him, part of the answer to this challenge relies on the development of innovative policing models and international cooperation and dialogue.

The next panellist was Hong Xue. She raised the importance of taking into account, in discussions on cloud computing, the perspective of developing countries - and remarked that the specific case of China, with its peculiarities regarding Internet regulation, is especially interesting to analyze. Xue stressed the fact that cloud computing is an important application in the Chinese Internet, in a country with a huge market and population. However, there is no real cloud computing system capable of ensuring the privacy of the user. Simon Davies started his presentation by remarking that cloud computing is a complex issue that raises additional concerns in comparison with other computational systems. According to Davies, when you start to fragment any service or any industry, transparency and accountability drop. Moreover, in regard to cloud computing, massive jurisdictional issues arise. As a result, unless there can be some means of ensuring transparency and accountability, cloud computing is something that essentially offers an extraordinary danger to the rights of the consumers.

Jean-Marc Dinant was the last panellist to speak, and provoked a reflection on the distinction between access providers and service providers. Dinant reminded the audience that the storage of data is an obligation only for access providers - however, service providers, which may harm the general principle of telecommunications secrecy, are also performing it. Dinant compared all the data stored by Google - a service which is used by 88% of the online population, to "the dark hole of the Internet," stressing that much more than what is acceptably allowed for any ISP is now being allowed for one single private company which provides online services.
A discussion took place on the limits and possibilities of different actors in the Internet market, especially small companies. Most of the panellist agreed that transparency, accountability and the ability to build trust among consumers would be the most important differentials in a market that is still being

formed. The importance of consumer protection was a concern shared by all the panellists. The role of regulation and specialized bodies able to deal with cross border disputes was mentioned, particularly when consumers cannot negotiate with international service providers. The fairness of this relationship was a concern for many of the presenters. Another point stressed by the panellists was the right of consumers to hold control over their personal data - what can be ensured by technological features and models, and on the other hand what needs to be guaranteed by legislation and regulation.

There was also an agreement that cloud computing magnifies some of the complex cross border issues, and, in this sense, the improvement of cross border cooperation, dialogue among countries on privacy protection and coherent e-commerce guidelines are very necessary. Also, international privacy agreements and standards are now more important than ever. The Civil Society Madrid Declaration was mentioned as a source of principles that could solve some of the cloud computing issues. Other legal issues on cloud computing arose in the discussion, such as international data transfers, consistent treatment, lawful access issues, export control, data breach notification laws, data retention laws, e-discovery, government regulation, jurisdiction and conflict of laws (Alhadeff). On the contractual side: Data ownership, intellectual property rights, limitation of liability issues, SLAs, Indemnities, Subcontracting, Dispute resolution, Audits, Notice/ and consent for transfer, where applicable were also touched upon (Alhadeff).

WS 265. Medicines on the Web: Risks and Benefits

Report by: Sabine Walser

Organizers: Council of Europe EDQM and the Criminal Law Division

Moderator: Hugo K. Bonar (Enforcement Manager, Irish Medicines Board, member of the Council of Europe Group of Specialists on Counterfeit Pharmaceutical Products, Ireland)

Panellists: Paul Zickler (Canadian International Pharmacy Association, Canada); Kin-ping Tsang (International Alliance of Patients Organizations), President, Retina Hong Kong); Griffith Molewa (Manager Law Enforcement, National Department of Health, South Africa Questions and discussion); Dr Nico Kijlstra (Health Care Inspectorate, Ministry of Health, Welfare and Sport, Vice-Chairman of the European Committee on Pharmaceuticals and Pharmaceutical Care), the Netherlands)

The workshop dealt with health protection of the internet user from counterfeit medicines and other illegal offers of pharmaceuticals and healthcare products via the internet through empowerment of the internet user, establishment of best practices and regulatory policies, and, where necessary, legal instruments for combating counterfeiting of medicinal products and similar crimes threatening public health, where necessary. The quality of medical counselling and pharmaceutical products obtained via the internet cannot be taken for granted; the above products could entail considerable risks. Moreover, criminal activities concerning the production, distribution, and use of medicines and healthcare products (including counterfeit and illegal medicines and healthcare products) are widespread and the internet is frequently misused for these purposes.

The Council of Europe aims at counteracting the advertising and selling of illegal medicines and healthcare products via the internet through a comprehensive strategy comprising specific policies and legal instruments, improving patient information, the quality of healthcare that can be obtained online. The Council of Europe is preparing an international binding legal instrument against counterfeiting of medical products and similar crimes involving threats to public health, a Council of Europe convention . The convention is expected to be adopted in 2010 by the Council of Europe Committee of Ministers. The focus of the draft convention is on public health protection from counterfeit medical products and medical products which are manufactured or distributed without proper authorisation and/or in breach of safety standards.

As is the case for a number of other Council of Europe conventions, and considering the global dimension of pharmaceutical crimes, this Convention could be open for participation by non-member states, giving to the convention a potentially universal vocation. The impact of the draft convention will be complemented by existing Council of Europe international treaties in the field, namely the conventions dealing with international co-operation against cybercrime and corruption.

Summary presented by the workshop moderator, Mr Hugo Bonar, Enforcement manager, Irish Medicines Board:

The Council of Europe workshop raised the dangers of buying medicines from the internet through unreliable medicines, compromised confidentiality of patients, unknown legitimacy of medicines, the variation of quality of health and product information, and medicines in foreign language labelling. It emerged from the discussions that all medicines need to be safe and of appropriate quality, regardless of the pharmacy from which they are obtained. This should also apply to the quality of pharmaceutical care activities. Mr Paul Zickler, MD, Canadian International Pharmacy Association (CIPA) stated that "...there was definitely a need for access to safe and affordable medications internationally. When conducted legitimately and with the proper regulatory oversight, distance-based pharmacy care can provide this access. Several jurisdictions currently license and regulate the practice of international medicine to ensure that appropriate safety standards are in place..."

In order to enjoy the benefits of safe and affordable medications by mail order trade/internet/international pharmacy which is as safe the workshop concluded on the following:

- Prescription-only medications should only be dispensed at a distance by licensed pharmacists from a regulated and authorised facility providing pharmacy services and pharmaceutical care activities.
- No dispensing of medicines without prior face to face interface with a licensed physician providing an original valid and verifiable prescription.

- No shipping of narcotics and restricted medicines via mail order across borders.
- Only medicines with a known source and distribution history should be traded.
- There should be only licensed suppliers that can be audited.
- Operators of mail order /internet/international pharmacy must have a good understanding of the risks and the benefits in order to be able to mitigate the risks so that the benefits can be reaped by the patient/consumer.
- A system for aftercare, including recourse for the patient, and a tracing system of medication should be established.
- The dispensing pharmacy should be regulated and responsible for the quality of its operation, services, and pharmaceutical care activities. A dispensing pharmacy dispensing a product to a patient across a border should respect the respective legislation of the country of destination.
- There should be a rapid alert system for defective or counterfeit medicines and a recall system based on internationally agreed to protocol.
- In mail order trade, the following principles should apply: the receiving state is responsible for the public health of that state and not that of the supplying state or a commercial entity.
- The consumer should have the right to buy medications that he can afford from other states that guarantee the quality, efficiency and safety of the product. The medications should be dispensed from pharmacies that are licensed, subject to inspection and that are staffed by licensed pharmacists. The workshop recognised consumers' and patients' legitimate needs and expectations which are to.

The workshop recognised consumers' and patients' legitimate needs and expectations which are to
- The benefits of buying medications on the net are privacy, convenience and availability. In addition the consumer can compare prices easily from a variety of products to choose from. The consumer will be more likely to be compliant with his medications if he can afford them and at the same time reducing his risk of morbidity/mortality by not taking his medications.

The workshop expressed concerns that
- Currently, patients do not enjoy sufficient access to medicines on the net due to inequalities in access to medicines and shortcomings in information transfer from producers to patients.

The workshop called for initiatives and provisions such as
- Increasing medication- related health literacy of consumers;
- Giving consumers and patients better access based on objective, accurate and transparent information, and necessary legal and regulatory framework and no imbalanced advertising;
- Establishing verified web sites, overseen by regulators, patients associations, and professional boards;
- Involving patient advocacy organisations as regards relaying medicines' information;

- Taking responsibility for controlling and eliminating the risks of misleading and wrong information to consumers (4);
- Working out collaboratively formats for the contents of the web sites between producers and distributors, patients' advocacy organisations and regulators;
- Requiring pharmaceutical manufacturers/mail order trade/E-pharmacies, and government regulators.

The workshop urged increased efforts of public health authorities as regards
- Fostering of partnership with internet service providers, and professional associations;
- Offering reliable and unbiased product information;
- Designing web sites that are user friendly, including valid information easy to read and easy to find;
- Educating and empowering the consumers through promoting balanced independent medication related information;
- Consumer protection through cyber inspectors in charge of establishing supervising conditions for sale and distribution and through focal points for international co-operation.

Underlined by several panellists, the workshop emphasised that
- The liberty to choose freely from the offers on the internet requires well informed citizens.
- Legal offers of pharmaceutical product services through the internet, would need international regulation in order to become safe and effective.
- The Council of Europe standards for good practices for distributing medicines via mail order, which protect patient safety and the quality of the delivered medicines, provide a model for good regulatory practices in mail order trade in medicines that protect the patient and the quality of the medicines distributed, was developed by the Council of Europe.
- The workshop invited the UN IGF to host a platform for a future internet health action framework: patients' advocacy organisations, bodies of health professionals; e-commerce, national governmental bodies and the relevant regulators and international organisations such as the WHO and the Council of Europe should be involved.

With a view to protecting people and health systems from criminals abusing the internet for intentional criminal conducts, the workshop invited the UN IGF
- To recognise that international criminal legislation is needed to cater for the potential public health risks resulting from these crimes and especially those arising through Internet trade and the growing market of counterfeit healthcare products;
- To support the Council of Europe in preparing and implementing in Europe and beyond the first international legally binding treaty, a Convention on counterfeiting of medical products and similar crimes involving threats to public health. The future Convention will also be open for participation by other states beyond Europe and is expected to be opened for signature in 2010.
- The future Convention could serve as a model for other regions to participate or to adapt according to local conditions and to use in

conjunction with the Council of Europe's Cybercrime Convention to ameliorate some of the worst risks to the patient and to tackle crimes emerging from the abuse of the Internet.

The following intentional acts will be criminalised by the future Convention:
- The manufacturing of counterfeits,
- The supplying or offering to supply of, and trafficking in counterfeits, - the falsification of documents,
- The unauthorised manufacturing or supplying of medicinal products and the placing on the market of medical devices without them being in compliance with the conformity requirements.

All medicines need to be safe and of appropriate quality, and the quality of pharmaceutical care delivered needs to be appropriate, from whichever pharmacy they were delivered. Consumers and patients expect to benefit from medicines on the net through being able to choose from different offers, competitive prices of medicines and healthcare, the ability to compare prices, convenience, anonymity also due to the stigmatisation of certain diseases, and convenient access.

However, to date, patients have not uniformly benefited from medicines on the net due to inequalities in access to information, and shortcomings in information transfer from producers to patients. Often, medicines obtained outside of regulated and legitimate supply chains pose, including certain offers via the web, significant health risks due to substandard quality of product and the pharmaceutical care, and criminal conducts.

Initiatives are required for
- Better access to balanced and accessible information,
- Balanced medication related health literacy,
- Provisions for verification of information on medicines on the web,
- Participative setting-up of standards for the presentation of specific information on the web.

In particular information about medicines on the net should be unbiased and user friendly, including valid information easy to read and easy to find. Public health authorities have an important role as regards consumer education and empowerment, verification of web information content and accessibility, setting standards, and cooperation across borders to contain risks. Legal offers of pharmaceutical services through the internet, to become safe and effective, should be regulated at international level. The Council of Europe standards for good practices for distributing medicines via mail order, which protect patient safety and the quality of the delivered medicine and healthcare products, can serve as a model.

International criminal legislation is needed to cater for the potential public health risks resulting from criminal activity in this area and especially those arising through internet trade and the growing market of counterfeit medicines and other healthcare products subject to similar crimes threatening public health. The Council of Europe is preparing an international legally binding treaty, a convention against counterfeiting of medical products and similar crimes involving threats to public health, which will also be open for participation by non-member states beyond Europe and is expected to be opened for signature in 2010. The UN IGF is invited to consider hosting a future Internet health action framework.

WS 288. *Child Online Safety Indicators: Measuring the Un-measurable?*

Report by: *Amal Nasralla*

Panellists: Laurent Bernard (Policy Analyst, OECD); Christina Bueti (Policy Analyst, ITU); John Carr (Secretary of the UK's Children's Charities Coalition on Internet Safety); Cristina Schulman (Program Manager for Cypercrime, Council of Europe); Anjan Bose (ICT Officer, ECPAT International); Amal Nasralla (Monitoring and Evaluation Director, MCIT, Egypt)

Purpose of the workshop:
- Share vision about significance of indicators for the work on e-safety;
- Identify a possible link between indicators development and undergoing efforts;
- Communicate initial efforts for developing child e-safety indicators;
- Raise awareness of some possible approaches

Although there are several endeavours devoted to Child On-line Safety, questions regarding sufficient and coordinated input and the efficiency and effectiveness of processes are raised. How can we measure the efficiency and effectiveness of Child Online Safety endeavours? Input indicators should be developed regardless of current activities. There is a need for outcome mapping of potential change at all levels. There is a need for indicators-based monitoring and evaluation process with standardized data collection mechanisms.

OF 531. *ITU Open Forum on Child Online Protection*

Report by: *Preetam Maloor*

Panellists: Sami Al Basheer Al Moshid (Director, BDT, ITU); Cristina Bueti (Policy Analyst, ITU); John Carr (CHIS); Dr. Hoda Baraka (Government of Egypt); Giacomo Mazzone (European Broadcasting Union); Natasha Jackson (GSMA); Dieter Carstensen (Save the Children); Maria Badia (Member, Committee on Culture and Education, European Parliament); Mrs Jutta Croll, Managing Director Stiftung Ditial Protection Chancen)

The Open Forum presented a strategic overview of the main components of a child online protection policy. Issues discussed:
- Promote voluntary initiatives in the private sector,
- Promote user education initiatives and capacity building and
- Build capacity
- Foster international cooperation in the area of child online protection

It is suggested to involve more the ICT industry and NGOs in ITU's work on COP.

OF 532. ITU Open Forum on Cybersecurity

Report by: Preetam Maloor

Moderator: Alexander Ntoko (ITU)

Chairs: Sami Al Basheer Al Moshid (Director, BDT); Malcolm Johnson
(Director, TSB)

Panellists: Koji Nakao (Vice Chairman, ITU Study Group 17); Venkatesen Mauree
(Mauritius); Adam Mambi (Tanzania); Mohammad Amin (IMPACT)

The legal, technical and institutional challenges posed by the issue of
cybersecurity are global and far-reaching, and can only be addressed through
a coherent strategy taking into account the role of different stakeholders and
existing initiatives, within a framework of international cooperation.   A
fundamental role of ITU, following the World Summit on the Information
Society (WSIS) and the 2006 ITU Plenipotentiary Conference is to build
confidence and security in the use of information and communication
technologies (ICTs). At the second phase of WSIS in Tunis in 2005, ITU was
entrusted to take the lead as the sole facilitator for Action Line C5, "Building
confidence and security in the use of information and communication
technologies (ICTs)".

The main objective of this Open Forum was to raise awareness of ITU
activities in the area of Cybersecurity, carried out under its mandate.
Alexander Ntoko presented an overview of the GCA framework. The
remaining panellists presented their work under a specific pillar (work area)
of the GCA: Adam Mambi presented his country perspective on Legal
Measures. Under Technical and Procedural Measures, Koji Nakao presented
the work of the Study Group on Cybersecurity. Mohammad Amin presented
the IMPACT initiative and its role in providing an Organizational Structure
as well as International Cooperation for the global coalition for cybersecurity.
Venkatesen Mauree elaborated on his country's efforts in building capacity
through the setting up of CIRTS for incident response.   There is a clear
interest expressed by Member States in participating in ITU initiatives in
Cybersecurity.

2. Openness and Privacy

WS 263.   Privacy, Openness, Online Advertising and Online Behavioural
Targeting Advertising

Report by: Katitza Rodriguez

Organizer: Katitza Rodriguez (EPIC International Privacy Program)

Rapporteur: Cristos Velasco (Director General, North American Consumer Project
on Electronic Commerce, Mexico)

Panellists: Marc Rotenberg (Executive Director, Electronic Privacy Information Center; Pamela Harbour (Commissioner, US Federal Trade Commission); Ellen Blackler (Executive Director Public Policy, AT&T Services, Inc., USA); Graciela Selaimen (Núcleo de Pesquisas, Estudos e Formção da Rits, Brazil)

A powerful global system of online data collection for targeted interactive marketing has become one of the principal features of the Internet. Throughout much of the world, individual user information is now routinely collected for profiling, tracking and targeting purposes, which has raised growing concern over personal privacy and consumer welfare. Sophisticated digital marketing technologies, including the use of neuroscience for the creation of online advertising, has also generated public debate, especially related to public health. While advertising plays a critically important role in the Internet and Web 2.0, the majority of users are not well informed about the potential impact personal data collection will have on their daily lives. There are, however, other online advertising models beyond behavioural targeting that may allow companies to reach Internet users without the same risks to privacy. And a regulatory structure that protects user privacy will actually instil consumer confidence in the online economy, benefitting businesses and buyers alike. Online advertising is a global industry, and its impact on Internet users and privacy is profound, affecting developing and more economically advantaged countries.

This workshop is a follow-up to the event held during the IGF 2008. It will start by summarizing the major developments on this topic around the world during 2009. It will discuss some of the online advertising and behavioural targeting models applied in search engines, online video, online games, and Web 2.0, and will discuss how personal data is being collected and how it is used. Balancing freedom of speech, privacy, online marketing and consumer protection, various alternatives will be explored, including a discussion of international policy frameworks that have been proposed to regulate privacy and online advertising.

Consumer privacy is under siege both, online and offline

Commissioner Pamela Harbour opened the panel by setting the scene on online privacy. She explained that the explosion of free, online content and services that collect, integrate and disseminate consumers' personal information (webmail, blogs, mobile applications, social networks sites) are increasingly becoming part of one's personal digital life. "While these technologies potentially offer valuable benefits, not all consumers are fully aware of the privacy implications of the services."

As consumers pay for free content and free services by disclosing their personal information, their data is increasingly being use to generate targeting advertising that subsidizes their activities, she stressed. Already, it is possible to assemble a digital dossier that captures individual interests and habits runs them through a predictable model and then, determine what that person will likely do in the future. "Consumer privacy is under siege both, online and offline. Behavioural advertising represents one aspect of the multifaceted privacy conundrum surrounding data collection and use."

Tipping Point

"I am troubled by the asymmetry between consumer perceptions and business realities." "Once your data is shared, it can't be deleted." (Harbour) Consumers do not know how their information is used and collected, and based on these premises, it is impossible for them to knowingly consent to either disclosure or use of personal information. She called this the "Tipping Point," a point where consumers become sufficiently concerned about the collection and use of their personal information. While consumers want to exercise greater control over such use, their attempts to exercise control become futile at some point because so much of their digital life has already been exposed over the Internet.

Notice and Choice are insufficient on the current market

She mentioned that the attempts by the industry to provide "Notice and Choice" to consumers are insufficient on the current market. "Disclosures about information collection, use and control are not meaningful if they are very deep in opaque privacy policies that only lawyers can understand." It is troubling that businesses "have failed to effectively communicate with consumers despite evidence that consumers are greatly concerned about their privacy." A recent academic report from the University of Pennsylvania concluded that 66% of American adults reject tailored ads.

Concentration of Power

When the US Federal Trade Commission approved the Google Double-Click Merger in December 2007, Commissioner Harbour wrote a dissenting statement that, among other things, highlighted the relation between competition and privacy. In particular, the issues rose by data collection and use provides the right opportunity for companies to develop pro-privacy consumer tools that may help companies distinguish themselves from their competitors. Firms that offer these controls may be vulnerable to criticism from advertisers who depend on constant influx of personal data in order to make products and services to work as intended. In the long term, Commissioner Harbour believes that consumers who are increasingly able to click away to the next competitor will embrace innovative responses.

In her dissent in the Google-Double-Click merger, she discussed John Battelle's "Database of Intentions" concept that is the aggregate results of every search ever entered, every result listed, and every path taken to the results. According to Battelle, a few select companies share control over that database. "My key concern in Google-Double-Click is that the merger entity will move closer to dominating the database of intentions." The network effects generated by combining the two companies may have long-term negative consequence for consumers.

During the European Union and US review of the Google-DoubleClick merger, Google indicated that they would not engage in behavioural advertising. However, in March 2009 Google reversed course. Furthermore, Google purchased Ad Mob to offer advertising in the mobile market. She mentioned that the US market is leading companies to find new sources of revenue and such sources are driven by larger amounts of data and the connection between them. She concluded by mentioning that companies must engage in more serious enquiries over privacy and competition issues that affect consumers, particularly as they move to cloud computing, smart grids and mobile services.

The new advertising environment has become increasingly consolidated

Marc Rotenberg provided a general background on the significant changes that have taken place in the advertising world with respect to new media. He mentioned that in traditional advertising, there was virtually no collection of personal identifiable information while in the new interactive environment; it is now possible to track and record the interests of consumers across the Internet. This has led to a dramatic transformation that has changed the relationship that previously existed between publishers, advertisers, and consumers of information.

He mentioned that the new advertising environment has become increasingly consolidated, and there are small numbers of companies that are collecting vast amount of information about the activities of Internet users. Mr. Rotenberg stressed, "on the absence of regulation, the market efficiencies make it possible for the dominant firms to gather more information, and more difficult for competitors to get access to the same information." They find their selves reliant upon the large ad serving companies to get access to information about customers that might be interested in their products.

He offered two possible solutions to resolve such concerns: The first solution is the creation of a regulatory model under which certain restrictions could be enforced. He provided as an example the use of cookies which are key elements in order to link independent commercial transactions. He commented that the current EU legal initiative to give users control over their cookies might prevent and stop companies from tracking personal behaviour on the Internet. The second solution consists of an approach that relies more on technology: creates systems that do not rely on the collection of personal identifiable information. He concluded his presentation by recognizing that online advertising has a role to play in the Internet, as it has played with another media. Mr. Rotenberg made a call to recognize the significant transformation that has taken place in the collection and use of personal data in the online environment. He recommended that policymakers and businesses consider at ways to allow new business practices and privacy to co-exist.

There is an urgent need to work on an Ecosystem wide industry solution

Ellen Blackler gave a brief perspective of her company and underlined the importance of relying on a multimodal relationship with customers since many of them have now an interest in the way their personal information is collected and used on the Internet. She proposed the creation of a new solution that would protect consumer privacy and find viable ways to engage customers based on their needs and concerns. She mentioned that many privacy policies of Internet companies are not adequate for the digital environment, and she also emphasized the importance of offering customers control over their own personal information. Ms Blackler commented on the importance of the role of the FTC to recognize the need to protect consumers from online targeting advertisers. She added that many of those companies do not actually have a direct way to interact or offer a trustworthy customer relationship in the online environment. She noted how difficult it is for customers to get familiar with all the privacy policies of Internet companies. She mentioned that there is the urgent need to work on an "Ecosystem wide industry solution" in order to offer protection to the privacy of users on a coordinated basis, and to find ways to label ads and educate consumers on why they are targeted on the Internet. She also expressed that there is a need to educate publishers about so they can choose the kind of advertising that publishers really want.

Opaque Privacy Practices: "We do not know when and how we are being observed, we do not what is going to be done with all the feedback we provide". Graciela Selaimen focused her presentation on the philosophical and theoretical approach of targeted advertising. She referred to the work of Dallas Smythe, in an article published in 1977 - "The blindspot of western Marxism." She selected two of the questions presented by said author in order to reflect on the phenomena of online behavioural target advertising.

Ms. Selaimen noted that databases could serve as instruments of knowledge, where the object of representation (e.g. the consumer) becomes observable, measurable, quantified, and in short, known. She referred to current techniques such as "neuromarketing", which study people's behaviour using the patterns revealed in electroencephalograms, eye-tracking equipment and intelligent video. She also mentioned that users are constantly feeding companies their personal information and preferences. Amazon, for example, is a company that plays a critical role today in maintaining systems of online productivity. Ms. Selaimen said that one of the major problems that exists in this dynamic is its opacity, in other words, "we do not know when and how we are being observed, we do not what is going to be done with all the feedback we provide"

She also observed that the configuration of personal identity is no longer in our own hands. Electronic profiles of individuals can be combined, dissected, bought and sold, and otherwise manipulated without the knowledge or consent of the individual subject. She mentioned that computerized databases are actually identity-producing engines. Ms. Selaimen concluded by sharing some concerns in relation to online advertising practices that are impacting subjectivity and violating human rights. One of them is the possibility that in a world that commodifies everything, privacy itself will become a commodity in the near future. The other is directly linked to defending our need to be human, not a commodity. She underlined the importance of human rights in contemporary information and surveillance societies.

After the presentations, the moderator allowed interaction with the audience where the panellists offered views regarding Google's ongoing projects to enhance consumer privacy in their online services. Other questions were related to the current challenges to offer consumers more control over their own personal information and data, as well as international and national frameworks and government enforcement to protect the privacy of citizens; and the regulatory challenges that remain to be faced in areas like virtual worlds.

Commissioner Harbour stressed that companies must engage in more serious enquiries over privacy and competition issues that affect consumers, particularly as they move to cloud computing, smart grids and mobile services. Mr. Rotenberg made a call to recognize the significant transformation that has taken place in the collection and use of personal data in the online environment. He recommended that policymakers and businesses consider how new business practices and privacy can co-exist.

Ms. Backler urge to work on an "Ecosystem wide industry solution" in order to offer protection to the privacy of users on a coordinated basis, and to find ways to label ads and educate consumers on why they are targeted on the Internet. She also expressed that there is the need to educate publishers about so they can choose the kind of advertising that publishers really want. Ms. Selaimen concluded by sharing some concerns in relation to online advertising practices that are impacting subjectivity and violating human rights. One of them is the possibility that in a world that commodifies everything, privacy itself will become a commodity in the near future. The other is directly linked to defending our need to be human, not a commodity. She underlined the importance of human rights in contemporary information and surveillance societies.

WS 275. *Content Regulation, Surveillance and Sexuality Rights: Privacy, Agency and Security*

Report by: Jac sm Kee

Organizers: Association for Progressive Communications, Women's Networking Support Programme, Alternative Law Forum, Centre for Internet and Society

Moderator: Jac sm Kee (Women's Rights and ICT Policy Coordinator, Association for Progressive Communications, Women's Networking Support Programme, Malaysia)

Panellists: Wieke Vink (Youth Coalition for Sexual and Reproductive Rights, Holland); Maya Ganesh (Independent Researcher, EroTICS Project, India); Jehan Ara (President, Pakistan Software Houses Association for IT & ITES [P@SHA], Pakistan); Simon Davies (Networking & Events officer, Outeverywhere.com and Director, Privacy International, UK)

The workshop was opened by the screening of a 10-minute documentary video short, directed by Subasri Krishnan and Namita A. Malhotra, as part of the OpenNet Initiative: Asia project. It highlighted the context of internet use, content regulation, surveillance, sexuality and sexual rights in India, Indonesia and Malaysia, and surfaced the complexity and fluidity of definitions, use and experience in this area.

The segment on India, the longest in the video, features a series of interviews with sexual rights and communication rights advocates to explore the social, political and legislative culture, traditions and transgressions around "obscenity", sexuality and pornography vis-à-vis the internet. Amongst the comments, Nishant Shah of the Centre for Internet and Society notes that the user of technology is immediately presumed as guilty and constantly placed under the onus of proving that s/he is "a good ethical subject" - i.e., not engaged in terrorism, pornography or piracy - in order to be entitled to the use of technology. The segment on Indonesia, entitled "Reckless teenagers in an age of technology" was a satirical look at young people and their sexual expression and activity online, explored through a music video mash-up. The final segment on Malaysia featured the press conference video of a popular human rights activist and politician who announced her decision to resign when intimate photographs of her were circulated without her consent. All three segments presented a provocative overview to the multiple dimensions of culture, private | public, law and expression on the issue of sexuality and content regulation of the internet.

The first speaker of the workshop, Wieke Vink, is from the Youth Coalition - an international organisation of young people (ages 15-29) working on the promotion of adolescent and youth sexual and reproductive rights. She reminded workshop participants about the fact that young people are active subjects who are leading and shaping the internet, not just passive consumers and users. Wieke importantly articulated that sexuality and the exploration of sexuality (by people of all ages, including the young), is a perfectly normal, natural and healthy fact of life. She also stressed the importance and value of the internet as a platform for connection, information, education, activism and peer support for young people on the issue of sexuality and sexual rights. Wieke noted that, "In debates about internet and sexuality, the importance of protection children and youth to dangerous online content is often referred to. But we also have to admit that watching porn online is in most cases not that harmful. What we could do, what we should do, is think creatively about age-appropriate access to pornography, and about developing content which is more gender-just, and frankly, about encouraging people to protect their sexual health, e.g. by using condoms – both in the online and offline world."

The second speaker Jehan Ara, is the President of the Pakistan Software Houses Association for IT & ITES (P@SHA). She disclaimed the artificial separation between different stakeholders' interests in the area of internet governance, and noted that she is at the same time, invested in this issue as a business person in the private sector, a member of civil society, and as a woman, since any effort to legislate on this area affects all of these aspects. Jehan shared P@SHA's experience in their engagement with the Prevention of E-crime Ordinance in 2007. Important lessons learnt from this experience include the fact that legislation on internet governance does not protect the interest of both citizens and businesses when it is framed in a vague and broad manner, and when there is no strong human rights framework that is grounding the legislation. Instead, this presents legislative burdens, especially when framed through notions of "security" from a protectionist standpoint, and when it overburdens the gatekeepers, i.e. providers of information and internet access.

The third speaker, Maya Ganesh, is an independent researcher working on the APC exploratory research on sexuality and the internet in India. Maya

297

extrapolated the value of the internet and online spaces for resistance and expression, and for the creation of identities. She examined how online spaces have been used to redefine offline spaces, to challenge limitations of boundaries, to organise and to resist against fundamentalisms, and cited the Pink Chaddi campaign on Facebook as a case study on sexual resistance and the reclaiming of morality. Maya also spoke about the blurring of the private/public vis-à-vis the digital interface, where intimacy and relationships are built.

The final speaker of the workshop is Simon Davies, Networking & Events officer of Outeverywhere.com - one of the oldest LGBT networking site in Europe (established 1996) - and the Director of Privacy International. Simon emphasised the importance of the internet and online spaces for communities who are in isolated environments to explore themselves, ask questions, build relationships and establish communities. Central to this is the ability for individuals to decide and selectively disclose and share personal information, especially to counter real risks and threats personal safety. Centring the right to privacy as a framework and approach, Simon shared a technical solution that was developed (different levels of personal information is randomly anonymised based on the user's choice to disclose) to ensure adequate levels of anonymity for the online networking environment to work as a space that protects and promotes the rights of its users, as well as provide them with the ability to decide and control their personal data.

In summary:
- When looked at from the perspective of sexual rights, it is clear that the internet and emerging ICTs hold tremendous value - especially to those who are isolated and have less access to power (including young people, sexually marginalised groups, disabled communities etc.) - to overcome/transgress cultural, legal, economic and physical barriers and boundaries.
- This is done through forming relationships, engaging in acts of intimacy, to organise and mobilise, taking action, to learn, to exchange and acquire information, to build communities etc - all of which are important parts of human development and existence.
- There does exist particular dangers and risks, such as excessive disclosure of personal information.
- In response, legislative burdens must not be placed on users (citizens) and the private sector (e.g. gatekeepers) in the guise of "security" - moral, cultural, criminal or otherwise. Important criteria: legislation must not be broad and vague, and must be grounded by a strong human rights framework.
- Other strategies include: shifting of information and connections from spaces to spaces, technology to people and partnerships between civil society and the private sector.
- Privacy appears to be an important framework to address many of these issues, whether as a principled approach, legislatively or through technical solutions.

Some of the points raised in the discussion were:
- Many policy makers share the concern on the fear for safety of children and national security. However, this concern is played out on restrictions

to the internet when in fact, the issue is not necessarily located or concentrated online. What is needed is capacity building on the level of law enforcement and the rule of law, and resources should be channelled to all these different responses, not just to the internet in a kind of paranoid reaction to children's safety online.

- When looking at sexuality and young people, the response is often that of panic and paranoia, which negates the fact that everyone, including young people, have rights. A shift of perspective needs to happen from paranoia to what can we do to protect the rights of a diversity of people with diverse sexualities, including that of young people. Rights need to be seen as applicable in online spaces as in the physical/material spaces/world.
- There are positive dimensions to sexuality including education and learning, which are important to highlight and surface. This is especially since when it is discussed in internet governance issues, it is often framed in a negative way (oppression & disease).
- Public health (including sexual health) and public education (including sex education) are important policy dimensions which need to be brought to the debates and discussions on internet governance. The internet has great potential to bring about increased knowledge and empowered knowledge, which can lead to improved practice, i.e. safety.

Conclusions

- The discussion and formulation of responses - whether in policy, legislation or technical solutions - on safety, security and internet regulation must be framed from the perspective of rights. This ensures that excessive burdens are not placed on various actors invested in the use and development of the internet, and that security is not used as a shortcut to distract from the real risks and dangers at hand.
- The internet governance debate will benefit from greater participation from the sexual rights movement, including that of young people, women and people of diverse sexualities, to better understand the actual value and risks that the internet presents to the exercise of rights. This is also to balance out the debate from focussing on the negatives and dangers to examining benefits and other forms of strategies and responses.
- It's noteworthy to explore public health and public education as important policy dimensions that should equally be taken into consideration when debating on policies on safety, sexuality and young people. Safety and security of young people when looked at from this perspective encourages openness instead of standing in conflict or tension with it.

WS 302. *Network Neutrality*

Report by: Vladimir Radunovic

Moderators: Vladimir Radunovic (Coordinator of Internet Governance Programmes, DiploFoundation); Ambassador David A. Gross (former U.S. Coordinator for International Communications and Information Policy at the U.S. Department of State); Chuck Kisselburg (Director of Strategic Partnerships, CommunityDNS)

Panellists: (part 1) Robert Pepper, (Vice President Global Technology Policy, CISCO); Thomas Lenard, (President and Senior Fellow, Technology Policy Institute); Jacquelynn Ruff (Vice President, International Public Policy and Regulatory Affairs, Verizon Communications); Ian Peter (Internet Governance Caucus); Nathaniel James (Executive Director, OneWebDay.org); Emmanuel Edet (National Information Technology Development Agency, Nigeria)

(part 2) Belhassen Zouari (CERT-Tunisia); Steve Purser, (European Network and Information Security Agency); Chuck Kisselburg (CommunityDNS)

(part 3) Dr. Amr Badawi (CEO, NTRA Egypt); Willy Jensen (Director General, NPT Norway); Vanessa Copetti Cravo (University of Rio Grande do Sul – UFRGS); Parminder Jeet Singh (Internet Governance Caucus); Jake E. Jennings (Executive Director, International External and Regulatory Affairs, AT&T); Michael Truppe (Council of Europe and Federal Chancellery - Constitutional Service Media Affairs Coordination Information Society Austria)

The workshop discussed the accuracy of a very term of Network Neutrality in opposition to a term of Open Internet. It further discussed economics and engineering aspects of networks and how network management regulation might affect those investments. It also discussed the end-user perspective, need for transparency and a freedom of choice. As a cross-cutting issue, the implications to the digital divide and development were examined. Needs for policy and regulatory approaches towards network management were questioned and discussed, including analysing several experiences on national levels.

The workshop involved a variety of stakeholders presenting different perspectives to the audience and listening to their opinions. It aimed at listening to the interests and concerns of technical community, incumbents, Telcos and ISPs, service and content providers, civil society groups, users, government representatives and regulators, etc.

The workshop was structured in three parts with specific goals:
- Mapping the field: -
  - engineering aspect;
  - economical aspect;
  - socio-cultural aspect and end-user perspective;
  - implications to a developing world;
  - policy aspect.
  Ultimately, outlining the areas of common agreement and putting in forefront the remaining confronting views of stakeholders involved.
- Identifying and understanding local or regional Internet substructures, threats and pressures faced: bringing in the security aspects of malicious data traversing the network and how organizations making up the Internet Substructure are impacted or may be able to have an impact on this debate.
- Discussing the basic principles:
  - regulatory views and existing practices and case-studies (Egypt, Norway, Europe, Brazil);
  - basic principles that all the stakeholders might sustain.

Part 1: Mapping the Field

The first part of the panel discussed core aspects of the debate, including the convenience of the very term of "Network Neutrality" and its essence and core principles. A discussion on appropriate network management was connected to the debate on rights of all parties involved. Concerns over approaches to regulation of Network neutrality brought into focus the aspects of investments, liability and innovations in network and applications as well as in economic models - including pros and cons of carriers charging content providers and models of packaging Internet offer. General consensus was achieved on several aspects, yet more clearly defining the remaining open issues.

The term "Network neutrality" was found by most speakers as potentially ambitious and misleading one, which should rather be replaced by "Policies for Open Internet". Nevertheless, voices were heard also that the word "open" might be even more ambiguous than "neutrality", and that one should rather keep the old term to better communicate the debate to wider range of users. Another term that was heard based on the discussions is "Appropriate Network Management". The bottom line most agreed upon, however, is that one should focus on a concrete question - or a set of questions to be responded to - rather than on a phrase. In that sense the term used should provide a normative base for deciding what is appropriate practice and what is not.

A general feeling of the discussion was that Network Neutrality should not be about the regulatory mechanism but about the principles instead. Consensus existed on basic principles:
• Rights of users to access any content, application or service
• Transparent and non-discriminatory network management.

The way the principles should be enforced was yet a separate discussion. It was also mentioned that core principles should be followed by content and service providers, not only the carriers, since growingly the access to information and content rely on them as well. In essence, it was suggested, principles of Network Neutrality should ensure equality of opportunities for everyone.

One of the foci of the global debate - the concept of network management - was not objected by any speaker: it was understood that network management is needed to improve performances and bring innovations, and especially to prevent congestion, latency and jitter. While the principle of traffic management as such was acknowledged, the practice of traffic management was disputed by some speakers, as it gives space for interest-based interventions by providers or governments, and may result with breaching the principle of access rights of users. To that end transparency was a principle generally agreed upon, while a clear question was set forwards for future debates: what is appropriate network management?

"Rights" was an important word of the debate. On the end-user side it was repeated that users have rights to access any kind of content, services or applications from any networks, without barriers and intervention from carriers or governments or third parties. Besides, rights of users to be able to switch providers easily were mentioned. Finally, it was emphasised the users should have a final say. On the other hand, the rights of carriers to manage traffic and offer managed network services to customers were outlined as well.

From the perspective of developing countries a principle of knowledge economy was understood as the underpinning one for further development: in order to compete equally with developed world, the developing world needs to be allowed to access the (online) knowledge equally, as well as to be able to compete on equal bases. Emerging content and service providers bringing innovations at network ends - especially those from developing countries - should not be prevented from competing due to their low initial market power. Non-commercial and non-competing producers of online content and services should as well have the equal rights to broadcast through any carrier to reach any interested user. Special concern was made on the rights of marginalised groups - people with disabilities being among those - to use content, services and applications (including high-bandwidth-demand ones) of their needs without any limits whatsoever.

As expected, a very important thread of the debate was on the need and level of regulations in broadband market when it comes to Network Neutrality. It was acknowledged that a high level competition is welcomed and would leave more choice for users. A self-regulation based on the competition only was, however, questioned by some speakers, on several bases:

- Internet should be user-centered; while business generally cares about satisfying users' needs for greater value of its offer and a comparative advantage on the market, it has own benefits as a primary goal, rather than the end-user needs.
- The rights of carriers are based on owning the infrastructure, but not owning the Internet, standards or services; greater values and user-rights should be safeguarded more firmly by authorities, especially in case of emerging telecom-related monopolies or oligopolies.
- The crash of an open-market economic system in the past years has raised fears that competition-based regulation might not be sufficient.
- The hierarchical (tier-based) Internet infrastructure influences business relations, creates dependence on the decisions of the top-level carriers and impacts the competitiveness of ISP at on the ground levels.

On the other side, a need for a more firm involvement of regulators and governments was disputed by several speakers on following bases:

- Broadband is a capital investment industry, and the regulatory interventions may increase risks.
- Rules should not preclude innovations in either technology or business models to run and be tested; it is likely the market-driven innovations would bring benefits for users as well (greater choice, lower prices, better quality)
- Governments' interference would as well endanger neutrality of the net.

A general zone of consent of all speakers was that a collaborative multistakeholder work should be done towards establishing principles and norms that actors - especially carriers - should follow (including transparency and non-discrimination). It was discussed that the regulators should embrace such principles and should act as mere safeguards, taking the enforcement action only if a problem occurs. A question was also raised if the regulators can use the existing authorities to intervene when needed, or if new regulations are needed to provide such authorities.

Economic models were another important thread of the debate. Statistics of global use presented suggested that the common users currently subsidise power users; instead, it should be that the entry level users are able to afford entry level, while power users pay for their power use. Two possible models were discussed to overcome the drawbacks of the current "all you can eat" model:

- "Volume charging" approach within which power users would pay more. While this approach (typical for electricity or water pricing) might be the fairest one, charging consumers would result with higher prices for some.
- "Two-Side Market" models within which carriers would charge content and service providers for their access to consumers. While these models (innovative on the Internet) may lower connection prices to end-users and potentially enlarge the pool of accessible and affordable applications, they might likely heavily impact core principles of access rights of users and might lead towards packaging the Internet offers.

A caveat was brought up by representatives of developing countries that the western (especially US) economic models may not be easily implemented globe-wide - in developing countries competition is weaker - if any, governments' relation to open-market is commonly different, and there are many "cultural specificities".

The debate over whether it should be allowed for carriers to charge content and service providers was particularly rich. On principal bases several speakers emphasised that any innovative economic model like this should not be legally precluded but rather given an opportunity for market to shape it in convenient way beneficial to all. Justifying such approach they outlined that the content and service providers do already pay to carriers for their high bandwidth connections but not to the access to consumers. In such a two-side market approach, they argued, the business would pay more, instead of the users - which might bring great benefits especially to developing countries, enabling greater accessibility and more users.

This model was strongly disputed by other speakers, arguing that it would not be practically feasible without endangering rights of users to access any content, application or service. Charging content providers would lead to a "pay more and you get the job" approach, possibly leaving out of a carriers offer those not willing to pay (enough), which would in return lead towards creating packages of offered services by carriers, directly influences the choice of end-users. A cable-TV was taken as example, extrapolating it to cases of packages offering Facebook but not MySpace, Bing but not Google, in-house VoIP but not Skype, and alike. Further, it was said, charging content and service providers might endanger innovation and diversity: even if a carrier would be price-sensible towards emerging and small service providers - it is in its interest not to reduce the value of its network by reducing choice - those that would not like to pay would probably be off the carrier's net. In order to preserve openness and diversity zero-prices would be needed for non-commercial groups, informal online learning platforms, presentations and broadcasts of cultural content - including music, arts or languages. This might have considerable impact on innovations and access in developing countries, and might result in requiring them to pay even more on the top of what they are already paying - subsidising the global net by being at the end of the economic chain.

Common view was taken that innovations on both infrastructure and applications side should be promoted. Different perspective existed, however, on how the basic principles of Network Neutrality impact innovations, and vice-versa. Having the emerging needs and habits of users, a "fit-for-purpose" Internet based on the applications was suggested. Concerns were raised, nevertheless, that such a concept might lead towards packaging the offer and limiting access rights of the users. Besides, innovations in services should not hamper innovations on the network ends (including open source) due to unfair payment models; also, innovation in developing world should not be hampered by models from developed world. A general impression emerged that no innovation - be it a technological or an economical one - should be initially precluded as long as it does not harm the core principles of Network Neutrality.

Lastly, a link between Network Neutrality and liability of carriers for illegal content was made. It was noted that, if carriers are to provide transparent and non-discriminatory traffic management, providers should be "reasonably free from liability of transmitting content and applications deemed illegal or undesired by third parties". It was also noted that no protocol or application should be banned on bases of what some people might use it for (as happened with P2P applications).

Part 2: Internet Substructures

The malicious community, global in nature, has become organized, committing various acts of cyber crime. While the basis of most criminal activity is financial there are other aspects that deal with revenge, some form of espionage or simple form of rivalry. Through such levels of organization and financial backing the malicious community has become more sophisticated with how they are able to launch and be successful with their attacks.

DNS providers are not affected by the Net Neutrality debate as their responsibility is to help Internet users connect with their application(s) of choice. As such DNS providers, by nature of their technical responsibility, are neither for nor against Net Neutrality. Network infrastructure, however, is directly impacted by cyber criminals. From a DNS perspective cyber criminals affect network infrastructure by either attacking DNS directly or by using DNS to launch their malicious attacks. If DNS is attacked directly the resiliency of the internet may suffer as DNS may be taken off-line in some areas of the globe, thus creating outages for initial routing. Such disruptions in, or attacks to Internet resiliency decrease confidence in Internet use by its user-base.

If DNS is used to launch attacks DNS may be indirectly affected by the increased volume of traffic. Such increases in traffic may flood some DNS providers, thus regionally impacting a DNS provider's ability to provide DNS services for areas experiencing the largest levels of criminal traffic. DoS (Denial of Service) or DDoS (Distributed Denial of Service) attacks are the main culprit of increased levels of traffic. DoS or DDoS attacks are where specific websites are targeted with a flood of data packets. The sudden flood of packets is too much for the sites to handle, essentially taking the site off-line. Not only will cyber criminals use DNS to carry out their attacks, the shear volume of traffic generated by such attacks can impact DNS providers with the unintended consequence of appearing to be in the midst of a regional outage. Such DoS or DDoS attacks are aimed at organizations in order for cyber criminals to inflict financial harm on the organization they are attacking, to gain superiority over the organization they are attacking, or hold the organization hostage until they pay to have the attack stopped. At any given time there can be close to 1,000 DoS or DDoS attacks happening around the globe. As such network providers have to handle all of the traffic associated with such malicious, criminal activity.

Another form of Internet traffic generated from the malicious community deals with spam, or unsolicited e-mails. In many cases such spam has lead unsuspecting users to sites with malicious intent. Such intent can result in the computers of such unsuspecting users to become infected with computer viruses. It is from these infected computers that cyber criminals are able to launch DoS or DDoS attacks. It is from such infected computers that cyber criminals are also able to launch additional spam campaigns. With regards to spam over 90% of all e-mails is spam. With all of the traffic, or data traversing the Internet associated with the malicious community, how might this impact organizations within the Internet Substructure? Might organizations within the Internet Substructure be able to help?

Education is the biggest defence against cyber criminals or members of the malicious community. CERTs (Computer Emergency Response Teams) help identify items that can have a negative impact to users of the Internet. Such items can be alerting users to bugs in software that may be exploited by organized cyber criminals. CERTs can also provide members of the Internet community with information on how to prevent computer infections and attacks from the malicious community. CERTs are being established in various countries around the globe. In Europe there is the desire to have a CERT in each of the EU Member States. Other countries may have multiple CERTs, where there may be a CERT for each of the country's industry sectors. CERTs serve as an excellent platform from which education can be launched. Such educational efforts will be used not only for Internet users of a specific country, but also to help other organizations within the country's respective Internet Substructure (such as ISPs), educate their customers on how to curb activity from the malicious community. By helping to educate a country's populace on how to curb the Internet's malicious community they are also playing a leadership role for those countries that do not have any rules, or framework regarding Net Neutrality.

Within developing nations infrastructure may be limited. Such countries may also have a limited or incomplete number of organizations to help form a healthy Internet Substructure. Where countries have one, or a very limited number of ISPs, an ISP's greatest challenge is to secure funding to provide bandwidth for its uses. Until secure in its funding a struggling ISP may have to operate based upon the wishes of its major funding providers, thus not able to implement an "equal access for all" policy as found with one part of the Net Neutrality debate. Under such circumstances a CERT, through its educational efforts in curbing malicious Internet activity, can have a positive affect on yielding additional bandwidth normally cluttered by cyber criminals.

Cyber criminals also gravitate towards countries that are considered weak in regards to its cyber image; meaning citizens or companies do little to implement standards used to fight cyber crime. Such weakness allows them to launch and maintain their attacks with least resistance. An effective CERT can discourage cyber criminals from conducting their attacks from what might be considered a cyber-weak nation.

Today's Internet is cluttered with packets from the malicious community. Having a cleaner Internet should free up bandwidth to carry traffic for new applications. We are already seeing needs for increased traffic that cross traditional boarder, cultural and sector boundaries. For example EID, or Electronic ID, censors have the capability of transmitting their information via the Internet as containers they are connected to are shipped to their final destination. As we see the emergence of smart technologies, such as smart electric grids or microchips residing in home appliances, all devices serve as a source for communication across the Internet. Such technologies, however, can be targeted by organized cyber crime. Through modification of the Lisbon Treaty we will soon see communication, once reserved among those within identified sectors, to occur among those across sectors. Social networks and blogs continue to proliferate and in some cases such blogging and social networking efforts are pushing cultural boundaries. As we saw with the recent election in Iran while some technologies were blocked other technologies emerged allowing information to flow across the Internet from Iranian citizens.

Cross border, or the international aspects of ensuring Net Neutrality can be difficult to enforce for multiple reasons.
- Countries or regions (such as the EU) can have different rules or interpretations of what Net Neutrality means. Some countries, particularly emerging countries, have no rules or guidelines regarding Net Neutrality. In the EU, for example, the Telecommunications bill was recently modified to make it easier to ensure everyone has full access to all applications across the Internet. This loosens the power existing "3-Strikes" laws have within EU countries. "3-Strikes" laws were designed to curb the downloading of illegal content by threatening users with disconnection from the Internet. Finland has gone as far as declaring access to the Internet as a "Civil Right".
- Based upon culture some countries will deem some data to be off limits to Internet users within their respective country. Such countries are, or have introduced filtering of specific sites based on content.
- There has already been a court case, launched in Australia, to have content removed from a website located in the US. While the case lost it points to

an example of how cross-boarder disputes may arise based upon content or applications that may exist legally in one country but may be counter to laws or culture of other countries.

Such instances have a direct impact on organizations that form the Internet Substructure as countries look to organizations within the Internet Substructure to provide such filtering. In other cases organizations within the Substructure are taking it upon themselves to address issues related to cyber crime. Examples include:

- Australia, through the Australia Internet security initiative (AISI), is asking ISPs to provide filtering to curb botnets.
- Australia, through its government-sponsored filtering program, is wishing to implement filtering through its ISPs using a government created filtered list of what is considered "undesirable".
- German government passed a law empowering the German police to issue a daily filter file to German-based ISPs. The focus of the list deals with filtering child pornography site.
- Dutch ISPs have come together to form a treaty to help fight botnets.
- DNS providers, such a CommunityDNS, have the capability of identifying sites which are used by the malicious community. Viruses on infected computers need to contact their respective control centres. In this case the DNS provider can help ISPs identify which computers on their network are infected.
- Georgia Tech recently received a grant to develop technology on how to thwart malicious activity within cellular networks.

While the debate on Net Neutrality continues on whether providers should or should not have the ability to prioritize data, cyber criminals are flooding our networks with spam and attacks. Such efforts undermine the resiliency of the Internet. Through education and common-sense security efforts people, governments and organizations can work together to curb criminal activity. Organizations forming the Internet's Substructure can work to provide the education and technology necessary for combating malicious activity, thus raising confidence in Internet usage as well as a country's cyber image. The question raised in this debate is from the security perspective should members of the Internet Substructure be able to drive intelligence into the Substructure to combat cyber crime?

Part 3: Basic Principles and Regulatory Involvement

Third part of the panel aimed at bringing in the regulatory perspectives of the Network Neutrality debate. The regulators expressed the view that the Internet has become a public sphere, and that their role is to safeguard the interests of all players, keep the market balanced and assure it is fair for all users. To that end the opinion was heard that all traffic should be treated equally in a value sense - though of course not identically. As an ultimate goal the principles of neutrality should assure the equality of opportunities for all.

While a broader view of the Network Neutrality principles encompassed anything related to free access to information, end user choice and access to services, transparent and non-discriminatory traffic management was reiterated as common ground by all speakers. For developing countries with limited infrastructure and thus bandwidths, such as Egypt, a fair usage policy is considered to be an important principle on users' side to avoid congestion - affordable prices and fair access to all are protected also by the OECD bit-cap scheme (bandwidth drops to 128kbps or so after a certain download limit of a flat-rate has been crossed). The importance of neutrality on international level was also emphasised - that the traffic from all countries should be treated the same way, with no preferences based on termination costs, which might otherwise disadvantage developing countries.

In some countries such as Brazil, discrimination of packages is not allowed except for technical and ethical aspect. Judging on the justification, nevertheless, has to be done on case by case bases, yet certain core principles would be of a great help not only for the regulators but also for the juridical authorities if needed. It was noted, however, that the very understanding of "ethical aspect" when it comes to preventing "objectionable" and even illegal content (except in case of child pornography) varies dramatically across the globe, and so does the understanding of the concept of Network Neutrality. Link back to a discussion on liability of providers was made again.

Norwegian principles - reflecting the approaches of European Union, United States and Japan mainly - were discussed as a solid base for possible international principles:

- Transparency principle: users are entitled for the Internet connection with a predefined capacity and quality of service.
- Non-blocking principle: users are entitled for the Internet connection that enables them to send and receive content of their choice, use services and run applications of their choice, to connect hardware and use software of their choice that do not harm the network.
- Non-discrimination principle: users are entitled for the Internet connection that is free of discrimination with regards to type of application, type of service, type of content, or based on sender or receiver address.

It was stressed jointly that regulators do have a role to play in the telecom market and services, though only as safeguards from a possible market failure, which might lead to harming the access rights of users and their choice. Besides, the regulators found themselves responsible to act in cases of network congestion, illegal conducts, security threats or breaches of user rights. In order to protect the interests of users and citizens, but also of service and content providers, it was explained, the regulators should bring up a lawful scene that would establish and promote competition on one hand but also put up the provisions for consumer protection on the other.

Discussing the ways regulators should act, the speakers have however not taken hard regulation and legislation as a most favourite way - on contrary, they esteemed legal procedures as too harsh and expensive. Instead, they invited for a multistakeholder-based approach to designing soft co-regulations, to re-assure consumers and business that market can be regulated without hard law. These co-regulations would nevertheless be binding agreements around core principles (such as the Norwegian ones). Any breach of the agreement and the principles within would firstly be put through a "name-blame-shame" pattern, encouraging self-corrective measures; ultimately, further absence of respect for the principles might be a trigger for turning the agreement into legislation. It was a general atmosphere throughout the panel that none would really embrace hard law.

Further discussions are needed on defining the appropriate network management, based on existing commonly acknowledged principles. Council of Europe has started working on developing guidelines and principles in form of practical tools for Internet Service Providers for network management. This initiative along with the work of the Norwegian authority were offered as examples of the inclusive and transparent processes leading to very concrete and useful documents ensuring equality of opportunities for all.

The workshop clarified a general consensus on the basic principles related to Network Neutrality - rights of users to access any content, application or service, and transparent and non-discriminatory network management, as well as the right of carriers to manage the traffic in accordance to these principles. A straight-forward challenge was posed for future discussions: defining appropriate network management.

A shift was suggested in terminology: using "Policies for Open Internet" instead of "Network Neutrality", yet was not unanimous. It was agreed that the term should reflect a normative base of deciding what appropriate traffic management is. It should also be able to convey the essence of the debate to the wider audience. While there is space for more deliberation on the term, it is likely both terms will be used equally in future.

Innovations were jointly supported as long as these do not endanger core principles and do not hamper other innovations. The innovations in economic models were carefully debated, while the model of carriers charging content and service providers came into forefront of discussions and will need further analysis and debates.

More should be explored on how each of these discussions impact developing countries. Besides, the impact of emerging trends - such as mobile services and cloud computing - on Network Neutrality should be analysed.

A key challenge that emerged from the workshop and that might present a basis for future debates is: What would be the right ecosystem that would respect core principles while also encouraging innovation and investments, mainly based on the competition? While the debate on Net Neutrality continues on whether providers should or should not have the ability to prioritize data, cyber criminals are flooding our networks with spam and attacks. Such efforts undermine the resiliency of the Internet. Through education and common-sense security efforts people, governments and organizations can work together to curb criminal activity.

Organizations forming the Internet's Substructure can work to provide the education and technology necessary for combating malicious activity, thus raising confidence in Internet usage as well as a country's cyber image.

The question raised in this debate is from the security perspective should members of the Internet Substructure be able to drive intelligence into the

Substructure to combat cyber crime? While different views existed on the level of involvement of regulatory authorities within broadband policy maters, a common standing was expressed that a collaborative multistakeholder work should be done towards establishing global principles and norms that actors should follow. These principles should be shaped through soft co-regulations, such as agreements, that would initially use "name-blame-shame" mechanism to protect the principles; though neither regulators nor business would have interest to see it, these might ultimately be transformed into a hard legislation if not respected by the actors.

Norway guidelines might be taken as a starting point for an agreement of a more global scale. Council of Europe recent initiative on producing practical tools for carriers and service providers may present a good global working framework. Further panels and debates should be organised within the IGF process - on global, regional and national levels - to raise awareness of all aspects of the debate to various stakeholders, to reach consensus on certain core global principles but also define eventual culturally-varying aspects, to analyse possible new economic models and their relations to core principles, to discuss emerging trends (cloud computing, oligopolies and service providers, search engines, Internet of things and NGNs, etc) and the implications to Network Neutrality principles - especially to developing countries.

WS 314.   *Human Rights and Principles in Internet Governance: Practical Steps Forwards*

Report by: Lisa Horner

Panellists: Rebecca MacKinnon (Global Voices/University of Hong Kong); Ebele Okobi-Harris (Director of Business & Human Rights, Yahoo! Inc.); Michael Truppe (Council of Europe Expert); Michael Truppe (Council of Europe Expert); Michael Remmert (Council of Europe); Katitza Rodriguez (EPIC); Natasha Primo (APC)

The ongoing evolution of the internet and associated networked communications has profound implications for human rights. New opportunities for fully realising our fundamental rights and freedoms have been unleashed by the development of new communication tools, platforms and practices. However, new challenges have also arisen, for example with the emergence of new forms of surveillance and censorship. There is an urgent need to develop strategies for protecting human rights in the internet age, whilst at the same time ensuring that internet governance fosters the continued development of an internet that supports the further realisation and expansion of human rights.

This workshop examined practical strategies for incorporating human rights standards into internet governance processes and policies. Discussants shared their experiences of working on a wide range of initiatives that are helping to protect and expand human rights online, drawing out lessons learnt and emerging best practice. The focus was on challenges and opportunities for multi-stakeholder cooperation to create enabling environments and tools for the protection and promotion of human rights in the internet age.

The workshop began with an opening presentation from the UN Special Rapporteur on the Right to Freedom of Opinion and Expression, Mr Frank La Rue. La Rue's comments provided a useful backdrop for the workshop discussions, highlighting the universality of human rights and the importance of understanding the dramatic impacts that the internet is having upon them. He commented that perceptions of freedom of expression have evolved over the years. The right used to be seen as a passive responsibility of the state, in other words not to interfere with individuals' right to freedom of expression. The right is now increasingly recognised as encompassing active responsibilities to enhance the free flow of information and put the necessary infrastructure in place for its full realisation. He highlighted the ways in which communication technologies are helping to raise awareness about human rights violations to increased numbers of people across the world more quickly than was previously possible, and how the internet is enhancing people's ability not only to develop opinions through gathering information, but also to speak out about those opinions. Finally, he stressed the centrality of the internet for helping to achieve social and economic rights; for helping to enhance development. It is therefore crucial for states to work in cooperation with other stakeholders to realise their responsibilities to ensure that all people across the world have the broadest possible level of accessibility to the internet.

The workshop then moved on to examine the experiences that stakeholders have had in trying to ensure that internet governance works to enhance rather than undermine human rights. A number of common points emerged from the discussion.

The relevance of human rights in internet governance

The internet offers tremendous new opportunities for realising civil, political, economic, social and cultural human rights. However, a wide range of current policies and practices in the internet environment also threaten human rights. Internet governance institutions, actors and processes have important roles to play in ensuring that human rights are protected and enhanced as the internet continues to evolve.

There is a strong need for practical approaches to address specific human rights and internet governance issues.

The workshop presented a number of practical initiatives that are helping different stakeholders to address human rights issues through internet governance. These have been most successful where they have focused on a specific problem, helping stakeholders to understand how their activities impact on human rights and identifying particular steps that they can take to address the issues. The focus of initiatives can be geographical (as in Kictanet), thematic (as in the GNI), institutional (as in the CSISAC) or sectoral (as in the Human Rights Guidelines for ISPs). Initiatives have to be based on an understanding and appreciation of the different incentives and priorities that different stakeholders have, causing them to understand and approach issues in different ways. Initiatives should therefore address differences in opinion directly, aiming to find common ground between different stakeholders to build on. They should also include all relevant stakeholders, particularly key gatekeepers, power holders and trend setters. For example, the Council of Europe identified ISPs as key stakeholders with the power to influence whether or not human rights are upheld online, and therefore decided to work with them to draft practical human rights guidelines. All successful initiatives discussed have had heavy involvement from influential, respected and well-connected individuals or institutions which has helped to lend them credibility and spur wider participation.

The importance of multi-stakeholder governance

Workshop participants agreed that getting governance processes and structures right is as important as governance policy and implementation. In the case of the internet, governance based on multi-stakeholder participation and cooperation is likely to be most effective. This because the internet environment is complex, supporting different interest groups and different uses, including those with public interest dimensions. Internet governance policy and practice therefore should be based on multi-stakeholder collaboration if it is to be effective, legitimate and uphold the public interest and human rights.

However, in order to function effectively and fairly, multi-stakeholder internet governance systems have to be carefully designed and managed from the outset. They should be able to draw on a diverse range of expertise and take into consideration the needs and perspectives of all who have a stake in the internet. During the workshop, a number of participants emphasised the importance of identifying the right actors to lead multi-stakeholder processes and of putting effective systems in place to ensure inclusive participation and transparent decision making. The Code of Good Practice initiative is currently drawing upon lessons learnt in this field to draft guidelines for internet governance institutions seeking to enhance participation.

The workshop also discussed how different stakeholders often have different but complementary roles in governance initiatives. For example, in the Global Network Initiative, human rights organisations provide businesses with a source of expertise on rights issues, whilst businesses share insights concerning the practical realities of negotiating between the demands of different stakeholders whilst doing business on the ground.

A number of workshop participants emphasised that governments have a particular role to play in ensuring that the public interest is upheld. Within the human rights framework, states are responsible for protecting and guaranteeing human rights, and this responsibility does not diminish in multi-stakeholder and self-regulatory governance systems. Some workshop participants highlighted the dual role that civil society organisations often have to play in multi-stakeholder governance arenas. Whilst negotiation and consensus building are integral to successful multi-stakeholder governance, many civil society organisations also wish to maintain their role as watchdogs over the government and private sectors, ensuring that ethical standards are upheld and advanced. This can require balancing the need to negotiate and compromise in multi-stakeholder policy making with acting on behalf of the wider public to insist that minimum legal and ethical standards are upheld.

Human rights provide a practical, moral and legal framework for internet governance.

The workshop demonstrated that human rights are not only universal moral standards, but that they also provide a practical framework for defining the rights and wrongs of internet governance. For example, human rights standards provided the GNI with a basis for defining principles and practical guidelines to help companies make decisions when operating in countries where human rights are threatened. They similarly formed the basis for the Council of Europe and EuroISPA's guidelines for ISPs.

The legitimacy of the human rights framework as a tool for internet governance lies largely in its acceptance at the international level, and in its enshrinement in international law. However, the focus of the workshop discussion was on using human rights as a framework for soft or voluntary regulation, showing how they can be used proactively to guide decision making rather than solely retroactively to litigate in cases of rights violation. A number of participants argued that making human rights practical and relevant for key stakeholders is key; legalistic language is not always helpful for businesses and other stakeholders in their day to day work, and the translation of international standards to apply to everyday dilemmas and issues is essential. Some participants expressed concern that these approaches might result in the erosion of human rights standards, and it was agreed that all initiatives should make sure that they build on and advance existing international standards, never inadvertently undermining them.

Transparency and human rights literacy are key underpinning principles

Transparency in decision making and policy approaches emerged during the discussion as a key principle that must be upheld if human rights are to be protected in and through internet governance. This is reflected in the GNI principles, Code of Good Practice, Council of Europe/EuroISPA guidelines and Charter of Human Rights and Principles for the Internet. Transparency in governance processes and decision making is essential for successful multi-stakeholder collaboration as it helps all stakeholders to understand each others' approaches and the influence they have over decisions. If the activities of businesses or other stakeholders affect internet users' human rights, they should be transparent about their policies so that users can make informed decisions about which services to use and how. However, for transparency to contribute towards human rights protection, service providers and other stakeholders need to understand how their activities impinge on human rights, and users need to understand not only what their rights are, but also how to exercise them. Many of the initiatives discussed therefore encompassed awareness raising and education components, and some also use litigation.

The workshop reaffirmed the relevance of human rights to internet governance and the importance of taking concrete steps to uphold human rights in and through internet governance. Through showcasing a wide range of practical initiatives being led by different stakeholders, the workshop provided an arena for sharing information, lessons learnt and best practice approaches that can be built upon and adapted to address different issues in different contexts. A number of participants commented that this process of information sharing was valuable, and should continue on an ongoing basis.

The workshop demonstrated that practical, multi-stakeholder and self-regulatory initiatives can have real impact in upholding and advancing human rights online. However, in order to be effective, such initiatives have to abide by key underpinning principles such as transparency and building on existing human rights standards. They also have to translate human rights into "implementation principles" that apply rights standards to specific internet governance and policy issues.

Whilst progress is being made, there remains much work to do to ensure that internet governance processes and practice protect and advance human rights. Greater coordination is needed between initiatives such as those discussed in this workshop, and more serious commitment is needed by institutions and actors across the three main stakeholder groups to participate in existing initiatives and implement new ones.

This workshop demonstrated that the IGF can and should be a venue for making progress in these areas. This progress would be accelerated if human rights and associated principles received more explicit attention within the main agenda of future IGFs and internet governance policy arenas. This workshop is part of a wider shift in policy debate from talking about the theory of human rights and internet governance in largely abstract terms towards identifying practical opportunities for multi-stakeholder collaboration and change. In order to maintain this momentum, future discussion and activity should address specific human rights issues faced by specific stakeholder groups, focused on addressing the following questions:

- How does the existing internet policy and practice of specific stakeholder groups affect human rights, both in terms of violating rights and affecting prospects for realising their positive dimensions?
- How can respect for human rights standards be incorporated into specific internet policy frameworks?
- What challenges are being faced by different stakeholders that are continuing to prevent human rights from being upheld in and through internet governance?
- What practical steps can be taken, and what roles can different stakeholders play?

WS 323.   Roundtable: Balancing the Need for Security and the Concern for Civil Liberties

Report by: Sivasubramanian Muthusamy

Chair: Alejandro Pisanty (Director General for Academic Computing Services of the National University of Mexico and Member of the Board of Trustees of the Internet Society)

Panellists: Prof Dr. Wolfgang Benedek (Director of the Institute of International Law and International Relations of the University of Graz, Austria and of the

European Training and Research Centre for Human Rights and Democracy in Graz); Steve Purser (Head of the Department of Technical Competence and Security, European Network and Information Security Agency); Prof. Simon Davies (Founder and Director, Privacy International and visiting Senior Fellow, London School of Economics); Bruce Schneier ("Security Guru" and Internationally renowned security technologist and Writer); Barrister Zahid Usman Jamil (Councillor of the ICANN Generic Names Supporting Organization and Member of the Multistakeholder Advisory Group of the Internet Governance Forum)

Governments are concerned about Cyberwarfare and related threats, business entities suffer from cybercrime in various ways while the average user faces various forms of security threats online. These threats are real but the measures against these threats are considered disproportionate and happen to cause greater harm sometimes than the threats to be warded off. Moves to address the security concerns often result in breach of privacy, This round table was organized to bring together different points of view on Security and Privacy and encourage a free and unrestrained debate to look for convergence in some areas between the two sides. The roundtable approached this broadly with a view to define and enumerate concerns on both sides and look for unseen common grounds.

Dr. Wolfgang Benedek: When 9/11 happened, the reactions were to tighten security and to introduce new kinds of regulations. Our title is large, Security Vs Civil Liberties and balance could be refuted in a certain way. Why should we balance absolute human rights against security interests? Article 17 of the International Covenant on Civil and Political Rights does not contain any qualifications. But Article 8 of the European Convention on Human Rights has certain possibilities for restricting rights, in particular for public safety and security. But in International covenants, under article 4 a state has to declare a state of emergency to introduce any restrictions. Article 8 of the European Convention on Human Rights, the qualification is that such measures have to be necessary in a democratic society. We have certain Standards developed by European court of human rights in Strasbourgh, on how to deal with such restrictions. Also the standards developed by the European Court are restrictive on such restrictions.

During the terror attack in 2009 in Mumbai, India, many International participants of the IGF Hyderabad had to take a flight from Mumbai to Hyderabad despite adverse travel advisories. There is a certain measure of insecurity that we have to take into account in our world of today. You can not fully avoid risks. The anti terrorist legislations which we have seen over the last few years are under the presumption that you can largely avoid risks and therefore you have to give away freedom in order to preserve security. We have given away quite a good part of our freedom but I am not sure of its effect on security. The hypothesis is that there is problem of proportionality between the measures of restriction and the gains on security due to the measures.

Steve Purser: One of the fundamental rights of citizens is the right to understand what is going on, but we don't understand what is going on in terms of security. We use a lot of acronyms which are not easy to grasp.

Citizens have to develop Electronic Common sense - a way of behaving in electronic world if we have to make progress.

Simon Davies: Privacy was nascent and almost invisible as an advocacy stream twenty years ago. Over the past twenty years people have developed a sense of privacy as a fundamental right, though not as an absolute right. There are restrictions on privacy, there always have been. There is nothing different today from what it was twenty years ago or a few hundred years ago. What I sense is the emerging social contract which involves right to know, right to understand, the right to be brought into the equation of the way society works. That is part of the way people expect society to go or the way Governments to behave. A fundamental problem is that while people want to assert their right to privacy. When people talk about the right to preserve their privacy, they are constantly told to justify their position. There is a slippage on the security end. one of the biggest problem we face in balancing security and civil liberties is that Security has become such a means to an end, security has become such an industry that it is almost self fulfilling. For Instance in England, the government claimed that it should collect all data related to cars going in and out of London. for national security purpose. The objection to this idea of high-jacking data from the congestion management system in the name of security without providing any evidence or adequate justification, without providing a matrix by which it could be judged, examined if it is a justifiable claim. while data protection rights are eliminated in the name of National Security. The objections were thrown out because the Government maintained that the citizens can get information about what the Government is doing therefore the rights are asserted The information that we get is that the Government is collecting the information.

This is a vicious loop and exemplifies the problem we are facing. National security and security in general are a means to an end, it is not quantifiable. Try getting the FBI or CIA to quantify their claim of national security for privacy exemption- it is extremely difficult. There is a disconnect between the expectations of citizens who want to assert their privacy rights and the expectations of many security professionals who believe that the mere mention of word security should give them a golden pass through the privacy conundrum. That is not an emerging problem it is a growing problem, the one that we have to deal with.

Bruce Schneier: We are here having this conversation, because the Internet in a sense is a very identifying technology. Someone who wants to send an email needs to know where you are. When you send a query to a search engine, the search engine needs to know where to send the information back to. Internet and Information Technology have a lot of identity embedded in, but it is sloppy, because it is the computer that is identified not the person. There is a lot of identity, but there is a disconnect between the computer and the person in the chair, a disconnect between the network and the person. This sloppiness is bothersome to a lot of people in government or corporations who want to use their data for political purpose or for marketing, for control. We have entered an era where national security is the pass to do anything, in a way that it was when there was a war on drugs was ten years ago that you can use that phrase to justify anything. There is a wide-spread belief that there is a situation of Security Vs Privacy, that in

316

order to have security you have to give up your rights to privacy. If you want more privacy, you have to give up security. This is meaningless. For instance the metal detectors in a building are a security measure, but they have nothing to do with privacy. The locks that we use in a hotel room are essential to security. that is nothing to do with privacy. There are dozens, hundreds of security measures that have nothing to do with privacy. Identity based security has to do with privacy.

There is a wide spread belief between governments and the corporations pushing these technologies that If we knew who everybody was we can pick out the bad guys. This is fuelling the desire for information which is pushing on our privacy. Already the police have extraordinary powers to invade our privacy but there are limits on that power. There is a warrant process, a disclosure process, a judicial process, all designed to limit the powers when they invade our privacy. that is a key thing to pay attention to. the only thing security vs. privacy if we look at one threat We live in a world where there are many threats. Terrorists are a threat, repressive governments are the second threat. unethical corporations are the third threat. nosy neighbours are the forth threat. When you look at all the threats you quickly realize that privacy is not antithetical to security, privacy is component of security. In order for us to be secure we must also have privacy. They are not in opposition at all.

By giving away our privacy in some misguided attempts to make us secure against terrorism, we are actually reducing our security against governments against multi national corporations against those who are in power. Privacy is empowering. Giving privacy to people raises their power with respect to government. That is why it is important and that is why it is part of security.

Zahid Usman Jamil: Corporations tend to want to identify users and collect a lot of data. From user perspective, in social networks, there is anonymity. One does not have to disclose information, or present national identity card. One can have multiple identities but Law enforcements can trace the IP address from the mac address.   Businesses have to maintain certain amount of credibility, certain amount of security for consumers about their privacy. To that extent it is imperative on the part of business to maintain privacy, the difficulty is when they are faced with national regimes, who wish to make use of the data that businesses have collected. This a challenge for business.   Do businesses avoid regimes that don't respect privacy? Too much regulation legislation affects innovation. It is not practical for business to avoid territories that are not completely free. It is important to make consumers feel secure about the privacy of their data.

Steve Purser: There is a need for a cultural change, need to develop electronic common sense, People need to need to develop a basic risk management strategy by which they can handle all risks on or off the Internet. Legislation is a clumsy tool, heavy handed tool, takes time to develop, and by the time it is developed it becomes obsolete. Legislation is national. Internet is global. Legislation does not satisfy needs. It is softer measures, proactive, preventive measures that will win the day

Bruce Schneier: If we examine the history of common sense, we find that it is slow to develop. New technologies can take 20 or 30 years before the new generation develops common sense. It is clumsier than legislation. It takes even longer. Legislation becomes obsolete by the time it is enacted, so it is clumsy. Common sense is clumsier than that. We live in a world that changes faster than ever before. A thousand years ago, one did not see anything new in all his lifetime. Now we see something new every year. We might be living in a world where common sense can no longer catch up. It changes so fast that it is impossible for people to integrate new risks, new trade offs, new socializations, faster than they change.

Twitter did not exist two years ago and there may be something new two years from now. By the time we develop common sense about twitter, it is too late, twitter may be gone. Younger generations are better at detecting nonsense on the Internet. We might be heading to an era where common sense becomes obsolete. We don't know what that means to society.

Simon Davies: The phase of change is such that common sense can not engage the problems we face, we face the interesting dilemma similar to the migration from agrarian to the industrial, to the cities, Legislation ultimately had to take over. Industrial health and safety for example had to be taken over by the state as a requirement. We don't want that to happen in the Internet. Perhaps we need to find another formula, perhaps we have to lean towards engineering solutions.

Prof Wolfgang Benedek: There is considerable difference between north and south, privacy as known in the North is not known the same way in the south.

Zahid Jamil: The European debate, the American debate on Security Vs Privacy, it is not a debate that translates well in some developing countries. It gets misunderstood, misused, misinterpreted in developing countries and actually affects freedom of expression. For instance it is not possible for Internet users in Pakistan to tune into Hulu videocasts on their laptops because these are prohibited from broadcasting in Pakistan. VOIP can not be used because it affects [telecom] business. Skype is blocked in many countries. Had there been a debate when began, some governments might have decided that the Internet would be undesirable because there is pornography, Users wont know what to do, because things are moving too fast from a southern perspective, Legislation about privacy would lead to legislation on morals.

Alejandro Pisanty: The legislation and rules that protect privacy are sometimes seen as a huge obstacle to protect people in enforcement of the right to safety and security. Privacy rules from telecommunication law in several countries make traffic data - for instance, who is calling who - confidential. If there is a kidnap or extortion going on, the police force can not get the traffic data in a timely manner to follow up and persecute the criminals. The procedures that the law and order agencies have to go through will allow time for a kidnapped person to be killed by the time the warrants are obtained to get the phone companies to release the necessary data related to a phone call or the IP address information for an email message associated with the crime.

Rebecca Mackinnon, Cofounder, Global Networks Initiative: In China measures ostensibly to protect children are used to control political content. Measures to fight terrorism are used to oppress minorities while at the same time there are legitimate concerns among people in china about crime on the Internet. So we do have these universal concerns but they play out in different regimes in very different ways. The danger of unintended consequences is that certain regimes use what is happening in the West as an enabling excuse to solidify their powers. So it is very difficult to have one size fits all type of legislation.

Legislation is an over-blunt instrument. Companies are caught between governments and citizens, In some places governments can be a force for good in law enforcement, but in some cases they are not. So an initiative such as the Global Networks Initiative which is a multi-stakeholder initiative of which Google, Yahoo and Microsoft at present form part of, becomes relevant in arriving at base principles on free expression and privacy. As these are applied, how each company approaches the base principles depend upon the specific circumstances in a specific country so the multi-stakeholder process arrives at benchmarks. In some cases legislation may be helpful, but in other cases government is part of the problem.

A gentleman from the Asia pacific region: In Asia Pacific most of the problems related to Security and Privacy come from Governments. Governments have their own explanations; National Interest is higher than personal interests. This gives governments the excuse to compromise on personal privacy.

John Laprise, North Western University Qatar: There is a semantic issue that exists within Us Government. There are two parallel privacy definitions On the one hand there is the traditional protection of privacy which is protection from intrusion by governments. At the same time there is a responsibility of the federal government to protect their citizen's privacy from intrusion by outside the country. In United States the later definition always triumphs the former definition. In the post 9/11 environment, measure to sift through external communication is done in the name of the second definition of privacy.

Audrey Ponk Intel Corporation: We need accountability mechanisms rather than overly burnt legislations. There is evidence of movement towards developing accountability mechanisms. How can we find accountability mechanisms that find a middle ground. One example is about how law enforcement agencies obtain crucial information in time sensitive situation, for example in a situation where a hostage could die if the information isn't available in time. There are cooperative mechanisms, accountability mechanisms that have worked in the past, in different jurisdictions globally, not to circumvent but to enhance the judicial process, so that corporations who hold private information or access to information can work together to get critical data in critical situations. release the crucial data By these

319

cooperative mechanisms law and order agencies have been able to obtain crucial information in time.

Alejandro Pisanty: Historically, mostly in Europe, Privacy was split into Private Life and Intimacy. It was found that it was very hard to protect them legally. Personal data is much easier to define and legislate. Personally identifiable data is in the hands of the State. This data is of two types, that which is mandatory as in tax return data and that which is provided to the State as optional Information or obtained by the State legally or illegally by surveillance, espionage and other legal and illegal means. Then there is data in the hands of private parties.

There are three kinds of law. The law in Europe which is extremely exacting and demanding with all kinds of rights embedded in the legislation for citizens. Users has all kinds of rights whether to allow or disallow transfer of the data. Another would be the US kind of view. In the US private data is handed out voluntarily to business establishments, like information disclosed voluntarily to the local mega store or video store, It is assumed to be voluntary. Many companies are sloppy about data protection. The market hypothesis is that one can choose the companies that are good at data protection, which is also equally sloppy as a hypothesis. in protecting the data. The third would be the law prevailing in the rest of the world, which is the law of the jungle. The split between intimacy and data protection looked right 30 years ago. Now even extreme examples of intimacy provide digital data recorded in a permanent form This gives rise to some very complex situations, whereby our intimacy has also become a provider of data.

Steve Purser: For every rule with a good example, there is one with a bad example. Context is enormously important. In security there are very few tools and it is a question of using the best tools. Lets talk in terms of alternatives. One is the idea of common sense which is limited. One is the idea of using legislation which is slow. The third is the idea of using software but human brain is more powerful than software. We need to develop Electronic Common Sense. We know that there can not be 100 percent security. If someone is to approach on the street and ask for details one is cautious, but it is amazing how much of information is shared in a chat room.

Wolfgang Benedek: When it comes to law enforcement, the mechanisms are there. Particularly after the Madrid and London bombings. In Austria, the police have to simply sign a form, these provisions are used mostly in case of saving someone from suicide. That would be a computer search and would require a warrant from a judge. But in Europe there are data retention directives that require data to be retained for a period of 6 to 24 months. Vast amounts of data are to be collected allegedly for anti terrorism, anti-crime measures. It goes beyond reasonable limits and disproportional to keep all this data This directive is challenged together by business, civil society and by governments. Austria has challenged it in court and have asked human rights groups to suggest ways of implementing the directives in the most human friendly manner. US has been secretly collecting swift and credit card data, and when discovered, US is negotiating with European governments to do this transparently.

Bruce Schneier: Social network sites avoid any mention of privacy as they want the users to share information. But they have very exacting privacy rules that are buried and they are very hard to implement. It is wrong to think that people will get better choices if companies compete on privacy. The goal actually is not to give people better choices, often the goal is to make better profits which they achieve by giving people fewer choices.

Zahid Jami: Data retention is a serious concern for business. It is a cost issue. If we concentrate on security aspects, it is important that we don't confuse the developing countries in the very high level of some of the discussions. It would be useful to come down to developing countries and make them aware. There are such a lot of obstructions created in evangelizing, informing or making aware developing countries the benefits of the Budapest convention on cybercrime. It is not a law enforcement agency tool, or for cooperation between governments. It has specific human rights articles that require safeguards, due processes, judicial oversight, all of which get lost in translation and not conveyed to the civil society in the country. There were specific clauses and articles that were removed from the legislation when these model clauses go down to developing countries. Nobody was made aware of it. This is a convention with some balance, this convention need to go down to the developing countries, It needs to be explained to business that the model clauses from EU on data transfer is a frame work. If the developing country does not have the legislation, the businesses at least have to subscribe to the model clauses. These are duties and obligations if businesses in a developing country have to do business with the European union.

Simon Davies: Companies have to some how ignore privacy One of the ways privacy isn't invaded through exception, in the name of public security. In the movie Batman the Dark Knight, Batman has built the capacity to look into all mobile phones in Gotham city. The dialog against the use of such technology is revealing. [dialogue deleted] Most privacy is systematically invaded Whether it is batman or real world, if citizens are to give away privacy, the authorities have to be more accountable, they have to give away some of their secrecy, legacy of being able to hold back. That would be an enduring formula for the protection of privacy. If we can keep that as a concept in mind, then many of the problems of privacy systematically will disappear.

Wolfgang Benedek: In the process of bringing the cyber-crime convention to developing countries, the human rights dimension is lost. The problem is that in the Cyber-crime convention it is said that the human rights part is left to the national governments. This is a structural flaw in the cyber-crime convention that human rights concerns are not included on the same level as security concerns. More has to be done in order to get the full concept across. We have some orientation, from rules. In International Covenants on Civil and Political rights, Privacy is not explained in any large way. APC in 2001 in its Internet Rights Chart tried to translate privacy into this environment This is being updated to bring it up to actual needs. Stakeholders are not against human rights.

Zahid Jamil: In developing countries there is one convention available, one standard. We have a model law from the commonwealth which is based on the Budapest Convention. We will take something out of the convention for privacy and human rights. That convention focuses on preservation and not on data retention. Second, it talks about judicial oversight, due process, and incorporates the UN convention on human rights and the European convention on human rights. These clauses have to be explained to the developing countries, otherwise it is only the Security protocols that are adopted and nothing else.

Investigating agencies ask for information. To what extent the law and order authorities are themselves accountable? Developed countries have tribunals to look into the use of regulatory powers but such accountability mechanisms do not exist in some developing countries. These are aspects that need to be looked into. There is a lot that each of us can do to protect our privacy. The framework of Rights against Obligations applies to citizens and not to Governments. There is a real imbalance.

Bruce Schneier: There are some rights that simply come as rights. That is the way the world has to work. If people are going to throw their private data without worrying about consequences, it wouldn't help. One obligation is to behave responsibly while giving out data. Another has to do with delegation.

Sara State Department, United States of America: The e-government Act in the United States requires the Government to disclose what it does with personally identifiable data collected. There are privacy impact assessments published which can be shared with developing countries.

Zahid Jamil: The best practices can be shared with the developing countries who can determine the level they want to implement.

Bruce Schneier: The number of exemptions to that act make it irrelevant.

Eric Iriarte Peru: United States was to sell some arms to Chile, which transparently appeared on the US government website. In Latin America there are no laws for data protection, laws are based on security. In Mexico there is very quick movement for access to information, without any privacy laws, which means access to information is sought without any cause.

Pranesh Prakash, Center for Internet and Society, Bangalore, India: A lot of debate is happening on a theoretical level. A lot of good ideas are coming out. These ideas have to be translated into good systems of governance in countries like India. Consumer organizations are trying to make human readable privacy signs such as that of the creative commons. Concerning citizen's privacy a lot of systems that have been discredited by Bruce Schneier such as Key escrow are sought to brought to India. There is a national ID scheme that many countries are freezing. In India open wireless is no longer allowed without being registered with Government. There have been debates on these issues, but these debates find actual recognition in the governance systems. That translation is very important.

The debates taking place across the pond have to be relevant for other countries and it should be made sure that it is not mistranslated. We need to think of data as the pollution problem of the Information Age. All processes produce it. It stays around. It has some secondary uses and has to be disposed off properly. Just like in the Industrial Age, in the rush for progress in the Information Age, we tend to ignore pollution, ignore the issue. The decisions we make today will have profound effect in the next ten, twenty, fifty years.

Are you afraid that our children will ask us tomorrow "Why didn't you forbid me to put my data in facebook? I can't get a job". Actually that is not true. There is the greatest generation gap since the Rock and Roll. That is the old generation talking. We already have CEOs who blog. Soon everybody will be on facebook. We can't tell our children not to do something. They are right and we are wrong. Security is not in general algorithmic. Most good security solutions need a lot of brain power. We need to look at alternatives and choose wisely. We have three social solutions. One idea of good practices, or electronic common sense. One is the idea of intelligent software, the third is legislation and each has its place and the key to issue is using them wisely.

The Internet is one of the large spaces where there is large freedom. This obviously makes government uneasy and find ways of control. In Europe there is a proposal to give one single identity to every Internet user who has to disclose it every time he goes online. We have to make sure that it does not happen. The security debate has a chilling effect on privacy and other civil liberties. We have to explain civil liberties to all stakeholders in a way that they are not afraid and make them see them as a common way of interacting in cyber space. When in future is so obsessed with exposing themselves, privacy would lose its important. People would be suspicious of non disclosure. I am wondering if we left the engineers out. I am wondering if we can do something in the next 12 months which involves the engineers. We have to get the engineers involved. That is one of the missing ingredients.

Can we ban the word security for a year? security is a very charged word. Can we use the phrase risk management instead? There are a lots of different words, security, risk, privacy, vulnerability. different shades of the same thing. We have to hit security head on. It is emotionally charged and you cant ignore the word, cant ignore the emotional charges. One of the reasons why we have nutty policies in my country is because people of afraid. Fear. That is another word. These words are important. The emotions are important. And the meaning right or wrong, erroneous or true are all important. This is hard, not easy, it is not new. The old notion of security is as old as multi-cellular life. The first thing that you will introduce to life forms is how to reproduce, how to eat and how to avoid being eaten. This is it.

Security is not black and white, it is shades of grey. As we move further and further into technological development we have to understand that we are less in control. There we see Bruce's point about data pollution a good one. The classic book on security says first list your assets, then value your assets and then protect your assets. A lot of companies don't even know their assets. And by the time they define their assets, it has all changed. Part of security is compromise. It is being able to live with a bit of fussiness and taking the best alternative that is open to you. I do like the analogy of risk management. It is essentially risk management of a particular sort.

Conclusions

- National security and security in general are a means to an end, it is not quantifiable.
- Citizens have to develop Electronic Common sense - a way of behaving in electronic world.
- We have given away quite a good part of our freedom but its effect on security has been less than proportional.
- Privacy is not antithetical to security, privacy is component of security. In order for us to be secure we must also have privacy.
- There is considerable difference between north and south, privacy as known in the North is not known the same way in the south
- The danger of unintended consequences is that certain regimes use what is happening in the West as an enabling excuse to solidify their powers. So it is very difficult to have one size fits all type of legislation.
- We need accountability mechanisms rather than overly burnt legislations.
- If citizens are to give away privacy, the authorities have to be more accountable, they have to give away some of their secrecy, legacy of being able to hold back. That would be an enduring formula for the protection of privacy.
- There is a structural flaw in the cyber-crime convention that human rights concerns are not included on the same level as security concerns. More has to be done in order to get the full concept down to the developing countries
- Developed countries have tribunals to look into the use of regulatory powers but such accountability mechanisms do not exist in some developing countries. These are aspects that need to be looked into
- The best practices can be shared with the developing countries who can determine the level they want to implement.
- A lot of debate is happening on a theoretical level. A lot of good ideas are coming out. These ideas have to be translated into good systems of governance in countries like India.
- We have to explain civil liberties to all stakeholders in a way that they are not afraid and make them see them as a common way of interacting in cyber space.

WS 346.   *Open Knowledge Environment in Bridging the Digital Divide for Innovative Research and Development*

Report by: Ma Jing

Organizer: China Association for Science and Technology

Panellists: GAO Xinmin (Standing Vice Chairman of Internet Society of China, Member of the Advisory Committee for State Informatization); QING Sihan (Institute of Software, Chinese Academy of Sciences); Dr. William Drake (Senior Associate, Centre for International Governance, the Graduate Institute of International Studies, Geneva, Switzerland); TAO Xiaofeng (School of Telecommunication Engineering, Beijing University of Post and Telecommunication); LIU Chuang (Director of Global Change Information and

Research Center, Institute of Geography and Natural Resources, Chinese Academy of Sciences); Lambert van Nistelrooij (Dutch politician, Member of the European Parliament. Member of the Christian Democratic Appeal); Wolfgang Kleinwächter (International Communication Policy and Regulation, University of Aarhus)

Through panel discussion, the following consensus was reached:
- The OKE was needed, as it will help developing countries in the innovative research, education and development;
- Much attention was paid to challenges of Internet governance dimension of open knowledge environment, especially in developing countries. Concerns on national security, intellectual property protection, technology transformation and capacity building were identified at the discussions;
- Experiences and cases on strategy and policy reform from China as well as European countries were presented. Diversity modes of Internet governance of OKE from the cases showed the gaps and possibility in enhancing OKE.
- It is necessary to continue more detailed discussions and exchanges regarding the Internet governance dimension of OKE, especially the principles and guidelines of OKE.

Discussions on principles and guidelines of internet governance of open knowledge environment in bridging digital divide will follow up. China Association of Science and Technology (CAST) will work with the partners to continue the discussions.

WS 361. Open Standards: A Rights-Based Approach

Report by: Pranesh Prakash

Panellists: Tim Berners-Lee (World Wide Web Consortium/Web Foundation); Renu Budhiraja (Department of Information and Technology, India); Sunil Abraham (Centre for Internet and Society); Steve Mutkoski (Microsoft); Rishab Aiyer Ghosh (UNU-MERIT); Aslam Raffee (Sun Microsystems)

There is a complex and entangled relationship between the rights of consumers, citizens, non-citizens, governments, competing corporations, etc., within which the promotion/adoption/enforcement of standards plays a part. For instance, governments have a duty towards their people to ensure that the data that they hold in trust for the people is easily accessible to them and can be reused by them. Still, governments are also the largest consumers of standards, and by adopting certain standards, force the public to make certain choices as well. Similarly, ensuring unhindered portability from one product to another comparable one, and interoperability of comparable devices and applications should be seen as part of that set of minimum rights of consumers, inclusive of governments, that corporations are obliged to respect. Part of the aim of the workshop will be to disentangle the relationships between some of these rights and map out some directions which a rights-based framework can take. To further establish the translation of these rights from principles to practice will be the goal of this workshop.
The workshop will help bring out the issues that are currently being faced and likely to be encountered in the future by governments, consumers and

the public, addressing specific areas such as the needs of the disabled community and perspectives of developing countries, and the possible solutions that governments and vendors can offer through implementation of open standards. The discussion would primarily revolve around issues of governmental procurement of software, open e-governance, portability, and interoperability, which affect everything from communications protocols, documents, multimedia, and databases, to hardware.

Importance of Open Standards in Government-held data

- Sir Tim Berners-Lee began by contextualising the entire debate, addressing the dynamic nature of rights and the differences that may arise in the case of competing and conflicting rights.
- The importance of open standards at the government level was then discussed. It was noted that governments have a duty towards their people to ensure that the data that they hold in trust for the people is easily accessible to them and can be reused by them. Governments, by adopting certain standards force the public to make certain choices as well.

Social effects of open standards

- Since technological standards exhibit path dependence, it is difficult to change over to another even if that other format is superior to the first.
- Thus, clearly, standards benefit when there is a 'natural monopoly' and the challenge lies in creating a monopoly in a technology without the supplier of that technology exhibiting monopolistic tendencies.
- This can only be done when the technology is open and developed openly, and has multiple implementations, of which the web standards and the W3C are excellent examples.
- If the technology or the process are semi-open, then because of the few intellectual property rights attached to the technology, some would be better off than others.

Citizens' Rights

- Citizens should not be required to pirate or purchase particular software to interact with the state. If e-governance solutions are based on proprietary standards, not all citizens would be equal.
- Propriety standards for e-governance solutions hinder citizens' access to information (e.g. South African Election Commission and Hurricane Katrina relief site requiring the use of a particular browser)
- Governments issuing compulsory license should be explored a possibility of ensuring open standards for their citizens.
- Government Interoperability Frameworks should be taken into account, and all government-to-citizen (G2C) information should be transacted via open standards.
- Proprietary standards act like pseudo-intellectual property rights, just as DRMs, by adding a layer on top of rights such as copyright. They can thus prevent the exercise of fair use and fair dealing rights because of an inability to legally negotiate the standards in which the content is encoded in a cost-free manner.

Governmental Concerns and Implementation

- Intra- and Inter-Governmental Interoperability and Risks of Vendor Lock-In
- Renu Budhiraja of the Department of Information and Technology identified the need to move towards a single-window government service for citizens, enabling them to interact easily with the government's various departments.
- While such an initiative must be centralized for it to be effective, it is crucial that its implementation be decentralized and suited to each district or localities' needs. This would ensure ease of access as well as efficiency.
- India's National Policy on Open Standards, to be finalized soon, outlines the principles based on which particular standards required for governmental functioning are to be chosen or evolved. It aims to ensure long-term accessibility to public documents, seamless interoperability between departments and reduce the risk of vendor lock-ins.

Problems with Reasonable and Non-Discriminatory Standards (RAND)

- Ms. Budhiraja also identified the problem in selecting between a superior technology, which is reasonable and non-discriminatory and a royalty-free standard and the government's position when, in a particular domain, a RAND standard is the only option and there is no royalty-free alternative standard.
- Sunil Abraham gave the example of the Smart Card Operating System for Transport Application (SCOSTA) standard in India, which reduced costs considerably, bringing it down from Rs. 600 per smart card to Rs. 30 per card, although a more expensive RAND standard alternative was also available. - Single v. Multiple Open Standards
- The question was raised: If interoperability is the ultimate aim, at the government level, should the idea of multiple open standards be given weightage?
- Multiple implementations of a standard promote competition, but multiple standards defeat the purpose of the standardization process and must be avoided.
- But having two standards with similar functions but different domains of operation does not make them multiple standards (e.g., XSLT and CSS). –

Market Maturity

- Sometimes, when a government department adopts a particular standard, it finds itself with limited product options, with a lack of vendors using that standard.
- Governments should lead the market, since governmental decisions also give signals to the market and help direct attention to the open standards.
  * Under-mature standards maybe designated as "preferred standards", thus helping push industry in a particular direction.

Organizational and Semantic Interoperability in eGovernance

- Steve Mutkoski of Microsoft identified the real challenges in e-governance interoperability as organizational and semantic interoperability and not so much technical interoperability.
- Since the transition from a paper-based to electronic medium did not see any institutional or organisational changes, governments continue to function with electronic data the same way that they did with paper-based data. They often lack strong privacy policies regarding the data that each of their departments holds.
- He stressed that sometimes standards are not enough to ensure interoperability. Transparency of implementations, collaboration with community, active participation in maintenance of standards, etc., would help.
- There is a need for continued public sector reform, with a focus on citizen-centric e-governance. Conclusions and further comments:
- Technological standards have grave social impact, and thus should not be left solely to technical committees
- Many citizens' rights are affected directly by the choice of standards at the governmental level. There are multiple instances where citizens have suffered when government agencies have resorted to using propriety standards.
- Multiple standards in a single domain are antithetical to the process of standardization, while multiple implementations aid in competition.
- Standards are not a singular solution for interoperability issues, but without open standards interoperability would not be possible. Open standards are necessary, but not sufficient.
- In the interests of their citizens, governments should lead the market, rather than let industry dictate proprietary standards.
- Governments should categorize open standards, with clear time-tables for shifting to open standards, to enable industry to meet governmental demands satisfactorily.

OF 541. Freedom of Expression and Access to Information in Online (Cross-border) Environments---International Cooperation in Connection with Critical Internet Resources

Report by: Elvana Thaçi

Organizer: Council of Europe

Moderator: Mrs Elfa Ýr Gylfadóttir (Head of Division of Media at the Ministry of Education, Science and Culture of Iceland. Member of the Bureau of the Council of Europe Steering Committee on the Media and New Communication Services)

Panellists: Mr József Györkös (State Secretary, Ministry of Higher Education, Science and Technology of the Republic of Slovenia); Mr Andrew McIntosh (Chair of the Sub-Committee on the Media and Rapporteur on Media Freedom, Council of Europe Parliamentary Assembly); Mr Antti Peltomäki, (Deputy Director-General of the Directorate-General for the Information Society and Media, European

Commission); Mr Jean-Jacques Subrenat (ICANN Board Director); Bertrand de la Chapelle (French Ministry of Foreign Affairs, France); Wolfgang Benedek (Institute for International Law and International Relations, Karl-Franzens-Universität Graz, Austria); Marco Gercke (Cybercrime Research Institute, Germany); Thomas Schneider (International Affairs Department of the Swiss Federal Office of Communication, Switzerland); Rolf Weber (University of Zurich, Switzerland)

The Open Forum explored the connection between a possible right to have access to the Internet and consequences for international law. A number of issues relevant to the implementation of the Resolution on Internet governance and critical Internet resources adopted by the 1st Council of Europe Conference of Ministers responsible for Media and New Communication Services in May 2009 were considered. The moderator laid out the framework of the discussions and addressed specific questions to each of the panellists concerning their institutional perspectives on the protection of human rights in online environments. Questions and comments were elicited from the audience.

Discussions explored a number of issues in relation to the protection of human rights in online environments, the stability of the Internet and responsibilities that states share in that respect. Different views were expressed with respect to the issue of access to the Internet as a basic right. It was reported by discussants that, in some countries in Europe, access to the Internet is understood as part of an enforceable right. It was suggested that this understanding should be taken up at the international level. Other panellists and speakers argued that, while desirable, the existence of this right is first of all a question of possibility to deliver on the public service value of the Internet. It was furthermore underlined that principles of international cooperation should be determined in order to be able to deal with malicious use of the Internet. Mr Peltomäki reported that access to information and freedom of expression are duly considered when developing regulatory policies in the European Union. In that regard, the telecoms package deals with a number of aspects of protection of human rights in online environments.

It was argued by some speakers and other discussants that ICANN is a global service provider and that its actions have indirect effects on human rights. Mr Subrenat noted that the implementation of fundamental freedoms is the responsibility of governments. The new Affirmation of Commitments underlines public interest as a key element of ICANN's commitment to accountability and transparency. In that respect, ICANN has a duty of public trust; the next important step is to define the standards against which the international community wants to measure ICANN.

Conclusions

- Access to the Internet is intimately related to the exercise of freedom of expression and the right to information regardless of frontiers as provided for in Article 10 of the European Convention on Human Rights.
- The use of the Internet is a central part of democratic life. Access to the Internet is part of an enforceable right in some countries

- This understanding gives rise to consideration of access to the Internet from a trans-boundary relations perspective and constitutes the premise for thinking international cooperation on cross-border Internet.
- Principles of international cooperation should be formulated in order to be able to deal with misuse of the Internet and to ensure the stability of the signal.
- There is a duty of public trust intrinsically linked to the management of critical Internet resources by ICANN. In that respect the criteria and the standards against which the community should measure ICANN action need to be defined.

DC. Freedom of Expression and Freedom of the Media on the Internet Dynamic Coalition Meeting

Report by: Lisa Horner

Panellists: Frank La Rue (U.N. Special Rapporteur on the right to freedom of opinion and expression); Sami Ben Gharbia (Advocacy Director for Global Voices Online); Johan Hallenborg (Special Advisor at the Swedish Ministry for Foreign Affairs); Mogens Schmidt (Deputy Assistant Director-General for the Communication and Information Sector, UNESCO)

The Freedom of Expression and Freedom of the Media on the Internet Dynamic Coalition meeting was attended by a broad range of stakeholders from the civil society, governmental and business sectors. Each contributor reflected on the main challenges and opportunities for freedom of expression in the internet age, outlined the work being done by their respective institutions and provided suggestions for the future direction and work of the dynamic coalition. Their presentations were followed by open discussion from the floor. A number of key themes and points of agreement emerged during the course of the presentations and discussion, outlined below.

The centrality of the human right to freedom of expression. All workshop participants stressed the importance of freedom of expression for the realisation of the humanity of all people across the world. One participant commented that, whilst freedom of expression used to be seen as the passive responsibility of states, the importance of realising the positive dimensions of the right is increasingly recognised. These positive dimensions include providing access to the means of communication, ensuring that people have the ability to both receive and document information, and ensuring diversity and pluralism in communications content. This point was echoed by other participants who stressed the importance of all three dimensions of the right to freedom of expression as defined in the Universal Declaration of Human Rights: the ability to seek, receive and impart information and ideas through any media, regardless of frontiers.

The internet has unleashed new opportunities for realising freedom of expression. Workshop participants agreed that the internet presents new opportunities to protect freedom of expression and to realise and enhance its positive dimensions. One discussant highlighted the rise of citizen journalism and activism, with the internet allowing people to document news and views on an everyday basis and to reach out to global audiences. Another commented that in the past, it took decades for crimes against humanity to come to public attention, whereas now the mobile internet has opened windows through which awareness can be raised about human rights violations in real time. The internet has made the human right to be able to seek, receive and impart information a tangible possibility for increasing numbers of people across the world.

Freedom of expression is under threat in old and new ways. Whilst the internet has given rise to new opportunities for freedom of expression, both workshop discussants and people participating from the floor stressed that significant challenges remain. Many of these challenges are not new, with legal systems, regulation and activities continuing to restrict and undermine freedom of expression across the world in both online and offline media. A number of participants raised the issue of defamation law all too often being used across the world to restrict legitimate speech, arguing that defamation should not be a criminal offence and should never be used to limit criticism of public policy or officials. One participant stressed the danger of the notion that ideologies and ideas can be defamed. Other long-standing violations of freedom of expression that were discussed include the direct censorship of communications content, violence against, or intimidation of, journalists and other forms of indirect censorship. One discussant described censorship practices as a form of terror, and expressed shock at its continued extensiveness and pervasiveness across the world.

With the emergence of the internet, these threats to expression remain, and in many instances have been exacerbated. For example, increasingly sophisticated censorship and surveillance mechanisms are being used, often unbeknown to internet users. Enhanced access to materials via the internet regardless of geographical location increases opportunities for "libel tourism" in which cases from all over the world are taken to court in countries whose laws have insufficient protections for free expression. Thus, whilst longstanding challenges to freedom of expression persist, the nature of these challenges often shifts in online environments, requiring new approaches amongst freedom of expression defenders. It was stressed that new human rights standards are not required, and that the limited circumstances in which freedom of expression can be limited legitimately are already clearly defined in international law. Rather, how human rights standards apply in different online scenarios needs to be clarified, for example with one participant asking whether online journalists should receive the same protections as offline journalists. New tools and strategies are also needed. One participant highlighted initiatives that are being led by citizen activists, including for example the building, translating and sharing of censorship circumvention tools that can be plugged into everyday internet applications.

Conclusions

Freedom of expression should be a central issue at the IGF. The workshop also discussed levels of awareness about freedom of expression at the IGF and the role that the Forum can play in ensuring that internet governance processes protect rather than undermine freedom of expression. One discussant noted that there appears to be increasing consensus amongst stakeholders at the

Forum that freedom of expression is a universal principle that should both underpin and be a goal of internet governance. In the opening sessions of the Forum, a large number of diverse stakeholders made comments along these lines, committing themselves to supporting the openness of the internet and expressing recognition of the universality of human rights. However, workshop participants generally felt that much work remains to be done in terms of raising awareness, finding practical solutions to issues and pressurising actors who violate freedom of expression to comply with human rights standards. Worrying statements are being made within IGF workshops and plenary sessions which betray a widespread misunderstanding of, and/or disregard for, human rights. For example, one participant reported that in one IGF workshop, "propagating rumours" was classed as a cybercrime of the same level of seriousness as child pornography. They argued that freedom of expression defenders have to be more proactive and maintain a more reflexive analysis of wider events at the IGF outside of workshops that are explicitly focused on human rights.

The dynamic coalition has an important role to play. All participants agreed that the Freedom of Expression Dynamic Coalition has an important role to play in protecting and advancing freedom of expression in and through internet governance. However, the precise nature of this role has yet to be defined. The workshop highlighted the difficulties that the coalition has experienced in maintaining momentum between annual IGF meetings, and discussed potential ways of addressing this problem. One participant stressed that, whilst the IGF as a whole is not mandated to produce outputs, the dynamic coalitions can and should be making practical recommendations, demonstrating how multi-stakeholder collaboration can work in practice. However, it was felt that the coalition should not be too ambitious, and that it also has to find ways to be proactive whilst at the same time respecting the different mandate of all member organisations. There was general agreement that the coalition could be a more valuable space for networking and sharing information amongst free expression advocates, acting as a clearing house for information and an early warning system for new expression threats. However, this would require committed participation by key human rights organisations and individual activists, coupled with outreach to new constituencies, especially in developing countries. Coalition members have committed to continuing discussion on these issues in the coming weeks, developing a strategy for effective working and enhanced impact.

DC. *Internet Rights and Principles Dynamic Coalition Meeting*

Report by: Lisa Horner

The annual meeting of the Internet Rights and Principles (IRP) Dynamic Coalition was held at the 4th Internet Governance Forum in Sharm el Sheikh. Owing to organisational and scheduling issues in the wider Forum, the meeting was rescheduled to the early morning on a day when Forum participants had difficulty clearing security to get into the venue. A number of participants therefore did not make it to the meeting or arrived late. However, despite these issues, the meeting was still relatively well-attended and productive. The meeting took the form of an informal and open discussion amongst participants. After a short presentation of the history of the coalition and projects undertaken over the course of the year, the discussion focused on the coalition's work to build a Charter of Human Rights and Principles for the Internet.

The IRP Coalition was founded in 2009 as a result of a merger between the coalitions for an Internet Bill of Rights and Framework of Principles for the Internet. The aim of the coalition is to promote understanding of how international human rights standards apply in the Internet environment, and to provide a coordinating umbrella platform for individuals and groups working on rights and Internet governance issues. The coalition has a broad membership of individuals from the civil society, government and business sectors. Members share information and debate issues via the coalition mailing list and work together on collaborative projects. Membership of the coalition has grown throughout 2009, and now has over 130 participants registered on its website, 360 fans on its Facebook page and over 160 people on its mailing list.

The coalition held a mid-term meeting in Geneva in September 2009 which focused on work done by some members to explore the relationship between values, human rights and principles in Internet governance. Whilst discussion continued at Sharm el Sheikh as to what exactly the term "principles" means in the context of the coalition's work, there appears to be a growing consensus that the focus should be on "implementation principles"; principles designed to apply human rights standards to specific policy and Internet use issues that have arisen with the evolution of the Internet. The coalition meeting discussed the nature of the IRP coalition and strategies for its continued work. It was stressed that coalition activities are rooted in the Universal Declaration of Human Rights, aiming to build upon it so that human rights are protected and promoted on the Internet.

Discussion during the meeting highlighted the need for coordination between the different dynamic coalitions operating in the context of the IGF. A workshop held by coalition members at the 2008 IGF brought the different dynamic coalitions together to discuss how human rights are relevant to their work. Each coalition now has a representative who has agreed to be the liaison person with the IRP coalition. However, more remains to be done to enhance cooperation and coordination, building a united front to push for better consideration of rights issues at the IGF. Coalitions are also being encouraged to participate in the authoring of relevant sections of the new Charter of Human Rights and Principles for the Internet. Meeting participants commented that dynamic coalitions are open spaces for collaboration and for the initiation of specific projects. The dynamic coalitions dedicated to addressing human rights issues have tended to be dominated by civil society, although there has been growing interest from government and business stakeholders.

Focused discussion on the Charter of Human Rights and Principles for the Internet

Discussion began with a brief background to the rationale and motivation behind this coalition initiative. The project is rooted in the early mission of the former Bill of Rights Dynamic Coalition to create a bill of rights for the

Internet. Whilst the coalition has been renamed, many of its members are still keen to work on such a bill. The coalition therefore accepted the Association for Progressive Communications' (APC) invitation to participate in a revision of its Internet Rights Charter. The aim is to interpret what international human rights standards mean in the context of the Internet, and to identify implementation principles that will help stakeholders to uphold these rights. Implementation principles consider issues at broad "layers" of the Internet environment, from infrastructure through to code, applications and content. Workshop participants discussed how the new Charter could be used as a tool for advocacy, and form the basis of a strategic plan for action and platform for multi-stakeholder collaboration.

Progress has already been made in drafting the Charter, using APC's original work as a starting point. IRP coalition members and APC network members have brainstormed ideas and principles in a Wiki. An expert group, led by Meryem Marzouki, Rikke Frank Jørgensen and Wolfgang Benedek, has been formed to review this work and produce an edit that is in line with international human rights standards and that builds on existing agreements and conventions. The wiki remains open for public additions until the end of 2009, at which point the expert group will begin its work. They plan to feed back to the wider coalition in Spring 2010. The expert group is currently looking for human rights experts and practitioners from developing countries to participate in its work, and interested parties are invited to get in touch via the coalition mailing list. Whilst the expert group will produce a "version 1.0" of the Charter, the idea is to produce a living document that can be revised as technologies and contexts continue to evolve. The overarching goal is to produce a practical, multi-dimensional Charter, with hypertext links to relevant case studies and material. As the Charter is a work in progress, stakeholders are currently being invited to endorse the process rather than the document itself.

Meeting participants were generally highly positive about the process of creating the Charter. They commented that the initiative was timely, and that Internet governance issues are rarely framed in terms of human rights. Some felt that the Charter shouldn't be restricted to the IGF arena, but exported to the wider Internet community. It could be a common reference point for different international policy spaces, and could really influence and inspire change. There was recognition, however, that the project is an ambitious one and will require considerable inputs of time, as well as human rights and technology expertise.

Steering Committee Elections

Following the coalition meeting, elections were held for the creation of a new steering committee with equal participation from the academic, civil society, private and governmental sectors. The results are due to be announced by the end of 2009. Max Senges has announced his intention to step down as Chair of the coalition, and a new Chair will be elected from the new steering committee members. The coalition has made good progress this year, but needs to expand its membership to be more effective and inclusive.

Access and Diversity:

Report of the Main Session on Diversity

17 November 2009

Chair:

Mr. Talal Abu-Ghazaleh
Chairman of Talal Abu-Ghazaleh Organization, Egypt and
Chairman, UN Global Alliance for ICT and Development

Moderator:

Mr. Jonathan Charles
Presenter, BBC World News

Panellists:

Mr. Gerry Ellis
Accessibility and Usability consultant, Feel The BenefIT

Mr. Shadi Abou Zhara
Activity Lead, WAI International Program Office, W3C

Ms. Cynthia Waddell, Executive Director, International Center for Disability
Resources on the Internet (ICDRI)

Ms. Andrea Saks
Convener of the joint coordination activity on accessibility and human factors,
Coordinator, Dynamic Coalition on Accessibility and Disability

Mr. Abdul Waheed Khan
Assistant Director-General for Communication and Information, UNESCO

Mr. Abdulaziz Al Zoman
SaudiNIC (.sa)

Mr. Dwayne Bailey
Research Director, ANLoc (African Network for Localisation)

Extracts from the Transcript of Proceedings

JONATHAN CHARLES:

Ladies and gentlemen, hello, good morning. Access and diversity---well, I
suppose it is two sides of the same coin, isn't it. In the case of access, it is
about getting some of the hundreds of millions of people who aren't currently

online involved in this large global conversation. As for diversity, we're all aware that the Egyptians have just announced over the past 24 hours they are about to file the first non-Latin domain name. They want dot masr, dot Egypt in Arabic. They are trying to bring the Internet to the 300 million potential Arabic users in the world, very few of whom are currently online, and many of whom may be unable to read the Latin alphabet. And in the past 24 hours, we also have been talking a lot about access for the 10% of the global population that are in one way or another disabled. Our chairman today is Talal Abu-Ghazaleh, but first an announcement from the secretariat.

MARKUS KUMMER:

Thank you, Jonathan. IPv6 is now functional in the Congress centre. It was not planned to begin with, as part of the network requirements, but in order to accommodate the requests that were made during yesterday's session on critical Internet resources, the host country network team has now set up an IPv6 network with SSID, if you prefer to use that network.

TALAL ABU-GHAZALEH:

Good morning. I would like to be candid and direct. I take objection to the subject of diversity because, as defined, it involves two parts only: diversity in language and diversity of disability. Diversity is much more and much wider than that. On language, I don't like to hear that Arabic has been recognized as one of the diversities, as it is a major historically respected language like Indian, Chinese, and others.   ICANN started as a U.S. gift, and we are grateful to the United States of America for making that gift free to the entire world.   And of course it had to start with what you call Latin, which is the English alphabet. But the Arabic alphabet is there, has been there, and is not a diversity. It is just another language, equal to the English language.   The Arabs and Indians take pride in having introduced characters and numbers; we invented the zero, which makes the Internet operate.   So we do not want to be seen in terms of diversity.

Similarly, disabilities are not a matter of diversity. It is just another kind of circumstance, another wellbeing in a different condition, like being a tall man, a fat man, an idiot, an intelligent person. Each is equal to any of us and is sometimes better than any of us. So the subject cannot be limited in this way. What about poverty? If I cannot have the means to learn of have access, I am much worse off than a person with a disability who may be in a country that provides the respect he deserves and is in a much better position than a person in a country where he cannot even know what a computer is like. Then we talk about infrastructure, and education... That's why we in the UN Global Alliance for ICT and Development are very proud that yesterday we launched a partnership with UNESCO on education and, among other things, we are looking at ICT indicators on a web-based transparent basis so that every country knows where they stand and what they are doing. But more than that, we are developing an open platform and an open source program for the entire world that will provide complete access to content. I was very proud that His Excellency Minister Tarek Kamel yesterday endorsed this project, and I will be working with his ministry and under his leadership in pushing this project in Egypt, in the Arab world, and in the entire world.

So let us be clear that when we talk of disabilities, we don't talk of an inferior person. And that access is the most important source of diversity. The people who do not have access but are without any disability are at least hundred times more in number than those who have a disability and do not have access because of this.

JONATHAN CHARLES:

Talal, thank you very much. I would have been very disappointed if you hadn't been provocative. We take for granted that when we click on a Web page we are able to navigate it. But that's not the case for everyone. So our first two speakers are going to show us why people need to think a lot harder about the way they design their web pages in order to make sure they conform with universality.

SHADI ABOUZAHRA:

For those of you who have attended Tim Berners Lee's keynote on Sunday, I think he showed the vast importance of universality on the web for people from different cultures, with different languages, with different devices, and with different abilities. So it's really about connecting humanity, and the web provides unprecedented opportunities for people with disabilities to interact, to access information, and to act as equal peers on the by providing content and using information. Gerry is totally blind and is going to show us how he uses his computer and what happens when a web site is developed accessibly, and what happens when the same website is not.

GERRY ELLIS:

Chairperson, ladies and gentlemen, thank you very much. As Shadi said, what I have here is a standard laptop, the same as any other person would use, with an extra piece of assistive technology software called a screen reader, which speaks text on the screen. What I'm going to show you is two versions of the same Web site. So let's see, it said "access to the city," and you hear the voice. So what do you do when you go onto a Web site? Firstly, you normally get a general overview of the site, but I can't do that. Normally, what I would have to do is read all the way from top to bottom, unless there are proper structures. So the first structure that I want to look at is the headings on the Web site. So what I'm going to do is go through a couple of headings and what you will hear is the heading being spoken and then it will say "Level Heading 1," "Level Heading 2", or "Heading Level 1," "Heading Level 2," so I know which are the important headings. So I'm just going to flick through a couple of headings to get a feel for the structure of this Web site.

So it said "Before and after demonstration, Heading Level 1," so I know that's a major heading. The next one says "Welcome to city lights," and I know that's still a major heading because it said "Heading Level 1." Let's try the next one. "Heat wave, Heading Level 2," so I notice that these are lower size headings and not big banner headings, which gives me a knowledge of the structure. The next thing that I want to do is what are the tabs on here, or what are the links. I can't click on a mouse, so I am clicking "tab" to go through a couple of links and you'll hear the content of the link. "Heat wave, full story," and you heard the word "link," so I now know that that is a link because it's properly structured. I'm going to go to the next one. "Man gets nine months in a violin case." I don't know how he fit inside a violin case, but that's neither here nor there. That sounds interesting to me, so I can just arrow down and listen to the text. So there's a picture of a violin case and it's open for inspection and it was a simple little explanation attached to that graphic. Even though my software can't read a picture, it can read that description. And, again, I can go linking again. Tab, violin case, full story, link. So that is basically how I can get around if it's well structured.

What I'm going to do now is link to an inaccessible version of the same site. It looks the same aesthetically, let's see if it's as functional and read the heading. "Dot, dot, city lights, dot, dot, dot." This is a bit confusing, but not too bad. If you remember, the first thing I did last time was I went through the headings to get a feeling for the structure, so let's see what the headings are here. "Before and after demonstration, Heading Level 1." So far, so good. Let's look at the next heading. It wrapped to the top because there are no more headings, so I'm immediately at a major disadvantage because I can't get that general feeling of what the Web site looks like. This is a first major inaccessibility, let's go through some of the links and hear one. Before, slash, nav, backslash, something or other. Total gibberish, from my point of view. It probably looks perfect if you can see the graphic, but because that graphic isn't properly tagged with the information that I need, it sounds like gibberish. I haven't a clue what that means. So now I'm tabbing to links which again you can see highlighted, but the information that I need from my clean reader is not there, so let's establish through a couple more of these. Tab, blank. I can't access that. So the accessible one is just as aesthetically pleasing, just as functional, but is much more accessible, and that's the message.

SHADI ABOUZAHRA:

Thank you, Gerry. What's important is the coding that makes it work for a screen reader or for other types of assistive technologies, so people with different types of disabilities can use other types of assistive technologies. But that is essentially the same means that we use to access, for example, with mobile phones, or with other devices. So it's an improvement that benefits all in the end, regardless which languages or technologies you are using. You can have the same visual appearance and same functionality, but with more quality that makes it work on a whole range of devices and for more people. At the W3C Web accessibility initiative, this is exactly what we developed, guidelines and solutions and standards and resources to make the Web accessible for people with disabilities. And this is an example of why standards in ICT are so important for people with disabilities and for the inclusion of accessibility requirements.

JONATHAN CHARLES:

We next hear from Andrea Saks, who is the convener of the joint coordination activity on accessibility and human factors, and the coordinator of the dynamic coalition on accessibility and disability. She was born into a family where her parents were both deaf.

ANDREA SAKS:

My father was one of the founders of the text telephony system that is still being used throughout the world. We are moving to new technology, and one of the legacies of that is something that's called real-time text, which we presented in an accessibility workshop yesterday.

I want to give the Egyptian authorities a compliment. This has been the most accessible IGF meeting to date. We have seen tremendous progress in developing places and accessibility for people with disabilities and we have captioning and sign language. I went on an Egypt airplane and they had sign language and they had captioning in Arabic, so somebody who is deaf could understand the emergency instructions and they had their prayer. There has been a lot of change but we need convergence. We need to work together. The western world always wants to tell what they call the developing world what to do. I don't feel that that is an answer. I think what we have to do is work with and have the projects originate in countries with the assistance of experts throughout the world to develop programs where people can get education and get out of the problem of not being able to have access due to disability.

JONATHAN CHARLES:

Andrea, thank you very much indeed. Cynthia Waddell, I will hand it over to you for your message.

CYNTHIA WADDELL:

This message by the dynamic coalition was put together mindful of the 650 million persons with disabilities around the world as well as the 2 billion members of their families that are impacted by the challenges of disability. When we speak of accessibility, I would like to point out it really has three different meanings. When we talk about accessibility we are talking about connectivity with the Internet, we are talking about affordability, and we are talking about accessible design. 80% of persons with disabilities live in developing countries, and most, unfortunately, tend to be at the margins.

So now I would like to present to you a summary, and not read a four-page document out loud. I would ask you to please refer to it. First I want to tell you that this message begins with the introduction that talks about how the dynamic coalition was formed at the Internet Governance Forum to ensure that information and communications technology accessibility is included in the key debates about Internet governance. The dynamic coalition seeks to build a future where all sectors of the global community have equal access to the information society. The message goes on to a section regarding rights and supports the United Nations convention on the rights of persons with disabilities, the purpose of which is to promote, protect, and ensure the full and equal enjoyment of all human rights and fundamental freedoms by persons with disabilities, and to promote respect for their inherent dignity. These rights include equal access to the Internet, and to electronic services and emergency services. Many people are unaware that ICT accessibility for persons with disabilities is a significant obligation of the U.N. convention and is supported by the Tunis commitment of the World Summit on the Information Society.

The message moves on to a section that promotes the use of internationally recognized and open standards that support accessibility. We believe that technical design standards play a critical role in the implementation of accessible ICTs. However, one chief concern is the problem of the prevention of barriers to participation that are created by a proprietary protocols. We then have a section that discusses the tangible and measurable benefits that come from implementation standards and accessibility support. I'd like to note that the benefits of assisting persons with disabilities also extend to older adults and actually improves access for everyone around the world. The message also points out the benefits of universal design as defined in Article II of the United Nations convention: "Universal design means the design of products, environments, programs, and services to be usable by all people to the greatest extent possible, without the need for adaptation or specialized design. Universal design shall not exclude assistive devices for particular groups of persons with disabilities where this is needed." Article IX of the convention states that the obligation of the signatories is to promote the design, development, production, and distribution of accessible ICT and systems at an early stage, so that these technologies and systems become accessible at minimum cost. The last two sections of the message address training and provide recommendations and pointers to resources we feel are helpful, and practical steps. We submit before you a list of such steps to enable the global community to benefit from an accessible ICT world.

JONATHAN CHARLES:

Cynthia, thank you very much. At the end of our first half of proceedings Talal is going to give a summary of where we are and also call on all of us to back the message from the Dynamic Coalition on Accessibility and Disability. Before we move on to our next section, which is multilingualism, this is the time where I want to take a little bit of a break to allow the audience to have its say on the speakers that we've heard so far.

FROM THE FLOOR:

I'm David Wood from the European Broadcasting Union. I strongly support the statement. Please put it in your bag, as when you go back home you will need to interpret nationally what the U.N. convention means for things like the Internet and this is going to be an invaluable aid to that. But please also remember that it is just a first important and critical step. It's talking about tools for multimedia Web sites, and the technology of Web sites is moving on and including a lot more video and television programs, and the new world is one of combining Web and television content. So there's still a job to be in developing tools for these new evolving environments. And about broadening thinking in the future, access doesn't just mean mechanical access, it also means access to society. It means the content of the Web site is important, too. And we do have to look beyond the tools and the mechanics of accessing to find out which contents people with disabilities need that we can provide.

JONATHAN CHARLES:

David, if I can just ask you, with a lot of these issues, it often comes down to money, doesn't it, particularly subtitling on the Internet. How is that going to be resolved by broadcasters?

FROM THE FLOOR:

As more and more television programs get shown on the Web, we have to find a way of transferring the subtitles, the video and audio descriptors that are used, and we need the technical tools for that from standards bodies like the ITU. But cost is a factor and we have to find some way of convincing management that this is money well spent.

FROM THE FLOOR:

Thank you. I'm Arun Mehta from New Delhi. I'm delighted that we have a chairperson who is so frank and I would be grateful if he and others on the panel would help me understand why the Millennium Development Goals of the United Nations and all the indicators for progress on these make no mention of disability.

TALAL ABU-GHAZALEH:

The Millennium Development Goals were set by a summit in 2000 with a target of 2015, and we are now two-thirds of the way through with very little accomplished as a global community. So the UN global alliance is undertaking a project now under the leadership of the Secretary General and his deputy, Mr. Shah, to set a practical approach to the goals. We will be submitting to the third Millennium Development Goals summit in 2010 a matrix with clear indicators of how ICT can be used for development in every sector of development, and that includes business, health, education, disability, everything.

SHADI ABOUZAHRA:

On the question of costs, this goes beyond the 10% who need captioning in order to understand the content because it helps so many more. Especially here at the IGF. Looking around the room, probably most of us are non-native English speakers, yet we are speaking English to be able to communicate with each other. My mother tongue be is Arabic. I very often miss words because of pronunciation and I use the captioning even though I can hear. So it helps me a lot, and I'm sure it helps many of you in the room. So in the long run you will save costs by implementing accessibility.

FROM THE FLOOR:

I'm Fernando Botelho and I specialize in low cost solutions for persons with disabilities and scalable projects. I just want to give an example. There is a huge challenge in making sure that persons with disabilities have employment opportunities around the world, and there are companies such as a captioning company in Argentina I discovered where the blind are even more productive than the average person when doing transcription.

FROM THE FLOOR:

My name is Frank La Rue and I am the special rapporteur of United Nations for freedom of opinion of expression in the world. I also happen to be legally blind, and proud of it. The accessibility of ICTs includes not only the ability to receive information but also the ability to express one's thoughts, and we should all have the possibility of this double way of communication, receiving and expressing freely. I also agree that the worst limitation is poverty, and technologies for people with disabilities will tend to be expensive. So I wonder whether, within the millennium goals or as a recommendation to the UN, we should make all communities and sectors, including people with disabilities, fully accessible to electronic communication to ICTs? Moreover, should there be sort of a world campaign to create a fund so each state can subsidize access to poor people or people with disabilities, and should there be a worldwide fund for the exchange of technology to the developing world?

TALAL ABU-GHAZALEH:

In the Global Alliance we are working on a statement on the right of every individual in the world to access and to be part of the knowledge society of the world. We should make it a right like any other human right.

ANDREA SAKS:

I hope to work with you, Mr. Chairman, in the dynamic coalition and also in the joint coordination activity of accessibility and human factors in the ITU, which I chair. We have to have convergence in standards and we have to work hard to work with people in different groups and the **U.N.**, and unfortunately sometimes it is all talk and no "do." We need projects in the countries to be able to accomplish accessibility for everyone.

CYNTHIA WADDELL:

Article XXXII of the U.N. convention and rights of persons with disabilities calls for international cooperation to facilitate research and access to scientific and technical knowledge, to provide technical and economic assistance, and to enable technology transfer. So accessible Web implementation and ICT assistance and international cooperation are already obligations for signatories to the convention.

FROM THE FLOOR:

I'm Gunela Astbrink from the Internet Society of Australia. The issue about poverty keeps on coming back. We had a workshop yesterday on capacity building on Internet accessibility policy development, on helping people in their own countries to develop skills to lobby governments and industry to improve accessibility. We're going to continue that discussion, but I'd like to

342

pose a challenge, namely how can business be more proactive in supporting people with disabilities to improve accessibility? Could there be some way of working with disability NGOs? It might be I.T. induction programs for staff, or making sure their products or at least their Web sites are accessible.

FROM THE FLOOR:

I'm Rohan Samarajiva. I represent a research organization called LIRNEasia. I think the discussion has been very positive in terms of mainstreaming disability access, but suddenly and we are hearing a conversation about more funds, more subsidies. I think when you mainstream something, it must be part of the business model because we have a real good example today of half the world's population being connected to electronic networks without subsidies. That's the most important thing. We've had universal service funds, where the money has not been expended, and where it has been expended, it has not been expended wisely and efficiently. Instead, the people who have been paying for the universal funds, the mobile networks, have been connecting the world's poor at extraordinarily low prices and without the support of universal service funds, for the most part. So I am somewhat disheartened to hear again a failed public policy solution being proposed, because I think it is much better, and you have much better mainstreaming through the business model that is being developed and implemented in the developing countries, where for below five dollars U.S. people are being connected and companies are making profits. Set standards for accessibility, for mobile networks, and for the mobile broadband. If you do that, it will be a sustainable solution unlike something where there are government bureaucrats in the middle and who are putting inefficiency and delay into the entire system.

FROM THE FLOOR:

Thank you very much. I'm Abdoulaye Diarra from Mali. The problem of access is a very real one at all levels, because there are many people with handicaps. We saw how someone who has poor sight is able to use software and that it can be awkward if that software does not exist. In our developing countries, these situations are far worse. We do not have the means to confront these very real problems for persons with disabilities. The ITU has set up many activities for persons with disabilities. We should look into these discussions so that there be standards relating to persons with disabilities to see how developing countries might be able to increase their access.

ANDREA SAKS:

We are attempting at the ITU to set up training and to be able to get people within a country to be able to use ICTs and we are thinking about using the Universal Funds mentioned previously. It is just not off the ground yet but we are thinking along those lines.

SHADI ABOUZAHRA:

To respond to the gentleman from Mali, one of the key aspects for people with disabilities is royalty free standards that allow affordable and low cost technologies to be produced.

JONATHAN CHARLES:

Thank you. Let's move on to the other topic that we're looking at today, which is multilingualism. A whole new world is about to open up with the change in domain names. Hundreds of millions of people, perhaps billions of people, who have been unable to enjoy the Internet may now have that opportunity, but it's not without challenges. Let me introduce our first speaker, Abdul Waheed Khan.

ABDUL WAHEED KHAN:

Language is a barrier, no question. If you recall, in the opening session I talked about UNESCO advancing the notion of knowledge societies based on human needs and human rights, and on the four fundamental principles of universal access to information and knowledge, freedom of expression, cultural and linguistic diversity, and quality education for all. If you look at those four principles, is communication a fundamental human need? The answer is obviously yes. Is freedom of expression a fundamental human right? Indeed, it is. Can you ensure cultural diversity? What is culture, if you take out language? I'm not saying language is the only aspect of culture, and my organization is known for celebrating cultural diversity. The world will be a very dull and boring place if we had just one culture, one language, one form of human beings.

When we talk about quality education for all, we know based on empirical studies that the children who receive education in their mother tongue do much better than those who are forced to learn in a language that is not their mother tongue. So language clearly can be abling and disabling, and it's part of everyone's identity. For education, for culture, for dissemination of scientific information, the tools come next but the means of communication is the language to begin with. What is flowing through these electronic devices, what is it that people are accessing once you have them? Whether the issue is universalization of primary education, gender equity, health issues, environmental issues, all those eight Millennium Development Goals, what is the common denominator? Flow of information and knowledge. Without that, none of these goals are going to be met. How can you share scientific innovations with a farmer if that information is not available in the language that he or she can understand? Can you educate the about 900 million adults that are still illiterate? More than a hundred million children do not still receive education in schools. So one of the barriers would be the language.

In the last 500 years, half of the world's languages have disappeared. And what is more disturbing is that it is estimated that in the next hundred years, nearly 90% of the world's 7,000 languages will become extinct if we do not take steps. This is a loss in opportunities, in traditions, in memory, in unique modes of thinking and expression. So it is important that action be take collectively, as a global community, which is what this forum is all about, for us to create an enabling environment through policies and strategies at the national level, at the regional level, and indeed at the international level, so that the languages will flourish in cyberspace.

Fortunately, we have the means. Digital preservation is now available, and UNESCO has adopted a Universal Declaration on Cultural Diversity that recognizes cultural diversity as part of common heritage of humanity and an endless source of new ideas and creative development. There is a strong correlation between cultural diversity and linguistic diversity. People who do not have voices to express themselves in the language that they feel comfortable with, is that not a barrier? Of course it is. Can that be a potential source of conflict? Of course it can be. So it is important to take steps and preserve the knowledge available in so many languages and to ensure that languages flourish.

ABDULAZIZ ALZOMAN:

I will be talking about domain names. We know that just recently ICANN announced the opening of accepting top-level domains in languages other than ASCII. Are we to deal with Arabic languages or Arab script based languages? Everyone knows the importance of IDN to our regions and communities. We have about 17% Internet penetration in the Arab world, and our region is seeing the fastest growth with respect to the number of users because the Internet was a little bit late to arrive. In Saudi Arabia we did a study and found that 80% of operating systems used in education are only in Arabic, and 73% are used by individuals in the household. So that means really the language is very important to the user. The Web site they are visiting are mainly in Arabic; 65% of the sites visited have 75 and more percent Arabic content.

Now, in our region, what we have done with respect to Arabic domain names? First, we listed a number of the linguistic issues regarding names and we discussed and reached conclusions through a long process with a number of committees. We did some surveys on the Internet, collecting feedback from the users, and we consulted a number of expert linguists. And all these results have been handed to a team for Arabic domain names and the Arab League, and they have published our recommendations and the language table for Arabic language on RFC 5564. So we have now working documents that reference all the language table for our domain names. Also, since 2005 we had a pilot project for Arabic domain names in which that we tested the usage and developed a number of tools like the IDN registry symbol, IDN registry, DNS checker, Web based WHOIS, and so on.

Still, we have a lot of challenges to overcome. When ICANN opened the IDN TLD test, dot test and the equivalent in Arabic, we did extensive tests for ten applications, mainly Web browser and email applications, and for four different operating systems as well as web-based email. We had 13 test cases, and we found most of them failed. They have a lot of problems dealing with the Arabic language. And we must expand our look to the whole Arabic script, because a number of registries and Web services will provide their registration in Arabic script rather than just only one language. So there are a number of issues we have to face that have not been dealt in the protocols, but rather have been left to the registries to look after. And this is a worry for us because a give registry might deal with these issues differently, so that we will have different registration systems that deal with different issues in different ways. And then the user will have different experiences with domain name registration in Arabic script-based domain names. I will just show you some of the examples. One of them is what is called zero width non-joiner control character. This control character is not visible on the screen by itself, but it has some effects on how the characters get connected together. But you can see the effect is there in the connections between characters. This could be a good ground for phishing, and that has not been solved at the protocol level, they just left it to the registry to look at. Another problem is the digits. We have a number of digits being used in the Arabic script. One is the Arabic-Indic and one is the eastern Arabic-Indic digits. They almost look alike on all digits except for three or four, so if you type these numbers the user could get confused because they have different codes, but the look are similar. So this is another problem from security point of view that has not been addressed in the protocol.

Moreover, in the screen you should have seen the digits written in Arabic and the digits written in Latin, but you have seen the same format. You have seen little difference just because the laptop I am using does not support Arabic letters. The Microsoft operating system deals with digits differently from other operating systems. Regardless of what you type, it will be displayed based on the system the language you define in the system, so you sometimes can't type the digits you want. Users of Linux or Macs will have different ways of writing the digits than the users of Microsoft. The biggest problem is confusingly similar characters. In the Arabic scripts there are a number of letters that are used in different languages like Farsi or Urdu that have the same shape but different codes. If you look to the Unicode tables, there are a number of letters that have similarity in shape and are used in different languages. And sometimes you can't even type in certain languages, because the keyboards are language based, not like script based. So I could have a domain name that friends in Pakistan or India or Malaysia will not be able to type because the keyboard they have, they have the letters but with different codes. So the solution is to have the variants, like all the confusingly similar characters combined together in one master key for domain names, so when you register one affect the other variants to that domain names.

DWAYNE BAILEY:

I am from South Africa. The vision of ANLoc is to empower Africans to participate in the digital age by removing barriers imposed on language by the limitations of technology. In South Africa we have 11 official languages, so in trying to implement and seeing how governments can implement multilingual names I am acutely aware of the problems and the benefits. The lack of access to information---and I mean access as in being able to use it, not that you have got a computer on your desk--- is life threatening. It threatens your ability to stay healthy, to access government services, whether your children will have a good education and a good job, and your socioeconomic and general welfare.

In a lot of the sessions I have been to, issues of language like how to do IDNs have been raised. My concern is that this is not at the forefront of our agenda. There are lots of languages in the world, 2,000 of them spoken by a billion

346

people in Africa. And about 200 of those languages in Africa have more than half a million speakers. There are 15 languages in Africa that have more than 10 million speakers each. And almost none of those are present in any significant way in the information age. So the people who need multilingualism the most are the people that we haven't reached yet, and the people that can benefit so much from the kind of information we talk about. If we look at the use of the Internet in Africa, and I don't have data for other continents, the predominance of languages that people are browsing in are English and French. So it seems to indicate that the people that are accessing this information age are people that are already enabled through access to a language like English and French and Arabic to be part of this, but that the rest are ignored. So clearly for the last billion, multilingualism is not an option, it's an imperative.

Regarding everything resting on multilingualism, the words and phrases I have heard over the last few days include: inclusive, knowledge societies, pluralistic, equitable, create, share, diffuse, preserve, linguistic diversity, flow of ideas, increasing knowledge. And all of these things are possible in a mono-cultural, monolingual environment. But in all the sessions I have been to, it's implied that all these benefits are meant for all of humanity. And it's impossible without multilingualism being a first priority. It's not going to benefit all of humanity if we don't make it a priority. And there's a lot we can do. There's an assumption that all languages can be typed, but there are languages that you can't type and capture at the moment. The software is not available in these languages and there is the assumption that it is, or else people haven't thought down that road about people who don't speak a certain language having to capture it on digital equipment that they can't use. And there is an assumption we can store these languages.

Multilingualism is not IDNs; IDNs are one aspect of multilingualism. There is a danger that IDNs could create silos, a multilingual world of monolingualisms. We need to think quite seriously about how we prevent that from happening and ensure the free flow of ideas.

At ANLoc we have developed keyboards that allow people to type African languages that they couldn't type before. We have developed extended fonts allowing people to see what they wrote, and we are translating the Firefox Web browser into ten languages. We are looking at a hundred locales across Africa that allows people to store documents and information in their languages. We are training people on how to translate and localize content, make it relevant for their environment. We are building tools that allow people to create and translate content. We are making spell checkers, because there is nothing as negative for a language as seeing it all underlined in red and your computer communicating to you that your language is irrelevant in the communication age. The consortium is working hard at making sure we can store all of these languages. And Microsoft is translating their operating system into African and other languages, while Firefox seeks to have 80 versions in different languages. And there are groups like Global Voices who are ensuring that blogs are translated and that there is a cross-pollination between communities. Organizations like Medan helping to ensure there is dialogue between the Arabic and the English-speaking world, and many others I have forgotten.

FROM THE FLOOR:

I'm Tarek Khalil, the president of Nile University. I would like to address a couple of issues that seem to be missing in the discussion, and I'm going to speak as a professor of human factors engineering. There are no absolute disabilities, there are functional abilities and they relate to the demands placed by the task required. In a sense, all of us are disabled if we are not relating to what is being presented to us. We have to put pressure on the designers of the technology, because it's the human/technology interaction that we are talking about, and human-centred design of the Web itself as well as of the information and the pages and everything that goes along with it. So the issues we have talked about in here are related to what we are present with, and it's a technology issue more than anything else.

FROM THE FLOOR:

My name is Reinhard Schäler and I'm director of the Localisation Research Centre in Ireland. We just set up a foundation called the Rosetta Foundation that will allow volunteer translators and technologists to come together to offer translation services to digital publishers. Translation is not just "nice to have," it's something that is a question of life and death it should really be elevated to a much higher level, like the fight against AIDS, malaria, and tuberculosis. The industry has given a lead here, there is a localization industry that is worth 16 billion U.S. dollars, but it works for the people who have money, for commercial purposes. So we need an initiative that does localization for political, cultural, social, and developmental purposes. And localization translation, or the lack of it, is not just a matter for the developing world, it's also for the developed world.

FROM THE FLOOR:

My name is Jean-Jacques Subrenat. I'm a member of the ICANN directorate, and I have two comments. The first one has to do with the use of the term "multilingualism." It's partially accurate, but we should be talking about linguistic diversity instead, because multilingualism is the capacity of a single person or an entity to speak several languages. So I prefer the term "linguistic diversity." The second point is that we are living in a new world with the introduction of IDNs and I simply wanted to point out here that of course we have to make further progress, and I'm grateful to the representative of Saudi Arabia for having showed very clearly, using examples, what difficulties are still outstanding and will have to be overcome. But I wanted to underscore how important it is for the communities such as those represented here at the IGF to express their views and advice. If the introduction of IDNs became possible, it is largely thanks to your insistence and your advice. It's thanks to that that ICANN managed to put that through.

JONATHAN CHARLES:

Thank you for that. I'm sorry we don't have time for any more comments from the floor. I'd like to thank our panel and to bring this first part of the debate to an end, I'd like to call on our chairman, Talal, to make a few closing comments.

TALAL ABU-GHAZALEH:

I would like to respond to the point on multilingualism. Yes, we indeed are talking about multilingualism because we want the Internet to be multilingual, so that we don't have a fragmentation of the Internet because I will then go for my Arabic Internet, my Chinese Internet, and so on. We need to have one Internet that can speak many languages.

With your permission, and if you agree, I would like an expression of applause at the end in support of what I would like to say. I move that we endorse by acclamation and for inclusion in the conference proceedings: One, to applaud with great admiration the Egyptian efforts towards the development of an Egyptian knowledge society led by the most able minister of ICT, His Excellency Tarek Kamel, and we want that to be minuted and conveyed in the proceedings to express how we all agree that is a great model of development in a knowledge society that we are seeing in Egypt. Number two, to adopt the excellent message on access by persons with disabilities presented by the Dynamic Coalition on Accessibility and Disability. It is a very clear, candid, and well studied document which addresses one of the diversities or barriers, but also addresses the many other barriers in disability. Number three, to encourage ICANN to accelerate its process on multilingualization and to make it a priority in order to ensure the continued coherence of the Internet.

In closing, I would like to not only thank our great moderator for an excellent job, but also to thank him personally because it gave me the privilege of sitting on the podium next to a media celebrity. Thank you.

JONATHAN CHARLES:

I had the privilege of sitting next to you. And thank you to you for taking part. Thank you to our distinguished panel. Stay where you are. The next section is on access and the panel will be coming up and the moderator and chairman, right now.

Access and Diversity:

Report of the Main Session on Access

17 November 2009

Chair:

Mr. Amr Badawi
Executive President, National Telecommunications Authority Regulation, Egypt

Moderator:

Mr. Hopeton Dunn
Director, Caribbean Programme in Telecommunications Policy and Technology Management, Mona School of Business, University of the West Indies, Mona, Jamaica

Panellists:

Mr. Ben Akoh
ICT Programme Manager, Open Society Initiative for West Africa

Mr. Pierre Dandjinou
CEO, Strategic Consulting Group SCG

Mr. Mohamed El Nawawy
Vice Chairman Telecom Egypt Company, Egypt

Mr. Ernest Ndukwe
Chief Executive Officer and Executive Vice Chairman, Nigerian Communications Commission

Mr. Ermanno Pietrosemoli
President, EsLaRed, Venezuela

Extracts from the Transcript of Proceedings

AMR BADAWI:

I'm Dr. Amr Badawi and I'm pleased to have an excellent set of panellists today. Our moderator will be Dr. Hopeton Dunn.

HOPETON DUNN:

Access was among the matters of highest priority throughout the entire WSIS process. In fact, it's a process that I participated in, and the Tunis phase documentation has very many and very strong declarations supporting access on a global scale. For example, the Tunis declaration states that we are resolute to empower the poor, particularly those living in remote, rural, and marginalized urban communities, to access information, and to use ICTs as a tool to support their efforts to lift themselves out of poverty. When we speak of access, we are speaking not only about the physical ability to connect with a network, but we are talking about a great range of additional means by which access is to be attained. We are talking, colleagues, about financial access, the ability of people to afford the content, to afford the connectivity. We are talking about the essential nature of literacy to access, including information literacy, all the cognitive skills associated with being able to use the network.

We are talking about access to relevant content. We are talking about access to institutional support, including political access and a voice. We are talking, as we did in the previous session, also about linguistic access and access by the disabled. So these considerations are the ones that help to frame our discussion today, and we are fortunate to have a very engaged and outstanding panel of presenters.

BEN AKOH:

The global debate on access has moved on from the infrastructure-based arguments that we've always had to issues of policy, regulation, and rights. Not that infrastructure is not important; infrastructure such as undersea cables have finally begun to arrive in some underserved coastal areas in Africa. There has been increased mobile phone proliferation, which have characterized most of the landscape in our countries. We've seen previously where copper cables didn't exist that mobile phones have been able to take the spaces and enable communications. The tele-densities in most of our countries, especially in the rural areas, continue to increase. Even with these advancements though there remain challenges, including the fact that landlocked countries still continue to struggle to access coastal cable infrastructure. Broadband remains a major challenge, still. Either traditional broadband as it is or broadband on the mobile phones as we are hoping will begin to happen. The rights to a landing station continues to pose problems for cable companies that are seeking to land infrastructure as they pass by coastal cities.

The cost of making phone calls and sending of simple SMS messages still is approximately 50% of the disposable incomes of most Africans or most underserved people. In literal terms what that means is it's a sizeable fraction of a day's wage of a Rwandan farmer. The difference between the current state of access and the future progressive opportunity for all states, which is the theme of this conference, remains with three critical and strategic moves, and those are: Policy issues, regulation, and rights. Appropriate steps have to be taken to address these three issues, and how we deal with them will determine what progress will be made in the coming years.

I will focus specifically on one of these issues, spectrum and its management, which is a fundamental component of access. I'll talk about it from three key perspectives. The first is reclaiming unused spectrum space. I don't think that up until now, there has been an initiative to make sure that we reclaim the spaces that may be available within the spectrum bands; it's important that we begin to make specific moves. Second, It's important to leverage the benefits of digital dividends of the switchover that will likely come in the future. And third, specific advocacy and policy recommendations need to be made on how this is to be handled.

On the reclaimed unused spaces, one of the things that we need to look at is managing spillovers and maybe guard bands. Spillovers are out-of-band emissions that happen within a defined frequency, so if you cross from one country to another there is a momentary period where the signal from one country tends to interfere with the signal from another border space. And there's a lot of infrastructure and cost that is put into managing that sort of issue. It's about time we begin to look at ways we can allow such spillover to happen and find better ways of managing cross-border spectrum harmonization. Guard bands, on the other hand, are bands that have been kept within a spectrum space to accommodate interference by alternate bands, which is important with the new advances in technology, with the new ways by which transmission and receiving devices can connect and negotiate how to connect with themselves. It's important that we find ways of reclaiming those guard bands as eventually they will make more spaces available within the spectrum.

On digital dividends, this is a benefit of digital migration and stakeholders have claimed that it will lead to more available spectrum spaces. Further, through innovation and compression, these spaces will be optimized, resulting in more available spaces. Effective technology such as agile or software defined radios will encourage further innovation and better and efficient utilization of this available spectrum. The bottom line is that there will be more spaces available for more applications, but this can only be true if and when specific measures and steps have been taken to effectively and collaboratively plan the potential spaces that will result from digital migration or switchover. Ultimately, the spectrum management mechanisms and methodologies, policies, and regulations of the past may not be sufficient for these future spaces. New mechanisms are required as the factors have changed somewhat. Basically, it's a specific case of pouring new wine into new skins.

So what proposals do we have? That these policies on spectrum and infrastructure should be looked at as a rights-based issue. Access to spectrum should and must be couched under themes such as access to information or even freedom of expression. Certain policy measures on cross-border spectrum needs to address public goods and rural development, as reclaimed spectrum bands can and should be reserved and specifically targeted to address broadband deployment in underserved areas. Secondly, we should begin to see this as a social responsibility issue. Social responsibility of the current spectrum administrators or regimes to their citizens, requiring that provisions are made to incentivize service providers who will utilize reclaimed and available spaces for broadband rural connectivity.

352

PIERRE DANDJINOU:

I will be talking on mobile broadband and whether the whole hype around mobile broadband is justified, especially in regions such as Africa. I'm going to take a holistic approach. Ben alluded to this better management issue. I'll try to deal with it as well, having assisted different countries in Africa to develop their own e-strategies, and having observed that most of those were shelved and not implemented, sometimes for lack of funding, but also for lack of a realistic agenda. We need to have a switch in the connectivity paradigm. Access to ICT has a direct and measurable impact on social and economic development. So if you consider that we have more mobile telephone users in Africa than Internet users, that may be the paradigm to switch to, that we should be talking more about national backbones not only for fibre, but also for mobile. That will open up more opportunities. We are talking about socio-economic development, but it is also about education, health care, and social inclusion. Broadband technology is there today, and various network standards may be used, such as GPRS, 3G, Wi-Max, LGE, and ASPA. And the business has come up with a common platform known as the Global Third Generation Partnership Project; 90% of the world's mobile subscribers are using this today.

Regarding mobile broadband development and adoption, developed countries have set their strategies. In the U.K., for instance, since October 2008 the aim is to have 100% broadband coverage, with a minimum speed of two megabytes. The European Union has outlined Internet innovation strategies that encompasses a right to the Internet and to broadband, and the use of liberated airwave to spread broadband access. So how about Africa? It was quite surprising that most thing we are reading today say that Africa and the Middle East are going to be where it is going to really happen, because those places have been kept away from Internet access for so many years, and the mobile uptake rate is phenomenal. It's quite interesting that in places like Mauritania, Senegal, and Kenya you have access to mobile telephony through the CDMAs that are being laid out. Places like Rwanda already are using part of this technology for e-health promotion.

Now, mobile broadband technology comes with a few issues like market structure. What model are we going to use in Africa or other developing regions? Certain that the single subscription equals single customer model that we have in developed countries will not be appropriate in Africa. The other prerequisite is the challenge of how we do free and manage the spectrum, which Ben commented on. There is a fundamental role for governments and regulators, and they need to facilitate and adapt. Most people will say that the liberalization of telecoms in Africa has not been a success, for many reasons. Having the right license fee structure is important; in many places the aim was to make it very expensive to buy licenses, while in other places there was just a simple administrative charge. In the long run now you have to consider what you are gaining, so we are calling for revisiting the right to license. The other thing is taxation that is holding back deployment in most places. Last but not least is the power issue; for operators of mobile in Africa, energy is a big part of the expense. So we cannot solve the issues if we don't have a holistic approach, and government, regulators, and all other stakeholders have to come up with strategies that include technology neutrality, security, and transparency, especially in managing the spectrum, tax policies, universal service funds, national and local content development, competition, and the energy issue.

MOHAMED EL NAWAWY:

I will address infrastructure and submarine capable infrastructure. Egypt is playing a predominant role in connecting the infrastructure that goes from Asia to Europe. With the boom in Asia, many more projects are coming up, and this connectivity role is becoming even more important. To date, nearly 300 gigs of traffic are going on these routes with just a modest amount of infrastructure in place. But over the next ten years, we are expecting to reach a good nine terabits of data. Just to put things in perspective, nine terabits of data is approximately two and a half times what is going over the Atlantic right now. Just a quick survey of what's out there: Certainly SMW3 and SMW4, substantially important consortium systems that have existed for some time. Perhaps SMW4 is the first system that was designed with the Internet in mind. It is shorter than SMW3, which was considered to be an innovation at its time, going into the strait around the Iberian Peninsula and reaching Atlantic Europe. This was a very important but modest system that was not really ready to handle Internet traffic. Newer systems are also coming up like IMEWE and EIG, both consortium systems. They are similar to SMW4 but shorter in path, starting in India, ending somewhere in Europe, although EIG followed the SMW3 path connecting to Atlantic Europe. And both are Internet ready, very dense systems with about 3.8 terabit capability. FLAG is a very famous system that starts deep in Asia-Pacific continues all the way to Atlantic Europe. All of these systems in common they have the fact that they pass through Egypt. Another private system is FALCON, which gives great Arabian Peninsula and Arabian Gulf coverage and meets the needs of south Europe and Suez. And finally, TEN has the capacity to be the first system in the world that is at ten terabits, it's designed predominantly for IP transit, and it connects Egypt to Europe---the first of a new breed of cables that is acting more like a conduit for traffic and for other infrastructure.

We have started looking at diversity in a more granular way. So rather than just look at the physical diversity across Egypt and the Mediterranean, we are also looking at how we access Europe. Accessing Europe from the east is becoming more important, especially after what happened in December 2008 when nearly six cables were cut in the Northeastern part of the Mediterranean. As a person who has worked in the Internet field for a long time, I am excited to see the first fibre system coming out of South Africa extending east to the north, connecting to Egypt in the south, dropping in about eight different coastal states, and providing connections to the longest coastline in the world, the Africa coastline. Egypt stands to be connected with dive fibre connectivity to approximately 60 countries in the world. So we take diversity very seriously and divide things in the Mediterranean in a simple way: is it north or south of Malta, which has a very unique position close to the Sicilian strait which is a very narrow passage of international water between Tunis and Sicily with a lot of cables. And this is why accessing Europe also through Greece and Turkey is becoming a very important addition in order to make sure that what happened in December 2008 will not be repeated.

354

Taking again a granular approach, below the Mediterranean, the fibre that goes across Egypt that carries this traffic is inherently very diverse. Many of those systems use different paths, a north and a south path to make sure there is protection. And, in fact, much of the world's IP transit is happening here, which relates to the fact that access does not just mean structure, it also means cost. The amount of Internet traffic that is passing through this fibre is really bringing up the issue that we plan to challenge the need for IP transit versus IP peering. With enough traffic happening in this region, we wonder if very soon this would become an important enough network access point for the rest of the world to consider to peer with us and help us reduce our cost and make things more affordable for everyone. By meshing this infrastructure, we can take things to another level of protection. You can imagine, rather than having two routes for every cable, you have as many routes as there are cables.

ERNEST NDUKWE:

Without access, there will be no Internet. And Internet is not real and cannot be experienced or valued by people that do not have access. It means being connected to the Internet at the right speed and at the right price, and linked to the right content at the right time and at the right place. I will restrict my intervention to the enabling infrastructure, especially regional and national backbones as well as security and safety issues.

Many developing countries lost out in the telecom revolution that happened before the advent of mobile communications, when the rest of the world developed copious installed capacities for fixed-line transmission and last mile or last meter infrastructure. With the commercialization of the Internet, the cable infrastructure became the access infrastructure in developed countries, linking homes and offices to the Internet employing ADSL technology. But for many developing countries today, last market, last mile, or last meter access to the Internet has to be wireless---UMTA, WCDMA, Wi-Fi, Wi-max, satellite transmission, and of course terminal systems like mobile phones, PDAs, and the like. It is also important that last meter access is developed side by side with national and regional backbone infrastructure to ensure affordable bandwidth costs, interconnection and peering.

Regulators and governments must encourage investment in building of large capacity, optic fibre infrastructure within their national boundaries and across the region. I recently tried to launch a campaign for fibre without borders as some countries in Africa, especially in Sub Saharan Africa, delay or deny rights of way for cross-border or cross-country fibre projects. Some countries even deny landing rights to companies seeking to land submarine cables on their shores. These are serious policy and regulatory issues that must be addressed if we want Internet for all. Africa needs optic fibre highways crisscrossing the continent, and if this happens it will help aggregate data traffic, reduce the cost of access, increase regional transit footprints, encourage regional peering, facilitate development of local content, and enhance the contribution of Africa to the knowledge resource on the Internet. Within national boundaries, it's also important that we encourage the build-out of fibre to even the remote parts of a country. In Nigeria we have a project called the State Accelerated Broadband Initiative, and the idea is to incentivize operating companies via subsidy to enable them to build fibres to those areas that they don't consider very commercially viable.

On the issue of security of access, I wish to approach it from a different perspective. In Nigeria we had a major cut of the link to the Sat3 submarine cable infrastructure. This is the single submarine cable that actually lies on our shore, though there are a number of new projects that will bring more there very soon. When this cut happened it affected voice and data traffic and disrupted critical business and social interests interactions, showing that unprotected critical infrastructure, whether state owned or privately owned, can have far-reaching consequences and even escalate to disaster proportions if not handled well. So I am advocating the need for governments and regulators to plan major protection initiatives, especially landing points and the like within their countries; the build-out of redundancies; and diversity in the provision of critical infrastructure, to include satellite communication links alternatives, even when cable transmission access are available.

HOPETON DUNN:

Thank you very much for those remarks. I am very sympathetic with the notion of making sure that the physical plant and the resources are protected, especially since I come from a region---the Caribbean---that is experiencing hurricanes on a regular basis which destroy much of the physical assets, and is now thinking about underground and other protective devices, and multimodal redundant capacity-building.

ERMANNO PIETROSEMOLI:

I will talk about how to achieve connectivity in developing countries with low-cost solutions. These are solutions that can be implemented directly by the communities that will benefit from them, and not necessarily by big corporation that sometimes do not have the incentive to serve rural and sparsely populated areas. For sparsely populated area, fibre is not the solution because it's not cost-effective to build connectivity in a rural area. Of course fibre is needed for the backbone and for international connectivity, but we need another sort of modality for serving these areas. Wi-Max is very promising but is still quite expensive, and so are the cellular solutions that are very good but not the best for a rural area. Wi-Fi solutions can be easily modified to provide connectivity to rural villages and even in extended regions at long distances. There are many examples showing that we can use the same Wi-Fi hardware with modification of the software and external antennas to reach much longer distances. To see how big a distance could be reached, we did an experiment in April 2006 that took advantage of a particular geography with a clear line of sight between a mountain that is 4,300 meters high and a hill that is 125 meters, and we were able to span a distance of 280 kilometres with just normal off-the-shelf Wi-Fi gear and external antennas. A year later, we were able to prove that it is feasible to use Wi-Fi gear to go over a path of 382 kilometres, and at the speed providing connectivity to a village of 8 megabits per second directional.

Of course you cannot find every day this topographically suitable situation to take advantage of such a long link, and I don't think this is going to be used commercially, but it gives you an idea of how far we can go. Another application of Wi-Fi technology is in Malawi where we built a network to provide connectivity of the Hospital of Mangochi to the College of Medicine in Blantyre over three steps with standard Wi-Fi equipment, just modifying the firmware and using external antennas of just 1.2 meters in diameter. So some of these solutions can be useful for developing countries. The major obstacle is the lack of awareness, so we have devoted most of our energy to spread knowledge by means of web sites like Wireless U, which is sponsored by several international organizations has a repository of material on low-cost wireless solutions that are available in several languages and freely downloadable. We also published a book that is called "Wireless Networking for the Developing World," a team effort by people from different countries and published in six languages. It too is freely downloadable, or can be obtained in paper for a nominal cost from the publisher because it's published under the creative common license.

HOPETON DUNN:

Thank you. I wanted for us to engage in a discussion now. We have maybe just under half an hour in which we'll invite comments.

FROM THE FLOOR:

I'm from Kenya and represent the private sector. Given the differences between developed and developing countries, do you think the developing countries should focus on basic and affordable technology to bridge the digital divide, rather than trying to keep up with the latest technology such as mobile broadband, which is too expensive for the majority of the population?

PIERRE DANDJINOU:

If possible, developing countries will invest in those basic outlets or equipment. Your question actually is calling for the necessity also of thinking about local industry, and this is something we are always arguing for. And the policies I was alluding to should include an element of innovation and appropriate investment in local industry.

FROM THE FLOOR:

My name is Rohan Samarajiva. I represent LIRNEasia, a research organization. What I have found a little surprising about the panel is while you are clearly and correctly focusing on the question of affordability and what governments can do to help us solve the problem, why are we not looking at the two experiences that we have had in the last 10 to 15 years? One which has been an extraordinary success and one which has been an abject failure. The extraordinary success is mobile telephony. Because we licensed large numbers of companies in certain countries, we now have a situation where in India we are connecting 15 million people a month. We have a situation where the affordability that you are you and I and everybody is so concerned about is becoming not a problem. In India, in Bangladesh, in

Pakistan, a mobile phone is extraordinarily affordable. The prices, the average revenues per user, are below $5 and the companies are making profits and investments. So this is a successful model. What we need to do is to develop government policies that will leverage this model, that will help us to extend this model to the broadband arena. Why is it possible to make profits and contribute to government revenues in south Asia at less than $5 U.S. per customer while in poorer countries, in Africa, in Latin America in particular, we have extraordinarily high prices, same technology, same GSM being used. That suggests that there has been a failure that can be fixed because we just need to learn from the south Asian experiment and see what can be extended.

And when it comes to universal service, which is the abject failure, there is no country that I know of where this has worked very well. We have $4 billion unspent in Brazil. We have $4 billion unspent in India. India made some very significant improvements in their universal service policies recently yet it cannot get rid of this money, and they ask us how to spend it. And we say, "Why are you taxing poor people?" "To keep money in funds." "That you are not using or you are misusing." So we need to focus on the business model, and on government action that can support it, rather than pure government action, which unfortunately is what I'm hearing most of the time.

FROM THE FLOOR:

My name is Anita Gurumurthy and I come from I.T. for Change, an NGO in India. What needs to be in the debate here is that local governments increasingly have begun to harness the power of broadband to improve the quality of governance. So where are marginalized populations standing in relation to this? It's been acknowledged the world over that public services can be a lifeline for the poor, especially for women, and local information transparencies, information architecture, are changing dramatically in many countries, including in India, via a lot of public investment and finance, which really needs to be emphasized and brought back. This was on the table in 2005 when we spoke about public finance modalities in WSIS. I also noticed that intermediary organizations like NGOs who have been working for the right to information, food security, health, and education have successfully used broadband for social mobilization in order to get the entitlements to poor women, et cetera. So instead of looking at mobiles versus broadband, we need to look at technical as well as policy architectures, and to promote local governments that are more accountable, transparent, and relevant to local populations.

FROM THE FLOOR:

I'm Mohamed El-Moghazi from the interior of Egypt. Regarding the Wi-Fi solutions that were proposed, how do you see the regulation since most countries are not allowing a huge amount of power to be used in those unlicensed bands. And how reliable are those links?

HOPETON DUNN:

We have a question from someone online: Are there practical measures to protect fibre optic cables? So we have a number of questions. Could we start with anyone wishing to respond in respect to mobiles and universal service?

ERNEST NDUKWE:

Rohan, you are quite right about the success of mobile communications. There's no doubt that that has been a major driver of connectivity for the mass market. That's why mass market links to the Internet have to be wireless, and mobile technology plays a very important role in that regard. But I'm also aware that we don't have a one size fits all because mobile signals have not reached some places and sometimes you might depend on other technologies to be able to reach remote locations. And the terminal equipment can also be a challenge, the phones that are able to do things like broadband and Internet sometimes are a bit on the high side as far as the ordinary person is concerned. But definitely we should take advantage of mobile technologies at fairly affordable rates in order to spread broadband to as many parts of the world's population as possible.

PIERRE DANDJINOU:

On the good question posed by the lady from India, that can be addressed by national policy spreading mobile broadband. We need to be more innovative at policymaking and incorporate all stakeholders, including the local governments, in national policies.

ERMANNO PIETROSEMOLI:

The experiments I mentioned were done with just 100 milliwatts of output power and just by fitting an external antenna, so power is not an issue. And as far as the license bands, we are using the unlicensed 12.4 gigahertz band, which is available just about anywhere. Some countries are more liberal in the use of that band than others, but it is in one way or other available anywhere. Furthermore, the same technology can also be used in different bands, and the allocation of special frequency bands for rural applications will be a very smart move if done with frequency agile radios, which opens the road for very low-cost solutions.

JOSE CLASTORNIK:

Hi. My name is Jose Clastornik. I am the Executive Director of the national Information Society agency in Uruguay. I wanted to mention the first one-laptop-per-child model implementation to be done on a national scale. Our intention was to give one laptop per child and for each teacher, to give connectivity to all schools and high schools, and to ensure that children had connectivity just 2- to 300 meters from their homes. We achieved this in two and half years using all methods of connectivity, from cable to satellite, Wi-Fi, mesh technologies, and so on. And although it was a government project, the work was done by civil society. One-fourth of homes in the country now have one or more laptops and there is free access in all cities or villages where you can find a school or high school. We doubled in each year the broadband connectivity of the country, which was already was one of the highest in Latin America.

FROM THE FLOOR:

I am Fotindong Cornelius from Cameroon and I work with the Minister of Posts and Telecommunications. We realize that with the liberalization of the telecommunications sector there has been a tremendous increase in the mobile tele-density of Internet connectivity. These are some of the results of privatization, but there are two challenges that still need to be addressed. In the rural and enclave areas, the mobile operators are reluctant to invest because there is little or no chance of profiting there. And you have the problem of developing a national backbone when the operators each wants to develop its own, so there will end up being parallel backbones. This affects the end user through the tariffs charged, and the government is tempted to review the liberalization policy. We also think that the landing of marine cables is an issue of sovereignty and should be handled by the government.

ERNEST NDUKWE:

I'd recommend that you don't reverse the liberalization process. What we have done in our country is to adopt what we call State Accelerated Broadband Infrastructure. You can incentivize your operators by some form of subsidy to extend this cable infrastructure to rural areas. Just bear in mind that many of the incumbent operators operated for over 50 years without getting to those rural areas, so government may not be the right provider of such infrastructure.

HOPETON DUNN:

Okay. I think that brings us to the end of the responses from the panel and the questions from the audience, given the time. I want to thank you for your participation, and also invite you to thank the panel for their presentation before we wrap up.

AMR BADAWI:

We heard some very interesting presentations today, very technical but to the point, and they bring us to some conclusions. We have a historic opportunity to be able to provide wireless broadband at reduced cost provided that the governments start managing that spectrum. Especially for governments the African and the Arab countries, where they have stark differences from what exist in Europe in terms of the broadcasting services available and the utilization of TV channels. If you look at the 700 megahertz band, you will find that in most Arab and African countries the utilization is extremely low, and that is really wasted band that could be very well used in providing broadband services. So I urge the countries there to get together and see what would be the best means to advance on that issue. The other thing is that, especially for rural areas, we should look at universal service funds that could reduce the cost of accessing the network. Marine cables will provide much cheaper international bandwidth to all developing countries, and that saving has to pass through to the customers. If the operators and the Internet service providers pass that to the consumer we will have a more affordable broadband. The fibre optic infrastructure should a national project to make sure that all the country is well connected, and governments should provide incentives for companies to provide these services. I would recommend that this be part of the declarations or statements listed by this conference.

Diversity and Access:

Reports of the Workshops and Other Events

1: Diversity

WS 110. Global Internet Access for Persons with Disabilities

WS 176. Open Content and Open Licensing in the Arab World:
Opportunities and Challenges Facing their Use and Applicability

WS 199. Arabic Script IDNs: Challenges and Solutions

WS 235. Virtual Worlds and Public Diplomacy in the Digital Age

WS 248. Spanish and Latin Content in the Internet

WS 274. The use of Internet in the Arab Region: Prospects and the Future

BPF 282. Access for Everyone includes Persons with Disabilities

WS 295. Lost in Non-ASCII Translation

WS 318. Promoting Cultural Diversity through Cultural Heritage in
Cyberspace

2: Access

WS 95.   Expanding Access to the Internet and Broadband for Development

WS 97.   Global State of Copyright and Access to Knowledge

WS 216. The Internet and Citizenship: Applying a Gender Lens

WS 234. Issues Regarding the Mobile Internet

WS 243. Broadening Mobile Content and Sustainable Access

WS 270. Public Policies for Improved Interconnection at Lower Costs

WS 286. Towards Access: Combining Intellectual Property, Competition
and Human Rights

WS 328. Access to Satellite Communications as a Key for Capacity Building:
A Reference Model Looking for Affordable Costs

OF 533. OECD Open Forum on the Importance of Internet Access and
Openness for a Sustainable Economic Recovery

BPF 540. Best Practices for an Accessible Web

1: Diversity

WS 110.   Global Internet Access for Persons with Disabilities

Report by: Alexandra Gaspari

Organizer: Dynamic Coalition on Accessibility and Disability (DCAD)

Moderator: Jonathan Charles (BBC World)

Panellists: Malcolm Johnson, Director (ITU Telecommunication Standardization Bureau); Andrea Saks (DCAD Coordinator); Arnoud Van Wijk (Real-Time Text Taskforce [R3TF]); Arun Mehta (Special Kid [SKID]); David Wood (European Broadcasting Union); Dipendra Manocha (Daisy Consortium); Cynthia Waddell (International Centre for Disability Resources on the Internet); Nirmita Narasimhan (Center for Internet and Society); Fernando Botelho (Botelho & Paula Consultoria); Gerard Ellis (Feel The BenefIT)

The International Telecommunication Union (ITU) and the European Broadcasting Union (EBU), in collaboration with the Dynamic Coalition on Accessibility and Disability (DCAD) organized the workshop as an activity of the DCAD and the European Broadcasting Union. The workshop highlighted the different aspects on how to make the internet accessible for persons with disabilities. The workshop pointed out the necessity to make the Internet accessible to all, regardless of individual capabilities of different users.

Organizations that are members of DCAD include, among others: the International Telecommunication Union (ITU), SKID, Council of Europe, Digital Accessible Information System Consortium (DAISY Consortium), Global Initiative for Inclusive Information and Communication Technologies (G3ict), the Indian Centre for Internet & Society, International Center for Disability Resources on the Internet (ICDRI), Internet Society (ISOC), Internet Society Argentina (ISOC-AR), UNESCO, Web Accessibility Initiative (W3C).

In 2006, the UN General Assembly adopted the Convention on the Rights of Persons with Disabilities, which obliges its signatories to provide public information in formats and technologies appropriate to different kinds of disabilities. The ITU, as the world's pre-eminent global ICT standards organization, is embracing the challenges of accessibility through standardization efforts and has long championed the principles of inclusion and Universal Design enshrined in the UN Convention.

This workshop explored several objectives and the main ones can be described as follows:

- Spread knowledge and increase the awareness of the work being carried out in ITU in the field of accessibility to the ICTs;
- Give visibility to the work being done in the field of accessibility to the ICTs;
- Highlight the necessity to make the Internet accessible to all, regardless of individual capabilities of different users;

- Promote awareness on accessibility at different levels within the United Nations system and other International Organizations to implement accessibility and encourage its implementation in their daily work.

The keynote address was given by Malcolm Johnson, Director of the Telecommunication Standardization Bureau, ITU. The TSB Director underlined that a momentum is building for initiatives that allow persons with disabilities to take their rightful place in society. Malcolm Johnson stated that industry and governments need to understand that persons with disabilities not only need to be included but have a right to be included in the new technological achievements and advances of our time. This is especially important for developing countries that look to the developed world and to ITU for guidance.

The panel was divided in different parts describing several issues like, what are the access challenges to meet, the Media content for persons with disabilities, the UN Convention for Persons with disabilities and the specific measures that can be taken in order to implement accessibility. The panellists, mainly DCAD representatives spoke and presented the different issues related to the global access to the Internet from the point of view of the persons with disabilities. Some of the strategies that governments can adopt to ensure a thriving assistive technology marketplace and affordable products were presented. Another presentation investigated, from the point of view of a disabled user of ICTs, the economic benefit of including the needs of people with disabilities in technological products and services. People with disabilities and older people gain disproportionately from the inclusion of the Universal Design, but that all stakeholders benefit.

It is expected that the UN Convention will make assistive ICT technologies as common as wheelchair ramps and audible signals for traffic lights. Assistive technologies include screen readers (which read content from websites out loud for the visually impaired), captioning or sign language on television for the deaf, cell phones that include features such as special volume control, large character touch pads and predictive text features and auditory SMS messages for the blind as well as the adoption of accessible website design by both the public and private sectors. Finding solutions to these challenges is not always a simple matter. On the one hand, equipment and software is now available that provides amazing breakthroughs for people with disabilities. On the other hand, there are many barriers to finding the most appropriate equipment, particularly at affordable prices.

WS 176.   *Open Content and Open Licensing in the Arab World: Opportunities and Challenges Facing Their Use and Applicability*

Report by: Rami Olwan

Chair: *Brian Fitzgerald (Queensland University of Technology)*

Panellists: Ziad Maraqa (Abu- Ghazaleh Intellectual Property and his involvement with Creative Commons Jordan as a co-project leader); Rami Olwan (Research Fellow at ARC Centre of Excellence for Creative Industries and Innovation, Brisbane,

Australia); Rafik Dammak (Creative Commons Tunisia and a researcher at Tokyo University); Ahmad Gharbeia, (ICT consultant form Egypt); Issa Mahasneh (Jordan Open Source Association)

Ziad Maraqa gave an introduction on Creative Commons as an open content license. He introduced the concept of Creative Commons and how does it work in practice. He explained how Creative Commons licenses are expressed in legal code, human readable and machine-readable. He also explained and compared between six Creative Commons licenses Attribution, Attribution-Share Alike, Attribution-No Derivatives, Attribution-Non-commercial, Attribution-Non commercial-Share Alike, Attribution-Non-commercial-No Derivatives. He finally gave practical examples of how CC is been applied in the Arab world and adopted by Al Jazeera in their repository site for the videos taken during the Gaza war and available under a Creative Commons attribution license.

Rami Olwan gave a presentation entitled "Open Content Licensing and Creative Commons- A Jordanian Perspective". The presentation tackled the meaning of open content and open content licensing and their importance to the Arab World and developing countries. He also went through the history of Creative Commons and its foundation in 2001 by prominent U.S academics. Jordan was the first country from the Middle East to adopt the project in the region since 2002. The Jordanian Creative Commons team translated the American licenses to Arabic and made the necessary amendments to make it compatible with the Jordanian Copyright Law and the civil law legal system. Mr Olwan finally noted the open content licensing in the Arab World is still in an early stage and there is a need to conduct public awareness and to do research on the enforceability of Creative Commons licenses. This in his opinion would make Arab users more interested in Creative Commons.

Rafik Dammak spoke about the Tunisian experience in porting Creative Commons license to the country. He mentioned that it is not possible to reuse the same translation done by Creative Commons Jordan in Tunisia because of the difference between the legal systems in both countries. He explained why Creative Commons team in Tunisia need to do the work again. This is because the translation has to be done in both Arabic and French in Tunisia. He further explained that Tunisia is currently debating issuing a new copyright law that is expected to be much different from the current applicable copyright law, and that will definitely delay the work of the Creative Commons team. Mr. Dammak concluded by the acknowledging the lack of awareness among Tunisian users of Creative Commons and confusion between open content and open source licensing. He suggested in rectifying this problem to obtain the support of the Tunisian government, as this would encourage open content licensing particularly Creative Commons.

Ahmad Gharbeia delivered a short presentation on what he thought was hindering the adoption and acceptance of liberal licenses by the public, the private sector and governments in the Arab world. He believes that the basic concepts of intellectual property need to be disseminated in order to harness the sharing culture, which already exists, and to encourage more creativeness.

Issa Mahasneh's presentation was about free culture and how it could be harnessed in the Arab world. Mr. Mahasneh believes that free culture means "a world where everybody can participate freely to transmit, share and obtain knowledge and that would promote creativity, innovation, free expression, public access to knowledge and civil liberties". He outlined the positive points in the Arab world and also the negative points that are against the spread of free culture movement in the Arab world. He finally recommended governments to be more interested in open content and free culture should be supported from within communities.

During the question time, a couple of questions were addressed to the speakers. An audience member from the Library of Alexandria asked on the importance of adopting Creative Commons by governments and how this would assist in the spread of the movement in the Arab world. She wanted to know whether it is important to Creative Commons initiative into a political framework, or just address the authors?

Rami Olwan answered that adopting Creative Commons licenses by governments would make the general public more interested in the movement and more willing to know how it could be used. He further noted that in Jordan, the Minister of Justice has supported the launch of Creative Commons Jordan. This proved to be helpful especially when it is from the highest authority responsible for the enforcement of intellectual property laws in Jordan. Mr. Ziad Maraqa has also answered the question pointing out how Creative Commons Jordan is working with several organizations in Jordan and outside in spreading the idea to the public. Issa Mahasnah added that in his onion it is probably not required the presence of the government, but most importantly to have all the work produced by government and public administration under some open license and accessible to everyone.

Another audience member asked on the importance of Creative Commons and what it tried to achieve. Rami Olwan mentioned the fact that professor Lawrence Lessig, founding member of Creative Commons believes that laws are restricting freedom on the Internet and are been used to lock down creativity and innovation. He created this system of licenses to rectify the situation. Mr. Ahmad Gharbeia has also provided his opinion on what is the main problem that Creative Commons is trying to fix from his experience as an ICT consultant.

An employee of the British library addressed the last question. He was interested to see if in the Arab World, academics and universities started to use Creative Commons license? He mentioned that it is very important that civil society is engaged with government around open access/content, and it is important to work with organizations like universities and cultural institutions that actually sit in between civil society and governments and have different drivers. In his experience with the UK and also in the European level, he noted that government officials are actually interested in these issues and they will listen, but it is important to know the internal focus but be external focused on the political level.

Rami Olwan acknowledged the importance of building this sort of connection between Creative Commons and academic institutions. He also hoped that more research is done on how Creative Commons could help the development of research and education in the Arab world. Issa Mahasneh also added that unfortunately academics in the Arab World and most professors and instructors are not completely aware of the open access and he hoped that Jordan Open Source Association to be more active in the future in spreading the idea. It is important also for other communities in the Arab world to encourage educational organization and governments themselves to adopt open access.

WS 199.   Arabic Script IDNs: Challenges and Solutions

Report by: Ram Mohan

Organizer: Arabic Script IDN Working Group (ASIWG)

Panellists: Abdel Aziz Al-Zoman (Director of SaudiNIC, Saudi Arabia); Sarmad Hussain (Professor and Head, Center for Research in Urdu Language Processing, National University of Computer and Emerging Sciences, Pakistan); Ayman El-Sherbiny (First Officer, ICT Policies, ICTD, United Nations ESCWA); Baher Esmat (Manager, Regional Relations, Middle East, ICANN); Manal Ismail (Director, International Technical Coordination, NTRA, Egypt)

The workshop discussed:
- The need for ASIWG, work done so far and recommendations of the group,
- The approach followed by ASIWG in problem solving, developing a common Arabic script table and compiling the Arabic script variant table(s) across Arabic-script-based languages,
- Policy considerations and criteria set by ASIWG for decision-making,
- Technical challenges and possible solutions,
- Importance of safeguarding end-user experience
- Status of IDNs implementation within ICANN
- The need and importance of cooperation & collaboration among the different language communities sharing the same language/script,
- Variant analysis, implementation and a proposed solution for automating variants handling at the registry level,
- Recommendations of the group with regards to the use of Arabic script in IDN ccTLDs as well as IDN gTLDs, and
- Invitation & outreach to other Arabic-script-based languages
- Importance of collaboration among the different language communities specially those using the same script to collaboratively work on issues such as how to identify variant characters and how to deal with those variants.
- Importance of the timing as now is the right time to ensure that recommendations coming from language communities are being considered before policies are finalized.
- Although registration rules and policies may differ from one registry to another, it is important to have some homogeneity and agreement on general policy issues for a consistent and predictable end-user experience.

- Importance of starting with the necessary minimum set of characters then, if needed, extending further when ready as the reverse will not be possible.
- Urging language communities to look at language tables already within the IANA database before submitting their own.
- IDNs are just the start, more effort need to be exerted to enrich the Internet with local content and to have the necessary tools and applications serving end-users needs.

WS 235.   *Virtual Worlds and Public Diplomacy in the Digital Age*

Report by: Leigh Jackson

Panellists: Sue Baxter (Department of Business, Innovation, and Skills, UK Government); Ren Reynolds (tVPN); Jovan Kurbalija (DiploFoundation); Nagwa El Gazzar (Misr International University); Lizbeth Goodman (Futurelab); Michael Thatcher (Microsoft Middle East & Africa); Dorette Steenkamp (Uthango Social Investments); Dave Taylor (Imperial College London)

This workshop provided an introduction to Virtual Worlds (that is, online multiuser environments) and their relationship with the practice of Public Diplomacy.

Key challenges:
- Virtual Worlds are still viewed by many policy makers as a minority entertainment form this underestimates both the scale and breadth of their use.
- Virtual Worlds challenge policy makers are they are difficult to categorise
- In terms of use they are an entertainment form, but also are used in commerce, science and education.
- Virtual worlds combine many media forms which are typically governed by separate laws, regulatory frameworks and governance bodies
- Virtual Worlds also tend to be global in respect of their development, hosting and use – this gives rise to a wealth of inter-jurisdictional issues

Key opportunities:
- Virtual Worlds preset a range of opportunities which have both direct beneficial outcomes and tend to have positive environmental impacts, these include:
- Public engagement e.g. drug and sexual heath awareness
- Learning & teaching e.g. hands on / creative learning
- Collaboration e.g. virtual meeting
- Science e.g. virtual laboratories
- For policy makers Virtual Worlds provide an ideal test case where intersecting policies can be examined in a practical context.

The workshop closed with a short Question and Answer session lead by Mr Ian Taylor MP. This concluded with a summary of some of the key challenges and opportunities for virtual worlds and public policy.

WS 248.   Spanish and Latin Content in the Internet

Report by: Olga Cavalli

Panellists: Prof. *Jorge Perez Martínez (Universidad Politécnica de Madrid - InternetGovernance Forum España - Fundación Telefónica de España); Ernesto Majó (LACNIC Jesús Jiménez, Instituto Cervantes); Vanessa Fusco (Ministerio de Justicia de Minas Gerais, Brasil); Adrián Carballo (International Relations Director, South School on Internet Governance); Juan Carlos Solines Moreno (Ecuador); Olga Cavalli (Director, South School on Internet Governance)*

The Spanish language and other languages spoken in Spain and in the Latin American region like Portuguese and Catalán are growing in number of users and in the relevance and quality of their content. They also mean a relevant tool for enhancing the local culture and local communities. The workshop purpose was to explore the latest experiences in the use of Spanish and other Latin languages in the Internet, focusing on concrete results in relation with community inclusion, content development and education involvement.

An extensive revision about the use of Spanish and other Latin languages like Portuguese was made, which was a very interesting exchange of experiences among the panellists and the attendees.   Organizers of the IGF of Spain recognized the importance of this issue and exchange some experiences about best practices and documents produced in these meetings.   Also Instituto Cervantes explained how the language is promoted in other countries where Spanish is not de local language.   LACNIC talked about their role in relation with the critical Internet Resources and also about the relevance they give to the diversity of languages, he commented that all employees of LACNIC speak English, Spanish and Portuguese.

Latest figures about spoken language were exchanged and it was remarked that the biggest Spanish speaking country in the world will be the USA.   The experience of the use of Portuguese as a tool for preventing cybercrime was also presented.   Finally a case study about publication of academic papers in Spanish in Wikipedia was presented.

- Spanish relevant content generation must be promoted.
- The same should happen with other Latin Languages in Internet.
- Spanish should become one of the official languages of the IGF

WS 274.   The Use of Internet in the Arab Region: Prospects and the Future

Report by: Hanane Boujemi

Panellists: *Hanane Boujemi (DiploFoundation); Adel El-Zaim (IDRC); George Victor (NTRA, Egypt); Jawad Abbassi (Arab Advisors Group); Anas Tawileh (Meedan); Rafik Dammak (University of Japan); Rafid Fatani (University of Exeter); ED Bic (Meedan); Dr. Mohammed Al-kanhal (King Abdulaziz Institute City of Science and Technology) ED Bice (Meedan)*

The Objective of this workshop is to debate about the usage of Internet in the Arab region and to what extents it is contributing effectively in integrating the Arab Internet user in the digital age. The scope of this workshop covers access to Internet in the Arab region from three angles. It discusses the case study of Egypt highlighting the role of the government in enhancing the use of Internet as a tool of development, the state vision and the initiatives in place.

The workshop has also given an insight of the facts and numbers about Internet users in the region and how the private sector is involved in promoting access. The other topic this workshop will be tackling is the role of Internet in research. It explores how the Internet is used in universities and research centres both under the access aspect and the application aspect. The majority of the universities and research centres are offered access, and are participating in international research networks but the level and quality of usage vary significantly. It would be important to know how researchers and students are benefiting from the usage of Internet. Finally, the workshop delivers critical analysis of Internet usage in the Arab region, the current situation and how it can be used lucratively. It also describes the role of civil society and gives a synopsis about Diplo's focus on capacity development challenges and community building of policy makers in Arab region.

- Emphasizing the importance of having online content originally in Arabic since the meaning could be lost in translation to encourage more access to the Web in the Arab region.
- Discussing filtering in the Arab region and to what extent it limits access to online content.
- The necessity of building and ICT knowledge industry to the Golf country since all the financial resources are available but no positive results reflect on the number of users having access to Internet.
- Launching initiatives that are compatible with the cultural backgrounds of Internet users in the region.
- Highlighting initiatives which components include developing search engines, automatic translation, linguistic tools, a digital library, book translation, an open content project, an Arabic interactive dictionary, and an Arabic corpus. Their goal is to analyze regulations and governance for digital content globally and establish a roadmap for Arabic content.
- Decoding why there is an increase in Arab users but significant increase is noticed as far online Arabic content is concerned.
- Setting the distinction between access to knowledge and access to understanding. The next phase of the Internet is going to enable access to understanding.
- Discussing the role of research and ICT capacity building in the region and its importance in bridging the knowledge gap.

The workshop also discussed fact and figures about Internet penetration in the region and the type of connection mostly used. It also highlighted various aspects of Internet infrastructure and the future for the region.

Report by: Zhong Rui

Organizer: Internet Society of China, China Foundation for Disabled Persons, and China Communications Standardizations Association

Moderator: Mr. Gao Xinmin (Vice President, Internet Society of China)

Panellists: Huang Chengqing (Vice-President, Internet Society of China); Sun Yongge (Director, Internet Society of China); Mr. Lambert van Nistelrooij (European Parliament)

The purpose of the forum was to call further attention to the special needs of those with disabilities, and motivate a range of joint efforts to build an inclusive information society. The forum gave a brief introduction on current status of people with disabilities in China, and showed the latest efforts to promote information accessibility construction from various aspects, such as legislation, government financial and technical support, civil society initiatives, enterprises' products R&D, and active participation by social public. Specific cases were introduced in line with each part of efforts, included the annual China Information Accessibility Forum, China Digital Library for Visual Impairment, Baidu.com, Taobao.com, Harbin E-time Digital Tech Development Co., Ltd etc. Besides, the forum showed a series of efforts to promote web accessibility standard development and application in China, for example, the "Information Accessibility - for People with physical disabilities – Technical Requirements for Web Accessibility". Meanwhile, the examples of ICT benefit to European people, especially the project of Ambient Assisted Living to assist the Old group were demonstrated in the forum. Participants from EU, Brazil, India, Turkey, Hong Kong, IGF Dynamic Coalition, and CDRI had active interactive with the speakers.

Main issues:
- More efforts from various levels should be done to create/promote the accessibility, especially from the perspective of government and civil society. More specific regulations or rules should be set to push forward the accessibility construction. Further education program should be organized to raise public awareness to concerns about the needs of people with disabilities. Related industry and companies should be given more encouragement on accessibility products R&D.
- International cooperation and exchange are extremely necessary to promote the accessibility standards more compatible and easy to share.
- China will continue to perfect the information accessibility standards setting, especially the standards on picture and video accessibility. To promote the implementation of information accessibility using by the main portals and the websites frequently visited by people with disabilities will be a long-term work.

Thanks for the IGF platform, through which all of us could exchange communications with information accessibility experts around the world and learn thoughtful and new experiences to advance local information accessibility.

WS 295.   Lost in Non-ASCII Translation

Report by: Peter Van Roste

Moderator: Baher Esmat (ICANN)

Panellists: Mohamed El-Bashir (.SD); Zhang Jian (CNNIC); Leonid Toderov (Coordination Center for TLD RU); Vaggelis Segredakis (Foundation for Research and Technology Hellas Institute of Computer Science); Manal Ismail (Egyptian Ministry of Telecommunications); Elisabeth Markot (European Commission)

The current restriction for top-level domain names to include only ASCII characters is one of the main obstacles that prevent billions of users from full and easy access to the benefits of the Internet. Therefore, the launch of Internationalized Domain Names at the top level has become of paramount importance. An Internet which speaks all languages at all levels makes businesses and people more competitive and mobile, enhances inclusiveness and diversity at the same time, contributes to bridge the digital divide and ensures that the cultural heritage is better preserved. This workshop aims at illustrating the advantages of having non-ASCII top-level domains. It will explain the process of their introduction and the expected impact on the non-ASCII communities through the inputs, remarks and statements of government, ccTLD and civil society representatives.

More details on the linguistic problems were given at a workshop organized by CENTR on IDN ccTLDs, where Manal Ismail from the National Telecom Regulatory Authority listed as issues:
- Left-to-rights script
- Change of characters depending on position in a word
- Delimiter role
- Two set of numbers
- Arabic diacrits as issues to be solved.

Manal also said that IDNs would not solve all language barrier problems, as content still had to be developed in Arabic and all-Arabic domain name registrations will be only gradual.   Linguistic problems for the Greek community were presented by Vaggelis Segredakis from the foundation for research and technology Hellas. Vaggelis explained the problems with variants and how this could create confusion for the end user.

More general presentations about IDN planning were also given in this session by CNNIC and the coordination centre for TLD RU.   The EU Commission underlined during the CENTR session the importance of multilingualism for the .eu registry where preparations to allow registration of second level domains in all EU languages are ready (start of registrations is Dec, 10th).

372

Promoting Cultural Diversity through Cultural Heritage in Cyberspace

Report by: *Hind Mostafa*

Chairman: *Dr. Fekri Hassan*

Panellists: *Dr. Reem Bahgat; Tulika Pandey; Dr. Rodolfo Ambrosetti; Dr. Tarek Shawki; Dr. Adel Danish; Heba Hussam*

The idea of cultural diversity falling into stereo type trap was also discussed in terms of how people generally perceive certain cultures to be better or superior to others. Dr. Shawki discussed several important aspects regarding the concept of Cultural Diversity and adopting advanced technologies to culture and shed the light on important initiatives currently taking place such as the Memory of the Arab World register, which aims to protect collections of heritage from countries in the region. He also praised the role of certain institutions such as Bibliotheca Alexandrina, Dar El Kutob and the World Digital Library for their massive efforts in the preservation of cultural heritage such as ancient manuscripts and also implied preservation of heritage would one way lead to better and more prosperous economic state. Finally, he discussed a new project initiative where he talked about schoolbooks projects and the perception of the "Image of the other" and the mark it leaves behinds in the minds of school children. The discussion was ended by a brief talk about the importance truly understanding the concept of cultural diversity.

Dr. Bahgat talked about issues related to promoting cultural diversity through cyberspace in order to reach the conclusion about understanding, respect and tolerance of cultures. Translation of different languages of a work is regarded necessary for cultural interchange and for cultures to be able to understand each other. A best example of this would be that of the CULTNAT websites that have been and are still undergoing translation into many languages. She also explained how translation should be extended to both tangible and intangible forms of heritage and the importance of "semantic" translation which is regarded very useful. In addition, she also highlighted the importance of using certain types of tools in order for the information to reach a wider array of audience such as "text-to-speech" tools to reach disabled people.

Dr. Tarek Shawki response: Dr. Shawky covered the topic of building knowledge to societies in which societies are able to create new knowledge to be based upon 4 pillars. He mentioned that between 2003-2004 there was an effort made to digitize existing manuscripts in Egypt to prevent them from getting lost, and at the same time an envisioned encyclopaedia with CULTNAT, with cooperation from Dar El Kutob was created via labs for capacity building, in which such work was put into digitalized high quality form. Once again, the light was shed upon the Memory of the World Register and how it would be regarded the safe haven for ancient documents and manuscripts that required protection. In addition, he also mentioned how the US Library of Congress approached the US to create the "World Digital Library". He also praised the role of certain Arab Institutions where in 2008

King Abdullah University for Science and Technology donated millions of dollars to finance the World Digital Library. In addition, Dr. Shawki stressed an important point related to the Heritage Program designated to actual sites where if they were to fulfil certain criteria they would be added to the World Heritage Sites Lists which is regarded to be very significant attracting tourists to it and providing it with great economic opportunities. He also discussed how the UNESCO has been working diligently on safeguarding endangered languages, as well as, folklore, music, and dances.

Ms. Pandey emphasized the importance of the concept of Cultural Diversity and what at means to her being an Indian, where she regards her country to be a best demonstrative example of that being divided into 35 provinces and for their being 11 official languages in the country. She went about discussing how each separate province has its own dialect, food, dances, and writing scripts and how well they all manage to co-exist. She also talked about the leading role her country has taken in the arena of electronic governance for information to be disseminated and to reach a larger number of people and how the Indian government is working hard to facilitate IT to reach far more areas in regions in the country that are needing it the most.

Ms. Hussam went about discussing and naming several projects and initiatives adopted by MCIT in order to protect and disseminate information. A few of the projects she highlighted where those related to illiteracy reduction in the country such as the "E-connect" which now digitalizes the illiteracy reduction curriculum to be accessed easily online. Ms. Hussam also shed the light other projects such as "Fekr Rama" which offers a great change of people to share their experience and knowledge and gives them access to articles. In addition to talking about the "E-heritage" project which is an Egyptian National Archive protection project.

Final Notes from the panel were points made regarding trying to preserve the knowledge and at the same time exchange it without there being too many limitations that prevent the dissemination and access of knowledge

2: Access

WS 95.   Expanding Access to the Internet and Broadband for Development

Report by: Karine Perset

Organizers: OECD and InfoDev

Moderator: Dimitri Ypsilanti (Head of Information, Communication and Consumer Policy Division, OECD)

Keynote: Rohan Samarajiva (Executive Director, LIRNE Asia)

Panellists: Tim Kelly (Lead ICT Policy Specialist, infoDev - World Bank); Olfat A. Monsef (Vice President of National Telecommunication Regulator, Telecom Services, Egypt); Anriette Esterhuysen (Executive Director, Association for Progressive

Communications (APC)); Jake Jennings (Executive Director International External and Regulatory Affairs, AT&T)

Dimitri Ypsilanti chaired the workshop, of which the aim was to explore how developing countries can take advantage of developments in broadband, what lessons can be learned from the successful growth of mobile services, what policies and regulatory frameworks are needed to promote access to networks, how this can assist with broader capacity building (e.g., science and technology, education, information sharing) and how to promote policy coherence to support the opportunities such networks create for development.

Rohan Samarajiva was the keynote speaker. He drew from research conducted in South and Southeast Asia in particular Bangladesh, one of the poorest countries in the world. He stressed that the biggest challenge facing the developing world in this area was to connect low-income groups, but that in turn, solutions to this problem would help with other wider development problems. He pointed out that while a common image of the Internet features a desktop or laptop computer connected by wire or wirelessly, awareness of the importance of the mobile phone as an alternative pathway is increasing. Millions of poor people are beginning to participate in the Internet Economy through their mobile phones.

Samarajiva questioned whether this participation was happening because of good policy or rather, despite bad policy. He described the "budget network telecom model" that is meeting the challenge of connecting the developing world. Akin to low-cost airlines such as EasyJet or RyanAir, this model has already been successful in driving the mobile success story in South Asia and is based on the exploitation of long-tail markets and controlling costs through business process innovations. Key feature are reliance on pre-paid billing and low cost. In South Asia (India, Bangladesh, Pakistan, Nepal and Sri Lanka), the total cost of ownership of a mobile is typically below USD 5 per month, compared with an average for developing economies of over USD 13. The budget telecom network model --with large numbers of users each with very low ARPU-- does not appear to have negatively impacted the profitability of local operators, with acquisition costs close to $1 and volatile EBITDA sometimes exceeding 50%. Competition is the necessary pre-condition to lower prices that lead to greater participation by the poor, both urban and rural, in terms of demand side numbers.

For broadband, Samarajiva stressed that international connectivity represents the main bottleneck and that there is a need to reduce international backhaul costs by breaking international monopolies. He also spoke to the importance of getting away from "all you can eat" unlimited Internet models, because poor people pay as they go, when the need arises and money is available. He also highlighted the importance of new services/applications, such as CellBazaar, an e-commerce platform in Bangladesh that enables users to search for goods but not yet to order, pay, obtain delivery, or generate feedback. In discussing the role of policy and regulation, Samarajiva stressed that solutions must fit institutional conditions, the importance of market entry and spectrum management, the importance of the availability and wholesale access to large pipes, and the need to pay attention to anti-competitive practices, such as vertical price squeezing. In his view, "old-style" regulation should be replaced by forbearance and regulators in developing countries should be "gentle" on quality of service (QoS). He expressed the view that it would be preferable to phase out universal service levies which are incompatible with the Budget Telecom Network Model and are in case slow to be disbursed. There is a need to rationalise taxes.

Tim Kelly, the first discussant, drew attention to the link between ICTs and economic growth. He stressed that this link appears to be much higher in developing countries than in developed countries: World Bank research shows that a 10% increase of broadband penetration in developing countries leads to an increase of 1.4% of GPD per capita. In addition, the relationship is much stronger with mobile than fixed networks, and so the developmental impact of mobile broadband could be greater still. With regards to the role of governments, Kelly spoke of governments promoting: i) efficiency, i.e., creating competition between and within platforms, citing the example of Korea's early license that provided open access to networks through local loop unbundling and established a national vision for broadband; ii) equity, by acting on the demand side, e.g., by providing subsidies for rural access or access in schools and public institutions, and; iii) taking into account environmental concerns, since broadband can substitute for the physical movement of goods and people. Kelly said he believed that mobile broadband would overtake fixed broadband in most developing countries because of the lack of existing infrastructure and the decreasing prices of mobile broadband. He agreed with Rohan Samarajiva on the need to address bottlenecks in international gateways.

Olfat Monsef, the second discussant, spoke about broadband availability and use in Egypt. With a population of 80 million, Egypt is focusing on availability and affordability of infrastructure through competition, as well as content development/ localisation of content into Arabic. Egypt has about 5 million broadband users compared to 17% narrowband penetration. Both fixed and mobile broadband access platforms are taking off, thanks to effective competition and the telecommunications sector contributes some 4.5% of GNP. Dr. Monsef underlined the importance of working on the supply side and the demand side in a policy coherence environment. Providing a future proof that capacity infrastructure should be planned while adopting national initiatives to promote applications such e-government and ICT in education and health.

Anriette Esterhuysen, the third discussant, stressed the importance of broadband for development and opportunity to learn from lessons of the past, e.g., from poverty reduction strategies (PRSs) that contained ICT components, or from ICT mainstreaming efforts that were successful at filling the connectivity gap. She emphasized the need for multi-stakeholder approaches, as well as the opportunity to look at how ICTs can help in other sectors, including health and education but also media or entertainment. In terms of public policy priorities, she felt that removing barriers at the last mile was still necessary and the role of governments in last-mile access, that governments can use ICTs to improve the services they deliver to citizens, and questioned whether using resources from universal service funds, e.g., to stimulate local content, might be useful. Esterhuysen pointed to several risks, including that governments develop their national broadband plans too quickly or that they threaten freedom of expression by planning censorship and monitoring in the face of terrorism or to protect children. She also pointed to challenges related to market structure and excessive integration / concentration whereby incumbent mobile operators also offer content, payment services etc.

Jake Jennings introduced the "digital prosperity check-list" endorsed by the Senior Leaders of APEC in 2008 that includes access, availability and investment. While the checklist includes numerous items, there are some low hanging fruits that developing nations could address, namely, permitting entry without any limitations on foreign investment, technology neutrality and security and privacy for e-health records, online banking and data retention / privacy requirements. He stressed that it is important to have an open Internet, but that operators should be allowed to manage their network, provided that they do so in a transparent manner. He also highlighted the many benefits from broadband deployment ranging from education, healthcare, energy use, climate change and economic development. In addition, he noted that the free flow of information improves citizenship and allows governments to operate in a more efficient manner.

The Chair, Dimitri Ypsilanti, launched the discussion by pointing out that while wireless platforms are the focus in developing countries, OECD countries are emphasizing FTTH technologies. This led him to wonder whether we would see a North-South Fibre divide. Samarajiva pointed out that technologies depend on use. For example, for a farmer to obtain prices of agricultural produce, a mobile phone could be the most appropriate because it could be used in the middle of a transaction or on the way to market. With regards to technological neutrality, Juan-Carlos Solines-Moreno, who was previously the telecommunications regulator in Ecuador, stressed that when given the choice, operators opt for GSM because it is cheaper. Jake Jennings from AT&T confirmed that operators were willing to spend more on spectrum, but that it is important for the operators to use the spectrum using the technology standard of their choice such as GSM, LTE or Wi-Max, in other words technology neutrality is crucial. For example, repharming unused spectrum from Defence departments can no longer be postponed and secondary markets can be put in place so that companies are able to share frequencies with other companies. Samarajiva mentioned that WTO provisions exist to make transparent spectrum inventories in every country.

Rohan Samarajiva stressed that universal service obligations were the equivalent of taxes whereby the poor people coming onto the networks are being taxed, as opposed to rich people who are on fixed networks. In such situations, economics teaches us to use non-distortionary general taxes if subsidies need to be funded. On security, a participant from Symantec asked whether with security statistically linked to penetration, any work was being done on skills development with regards to security issues. Jake Jennings replied that AT&T was entering partnerships for online safety, and that users need to be confident that the Internet is safe and secure. Furthermore, in order to provide a safe and secure Internet operators need have flexibility to manage their networks. For example, some countries prohibit encryption which limits the ability of operators to offer a safe and secure Internet service.

On illiteracy, participants pointed out that while the success of the mobile model relied on voice and voice recognition technologies, a new generation of keypad-literate people is emerging.

The OECD/ infoDev workshop on "Expanding access to the Internet and broadband for development" focused on the spread of mobile throughout the developing world based on prepaid services and the budget telecom network model, which exploits long-tail markets. Participants discussed the importance of effective competition, of access to spectrum, of removing bottlenecks in international connectivity, and discussed the merits of rationalising taxation in the ICT sector, including by phasing out universal service levies. About 80 people attended the workshop.

WS 97.   *Global State of Copyright and Access to Knowledge*

Report by: Bassem Awad

Moderator: Dr. Bassem Awad (Chief Judge at the Egyptian Ministry of Justice and IP Expert)

Panellists: Mr. Tobias Schonwetter (Faculty of Law, University of Cape Town, South Africa); Dr. Perihan Abou Zeid (Faculty of Legal Studies and International Relations, Pharos University, Alexandria Egypt); Pranesh Prakash (Programme Manager, the Centre for Internet and Society, Bangalore, India); Jeremy Malcolm (Project Coordinator, Consumers International, Kuala Lumpur, Malaysia); Lea Shaver (Associate Research Scholar and Lecturer in Law at Yale Law School, New Haven, USA)

Although the Internet's reach is global, copyright laws remain tethered to national borders, providing different terms of protection, exceptions and limitations, and enforcement mechanisms. This has resulted in a patchwork of rights of access to copyright materials across the world, incorporating little regard for the special needs of users in developing countries. This in turn has produced both uncertainty amongst consumers about what the law allows, and contributed to their disenchantment with a legal system that often does not allow permit them reasonable access to materials that they need for their educational and cultural advancement. The Access to Knowledge movement is a global Internet-linked movement aiming to improve consumers' access to materials protected by copyright, including learning materials, through various mechanisms including law reform, education, and by addressing access barriers such as cost, availability and access to ICTs. This workshop will introduce two multi-country research programmes, one of the African Copyright and Access to Knowledge (ACA2K) Project, and the other of Consumers International (CI). These studies approach the study of copyright at the doctrinal and practical levels. The former encompasses national copyright laws, related access and case law. The practical component involves qualitative impact assessment interviews with different stakeholders to determine the impact of the legal framework on access.

Our first panellist was Lea Shaver of Yale University's Information Society Project, who dealt with the purpose of copyright law. One popular view is that its purpose is to maximize revenues for copyright industries such as publishers, movie houses and retailers, which makes sense to regulators as a source of growth and foreign exchange. But in fact the purpose of copyright is to encourage creativity and the diffusion of creative works. Copyright should therefore not be an industrial subsidy, but a tool for access to knowledge. If copyright law gets in the way of creativity and access, it is frustrating this purpose.

Thus Lea's first main point was that in assessing copyright law our touchstones should be access, affordability and participation. Our tools to uphold these values can be framed in terms of consumer protection, human development and human rights. Copyright shapes affordability and access because as the scope of rights expands, the more control is centralised and the less competition. It also shapes participation, because under current law the amateur who wants to build upon existing works is at a disadvantage, and risks running afoul of others' rights. Her second point was that we are seeing a shift in the economics of knowledge distribution. This has massively changed the ecosystem in which text and creative works travel. Distribution and format shifting is now much easier and cheaper than before. Yet copyright protection is ever increasing, and this cannot be justified by the need for additional incentives for creativity. Rather, it reflects the problem of rent-seeking ("the Disney effect" - so termed for the extension of the copyright term to avoid Disney's loss of its early Mickey Mouse assets). However Lea closed noting that there is a counter-movement emerging of organisations seeking to invoke the public interest in access to knowledge. This movement has gained traction following the passage of the TRIPS agreement which set new high standards for global IP protection. It is in this context that the importance of the research on A2K can be understood. In summary, copyright law should not simply maximising incentives at the expense of other public values.

Our second presenter was Dr Perihan Abou Zeid from Pharos University, Alexandria, Egypt. She introduced the ACA2K project, which aims to probe the relation between copyright law and access to knowledge with regard to education and learning materials. Working with the ACA2K project are 30 experts in 8 countries: Uganda, Mozambique, South Africa, Egypt, Morocco, Ghana, Senegal and Kenya. The project methodology consists of two main phases: a research phase comprising doctrinal (legal) research and quantitative (impact) analysis, and a policy engagement and dissemination phase. The first phase has now been completed, and dissemination is now in progress, with findings having so far been presented to WIPO's Standing Committee on Copyright and Related Rights. Dr Abou Zeid then moved on to discuss the A2K environment in Egypt specifically. Egypt is a civil law country (thereby recognising both moral and economic rights), governed by a 2002 Copyright Act. Its coverage for rights holders is quite broad. There is a copyright exception and also a compulsory license provision for educational purposes, but e-learning and distance learning are not covered by this. There is a separate exception allowing photocopying for personal use, adapting the three-step test, but many libraries impose their own quota restrictions outside of what the law requires, with varying levels of enforcement.

Other exceptions include translation of books not written in Arabic, and reproduction of single copies by libraries and archives on request or for archival purposes. There is no disability exception however, and unusually, Egypt requires a license to be obtained even to reproduce works that are in the public domain. Moreover, there are anti-circumvention provisions, with penal sanctions.

Dr Abou Zeid's conclusion relevant to the Internet Governance Forum was that ICTs are not about technology, they are about knowledge. ICTs are being used to extend protection to knowledge that is not protected by copyright already. There should therefore be exceptions and limitations to TPM (Technological Protection Mechanisms), just as there are to copyright law. Amendments covering distance learning, ICTs and disabilities are also needed. Meanwhile, the main channel to secure access to knowledge in Egypt is the non-enforcement of copyright law!

Tobias Schonwetter from the University of Cape Town, South Africa was next to speak. He described the methodology of the ACA2K project's work, which involved both a survey of legislation and a review of secondary literature and interviews with relevant stakeholders. The research output involved 8 country reports and policy briefs, and a stand-alone comparative review. There have been two WIPO briefing papers, and statements read at WIPO about the project's research, as well as book chapters and journal articles. There will also soon be a book to be published in 2010 under a Creative Commons license. Tobias and his team looked at the South African Copyright Act with respect to matters such as orphaned works, library and archive exceptions, moral rights, provisions for the sensory disabled, and distance education and e-learning provisions. The team also looked at other legislation besides the Copyright Act that impacted on access to learning materials, as well as the government's FOSSi policy, and global and regional treaties.

The copyright law in South Africa is a 1978 Act which does not take into account the new digital environment. Format shifting, for example, remains an infringing act. The exceptions and limitations are few, and there is uncertainty about their use. The anti-circumvention provisions are contained elsewhere in the law, and may nullify even some of the exceptions the Copyright Act does provide. The team found that the copyright environment in South Africa does not maximise effective access to learning materials. It made legal recommendations addressing the issue of orphaned works, and advising that copyright term should not be expanded from its current 50 years. Another weakness is that there is little case law in South Africa that might clarify ambiguities in the law. Although there is a body of secondary literature, South African academics are not very actively involved, with most input coming from copyright holders and libraries. Tobias concluded by briefly mentioning the situation in other countries, which had a variety of different legal traditions, and more or fewer exceptions. Most countries granted greater protection to rights holders than international law required. No countries dealt with distance and e-learning, and only one (Uganda) dealt with the needs of the disabled. He hoped that the extended dissemination phase would assist other projects to build in ACA2K's work.

CI Project Coordinator Jeremy Malcolm next introduced Consumers International's current research activities on A2K. These include the IP Watch List for 2009 and 2010 rating how friendly various countries' copyright laws are for consumers, a consumer survey on A2K access barriers, and targeted national research in Australia and Israel investigating the effect of consumer-friendly copyright limitations and exceptions on overall welfare. The results from the 2009 IP Watch list suggest that the biggest problems in copyright law worldwide are the lack of support of any country for non-commercial creativity and sharing. From the consumer survey, it is suggested that consumers would pay for better quality originals of copyright works if they were fairly priced. And the interim results from the national research suggest that consumer-friendly copyright exceptions may increase respect for the law. The overall conclusion from these research findings is that legal systems worldwide are not meeting consumers' needs for access to knowledge. A better legal system, the research suggests, would support non-commercial sharing and reuse of material, which in turn would drive down costs and increase sales of licensed material, and could also increase consumers' respect for the law overall.

Finally Pranesh Prakash from the Centre for Internet and Society, Bangalore took the session full circle by asking, why are we talking about A2K? He answered that it effects almost all areas of concern to consumers - education, industry, food security and health. IP has been said to be the oil of the 21st century. By creating barriers through IP, there is less scope for expansion of knowledge. In India, there is a new copyright amendment that will introduce Drums, and increased criminalisation which classes video pirates in the same category as slum lords, drug peddlers and terrorists, including preventative detention.

One tool to help change the mindsets of the public is the Consumers International IP Watch List, which can help policy makers and academics and advocates compare the best and worst practices of various countries. For example in a session earlier in the IGF, Carlos Afonso from Brazil had used it to demonstrate the weakness of Brazil's laws, in that it had achieved an "F" score from the Watch List on education. The Watch List is published in response to the USTR Special 301 Report, and helps countries learn to push back against that report, as Israel and Canada have done so far. As for India, its government has said that whilst IP is important, the right to health is even more important. Now even industry is pushing back in India.

Pranesh suggested that the ranking of countries needs to be addressed in future to avoid giving an "A" ranking to a country simply because it is the "best of a bad bunch", which could be counter-productive. The Watch List should also take into account unrealised possibilities to expand access to knowledge. Dissemination and reach-out to policy makers is also important, as is the assessment of impact. Pranesh concluded by observing that copyright is characterized as striking a balance between the interests of creators and consumers, but that this rhetoric is misplaced. In fact creators often benefit from freer sharing by users. Knowledge is an input into creation, not just an output from it. Therefore it is important to counter IP expansionism using various tools such as freedom of speech, competition law, consumer law and privacy law, as appropriate in various countries, to eventually produce a change in mindset.

During question time, an audience member from Jordan asked what was the outlook for countries such as his, which had recently signed an FTA (Free Trade Agreement) limiting its sovereignty over standards of IP protection? Lea Shaver noted that Jordan had effectively been coerced into this agreement, and that other countries, particularly those with small negotiating teams, need to be very careful to avoid the same fate. Jeremy Malcolm responded that the laxity of enforcement in Jordan was actually one of the few points in favour of access to knowledge in that country, as in Egypt. However Lea pointed out that the ACTA treaty, once signed, would be likely to raise global levels of IP enforcement, including liability for materials transmitted over the Internet. This worried her, as no computer algorithm can detect fair use, and the result will be a restriction on legitimate knowledge sharing.

Pranesh Prakesh noted that countries in Jordan's position should realise that foreign direct investment is not always linked to stronger IP - even OECD and WIPO studies go to show this. Finally Tobias Schonwetter stated that once an FTA is signed, it is tough to get out, but foreshadowed that perhaps once the prevailing mindset changes, both countries might allow renegotiation.

WS 216. The Internet and Citizenship: Applying a Gender Lens

Report by: Anita Gurumurthy

Organizer: IT for Change, APC Women's program and Sulá Batsú

Moderator: Anita Gurumurthy (IT for Change/India)

Panellists: Heike Jensen (Humboldt University in Berlin/OpenNet Initiative Asia); Margarita Salas (Sulá Batsú Cooperative/Costa Rica); Olga Cavalli (Government of Argentina)

The workshop analyzed the interface between citizenship and the Internet through a gender perspective. The theme brought inquiries in three dimensions:
- Within the Internet itself, considering the impact of the present paradigm and emerging trends on inclusion of women, particularly marginalized ones;
- At a global citizenship scenario, understanding the trans-local nature of the Internet;
- Within national contexts, examining how the Internet re-situates the citizen and redefines citizenship vis-à-vis the state and the market.

Heike Jensen addressed the issue of citizenship on the Internet within the context of censorship, particularly focusing on the aspects that hinder women from participating in public spheres. Margarita Salas spoke about how the feminist movement strategically used digital technologies to resist from the Free Trade Agreement with Central America and Dominican Republic

(CAFTA) and make visible women's proposals and concerns. Olga Cavalli considered the existing barriers that impede women from using technology and developing a career – the lack of motivating teaching methods in elementary education and a cultural issue that reinforces the idea that women are not smart enough to work as scientists or engineers.

The use of digital technologies by the feminist movement in Costa Rica to fight against CAFTA proves that in a context of power imbalance where the government, the private sector and the mainstream media control the resources to communicate, it is crucial to use the Internet as a virtual meeting point, and then have the content uploaded, downloaded and distributed throughout communities. This example shows that we do not need to be connected to harvest benefits from the Internet, as long as there are collective uses in place. In Costa Rica, women opened up their own spaces and made their voices and opinion heard in a way that would not be possible using only mainstream media. The presence of female leaders became visible and they were established as figures of knowledge. The feminist movement also established important alliances with other sectors, which recognized that the feminist vision coincides with many social movements' perspectives.

Censorship is a key element to be analyzed, as highlighted Heike Jensen. It shapes the public spheres and impacts possible forms of citizenship on the Internet. Censorship can take various forms: direct (laws and their applications and state violence) and indirect (administrative requirements to operate the media, market and financial conditions, architectural and infrastructural circumstances, and social norms). However, eliminating these blocks is not in the self-interest of the state nor the market. How can these imbalances be stopped from consolidating? To what extent does the transnational public sphere offer a space to build pressure, and how is this related to the local and the national?

The drawing of political/administrative boundaries is a key issue and feminists need to debate which boundaries they find useful. The principle of subsidiary may be a useful one to retain, since not all issues are or should be global ones. Boundaries are necessary. Could they be based on local contexts? How should they shape public spheres and should these spheres be based on any medium such the Internet? How would these spheres tie into one global public sphere? These questions should be approached in a historically informed way, and with reference to the public sphere and its censorship dimensions, in order to tackle the gendered complexities of 'Internet and Citizenship'.

The involvement of women in technological areas is seen by Olga Cavalli as a strategy to qualify human resources and hence contribute to the development of the country. In unequal regions such as Latin America, IT for Development programs are still isolated. There is not a general digital inclusion policy in place, and even less, a women's digital inclusion effort.

WS 234.   *Issues Regarding the Mobile Internet*

Report by: George Sadowsky

Panellists: Tim Berners-Lee (Chair, World Wide Web Consortium U.K.); Stéphane Boyera (Manager, Web for Society Program, Web Foundation France); Nii Quaynor (Professor of Computer Science, Cape Coast University Ghana); Leslie Martinkovics (Director International Public Policy & Regulatory Affairs, Verizon Communications Inc. U.S.); Yoshiko Kurisaki (Research Analyst, People, Society and Technology Switzerland, Basic Human Needs Telecom Japan)

The mobile Internet has arrived, increasingly in the form of a web browser, limited or full function, embedded in a mobile telephone. The uptake of mobile telephony in the developing world and the dramatic decline in the cost of processing power virtually guarantees that there will be hundreds of millions of mobile web devices available within a few years, with data services provided with broad geographic coverage.

The growth of the Internet will have a major impact on the developing countries, where mobile phone use is expanding rapidly. It is possible that very soon the mobile phone will become the principal method of Internet access within those countries. People and organizations involved with economic and social development can use this leverage to provide services to hundreds of millions of people heretofore not connected, but only if the regulatory framework is supportive and only if standards are in place to assure interoperability in this new dimension of Internet expansion. This new environment raises issues of the role of telecomm regulation and interoperability and cross-regulatory issues with the financial sector as m-commerce and m-banking applications migrate to such devices. The borderless nature of the Internet will exacerbate problems as these devices move around the world.

It is now clear that one of the major drivers, if not the major driver, for the expansion of Internet services is the mobile Internet platform. This platform is applicable to both development and developing countries, but its major impact will be in the developing countries since the cellular infrastructure is expanding mush faster than the fixed line infrastructure and even the wireless infrastructures associated with the Internet. NGOs have been quick to take advantage of simpler cellular-based strategies such as SMS, and are aware of and are starting to understand how to exploit more advanced mobile information environments to support civil society activities.

At the IGF meeting itself, Tim Berners Lee, the inventor of the World Wide Web, announced the formation of the Web Foundation, dedicated to research and applications of the Web. A primary thrust of the Foundation is to study the exploitation of the Web for society and societal progress. The Foundation's major focus in this area will involve the mobile web, as it is the platform that is rapidly expanding to encompassing more of the non-connected, i.e. the poor and disadvantaged in developing country environments.

Initial experiments in mobile banking have now evolved into production systems, viz., in Kenya, the Philippines and South Africa. Models of such m-banking vary, and are now being examined and are spreading. Depending upon the nature of services offered and the territory over which the service extends, financial regulators are very likely to become involved. Such joint regulation of a financially based communications service is likely to become more important in the future as the services become more plentiful.

There was general agreement that mobile Internet is a powerful new platform that will have major impact in almost all countries, and that the governance issues that surround it should take into account and be sensitive to the developmental implications of the technology and its potential to provide near ubiquitous services to all sectors of society.

This dimension of Internet development is increasing in importance, and increasing attention should be given to it in terms of development, applications, empowerment, and effective guidance and regulation.

WS 243. Broadening Mobile Content and Sustainable Access

Report by: Osama Manzar

Organizer: Digital Empowerment Foundation, NIXI, India

Panellists: Peter Bruck (Chairman, UN's WSA); Tulika Pandey (Additional Director, Department of Information Technology, India); Rajnesh Singh (Manager – Asia, Internet Society); Shahzad Ahmad (Co-founder, Bytes for All); Effat Al Shooky (Advisor to the Ministry of Comm & IT, Arab Republic of Egypt); a representative from Bangladesh; Rajesh Chharia (President, Internet & Mobile Association of India); Murali Shanmugavelan (Head of the Information Society Programme, Panos London); Dr. Pavan Duggal (President, Cyberlaw Asia & Cyberlaws.net)

Mobile phones are the best representation of convergence of Information & Communication Technologies and have overtaken Internet in its pervasiveness – occurrence, commonness, incidence, frequency and last but not the least popularity around the globe. Today a mobile phone multiplies in its functional roles of – a phone, a gaming device, a watch and alarm, a calendar, a memo pad, a geo-positional tracking aid, an IPOD, a camera, a video camera, a web browser, a device for online purchase and utility bill disbursal and this is not the end of the list. In its new avatar mobile phones have become a gadget for the young and the old, the lads and the ladies. Needless to say it has become our seventh sense, a habit and almost a necessity for billions across the globe. In countries like India, every month, 10 million mobiles are added, and the latest penetration has already crossed 400 million.

Mobile content naturally refers to all the application software and interfaces for the various functional operations. Lately, its utility for provisioning of e-services of education, health, government to citizen services and entertainment has caught everyone's imagination. Naturally, it entails a greater need for need based content. An instance is usage of Mobile for agricultural marketing purposes in country like India, Uganda... As the information flow increases due to the mobile phone coverage expansion, the cost of crop marketing decreases, particularly more so for perishable crops, such as banana, in remote areas because the increased information allows traders to collect perishable products more efficiently.

A study in Uganda found that the proportion of banana farmers who sold banana increased from 50 to 69 percent in the communities more than 20 miles away from district centres after the expansion of the mobile phone coverage. This explicitly highlights the socio-economic empowerment facilitated by mobile based information linked directly to market price points. The single device with a simple m-service replaces the complex interaction between agricultural scientists/advisors, farmer, trader and the end buyer of the produce saving on transport costs, cost inflation due to middlemen, and in return provisioning the availability of alternate face-to-face channels for information exchange and direct access to market.

There are instances at large in countries like Philippines, where more and more people are using mobile phones to take out and repay loans, pay bills, buy goods, make donations, transfer cash and even purchase fast-food burgers and according to the Asian Development Bank, the service is available to more than 95 percent of the population. In Bangladesh, need based content is generated through mobile applications for micro finance activities and credit services delivery. India too is lately seeing such services being welcomed.

Workshop Objectives:
- Understand the scope & challenges in effective and useful content services delivery through mobile applications;
- Understand the feasibility of using the mobile tools to bridge information and communication divides;
- Highlight cases of effective mobile applications for community content and info requirements and take cue from it;
- Chalk out strategies to encourage mobile content creation, application, delivery and usage between producers and consumers in larger demand-supply framework;
- Understand key legislative and policy elements in this context;
- How International best practices could be a learning example to each other

The larger issue that this workshop aimed to raise is appropriate and need based mobile content generation and delivery for inclusive growth through bridging information gaps. The focus was on visit mobile content that largely restricts effective and optimum usage of mobile applications. Continuous enhancement of utility based content of the mobile to meet regular and need based content for the marginalized groups and communities located in remote surroundings and countryside is the need of the day. More importantly the m-services shall gain the confidence of the user communities on the mobile tool as 'ICT application for the masses' if they are contextual and in local language. Until now English has remained the standard for all mobile devices and services through these. However, on the hindsight, because of English as lingua franca for mobile devices, English language is being learnt in developing countries like India easily and without any additional cost.

Thus, the larger issue is of mobile communications for inclusive growth with greater focus on need based and user oriented mobile content for addressing information and content gaps. There is need to rethink about mobile content applications from multiple stakeholders perspectives. The question is how mobile application can effectively fit into the larger public service delivery network. This means, a consumer who seeks a health query on his mobile receives an instant and reliable response. Strategies for formulation of international standards for the keypads, visual interface and mobile operating systems that ensure interoperability will go a long way to reinvent mobile phones as an effective public service delivery platform. The workshop focused on the larger issue of mobile communications for inclusive growth with greater focus on need based and user oriented mobile content for addressing information and content gaps. There is need to rethink at mobile content applications from multiple stakeholders perspectives. The larger question discussed was how mobile application can be effectively fit into the larger public service delivery network.

Internet, Navigation map, banking services, SMS alert and social facilities by SMS bring out as the positive points for the need to broaden mobile content access to serve content and information needs

- Internet through mobile will be more useful and content exchange platform
- People try to access Navigation map to locate the known place.
- People like to get Banking Services to check the balance and for money transaction
- SMS Alert for bank transaction and parent meeting in baby's school or pay the telephone bill and etc.
- Social Facilities like News, Movie, restaurant, taxi services and etc.

Bring out 5 key challenges towards the same

- Precaution for Cyber crime
- Required standard National Legislation; Different country is different stages in development of national legislation
- In an era of IT people like to get facilities of banking service; it is good to save the time, risk for hacking the user ID and password.
- SMS for small text, if the text is complex and long content then how it will be share.
- Roaming charge should be removed. Specially in India when you cross one state to another state then you have to pay roaming charge.

Music, Internet, Phone bill pay, twittering. Playing game, alert service, navigation map and etc those are widening usage of mobile access to meet content needs and their possible replication and extension

- People use predominantly Voice and SMS through mobile to communicate each other.
- As Internet is one of the tool of information technology, people access Internet in any where and any place
- Users are accessing email and sending through mobile

- SMS ad like real estate, astrology, caller tune and etc. are used by commercial fellow.
- People are using mobile mostly for downloading and listening the music
- Mobile banking is used to check balance the account and other monetary transaction
- Mobile is used to pay the Phone bill
- Mobile camera is using for photography and ideograph
- Alert service for different prepaid and post paid plan and banking transaction and etc.
- People playing and down loading the game through mobile
- Twittering is another way to access the information through mobile
- People are taking help the mobile to navigate the location
- Mobile is using to get up the people as a Morning alarm and reminder
- People also subscribe the news channel to get update information

Bring out 5 key Different policy elements like awareness programme, ICT for Rural people, high speed Internet, alert services and free of cost alert service that will augment this process of effective mobile application usage – especially in developing countries and the regions where the practice of communication is largely oral
- Awareness programme in local, regional and global level is one of the important areas. Except tech savvy, general mass community use mobile device for phone and SMS. Let them to know how to content exchange through mobile.
- Rural people have mobile connection. Now it is needed to take initiative to teach them how to get all IT enabled information through Mobile device.
- Alert services for security like bombing, firing, traffic jam and etc
- There is no broad band and other facilities for Internet in remote place. So High speed Internet service should be available through mobile and even it should be available in city
- Different alert services will be free
- Knowledge share between different producers in regional level

WS 270.   Public Policies for Improved Interconnection at Lower Costs

Report by: Ruth Puente

Panellists: Augusto Gadelha (Secretary Brazilian Minister of Science and Technologies); Roque Gagliano (Policy Manager, LACNIC); Nishal Goburdhan (CTO AFRINIC); Jacquelynn Ruff (Verizon Business); Malcolm Hutty (LINX-London Internet Exchange Point); Valeria Jordán (Economic Commission for Latin America and the Caribbean); Lorena Piñeiro (Chilean Council of Transparency)

Today's Internet inter-connection discussion includes a higher number of actors that participate in elaborate discussions that ultimately generate the reduction of the access cost. These changes have also been driven by a change in the users habits and traffic pattern, from a web-page only Internet to a network dominated by peer-to-peer applications. In this complex scenario the issue this workshop addressed how to generate effective public policies that improve the quality of the interconnection of today's Internet while lowering the costs for the end users. The workshop was organized in two sections. During the first section the topic of the workshop was introduced by two speakers and in the second section a panel of commentaries discussed the possible measurements from governments.

Today's Internet inter-connection discussion includes a higher number of actors that participate in elaborate discussions that ultimately generate the reduction of the access cost. These changes have also been driven by a change in the users habits and traffic pattern, from a web-page only Internet to a network dominated by peer-to-peer applications. In this complex scenario the issue this workshop addressed how to generate effective public policies that improve the quality of the interconnection of today's Internet while lowering the costs for the end users.

The workshop was organized in two sections. During the first section the topic of the workshop was introduced by two speakers and in the second section a panel of commentaries discussed the possible measurements from governments.

Roque Gagliano gave an introduction to the interconnection topic, giving the technical aspects that it implies and also describing the current complex environment with all the actors involved in the interconnection field, stressing which actors are more active and how infrastructure has changed since the discussions at the WSIS. Ten years ago developing areas and particularly Internet traffic in the Latin American region was characterized by its asymmetry and the dependency to international connection from outside of the region. Traffic between countries would normally take a path through the USA. The cost on the international link included both the submarine cable capacity and the Internet port at the destination.

Today local networks have grown and we find a more complex environment with many actors playing in the interconnection game. The following actors were identified during the workshop:

- Transit providers or big networks that takes the IP packages and can deliver them to any destination in Internet. Transit providers may have local, regional or global infrastructure.
- Local ISPs. These organization are normally taking care of facilitating the access to the end users. Local ISPs can provide access using a variety of mediums such as DSL, cable, wireless and FTTH.
- Content Providers, such as media companies (ex. ABC, YouTube, NBC, etc) are where the content is generating. In today's Internet Content Providers have many times global presence and look for interconnecting to ISP directly instead of using transit providers.
- Content distribution networks (CDN) are a new player that are playing a central today in the distribution of content in Internet, particularly multimedia content. These networks have global presence and can be hired to distributively push content by content providers. As these companies are aggressively looking for new nodes they act as local warehouses of content.
- Internet Exchange Points (IXP) are a meeting point that facilitates the interconnection by reducing the transport cost. They also serve as a natural location for critical infrastructure such as Root Servers copies.

At the end of this presentation the following examples of possible policy actions by local governments were given, particularly considering:
- Support to Internet Exchange Points.
- Secure access to infrastructure capacity such as Datacentres, metropolitan networks, diverse options of international fibre connections and local backhaul to the cables' landing stations

Dr. Augusto Gadelha exposed a use case, describing the Brazilian experience in the interconnection arena. The issue is: Making connections cheaper. CGI.br. Steering Committee of Internet, is a multi-stakeholder organizations which includes governmental, industry and academia. Dr. Gadelha remarked some of the Internet Problems in Brazil:
- The Digital Inclusion problem and the use regulation to reach the under populated areas.
- A market with little competition and defensive attitude from the leading companies
- The undersea cables connecting Brazil with USA land only in Rio de Janeiro and São Paulo cities, even though they traverse most of the country.
- No legislation requiring the exchange of traffic between ISPs.

The PPT Metro program of the CGI encourages companies and government to participate in Internet Exchange Points all over the country. Thanks to the IXP, participants can use large capacity and reduce cost. Particularly Internet transit providers can sell traffic without the need of local infrastructure. One of the measures that are under study is the reduction of taxes for serves and datacentre infrastructure.

After the main presentations there was a multistakeholder panel of commentators, moderated by Lorena Piñeiro, Responsible of the International Affairs of the Chilean Council for Transparency. Here the principal comments from the panellists:

Malcolm Hutty described the experience of an IXP that has been running since 1994. The London Internet Exchange Point has over 350 network operators and exchanging at a peak times over 540 gigabits/sec of traffic, lot of traffic even in global standards. In 1994 the Internet Connection in UK looks like this: In order to send traffic to one network operator in the UK, traffic would have to go by NYC through expensive international links for the ISPs. The goals that was achieved with the creation of LINX: keep the Local traffic locally, build local capacity. As a consequence, the cost of local traffic went down, making economically viable to invest in local infrastructure. Local infrastructure was invested in network capacity, local content and services, and that bring customers revenues from Internet , business for further investment. Driving down costs so the prices can come down. International carriers links, and traffic costs, has gone down because the market has grown. Lot of networks come to LINX to interexchange traffic. The value of IXP is driving down the costs to support the business case for investment to create further infrastructure.

Nishal Goburdhan, CTO AFRINIC, gave a view from a developing country, particularly as an ex- CTO of ISC in South Africa. 3 keys for interconnection:
- Regulation should act in a way that encourages competition, provides a free, open and fair market for everybody.
- IXP is critical in aspects like: Access and affordability. Nothing better affects the interconnection among ISP and Internet that an IXP in terms of Root Servers, copy, projects, root server copy program, critical Internet resources. It should be invested in rural areas to improve the access.
- Promotion of local content, implies local talent and getting people involved (ex. Web. 3.0).

Market for the locally stuff, similar benefits of having a Local Factory. We are connecting people.

Jacquelynn Ruff, Vice President International Public Policy and Regulatory Affairs for Verizon Communications, gave her perspective from a global backbone provider, Global services provider. The most important policy trend for lowering the cost of Internet connectivity is to bring the connectivity close to the home and the development of IXPs. A few other Policy trends:
- Keep traffic closer to home, you don't have to rely much on International connectivity but there will always be an international piece to be part of global Internet.
- We need to see all the pieces in the chain of Internet traffic: International transport or the submarine cable landing stations or the backhaul and connectivity inside the country.

2 relevant pieces in interconnection:
- Development of more cables. Getting more cables to a country, landing stations, more competition in the undersea cables coming in the country make significant impact in the prices. Last years more cables come into India, more players in the cable landing stations, the government impose some ceiling on the costs of some private international lines.
- Landing stations, different actors operates in the landing stations, using capacity. Is it possible to make interconnection there? Can you collocate your equipment and so on? those are regulatory policies. India and Singapore provide models in this aspect, landing stations are a good place to compare best practices. Some times there are strict requirements, requirements that limit some stakeholders to have an international license and impede growth of investments, high taxes on equipment. Implies opportunities as a point of presence in countries: Verizon can decide having a hub in one country or another.

Valeria Jordan, Coordinator of Information Society Programme at the Economic Commission for Latin America and the Caribbean, informed about the current situation in LAC region and made recommendations of public policies regarding interconnection. Public policies must address: the expansion of Internet access, the growing demand for broadband Internet to use multimedia and peer-to-peer services If we consider the particularities of the LAC region we find that:
- There are few policies and regulation on Internet interconnection in LAC region and it is worldwide connected mainly through U.S. Using

international links to route local traffic increases: connection time to access local content and service costs.

- Most of the regionally accessed content is created and hosted in U.S., most of LAC produced content is hosted in U.S. because it is cheaper than local hosting
- There is no good interconnection among LAC countries: Great delay in intra-regional traffic.

The main action points identified were:

- IXPs at local and regional level can contribute to improve the connection capacity and to create and host local content
- The establishment of IXPs is a strategy that should be considered in ICT development agendas

At the end of the session there was a period for questions and answers. Interconnection discussions have change greatly since the WSIS. This workshop helped policy makers to identify the new actors and trends in order to implement effective policies that help reducing costs

WS 286. *Towards Access: Combining Intellectual Property, Competition and Human Rights*

Report by: Abbe Brown

Moderator: Dr Abbe Brown (University of Edinburgh)

Panellists: Lea Bishop Shaver (Yale Law School and A2K Program Director, Information Society Project); Dr Nagla Rizk (American University in Cairo); Ren Reynolds (Virtual Policy Network); Professor Charlotte Waelde (University of Edinburgh); Dr Christopher Stothers (Milbank Tweed, University College London)l Professor S.K. Verma (Director, Indian Law Institute, New Delhi)

A discussion of the extent to which, and how, the fields of IP, competition and human rights can be combined to pursue the objectives of the IGF and WSIS, notably in relation to access to essential technologies.

Introduction

There are many fora in which IP can be considered outside the IGF, notably the World Intellectual Property Organization. IP can have a positive impact on encouraging innovation, but IP owners also have the power to restrict access to information and to technology, which is inconsistent with the WSIS and IGF goals. Various steps have been taken to address this, for example through the Doha declaration at the WTO in respect of TRIPS and the WIPO Development Agenda. Yet there are also attempts, notably through trade agreements and the proposed ACTA agreement, to extend the power of IP beyond the standards set out in the TRIPS agreement. IP, and its treatment, should therefore be part of the landscape when considering how best to pursue the WSIS and IGF goals.

Human rights and competition should also be part of this landscape. IP can be argued to be consistent with competition, as both seek to encourage innovation, and also with human rights, as IP can be means of rewarding innovation and delivering other human rights, for example through the development of medical treatments.

Yet competition and human rights may also have a role in limiting the power of IP when it goes too far, for example in relation to digital rights management. There may be a greater need for human rights and competition if/as the Internet develops more into an Internet of things, and on to an Internet of bodies, all under the power of IP owners. There can be strong ethical and philosophical objections to this, particularly if network effects mean that little choice is available to those who may have wished to use other options. IP owners may have a large amount of power, but this should not mean that IP should dominate debate regarding innovation and access - particularly if, as can be seen from work in open source and access to knowledge, there is an increased societal willingness to share. The IP focus can mean an emphasis on property, rather than on rights. A new balance may be required. There are also arguments that some new types of information (e.g. avatars in virtual worlds, Internet of bodies) should not come within the IP regime.

Human rights focus

There is a strong link between property and rights, for example through the work of Kant. IP can prevent fulfilment of human rights to life, health and expression – say, if IP owners enforce their rights in respect of patents for pharmaceuticals or climate change technology, or copyright in respect of software which has become an industry standard. IP can be used to reach over forms of cultural control. From a theoretical perspective, it can be difficult to identify human rights and their scope. International and regional human rights instruments do provide a clear starting point. Courts throughout the world (e.g. England, United States and South Africa) have, as required by the relevant legislative and constitutional regimes, considered instrumental human rights alongside IP. In some cases, the courts have been prepared to use human rights to limit the power of the IP owner (e.g. Ashdown (England) and Laugh it Off! (South Africa).

Article 15(1)(c) International Covenant on Social Economic and Cultural Rights 1966 can also support more access to information and sharing in cultural life, and challenge the expansion of copyright. This is key as the barriers to access to knowledge are now more legal than practical – persons in developing countries, in a range of languages and with disabilities can obtain access to what they need – but often IP owners will not let them. This is particularly evident in the discussion regarding digital rights management and the proposal for a Treaty on Improved Access for Blind, Visually Impaired and other Reading Disabled Persons.

There are also arguments, however, that IP should be protected as a human right, as a form of property (e.g. decision of the European Court of Human Rights in Budweiser). Further, in the majority of decisions courts balancing IP and its limits, with human rights and their limits, have considered that IP does produce an acceptable solution (e.g. Levi (England), Eldred (US)). Litigation does continue, however, and the decision of the US Supreme Court in Bilski may be of interest.

Yet even if one moves the debate regarding access to knowledge and cultural life from the IP arena to the human rights arena, the discussion can remain frustratingly familiar. And in countries which do not have a strong culture of human rights, introducing a human rights perspective or dialogue may be positively unhelpful.

Competition focus

The Internet can enable markets to operate in a manner which is closer to perfect competition than may be so in the analogue world; yet it also means that there is a closer link between goods, knowledge and control. There can be more development of public goods, which though expensive to develop can be shared at little cost; and also embedded goods, where the IP owner can have a large amount of power, which can have a negative impact on development.

When a market is not operating effectively, this can provide a role for competition. There is, however, no international competition agreement, which means that progress based on competition will be (even) more uncertain than that in relation to IP and human rights. Several countries – notably US, EC, Australia, India and South Africa – do, however, have legislation which prohibits abuse of a dominant position (or similar conduct). Exercise of IP could be argued to be abuse of a dominant position, and reference could be made to the essential facilities doctrine. In the EC, decision makers have been prepared to require IP owners to license interoperability information which has become a de facto standard (IMS, Microsoft). But this will be done only in exceptional circumstances, and competition arguments do not always succeed (e.g. Rambus in US and EC); and when competition points are pursued in IP infringement actions in England, they are viewed critically by courts and have not yet been the subject of a full decision. Thus irrespective of the attractiveness of the scholarly or policy argument, there are practical challenges.

Competition also may not be attractive when a state does not have an established market economy and when courts, regulators and businesses do not have the relevant tools and experience. Nonetheless, competition has been used to significant effect in work in access to knowledge in developing countries. It was argued that goods (possibly all goods, or only those where the IP owner is in a monopoly position) should be available for the common welfare; and that if this not done, then a compulsory licence could be imposed.

- A contribution can be made by looking outside IP to address the problems which can arise from the exercise of IP.
- Human rights and competition could have a key role in fettering and managing IP. Looking to competition may, for example, assist in unlocking the impasse which courts and policymakers have reached

between human rights and IP; and human rights could assist in relation to competition and IP. Compulsory licensing could be a helpful tool.

- Further action should not, however, be pursued at global level, for two reasons: the debates, which have been seen to be finely balanced, will simply continue in a new fora, without any progress; and solutions should be better focussed on the national and regional, within the local factual, legal, constitutional and societal parameters (while subject to TRIPS and international human rights).
- There is also a place for other principles: a development focus, or consumer protection, may assist more in some situations than human rights or competition. Both these other principles could be argued to be relevant to assessment of "abuse" of IP, within articles 8(2) and 40(2) TRIPS.
- Further work should proceed at a national and regional level, with a focus on legal solutions. This should be carried out alongside the wider and valuable work of civil society in pursuing the WSIS and IGF goals. This could, like the WIPO Development Agenda and Access to Knowledge activities, contribute to new attitudes being taken to IP by courts and decision makers. Links should be maintained with established IGF dynamic coalitions, scholars, activists and policymakers to ensure that fields other than IP are taken into account as robust legal and policy bases for any challenges to IP.
- Given the outcome of the workshop, seeking to establish a dynamic coalition is not the most appropriate course. It would be helpful, however, to hold a further workshop in Vilnius in 2010 to build on the dialogue carried out in Sharm El Sheikh, and to consolidate links made.

This workshop provided an excellent opportunity for a group of panellists and participants who were experts in different fields, were from all over the world, and had very different starting points, to explore an important legal and practical issue. Many thanks to all involved (in person and via remote access, in real time and subsequently).

WS 328. *Access to Satellite Communications as a Key for Capacity Building: A Reference Model Looking for Affordable Costs*

Report by: Marina Russo

Panellists: Betsy Dugas (New Humanity NGO, USA); Jenny De Boer (TNO, The Netherlands); Dr Bernard Key (ACIM association, Man, Cote d'Ivoire); Prof Martin Nkafu Nkemnkia (LATS association, Fontem, Cameroon); Marina Russo (ActNow Alliance of NGOs, Italy)

Aim of the workshop was to discuss with participants from Governments, private sector and Civil Society the first results from the "Capacity Building through ICT" (CBICT) initiative and evaluate together potential solutions to the issue of providing satellite access for Sub-Saharian-Africa (SSA) communities at sustainable costs. The workshop has been structured through 6 sections:

Introduction: explaining the aim of the workshop and introducing the main issue of Access and of Satellite Communications as a mean to provide fast connectivity in remote areas of developing countries; and the basic concepts of Capacity Building and Sustainability.

CBICT initiative presentation: CBICT initiative started in 2008 by European Space Agency (ESA) in the frame of the Advanced Research on Telecommunications Systems Programme (ARTES Element 1) and carried on by a consortium lead by TNO organization, supported by Avanti Communication ltd and by two NGOs (IICD and ActNow Alliance), recently produced a "CBICT Reference Model": a structured set of guidelines aimed to support capacity building projects. This model has been initially developed from existing CB projects: gathering lessons-learned, taking into account both technical issues and human and organizational aspects and bundling all the collected elements with the experience of members of the consortium. In 2009 the model has been applied to two projects: one in Mali (Health and Governance sectors) and one in Cote d'Ivoire (Education and Civil Society sectors) in order to update it with local experiences, and collect lessons learned and recommendations.

The experience in Man, Cote d'Ivoire: The Man geographical and political situation has been described. The actual project started since 2004 when Dr Mirco Nacoti, from MSF, provided the support from Italian association Sguazzi to setup a library at the Man CHR hospital, open to the whole community, in collaboration with the near Centre for Informatics of Focolare Movement (CIF). The project has been described in detail, showing both the short and long term objectives, the financial and logistics contributions, the partnerships in Ivory Coast and in Europe, the main activities. The impact of satellite technology (installed in April 2009) on the project has been also described and analyzed, after these first seven months of daily usage.

The experience in Fontem, Cameroon: The geographical and economical background of Lebialem region has been described, so explaining the social needs that were at the origin of LATS association foundation and specifically of the ICT introduction in the main Institutions at Fontem (schools, colleges, hospitals, local government offices, private companies) for capacity building. In October 2008 this project introduced satellite technology integrated with Wi-Fi for the distribution of connectivity. The success of this initiative has been produced by the join efforts of different partners: European Space Agency providing free satellite access for the first years, the Regione Lazio providing support for the twinning of schools, ActNow alliance providing the technical expertise and all local institutions involved with LATS. The future plans see LATS and its Partners working with the aim of introducing renewable energy sources for project sustainability and disseminating Internet in new areas of the Lebialem region. The Cameroon Ministry for Education recently authorised LATS to provide computer laboratories and Internet access for all the schools of Lebialem, assuring local funding for this purpose.

Approach, results and future challenges: The common elements of the approach followed in both project are: a) "multi-stakeholder, bottom-up", in order to build trust-based relationships, sense of ownership, awareness, mutual enrichment and provide better sustainability (both social and financial) focusing on real common needs; (b) "technology integration, modular open solutions", looking for low-cost and reliable HW technology, providing modular design of open, easy to adopt, understand, manage and repair components, replicable and customizable solutions; with a preference for open SW programs and applications, in order to promote local development and production of specific customized solutions. The first accomplishments have been showed and discussed, together with the main lesson learned. The open challenges have been presented, so introducing the last part of the workshop:

Dialogue with participants: About 15-20 people attended the workshop; the final discussion has been really participated and many questions arose, involving all the participants. The most relevant questions and discussions mostly based on two main issues: sustainability of satellite communication and involvement of Governments.

ICTs can play a substantial role to promote the social and economical development of SSA Countries, still a recent study from egov4dev.org states that e-government initiatives in developing or transitional countries are: 35% total failures, 50% partial failures, only 15% successes. ESA is promoting the use of ICT, in particular integrating satellite communications, in order to enable the adoption of e-Applications for capacity building in the less advantaged regions. The lessons learned from the CBICT projects in Cameroon, Cote d'Ivoire and Mali confirmed the relevance of the adopted methodology, based on a multi-stakeholder, bottom-up approach, on open modular integrated technical solutions and on a continuous learning process.

The main guidelines can be so summarized: pay attention to the real needs of the users and to the local environment, both in terms of territory and human organization; plan with accuracy people training, involving not only technicians, but all the relevant stakeholders; start a process that local users can really manage, avoiding the creation of new dependences; facilitate the involvement of local leaders, capable to work in team with different organizations; assure adequate timings for the execution and the operation; adopt a multi-stakeholder approach: only a truly collaboration among civil society, private sectors and public administration can assure sustainability and an enduring success.

The problems met showed the need for additional projects efforts, mainly in two directions:
- Deepen people and organizations relations in order to increase local cooperation;
- Expand the connections with other local organizations and institutions to provide future sustainability.

The open challenges require to work on three different sectors of Society:
- Market: looking for low-cost /affordable solutions/services, in order to facilitate and support the setup of local solution providers, working with global institutions to find new partners;
- Governments: institutions involvement is necessary mainly for facilitating processes (i.e. supporting health and education initiatives) and relations with international players; and also for regulatory issues and law enforcement;

- Civil society: cooperation and communication is the key, it is necessary to share initiatives and resources in a holistic approach, working on local organization, autonomy and identity reinforcement.

One of the most crucial aspects for sustainability of capacity building initiatives is "partnership". Partnerships are crucial for project sustainability. The experience made with RM usage and in the post project phase identified that new relationships, especially inside each region, must be put in place, in order to expand the group of stakeholders, so increasing project sustainability.

The main actors to be connected with will be: Nearby universities professors and students, mainly in the health, science and ICT sectors, in order to support the design and the development of new applications, specifically oriented to the needs of local communities, and also with the objective of creating local places for the production of original contents; local entrepreneurs, interested to contribute to the CB initiatives, in order to reinforce their market share and create a positive and successful environment for local business;

Nearby ICT suppliers, providing spare parts, with the main objective of creating an adequate demand to sustain (and facilitate the creation of) analogous initiatives; nearby civil society organizations, groups and NGOs, in order to share resources and create a wider network of users, so empowering communities; local public institutions, regional administrations and national governments, in order to lead, sustain and/or facilitate (both from a political and an economical point of view) internal processes to support initiatives in the health, education and governance sectors and the relations with international players (e.g. communication providers, financial institutions, U.N. organizations). They are also crucial in managing regulatory issues and in the law enforcement.

Other interesting hints emerged from workshop participants. About the involvement of private sector, a participant from a Dutch company (Nada Gombra from Interliaise) presented an experience in Benin, where low sustainable prices for computer training have been provided thanks to a ten year's agreement of local government with a private company and the support of investments from Dutch government. About the involvement of local governments, another participant asked who and how they have been involved in the presented projects and which are their positions toward ICTs initiatives. Martin Nkafu explained that many public offices are still without any connectivity in Lebialem region and that the interest is very high: the process of involving the public sector can be a long one, but its activation is a direct consequence of a successful project, as it is demonstrated by the new initiative of Ministry of Education assigning to LATS funds to provide ICT and connectivity to the schools in the region. Also in Ivory Coast the project has been possible thanks to the Ministry of Health asking for a special permission to use satellite services from ESA for humanitarian purposes (no licenses for satellite receive/transmit are actually assigned to foreign hubs).

About the role of satellite communications in capacity building, a participant from UK Parliament (Ian Taylor) agreed with the presented method and approach for capacity building initiatives, noticing that even if it may be a long process, it is fundamental to address since the beginning the basic issues of getting people involved, aware and properly skilled, promoting continuous learning and technologies integration. As an example of this approach, in November it has been completed in Cameroon a distant learning course on GIS technologies and geographical data acquisition and management: this is a first step of a training aimed to use satellite technology not only for access but also for applications development, mainly in the area of territory management and control (local governance).

OF 533.   OECD Open Forum on the Importance of Internet Access and Openness for a Sustainable Economic Recovery

Report by: Karine Perset

Chair: Richard Beaird (Senior Deputy Coordinator for International Communications and. Information Policy, Department of State, United States)

Panellists: Constance Bommelaer (Senior Manager, Strategic Global Engagement); Taylor Reynolds (Communication Analyst, OECD); Jacquelynn Ruff (Vice President, International Public Policy and Regulatory Affairs, Verizon Communications, Representing the Business and Industry Advisory Committee to the OECD [BIAC]); Willie Currie (Communications and Information Policy Programme Manager, Association for Progressive Communications, Representing the Civil Society Information Society Advisory Committee to the OECD [CSISAC])

Richard Beaird opened the Forum by recalling that policy makers are responding to the economic crisis using a variety of stimulus packages as well as reforms aimed at producing a sustainable recovery. In particular, Governments are using investment in infrastructure including, as a key component, investment in broadband IP networks. Some of the criteria being taken into account include the immediate potential for such projects to improve services in underserved regions and to provide employment. It is also recognized that broadband IP networks are critical for longer term economic and social development. In OECD countries networks are primary owned by the private sector, which is also responsible for the vast bulk of investment in networks. This raises several questions about how governments can best accomplish their goals without displacing or disrupting private investment. What criteria / principles should be applied in assessing where to allocate resources, encouraging further investment by the private sector and promoting open and competitive choices for users?

Constance Bommelaer stressed the role of governments in encouraging the transition from IPv4 to IPv6. For her, the 3 key challenges facing the Internet are: i) scaling the Internet and IP addressing, in particular encouraging the transition from IPv4 to IPv6; ii) increasing trust, and; iii) encouraging multilingualism though internalized domain names (IDNs). None of these challenges can be developed by one party alone. She stressed that the "Internet model", based on principles of openness, was the key, and that ICT and the Internet are transforming the way innovation and information sharing is done.

Taylor Reynolds, likening it to electricity in the 1950's as a platform that enables other sectors such as transportation, education, health or electricity to develop and grow. He emphasized that telecommunications firms are among the large investors but that governments have a role to play in helping to expand networks with public investments. In his opinion, cost-based non-discriminatory access should be given to market users and the social benefits of extending access to rural/remote areas should be taken into account. In his view, when governments invest in networks, they need to consider topology and technology of broadband networks, since the level of competition is tied to topology and technology.

Willie Currie, representing the Civil Society Information Society Advisory Committee to the OECD (CSISAC) explained that APC had worked on national ICT strategies and that it was helpful to have access to this research. He ventured that it could make sense for governments to look at the logical infrastructure and the impacts of IPv4/IPv6 as an instance of market failure and investigate various options including regulatory options (e.g., requiring ISPs to implement by a given deadline), government procurement or tax incentives and subsidies for IPv6 transition.

Jackie Ruff, representing the Business and Industry Advisory Committee to the OECD (BIAC), noted that in looking at the economic crisis, there were few certainties except for the positive role of ICTs in the recovery. She emphasized BIAC's Declaration at the Seoul Ministerial that identified the following requirements for ICTs to continue to contribute to ICTs and growth: i) innovation, enabled by technology: ii) education; iii) increased user choice of applications, provided through a wide variety of platforms; iv) better access to healthcare, through remote applications and governments stimulating demand; v) better respect and empowerment for all stakeholders; and; vi) increased trust and confidence in the Internet, especially for the young. She stressed that government funding for infrastructure, because of its finite nature, should avoid crowding out markets or favouring technological solutions. For example, the US Government is investing 8 billion USD in broadband but it is estimated that to get very high speed broadband in the United States would require another 30 billion USB. She pointed out that Verizon has installed FTTH in 15 states.

In discussion, participants stressed that IP addresses are a pre-requisite for broadband penetration and that there is an important role for the OECD to play, alongside other organizations such as APECTEL, in helping with education and awareness building on the transition from IPv4 to IPv6. Speakers felt that additional research was needed into what should be done to encourage the deployment of IPv6. In addition, they put forward the idea that the copper in telecom networks was put in place 50 years ago and used in many unintended ways: today, we are in the process of upgrading to the networks that will be foundation for the next 50 years.

Participants at the OECD Open Forum discussed the role of the Internet and broadband in the economic recovery as enabling other sectors -healthcare, education, or smart transportation and electricity grids- to develop. They agreed a multi-stakeholder approach is needed to address current challenges, in particular the global deployment of the newer version of the Internet protocol (IPv6) and ensuring the Internet remains open to innovation.

BPF 540.   Best Practices for an Accessible Web

Report by: Alexandra Gaspari

Organizers: International Telecommunication Union and the Dynamic Coalition on Accessibility and Disability (DCAD)

Moderator: Jonathan Charles (BBC World)

Panellists: Peter Major (ITU); Jorge Plano (ISOC Argentina); Dipendra Manocha (Daisy Consortium); Shadi Abou-Zahra (Web Accessibility Initiative (WAI))

The workshop highlights the necessity to make the Internet accessible to all, regardless of individual capabilities of different users. The program of the workshop focused on the different aspects of web accessibility for persons with disabilities. Most of the panelists were persons with disabilities themselves. The DCAD promotes working directly with persons with disabilities in order to benefit from their real-life experiences. Organizations that are members of DCAD include, among others: the International Telecommunication Union (ITU), SKID, Council of Europe, Digital Accessible Information System Consortium (DAISY Consortium), Global Initiative for Inclusive Information and Communication Technologies (G3ict), the Indian Centre for Internet & Society, International Center for Disability Resources on the Internet (ICDRI), Internet Society (ISOC), Internet Society Argentina (ISOC-AR), UNESCO, Web Accessibility Initiative (W3C).

The Web is fundamentally designed to work for all people, whatever their hardware, software, language, culture, location, or physical or mental ability. When the Web meets this goal, it is accessible to people with a diverse range of hearing, movement, sight, and cognitive ability, and provides unprecedented opportunities for people with disabilities to equally participate in the information society. This workshop explores best practices in Web accessibility including in standardization, implementation, and business case development. The goal is to promote one Web that is accessible for all users including people with disabilities.

The keynote address was given by Sami Al-Basheer, Director of the Telecommunication Development Bureau, ITU. The BDT Director underlined the mandate of Telecommunication Development Bureau (BDT) which is to ensure that all people participate fully in the Information Society. For persons with disabilities, the BDT efforts extend beyond simply ensuring that users are online or connected to networks. It is essential that persons with disabilities are able to access the content of a website and that websites do not pose barriers to use by persons with disabilities.

The panellists presented the different issues related to the web accessibility and the most current problems and errors that persons with different abilities encounter in the daily activities. Most of the websites are developed without taking care of accessibility hence they tend to include many barriers. One presentation has shown some of the most common mistakes that provoke barriers. A panellist from W3C shared information about some of the standards for web accessibility their industry group has already developed. A representative from the Daisy Consortium talked about how digital talking books can enable users to hear and navigate written materials presented in audible form for use. Finally, the last speaker shared his analysis on how official government websites respond to the need for accessible websites.

Ensuring web accessibility benefits persons with and persons without disabilities. Promoting web accessibility provides social, technical and financial benefits. Web accessibility ensures equal opportunity for persons with disabilities just as it offers benefits for the families of persons with disabilities and the increasingly growing number of elderly web users. Accessible website can have unexpected beneficiaries, for example those who are illiterate. Promoting web accessibility at the early stages of web design can save money later when private companies and governments seek to ensure their websites are accessible.

Internet Governance in Light of the WSIS Principles:

Report of the Main Session

17 November 2009

Chair:

Mr. Ahmed El-Sherbini
Deputy to the Minister for International Cooperation, Director of the National Telecommunications Institute, Egypt

Moderators:

Ms. Anriette Esterhuysen
Executive Director, Association for Progressive Communications

Mr. Bill Graham
Global Strategic Engagement, the Internet Society

Ambassador Jānis Kārkliņš
Ambassador of Latvia to France and Permanent Representative to UNESCO

Extracts from the Transcript of Proceedings

AHMED EL-SHERBINI:

The IGF was created by the Tunis Agenda and mandated to promote and assess on an ongoing basis the embodiment of the WSIS principles in the Internet governance processes. We would like to assess the past four years, whether the WSIS principles were taken into consideration in the governance of the Internet. We have three hours, and this session is an open forum for dialogue rather than presentations. We have three able and distinguished moderators. Ambassador Karklins will now explain the structure of the session.

JANIS KARKLINS:

We do not have a pre-assigned speakers list, so we are counting on very active participation by all you. I don't know what the dynamics will be. Participants who would like to make substantive interventions should take no more than five minutes. Participants who would like to react to something that has been said should not take more than three minutes the first time, and any subsequent reactions should not take more than two minutes. The style and tone of comments should follow rules of politeness and dignity and should avoid being offending so the debate will be extremely positive. Along the way, we will invite the organizers of workshops that are relevant to our debate to report on the main thrust of their discussions. This session will take place in three parts. In the first part we'll concentrate on the principles that have been adopted in Geneva and Tunis. The second part will be devoted to how Internet governance influences the evolution of an inclusive, non-discriminatory, development-oriented Information Society. And the third part will be conclusions. Bill Graham will be taking notes throughout and will do a concluding summary of the debate.

The session is intended to provide guidance to all of us, and particularly to governments who will be assessing the continuation of IGF and the implementation of the WSIS principles in the U.N. system. Let's start by recalling the working definition that was developed by the Working Group on Internet Governance during the preparations for the second part of world summit: "Internet governance is the development and application by governments, the private sector and civil society in their respective roles of shared principles, norms, rules, decision-making procedures, and programs that shape the evolution and use of Internet." This working definition underscores the inclusiveness of governments, the private sector, and civil society in the mechanisms of Internet governance. It also acknowledges that with respect to specific issues, each group may have different interests and roles, which in some cases may overlap.

The WSIS principles are contained in both the Geneva Declaration of Principles and Tunis Agenda for Information Society. Tunis paragraph 29 states, "We reaffirm the principles enunciated in the Geneva phase of the WSIS, in December 2003, that the Internet has evolved into a global facility available to the public and its governance should constitute a core issue of the Information Society agenda. The international management of the Internet should be multilateral, transparent and democratic, with the full involvement of governments, the private sector, civil society and international Organisations. It should ensure an equitable distribution of resources, facilitate access for all and ensure a stable and secure functioning of the Internet, taking into account multilingualism." These are high principles that we thought were applicable to the Internet governance. So what impact have these principles had on the operations and decision-making of different institutions, organizations, and stakeholders? Are these principles still relevant today? Should they be amended? Should they be enlarged? What are examples of application of those WSIS principles in the daily life or work of different organizations? I invite you all to answer those questions.

FROM THE FLOOR:

My name is Christian O'Flaherty from the Internet Society. I am going to make a brief description of the workshop of Internet core values which was held this morning. It was very diverse and represented many points of view, and I'm going to summarize some of the topics we covered. We must keep one root DNS for consistency. Free standards and open access to this information are required. Also important is freedom of choice for the user of any platform, software, or system. There are concerns about returning to a lack of compatibility. We need a universal Internet where the real value is the users experiencing freedom, friendship, fun, community, et cetera. The Internet model with bottom-up processes, collaborative efforts, self-organizing procedures was contrasted with the usual government style. And it was mentioned that some of these core attributes are under threat.

FROM THE FLOOR:

I'm Michael Remmert of the Council of Europe and I would also like to speak on behalf of the United Nations Economic Commission for Europe and the APC, as our three organizations are proponents of an initiative to launch a code of good practice on information, participation, and transparency in Internet governance. If it is endorsed by Internet governance entities and implemented, the code could contribute to the implementation of the WSIS principles. We have been working on this since the IGF in Rio de Janeiro in 2007. It proposes that all information which is relevant to Internet governance and decision-making should be open and publicly available; that Internet governance entities should broadly publicize opportunities for participation in the work and policy-making of their organizations; and that the development and administration of Internet policy and standards should generally be open, transparent, and inclusive. All these goals reflect the principles that have been agreed on by the WSIS, and we believe that this code would translate those principles into operational benchmarks for both organizations that have been born out of the development of the Internet, and also those who have had different public-policy traditions and working methods but increasingly are involved in setting standards and policies for the Internet. Against those benchmarks the implementation of the WSIS commitments and principles could be measured. For all those who are interested to learn more about this initiative and who would like to comment and discuss the initiative, I would invite you to a workshop tomorrow.

FROM THE FLOOR:

I am the chairman of the board of ICANN. ICANN is the international body set up by the Internet community in 1998 to meet the mandate of the U.S. government. It's often said that ICANN was actually set up by the United States government. It was not. It was set up by the Internet community in response to the government's White Paper. ICANN is responsible for the coordination of names, numbers and protocols. Looking quickly at the principle 29 that we had on the screen, it relates to the international management of those. We are careful to avoid the word "governance" in relation to what we do. It's the coordination or international management of those three elements of the critical infrastructure.

ICANN is composed of a wide range of organizations, individuals, NGOs, and corporations with the full involvement of governments from all over the world. We are transparent, and this is written into our bylaws. We have to be democratic; we listen to all voices and then have voting systems that take them into account. We have a Governmental Advisory Committee that has been growing stronger and stronger since the inception of ICANN and makes substantial contributions to the development of public policy, most recently in relation to the launch of IDNs for ccTLDs. In addition we have significant involvement by the private sector. We have contracts with 935 organizations that act as registrars in the management and retailing of Internet domain names in the generic name space. We also have huge involvement from civil society, which plays a substantial role. International organizations also play a part. We have as members of the technical liaison group, for example, the ITU, the W3C, and one of the European technical standards bodies. And they participate in other mechanisms as well. These things have been hard wired into the DNA of ICANN since its inception.

ICANN's commitment to these standards is a journey, and we constantly strive to improve. On Janis's question of how have things changed since the Tunis Agenda was developed in 2005, we divide our accountability up in a number of ways, beginning with accountability in the public sphere. We have a number of legal requirements for transparency, and have created an information disclosure policy. We have dispute resolution frameworks. We are required under the bylaws to make decisions by applying documented policies neutrally and objectively, with integrity and fairness. We are required to act with a speed that is responsive to the needs of the Internet, obtaining informed input from those entities most affected. And we are required under the bylaws to remain accountable to the Internet community. We have a disclosure policy so that information contained in our documents is set out and made very clearly available. We have classes of documents of course that are not available, and they deal mostly with personal matters, private matters, people's incomes, et cetera. There is also a process for applying for those documents, and, if you are turned down, of complaining that you want access and having that decision reviewed. We also have three dispute resolution mechanisms about that, including an approach to an ombudsman, applying to the board for reconsideration, and then applying to an independent review panel for consideration as to whether or not we have complied with our bylaws. On financial accountability, we do the usual things that you would expect of a corporation. We have independent external audits, we publish accounts, we have a Board Finance Committee that supervises those processes, and there's full reporting by way of the annual report and the financial accounts. Finally, let me come to the audit we conducted of our transparency in 2007. We got the One World Trust to conduct an audit. We published the terms of that, and their response, and then we published our response. So it's something that's deeply embedded in the DNA of ICANN, and we are constantly struggling to improve.

FROM THE FLOOR:

My name is Dmitri Ypsilanti and I work for the Committee on Information, Computer, and Communications Policy at the OECD, which looks at Internet issues, communications policy issues, security and privacy. I would like to talk about multistakeholder participation. For several decades, we have had a Business Industry Advisory Committee (BIAC) and a Trade Union Advisory Committee (TUAC) that participate fully in the work of virtually all committees of the OECD. I think what's important about the WSIS principles is that it brought to the forefront for policymakers the fact that there are other stakeholders out there. And as a result, in 2007 we invited both civil society and Internet technical community to work with us, in addition to business and trade unions, in the work and on the background documents leading up to our ministerial meeting on the future of the Internet economy, which took place in June 2008 in Seoul, Korea. At that meeting itself, before ministers met, we had encouraged both civil society and the Internet technical community to hold their own meetings in order to provide input into the final declaration that Ministers were expected to adopt. And this happened.

In the Seoul declaration, which was signed by 30 OECD ministers plus nine ministers from non-OECD countries, Ministers did call on the OECD to ensure that they took a multistakeholder approach in its work, in particular in following up on the Seoul declaration. As a result, after that ministerial meeting, civil society and the Internet technical community became full participants in our committee. There were certain principles that we did ask them to adhere to. We asked them to self-organize, and that when they come and work with us, they consult amongst themselves and then speak to the extent possible with one voice, so we didn't have to deal with multiple and potentially contradictory comments. So now, we have two other bodies in addition to those I mentioned earlier, BIAC and TUAC. We have ITAC, the Internal Technical Advisory Committee to the OECD, and we have the CSISAC, the Civil Society Information Society Advisory Committee. They've been participating fully in our work since the beginning of this year, and I think our secretariat and member countries have benefitted.

ANRIETTE ESTERHUYSEN:

Before I go on to the next speaker, it would be very interesting to get the reaction from some of the stakeholder groups who have now been participating in some of the institutions we've heard about, so if there are people that want to share their experiences, please add your names to the speaker list.

FROM THE FLOOR:

My name is Shadi Abou-Zahra. I work for the World Wide Web consortium, W3C, and I just want to share a bit of the experience of W3C in working with different stakeholders and the participation, in particular, of people with different backgrounds. So W3C develops standards that actually operate the Web, such as HTML and others. It's a consensus-based and open forum in which core staff and working group participants work together and collaborate to develop those standards. We are a truly international organization, operating from different host sites, from different places, and we've learned that this multistakeholder approach, bringing businesses, governments, private people, research, and more together at the table really produces standards that work better for all. We work with people from different backgrounds and cultures; I come from Egypt, I work in France, I live in Austria, and my boss is in the U.S. We produce royalty-free standards that really contribute to affordable solutions, so that people throughout society can use the technologies and are not locked into specific vendors or specific products.

The involvement of people from different cultures and backgrounds is absolutely important. For myself, as a person with a disability, the involvement of people with disabilities and older people in the standardization process has helped us produce better standards with better usability for all. And we see that a lot of our technical standards being used in policies that relate to people with disabilities. We think that the IGF has contributed to awareness-raising and to more inclusion of people with disabilities, but there's a lot more to do.

FROM THE FLOOR:

I am Bertrand de la Chapelle from the government France. I think it's an excellent idea to have a session on this because the question we're addressing is related to a very small set of words, "in their respective roles." Both in the definition of Internet governance and in several other parts of the documents adopted in Tunis, this notion that there are specific roles for the governments, the private sector, civil society, and international organizations is invoked, and it's the core of the multistakeholder question. What the IGF is doing, what the WSIS asked us to establish, are modalities of interaction that are not available anywhere else. It is our common task, especially in the IGF, to discuss and to test new modalities of interaction. I've had the opportunity in other IGF main sessions to explain that the respective roles of the different categories of actors can and should vary according to the issue, the venue, and the stage of the discussion. This is an opportunity to elaborate a little bit on this notion.

We deal with issues that are very technical, very political, very commercial issues, or that combine all those dimensions. And it is clear that some will have a heavy government involvement, some will have heavier business involvement, and some more technical or civil society involvement. However, the multistakeholder principle guarantees that on all issues, at least some proportion of interaction is required. The venue counts too. You have intergovernmental organizations, standards organizations, business communities, and each of them is dealing with certain issues, and the balance of responsibilities among them will vary as well. And finally, the balance of responsibilities depends also on the stage of the discussion. When you are at the decision-shaping stage or even at the issue-framing stage, the process must be as open as possible. When you evolve into the drafting stage, it can become more limited to specific stakeholders that have a major stake. And when you get into the adoption and validation stage, sometimes you have a smaller range of actors, sometimes it can be endorsed only by governments, or by governments and specific commercial business actors, or by a broader range of actors. The point is that Internet governance is an ecosystem of organizations, and what we are experimenting here in the IGF is actually a multistakeholder interaction protocol. How we do interact with one another. The IGF is not an organization. It's not an event. And it's basically a format. So the benefit of the WSIS principles is that it forces us to define what are the respective roles and the modes of interaction.

JANIS KARKLINS:

Bertrand, what has changed in France in the past four years, in terms of how you approach Internet governance issues? Is there just government involvement or do you have a process which involves also other stakeholders?

FROM THE FLOOR:

We have had a forum on Internet rights in France since 2000 that is a multistakeholder space for dealing with issues of access and regulation at the national level. And since the launch of the IGF, consultations have taken place to prepare for these meetings. Just the mere act of inviting the different participants in the IGF to discuss the next agenda is important. And we have been instrumental in helping the emergence of the EuroDIG, the regional IGF, in partnership with other actors from civil society and the Council of Europe. Moreover, my minister presented in the opening session on Sunday on the right to delete information about one's self, or the right to have one's information deleted after a certain period of time. We had a multistakeholder workshop a week ago on that topic to prepare for here, then she came and proposed this. We will have a follow-up nationally, and this is how this feedback loop is functioning. And in general terms, this is also forcing us to have more interaction among the different ministries and with the other actors to prepare for IGF and ICANN meetings.

FROM THE FLOOR:

My name is Kurt Eric Lundquist and I'm not speaking on behalf of my company, but rather as a long-time participant in the Internet Engineering Task Force. I do not represent the IETF, but I have chaired many working groups and worked there for a long time there, and I want to use it as an example of a multistakeholder and open and transparent process that existed before the Tunis Agenda and the IGF. The Internet is built on the standards developed by the IETF, where everyone who participates represents themselves as individuals. People can bring their ideas and innovations, whether they have been developed in a private, corporate, or governmental environment, into the standards process, and then have them vetted and maybe hopefully standardized and later implemented. All of this vetting is done on purely technical merits. The IETF process is highly inclusive, and anyone can join and participate on equal terms. You don't have to represent anyone. You don't have to be a member of any organization. And you can not only bring in work, but also comment and address work in progress. All the documents are freely and openly available on the Internet, and all of the discussions are conducted on mailing lists that are free to anyone to join. The IETF does hold meetings three times a year, where the ISOC provides fellowship programs for participation, but no decisions are allowed to be made at the face-to-face meetings. They actually have all to be done on mailing lists so that everyone is be able to equally participate. And the standards are freely available on the Internet for anyone to make use of without any restrictions, including the work in progress documents. This openness of the standards has enabled people to innovate and build new products, services, and businesses on the Internet, and this has made the Internet the success story it is today.

JANIS KARKLINS:

How has the work of the IETF changed in the last four years? While IETF initially was a gathering of technical gurus with ponytails and jeans doing stuff that nobody understands, the government representatives, has there been any increased participation by government representatives, in particular from the developing countries? And if the answer is positive, do you feel that their contribution has been useful? And if the answer is negative, why do you think they do not participate in IETF work?

FROM THE FLOOR:

One participates in the IETF as an individual, so it's hard to do statistics on who people actually represent. I do believe, however, that the governments and also developing countries have started showing a lot more interest in what's happening in the IETF and that they are participating. They have submitted work items and have worked on the standards. So is that a result of the Tunis Agenda or not, it's hard to say, but it's clear that as the Internet has become more important, they are working inside the IETF. But the IETF adopted the Tunis principles before the Tunis principles existed, so I think it's hard to say that they helped, but they certainly built on what was already there.

FROM THE FLOOR:

I am Abdul Waheed Khan, Assistant Director-General of UNESCO. Following the second phase of the World Summit on Information Society in Tunis, at UNESCO we had very extensive debate whether or not we should participate in the IGF. And the debate was, "Well, it's a governance issue and what has UNESCO to do with it?" But then we argued that our proposal for building inclusive knowledge societies included four principles: Respect for linguistic and cultural diversity, freedom of expression, universal access to information and knowledge, and quality education for all. Now, if we really want to advance the notion of knowledge societies and uphold the principles, then how can we not remain engaged with IGF? So we began to participate as observers, and I think over a period of time we have made a case for openness of the Internet governance to ensure, first of all, freedom of expression. Any attempt to block free flow of ideas, clearly UNESCO stands firmly against it. So we have participated in all the IGFs, and as a result we have encouraged member states to develop strong policies that promote and facilitate language diversity on the Internet, we've promoted the creation and dissemination of content in local languages, we've encouraged multilingual access to digital resources in cyberspace, and we've promoted harnessing ICTs for the preservation of endangered languages. We've worked in cooperation with other international organizations to establish policies, regulations, technical recommendations and best practices relating to multilingualism and multilingual resources and applications, including innovations in language computerization. In fact, this afternoon, I'm signing an agreement with ICANN to promote the multilingual part of UNESCO's work.

JANIS KARKLINS:

Thank you, Dr. Khan. I believe that especially now, with the introduction of IDNs in the ccTLD space and hopefully later in the gTLD space, UNESCO assistance to all those working on the multilingual Internet will be very much needed and you have a lot of years of hard work in front of you.

FROM THE FLOOR:

My name is Byron Holland and I'm the CEO of dot CA. We're very operational in nature, but I believe many of the WSIS principles are woven into the fabric of our operations. We operate within the ecosystem of the Internet and the IGF but fundamentally it's because it is our business, and the business of my colleagues in the cc world. Really, what we do to a great degree is translate principles into policy, and then policy into process on the ground. It's certainly not without its challenges. Engagement of our domestic stakeholders can often be a real challenge. We commonly get the refrain that, "Well, I turn it on and it works so who cares about discussing its governance?" Everybody in this forum does care, but on the street, the end user, often that's not the case. Getting the average user to engage in discourse and dialogue on the governance of the Internet is a real challenge, but we continue to do it. I have a few concrete examples of how we put the WSIS principles to work. Recently, we did some work with the International Institute of Sustainable Development and did an outreach and survey into issues that did matter to end users and various stakeholders regarding Internet governance. It ended up being very successful and gave us a real sense of what some of the concerns might be. And that hopefully is going to form the basis of an ongoing domestic dialogue that we can then bring to this forum at future dates to provide more educated input. We communicated with registrants, registrars, law enforcement, the sustainable development community, private sector, other civil society members. So it really was a very wide-ranging consultation and engagement to get feedback from the full spectrum of the Canadian Internet landscape.

As some may know, we introduced in the past year fairly strong privacy protections in the WHOIS. In our domestic landscape, we must do that. So for all individuals, we have privacy coverage within the WHOIS. That was the result of actually a multiyear consultation and engagement, again, of many different stakeholders within the Internet landscape in Canada. Certainly law enforcement, as you can imagine, privacy advocates, registrants, registrars, various end users, et cetera. And the policy we developed really came out of that engagement and it's the policy that we have on the ground in effect right now. Many people here will remember Conficker, the worm that made its name known last March. We were one of the early cc's to get very involved in that process, to take a very proactive stance and work with many stakeholders to create a policy that was collaborative, and then also to distribute the message out into the public arena So the WSIS principles are something that we deal with and have in effect every single day.

JANIS KARKLINS:

Let me ask you, suppose there hadn't been a WSIS. Would you have been following the same principles in your daily operations?

FROM THE FLOOR:

I think that if we wanted to remain successful, we would have to. And we were following some element of them prior to the WSIS principles in the early 2000s when our WHOIS engagement started. We were bringing in multiple stakeholders, but certainly WSIS has expanded upon it, and to some degree clarified some of the principles.

FROM THE FLOOR:

I'm Guru Gurumurthy from IT for Change in Bangalore India. We had a very interesting workshop today morning titled "Multistakeholderism at the IGF, Assessing Impact on Participation." In true multistakeholder spirit, our participants came from various sectors and there were slightly differing points of view that will be of interest to here. We began with a small study of actual participation at IGF at Rio and at Hyderabad being presented by the first panellists. It's from data available publicly about the people who actually participated, what sectors they came from, what were their nationalities. And about actual participation, the words being spoken, because transcripts are publicly available, so what is the word count. It does not necessarily mean that volley equates to impact, but it gives us an idea nevertheless. So the nationalities were broken up based on the UNDP Human Development Index (HDI) classification. So there were four groups, HDI 1 through 4, where 1 is the most developed and the 4th is what I'll call the least developed countries. So the analysis was not very surprising. The numbers say that participants, both in terms of individuals as well as organizations that were present, came overwhelmingly from the developed world, which is HD1 and HD2, and if you were to exclude the host country because we always find that in each of these IGFs, host country participation tends to be very high, more than 70% of the organizations who participated in IGF 2 and IGF 3 came from the 20% of countries in the world and were largely from HD1 and HD2. Even within the developing world, the participation of the least developed countries was very minimal. In fact, one noticed that at the IGF at Brazil, there was not even a single speaker from the least developed countries in any of the main sessions. This is in terms of the number of organizations. If you look at the number of individuals, the finding is even more skewed, because from the developed world many more individuals come per organization than from the developing world. So this was just an initial study to give us a feel and the panellists said that they would do more on the lessons learned in terms of who is chairing the various workshops and the dynamic coalitions.

I'll just go to the other speakers. There was the Greek ambassador who spoke about another aspect of this multistakeholder participation at IGFs. There are many themes because different stakeholders are perhaps interested in different kinds of things, and sometimes it becomes quite fragmented, which we are also seeing perhaps at Egypt, that there are so many different processes but how are they tied in together? How do workshops come and relate to the main sessions? And how together do they represent what is the thinking at the IGF is something that we really need to concern ourselves with, so that there is a more formal linkage. In the traditional processes of global governance, there is a linkage but even in subsequent policymaking, it's much more clear than it is now. At the same time, he also felt that because there are different sector people participating, it may not be that there is agreement at the venue itself, but there is a subliminal impact in people's minds and when they go back maybe changes are happening over a long period of time. The participants from the business sector said something very interesting, that for them it is even more skewed because small businesses from the developing countries have even less ability to participate than civil society from the developing countries. And that the IGF principle of multistakeholderism is impacting other institutional spaces as well.

People felt that while participation from the developing world is very poor, we need to have its voices here. Technical capacity-building gets brought up a lot, but capacity-building needs to extend to the political aspects as well. How do people from developing countries understand and articulate their own interests and make sure that they are taken care of here? Another issue was that we need to have funding support for people from the developing countries, and public funding was seen as important. I'll conclude by recalling that the first panellist said that if you're talking of democracy, it's very important to talk about substantive participation and not just formal participation. We may have very been successful in terms of formal participation. We still have a long way to go when it comes to substantive participation, and we need to be very focused on this because otherwise we will reduce the exclusion in one way but we will increase it in another way.

FROM THE FLOOR:

Hello, I'm Sami El Basheer, head of the development sector in the ITU. I am delighted to see this dialogue and to remember in '98 when the ITU adopted the famous resolution which started all this process and then organized both phases of the WSIS. Nobody challenges the multilateral governance of the Internet. The statement of the WSIS was very clear that we all have different roles to play. I would like to emphasize that the ITU is promoting telecommunication ICT infrastructure worldwide, and promoting the Internet as an important means of communication and forming the Information Society. We have 11 workshops during this IGF. We are active, and we want to be even more active. And I hope next time we'll see some of the ITU officials as panellists at the next IGF, because it's an irony that we started all this and now we are competing for a spot to speak.

We are very active in cyber security around the world. We are working with our members. All our work is driven by our members, which are the governments and 750 sector members. The idea of involving the civil society, it's still on the agenda of the ITU, and I think everybody knows it will be discussed at the next Plenipotentiary in Mexico. But I assure you that in many of our initiatives, especially on development, we work with many civil society entities and NGOs to promote the use of Internet. We have an excellent relation with ICANN, and like my colleague from UNESCO and others, we are working to have a Memorandum of Understanding with it to put behind us any misunderstanding that may have occurred.

JANIS KARKLINS:

Thank you Mr. El Basheer for your clear statement of friendship with ICANN. It's really appreciated, and I think that we should continue in that spirit for years to come. But if you would allow me, you may recall the question I asked the representative to IETF; is there any particular reason why government representatives do not participate in IETF? And are you are drawing on IETF experience and knowledge in different working groups of the standardization sector? Because certainly, you are addressing sometimes questions which are, if not the same, very similar.

FROM THE FLOOR:

I think that very limited numbers of developing countries are participating. I think it's clear from the WSIS outcome that the international community did not reach a consensus on how to run the Internet, that's why they came up with this arrangement of the IGF. That's why we are still discussing this. Another thing we have to remember that in the ITU, you have private sector driven proposals, but the governments are there and are sitting in management of the spectrum and in other issues of the ITU. I think it's as simple as that. It doesn't need too much effort to realize that the governments still don't feel that the IGF is the right place to govern the Internet, but it is a multistakeholder forum to discuss what we are doing.

FROM THE FLOOR:

I am John Curran, the President and CEO of the American Registry for Internet Numbers (ARIN). ARIN is one of the five Regional Internet Registries (RIRs) that collectively manage the Internet resource pool for all organizations worldwide. I am here to report on the experiences of the five RIRs in making use of the principles contained in paragraph 29 of the Tunis Agenda. Many of those principles have always been part of the RIRs. This includes transparency, multilateralism, and democratic principles. But I will say that the presence of those principles in the Tunis Agenda has made it easier for collaboration between the RIRs and other bodies, both civil society, government, and international organizations. We have undertaken a program of outreach, in some cases joint workshops, in some cases particular collaborations with people going to speak on each other's panels. And as a result of the principles that are contained in the Tunis Agenda, this collaboration has been much easier. We look forward to continuation of those principles and would welcome being able to continue to do collaboration with organizations like APTEL, CTU, and the OECD.

FROM THE FLOOR:

I'm Fouad Bajwa from Pakistan. The IGF is going to continue to be the result of open consultations, and will be an open dialogue forum that is constituted not through organizational divisions. The IGF facilitates open dialogue and opportunities for creating partnerships, and can draw attention to issues and put them on the agenda for international dialogue. The IGF topics are not fixed, and we have the opportunity to change them according to our needs. If we look at the Geneva Declaration of Principles, the world has a common vision of the Information Society. And we have a development agenda which is evolving slowly. So in the near future with the continuation of the IGF, human rights and the development agenda topics will come into the main sessions. And as I would like to say, that please don't forget we, the people of the developing world, are here. We may not be participating as much as in the international system. For example, my experience in ICANN has been that I've seen few staff members from my part of the world, or board members from the whole of the developing world. There is a requirement for more participation from the developing world, and there should be partnerships outside the IGF which can help ensure this.

FROM THE FLOOR:

I'm Olga Cavalli from Government of Argentina, and I'm speaking in my role as coordinator of the Internet governance working group of the Information Society of the Latin America and Caribbean ALAC 2010. This group follows a multistakeholder approach that we learned in WSIS. The group was created as a special request made by Argentina to exchange ideas and best practices about Internet governance in the region, and to increase the participation of the region in the whole Internet governance process. Now the group is conducting a survey of the Internet governance-related organizations and will upload this information to a map that will be built on a special Web site. We will make this also with our local chapter of Internet Society in Argentina. At the national level, there has been significant consolidation of the multistakeholder approach, and I want to mention to you two examples. The most important ones are the development of the national digital agenda, and an evaluation of the convention on cybercrime by the Government of Argentina. About suggested updates or changes to the IGF, I would say more focus on development would be good.

ANRIETTE ESTERHUYSEN:

Olga, do you think this would have happened in the Latin American intergovernmental process if not for the WSIS principles? And has it improved or changed the outcomes?

FROM THE FLOOR:

It wouldn't have happened without the multistakeholder approach established in 2005 by WSIS. It is not easy for governments to handle the multistakeholder approach, but it's a process. You can start from something and build upon there. This is only a personal opinion.

FROM THE FLOOR:

I'm Constance Bommelaer from the Internet Society. I wanted to echo what Dmitri Ypsilanti said earlier about the Internet Technical Advisory Committee to the OECD. This opportunity for us and civil society to join the work of the OECD was unforeseen. It was the result of the Seoul declaration that acknowledges the WSIS principles and encouraged member states to work collaboratively with all stakeholders. It all happened in less than a year thanks to a very welcoming OECD staff, and now these new constituencies are able to join all the working parties and contribute to crucial policies on information security, privacy, critical infrastructures including IPv6, and even Internet innovation and economic issues. The ITAC is open to any Internet technical or research organization, and its working methodology is based on a charter and on rules of participation set by the OECD. If you would like to know more please visit www.Internetac.org.

FROM THE FLOOR:

I'm Mr. Aldarrab from Saudi Arabia. I'd like to make two points. One is related to the point made by my friend from France concerning the magic words, "in their respective roles." He said that these respective roles are not clear, but Article 33 in the WSIS states that the WGIG report enhanced our understanding of the respective roles, and there we can find a list of roles. And on the participation of developing countries in the IETF, there are a number of issues that make governments less involved. A key one is financial; many developing countries face difficulties so it is not so easy for them to participate. If you remember in the WSIS, one important element concerned financial mechanisms. We need financial solutions, and the transfer of technologies and know-how. Unfortunately, I have heard that the Digital Solidarity Fund that was a result of the WSIS has been dismantled.

FROM THE FLOOR:

My name is Art Reilly and I am here on behalf the International Chamber of Commerce (ICC) and its Business Action in Support of the Information Society (BASIS). I work for Cisco. The business community supports the WSIS principles of multistakeholderism, transparency, and democracy in Internet governance. But the underlying principle is that the Information Society should be people-centric and development oriented, and we need to focus on that. Multistakeholderism is excellent, but that means that we are dealing with individuals and their needs, and we not lose sight of that. I was impressed this week to hear a representative from Ghana talk about their need for affordable, low-cost Internet connectivity and for us to have a detailed discussion of what are the elements that could do that. This is something we all look for, to increase the number of people on the Internet. The business community is very proud of the role that we play with the other stakeholders in achieving over the last four years a condition where there are now more than 2 billion more people connected via mobile than there were at the time of WSIS. And that there are now more than 700 million people connected to the Internet. Each of those businesses are very proud to be part of the process of connecting people, person by person. Business also is a big contributor to the content on the Internet, so we are proud of that role as well.

One of the activities of the IGF that we think is critical is capacity building. We are proud to bring our experiences to this forum and share them with others, and they can, in turn, impart to us their experiences. We can take issues back home and begin to work with them internally and improve things going forward. We have organized in BASIS to outreach to businesses around the world, in developing countries as well as developed countries, to include them in the preparation of issue papers and participation in these discussions. We have represented the business community here at the IGF, but also in the Global Alliance for ICT in Development, in the WSIS action lines, and in the U.N. Commission on Science, Technology and Development, to bring our expertise and gain from the insight of others. We have also participated in the regional IGFs and consultations associated with those, and we outreach to our individual affiliates in about 100 countries around the world to encourage them to understand these issues and to do advocacy with their respective governments on creating an enabling environment that underlies Internet governance processes. We participate in this forum that is multistakeholder, non-decisional, and gives us the opportunity to talk about these issues freely and without negotiated texts, and we look forward to continued participation.

FROM THE FLOOR:

I'm Heather Dryden from the Government of Canada. We really value this interaction. The WSIS was about raising awareness of ICTs at high levels, and the underlying principle was development and capacity-building, so I'm pleased that a number of previous speakers gave emphasis to that. I am happy to report that the Canadian government has provided funding to the International Telecommunication Union in the amount of Can $450,000 so that developing countries can participate here. This is the value that we place on this kind of format. The Internet demands flexibility and adaptability, and with the clear multistakeholderism emphasized in the WSIS documents, the discussion forums and the Internet organizations related to these issues need to remain flexible and adapt. There's really no stakeholder group or organization that can afford not to. This is consistent with the comments that have been made about the future of the Internet, and needing to embrace future and new challenges. It was a delight to hear from our colleague from Netnod talking about the involvement of governments in the IETF. A working group has been created in ARIN recently for governments to participate, which is simply a recognition that there are issues of interest and relevance to governments. That's not going to change. Not all issues are going to be of central relevance to governments, but this is one of the ways that governments have been able to become better involved in ARIN. And of course the Governmental Advisory Committee at ICANN is yet another instance of governmental involvement. And what I would like to emphasize related to this is those governments that participate are adapting. They are trying to find new ways of doing things. That's certainly how Canada views that matter. There needs to be a recognition of this as we meet future challenges related to the DNS.

JANIS KARKLINS:

Thank you. Let us now move to the next part of our discussion related to Paragraph 31 of Tunis Agenda. If the Secretariat now could put the text on the screen that we could read it together. Paragraph 31 says: "We recognize that Internet governance, carried out accordingly to the Geneva Principles, is an essential element for people-centred, inclusive development-oriented and non-discriminatory Information Society. Furthermore, we commit ourselves to the stability and security of the Internet as a global facility and to ensuring the requisite legitimacy of its governance based on the full participation of all stakeholders, both from developed and developing countries within their respective roles and responsibilities." And in order to trigger debate, maybe we should we should think about a couple of questions we would like to seek answers during the next 50 minutes or so. I would propose the following questions: What is the meaning of the term, "Internet governance for development?" What are some examples of impacts on development from governance arrangements?

FROM THE FLOOR:

I'm William Drake from the Graduate Institute of International and Development Studies in Geneva. We had a workshop today called "Implementing the WSIS Principles: A Development Agenda for Internet Governance." The workshop was cosponsored by eight different organizations, including two governments and one international organization, the Council of Europe. I did not manage to achieve gender equity, as seven of the eight speakers were women, and five of them were from government. There's been concern among many participants that there's been inadequate discussion in the IGF over the years around precisely the kinds of questions Janis was just posing, like how do we think through the impact of Internet governance arrangements on people-centred development. There's been a lack of systematic, focused dialogue on these kinds of issues, as well as a lack of real analysis by academics like myself. The consequence has been a missed opportunity to build support for a multistakeholder process focusing on developing country concerns, and to promote developing country engagement in the IGF.

One option for trying to address those issues is the notion of a Development Agenda. By a Development Agenda, I mean a holistic program of analysis and action intended to mainstream development considerations into decision-making across the range of important global Internet governance mechanisms. In the first instance, a Development Agenda would be an analytic enterprise, involving monitoring trends, aggregating information, and conducting analysis to assess progress against some agreed baselines in terms of how effectively these mechanisms are actually promoting or addressing developmental concerns. At the same time, one could also imagine such an agenda moving on beyond analysis to identifying and generalizing good or best practices, and perhaps even making some consensual adjustments to enhance the development awareness of Internet governance procedures and policies. Development Agendas are already being pursued in related international arenas, such as intellectual property and international trade in the WIPO and WTO, but we've had no parallel process in Internet governance. Of course Internet governance is very different from the two arenas I just mentioned because it's highly distributed, involving many different types of institutions and processes---governmental, nongovernmental, and multistakeholder---and that means that you could not pursue exactly the same kind of Development Agenda that you would have in a centralized body like WIPO and WTO. IGF does not have members, it doesn't have a rule-making role, and we don't make hard commitments and allocate budgets and so on here. But we could be using the IGF as a vehicle to sort through the issues, to identify those that do bear on development, to gather and share information, and to identify and encourage best practices. This is a parallel concept to the approach that the APC, the Council of Europe, and UNECE have pursued with regard to the procedural aspects of Internet governance, promoting transparency and inclusive participation. Development is a horizontal, cross-cutting norm that should inform all Internet governance activities, and we could be assessing how well that process works. Accordingly, I've organized workshops at Rio and Hyderabad to flesh out the concept of a Development Agenda, and in this meeting what we did was to make the link to the WSIS principles on Internet governance, which can be read as saying that Internet governance should advance development and that the IGF has a mandate to promote and assess that kind of activity on an ongoing basis.

The meeting considered four possible elements of a Development Agenda. The first is capacity-building, which could be more systematized with more information shared about what options are available, who's doing what and so on, best practices, et cetera. The second concerns institutional and procedural issues, such as possible barriers to effective participation in intergovernmental, private sector, and multistakeholder processes, and ways to overcome those. The third comprises substantive policy issues in the governance of infrastructures, in issue-areas like naming and numbering, security and technical standardization, and the identification of those most directly relevant to developmental trajectories. The fourth involves substantive policy issues in the governance of networked information, communication, and commerce. That's to say issues pertaining to the use of the Internet for transactions, like information security, intellectual property, and electronic commerce. So we've had an exercise over the course of the three workshops at Rio, Hyderabad and here, where we tried to identify what are some of the key issues that a Development Agenda might try to take on board, and then we also talked today finally about ways to take this concept forward in the IGF and global institutions and processes, and in terms of research and capacity-building.

The main conclusions were as follows. With regard to the IGF, there was strong support among the 60 or so participants in the room, and this resonates with the results of the previous two workshops as well, for the notion that development should be a main theme session in the IGF. We've been talking about the traditional five for a while now, and it might be time to have development in there. It also could be possible to organize a coordinated cluster of workshops, best practices forums, and open forums, where perhaps institutions would talk about what they do to promote development objectives, how they work with developing countries, et cetera. National and regional IGFs are increasingly important, and certainly we would want to see if there are ways to try to bring development considerations into those in a more systematic way and then percolate the results back up into the global IGF. And there was also discussion of having a dynamic coalition to sustain the dialogue. People have shown interest in this in the past, so we will consider how feasible that might be. Finally, there are initiatives that could be pursued in this context. Within ICANN, those of us who participate in the non-commercial stakeholder group have been discussing the possibility of forming a development interest group that would focus on relevant aspects of issues in the Generic Names Supporting Organization. There are other parts of ICANN that might want to take these issues on board as well. And in terms of research and capacity-building, I will probably try to organize something. We already do a bit of this in the international summer schools on Internet governance.

ANRIETTE ESTERHUYSEN:

Bill, I was in your workshop this morning and there was a very interesting question from George Sadowsky, who said that he understood that the IGF was about development, and that it was, in fact, a priority theme. He questioned why have we come to this point where there's a strong feeling among many people that the development agenda and development issues should feature in main sessions. I invite somebody from a developing country to say how it feels to them, to what extent is development a priority in the IGF, and how does it feel to be a developing country participant here, and why do we need to place this special emphasis on it?

FROM THE FLOOR:

I am Fotindong Cornelius from Cameroon. I work for the Minister of Posts and Telecommunications. I think that the idea of laying emphasis on the aspect of the government in IGF is very important for developing countries, because we are still trying to get the basic access to the Internet. So we would have expected more development workshops and for development to appear in a main session.

ANRIETTE ESTERHUYSEN:

We also talked about the importance of continuity because access has, in fact, featured in the IGF, but unless one participates in every single meeting it's difficult to get a sense of the progress.

FROM THE FLOOR:

I'm Lisa Horner from Global Partners. I'd like to speak a little bit about the extent to which Internet governance institutions and processes are contributing to a people-centred, inclusive, development-oriented, and non-discriminatory Information Society. As the only internationally accepted framework of standards and principles on what means to be people-centred and on what "development" means in practice, human rights provide an appropriate benchmark to measure progress that is being made and also an appropriate basis upon which to develop norms. The WSIS declaration itself reinforces the importance of upholding human rights, both civil and political rights and economic, social, and cultural rights. So I organized a workshop on, "Human Rights and Principles in Internet Governance: Practical Steps Forwards." It showcased the various initiatives that are being taken by different stakeholders from the bottom up to foster an Internet that supports and promotes human rights. These included the Global Network Initiative, my own organization's Freedom of Expression Project, the Council of Europe's Guidelines for ISPs, APC partner organization networks that are working at the national level, and other projects that provide practical guidance on how to actually incorporate human rights standards into Internet governance policy and practice. Stakeholders in the workshop commented that the human rights framework is an essential tool for a people-centred information society and Internet, and that the translation of human rights standards into practical principles and guidelines for specific issues and dilemmas is a promising way forwards.

The dynamic coalitions on Internet rights and principles and on freedom of expression have made important steps forwards over the past few years, but there does remain a lot to be done. The dispersed range of Internet

420

governance institutions, actors, and processes, and the multifaceted nature and multilayered nature of Internet governance makes it difficult to ensure that human rights do underpin Internet governance, which is often seen as a technical domain so the social implications of policies aren't always taken into consideration enough. So therefore, I'd like to say that we need more initiatives by all of the stakeholders at different levels from the bottom up to uphold and realize human rights through Internet governance, drawing on best practice examples like those explored in our workshop. We need better coordination between Internet governance institutions, for example between those concerned with social dimensions and those concerned with technical dimensions. We also need more meaningful multistakeholder collaboration, including spaces for civil society groups and Internet users from across the world to have meaningful and useful say in how the Internet is governed and operates on day-to-day basis. In the dynamic coalitions, we'd love to hear particularly from business stakeholders and from Internet governance institutions about how we in civil society and the user communities can help you to expand the ethical dimensions of the Information Society.

FROM THE FLOOR:

Yeah. Thank you. Y.J. Park from Delft University of Technology. I have been very impressed by how wonderful the multistakeholder principle is from ISOC, ICANN, OECD, W3C, IETF, RIR, and others, and is it really a wonderful principle for all? I felt like I was in a religious meeting that shares each other's experience of how the multistakeholder god came to each other's spirit and how great it was to observe all the changes the multistakeholder principle god wrote about. So I was quite afraid of saying my own experience that was not quite similar to people are sharing here. I wish the same god also came to me and saved me like god did to you. However, the god did not come to me. At least not yet. I'd like to share my own experience of multistakeholder principle in the context of a development, not as religion but as one of the WSIS outcomes. This morning, I could have a chance to talk one of the private sector members from USA. He said to me he just was coming from APEC CEO Summit in Singapore, and was very much surprised by the fact that there are very few Asian governments in this forum. Why? Governments in Asia, together with governments in many developing countries, do not take this equal footing multistakeholder principle seriously. As even the Canada delegation expressed, governments still make a lot of efforts to adapt to this new rule. At least some governments are trying to be in this process. However, the majority of governments in the world are not engaged with this critical Internet governance debate. Should we go without those governments? Is it a right thing to continue marching all together with those who converted to the rule first in this room under the flag of leadership of multistakeholder parallel or should we spend more time for those governments to take on board. If so, why should we do? National governments are critical in terms of standing up national policy and implementing both national and global policies. Without national governments' participation, multistakeholder principle is not meaningful enough. I'm glad IGF community is very sensitive to human rights and many other rights issues promoting development. I hope IGF community should also increase the rights of national governments' participation as well as civil society from developing worlds' participation, as my civil society colleague addressed. Lastly, as Guru addressed, we also have to support political capacity-building, as well as economic capacity-building, for those who will not ready for the new rule of the multistakeholder principle.

FROM THE FLOOR:

My name is Peter Bruck. The World Summit Award operates as an activity in over 160 U.N. member states, looking at best practice for Internet contents and innovative applications and using a mechanism of an open and fair and transparently judged competition in order to develop the content industries and the good use of applications. I was recently in western Africa and talked the people there who are producing contents, have Internet agencies and so on. I was struck by the enthusiasm and the creativity of the young entrepreneurs who will offering very valuable services to the community developing local media and so on. And then I talked to them also about the economics of the situation, and if you want to have a proper ISP access, broadband capacity, in those countries, you have to pay $12,000 a month. And when I came back to Central Europe, I looked at the bill that we have in some of our units, and we pay for the same connectivity 315 Euros a month. So when we look at the question of Internet governance in relationship to development, my questions is: Would it not make a lot of sense to take the cost issue and the dramatic inequality in terms of cost more into account? And I say this in light of the fact that when we look at the Tunis Agenda, prior to Internet governance there's a whole section on the financial mechanisms and the issue of how to finance the Internet and so on. This was an important issue and we had the setting up of a digital solidarity fund and other initiatives. When you talk about governance and development and you are not taking into account the glaring inequalities in terms of the economics of the situation, we are remaining completely idealistic.

FROM THE FLOOR:

I am Vladimir from Diplo Foundation. We should remember one important thing, which is capacity building within the governments. One of the lessons that Diplo has had with capacity building is the importance of involving younger governmental officials in the process. And you can see all the new fellows that are around from developing countries. In that sense, building up the IGFs on the national level is one of the best results that we had of the follow-ups of the IGF. We have ten hubs around the world participating remotely, and I'm following their discussion on Skype now. This remote participation was a direct result of capacity building. Another thing is the youth corner, which you can see in the IGF Village, where you can test your digital native level.

JANIS KARKLINS:

I want to come back to the question of connection and access costs. That was a huge issue during world summit, and there were a number of reasons mentioned that contributed to high costs in the developing world. Some of them were the lack of an enabling environment, monopolies, a lack of private or public investments in infrastructure, the low density of users, and a lack of local content which raised the prices and increased international traffic. So I would like to ask the ITU director of development, Sami El Basheer, if you can dwell a little on the situation now and what's the difference from when we discussed it four years ago.

FROM THE FLOOR:

In the developed world broadband costs went down due to more sophisticated networks, fibre optics, and mobile broadband. In the developing world, most Internet connections depend on fixed networks that are usually not as capable, so the cost of mobile broadband is high. That's why the ITU and other stakeholders are working to promote accessibility and connectivity in the developing countries regions where a lot of work and investment still is needed.

JANIS KARKLINS:

I know that you have many programs in that, and we can see from statistics that there is certainly an increased number of Internet users in the developing world, despite the high cost. So perhaps with the increased density of use, the costs may go down simply because of the volume. I see that Professor Brook wants to intervene.

FROM THE FLOOR:

The ITU published this spring its statistics, and that report is very comprehensive and breaks down at the country level the cost issue. The indicators are excellent in terms of monitoring the situation. My intervention before was along your line of thinking, Janis, that we need to take into account the cost and economic issues when we talk about Internet governance and development, because otherwise we are decontextualizing what we are talking about. In developed countries the mobile Internet has brought about a real revolution in terms of what contents, what kind of applications can be used. They are knowledge-intensive applications, they are content-rich applications, they are complex applications, and they are really user-centric in a way which really adds value. This is what I want to see being fostered and facilitated in the developing countries. And the monopoly situation is just one of the market structure factors which really impede access to Internet, mobile or fixed.

FROM THE FLOOR:

I am Raul Echeberria, the CEO of LACNIC, the Latin American and Caribbean registry, and also the chairman of the Internet Society. I have spoken many times this week in English. But we have translation services, so I will switch to Spanish. So we worked very much on the cost of access for developing countries. We have to take into account different factors, not only the international links. We have to make sure that decision-makers understand to what extent they can intervene in the situation to change it in Latin America. One hundred percent of the service providers are active in this sphere, and our organization has played a key role in Latin America. We have an IXP in Ecuador, and there were different initiatives launched with Google, with other companies for content distribution. So there are many companies that are going to Latin America now to change the state of affairs. Access to high-speed Internet through underground cables and fibre optics is also important. So the Internet has evolved over the last few years. Models are becoming more complex, and we can change the state of affairs by acting on different issues. We have to look at local content. We have to underline IXPs and their importance. We have to see how underground cables can be used. We have to give providers incentives to put these networks into place. All this will contribute to cost decreases.

ANRIETTE ESTERHUYSEN:

I want to read a comment from a remote participant, Miguel Alcaine, who is deputy Ambassador from El Salvador to the U.N. in Geneva and a member of the Multistakeholder Advisory Group of the IGF. He says, "I want to support the idea of transforming the development orientation of the IGF into something specific and practical. Abandon for a while the overarching nature and concentrate ourselves in discussing specifics about IG and development." And then we have a question, also from a developing country participant, from the remote hub in Ghana. His asks how we can get developing countries governments involved, more involved, in Internet governance processes.

JOHN NJOROGE:

My name is John Njoroge. I am from Kenya, and I am an ISOC Ambassador to the IGF. Developing nations should be accorded more support in relation to the IGF. Developed nations should empower and encourage developing nations in this agenda.

FROM THE FLOOR:

I'm Mactar Seck from the U.N. Economic Commission for Africa. I will speak in French. I wanted to explain the African experience that we have garnered with infrastructure and access. We have seen many strides made in the area of access. Governments' awareness has been raised, and computer equipment has been made tax exempt and is sometimes distributed free of charge--- laptops, for example. Higher educational institutions in some countries have 100 percent Internet connectivity. Equipment is being provided to make sure that citizens have access to social services. About ten African countries have provided such infrastructure. We know that infrastructure is something that they themselves can create, and they organize themselves together with the private sector and the development partners. I am referring to satellites, underwater cables, et cetera. In five years' time, the whole of Africa will be connected. But this has to be viewed against the background of certain regions, countries. There is a digital divide, and I think that IGF has to underscore this point. Another point is that the Internet is used sometimes to impede or stop freedom of expression. This is a very important, and we need to give some thought to that.

FROM THE FLOOR:

I'm Jeremy Godfrey from the government of Hong Kong, and I wanted to talk about how to widen participation, not just from developing countries

424

governments. I have been a member of the GAC for 18 months, but an absentee member in part because of the time commitment needed to participate effectively. I wonder whether or not that may also apply to representatives from developing countries governments and possibly even to people from civil society and from the private sector who might also have a contribution to make, but who haven't got the religion Y.J. mentioned and find that the cost of participating is too high. So it's been very good to meet with Janis and other people here at IGF and discuss these issues. People have talked about capacity building, and the lady from the Canadian government talked about helping people with the financial costs of participation, but we also need to look at some of the processes we use to enable people to contribute.

FROM THE FLOOR:

I'm Parminder Singh from I.T. for Change. Ambassador Karklins and the ITU representative listed issues in WSIS about access, and that reminded me that the biggest issue concerned interconnection charges, and we seem to have not done anything on that over these years. I would like to know whether there's a feeling that the problem has gone away, or we could not pull together the political will to address the issue. The WSIS documents talked about the ITU doing some study or work on interconnection charges. It seems we cannot summon the political will to take on a particular government's regime which informs all Internet governance systems, which is market fundamentalist. It is in this relation that I see WSIS principles, which gave political guidelines that stand alongside the market principles to guide Internet governance regimes. We have already kind of abandoned the interconnection charges issue, but network neutrality is another issue which is facing us and we refuse to look at it in terms of any kind of social/political principles, and there are enough of these in the Geneva Declaration of Principles to guide us along. Open and free sharing of knowledge is one of the core principles mentioned in the Declaration of Principles, and that gives us a way to take on network neutrality. There was a lot of examination done about how organizations involved with Internet governance assess themselves on the basis of multistakeholderism but not on the basis of substantive principles. One example is, does ICANN think about having an Access to Knowledge constituency at the same level as their IP constituency, which would start changing the manner in which those organizations do work.

ANRIETTE ESTERHUYSEN:

I think what we've heard, particularly from the government of Argentina, was how you had to do it in order to really understand the benefit of it. And also that if it wasn't for the WSIS, the governments of Latin America might not have started on that road. My reaction to the input was that there have been serious efforts to apply the WSIS principles and to reflect on whether it's been valuable. I think the extent to which we're achieving it is still very new. There's sense of beginning to grasp whether we're getting there, but there's still a lot of disconnects between developing countries and the global processes, and perhaps some disconnects between certain stakeholder groups and institutions. Also, when we talk about capacity-building, this includes institutional capacity-building. It's not just about building capacity of governments and individuals to participate in global processes. We've seen what local and regional institutions like LACNIC have achieved and need to keep that in mind. The process of transformation cannot just take place in the global arena, it also needs to take place in national and regional spaces.

JANIS KARKLINS:

Thank you, Anriette. Now I turn to Bill Graham for a summary and then to the chair for concluding remarks.

BILL GRAHAM:

This was a useful session, and it's one we were required to do by the WSIS. A lot of useful information came out, and some good suggestions about what we should look at in the future. The first session I wouldn't characterize as a religious revival meeting, but it indicated that even before the WSIS there was a commitment to what eventually became the WSIS principles. So the WSIS principles didn't arise suddenly out of a few months' meetings in Geneva but, in fact, there was already a developing trend in the world towards more transparent, more democratic, multistakeholder processes. The IGF like the WSIS before it is part of an ongoing evolution, and I don't think that evolution is finished. It was very good to hear specific examples of work that is being done that clearly responds directly to the WSIS principles. I'd point at the Council of Europe initiative on a code of principles for participation, which is a good piece of work. The OECD bringing in the technical community and civil society was an interesting example of best practices.

Certainly there was useful discussion of areas where work still needs to be done. Multilingualism is one of those. Some institutions identified problems that various stakeholders still have with full participation. The presentation by the ITU says that they, as a multilateral institution, don't feel yet that they're fully accepted in the framework of the IGF. That's something we need to note and mark down as requiring work next year, as well as ways to be more inclusive of participants from the developing world. There is no doubt that the developing world is making progress in many cases to increased multistakeholder participation, more open processes and so on. The government of Argentina gave us some examples. I also would point to the comments from France and Saudi Arabia on the importance of the WSIS statement about respective roles. We heard too from business that they have increased their outreach and credit that to some extent to the WSIS. We heard from civil society and technical organizations that they are increasingly engaged with other stakeholders in a multilateral and transparent fashion. We heard more examples from those sides than we did from governments, although it was quite clear that some governments are making an effort to adapt, such as Argentina and Canada.

On the discussion of people-centred and inclusive development in the second section of the session, Bill Drake pointed out that three years of workshops have gone on before there was a main session on this topic, and I was impressed myself by how far those workshops have gone to clarifying the thinking around the concept of Internet governance for development and the specific things that should be focused on going forward. We heard, first in the

426

report from Bill but it came up later several times in the discussion, that although this is a session on the WSIS principles and Internet governance, it needs to be a start, and specifically people-centred development needs to be drawn out as a separate main theme, rather than being an overarching theme as it has been for the first four years. So I think that's an important remark. We heard about benchmarks for people-centred development. Human rights was put forward. Again, lots of talk about how governments can be encouraged to be more engaged, particularly from the developing world. We heard suggestions of increasing capacity-building for government officials in national governments, particularly young people. We heard that even though that is still in its infancy, that kind of capacity-building in some governments is picking up.

One thing we all realize is that participation in open mechanisms is not a simple thing. It's complicated and time-consuming. And there were questions about whether it could be simplified to make that more accessible for government officials. And a number of speakers spoke about the need to think more thoroughly about economic realities and not simply concentrate on idealistic views of participation, and to look at some of the economic factors that work against participation. Finally, there was discussion of the Digital Solidarity Fund and whether there might be other mechanisms to support the ongoing development of these WSIS principles in Internet governance very broadly, and in the IGF specifically.

AHMED EL-SHERBINI:

Let me thank our three very able moderators for giving us a very lively, interactive session. There are two main points that I would like to highlight. One, there is definitely a serious effort being exerted to adhere to the WSIS principles in the Internet governance ecosystem, but there is still a lot of work that needs to be done to get everybody on board and to adhere to the all WSIS principles. The second point that is that there is a need for more serious engagement of the developing countries in the IGF activities, and from here I call on the developing countries governments to get more involved, to make use of this forum, to get their voice heard, to get their opinions debated, and I call on the IGF Secretariat to devise ways to motivate the governments of developing countries to get more involved in the IGF.

Internet Governance in the Light of WSIS Principles:

Reports of the Workshops and Other Events

1. Development

WS 90.   Mitigating the Financial Crisis with Open Source Applications

WS 109.   Greening the Internet

WS 207.   Ensuring Continued Investment and Digital Growth in a Climate of Global Economic Challenges

BPF 236. The Internet in Sweden: Present, Future, Research

WS 237.   Using ICTs and the Internet to Meet Environmental Challenges

WS 279.   Research on Access to Knowledge and Development

WS 291.   Internet Governance: Economic Recovery and Growth

WS 304.   Measuring the Impact of Internet Governance on Sustainable Development

WS 316.   Implementing the WSIS Principles: A Development Agenda for Internet Governance

WS 319.   Workshop on Fundamentals: Core Internet Values

OF 529.   Commonwealth Internet Governance Open Forum

2. Capacity Building

WS 1.   Nigeria Digital Sense Forum-09

WS 87.   2CENTRE, the Cybercrime Centres of Excellence for Training, Research and Education

WS 135.   Teaching Internet Governance: The Experience of the Schools of IG

WS 139.   The Challenges of Becoming Literate to Foster Participatory Cultures

WS 150.   Global Capacity Building for Internet Governance

WS 164.   Partnership in Action: International Examples of Good Practice

WS 186.   Online Education: Maximizing the Efficiency

WS 230.   Youth and Internet Governance: the Way Forward

WS 276.   Assessing the Role of the Participative Web in Youth Empowerment: A Regional Outlook

WS 277.   Internet Governance: Activating and Listening to the Voice of Teens

3. Participation

WS 96.   Code of Good Practice on Information, Participation and Transparency in Internet Governance

WS 200.   Remote Participation: Mapping the Field, Evaluation and Multistakeholder Involvement

WS 212.   Multistakeholderism at the IGF: Assessing the Impact on Participation

1. Development

WS 90.   *Mitigating the Financial Crisis with Open Source Applications*

Report by: Lillian Sharpley

Moderator: Dr. Viv Padayatchy

Panellists: Christian Roland (General Secretary of Club des hommes et femmes d'affaires du libre en Afrique; VP of FOSSFA, and COO of ASSIST); Samer Azmy, (FOSSFA Council Member); Michuki Mwangi (Internet Society); Dr. Viv Padayatchy (General Manager of Cybernaptics Ltd; Chairman of Board at AfriNIC); Ben Akoh (Information and Communication Technology and Media Program Manager at the Open Society Initiative for West Africa)

The workshop aimed to create awareness on open source application/technology and how this can be used to reduce the financial burden on an organisation's IT infrastructure, especially with the challenges that have been brought about by the global financial crisis. Emphasis was placed on Africa and developing nations.

There was a panel of five speakers who:
- Defined open source software, its background and how it is managed;
- Explained the difference between open source software and proprietary software;
- Provided alternate solution to proprietary software using open source and suggested specific solutions for common business processes. –
- Showed a cost-benefit analysis of open source software and proprietary software;

- Provided case studies of open source software deployments in government sectors.

At the end of the presentations, the audience was allowed a period to ask questions and share ideas and recommendations. Below are the key issues that were raised by speakers and participants during the panel discussion:
- Governments should be encouraged to maintain technology neutral policies to allow both proprietary and open source to allow fair competition.
- Marketing strategies should become more of a priority for open source developers and distributors, putting more emphasis on the end-user and less on the technical aspects.
- Open source is mature enough to offer alternate solution.
- There should be in increased understanding that Open Source is not necessarily free as there is a cost associated with implementation and maintenance.
- More funding should be made available to open source application developers, as this is a very important aspect to encourage them to continue with their open source projects, just as was seen with the Python Project, which was made possible because of funding and is now a success.
- Regarding the business aspects of implementing open source, there are no vendors and support and business training is required. Again, emphasis should be placed on the end-user who is not always technical. It was noted that vendors exist on the proprietary side and marketing is being done to the end-user in a less intimidating manner.
- It is a myth that open source is unstable, citing the decision of the French Police Department to switch to Ubuntu, operating system.
- The cost of license management is not only financial but has a legal obligation.

It was agreed that FOSS should continue to be a topic of discussion at IGF to continue to increase awareness about a cost effective solution for business operations; to increase the understanding of FOSS; and, to increase the support of FOSS software developers. Other conclusions were:
- FOSS faces challenges in Africa that needs to be addressed in more organized way.
- FOSS needs more support in Africa.
- FOSS awareness in Africa is one of the main challenges.
- Governments should be encouraged to maintain technology neutral policies to allow both proprietary and open source to allow fair competition.
- Marketing strategies should become more of a priority for open source developers and distributors, putting more emphasis on the end-user and less on the technical aspects.
- Open source is mature enough to offer alternate solution.
- There should be in increased understanding that Open Source is not necessarily free as there is a cost associated with implementation and maintenance.
- More funding should be made available to open source application developers, as this is a very important aspect to encourage them to

continue with their open source projects, just as was seen with the Python Project, which was made possible because of funding and is now a success.

- Regarding the business aspects of implementing open source, there are no vendors and support and business training is required. Again, emphasis should be placed on the end-user who is not always technical. It was noted that vendors exist on the proprietary side and marketing is being done to the end-user in a less intimidating manner.
- It is a myth that open source is unstable, citing the decision of the French Police Department to switch to Ubuntu, operating system.
- The cost of license management is not only financial but has a legal obligation.

WS 109. Greening the Internet

Report by: Preetam Maloor

Moderator: Arthur Levin (Head, ITU Telecommunication Standardization Policy Division)

Keynote: Malcolm Johnson (Director, ITU Telecommunication Standardization Bureau)

Panellists: Catherine Trautmann (Member of European Parliament); Joseph Alhadeff (Vice President for Global Public Policy, Oracle); Catalina McGregor (Deputy Champion Green ICT, UK Government); George Sadowsky (Director, ICANN); Alice Munyua (Convener, Kenya ICT Action Network); Tony Vetter (Project Manager, IISD); Nezar Sami (Director, Information Systems Department, Nile University)

Internet based-applications are a key to unleashing many opportunities for real solutions to climate change, such as smart homes, smart appliances, smart transportation and smart energy grids. Many companies today are already recognizing that going Green is not just "nice to do", they are doing this as it makes good business sense. The ICT industry has been making progress in energy efficiency and the use of renewable energy, and best practices can be already shared. Even new technologies such as NGN, are innately green compared to their predecessors. The ITU-T through its SG-5 is examining possible standards to measure and reduce the impact of ICTs on the environment to help advance the Green ICT. Energy efficiency is the easiest and quickest thing companies can to do reduce their consumption. Some obvious examples can be found in new types of data centres, and innovative techniques such as water cooling, air cooling, flywheel storage, virtualization of servers, etc. Virtualization and cloud computing have now added an interesting dimension to increasing efficiency through the Internet.

The Panellists spoke and presented on a wide range of issues concerning the Internet and Climate Change and agreed on the importance of including ICTs and the Internet in any future global agreements on climate change. Issues addressed included policy and regulatory frameworks, the need to build more energy efficient data centres, sustainable development, trends toward more energy efficient networks of the future and green universities. Ms. Munyua presented research from Kenya on e-waste that showed the dangerous effects from toxic ITC equipment that is shipped to the country.

WS 207. *Ensuring Continued Investment and Digital Growth in a Climate of Global Economic Challenges*

Report by: Daniel J O'Neill

Moderator: Daniel J. O'Neill (GIIC Executive Director)

Panellists: Anders Halvorsen (WITSA Director of Public Policy); Graham Vickery (Head, Information Economy Group, OECD); Masanobu Katoh (GIIC Commissioner and Senior Vice President, Member of the Board, Fujitsu, Keidanren); Waudo Siganga (National Chairman of the Computer Society of Kenya, World Information Technology and Services Alliance Vice Chairman and Board Member); Virat Bhatia (AT&T and Federation of Indian Chambers of Commerce and Industry); Richard Beaird (Senior Deputy United States Coordinator, International Communications and Information Policy US Department of State)

The Workshop examined the challenges facing all economies at this time, with a special recognition that policy and regulatory decisions are critical in developing economies to address the continued need for investment in high speed networks, Internet access and services, and supportive policies for growth and development. Using a multi-stakeholder approach in workshop organization and delivery, aimed to identify initiatives of the private sector and of governments, including the important roles of governments "as users". Participants were invited to discuss initiatives involving e-health, e-government; e-education and ICT and the Environment. Emphasis was placed on highlighting relevant policy drivers that are supporting continued digital growth in the current economic environment. The workshop aimed to identify key policy themes as its objective. The workshop feature participants from different perspectives and geographic regions discussing why continued investment in high speed networks and increased Internet access is critical to ensuring continued growth and development by providing the necessary access and opportunity for economic expansion.

Anders Halvorsen, set the stage by informing the group that -based on recent data from IHS Global Insight-, after three quarters of contraction; the world economy began to recover in the second quarter of 2009. Leading indicators were improving across regions and the global inventory correction was winding down. Financial markets stabilized, but credit remained tight. A moderate recovery was likely in 2010 and strengthening growth in 2011–12. The speed of regional recoveries was expected to vary, with Asia leading, the Americas in synch with the global cycle, and Europe lagging. The recovery was expected to be weak—at least initially. Despite fears, wage and price inflation would likely remain tame. The dollar would weaken, but not collapse.

Mr. Graham Vickery presented the workshop with a technology policy viewpoint of the use of ICT in the economic crisis. He presented survey data showing that 12 of 14 countries responded to a survey said they had increased their ICT policy priorities for economic recovery. The three main areas cited for these increases were: ICT skills and employment; broadband and technology diffusion to business. The second component of Mr. Vickery's presentation was on the government and industry initiatives on green ICT. On the government side, the review of 92 government programs showed a vast majority of these programs designed to directly impact the use of energy. In terms of targeting areas for "enabling impact" of government green ICT initiatives, the focus was more wide spread on the use, distribution and manufacturing elements of technologies associated with global warming and energy use. In terms of drawbacks to the development of these green initiatives, there seem to be few programs that have instituted measurable for evaluation – governments tended to do a better job establishing these goals than industry.

Masanobu Katoh made a report on recent progress towards a human centric networked society and new challenges for the future. Cloud service capabilities through advanced ICT are required to handle the significant increase in diverse data flows. Whereas cloud computing entails advanced networking between servers, middleware, new applications, data centres and supercomputers, in the real world, "human centric" interfaces connect us to what we really care about; goods, resources and information. ICT enables us to connect to our real-world surroundings. Cloud based services create new business opportunities. One exciting such new technology is the Fujitsu's model Raku-Raku Phone, which offers advanced accessible technologies to improve the intelligibility of mobile communications. A "slow voice" feature ensures that incoming speech is slowed down on the receiver to aid in hearing, and a "clear voice" feature provides that incoming and outgoing speech is enhanced for clarity. Mr. Katoh explained that supercomputing technology makes high-level simulations a new possibility, while supporting cloud based services to contribute to the advancement of industry. In one such instance, through a collaborative research with the University of Tokyo, Fujitsu is helping to build a first Multiscale / Multiphysics Heart Simulator. Through exascale computing, real time replication of a human heart's operation will be possible. In conclusion, Mr. Katoh stressed that through "human centric" networks connected to our real world, ICT provides high-value solutions to address universal challenges.

Mr. Waudo Siganga informed the group that the November 1-3, 2009 WITSA Global Public Policy Summit (GPPS 2009) resulted in a "Bermuda Declaration for the ICT Sector". The Declaration encourages business and government alike to embrace ICT and place ICT in their plans and programs as a strategic economic driver for recovery and future sustainable economic growth. In addition, Mr. Siganga added, carefully crafted and flexible public policy attracts and facilitates innovation, trade and investment, information flows, and infrastructure. Specifically, the Declaration stated that:

- ICT is a proven driver for global economic activity and growth.
- The economic growth generated by the development of the ICT sector will benefit all economies.
- Access to ICT and the knowledge and information provided by the Internet is an important part of an inclusive information society and is essential for broader sustainable economic growth.

- Public-private partnerships are a critical part in building ICT infrastructure and an information society.
- There should be an open trading system between nations free from barriers for ICT products and services. We urge WTO Members to reach the compromises needed to achieve a successful conclusion to the Doha Development Agenda with an ambitious and balanced outcome, including comprehensive results in services.
- Harnessing the power and benefits of ICT for society will not come automatically. Only if business and governments work together with other partners, including their education systems, can people everywhere be assured of access to ICT tools and the knowledge and empowerment they deliver.
- International strategies to tackle climate change need to make full use of ICT as one of the most powerful tools available, and one of the only ones that can produce dramatic changes without negative effects on prosperity or individual lifestyles.
- With the pressure on global public finances, Governments should recognize the use of ICT and technology-enabled change as tools to address their operational costs and efficiencies.
- The continued success and growth of ICT depends on trust and confidence; privacy and security should be appropriately integrated into ICT programs, systems, and products from the beginning."

Mr. Virat Bhatia made the point that –in the absence of trade barriers- ICT can be an enabler in both developed and developing markets, in times of growth and in times of decline. In rural India, over the past two years, more than 250 million new mobile phones were sold. The most popular such phone is a $15 Nokia pre-paid phone. Customers in rural India can get by with as little as $5 in monthly prepaid charges, revolutionizing the way business is conducted in these areas. A new generation of Indians are now connected, spurring growth of mobile banking and other electronic payment services throughout the countryside. As much as 98 percent of mobile connections in India are prepaid, characterized by affordability and absence of debt. In a country with a mere 13 million Internet connections, mobile penetration now has surpassed 500 million customers. The exponential growth of the Indian mobile market has taken place due to technology innovation and affordability, as well as sound business practices. Notably, growth in this low-wage market has been remarkably strong without any form of government subsidies or other involvement. Mr. Bhatia was optimistic that similar growth could be achieved in other developing country markets around the world. However, the level of investment needed in developing countries was more likely to come from a few large investors rather than many smaller actors. Governments have a very important role in building a legal framework that supports foreign direct investment, and in removing trade barriers.

Mr. Richard Beaird supported Mr. Bhatia's notion that affordable technology solutions, such as the $15 Nokia pre-paid phone in India, offers the best hope for growth of ICT products and services in developing country markets. Public policies must take these developments into account. Countries must find the right public-private partners in order to ensure economic recovery. Universities, the private sector and governments are all important players in the road towards economic growth and innovation. Mr. Beaird stressed that broadband development was critical for long-term growth and innovation. Broadband is central to eGovernment and all other e-services. As we are entering into the cloud computing era, Mr. Beaird explained that opportunities will emerge in developing as well as developed economies. With diverse demographics around the word, ICT businesses can thrive in markets selling $15 phones as well as $300 smart phones. Industry also needs to look at cloud computing as broadly as possible, so as to benefit customers and enterprises in the developing as well as the developed world.

Interaction with the audience of 30 people focused on the viability of public-private partnerships as a means to encourage continued ICT investment in the current economic climate. Mr. Graham Vickery pointed out that, in OECD countries, investments in ICT are made predominantly by the private sector. In building public-private partnerships, the parties need to carefully set both technical and performance goals.

Mr. Waudo Siganga agreed. Mr. Siganga added that governments are often major sponsors of major infrastructure projects, and that the lack of adequate regional ICT infrastructure to support high-quality and high-speed Internet connection in Sub-Saharan Africa is recognized as a major obstacle for setting the region's economic and social development in motion. Consequently, a number of initiatives are underway to create regional – and national - backbones, and some of these initiatives are private-public partnerships. The need for these regional backbones has been made even more urgent in light of the Tunis Agenda for the Information Society, adopted by the UN World Summit on the Information Society in November 2005, which asks multilateral institutions and bilateral public donors to consider providing more financial support for regional and large-scale national ICT infrastructure projects. Without access to affordable infrastructure, there will be little chance of building an information society. As part of the global agenda to improve communications and data transfer technologies, South Atlantic 3/West Africa Submarine Cable (SAT3), a high capacity optic fibre, was laid along the Western coast of Africa, from Morocco to South Africa. Similarly, a cable has been laid along the entire North African coast up to the Red Sea. The Eastern Africa Submarine Cable System (EASSy) is another initiative to connect countries of eastern Africa via a high bandwidth fibre optic cable system to the rest of the world. It is considered a milestone in the development of information infrastructure in the region. EASSy is planned to run from South Africa to Sudan, with landing points in nine countries, and connected to at least ten landlocked countries – who will no longer have to rely on expensive satellite systems to carry voice and data services. The project, partially funded by the World Bank, was initiated on January 2003, when a handful of companies investigated its feasibility. The cable is fully funded through public and private means and will be ready for service in the second half of 2010.

Mr. Virat Bhatia pointed out that public-private partnerships, such as embedded in many economic stimulus programs, are not without faults. Mr. Bhatia mentioned that, in many stimulus programs, only a very small percentage of allotted funds have been actually spent on targeted projects. Using his own company's experience in the Indian mobile market as an example, Mr. Bhatia believed that economic growth can be facilitated by corporations as long as unhindered access to markets are ensured.

Mr Katoh believed governments could play a pivotal role in developing partnerships in some additional areas, notably in next generation networks and exascale computing. E.g. a new initiative, dubbed the Institute for Advanced Architecture, is set to lay the groundwork for an exascale supercomputer that would be more than 1,000 times faster than any current offering. If achieved, it would represent a thousand-fold increase over that scale, possibly by 2018. Dick Beaird urged workshop participants to consider the trade implications for the emerging era of cloud computing, including whether current trade rules are adequate in this regard.

Looking forward, the growth of Cloud Computing Based Network Services will be shaped by market forces and technology innovations. These are largely evolutionary in nature, playing out over the course of years. These advancements, however, will not take place in a vacuum. Public policy decisions may have an immediate impact. Dominating the discussion are security, privacy, spam, competition policy, spectrum availability, and standards. How society deals with these challenges will determine whether the cloud computing and next generation networks (NGN) are able to reach its fullest possible potential. Meanwhile, users are likely to enjoy a variety of new services and lower costs for existing products. Increased IT productivity, the combination of once distinct products, and industry consolidation could cause a digital deflation, reducing IT spending and employment. GIIC and WITSA may choose to explore these challenges further at the next Internet Governance Forum in Vilnius.

BPF 236. The Internet in Sweden: Present, Future, Research

Report by: Anders Johanson

Organizer: PTS, The Swedish Post and Telecom Agency

Moderator: Paul Kane

This workshop gave a concert picture of leading Internet implementations, high usage, leading quality and balanced control mechanism. Several public private partnership development projects like "Ambient Sweden" were presented and discussed in the workshop as well as research work on Mobile Life and services on 100 Mbit mobile networks. The session deals with best practices, particularly in Sweden.

Sweden currently holds the Presidency of the EU. As a country Sweden has a population of 9.2 million people. Sweden's GDP is 454 billion dollars which has a per capita income of about 36,000 dollars per year. The government is a constitutional monarchy and a vibrant parliamentary democracy. The country has a highly independent, local government structure, comprising of 24 regions. Each region has a high level of autonomy under the nation-state laws. In terms of exports the electronic sector leads the way with electronics and telecom equipment, machinery, cars, paper, medicine, iron and steel.

Industries are obviously Volvo, Eriksson, Electrolux and Idea. The Nobel Prize is given out on the 10th of December of each year.

Sweden is one of the top five nations in the world concerning Internet penetration and Internet services. The Swedish telecom regulator authority – PTS - has worked out strategies and goals for the robustness of Internet in Sweden, and has the governmental responsibility to overlook the implementation and usage according to Swedish law along with extensive multi stakeholder co-operation. Examples were shown how the strategies and goals are being full filled by private public partnerships.

The mission of the project Ambient Sweden is to make Sweden a leading Internet nation in 2015. The steps through implementing ten focused topics from October 2008 to December 2009 were described. Human resources from industry, government, operators and academia are actively involve in the projects. SICS is one of the most famous Internet research institutes in Sweden, used by operators manufactures and government in Sweden. SICS showed what applications can benefit from the new mobile technology LTS when users will have up to 100 Mbit capacity in their mobile phones in the future. This research is part of Ambient Sweden and Mobile Life, combining technology with users and society. The vision is that you will always be connected to Internet by your mobile phone.

- It was interesting to learn how a nation on a private public partnership (PPP) are planning for a national task to became a leading Internet-nation
- The workshop were interesting, covering the current issues of today, the plan for the future and Sweden cooperating with other nations
- The emphasis in Sweden is very much one of strong partnerships where government, the regulator is there to assist parties, to inform parties of the duties they should undertake.
- The regulator PTS, importantly, create the forum where parties can exchange information in a secure way without worrying that the information exchanged could be used against them in an anti-competitive, or hostile way.
- Public/Private Partnerships are well established within Sweden and that is one of the ways they are driving the well being of their economy.

Good experiences on how a nation can develop it's robustness for a stabile Internet and plan for further challenges

People at the meeting comment that the goals for the project Ambient Sweden were both technical and social, and noted that there were challenges in the balance among several goals.
- The Ambient Project and Östen kindly said he and the group are willing to disseminate information to interested parties, interested countries wishing to emulate what they were doing in Sweden.
- The driving factor is the Secretariat, the actual core function who actually solicited parties to join the group.
- The Secretariat proactively invited industry, government and others them to participate as well as bringing people. The research part covered research from several areas such as Internet of things, Sweden as a part of EIT ICT Labs, the KIC (Knowledge and Innovation Communities) for the

future information and communication society. All this aims at radical transformation of Europe into a knowledge society with an unprecedented proliferation of Internet based services.

The multi stakeholder approach through public private partnerships was identified as a key success method to develop and integrate Internet usage in all parts of the society. It was also clear that different stakeholders like industry, operators, government, academia and users by building partnerships, confidence and trust can learn from each other and create new knowledge. Several examples of this were shown.

WS 237. *Using ICTs and the Internet to Meet Environmental Challenges*

Report by: Siv Mørch Jacobsen

Moderator: Dr. Hossam Allam, Regional Programme Manager, Centre for the Environment & Development for the Arab Region & Europe (CEDARE)

Panellists: Heather Creech (Director of Global Connectivity, IISD); Finn Petersen (National IT- and Telecom Agency, Denmark); Ignacio Campino (Deutche Telecom); Graham Vickery (Head, Information Economy Group, OECD);

The aim of the workshop was to debate which actions to take in order to utilize ICTs and the Internet to meet environmental challenges. To discuss policies and next steps for improving environmental performance, making more effective use of the Internet in meeting environmental targets, and harnessing the ICT sector's potential for sustainable growth and employment, speeding a green recovery and underpinning green growth in a time of economic turmoil.

Heather Creech emphasized the importance of researching third order/systemic changes, as increased global connectivity causes economic and social transformation.
Several specific issues to tackle were outlined:
- Better analysis of systemic effects is needed including methods to measure systemic effects.
- Application of ICT-enabled networked governance approaches to sustainable development policy-making and implementation.
- An integrated approach to issues and policies at national and international levels.
- Sustained attention to capacity in the South: Revitalization of bilateral, multilateral ODA agencies on ICT: What does "mainstreaming" ICT mean?
- R&D on how to drive "green intelligence" out to the edges where the individual is.

Finn Petersen explained about the Danish approach. In spring 2007 The Ministry of Science, Technology and Innovation started to explore the relation ICT and climate. Use of ICT was estimated to be accountable for 2 percent of the total CO_2 emissions. It was discovered that the negative impact on the climate from use of ICT could be reduced and that smart use of ICT has great potential in reducing the overall impact on the climate. The Action plan for Green IT in Denmark was published in early 2008. ICT is not only a part of the problem, but also very much a part of the solution to the climate challenge. Clear targets needs to be set. Smarter and cleaner environmental and economic strategies and policies will help tackle global warming. This will also contribute to "green growth" in the economic crisis and recovery.

Ignacio Campino stressed the importance of acting now, as the earlier we start, the easier it will be to combat global warming. If global warming can be stopped by a temperature not exceeding 2°C against the pre-industrial temperature, then dangerous damages can be avoided. This means, according to resent research, that the emissions by 2050 have to be halved compared to 1990. The later the peaking year is reached, the more expensive the reduction. Dr. Campino mentioned logistics and mobility, building management, production and industry as well as power supply and networks as areas where the potential is specifically great.

Graham Vickery presented highlights from the OECD report: "Towards Green ICT Strategies: Assessing Policies and Programmes on ICT and the Environment" released in June 2009. The report shows how governments and businesses have a wide range of initiatives dealing with the impacts of ICTs on the environment and climate change. By far most of the initiatives concentrate on greening ICTs rather than tackling global warming and environmental degradation through the use of ICT applications. Mr. Vickery also stressed, that measurable targets for evaluation of policies and programmes are necessary to improve.

WS 279.   Research on Access to Knowledge and Development

Report by: Nagla Rizk

Moderator: Lea Shaver (A2K Director, Associate Research Scholar and Lecturer in Law at Yale Law School)

Panellists: Carlos Affonso Pereira de Souzan (Vice-Coordinator, Center for Technology and Society at Getulio Vargas Foundation, Brazil); Hossam Bahgat (Director of the Egyptian Initiative for Personal Rights); Sherif El-Kassas (Associate Professor at the Department of Computer Science and Engineering, American University in Cairo); Sherif Kamel (Dean, School of Business, American University in Cairo); Nagla Rizk (Associate Professor of Economics, American University in Cairo); Tobias Schonwetter (Faculty of Law, University of Cape Town, South Africa)

The Access to Knowledge Global Academy (A2KGA) held the workshop. Panellists presented research results from partnering academic institutions within A2KGA. These are academic centres dedicated to policy-oriented research, education, and advocacy in the area of access to knowledge and development. They are engaged in capacity building within the access to knowledge framework, seeking to ensure that the potential for knowledge-based development is maximized through programs, technologies, and business models that enable knowledge to be shared widely and to flourish in conditions of freedom, promoting human development. Panellists presented research results from Brazil, Egypt, South Africa and the United States. Research results from other member countries (Argentina, Chine, Ethiopia and India) were cited by the moderator. Presentations were made over 60 minutes, followed by a 30 minute Q&A session.

The purpose of the workshop was to share outcomes of cross-national research on access to knowledge. This cross-national research looks at knowledge in its wider sense, going beyond access to data to encompass the utilization and promotion of knowledge and knowledge-embedded goods, tools and skills. At the heart of this work is the belief in knowledge as an integral component of sustainable human development. The workshop provided a wider perspective on the utility and importance of the access to knowledge framework and its relevance to the developmental needs of the global south. A relatively unfamiliar topic in Egypt, access to knowledge was discussed in the workshop as a framework for the relationship between intellectual property and development.

The workshop focused on three themes within the A2K framework: Access to Education (A2E), Open Source Software (OSS) and Access to Medicines (A2M). These three themes are common in A2K research in the different countries represented on the panel. Of particular importance is the comparative approach to these issues, highlighting the uniqueness of individual countries while distilling common themes in some or all of the countries under study. This emphasizes the belief that intellectual property should not be dealt with as a one-size-fits-all, but rather nuanced to respond to the developmental realities of each country. It is fair to note that while studies included more detail than could be presented in one hour, the presenters made it a point to give the audience a flavour of the research done in each country, even if the emphasis and detail came out different for each country and respective theme.

Access to Education (A2E)

Nearly all A2KGA participating countries have conducted research on educational copyright and regulations. Research in China and Ethiopia shows that the current laws are inadequate in enabling access to education. The following paragraphs summarize the research of South Africa, Brazil and Egypt.

In South Africa, The Freedom Charter sets out learning and access to books as essential aspects of a democratic society. The Access to Knowledge in the South Africa study reveals that access to learning materials (A2LM) is a central factor in A2K. It was found that most South African academics tend to favour a less strict copyright regime. Moreover, South African Copyright Act and Regulations are outdated. In fact, the Copyright Act neither makes use of existing copyright exceptions and limitations nor properly addresses the digital environment. Also, provisions benefiting sensory-disabled learners and distance education are insufficient. The six case studies covered in the South Africa study reveal that South African A2K initiative are short-lived and hence lack capacity building aspects for a long term access to knowledge framework.

Research on access to knowledge in Brazil depicts the general picture of copyrights in Brazil, arguing that strict copyright laws in Brazil have forced people to resort to illegal methods of accessing knowledge goods. Unlike South Africa where exceptions and limitations exist, there are no copyright exceptions for access to educational material in Brazil. Nonetheless, Brazilians have found many legal as well as illegal channels of access to knowledge. The A2K channels in Brazil include the use of P2P software, creative commons licensing as well as the use of cyber cafés in the poor areas, which rely on illegal infrastructure and Internet connection. The study describes the model of Techonobrega Music, where artists sell their music to street vendors at a low price, providing a unique model of integrating street vendors in the chains of production. Finally, collaboration in access to knowledge in Brazil is the reason behind the noticeable development of the Portuguese Wikipedia.

The Access to knowledge in Egypt study reveals that for the past 24 years various initiatives and programs in Egypt have targeted ICT diffusion and e-readiness. The study highlights that ICT can be a path to access to knowledge; however, this requires enabling policies and emphasis on education. Further, the speaker explained that knowledge itself is key to the improvement and development irrespective of the sector or field. It is worth noting, that diversity and language are important issues when discussing A2E in Egypt.

In conclusion, more work is needed to expand access to educational materials and technologies in countries of the South. There is also a need for including and utilizing exceptions and limitations to copyright for educational purposes.

OSS as a Platform for A2K

Research in Argentina and South Africa reveals various benefits of adopting OSS tools. These studies highlight that the variation of legal frameworks poses problems for adopting OSS tools. They argue for the benefits of OSS in their respective countries. The following paragraphs summarize the research presented for Egypt.

The chapter on the software industry in Egypt adopts a bottom-up approach via on the ground research interviewing different players from the proprietary as well as OSS providers, in addition to consumers and policy makers. The authors present two opposing trends within the software industry. On the one hand, the Internet and technology have created transparency and allowed for different market players and free flow of information. On the other hand, the unique characteristic of the production of knowledge with high production cost for the first unit and zero cost of duplication opened the door for large multinational owners of intellectual property. In fact, the latter gave rise to business structures of monopolistic nature. The new economy thus experienced opposing forces where information technology changed the boundaries between firm and market, encouraging small firms while simultaneously expanding mergers and acquisitions into larger structures. The tension between proprietary and open source software falls at the heart of these two opposing forces.

The authors examine models of software providers that are common in Egypt, explaining how most stand to benefit from OSS. They also explain how in reality OSS industry in Egypt is stunted, calling it "an infant exposed". There is lack of competition as much as there is scope for OSS platforms to promote human development. The authors conclude that the OSS industry is an issue of competition rather than one of intellectual property. They call for the creation of an enabling environment that provides scope of business build around OSS. Future research in this area should investigate software production and means of adaptability to the Egyptian local market.

Access to Medicines

The Access to medicine research in Egypt looks at the impact of intellectual property laws on people's right to affordable medicine. The research investigates the tension between health and trade on the one hand and the IP laws on the other, calling for a human rights approach to access to medicines in Egypt. The authors argue that a human rights-based approach is the most powerful way to guarantee affordable access to medicines in Egypt. This, however, would require the Egyptian government to actively address the primacy of the right to health, despite potential conflicts with IP regulations. In order to promote, protect and fulfil the right to health, the government should apply the provisions in TRIPS agreement.

The study highlights that Egypt is the biggest consumer as well as producer of drugs in Middle East, which creates sizable benefits for pharmaceutical companies and adds pressure on policy makers. The authors analyze three court cases to highlight the different attempts to influence the IP regime. They conclude that foreign pharmaceutical companies will continue to have vested interest in restricting generic competition. This would require the development of a coherent human rights argument regarding the legal priority of access to medicines.

Additionally, Egypt should establish more interaction between different governmental bodies in order to adopt a more coherent stance in FTA negotiations. Such interaction would also include key stakeholders from other sectors such as specialized agencies, the private sector and civil society. Egypt should also be more transparent in the negotiation of IP and trade treaties. This requires the active participation of civil society.

Below are conclusions reached based on a vibrant discussion and audience comments following the presentations.

Dialogue with Policymakers. Panellists as well as workshop participants recommended that access to knowledge research findings and policy recommendations be communicated to policy makers within countries. Indeed, this will be the first item on the agenda of the Access to Knowledge for Development (A2K4D) Center, to be inaugurated at AUC next February. This point is particularly relevant to OSS in Egypt. It was rightfully noted by the audience and agreed to by panellists that there is little demand by the Government of Egypt for OSS. This calls for raising awareness as well as providing training and education on OSS. Finally, it is worth noting, some of the research findings in Brazil and South Africa are already being reflected in ongoing policy reforms

Connection to global A2K players. Panellists agreed to a comment from the audience on the importance of furthering strong connections with the global A2K movement. This is something that members of A2KGA have been active with, perhaps individually given its recent establishment. Indeed, this workshop is our first group presentation as one team. It will be the first of many proactive endeavours as one team on the global scene.

Regional connections. On the regional level, it was announced that the Access to Knowledge for Development (A2K4D) Center at the American University in Cairo will act as a regional hub for access to knowledge research in the Arab world. Additionally, A2K4D is to identify potential partners throughout the region to carry out further research. An invitation for collaboration in this respect was also made at the conclusion of the workshop.

Translation to local languages. Additionally, it was emphasized that translation of the cross-national research to native languages of researchers would widen the impact of the research results within each nation. Panellists agreed; A2KGA members will pursue this recommendation.

Comparative research. Comparison and analysis of cross-national research outcomes would help identify best practices and lessons learned within the framework of access to knowledge for development. This could be accompanied by an ongoing online platform for discussions amongst researchers on access to knowledge. Indeed, this was discussed during the last meeting of A2KGA in August 2009, and is already on the research agenda of A2KGA.

Role of libraries. it was highlighted that libraries and archives could play an important role in providing access to knowledge. This could be facilitated through the enlargement of copyright exceptions and limitations across the board.

WS 291.   *Internet Governance: Economic Recovery and Growth*

Report by: Luz Rodriguez

Organizers: ICC BASIS, and Government of Lithuania Information Society Development Committee

Moderator: Herbert Heitmann (Chair ICC's Commission on E-Business, IT and Telecoms (EBITT), Chief Communications Officer, Global Communications, SAP)

Panellists: Joseph Alhadeff (Vice President Global Public Policy and Chief Privacy Officer, Oracle, USA); Mohamed Elnawawy (Vice President for Corporate Strategy, Telecom Egypt, Egypt); Desiree Miloshevic (Visiting Industry Research Associate, Oxford Internet Institute, United Kingdom); Aurimas Matulis (Director, Information Society Development Committee under the Government of the Republic of Lithuania); Nermine El Saadany (Director of International Relations Division,

Ministry of Communications and Information Technology, Egypt); Former Ambassador David Gross (Partner, Wiley Rein)

Panellists and participants had an interactive exchange on how addressing Internet governance issues appropriately can stimulate economic recovery and growth. Economies can be boosted by putting in place the necessary legal, policy and regulatory approaches that promote innovation, infrastructure and investment in the Internet and ICTs.

The panel began with the results of the Oxford Internet Institute Policy Forum discussion paper "The New Economic Context of Internet governance" that showed that there was no immediate evidence that the economic downturn has caused any changes or call for changes in the roles of stakeholders in Internet governance processes. Nonetheless, Desiree Miloshevic questioned whether there will be more regulation or more liberalization as a result of the economic crisis. She believed that the recent signing of the Affirmation of Commitments between the US Department of Commerce and ICANN is an example indicating that the response will be greater liberalization. She urged governments to support the Internet as an essential driver of economies, stating "it's the oil that makes everything move smoothly." She discussed a case study that examined the United States Stimulus Bill aimed at creating jobs and as a sign that a stronger Internet sector was perceived by policy makers as a key facilitator to the economic downturn. A remaining question is who will make next investments- private sector or government. Participants also considered whether there was a difference between governments' use of stimulus plans, where those in mature markets may implement policies to protect existing industries during economic downturns while those in emerging markets may support investment in ICT as a source for future growth. Panellists cited figures that support these claims- 25 million jobs can be created globally due to ICTs, especially mobile broadband. This is because of multiplier effects, as an example, for every 1 ICT job created in India, 4 non-ICT jobs are created.

Joseph Alhadeff described the "I's" that are part of the APEC checklist: infrastructure, innovation, investment, information flows, intellectual capacity, integration (trade), implementation and inclusion that are key elements of an environment that enables ICT-driven economic growth. Nermine el Saadany discussed Egypt's experience. Her ministry has been working with the private sector, using a bottom up approach to policy development, listening to their views to develop their development strategy. Panellists suggested that Egypt was successful because they put in place the right foundation. "You can throw money at technology but without the right foundation it won't take- you need to optimize investments," stated Joseph Alhadeff.

Aurimas Matulis shared how his office, which is charged with coordinating the information society in Lithuania, implements projects related to infrastructure development. He has found that cooperation with the private sector in explaining how and what to access as well as the advantages of using ICTs has improved issues related to lack of skills and knowledge and improve the ability of ICTs to drive economic growth. In Lithuania, state financed rural fibre connections have also played an important role in building an environment for small and medium enterprises to offer services. This is particularly important for countries like Lithuania, where one third of the population lives in rural areas. Recently, more than 20 small new Internet Service Providers (ISPs) have started in rural areas. As a result, while the overall economy shrunk 20% in 2008, during the crisis, the percentage of people connected to the Internet grew by 11%. Proper state regulation also contributes to the growth of ICTs. For example, the Lithuanian regulator is flexible providing licenses for Wi-Max and other technologies and provides them free of charge.

Mohamed Elnawawy discussed the importance of adequate infrastructure, using the direct fibre connections to Egypt and Africa as examples. Although there is currently a moderate amount of infrastructure currently connecting the south to the north, forecasts show a large increase in the near future. He discussed the need for diverse connections, specifically to avoid outages due to accidents such as cable cuts that recently occurred that could pose extreme detriment to economies.

Participants questioned why, when there was strong commitment to the relationship between ICTs and growth so few most senior political leaders are focused on this issue, Ms. El Saadany thought political will and empowerment was necessary. She cited the positive example of Egypt, where the highest levels of government are committed to promoting development by improving ICT infrastructure and access. In this case the political empowerment stems from the fact that the Prime Minister is a former ICT Minister- political empowerment. She also discussed the need for private public partnerships which can't happen without senior leader support. Others cited the Global regulatory symposium, an annual event that discusses how future policies should be developed, as an example of government leadership looking at the role of ICTs.

A participant from Kenya encouraged global business organizations to support local business associations by reaching out to their members through capacity building programs. He thought this would inform private public initiatives and help industry communicate their needs better to governments. Participants also discussed what companies are doing to build capacity, including establishing local partnerships to offer training academies. It was emphasized that training needs to start at earliest levels of education-linguistic, etc. and that there was an equal need to teach the teachers as technology evolves.

The panel concluded that to spur economic recovery and drive growth, there must be awareness among world leaders to the advantages of getting Internet policy right. The workshop highlighted many promising examples of highly flexible regulations stimulating economic growth, but panellists felt there was more that could be done to bring other sectors into the loop.

WS 304. *Measuring the Impact of Internet Governance on Sustainable Development*

Report by: Tony Vetter

Panellists: Heather Creech (Director, Global Connectivity, IISD); Dr. Hossam Allam (Head, ICT4D, CEDARE); Susan Teltscher (Head, Market Information and Statistics Division, ITU-D); Alan Finlay (Consultant to APC)

Mechanisms are needed to monitor the impact of Internet policy and governance choices. How do we determine whether these choices are helping to achieve the broader sustainability goals of humanity? What do Internet policy makers need to measure to find out whether they are "getting it right"? This workshop provided an opportunity for participants to explore the range of indicators needed to monitor whether Internet policy and governance choices are leading to an Internet that is supporting social, environmental and economic goals, as well as innovations in accountability and governance. The workshop was organized to be interactive, using a breakout group format to engage participants directly rather than rely on a traditional panel format.

Report from Environmental indicators breakout group

- This breakout group had something of a clean slate in that not a lot of work has been done yet on Internet and supporting technology environmental indicators. Here are some of the ideas for such environmental indicators that were discussed.
- Tracking ICT re-use vs. recycling vs. disposal rates
- Percentage of material used in ICT manufacture that is recyclable at end-of-life - Average life span of ICT products prior to recycling or disposal
- Carbon footprint reduction resulting from e-service use
- Public awareness of ICT re-use or recycling options
- Availability of environmental content on the Internet
- Corporate greening of ICT infrastructure
- Incentives for greening ICT infrastructure

Report from Economic indicators breakout group

- There is a need to develop indicators that explicitly address the impact of ICT on GDP. Could potentially look at:
- Volumes of ICT exports and imports
- Employment rates in ICT related industries
- Income generation in ICT related industries
- Need more research into implicit measures of ICT on GDP. For example
- Measuring the impact of ICTs on efficiency
- In-depth analysis of ICT impact on productivity in other sectors – services, etc.

Report from Social indicators breakout group

- It was necessary to attempt to classify the issues before identifying gaps for further work.

- Initial classification organized as follows:
- Gender
- Access to the Internet on gender
- Internet literacy - Access by gender
- Gender specific content
- Education
- Quantity or quality of access
- Universities that have access
- Health
- Telemedicine facilities
- Solidarity
- Amount and speed
- Disaster management and relief
- E-government
- Quantity
- Access
- Timeliness

An initial general observation made by Heather Creech was that the indicators advanced by each of the breakout groups appeared to parallel the Millennium Development Goals (MDGs) in many ways. It was agreed that this was worth exploring further.

In terms of Internet and supporting technology environmental indicators, Susan Teltscher commented that not a lot of work has been done there yet and that this is an area where it would be important to focus more discussion. She expressed interest in taking initial learnings from this session to such discussions. She also noted that monitoring the availability of environmental content on the Internet as a measure of the success of awareness raising efforts had promising implications for furthering environmental objectives. Regarding Internet and supporting technology economic indicators, Susan noted that in the case of the indicators forwarded by that breakout group, we already have well developed definitions for those which would make it easier to move to the data collection phase. Once the data is available country level academics and policy researchers would do the analysis.

Susan acknowledged that identifying workable Internet and supporting technology social indicators is a significant challenge. She commented however that some notable progress had been made on this front by UNESCO in their work developing and using indicators of ICT use in education. This work identified ten core indicators and about thirty more through their work with developing countries to look at the impact of ICT use on education. Susan also pointed out that the World Health Organization is conducting its second global e-Health survey to gather evidence on trends and uptake of the use of ICT for health. In general terms Susan commented that speed and quality of access are very important technical indicators when monitoring the impact of Internet and supporting technology social indicators. On the topic of the MDGs, Susan recalled that at their very early stages of development there was work done to link ICTs to the MDGs but that effort was eventually dropped. The reflecting on the discussions at this workshop she commented that it might be worthwhile picking that up again.

Hossam Allam commented we do not currently have a good development index that includes Internet and supporting technology indicators. As an example, Hossam suggested that we should be looking to incorporate Internet and supporting technology indicators into indexes such as the Human Development Index (HDI).

Alan Finlay cautioned that the point of entry issue for this workshop is huge and it is important not to set the bar too high. Alan pointed out that surveys are a key instrument for collecting relevant indicator data. A case in point, monitoring progress on environmental objectives has more to do with changes in behaviour, not the take up of ICTs. Where do you development these indicators, in the ICT sector or the environmental sector? It is important to focus on measuring human impact.

After the workshop the co-organizers met to explore how these observations might inform further work in this area. There was some discussion regarding the increasing acknowledgement the impact that ICTs have on the environment, including their contribution to the problem of climate change, as well as a tool for addressing environmental issues. It was noted that an analysis by The Climate Group in partnership with the Global e-Sustainability Initiative (GeSI), and McKinsey suggests that smart solutions enabled by ICT could save 7.8 Gt CO2e in 2020, or 15% of global emissions in 2020. However co-organizers all felt that there has as of yet been little action to developing a coherent and structured approach for advancing the development of ICT statistics that could be used to monitor the impact of ICT on the environment and climate change, as well as the effectiveness of ICT applications upheld for their environmental management and impact mitigation potential.

It was agreed that the availability and agreement on such statistics will become increasingly important to developing countries as they rapidly develop their ICT infrastructures and user communities. Effective indicators to monitor the impact and benefits of their management of this growth will be critical as they join the rest of the international community in tackling the problems of climate change, reducing the impact of ICT production and consumption on the environment, as well as developing intelligence strategies for managing their environment using ICTs.

IISD took the action to further explore with the co-organisers the potential for North and South partners working on the use of ICTs for environment and climate change to join forces with those working on the development of ICT indicators in a coalition. Such a coalition could explore working together on a scoping study on this topic which could be used to engage with the Partnership on Measuring ICT for Development on a broader program of work; opening the way for a more integrated suite of indicators measuring ICT for sustainable development.

WS 316.   Implementing the WSIS Principles: A Development Agenda for
            Internet Governance

Report by: William J. Drake

Organizer/Moderator: William J. Drake (Senior Associate, Center for International
Governance, Graduate Institute for International and Development Studies, Geneva,
Switzerland)

Panellists: Anriette Esterhuysen (Executive Director, Association for Progressive
Communications, South Africa); Derrick Cogburn (Associate Professor of
International Relations, American University, and Senior Scientist and Chief
Research Director at the School of Information Studies, Syracuse University, USA);
Olga Cavalli (Advisor to the Ministry of Foreign Affairs, and representative to the
Governmental Advisor Committee of ICANN, Government of Argentina); Christine
Arida (Director for Telecom Planning and Services, Egyptian National Telecom
Regulatory Authority (NTRA), Government of Egypt); Alice Munyua (Convenor,
East African IGF and Kenya ICT Action Network, Communications Commission,
Government of Kenya); Hong Xue (Professor of Law and Director of the Institute for
Internet Policy & Law, Beijing Normal University, China); Fiona Alexander
(Associate Administrator [Head of Office] for International Affairs, National
Telecommunications and Information Administration, Department of Commerce,
Government of the United States); Elfa Yr Gylfadottir (Adviser, Office of Cultural
Affairs, Ministry of Education, Science and Culture, Iceland)

The Tunis Agenda's WSIS principles on Internet governance comprise both
procedural and substantive prescriptions. The former state that governance
should be conducted in a manner that is multilateral, transparent, democratic,
and fully inclusive of all stakeholders. The latter state that governance should,
inter alia, ensure an equitable distribution of resources, facilitate access for all,
and be an essential element of a people-centred, inclusive, development-
oriented, and non-discriminatory information society. Taken together, these
latter principles suggest that Internet governance should help to advance
development objectives. In addition, the Tunis Agenda mandates the IGF to,
"Promote and assess, on an ongoing basis, the embodiment of WSIS
principles in Internet Governance processes." Implementing the substantive
WSIS principles and this element of the IGF mandate would require that
stakeholders use the collaborative opportunities afforded by the IGF to assess
and encourage governance mechanisms' contributions to development. But
unfortunately, the development dimension often has been overlooked in
discussions of the WSIS principles and the IGF mandate.

Accordingly, this workshop sought to help redress the problem by fostering a
dialogue that took seriously the concept of IG4D and by exploring ways to
promote its realization in both the IGF and Internet governance mechanisms.
More specifically, the workshop considered the possible establishment of a
development agenda for Internet governance that would facilitate
implementation of the WSIS principles and the IGF mandate. A development
agenda is a holistic program of analysis and action intended to mainstream
development considerations into the procedures and policy outputs of global
governance mechanisms. While there have been concerted efforts to pursue
such agendas in the multilateral institutions dealing with issues like

international trade and intellectual property, there has been no broad-based discussion of a corresponding initiative for global Internet governance.

This was the third in the series of IGF workshops intended to foster such a discussion, each of which has built upon and gone beyond its predecessors. The first workshop, "Toward a Development Agenda for Internet Governance" was held at the IGF in Rio de Janeiro in 2007. Participants considered the general desirability of pursuing a development agenda and agreed that a properly configured and consensual initiative could help to promote an open, accessible, diverse, and secure global Internet. The second workshop, "A Development Agenda for Internet Governance: From Principle to Practice" was held at the IGF in Hyderabad in 2008. Here participants began to explore the possible substantive focus and operational aspects, and inter alia affirmed that the IGF is the most appropriate venue in which to elaborate a cross-cutting and flexible agenda that could encourage development-oriented enhancements within Internet governance institutions. The third workshop, held at the IGF in Sharm el Sheikh, sought to advance consensus building on the substantive focus and operational aspects of pursuing an agenda in light of the WSIS principles mandate.

Because the workshop enjoyed an expanded three hour time slot, it was possible to engage a wider than usual range of speakers. The panellists included seven females and one male---five governmental and three nongovernmental representatives, from seven countries around the world. In addition, the increased time allowed ample opportunity to probe the issues deeply and to have a robust discussion with the sizeable audience. Two online platforms were used in parallel, and about a dozen people participated thereby from around the world. All the online participants' questions were read out by the moderator during the open discussion portion of the program and addressed by the panellists.

The workshop proceeded as follows. To set the stage, the moderator began with an overview presentation that summarized the evolution of the discussion to date, both in the previous IGFs and related events organized in Geneva and by the Global Internet Governance Academic Network (GigaNet); outlined four possible substantive elements of development agenda; and proposed two possible options for taking the process forward in the IGF and beyond. The speakers then drilled down into the details of these elements and options and offered comments on related matters as well. This was followed by an extended Q&A segment with the audiences in the room and online.

With regard to the substantive focus of a development agenda, the first possible element discussed was capacity building. Panellists and audience members shared examples of initiatives underway and of challenges encountered in seeking to enhance the ability of developing countries to participate effectively in global Internet governance. Other points raised included the importance of building the skills and knowledge of both governmental and nongovernmental actors; tailoring capacity building to different governance institutions and local environments; leveraging widely available and low-cost technology and applications for distance education and empowering online collaborations; and recognizing that capacity building is a necessary but not sufficient condition of effective participation, as it must be blended with other steps (such as those discussed next). A development agenda could include mechanisms to aggregate and make more accessible and usable information on the various initiatives and experiences, to identify good practices, and so on.

The second possible element discussed concerned institutional and procedural improvements to reduce barriers to effective participation. Workshop participants noted that developing country representatives from government, the private sector, the technical community, and civil society can encounter a variety of formal and informal barriers in intergovernmental, private sector, and even multistakeholder governance arrangements. These may include, inter alia, restrictive rules on admission, speaking and document submission; the location, cost, and timing of meetings; organizational culture, language, and working methods; and asymmetries in knowledge, technology and power that can frustrate efforts to influence agendas and outcomes. Here too, it was agreed that development agenda could helpfully organize and present information on conditions and experiences, identify good practices, and encourage improvements.

The third element discussed concerned the substantive policy issues on infrastructures and critical resources that a development agenda could address. The global governance mechanisms that have the strongest and most direct impact on the Internet---i.e. those for names and numbers, technical standards, and network security---are responsible for managing a range of issues that can entail distinct developmental concerns. However, as participants noted, these concerns usually are not the focus of concerted deliberation and action. In contrast, some ICT global governance arrangements---e.g. those for telecommunications, trade and development assistance---often are more explicitly focused on developmental concerns, but they have weaker and more indirect effects on the Internet. In this context, a number of workshop participants dwelled in particular on related challenges concerning access to and pricing of network infrastructure, international interconnectivity, and the like.

The fourth element discussed concerned policy issues raised by public use of the Internet for information, communication and commerce. The global governance mechanisms that have the strongest and most direct impact on use of the Internet---e.g. those for intellectual property, cybercrime, digital trade and global electronic commerce, and cross-border information flow and content---also address a range of issues with important developmental dimensions. In particular, intellectual property and access to knowledge attracted sustained commentary from workshop participants, some of whom expressed concerns that developing countries' prospects could be sharply limited by current and proposed governance frameworks. Concerns were also raised about the comparative weakness of other relevant governance mechanisms, such as those for privacy and consumer protection and spam reduction, and the implications thereof for developing countries. In sum, workshop participants identified a number of substantive policy issues that could be productively monitored and assessed in order to encourage governance institutions to blend a development perspective more fully into their processes and outcomes.

The workshop discussed two broadly framed options for taking a development agenda effort forward. The first was to promote the idea within the relevant global institutions and processes. Not surprisingly, much of the discussion on this point concentrated on the IGF. Among the ideas raised were to make development an ongoing main session theme; organize annually a cluster of interrelated workshops, best practice forums, and open forums; related coordination with national/regional IGFs; and establishment of a dynamic coalition. Also discussed was the promotion of a development perspective within Internet governance decision making bodies; for example, an interest group is in formation among some non-commercial stakeholders in ICANN's Generic Names Supporting Organization. The second option discussed was to advance the development agenda concept through scholarly/policy research institutions and collaborations, and to encourage its incorporation into the work of some of the leading capacity building programs.

WS 319.   Workshop on Fundamentals: Core Internet Values

Report by: Sivasubramanian Muthusamy

Moderator: Lynn St Amour (President and CEO of the Internet Society)

Panellists: Ian Peter (Ian Peter Associates; Coordinator of the Internet Governance Caucus); Daniel Dardailler (Worldwide Web Consortium); Rt. Hon' Alun Michael (MP, United Kingdom); Nathaniel James (OneWebDay); Markus Kummer (Executive Director of the Internet Governance Forum); Alejandro Pisanty (Member, Board of Trustees, Internet Society)

What is the Internet? What makes it what it is? What are its architectural principles? What are the core values? And what is happening to the core values in the process of its evolution? What is it that needs to be preserved and what changes are inevitable? What does the Internet Community say as what can't be changed? How could changes and improvements be brought about without compromising on the core values? How would the different positions between stakeholders be reconciled to commit to the core Internet values? The workshop has been organized to answer these questions and define the core Internet values.

Lynn St. Amour: Internet is much more than a technology. Its origin was not a single act of invention, but very much a process of collaboration and cooperation, based on shared values, processes, practices and ideals that actually underline the Internet, in addition to the technical developments. The Internet Model is characterized by open standards, transparent governance, community-driven processes. with architectural principles governed by a common set of operating values. The model relies on processes and products that are local, bottom-up, and accessible to users around the world.

Daniel Dardailler: On a technical level, Internet is a layer and the Web is an application on top of that layer. The Web is completely independent of the Internet. On the Internet everything is extensible and independent of each other. In comparison with other technologies such as telephone, the Internet is based on open standards, everybody is able to participate in the design process.. These are the principles that came with the development of the Internet. We have one root and need to maintain that because multiple roots would break one of the essential principles The Web is sending data through a pipe and we don't want the data to be looked at by the careers, by the ISPs, for example. We don't want the data to be fast-laned or restrained. This principle of network neutrality is important. Web is the user interface. It is the top of the stack over which applications reside. There are specific principles that govern the worldwide web. The web is accessible to all users, irrespective physical disabilities of the users, and irrespective of the type of devices used to access the web. On the web, content is separate from presentation. The web has a lot of principles -architectural principles that define a resource, address. Even for filtering there are principles. There should be meta data and the filtering should be done objectively. The central principle is the principle of choice: we want users to be able to buy whatever platform, browser, etc. from different places of their choice. With the phone system, it is not like that. The Internet has been on the forefront of choice and participation

RT Hon Alun Michael: We need to grasp three nettles (A nettle is something that if you grasp it leaves you alone, but if you brush against it, makes you turn out in a rash).
- We are dealing with a future not yet conceived, so existing management techniques of the past and present are likely to prove inadequate - i.e. the management tools of the industry, management tools of the government, management tools of the International community, and management tools of legislation- they are far too slow to keep up with the developments and changes of the Internet.
- Core Internet values laid out by Vint Cerf are largely technical values, but Internet is used by all of society and it affects the whole of society - even those who are on the other side of the Digital Divide. It is not just about the architecture of our online city, Cities very often don't turn out as their original architects intended, once they are populated. So, it is not just about technology, but about the behaviour of the inhabitants, in this case, the Internet Users who are now defining the Internet
- We not only have to listen to young people, we need to hand-over to young people (we need to give them a day on the main stage) Young people who grew up with Internet approach the Internet in a totally different way and their talents could be made use of and they could be engaged in a positive way.

IGF needs to help communicate with policy makers, who might not know what this workshop is talking about. Do legislators understand what they are doing? Most legislation is a reaction to demands, requirements and problems, rather than designed to bring about a particular outcome. And on the other side, does the IGF community understand policy makers and legislators? the pressures on Ministers? the Media Voices that very often go for quick solutions by headlines and demand that something be done? Are policy makers overwhelmed by the exaggerated concerns of cyber-security? All that they need to do is to listen to an average speaker from the FBI who would frighten the living daylights out of those who listen to them.

It is true that there are enormous dangers. What is required is proportionate response, which is scientific, evidence based and people based. There certainly is the danger of disproportionate responses in legislation. Are there dangers of over-regulation? Yes--it happens on nearly everything: "Laws rarely prevent what they forbid" If the Internet Community provides answers to some of the people related issues, then there is the opportunity for much better governance in the real world as well as online governance. Proposals to fix a problem threaten the core values of the Internet, but if experts, or, those who care about the core values do not provide answers to problems, there would be crude regulation. We need to show that a cooperative approach works and that core Internet values deliver a healthy community. We have to deliver solutions instead of relying on the last refuge of the policy makers.

Nathaniel James: Article 19 states that everyone has a right to freedom of opinion and expression, through any media, regardless of frontiers. Real value of Internet is in it being a human network of users. A discussion of core Internet values must begin with the human value of users. Do users value the End to End principle, the Open Innovation system, a unified and secure root, the IP address system ? Most of the users do not know about these principles and values. They value the Internet as an expression of their deeper values and aspirations - expressions, collaboration, dissent, freedom, democracy, family, friendship, community, opportunity, justice and fun, of respect the deeper values of Internet. Internet Community is a network of lawyers, experts, engineers, business and NGO leaders, but unfortunately democracy of experts is not a democracy at all, but a technocracy. Democracy requires strategies for grass root engagement. We need to frame Internet controversies over privacy, identity, security etc., in the context of deeper human values. We must begin by reaching out to other sectors – human rights, social services, health sectors and helping understand how Internet Governance has an impact in the realization of their core values.

Markus Kummer: IGF is less of a technocratic gathering than some of the specialized gatherings are - e.g. ICANN which discuss specialized matters that are arcane to the outside world. - IGF has a mix of societal and technological questions. Governments work differently than the Internet Community. Governments and the world of Inter-governmental organs and world of treaties are based on a system that came out of the Westphalia Peace Conference of 1648, on the principles of sovereignty, hierarchy, pyramids. Internet is the opposite of all that-- it is borderless, it is bottom up, it is a network of networks, it has very flat hierarchies, it is about cooperation, collaboration, not about giving orders to subordinates. IGF is an attempt to bring these two cultures together.

Nation state has a very well-structured way of operation. On the Internet, networks are forming independently of formal hierarchy. This is an interesting development. Governments are struggling with this and how the Internet undermines the existing processes. It becomes difficult to combine the sovereignty of the nation state with the freedom of the borderless world. The IGF has adopted the principles of the Internet--open, collaborative, transparent and the intelligence is at the edges.

Alejandro Pisante: Internet was conceived as a means of communication between computers. Before Internet computers that shared the same protocol communicated within their networks, but not outside their networks. Internet got various networks to communicate with each other with a common protocol. The computers became inter-operable and this was done by merging standards. It was necessary to make the protocols extra-simple to make the computers communicate across networks.

Standards were developed without hierarchy--as the Internet network had no hierarchy. For instance the Request For Comments (RFC) which as a part of the Internet standard making process, are always provisional, always subject to improvements. One of the principles outlined in Interesting concepts that originated in RFC760, extended in RFC 1122 was "Be liberal with what you receive and conservative with what you send» This was a technical standard at that time, but later became RFC 1855 which is netiquette translated to human behaviour of not complaining about receiving what one doesn't like and not sending out unnecessary communication. This is a very fundamental principle that is built into the technology, protocol. Openness on the Internet is about your computer being open to receiving all sorts of communication which translates to the user being tolerant and open to receive communication, and the network being open to communication. 'openness' has technical and human/organizational dimensions (i.e. "layer 8" discussions such as network neutrality) and is one of the values that is under threat. This is tolerance of communication, one of the core values under threat. "layer 8" is human and organizational restrictions imposed over network communication.

The network operators are to treat all packets as equal. They are not to give preference to their own or favoured traffic, as in the case of an ISP who owns a television company giving preference to its television content over other content on the Internet. The Internet is distinct from the "owned network" model, such as that of phone companies who owned the cables, equipment and even the telephones. The telcos are trying to take the Internet back to the owned network model through the NGN (and sometimes 'new' is actually going back to the old, what is called 'change' is change backwards.) To really continue this innovation in communication, allowing smaller companies and smaller civil society organizations their respective roles and not let these be crushed by constraints that are artificially built into the technology, or operated without being inbuilt.

Ian Peter: A 1983 study looked at mass media, and came up with the idea that the purpose of all this media is the development of human kind. We can apply that to the Internet. Internet is a tool for our development. As a tool for our development it is an extraordinarily powerful one, an extraordinarily useful one. Technologies have a way of evolving: examples include radio, telephone, Internet, how TV is watched. Telephone was invented as a music device. Radio began as ham radio for people to talk to each other. Internet started as mainframe computers talking to one another, then personal computers were added and now the most dominant device is the mobile device. We don't watch television the way we used to. In Hollywood, the era of the blockbuster is finished. The Internet community understands this: the principle of constant change is the only constant principle that should continue for the Internet The principal of constant change is the only principle that should continue for ever In the middle of this change what do we need to protect?

Interdependence of applications and permissionless innovation
- Open Standards - vendor neutral - (I can use any computer)
- Accessibility
- Globally inclusive
- User choice
- Easy of use
- Universality - trans boundary - (I can use it anywhere)
- Freedom of expression - (I can say what I want)
- The ability to change rapidly
- Trustworthy and reliable

The Internet model is open, transparent, and collaborative and relies on processes and products that are local, bottom-up, and accessible to users around the world. This needs to be preserved. We need to preserve the system of a single root. The principles of network neutrality and platform independence must also be preserved. We need to involve young people who grew up with the Internet and are bound to approach the Internet issues in a totally different way and their talents could be made use of and they could be engaged in a positive way. IGF needs to help communicate with policy makers. On the other side, the IGF community needs to understand policy makers and legislators as also the pressures on Ministers

People have to become Internet-wise just as people need to become street-wise. On Security issues, what is required is proportionate response, which is scientific, evidence based and people based. "Laws rarely prevent what they forbid" We need to show that a cooperative approach works and that core Internet values deliver a healthy community. The Internet Community has to deliver solutions instead of relying on the last refuge of the policy makers. The panel proposed to continue discussing this topic by forming a dynamic coalition for the next few years. The panel commented that IGF and ICANN are complementary, and should not seek to duplicate functions.

OF 529.   Commonwealth Internet Governance Open Forum

Report by: Subhodeep Kundu

Panellists: Joseph V. Tabone (Chairman CIGF); Anthony Ming (Commonwealth Secretariat); Alice Munaya (KICTANet); Fred Ruth Murray-Bruce (Nigerian Communication Commission); Jahid Jamil (Domain Name Dispute Resolution Center, Pakistan)

Mr. Joseph opened the forum with a key note address about Commonwealth Federation & Commonwealth Internet Governance Forum. He highlighted the role of CIGF for the future of IGF and the purpose of the travel bursary to the 18 CIGF Travel Bursary recipients. Mr. Ming described the structure of Commonwealth Federation by describing the representation of 2 billion people, 53 countries in Commonwealth and most importantly highlighted the representation of 30 % of the world population and most importantly the youth consists 50% of it. He explained the shared value of governance, human rights & collaboration in Commonwealth. He also briefly described origination of Commonwealth Connect in 2005 at Malta and how CHOGM endorsed the revolution of report prepared by a coordination committee, which resulted in the creation of Commonwealth Connect by following the principles of share, learn & improve. He mentioned that how IGF would be instrumental in finding the gap in telecom & IT infrastructure and providing inputs, as well the role as the enabler for digital divide. He mentioned that the Secretary General(CW) has created a new strategic advisory committee by bringing Mr. Kiran. Karnik as the head of it and emphasising accelerated multistakeholderism.

Ms. Munaya explained the transition of East Africa's participation in IGF and Kenya's virtual support for the continuation of IGF beyond 1010 by conveying their interest to host the IGF2011 at Kenya. She highlighted the importance of: Cost of Internet access, broad band policy, IPv6 transition process, and harmonisation of equipments. Ms. Murray explained about the West Africa's participation in IGF and how Nigeria proactively taking forward IGF. She mentioned that IGF is about accessibility to capacity building and Commonwealth has greater voices than the individual countries and thus upheld the values of sharing & collaboration. Mr. Jahid elaborated, how the Commonwealth & the SAARC countries can share knowledge, best practices & know how to the respective countries and about Pakistan's progress in ICT policy & regulation. He highlighted the pain areas regulation & governance.

- Pain areas regulation & governance.
- West Africa's participation in IGF
- Transition of East Africa's participation in IGF
- Structure of Commonwealth Federation & Commonwealth Connect programme

Among several issues & discussion the some of the points that got importance's and the voices:
- Digital divide seems to be common in every where irrespective of demography & geographies.
- Capacity building programme required
- Accessibility
- Security

2. Capacity Building

WS 1.   Nigeria Digital Sense Forum-09

Report by: Nkemdilim Nweke

Organizers: Digital Sense Africa (DSA) an initiative of Remnek Kommunications Ventures (RKV) in collaboration with the Nigerian Communications Commission (NCC)

457

The participants of the Nigeria Digital Sense Forum held at the Golden Gate Ikoyi-Lagos on "Internet Governance: Creating Opportunities for All Nigerians" on Thursday, November 5, 2009, organized by Digital Sense Africa (DSA) an initiative of Remnek Kommunications Ventures (RKV) in collaboration with the Nigerian Communications Commission (NCC), called to mind that a harmonized voice within the Nigerian Internet community is critical to the development of Internet in the country and the sub-region and the continent in entirety. Also, they called to mind that harmonized voice among Nigerian Internet community will provide Nigeria the opportunity to have a united front before confronting the world at the Internet Governance Forum (IGF) scheduled to hold in Sharm El Sheikh, Egypt between November 15 and 18, 2009.

The event was presided over by the Chairman of Linkserve, the pioneer Internet service provider in Nigeria, Chief Chima Onyekwere, while Among the IT personalities that attended the one day preparatory forum and contributed were Chief Chima Apugo Onyekwere, Chairman Linkserve, Dr. Emmanuel Ekuwem, President, Association of Telecommunications Companies of Nigeria (ATCON), Mr. Lanre Ajayi, President, Nigeria Internet Group (NIG), Mrs. Mary Uduma, Vice President, Nigeria Internet Registration Association (NiRA) and a Director at the NCC and represented the Regional Liaison Manager for Africa at the Internet Corporation for Assigned Names and Numbers (ICANN); Mr. Mohammed Rudman, Managing Director, Internet Exchange Point of Nigeria (IXPN) Limited, Mr. Titi Omo-Ettu, Chief Executive, The Executive CyberSchuul, Mr. Gbenga Sesan, Executive Director, Paradigm Initiative Nigeria (PIN) and Ms. Boma Kalaiwo, Director, Lagos Operations, Federal Radio Corporation of Nigeria (FRCN), who represented the Honourable Minister of Information and Communications, Prof. Dora Akunyili.

The Nigeria Digital Sense forum 2009, identified security as a major issue of concern for the Nigerian Internet community. Additionally, we call to mind that the global Internet Governance Forum afforded the Nigerian Internet community to come together alongside other communities from around the world to ensure optimization of Access, Openness, Security, Diversity and Internet Governance. Equally, we call to mind that the release recently by the United States' Affirmation of Commitment to the global Internet community via the Internet Corporation for Assigned Names and Numbers (ICANN); is a welcome development that could endear the trust of those hitherto not comfortable with the arrangement which began with the US Department of Commerce (DoC). Hence, in alignment with the outcome of the West African Internet Governance forum, held in Accra-Ghana, especially in the areas of encouraging African countries to take the issues of Internet Governance more seriously by ensuring engagement of stakeholders at IGF level.

Therefore:
- It was agreed that members of the Nigeria Internet community must be encouraged to participate at the forthcoming Internet Governance Forum and actively too.
- Make pronouncement with respect to the security of the Internet and discrimination thereof, especially meted out on honest and God fearing

Nigerians who are more interested in engaging positively with the world on the Internet.

- The discrimination against Nigeria's based Internet Protocol (IP) address should stop because it is negatively affecting the majority of Nigerians who are confidently engaged on the Internet.
- Both the government of Nigeria and Internet community in the country should strive in enlightening the populace and the world over on the keenness of the majority of Nigerians in deploying Internet for ICT for Development (ICT4D) growth.
- Nigeria's Internet Service Providers (ISPs), especially members of the ISP Association of Nigeria (ISPAN), Association of Licensed Telecom Operators of Nigeria (ALTON) and Association of Telecom Companies of Nigeria (ATCON), should connect without further delay with the Internet Exchange Point of Nigeria (IXPN), so as to encourage local Internet to remain local, which has multiplier effect, including saving money for both the ISPs and customers – the end-users.
- Nigeria should canvass for a root server to be located in the country to further push and retain local traffic locally.
- Also, members of the ISP Association of Nigeria (ISPAN), Association of Licensed Telecom Operators of Nigeria (ALTON) and Association of Telecom Companies of Nigeria (ATCON), should ensure compliance by ensuring registration of their domains in the country code Top Level Domains (ccTLD), .ng.
- This will make the .ng commercially viable and eventually give the ccTLD the need popularity it needed to be feasible among equals.
- Nigerian participants at the IGF 2009 must ensure that alienation of Nigeria's IP address (IP blocking) is stopped and that Nigeria has the population to push its desire and voice to be heard in Egypt and at all conferences in relation to Internet and its governance even beyond IGF.
- There is need to refocus Nigerian youths engaged in online fraud (cybercrime) otherwise known as „Yahoo, Yahoo□ by way of granting them amnesty followed with skilled training and adoption into the mainstream, in order to positively utilize their talents.

Enjoining Nigerian stakeholders to:
- Ensure maximum participation at all times, at Internet Governance related forum.
- Strengthening the partnership of the forum through collaboration with relevant Ministries, Departments and Agency of government, mostly at the federal level including the National Information Technology Development Agency (NITDA), National Broadcasting Commission (NBC) among other public private partnership.

WS 87. 2CENTRE, the Cybercrime Centres of Excellence for Training, Research and Education

Report by: Jean-Christophe Le Toquin

Moderator: Jean-Christophe Le Toquin Director, Internet Safety, Legal and Corporate Affairs, Microsoft Europe Middle-East and Africa

Panellists: Dr. Joe Carthy (Head of School UCD School of Computer Science and Informatics University College Dublin); Alexander Seger (Head of Department of Economic Crime and Information Society Directorate General of Human Rights and Legal Affairs Council of Europe); General Amir Alphonse Sadek Tadros (General Department of Information and Documentation – Interior Ministry of Egypt)

The audience was made of 60+ experts. The Q&A session lasted 45-50 minutes. Questions from the room came from:

- Various geographies: Pakistan, Bangladesh, Egypt, Nigeria, Zambia, Belgium, France;
- Various backgrounds: ministry of information, legal advisors on cybercrime, NGO (freedom of expression), academia.

In developed and developing economies, Law enforcement has insufficient training options in IT forensics and cybercrime investigations and rely on courses provided by INTERPOL or foreign national law enforcement.

In addition, a number of countries have developed their own law enforcement cybercrime training programmes either alone or in conjunction with academic institutes. Law enforcement has also been provided with and availed of a large number of training courses, seminars, conferences and hands-on training provided by different industry players in locations throughout the world. Both groups of actors – law enforcement and industry – have arrived at the realization that ad hoc training provided on request or as part of ongoing but irregular support services do not provide sustainable, scalable, standards based, measurable skills delivering the requirements of the cybercrime forensics investigator today.

In order to continue the development and delivery of effective cybercrime training to law enforcement on an international level, it is necessary for them to partner with learning organisations and industry to create a network to take responsibility for the programmes and academic oversight, and where possible, offer of appropriate academic qualifications. Law enforcement and industry face the same challenges, both in countries with developed or developing economies: they do not have a scalable and sustainable program to educate their staff in investigating or addressing cybercrime.

A program like 2CENTRE, which aims at building capacity for law enforcement at national level, while at the same time building international cooperation between national centres of excellence against cybercrime, met the interest of the participants.

WS 135. Teaching Internet Governance: The Experience of the Schools of IG

Report by: Olga Cavalli

Organizer: Olga Cavalli (Professor Universidad de Buenos Aires)

Panellists: Olga Cavalli; George Victor Salama (National Telecom Regulatory Authority, Egypt); William J. Drake (Graduate Institute International and Development Studies, Geneva, Switzerland); Wolfgang Kleinwächter (Professor

University of Aharus, Denmark); Avri Doria (Professor Lulea University); Sandra Hoferichter - Euro SSIG)

Internet Governance is a cross-cutting theme and there were no specific teaching programs that covered all aspects of Internet Governance from an integral perspective. The Workshop objective was to describe the experience of the three Summer Schools on Internet Governance that took place during 2007 and 2008. Many of the former students of the different IG Schools are now deeply involved in different IG processes like ICANN, teaching or in Government roles ruling the Internet.

The value of the IG schools is bringing younger participants broadening the participation especially from representatives from developing countries, all with a multistakeholder approach and with a multi-background experience. The workshop reviewed the existing experiences and new improvements to be implemented in the IG schools after the three successful experiences. These were the main issues identified:

- In each School local and regional aspects are specially considered, in order to make it a relevant learning space for young professionals interested in IG.
- For faculty members is challenging to finding a correct level of complexity in their presentations as the students have different backgrounds and knowledge base.
- Logistics and preparation is a main part of the success, and is a complex task to do, specially the stage related with the selection of the fellowship candidates that will attend the Schools.

The three experiences, Europe, Arab Counties and Latin America, have resulted successful experiences in relation with the local and regional impact and with the high involvement of new participants in the IG process.

WS 139. The Challenges of Becoming Literate to Foster Participatory Cultures

Report by: Lee Hibbard

Organizers: Dynamic Coalition on Media Education, Cyber Peace Initiative, UNDP Egypt's ICT Trust Fund and the Council of Europe

Panellists: Samy Tayie (Professor of Public Relations and Advertising, Faculty of Mass Communication, Cairo University, Egypt); Ibrahim Saleh (Officer of the Academic Council on the United Nations System); Sheba Mohammed (Policy Analyst, Trinidad and Tobago); Malte Spitz (European Youth Forum); Andrew McIntosh (Parliamentary Assembly of the Council of Europe); Hosein Badran (Regional Chief Technology Officer and Distinguished Systems Architect, Cisco Systems International, Egypt); Yasser Kazem (Director of the E-Learning Competence Center of the Ministry of Communication and Information Technology Egypt); Ahmed Hefnawy (Converging Services Manager, National Telecom Regulatory Authority, Egypt); Nevine Tewfik (Director, Cyber Peace Initiative, Egypt); Divina Frau-Meigs (Dynamic coalition on media education); Lee Hibbard (Council of Europe)

Millions of people are using the Internet throughout the world today. The Internet has an enormous potential for improving the quality of life of its users in many different ways. Promotion of Internet literacy is vital for societies that depend on digital information. A number of projects are aiming to promote Internet literacy among the population, especially for children. But what are the risks of using the Internet without having previously acquired the appropriate skills and knowledge? How can individuals be trained to use the Internet? What should the role of different stakeholders be?

The challenges and risks to users were considered from a variety of regional perspectives. This examination showed that there were differences between developed countries and developing ones, in their understanding of risks and challenges. For the MENA region, issues of access and dependency on foreign content were a major concern. The imbalance was also felt in the Caribbean area as well as the Latin American region: some cultures are downloading cultures whereas others are uploading cultures. So participation in the culture of the digital networks is crucial for providing regional and national content. These challenges were less felt by the European region contributors: media rich in content and access, they were more concerned with inclusion and media rights in the context of human rights (freedom of expression, privacy, dignity,…).

But in spite of these differences, there was a general perception that, for Internet to become a tool for empowerment, there was a need to prevent the digital world from becoming a source of alienation as there are risks of loss of identity and addiction, not to mention spam and unsolicited marketing, as well as risks of content becoming only entertainment-driven. The general consensus was that there was a need to foster participation in the digital networks, combining it with the protection of young people from harmful content and with state provision of quality content to ensure that people engage with the media and feel motivated to contribute in ways that make sense to their personal needs. Becoming e-literate was also perceived as a means of creating trust in the media in regions where there is a lot of malaise about the media, as they are perceived as too dependent either on the State or on Corporate interests.

The e-competences needed for effective participation in digital cultures were discussed within the larger context of media literacy. The Internet was considered as part of the media family, with a specific function, interactivity, leading to participation and citizenship enhancement. Becoming literate with Web 2.0 technologies was considered as a turning point in media literacy, because of the possibilities of putting the learner at the centre of the process, with tools and platforms that foster user-aggregated content. There was a general feeling that letting young people use the media was not enough. The e-competences identified by most participants, especially young people, focused around the need to understand and master processes of navigation, search and retrieval, mixing and remixing of data, collaborative production, joint-authorship, etc.

This implied also considering the human rights that were solicited by such processes and activities. Freedom of expression was mentioned, together with privacy, intellectual property and child protection. It was however perceived that e-competences had to be promoted as "self-competences" that could have an impact on lifelong learning and critical knowledge acquisition. Such self-competences were seen as one of the best filters again harmful content as well as a means to foster motivation in participation as well as trust in the digital media.

The different stakeholders made proposals as to their role in empowering individuals, within an Internet governance framework. There was a sense of urgency as people imagined the worst-case scenarios, such as doing nothing to foster e-literacy. Besides those who worried that Google use would be e-literacy by default, people considered other options: becoming literate might help some countries leap-frog into participatory cultures; becoming e-literate might happen while being illiterate... The Internet governance framework was solicited so as to foster a global feeling of sustainability and solidarity around media literacy, each region benefiting from the sharing of experiences with others. Multi-stakeholder partnerships were considered as vital for scaling up and many examples were mentioned.

The representatives of governments and states agreed that media literacy should be promoted bottom-up and not top-down, by persuading operators and legislators to showcase the best practices and the existing communities of practice, so as to reach young people and adults alike. Business representatives, providers and operators, recognized their crucial role in providing easy and cheap access to the full web experience; they also insisted on their capacity to raise awareness about media literacy issues, especially among young people. Civil sector representatives, educators and NGO members, insisted on the need to move from access to active use, and to integrate the recent developments in mobile telephony, so as to embed e-competences more deeply in the daily practices of young people.

This workshop, co-organized by the Dynamic Coalition on Media Education, Cyber Peace Initiative, UNDP Egypt's ICT Trust Fund and the Council of Europe, was very well attended and many contributions of value came from the floor as well as from the panellists, with noted comments from youth representatives. It examined the challenges and risks of using the Internet without having previously acquired the appropriate skills and knowledge. It then discussed the meaning of those e-competences in order to foster effective participation on the digital networks. It concluded with a common examination of the role of different stakeholders.

The three convenors of the workshop wrapped up the major conclusions and suggestions for future action:
- Connect with human rights and issues of respect, dignity, freedom of expression and privacy
- Connect with e-learning and emerging issues of cross-literacy and media convergence
- Connect with policy-making, within a global Internet governance framework
- Raise awareness for media literacy, with initiatives like the Dynamic Coalition for Media Literacy or the Cyber Peace initiative
- Provide assessment tools, benchmarking frameworks, public policy solutions, private-civic-public experiments.

WS 150. Global Capacity Building for Internet Governance

Report by: Rajeshree Dutta Kumar

Panellists: Dalia Zaki (Programme Assistant, UNDP, Egypt); Tracy Hackshaw (Internet Society Ambassador, Trinidad & Tobago)

In recent years, developing countries, civil society organisations, and concerned academics have sought to promote broad development agendas in the international institutions and policy debates dealing with such issues as trade, debt, and intellectual property. But in the field of Internet Governance (IG), such parallel initiatives have yet to take shape in adequate numbers and frequencies. Accordingly, the purpose of this workshop session was to begin a multistakeholder dialogue on the nature of a possible development agenda in Internet Governance.

An interesting cross-section of the Internet Governance community was in attendance including representation from the Ministry of Communications & Information Technology in Egypt, the Department of Information Technology from the Kurdistan Regional Government in Iraq, the Internet Corporation for Assigned Names & Numbers (ICANN), the Directorate of e-Government in Kenya, the Commonwealth Secretariat/DiploFoundation and Interliaise from the Netherlands.

The panellists decided to organize more of a roundtable setting with full interaction facilitated by Mr. Hackshaw and Ms. Zaki. Ms. Zaki introduced the session by pointing out that in order for Global Capacity Building in the area of IG to be successful, key public policy issues need to be examined in the areas of:
- Infrastructure and Management of Critical Internet Resources
- Privacy & Security
- New Economic models/e-Commerce
- Networks - linking telecentres
- Video & Visual methods of knowledge transfer
- Training the Trainers
- United Nations organisational support

Mr. Hackshaw added to this list, observing that non-traditional areas were in dire need of support and exploration including:
- Relevance & Localisation of Content
- Mobile & the emergence of significantly high levels of mobile penetration in the developing world
- Digital Convergence
- Youth, Gender & the Environment

With the above in mind, the following questions needed to be answered: Which of the many issues involved in Internet Governance should be given priority in the near-term? Could new approaches to these individual issues collectively constitute a holistic and coherent development agenda, and what would be the benefits and risks of pursuing such a framework? How can these concerns best be taken forward within the distributed array of governmental, intergovernmental, private sector, and multistakeholder governance mechanisms?

As the roundtable discussions moved forward, the following key points emerged in response to the posed questions:

- Even if IG or ICT standards or policies are developed, which body will ensure that they are enforced? Mr. Hackshaw referenced ISOC's Internet Ecosystem in providing a snapshot of the various actors involved in IG
- Training and capacity building were urgently needed in the area of Cybersecurity.
- It was stressed that capacity training and not just training was what was required in the developing world i.e. focusing on materials dealing with traditional media and new media.
- Where will the budget and funding for the expansive requirement for Capacity building come from? Top down? Bottom Up?
- In the developing world, ICT and IG issues are not necessarily aligned with national priorities such as a clean and regular supply of water, affordable and adequate health care, etc. Any capacity building effort must take into account the different needs and priorities of different countries - a "catch-all" solution is highly unlikely to be sufficient
- Related to the points raised above, it was noted that ICT and IG issues did not currently form a visible part of the United Nations' Millennium Development Goals. To this end, it is extremely difficult to (a) obtain/raise national or governmental support and funding for ICT/IG issues and (b) obtain external multi-lateral funding for same

So, how do we take this approach forward? At the conclusion, there was a significant perception that a fully participative multi-stakeholder approach including Civil Society, Faith-based organisations, Business, Government representatives and Academia somewhat akin to the concept of IGF itself was required. Whether this approach is meant to drill down to the local or even grassroots levels remains a great unanswered question.

WS 164. *Partnership in Action: International Examples of Good Practice*

Report by: Martin Boyle

Chairman: Ian Taylor (MBE, Member of the UK Parliament)
Panellists: Lambert van Nistelrooij (Member of the European Parliament from the Netherlands: Ambient Assisted Living, a programme to improve life of elderly through ICT); Osama Manzar (Founder, Digital Empowerment Foundation: Examples from South Asia); Lesley Cowley (CEO of Nominet: Nominet Best Practice Challenge); Henry Warren (Gemin-i.org, Rafi.ki Project); Will Gardner (CEO Childnet International: Hearing the voices of young people); Cheryl Langdon-Orr (Director of auDA, co sponsor of the Australia-New Zealand Best Practice Awards); Andrew Miller (Member of the UK Parliament: Make It Happy programme)

This workshop aimed to highlight the exciting projects that have been recognised by the Manthan Project in South Asia, the UK Best Practice

Challenge and the Australian & New Zealand Best Practice awards as making the Internet a better, safer, more accessible and more entertaining place.

Speakers outlined the motivation for the different initiatives. They emphasised the importance of learning from others and for promoting the exchange of ideas. The awards also help recognise achievements from the organisations that have made a real difference in their communities. The Australian and New Zealand Internet Best Practice Awards work focus on security, access, openness and diversity, four key themes in the IGF, as well as a best youth initiative.

The UK's Nominet Best Practice Challenge started with a similar focus on four IGF themes, but has evolved these to cover six areas of interest: development, security, personal safety, raising industry standards, the Internet for all, and open Internet. The Manthan Awards predates the IGF – it has been in existence since 2004 – and looks for best practices in e-Content and Creativity. Originally looking at India, it now addresses eight countries in south Asia: India, Pakistan, Bangladesh, Nepal, Sri Lanka, Maldives, Bhutan & Afghanistan in 13 categories.

Lambert van Nistelrooij MEP introduced the Ambient Assisted Living Joint Programme. This is a joint research and development funding programme implemented by 20 European Union Member States and 3 Associated States. The objective of the programme is to enhance the quality of life of older people through the use of Information and Communication Technologies. The motivation is the demographic change and ageing in Europe. The concept of Ambient Assisted Living is;

- To extend the time people can live in their preferred environment by increasing their autonomy, self-confidence and mobility,
- To support maintaining health and functional capability of the elderly individuals,
- To promote a better and healthier lifestyle for individuals at risk,
- To enhance security, prevent social isolation and support maintaining the multifunctional network around the individual, and
- To support carers, families and care organisations.

Osama Manzar highlighted the case of Barefoot College which won the Manthan Award in 2006 and has been showcasing its work at all the subsequent award ceremonies. The Barefoot College is a non-government organisation that has been providing basic services and solutions to problems in rural communities, with the objective of making them self-sufficient and sustainable. These "Barefoot solutions" cover areas like solar energy, water, education, health care, people's action, communication, women's empowerment and wasteland development. It has developed contacts to use the Internet to sell rural handicrafts, now generating an income of Rupees 6 million. The University of Colombo had won an award for work on a Patient-Centric Telemedicine Solution. Osama also highlighted their work on developing a repository of case studies.

Andrew Miller MP briefly described the UK Parliament initiative Make IT Happy: this is a UK wide competition for primary school students aged 9 to 11. In 2009 the challenge was for the children to show how they would use IT to make people happy. For 2010, the award will be for schools that show how they have helped their community learn about the exciting possibilities of the Internet. Cheryl Langdon-Orr outlined the range of applications that the Australia-New Zealand Best Practice Awards had seen, including from local State and Federal government. She highlighted the work of Hector's World on addressing cyber bullying and the New South Wales Rape Crisis Centre.

From the Nominet Best Practice Challenge, Henry Warren described the work of Rafi.ki (www.rafi.ki), the winner of the best development project: it provides a secure online learning community that lets school pupils talk to children in schools all over the world, with schools in over 114 countries engaged. This included auto-translation services. Will Gardner outlined the work of Childnet International's KIDSMART web site (www.kidsmart.org.uk), winner of the personal safety on-line award, which offers a wide range of interactive activities for young people to educate themselves about online safety issues.

During the discussion, it was suggested that sharing best practice needed to be made more central in the work of the IGF: "bringing it centre stage" was how one commentator put it. It was suggested that examples needed to be made more accessible. Will Gardner spoke about how Childnet had brought children into Parliament to talk about their views about the Internet, raising issues of interest and concern to them: he noted the importance of this work to improving accountability. This approach had also been adopted at the IGF with the work of the Cyber Peace Initiative and Childnet International to engage the voices of young people (Internet Governance – Activating and Listening to the Voice of Tweens). It was suggested that best-practice examples could usefully be brought in to other workshops in the IGF and to the work of Dynamic Coalitions. A number of speakers highlighted the value of having a repository of best-practice examples and thought that it would be valuable to develop such a reference facility. It was noted that the Manthan Award has already been working on this.

The workshop agreed that there was value in:
- Developing a database of examples of good practice identified through some form of review process. This would not necessarily need to be done through the IGF;
- The IGF should build more on best practice, looking at possible solutions to issues and concerns. This could be through using case studies and examples in thematic workshops and the work of Dynamic Coalitions; and
- Work was needed to make the identification of good practice and its presentation more effective: it needed to be in a way that could be understood and drawn on by the business community and civil society more easily.

WS 186.   Online Education: Maximizing the Efficiency

Report by: Ginger (Virginia) Paque

Moderator: Divina Frau-Meigs (Director, Master's programme "E-learning Engineering" at Sorbonne University, Expert with the Council of Europe, France)

Panellists: Carolina Rossini (Berkman Center for Internet and Society, Brazil); Charity Gamboa-Embley (Literacy Lubbock, Phillipines); Pablo Molina (Georgetown University, Washington, DC); Priyanthi Daluwatti (The DiploFoundation Capacity Development Program)

To provide more inclusion, especially in the times of economic crises there is a growing need for online learning - a cost-effective and innovative alternative to the conventional in-situ meetings often accompanied by high travel costs. Online education offers myriad of new opportunities both for professionals and "digital natives". This workshop explored actual challenges, advantages and techniques of effective online education differences comparing to traditional and contemporary in situ educational techniques, with emphasis on Open Educational Resource possibilities.

The Moderator and panellists discussed the possibilities offered by Open Educational Resources and the need to continue to develop and use these tools. The online education workshop at the IGF brought together thinkers and innovators in the areas of distant education and open education. Apart from the necessary distinctions of concepts, and a dive into the concept, methodology and justifications of Open Educational Resources, the group debated with a small but attentive and participative audience the impact of Internet governance, cyberinfrastructure and open standards in education policy.

The concept of improving the quality of education pertains to training teachers in OER, the exploration of newer pedagogical models and a much broader framework for teacher and learner empowerment. This notion was established through a training program on open education for educators across the globe by Mozilla Foundation, CC Learn and P2P University on open content, open technology and open pedagogical skills. The various examples suggest that online educators should to modify their teaching practices to harness the competences required by the digital networks, like play, simulation, pooling of resources, navigation, etc. This will empower users as they already master some of these competences in an implicit, intuitive way. Building on these competences can then truly lead to the co-construction of knowledge, with full participation of both trainer and learner.

The DiploFoundation Capacity Development Program was cited as an example of a program that provides the intensive discussion and interaction among participants to share professional and regional experiences which allows them to contribute to group knowledge building. The result is an effective programme promoting a multistakeholder-based community of individuals from developing countries learning and engaging in issues of Internet Governance.

Open Educational Resources received special attention from those from the audience coming from developing countries in search for new models of education more akin to the Internet culture of collaboration. The question of access was raised, not so much as access to infrastructure but as access to infostructure and to quality content, validated by peers as well as teachers.

Further mention was made to attach OER to media education as a means to enhance information sharing on line as well as communication competences for participation. Ideas about connecting OER to the whole movement of human rights based Internet also raised interest. We hope we have achieved a core understanding of the main concepts and opportunities OER brings, in order to spark further discussion in regard to the adoption and expansion of OER.

WS 230.   Youth and Internet Governance: the Way Forward

Report by: Rafik Dammak

Panellists: Amr Elsadr (Net Amans); Agnieszka Wrzesien (SaferInternet.pl Project); Noha Fathy Mohamed (Gloabl Youth Internet Taskforce); Mohammed Fathy (UN-GAID Youth eleaders Committee); Marilia Maciel (Brazil); Johan Ekman (European Youth Forum); Pascal Bekono, Markku Rasanen (Finland); Jyry Suvilehto (Electronic Frontier Finland); Eugene Daniel; Fatani RAFID (Saudi Arabia)

This workshop was organized to discuss the main emergent issues faced by youth and push for further discussions and proposals: the creation of a cybersafety taskforce for youth , the formation organization of a Dynamic Coalition for youth involvement, participation of young citizens in democratic processes of their countries through social media on the Internet, involvement of young leaders with innovative solutions, and a more general debate on youth and social media and Internet use. As format the workshop was divided according three main themes followed by a Q/A session: Cyber safety, Youth participation and Youth in social media and Internet use. Each panellist had only 5 minutes to present in order to have more time for listening the public feedback.

Agnieszka Wrzesien: Online safety for children and young people has become a growing social concern recently. While it is obviously impossible to eliminate all Internet risks, awareness-raising and educational programmes seem to be the best methods to empower children and young people to stay safe online. In this respect the role of adults is of fundamental importance, however we must remember that young people themselves have a crucial role to play in conveying online safety messages to their peers. As new technologies are the domain of young people, much hope is put into peer-to-peer mentoring. Young people with leadership skills can effectively work in their peer groups by promoting safe and positive use of the Internet and new technologies. They also play an important role in promoting online mechanisms (Helpline services) where children and young people can raise concerns about different dangerous situations they encounter online and seek support and guidance. A Polish example of www.helpline.org.pl was mentioned.

Amr Elsadr: The presentation was a brief description of the history of Net-Aman, the Internet safety focus group of the Cyber Peace Initiative launched by the Suzanne Mubarak Women's International Peace Movement at the International Youth Forum in Sharm El Sheikh, Egypt in 2007. The presentation time allowed was only about five minutes, so most of the presentation was prepared in the form of pictures telling the story of Net-Aman, the inception, capacity building in different disciplines (Internet safety, youth empowerment, entrepreneurial activities for young Egyptians, and Internet governance), and some of the activities engaged in including working with public schools and the Internet safety conference in Cairo in 2008.

Noha Fathy: She presented her proposal on the creation of Global Youth Internet Taskforce which aims to help making the Internet a safer place for children and young people in the course of enabling and empowering youth to play a vital role and share their part of responsibility. The G-YIT is a non-profit organization that aims to build up a multi-stakeholder partnership between Youth and Adults with objectives like Raising awareness among youth on Internet safety issues and Designing training and learning programs

Mohamed Fathy: During the Global Forum on Youth and ICT for Development held last 24-26 September 2007, in Geneva, Switzerland, youth participants from around the world proposed the establishment of a Global Youth Coalition / Network that would support the agenda of the United Nations on harnessing information and communication technologies for the achievement of the Millennium Development Goals (MDGs). The Global Youth Coalition is enabling the youth to exchange knowledge and experiences on ICT for development and youth issues, as well as spearhead initiatives and programmes in the regions. It will also allow the youth to communicate with other organizations and stakeholders working on the MDG agenda for youth and ICT. The work of the Coalition is governed and coordinated by a Committee of e-Leaders for ICT and Youth, a body under the UNDESA-GAID Strategy Council, composed of regional youth representatives and other successful youth leaders from various fields. The Committee of e-Leaders for ICT and Youth is composed of active and committed regional youth representatives from Africa, Asia and the Pacific, Europe, Latin America and the Caribbean, North America and the Arab World.

Marilia Maciel: She talked about the use of Internet for political participation of young people in Brazil. She mentioned that youth had a pivotal role in Brazilian political life, but according to researches, nowadays young people do not participate or believe in traditional channels such as political parties or unions. She said that political involvement online is starting to increase the levels of youth involvement. She briefly commented on the cases of the "#foraSarney" movement on Twitter and on young people's participation on the process of building a civil framework of rights regarding the use of the Internet in Brazil, through an online collaborative platform: (http://culturadigital.gov.br/marcocivil).

Markku Rasanen: His aim in the presentation was to describe ways, how young people can use the Internet to be more active politically, and bring their opinions through, by using the Web. This was mainly accomplished by telling his own example of his campaign against the Finnish Railway monopoly, because of their cut in the student discounts for certain group of students.

Pascal Bekono: The presentation aims at bringing out some feedback on Internet Governance Issues regarding youth and state the global situation of youth and Internet Governance in Africa. It also presents some recommendations to empower youth participation towards IG global agenda and it uses some results from the youth and Internet Governance e-consultation organized on November 2009. In his speech, he highlighted youth participation on IGF from Athens to Hyderabad. Using some priorities like participation, access, capacity building, etc., specified in the youth and IG strategy document, he has presented the current situation in some regions. For instance, access to infrastructure is the main problem faced by youth developing countries (around 3-5%), while in developed countries access is more than 60%. He has presented experience of Regional IGF meetings and summers schools which really are really benefit and should be reinforced and supported for capacity building of youth in developing countries. He has also recommended the Cyber Peace Initiative project implemented in Egyptian as a model which has to be modelled by others countries. Youth in social media and Internet use Jyry Suvilehto He presented a citizens' rights NGO's viewpoint (Electronic Frontier Finland) on governments restricting the Internet in ways that he attempted to point out as being ineffective or otherwise not beneficial.

Rafid Fatani: He discussed Internet filtering in Saudi Arabia. He highlighted the Saudi government is in charge of regulating content, especially surrounding cultural, religious and national security issues. He added that this content censorship extends far beyond the Internet in a typical top-down government approach. Social Web sites in Saudi Arabia are sometimes censored, which he said is a new phenomenon. Political blogs in particular have been under fire and adding that since public demonstrations are banned in Saudi Arabia, many people turn to the Internet to campaign for their causes.

Eugene Daniel: The reason for forums like the IGF, are to best advance our usage of the Internet, but what good will it do to discuss the future without educating those who will be here to utilize it. There needs to be an education of the youth on the serious issues concerning the current and future state of the Internet, both negative and beneficial. Youth need to be both informed and involved in the current processes in determining such issues. Although many youth today know how to utilize the Internet, there is a lack of knowledge in its inner screen operations. Without equipping the youth with this knowledge, the discussions formed in these global forums will prove to be null and void.

The main recommendation was to create a dynamic coalition for youth and Internet Governance and there are a clear interests from the panels and participants from the audience. The workshop provide an opportunity to be in contact with youth from Asia for further collaboration and involvement on the to be formed dynamic coalition. There is also an appeal for more youth participation and representativeness on IGF like former experience of Youth caucus in WSIS process. An important point was the dynamic created by an active participation of the audience since we allocated a consequent Q/A session. Many participants intervened especially about children protection and youth empowerment.

WS 276.   Assessing the Role of the Participative Web in Youth
           Empowerment: A Regional Outlook

Report by: Dr. Hosein Badran

Moderator: Dr. Hosein Badran (Chief Technology Officer-MEA, Cisco)

Panellists: Ken Corish (South West Grid for Learning UK); Ruth Harris (European
Commission, Safer Internet Forum on Internet Safety); Charles Nagy (Chief
Technology Officer, Silatech, Qatar Foundation); Salam Yamout (Program Manager,
Partnership for Lebanon, Cisco); Dr. Yasser Kazem (Director e-Education, MCIT and
Cyber Peace Initiative)

This workshop aimed at providing a critical view of key developments and
challenges affecting the youth empowerment, through education and skill
development using the potential of the participative web in the region. The
workshop explored actual projects that have relied on web 2.0 tools.
Experiences in the Middle East and North Africa region were discussed to
identify the issues and challenges and to promote and assist other initiatives
around the world. Several approaches and case studies were explored by
panellists, including:

• Combining Cyber security and youth empowerment to best utilize the
   Internet as both an education and skills enhancement tool
• Education and Safeguarding providers
• Walking the tight rope; Balancing access with safeguarding for children
   across the UK
• Initiative of Silatech, which is part of the Qatar Foundation sponsored by
   Shaikha Mouza First Lay of Qatar. Silatec initiative addresses the gap in
   youth employment by developing the necessary technical and business
   skills through utilization of Web2.0 and collaboration tools
• Partnership for Lebanon Initiative and national Broad Band infrastructure
   modernization project to enhance youth skill development and
   employment opportunities as well as private sector evolution.
• Experience from EU Commission – Safer Internet Forum

Silatech/Qatar Foundation presented their vision of preparation of youth to
the job market, through the utilization of web2.0 technologies. The initiative
will cover several Arab countries, in addition to African countries, e.g.
Zimbabwe. Three main dimensions were identifies: mind set (e.g. gender
issues), policy (how to modify existing policy constraints), and access
(available skills, technology readiness in country). Target youth age is
between 18-30 years.

Dr. Yasser covered different aspects of Egypt Education Initiative, including
the introduction of ICT content in university curriculum, establishment of
Egypt Learning Center, providing ICT knowledge to high schools throughout
Egypt. So far more than 600 schools have been enlisted, target is 1000 schools
over the next short period. This initiative covers training of both students and
teachers on basic ICT knowledge, content developed through partnership
with Cisco Network Academy program. Recent expansion of the EEI initiative
includes content development as well.

Partnership for Lebanon initiative was presented by Salam Yamout. This initiative aims at modernization of the country telecom sector, through the development of regulatory frame work and modern broadband telecom infrastructure, as well as market readiness for the adoption and use of broadband telecom access. On the youth and web2.0 front, the initiative established annual youth camps attended by about 50 youths each time from different back grounds. They used web2.0 and social networking tools to communicate and develop IT skills. PfL also established a Community Center project for dissemination of ICT and Internet access knowledge in the community at large. A third dimension of youth empowerment was the engagement of youth in the development of a country Broadband Manifesto that outlines the importance of BB capabilities and the aspirations of youth in this regard.

Ruth Harris presented the experience within the EU Commission. She focused on recent developments on the front of peer creation of resources, and on web content creation with active participation form student and youngsters. At the same time it is quite important to protect organizations and provide secure and safe communications for youth on the Internet. An important angle is how to reach and address the needs of vulnerable children.

Ken Corish reviewed the current legislative situation in the UK affecting youth participation and learning. One size fits all solution is not adequate in addressing students education and learning needs. It is quite important to take pupils opinion through youth panels and peer mentoring. The importance to raise both pupils and teachers confidence in utilizing web2.0 technologies and managing awareness on on-line safety aspects.

Conclusions

- Importance of education for teachers on relevant technology aspects of social networks and Internet safety. In some cases, students are more familiar with new tools than teachers.
- A critical challenge is the speed of curriculum development and adoption of new educational content due to lack of understanding of both teachers and parents.
- importance of reaching out to parents to so they can cope with change in youth needs and the challenges they are seeing when accessing the Internet.
- the need to have content in local languages on the Internet was stressed through an intervention from a representative of the Kenyan government.

WS 277. Internet Governance: Activating and Listening to the Voice of Teens

Report by: Lucinda Fell

Organizer: Childnet International and the Cyber Peace Initiative

Panellists: Lucinda Fell (Childnet International); Ellen Ferguson (Childnet International); Mohammed Fathy (Cyber Peace Initiative Youth Panel taken from the

473

SMWIPM Youth Camp); Andrew Miller (MP); Alun Michael (MP); Karim Al-Fateh (Intel)

The workshop was convened by Childnet International and the Cyber Peace Initiative to communicate two methods of how to promote Internet governance and safety awareness with teens. The aim of the workshop was met through analysing the processes adopted in two national projects, featuring two different models of youth participation and engagement and to model best practice sharing key observations to aid other delegates in replicating similar projects in future years.

The workshop also placed at its heart an International team of 'teen youth panellists' from the Cyber Peace Initiative's Youth Camp who shared what their experiences of Internet Governance were, covering the themes of access, openness, security, diversity, rights and digital citizenship, The camp also coincided with the special importance given to teens' involvement and empowerment, as a capacity building effort to form future savvy young cadres in Internet issues and safety concerns.

The youth panel were active participants in the session bringing a fresh and challenging perspective to the topics of discussion and an honesty and openness about how various technologies are used.

With just 1 ½ hours to conduct the session in, it was important to set the scene and to outline the best practice identified and achieved by the partners. Both partners showed engaging and comprehensive presentations, and prior to moving on to the discussions with the youth panel, Childnet showed a video communicating the voice of youth in the UK which was representative of the 1,500 plus young people who were engaged in the UK as part of the Youth IGF Project.

Hearing the voice of youth on film led into presentations from 7 pre-selected youth panellists who gave two minute statements on their experience of Internet Governance. The participants covered different aspects of Internet Governance and agreed that taking part in the Cyber Peace Initiative's IGF 2009 Youth Camp had given them the opportunity to question themselves on the topics which they had not previously done and also to share the experience of young people in their country.

Following the presentations the discussions were varied and the issues that were covered in particular included different online experiences, Internet rights and responsibilities, privacy and disparity and access and representation. The participants felt that children and young people should be afforded the same rights online and offline and that there shouldn't be a distinction between these rights. They highlighted the right to an Internet that represents them and their culture. They acknowledged that there were many young people globally who weren't able to access the Internet and that they believed this should be addressed. As well as discussing rights, the notion of online responsibilities were also discussed and just as it was acknowledged that rights should be consistent both online and offline, there was an acceptance that offline laws such as copyright should also be respected online.

The contradiction between the desire expressed by young people for freedom and their belief that they have an automatic right to be safe was discussed. The phenomenon of social networking was widely discussed, and a number of the concerns raised under the discussions on security centred on concerns regarding the privacy of information. The youth participants outlined their concerns about social networking and the issue of privacy, but also the potential for these sites to be used in communicating key messages to other young people and the fears and lack of understanding that sometimes accompanying Internet use.

The workshop heard from the young people that while very often they are held up as the experts in this field, and undoubtedly they do have a degree of expertise that is instinctive, this is also a new environment for young-people and very often they too are learning on the job. However, the youth panellists agreed that while young people may have not engaged widely on the topic of Internet governance in the past - they do want to continue to engage in the future of the IGF. They also stated that the burden for engagement and youth participation should not rest on youth alone and that parents and teachers also need to be more informed about the Internet experiences of young people and they called for greater participation in the IGF from the user perspective.

The youth participants felt that moving forward young people should be integrated into the heart of the IGF, and would like to see youth representatives on the various IGF committees. They sought real action and input following the session and an insight into strategy discussions, both at the IGF and also with the Internet industry. The chair's concluding remarks from the session reiterated the mile-stone that had been reached in including young people in the discussions at the IGF, but proposed that this is just the start in working towards the meaningful inclusion of young people in the IGF process. There was a commitment from those present in the session to continue to progress the work of youth inclusion in discussions around this topic leading up to the IGF 2010 in Vilnius with the golden aim to be to get the voice of youth heard from the main stage.

3. Participation

WS 96. *Code of Good Practice on Information, Participation and Transparency in Internet Governance*

Report by: Anriette Esterhuysen (APC), Michael Remmert (CoE)

Organizer: Council of Europe, the United Nations Economic Commission for Europe, and the Association for Progressive Communications

Panellists: Michael Remmert (Council of Europe); Anriette Esterhuysen (Association for Progressive Communications); David Souter (ICT Development Associates, project consultant); Jeanette Hofmann (London School of Economics, IGF MAG); Brendan Kuerbis (Internet Governance Forum); Constance Bommelaar (ISOC); Kieran McCarthy (ICANN)

The workshop provided an opportunity for IGF participants to discuss a draft Code of Practice on Information, Participation and Transparency in Internet Governance and to contribute to the next phase of the Code's development. The draft Code has been prepared by the Council of Europe, the United Nations Economic Commission for Europe and the Association for Progressive Communications, following earlier discussions at IGF2 (Rio de Janeiro) and IGF3 (Hyderabad). It builds on the experience of existing Internet governance entities and of participation mechanisms in other governance domains, such as the UNECE Aarhus Convention. It seeks to provide a platform to enhance information and participation in all Internet governance bodies, and thereby further improve their transparency and accountability. The session was organised as a workshop with discussion groups, rather than a series of presentations.

Wide-ranging discussions have been held during the preparation of the draft code, in particular with ISOC, IETF, W3C, ICANN, NRO, the Regional Internet Registries and ITU-T, all of whose information and participation arrangements and practices were assessed in a report published by the workshop sponsors during the May 2009 IGF consultation meeting. Participants from most of these entities, and other stakeholders, contributed to discussions during the workshop.

Following an introduction to the draft Code, participants in the workshop divided into two groups, led by (1) Jeanette Hofmann (London School of Economics, IGF MAG) and Brendan Kuerbis (Internet Governance Forum) and (2) Constance Bommelaar (ISOC) and Kieran McCarthy (ICANN), which discussed the following two questions:

- Do you welcome the code of practice in principle?
- What additions, deletions or changes would you suggest to the draft text?

The outcomes of these discussions were reported to the workshop as a whole, and followed by a general discussion on the most appropriate ways forward for the draft Code and the role it could play in fostering more inclusive engagement in Internet governance.

The draft Code was commended by participants in the workshop as a positive initiative in itself, as a framework through which Internet governance entities could examine their current practices, and as a platform on which they could build transparency and inclusiveness in future, as the Internet continues to evolve and as it extends its impact within society, economy, culture and government.

Participants made a number of valuable suggestions for development of the Code's content and presentation, which are being considered as the Code is finalised. Participants also discussed opportunities for a number of Internet governance bodies to engage with the Code during the period between IGF4 and IGF5, reviewing their own practice and looking into ways in which this might develop in response to the information and participation needs of stakeholders and the changing environment for Internet policy, standards and governance.

The sponsors of the draft Code are actively following up these discussions with ISOC, ICANN, W3C and other Internet governance bodies. They intend to finalise the Code and hope to implement a number of initiatives with specific IG bodies before IGF5 meets in Vilnius.

WS 200. *Remote Participation: Mapping the Field, Evaluation and Multistakeholder Involvement*

Report by: Marilia Maciel

Panellists: Markus Kummer (IGF Secretariat); Jovan Kurbalija (DiploFoundation); Nermine EL Saadany (Ministry of Communications and Information Technology, Egypt); Olga Cavalli (Ministry of Foreign affairs, Argentina and University of Buenos Aires); Shadi Abou-Zahra (Web Accessibility Initiative of the World Wide Web Consortium); Virginia Paque (Remote Participation Working Group); Marília Maciel (Remote Participation Working Group; Center of Technology and Society)

At the IGF Hyderabad, the Remote Participation Working Group and the IGF Secretariat coordinated with local partners in the creation of IGF hubs and gave support for Remote Participation in the IGF Since then, the debate about remote participation has gained momentum. Nonetheless, stakeholders must review:

• How they can benefit from the improvement in remote participation possibilities at the IGF;
• What heir role is in the projects that aim to enhance remote participation;
• How stakeholders can work synergistically in order to implement remote participation. The workshop will discuss remote participation both from a policy (what should be done) and a best practices approach (what has been done).

Policy:

• Mapping the field of remote participation. Identify the impelling/institutional arrangements (global and regional) where remote participation is most needed. Identify additional prospective stakeholders that should be involved in this initiative and how to engage them.
• Inclusion of people from developing countries
• Inclusion of people with disabilities.

Best practices:

• Best practices at the IGF: an evaluation (including remote hubs)
• Guidelines for RP at the IGF: a step towards a code of best practices in the field of remote participation?

Marília Maciel introduced the debate. She said that the workshop happens in a special moment in the history of the IGF; a moment of reflection and evaluation. It is important to discuss if remote participation has helped the IGF to fulfil its main goals and how it could be further improved in the future. Markus Kummer said that a conference about the Internet would not be complete without providing the opportunity for remote participation. He emphasized some improvements, such as live captioning from the main room. In his opinion, one of the issues that should be discussed is how to bring remote participants to the debate in an efficient and timely manner. He stressed that it is important to have good moderation for remote participation. Technology is important, but the human factor is essential. The remote moderators, the volunteers who connect to remote participants are the key to the success of the initiative. Hubs are a very good initiative, which make easier to identify remote participants. Live video interventions from the hubs should be further encouraged. In order to do that, technology and moderation should be improved

Nermine El Saadany mentioned that different kinds of constraints hamper participation in conferences such as the IGF. Finding a way to communicate with remote participants helps to overcome the information divide. She said that capacity Building is a fundamental precondition for remote participation. There should be people informed about the IGF so they will have the ability to interact and contribute meaningfully and also be interested in taking part in initiatives, such as the hubs. She agrees with the importance of the human factor, highlighted by Markus Kummer.

Jovan Kurbalija called attention to the fact that remote participation in the IGF is part of a broader attempt to open the international meeting for people that could not otherwise participate. At first arguments for inclusion were based on ethics. Nowadays there is a real necessity of bringing other perspectives. In order to be effective, the regime should bring as many people as possible and involve broader communities in the policy process. The IGF is setting good practices in the field of remote participation that could be followed in other fora.

Olga Cavalli commented on the importance of remote participation to developing countries, especially to South America. The long distances and the lack of awareness hamper more participation. Remote hubs give the opportunity to raise awareness and reinforce capacity building. However, for this potential to be fully enjoyed, the hubs should be carefully organized. It is the responsibility of the hubs and its organizers to be accountable and prepare the local meetings in advance in order to be able to make good use of the opportunity given.

Shadi Abou-Zahra stressed the importance of the human factor and that it is necessary to find out how to bring in remote participants while taking into account the participants who are physically present. It is an ongoing learning process. He commented on the ethics of remote participation in W3C. The team works from different corners of the globe and has to adjust to the methodology. For instance, one different person is appointed to transcribe each meeting. It is useful for deaf people and also to provide a written record of the meeting. He called attention to the necessity of building a system of remote participation that could be used not only in the IGF itself, but also in other occasions, such as on the meetings of the dynamic coalitions.

Ginger Paque called attention to the infrastructure and the people who made remote participation possible. Remote participation includes the ones that have constraints to participate. Those who are not in the IGF are exactly those who need more to be there, in order to close the digital divide and the access to knowledge and diversity. She said that supporting remote participation is making an investment that will benefit all of the attendees, who potentially will need it at some point. Remote participation is also an inclusive and sustainable green option. She also said that there is an overlap among the topics of remote participation and the topics of access to people with disabilities. There is also an overlap of the mechanism that are important for both groups. Live captioning, for instance, is important for people with disabilities and also for remote participants if they do not receive good audio quality. With live captioning they are able to continue following the debates.

Marília Maciel said that there is an increasing potential of web tools to promote remote participation. It is important to think about how to integrate different web tools for participation. There should be a broader planning to analyze how these pieces fit together (official platform for remote participation, the use of twitter, facebook, etc). She said that if we compare remote participation in 2008 and in 2009, we can conclude that that more hubs registered in 2009 and that the hubs are more widespread worldwide. She made some suggestions for improving remote participation: a) more multistakeholder involvement. MAG could help to put in touch with strategic partners   b) institutional follow ups: learning from past experiences c) improve procedural guidelines in the process of remote participation: planning, structure, larger team involved.

Conclusions

- All speakers agreed that the human factor is essential to the success of remote participation. The importance of remote moderators was emphasized.
- Remote participation is a necessity. In order to be effective, the IG regime should bring as many people as possible and involve broader communities in the policy process
- Live captioning proved to be important. It would be good to have live captioning for all rooms, but this increases technical complexity and should be evaluated
- One issue to be further discussed is how to bring remote participants to the debate in an efficient and timely manner
- Live video interventions from the hubs should be further encouraged
- Capacity building should be strengthened. It is an important pre-condition to improve remote participation
- It is the responsibility of the hubs and its organizers to be accountable and prepare the local meetings in advance in order to be able to make good use of the opportunity given
- We should create a system of remote participation that could be used not only in the IGF itself, but also in other occasions, such as on the meetings of the dynamic coalitions
- It is important to think about how to integrate different web tools for participation. There should be a broader planning analyzing how these pieces fit together (official platform for remote participation, the use of twitter, facebook, etc).

- One suggestion to integrate the tools mentioned above was to have a central site (probably IGF website) that would be a focal point where all the feeds and posts from all platforms would be exhibited
- More multistakeholder involvement is needed. MAG could help to put in touch with strategic partners
- Improve procedural guidelines in the process of remote participation: ex. planning, structure, larger team involved
- It would be useful to know more about the remote participants, to have an idea of their profile. One suggestion is to ask remote participants to register as well.

Finally, three comments should be made about the workshop:
- It succeeded to achieve gender balance, with the presence of 4 women and 3 men as panellists
- It showed a good level of regional balance, with representation from Europe (2), Latin America (3) and MENA (2).
- A successful case of remote presentation, made by Ginger Paque

WS 212. *Multistakeholderism at the IGF: Assessing the Impact on Participation*

Report by: Parminder Jeet Singh (Workshop Moderator/IT for Change/India)

Panellists: Felipe Santarosa (Government/Brazil); George Papadatos (Government/Greece); Karen Banks (APC/UK); Jennifer Warren (Lockheed Martin Corporation/USA); Murali Shanmugavelan (Panos London/UK)

IGF is a particular experiment in the area of global governance, whereby an 'official' global body – mandated by a world summit – is constitutively multistakeholder, going beyond the typical inter-governmental model in the international arena. However, multistakeholderism can only be seen as an instrument of enhanced and more democratic political participation, and not an end in itself. This panel aimed at assessing whether and how IGF's unique multistakeholder model has actually impacted participation in global Internet Governance processes. Such examination discussed the issue of participation with respect to different groups and sections of the global society. The workshop produced outcomes to feed into the IGF review process.

Multistakeholderism is a vital part of the IGF that brings a crucial contribution into the space of global governance. The moment is propitious to discuss the principle and the implementation of Multistakeholderism since the IGF itself is being reviewed and the next steps are being defined. It is positive to observe that IGF participants come from various sectors and represent slightly differing points of view and interests.

Based on speeches' transcripts and the list of sectors and countries represented at IGF in Rio de Janeiro and Hyderabad, panellists presented a study on actual participation in these previous IGF's meetings. According to the four groups defined by UNDP Human Development Index (HDI) classification, where 1 is the most developed and 4 the least developed countries, it was possible to verify that IGF's participants came overwhelmingly from the developed world (HDI 1 and HDI 2), both in terms of individuals as well as organizations. By excluding the participants from host countries to avoid skewed results caused by a high number of attendees who do not travel when the event is in a different place, the study concluded that more than 70% of the organizations that participated in the second and third IGF Meetings came from the 20% of countries which are classified as HDI 1 and HDI 2. Even within the developing world, the participation of Southern countries is minimal, i.e., at the IGF Meeting in Brazil, there was not even a single speaker from the least developed country world in any of the main sessions.

Considering the number of individuals, the result is even more skewed: organizations from the developed world can send more people per organization than institutions from the developing world. Another aspect of IGF multistakeholderism discussed at the workshop was the challenge to avoid fragmentation and tie together a diversity of processes and issues brought by different stakeholders. How do workshops relate to main sessions? How do they represent together a unique IGF thinking? Panellists raised the need to have a more formal and firm linkage that reflects the nexus that can be seen in the traditional processes of global governance and that can be observed even more clearly in subsequent policymaking.

Panellists also argued that the participation of different sectors (with different interests) may not lead to an agreement at the venue itself. However, a subliminal impact in attendee's mind can generate changes over a long period when they are back to their home-countries. A representative from the private sector highlighted the difficulties in promoting the participation of small businesses from developing world. However, it was also observed that the multistakeholderism element has an impact not only within the IGF itself, but also in other institutional spaces such as the U.N., that starts to open its structure to have MSP as an intrinsic part of their work.

A civil society participant stated that IGF's multistakeholderism principle has also an impact within countries that start adopting the practice of getting people together and promoting dialogue among them. An important aspect suggested to improve the implementation of the multistakeholderism principle is to invest in capacity-building and funding support in order to guarantee actual participation of the least developed countries. Without developing world voices, the debate is much poorer.

The initial study presented at the workshop brings lessons to ensure the actual participation of developing countries in future workshops and dynamic coalitions. It is of great value that the impact of participating in IGF Meetings can generate changes for a long period in terms of policymaking. It demonstrates a linkage among different participants that may seem too fragmented during the event. It is important to formalize this process of connection within the venue (among different sessions) and subsequently to it (when participants go back to their home-countries).

To invest in capacity building was mentioned as an important demand to promote the participation of developing world's countries and hence enrich the debate at IGF. However, technical capacity-building is not enough. This effort must be extended to political aspects in order to assure that people from the least developed countries are able to understand and articulate their own interests and that these issues will be addressed at IGF. Following the same argument, it is crucial to have funding support, particularly public funding, to promote developing countries' participation at IGF. As stated by one of the panellists, in democracy, substantive participation, not just formal participation, is important. Although IGF may have been successful in terms of formal participation, there is still a long way to go regarding substantive participation. If IGF does not focus on this principle, we may reduce the exclusion in one way, but increase it in another.

The conclusions of this workshop were presented in the main session Internet Governance in Light of the WSIS Principles since the principle of participation is a critical emphasis of the WSIS.

Taking Stock and Looking Forward:

On the Desirability of the Continuation of the Forum--

Oral Statements

18 November 2009

Chairman:

Sha Zukang
United Nations Under-Secretary-General for Economic & Social Affairs

Speakers:

Bob Khan
CEO and President of the Corporation for National Research Initiatives

Vint Cerf
Vice President and Chief Internet Evangelist, Google

Samuel Poghisio
Minister for Information and Communication, Kenya

Rajesh Chharia
President, Internet Service Providers Association of India

Felipe Costi Santarosa
Head of the Information Society Division, Ministry of External Relations, Brazil

Akram Chowdhury
Member of Parliament, Bangladesh

Malcolm Johnson
Director, International Telecommunication Union (ITU) Standardization Bureau

Talal Abu Ghazalah
UN GAID Chairman

Ambassador Ferry de Kerckhove
Ambassador of Canada to Egypt

Chen Yin
Head, Delegation of China

Maria Häll
Deputy Director IT Policy, Ministry of Enterprise, Energy and Communications, Sweden, Representing the EU Presidency

Mogens Schmidt
UNESCO

Masanobu Katoh
Keidanren, Japan

Rod Beckstrom
CEO and President, ICANN

Abdullah Al Darrab
Saudi Arabia, Government

Bill Graham
Global Strategic Engagement, The Internet Society

Waudo Siganga
WITSA Vice Chairman for Africa, Chairman, Computer Society of Kenya

Ayesha Hassan
Senior Policy Manager, E-Business, IT and Telecoms, ICC BASIS

Richard Beaird
Deputy Coordinator, International Communications and Information Policy, Department of State, United States

Vladimir Radunovic
DiploFoundation

Parminder Singh Jeet
IT for Change

Andrew Miller
Member of the UK Parliament

Konstantin Kladouras
ETNO, Chairman ETNO IGV-Working Group, Head of Regulatory Strategy Section

Olga Cavalli
Adviser for Technology, Ministry of Foreign Affairs, Argentina

Lambert Van Nistelrooij
Member of the European Parliament

Liesyl Franz
Vice President, Information Security and Global Public Policy, TechAmerica

Mactar Seck
United Nations Economic Commission for Africa

Johan Ekman
Bureau Member, Institutional Relations, Council of Europe, European Youth
Forum

Peter Voss
Head of Division, International Policy for Information & Communication
Technologies, Federal Ministry of Economics and Technology, Germany

Anupam Agrawal
Chair, Kolkata Chapter of Internet Society, India

Bertrand de La Chapelle
Délégué Spécial pour la Société de l'Information, Ministère des Affaires
Etrangères et Européennes, France

Ana Cristina Amoroso das Neves
Head International Affairs, Knowledge Society Agency (UMIC), Ministry of
Science, Technology and Higher education, Portugal

Willie Currie
Communications and Information Policy Programme Manager, Association
for Progressive Communications (APC)

Giacomo Mazzone
World Broadcasting Union

William J. Drake
Senior Associate, Centre for International Governance Graduate Institute of
International and Development Studies, Geneva

Thomas Schneider
Coordinator international Information Society International Affairs, Federal
Department of the Environment, Transport, Energy and Communication,
Federal Office of Communications OFCOM, Switzerland

Charles Mok
Chairman, Internet Society Hong Kong

Y. J. Park
Delft University of Technology

Zahid Jamil
Senior Partner and Barrister-at-Law, Jamil & Jamil

Sue Baxter
Head of UK delegation. Head of EU & International Competitiveness Unit,
Department for, Business, Innovation and Skills

Gao Xinmin
Vice President, Internet Society China

Lillian O. Sharpley
NRO (AFRINIC Communication Manager)

Wolfgang Benedict for Ian Internet Governance Caucus Peter

Jyrki Kasvi
Member of Parliament, Vice chair, Committee for the Future, Finland

Heather Creech
Director, Global Connectivity, International Institute for Sustainable Development

Frédéric Riehl
Chair, UN Commission on Science and Technology for Development; Director, International Relations, Federal Department of the Environment, Transport, Energy and Communication, Government of Switzerland

Christine Arida
Director of Telecom Planning and Services, National Telecom Regulatory Authority, Egypt

Extracts from the Transcript of Proceedings

MR. SHA ZUKANG:

We are gathered here to discuss the future of IGF. Heads of state and government in Tunisia in 2005 gave IGF a provisional life span of five years. The Tunis Agenda specifically called upon the Secretary-General of the United Nations, "To examine the desirability of the continuation of the forum, in formal consultation with formal participants, within five years of its creation, and to make recommendation to the United Nations membership in this regard." In the last few days, we have heard some clear views on the issue of our extension of the mandate of IGF, starting with the Prime Minister of Egypt. But let us be open and honest and recognize that not all positions and views are so easily expressed, nor so quickly understood. Today's consultation will be a formal one, focusing only on the examination of the desirability of the continuation of the forum as is called for by the mandate indicated in the Tunis Agenda for the Information Society in paragraph 72, 73, and 77. We will have a series of speakers representing various stakeholder groups who have asked in advance for a speaking slot.

This meeting has been prepared through a consultative process, both in physical meetings in Geneva and here in Sharm El Sheikh, as well as through our online process. The result of the online process has been reflected in the synthesis document prepared by the IGF Secretariat. This document has been translated into all six U.N. languages and can serve as input to our discussions. In the past few days I consulted widely and now have a better understanding of the positions of some of the stakeholders in attendance. However, it is today's discussion that matters most in this formal consultation. If you believe the forum is valuable, I would encourage you to say so and tell us in what ways. If you believe it can be improved, I would encourage you to say that and tell us how. If you believe that IGF has fulfilled its purpose, I would encourage you to speak out against an extension of the mandate and tell us why.

Later, I will report to the Secretary-General. He will make recommendations in his report to the General Assembly next year, taking the openings expressed in these consultations into account. I'm sorry not everyone who asked for a speaking slot can be accommodated today, and I appreciate your understanding. But we are limited to less than three hours. All written statements sent to the IGF Secretariat by the end of today will be included in the formal consultation. Speakers today should speak for maximum of three minutes. Without further delay, I now open the floor.

ROBERT KAHN:

In one fundamental aspect the IGF has been quite successful, and that is by providing a means for discussion of issues and exchange of views between individuals and organizations from all over the world. I'd like to publicly acknowledge the role that both Nitin Desai and Markus Kummer have played in shepherding the process from the beginning, that's been one important reason for its success. The IGF has provided a neutral venue in which important Internet issues can be discussed, not only in the sessions but by the personal contacts in the halls and in between the sessions, which are an integral part of the forum. The IGF plays an important and valuable role, and it should definitely be continued. It's particularly interesting to me because I never expected to see the Internet, which began as a small research project, take on such hold in so many countries around the world. I have one specific recommendation to make, which is that in the future, in addition to dealing with the issues that arise in these deliberations or that arise through the many pre-forum consultations, that a focus be put on developing issues and approaches in certain specific sub-areas of interest to the participants now and in the future; that we have not only a general area, but that we also have several topical areas at each meeting so that it will be possible to attract a broader community of interest than has currently been participating. The IGF cannot and should not attempt to address every possible area, but it can help to move the discussions forward by addressing a broader set of potential areas than are now being addressed. So I look forward to participating in future IGFs, and I strongly urge that the IGF be continued.

VINT CERF:

The IGF has been a remarkable assembly of people deeply concerned about the Internet and its use on a global scale. We all recognize now that there is enormous utility in this system. The information that's accumulated on the World Wide Web has proven to be extremely valuable. On the other hand, we also recognize that there are abuses of the Internet which we must attend to, ranging from annoying things like spam to much more serious problems like fraud. The IGF is an ideal setting in which to raise issues along these lines as well as issues related to cooperation for the improvement of electronic commerce. For example, decisions about the legal significance of the digital signature so that we can conduct contracting activities and have a mutual understanding of the enforcement of these contracts that have been signed digitally in cyberspace. If there are disputes between parties, it's important that we have intergovernmental agreements about the enforcement of the provisions, contracts that are so executed. Also, a party that is abusing someone might be in one country and the victim in another. The only way that we are going to deal with such international difficulties is to have a more common framework in which we agree as to the activities that are considered to be socially unacceptable. And here I believe the IGF can play a very important role in surfacing different views of these kinds and allowing us to discover venues in which these matters might be best resolved.

The IGF is not a decision-making activity. Although some people have criticized that, in my honest opinion, this lack of decision-making is what makes it important. It's a place where all sides can be exposed. It's a multistakeholder activity. We get inputs from the technical community, from civil society, from governments, from the private sector, all of which inform us about the problems we face and the possible solutions that might be available to us. This non-decision-making effort allows many of the opinions that might be in conflict with each other to be heard, and it am allows many of us to come to some conclusions about constructive steps forward. So I would urge all of you to take a very positive view, to participate in and support these meetings, and use them as a tool for making the Internet a better, safer, and more effective place in which to conduct our global affairs.

SAMUEL POGHISIO:

After four years of IGF, it's time to reflect on what we have achieved so far and the future of this forum. As we deliberate on the five-year life span it's important for us to think of the need for continuation of this coordinated mechanism to harness contributions from all Internet stakeholders. Kenya has established this process at a national level and has also pioneered the same at the sub-regional and regional level, and we've found that with inspiration from the national IGFs, we are able to identify local level Internet governance issues that then form the building blocks for the East African IGF, which is now on its second year. And we've found that the level of sensitization of various Internet governance issues is high. We are now very much aware of the issues from management of critical Internet resources, more specifically strengthening our country's code Top Level Domain, to develop the strategies for handling cybercrime and creating universal, affordable access to ICTs. This has been an important lesson for us, and we see an even better opportunity in the future. We support the extension of the IGF and particularly the multistakeholder processes underpinning it, and we believe it is important for us to continue the constructive discussions and the debates and open exchange of ideas. However, there are a number of things that we may want to see changed. One, the allocation of adequate resources to the IGF Secretariat and its ability to function. Two, the support for regional and national IGFs, with clear mechanisms of inclusion and integration with the global IGF. The East African IGF wishes to help the IGF achieve more practical and useful outcomes growing from local and regional lessons, e.g. deep analysis of discussions on thematic areas to provide a framework. This will not only allow for broad and structured discussions, but also harness the potential for all to get value out of our process. Lastly, Kenya is proud to be hosting the ICANN 2010 Africa meeting in Nairobi in March 7th through 12th and we look forward to hosting you all at the 2011 IGF. I thank you.

RAJESH CCHARIA:

IGF is important because it represents a multistakeholder consultation process and needs a formal mandate. These inputs are critical for the balanced growth and management of Internet resources, not just within countries but across the world. Not other forum provides a similar opportunity, ever. IGF occurs once a year, which is the minimum that we need given the rapid innovation in the Internet and mobile worlds. Any change in frequency would leave very large gaps and the continuity of the IGF would suffer. The importance of the IGF to the emerging countries is even more important. For example, India and China already have more than 1 billion mobile users. By 2014, this number could reach to 2 billion even, which will be 30% of the total world's population. Add to this the rest of the emerging nations such as Egypt and the scale and speed at which these technologies are changing and the socioeconomic realities would mean that IGF and more such forums should be set up for engaging governments, service providers, technology companies, NGOs, civil societies and academicians. The IGF should be continued in the current form and held at least once a year, preferably in an emerging country. We should give it an automatic extension of a minimum five years right away.

Two small modifications would help. The first is to expand the stakeholders community further to bring in health, education, employment, banking sectors, since they will next be impacted by an ICT, and this way we will be able to connect our rural portion also with the Internet. Second, structure the workshop in a manner that it is slightly easier for the participant to choose by combining similar themes and adding the new ones. What are the lessons from the IGF? The Internet and mobile revolution which everybody knows are probably the first real chance for the entire world to experience democracy in its purest form. The next set of beneficiaries of the Internet are going to be the lower middle class and the poor in the emerging economies and for their sake this dialogue must continue. The governments must take the role of facilitating large-scale private investment in infrastructure to provide access as a key priority. A topic which has been discussed in the IGFs but on which concrete steps are still pending is online child and woman abuse and pornography. In Rio, we discussed about international monitoring All stakeholders have a responsibility to look into this serious cancer of our society and take immediate action by inducing a chemotherapy type action so that our future generation will remain clean.

FELIPE COSTI SANTAROSA:

Brazil is one of the countries that has had the honour of hosting a meeting of the IGF in Rio de Janeiro in 2007. Our country, including government, civil society, private sector, and academia, has been a very active and enthusiastic player in IGF. Either in person or remotely, Brazilians have shown a consistent and increasing interest in the IGF. Brazil adopts a multistakeholder Internet governance model at the national level, and in the Brazilian Internet steering committee representatives of all stakeholders play a key role. Their engagement in the IGF is a consequence of their involvement at home. This explains why the Brazilian government, as already declared by Vice Minister Augusto Gadelha at the opening session of this forum, favours the renewal of the mandate of the forum. We firmly believe in the multistakeholder process. Moreover, our own experience tells us that IGF can go beyond promoting debate. It can and should provide advice that helps incorporating the World Summit principles in Internet governance processes at the global, regional, and local levels. It's our conviction that during its first period of five meetings, the IGF will be able to fulfil its mandate and issue guidance on a limited set of issues on which convergence can already be noticed. Turning to another point, as determined by the Tunis Agenda, Paragraph 72f, IGF should strengthen and enhance the engagement of stakeholders, in particular those from developing countries in existing and/or future Internet governance mechanisms. This task cannot be carried out, if the existing inadequate balance between developing and developed countries in the IGF persists. I'm not only referring to attendance at the IGF themselves, but also participation in the preparatory meetings in Geneva.

The Brazilian government fully supports IGF and favours its continuation, but in light of our previous observations we believe it can be improved, particularly in two areas. One, the IGF must enhance its ability to provide outputs that could point to guidelines and best practice that, though not mandatory, should show countries, multilateral organizations and the U.N. Secretary-General how to promote cooperation on the key issues. This can be achieved by streamlining its reporting procedures so as to have a more user-friendly output that can be brought to the attention of the United Nations, relevant international organizations, governments and other stakeholders. Two, a renewed IGF ought to become yet more inclusive and able to finance the participation of a greater number of stakeholders from developing countries, in particular from the LDCs. This can be achieved in different ways. One would be for the IGF to become partly financed from within the regular U.N. budget.   These are just preliminary ideas and the Brazilian government remains open to a consultative debate on these issues.

AKRAM CHOUDHURY:

I bring greetings from Prime Minister, Sheikh Hasina, who in the 2008 election campaign developed a manifesto for digital Bangladesh. The IGF helped us get a lot of feedback and ideas on that. We feel that IGF should concentrate more on Internet diversity, child cybercrime, commercial security, and individual security, and that the IGF should be continued. In Bangladesh, 300 million people, 150 in the country and 150 outside the country are speaking in Bangla language, so I demand that a Bangla domain be introduced very soon, and that the authority of name assignment and number should not be monopolized, it should be democratized. More participation of Parliamentary members should be ensured in the next IGF forum. And there should be a separate panel of these members sharing their ideas of how they have digitalized their Parliament. There's good news that our speaker, Abdul Hamid, yesterday announced that the Bangladesh Parliament will be digitalized gradually and all members will be given laptops to bring it to the

House so that they can use the Internet. This will make them more effective and, transparent and accountable to the people.

MALCOLM JOHNSON:

Thank you, Mr. Chairman. As you know, the ITU has a membership of 191 governments and over 700 private sector entities and nongovernmental organizations, many of which have participated here this week. Our membership hasn't discussed the future of the IGF. However, the ITU Secretary-General and his elected colleagues will recommend to our membership to support the continuation of the IGF in its present format for the reasons that many speakers have expounded over this week. This is not to say that improvements cannot or should not be made. The IGF has evolved from the first event and will continue to do so. In particular, the number of events running in parallel should be drastically reduced. Eight different events starting at the same time is far too many. ITU has itself contributed to this; we organized 11 events here, but we intend not to hold so many events at the next IGF. I'm pleased to say that our events have been well-attended. But we have seen that in many other events, there's been very small participation, and this isn't really fair to the organizers or the presenters. It also means that it's very easy to miss important discussions going on in the main session. Why do we have side events in parallel with the important discussions in the main session? Why not concentrate on one or two themes for each IGF? So this leads us to question the effectiveness of the organizing structure, including its transparency and accountability.

TALAL ABU-GHAZALEH:

As co-chair of the United Nations ICT Task Force, I enthusiastically promoted the establishment of the IGF at our forum in Berlin in November 2004. I have continued to fully support IGF as GAID chair, and as the TAG Organization's chair. The TAG Organization proudly served on the United Nations Working Group on Internet Governance. Today I wish to applaud IGF's success under its able leadership, noting that IGF and GAID are twin brothers born out of the WSIS process and in the spirit of support for IGF I wish to suggest that IGF and GAID would have a lot to gain by combining their agendas through the development of a creative formula. There could only be added value in such synergy, coordination, harmony, and partnership. Just like ICT and the Internet are coherently interlinked, so should be the IGF and GAID. And in the process, I would look forward to losing my job as GAID chair. I would appreciate if this statement be considered as part of the proceedings.

FERRY KERCKHOVE:

I would like to make five statements on behalf of Canada. First of all, the transforming power of the Internet has been recognized by everyone. It penetrates all spheres of society's life at the community, national, and international levels. It is an essential development factor. And so it makes perfect sense that the instrument of consultation in governing the Internet be multistakeholder and unite all aspects of society, and this is why this forum has to become a different one than typical management forums in that it doesn't have decision-making power. We should not change the existing structure, or try to change this IGF into something that it is not. We have begun an evolutionary process in which we are adapting to and in which each person should find his or her role. This is why Canada speaks formally in favour of continuing this forum for the next five years. When it comes to the debate on the IGF mandate, there should not be negotiated outcomes. The IGF has a multiplicity of outputs with significant impacts on Internet governance. I don't deny that for national or international bureaucrats accustomed to the rigidities of forms and format, it can appear irritatingly messy. But we are prepared to take a bit of mess in exchange for the extraordinary capacity building potential that this forum offers thanks to its multistakeholder structure, its flexibility and its transparency. And I am grateful that the IGF is independent of assessed contributions and relies on voluntary funding from diverse sources, thus adding to its independence from influences. The IGF should not be judged by its structure or its links with governmental agencies, but rather by its practical contributions on issues like security, child pornography, all issues that we discussed here. The Internet is a personal liberating instrument. It is at the basis of the democratic principles that were in the WSIS. It is a grantor of freedom of expression and universality of the rights of the person. Canada supports the revolution of the Internet on a national level and we understand the role that governments are to play in this sphere. This is why we appreciate the principle of reinforced cooperation and we have the responsibility to contribute to reinforcing access and development. Canada attaches great significance to the importance of the system, and we don't want to experiment here with international institutions that have political interests. We have to make sure that the mandate is clear for this IGF.

CHEN YIN:

The Chinese delegation has noted that as mandated by WSIS, IGF has conducted productive and effective activities in promoting dialogue and exchange among the multi-stakeholders, and will conclude its mandate within its five-year life span. We would like to congratulate and appreciate the excellent work done by IGF Secretariat, MAG, and all the hosting countries including Greece, Brazil, India and Egypt. We also would like to point out some of the IGF's shortcomings. First of all, the current IGF cannot solve in substance the issue of unilateral control of critical Internet resources. Secondly, the developing countries lack the resources to participate in IGF meetings, and the priority of development agenda has been downplayed. Thirdly, the issues discussed in IGF have duplicated the work being explored and covered by other UN agencies and international organizations. Therefore, the Chinese delegation thinks that without reform, it is not necessary to give the IGF a five-year extension. We note that relevant parties, developing countries in particular, hope that Internet governance issues can be discussed at the U.N. level. We support the views of Saudi Arabia and other developing countries in their proposal to set up an Enhanced Cooperation mechanism within the U.N. framework.

If the mechanism of Enhanced Cooperation needs the extension of IGF for the purpose of exchanging views among multi-stakeholders, the IGF should carry the following reforms. First, in accordance with the Tunis Agenda, it should focus on how to solve the issue of unilateral control of critical Internet resources. Secondly, the representation and voices of the developing countries should be increased in the IGF, and the development issue should be placed as the first priority. Thirdly, we should seriously consider the possibility of incorporating IGF financing into the regular U.N. budget, and provide assistance to developing countries for their participation in the IGF meetings. Fourthly, we should follow rigidly the Tunis Agenda so that the reformed IGF should not duplicate the work and mandate of other organizations. Fifthly, a Bureau should be set up with a balanced membership of various parties and geographical regions, and its term of reference and rules of procedures should be formulated by the United Nation. Sixthly, on tenure of the future IGF, we deem it necessary to review the extension of the IGF every two or three years. In the view of the Chinese delegation, the setting up of a mechanism for Enhanced Cooperation with a reformed IGF will effectively promote the global Internet governance process and facilitate the achievement of Millennium Development Goals.

MARIA HÄLL:

I am speaking on behalf of the EU Presidency. Mr. Under-Secretary-General, at the opening ceremony you asked us three questions. First, whether we thought the forum should continue. The answer is yes. The multistakeholder format and the IGF is a place for open discussions on all issues without binding outcomes or oversight functions. These pillars are vital preconditions for the free and open exchange of views in the IGF. Having no negotiation outcomes does not mean there are no results. You Mr. Chairman correctly stated at the opening ceremony, "While the IGF does not have decision-making powers, it inspires the ones who do." I can assure all of you that the influence of the IGF on the policy-making by the European institutions has been considerable, and I know that this is true for our colleagues in the Council of Europe as well. This is exactly what we want, a place for civil society, business, the technical community, and governments to engage in dialogue. The IGF has delivered on all the issues listed in its mandate in paragraph 72 of the Tunis Agenda. This is far from saying that the job is finished; the mandate refers to long-term processes that the IGF must continue to address.

Secondly, Mr. Chairman, you asked whether the forum should be improved. Of course, it could be improved. It is in the process of growing and maturing, and every year it gets better. As stated by Mr. Nitin Desai in his speech on Sunday, the forum is made up by its participants. It evolves progressively as the knowledge and experience base of its participants develops. This is why it's important to enable and increase participation from developing countries. As illustrated by the event with the First Lady this morning, the IGF does produce results, and in this case, it has contributed significantly to improving child online protection. Thirdly, Mr. Chairman, you asked us whether the process towards enhanced cooperation should be a part of the IGF or elsewhere. Enhanced cooperation is developing---just think of the environment in 2005 compared to now and you will agree with me that cooperation has been enhanced and that the IGF plays a key role in bringing the relevant parties and issues together. The high level of participation and the fact that states from all regions have offered to host the IGF shows the value attached to this forum by all stakeholders, including governments. If there were no value in this forum, it would not have spun off the national and regional IGFs. Mr. Under-Secretary-General, let these facts guide the Secretary-General's recommendations. The E.U. looks forward to fruitful and inclusive discussions at the first rendezvous of the CSTD in May next year.

MOGENS SCHMIDT:

Let me congratulate you, Mr. Desai and Mr. Kummer, for the great leadership you have lent to the IGF process for the last four years. It has been greatly appreciated by all of us. UNESCO has been an active participant in this process from the outset, and se look forward to continue to play an important role in the, hopefully, extended period of the IGF. UNESCO has consistently highlighted that Internet governance must be based upon the principles of openness, freedom of expression, diversity, and universality or interoperability. You may even say that it is only openness and universality that can guarantee that every citizen in the world over time can benefit from the fantastic resource the Internet is for acquiring, sharing, and creating information and knowledge. Only universal and open technical standards can ensure that diversity and pluralism can continue to unfold on the Internet, and that connectedness can become truly universal. UNESCO's rich mandate encompassing education, science, culture, and communication and information is a useful soundboard for our IGF activities within such areas as freedom of expression, linguistic diversity, increased access and accessibility, privacy issues, and information and media literacy. The IGF has offered a much needed opportunity to discuss all these issues, and it has had success in impacting on existing government structures because it is multistakeholder. This and the fact that the IGF is, indeed, a forum, a platform for the discussion and sharing of ideas, opinions, and experience, has very much contributed to its success, and UNESCO strongly supports the IGF maintaining this forum character. We also hope that we can ensure stronger participation from the developing countries in the next phase of the IGF. UNESCO is ready to fully participate in what has been called enhanced cooperation, and is right now preparing major agreements with a number of international organizations like ICANN. Last month, UNESCO's 103-country general conference unanimously made a plea for UNESCO to strengthen its involvement in the international debate on Internet governance. Please be assured that we will do so next year in Vilnius, and in what we hope will be a whole new series of Internet governance fora.

MASANOBU KATOH:

I chair the international subcommittee of Keidanren, the largest cross-industry association in Japan. Keidanren has been involved in IGF activities from the beginning, submitting position papers, attending meetings, and organizing local IGF meetings in Tokyo. We find the IGF process very important and useful. Although it does not have decision-making power, open dialogues within IGF undoubtedly influence the policy and the behaviour of government, private companies, and civil society. We strongly hope that the IGF process will continue beyond its original mandate of five years. We propose continuation of IGF not simply because it is a useful multistakeholder forum, but also because we have many remaining and new issues to discuss. For instance, thanks to the development of the Internet and

ICTs, we are coming to the age of cloud computing, in which people will not need to own computers, software, or datacentres. By accessing a network, you can achieve anything you need. This whole world of cloud computing may give a new opportunity to those who did not enjoy the benefit of Internet in the past. At the same time, it may raise more complicated questions about privacy, security, and broadband access. We have discussed such issues in past IGF meetings, but because technology changes at Internet speed, we need to catch up. In conclusion, IGF has accomplished many things, but we have many new issues coming in the future, and we need to discuss them at future IGF meetings.

ROD BECKSTROM:

Our world has been made smaller by our technological advances. 4,000 years ago, incredible technology was exhibited in the pyramids. They were remarkable in what the showed about the engineering, construction and machinery of the day, and people from around the world came here to see them. Many millennia later the telegraph came and made the world much smaller, with news spreading instantly. Then the telephone came, connecting human beings with voice around the world. Then the radio came, and we could hear any person speak to millions of people around the world. And then the television came, and we could see other parts of the world. And then the Internet came, thanks to Bob Kahn, Vint Cerf, and other scientists, and it changed the world.

First we saw e-mail, just like the telegraph text. Then we moved to publishing with the Web, Tim Berners-Lee showed us. Then we moved to Skype and phone calls. Now we're moving to video, and now we're moving to something that the other electronic forums never had: social media. Youth are leading the way in this revolution, and we are not here to enable them, we are here to learn from them and to stay out of their way as the Internet continues to spread globally. So I had a chance to ask some people what they thought about the IGF, because they are not speaking on this dais. A man named Anwar said, "What I have learned is that there are so many different perspectives and controversies taking place;" and that while it is a rich debate, people aren't looking at how they fit into the ecosystem, but rather at what they could get out of the ecosystem. And then I spoke to Leila and she said it was about learning the tremendous responsibility that each of us feels as we're at this event. And then I really learned a lot when I spoke to Maha who said the best part of the event was the friendship and the community amongst the other participants. So what I would say is that in my organization, we have learned a tremendous amount from this forum. Thank you. We would like to see it continue. Most of the members of the communities that we're involved in are extremely positive about this forum. And most importantly, the youth have said they would like to see this continue. So yes to the future, yes to the youth, and yes to the Internet.

ABDULLAH AL-DARRAB:

The IGF is now four years old, and the question is what has it achieved so far. To answer this question, we have to be very open and frank, and each one of us should accept the ideas and opinions of others. There is no doubt that the as a forum for discussion, the IGF has achieved a lot of benefits. I would like to mention only a few of these. It has helped in bringing together all those interested in the Internet to discuss several issues related to governance. There are differences in opinions on critical Internet resources and so on. The forum meetings have been an excellent chance for me to meet people from all over the world. But there are some negative aspects. The participation of the different stakeholders from the developing countries is very limited, so such discussions do not reflect the true interest of all the stakeholders. This forum should be the arm that helps enhanced cooperation, which has not seen the light until now even though it was supposed to start before this forum according to Article 69 of the Tunis Agenda. Enhanced cooperation should start down another path from that of the IGF. I believe that the IGF as it is was a very good experience for all of us, but that it has also proved that the forum without enhanced cooperation is like asking a person to run who has only one leg. The most important objective of this forum was to help developing countries to bridge the digital gap. If we assess it from that point of view, the results are not encouraging, as the gap is getting even greater. These observations do not undermine what been achieved in this meeting, and I would like to thank the Egyptian management of this forum.

BILL GRAHAM:

The Internet is successful, in part, due to its unique model that relies on processes and organizations that are local, bottom-up, and accessible to users around the world, and that work together in a vital, responsive, and cooperative manner. The IGF has become an important element in this ecosystem. When we consulted our members and chapters all around the world earlier this year, they encouraged us to call upon the United Nations to extend the mandate of the IGF in its current form for another five years. The IGF brings together people who might not otherwise meet and inspires them to work effectively in support of people-centred development, a key goal of the WSIS. It feeds work in communities, countries, all regions, and at the global level.

The Internet Society believes that we must learn to think in terms of outputs *from* the IGF, not outputs *of* the IGF. Outputs come from the IGF when stakeholders learn, build relationships, and return to their homes and organizations to work together in ways they would not have done otherwise. We should not lock the IGF into a traditional institutional structure that would necessitate creating new bureaucracies and processes, and would make it less adaptable, responsive, and effective. In addition, there are significant costs to making the IGF a success, and our country hosts have made huge financial contributions. Some not-for-profit organizations, including the Internet Society, make regular contributions to the Secretariat, as do some businesses and a handful of governments. Others provide in-kind donations or support attendance at IGF meetings. We recommend that this voluntary and multistakeholder funding model be continued in the next mandate. The Secretariat must have greater stability and assurance in order to do its job, and we call on others from all stakeholder groups to help sustain the IGF in this material way.

WAUDO SIGANGA:

World Information Technology and Services Alliance (WITSA) members are from 72 countries representing some 90% of the world ICT market, and over 50% of them are from developing countries. WITSA supports continuation of the IGF beyond its initial five-year mandate, and maintaining the structures and processes in which all stakeholders interact on an equal footing. We are committed to working with other stakeholders to deepen and broaden participation from developing countries, and believe that the IGF has already demonstrated that it is flexible enough to allow for change, as is evidenced by the emergence of national and regional IGFs. Its value lies in its open nature, allowing all views to be expressed and the full range of experiences and expertise to be shared. In this way, we all continue to learn more about how to use, expand, and protect the Internet. The IGF should remain consistent with its original mandate for facilitating dialogue and sharing best practices and should not engage in the negotiation of formal documents or outcomes. Moreover, WITSA supports the continuation of an independent IGF Secretariat with an appropriate level of staff and funding to support the IGF's events and maintain continuity between its annual meetings. WITSA applauds the current Secretariat's efforts to serve all stakeholders fairly and equitably through their consistently excellent output, including the provision of online content, Webcasts and audio casts, and real-time transcriptions of the IGF sessions.

AYESHA HASSAN:

International Chamber of Commerce members include hundreds of companies and associations from across sectors and countries and of all sizes. Business around the world fully supports the IGF with its current structures and we urge its continuation. The IGF is addressing the items in its mandate in Paragraph 72 of the Tunis Agenda and facilitating multistakeholder dialogue that is inclusive and meaningful. It has also continually evolved and improved. I would like to highlight some of these items and the comprehensive ICC/BASIS input to the review questionnaire. Substantive discussions have taken place on all issues, including those that foster the sustainability, robustness, security, stability, and development of the Internet, and accelerate the availability and affordability of the Internet in the developing world. The IGF provides excellent human and institutional capacity-building opportunities on a wide range of complex issues and the policy approaches and choices that impact them. And every year, new issues are being brought into the process. One cannot help but come to an IGF and leave having gained insight and knowledge. Every IGF brings together organizations engaged in cross-cutting international public policy issues and participants learn about their work programs and activities, the status of discussions on particular issues, and those on the horizon. A wide range of stakeholders who connected at the IGF are now actively involved in the work of other organizations. This is an important value-add for all. It's not easy to measure, but it is still very real. Many stakeholders have commented that this is a one-stop shop for them to get information, make contacts, share experiences, and develop their understanding. Excellent outputs include the real-time transcripts of the sessions, the Chairman's Reports, the substantive inputs, and the synthesis and background papers. This unique forum allows us to discuss all relevant topics candidly. It maximizes participants' time by increasing their understanding instead of negotiating texts. And it is a catalyst for change---we have become more receptive to each other's perspectives and concerns, and as participants have adapted to this open environment, we have seen the level of rhetoric reduced and more informed decision-making by all. We believe that the IGF processes and structures are effective, and address the tasks at hand. We commend the leadership and hard work of Mr. Nitin Desai, Mr. Markus Kummer, and the IGF Secretariat. In conclusion, I would like to emphasize that ICC/BASIS members support the continuation of the IGF with its multistakeholder approach that leads to more informed policy and business choices. The IGF is having an impact, and real outcomes.

RICHARD BEAIRD:

The United States of America reiterates its commitment to the results of the WSIS, and in particular to the convening of the IGF. We appreciate the opportunity afforded by the IGF Secretariat to submit comments and views on the possible continuation of this forum. We will also submit our support in writing to ECOSOC through Under-Secretary Sha. The IGF has proven to be a valuable venue for information sharing and international dialogue. Its flexible structure, which includes open forums, workshops and main sessions, has evolved into a dynamic mechanism that facilitates the exchange of information and best practices among all stakeholders. Consequently, the United States supports the continuation of the IGF beyond the initial five-year mandate. We believe that the current work methods of the IGF are fully consistent with the principles agreed at the WSIS in Tunis. The United States commends the Secretariat, as well as current and past Multistakeholder Advisory Group members, for their tireless efforts. We hope that the cross-cutting themes of development and capacity-building find renewed emphasis in the IGF process. Finally, we wish to congratulate our Egyptian hosts for this, the 4th IGF. It has been a great success.

SHA ZUKANG:

Next I'll give the floor to Vladimir Radunovic of the DiploFoundation to screen a short film. [The film is displayed, then presentations resume.]

PARMINDER JEET SINGH:

I.T. for Change is of the view that the IGF is an innovative experiment in global governance. We would like the IGF to continue beyond its initial five-year term. However, we also believe more efforts are required to ensure that the IGF fulfils all parts of its WSIS mandate. The inclusion of nongovernmental actors on par with governmental actors is a key principle of the IGF and under no circumstances should this be diluted. The present support structure and institutional location of the IGF should not be disturbed. The IGF maintains a fine balance among stakeholders and institutions in the Internet governance ecology. The UNDESA has given fine support to the IGF and helped to maintain its independence and neutrality. Moving the location of the IGF into any of the institutions directly concerned with Internet governance will disturb this delicate balance and may harm the global public interest. An institution like the IGF should be supported by U.N. funds and should not rely on private funding or even on funding from a few countries, since global Internet governance issues entail geopolitical contestation. We agree with the Under-Secretary-General's statement in the opening session that the IGF should not make public policy, but that its activities should feed into global policymaking processes. To do so, the IGF requires structural improvements while keeping within its Tunis mandate. There should be a clear identification of key issues to be handled in an outcome-oriented way every year, while a broader set of issues can continue to be handled in the workshops. These key issues should have dedicated working groups that can do intensive preparatory work throughout the year, and IGF intersessional meetings can also be held for this purpose. With adequate preparation, including through research and background papers, these key issues should be taken up in a focused manner at the annual IGF meeting. After the IGF meetings there should be adequate follow-up work on these issues, which could later become some kind of outcomes. The Multistakeholder Advisory Group has to transform from a program committee to a more empowered entity that can interface with other organizations and can advise and make recommendations on the IGF. The working and output model of the Working Group on Internet Governance can be a good example to look at for this purpose.

ANDREW MILLER:

I firmly believe, as does my delegation, in a new mandate for the IGF. We want to thank Nitin Desai and Markus Kummer and his team for a fabulous job, and also our hosts here in Egypt. Just ones small criticism, if I may be so bold: one of the problems is that we all end up trying to get too much in, and I regret to say that I have to leave this room to now go back to a panel that I've got to address. A minor criticism, but a fabulous event and let's look forward, not just to Lithuania, but to Kenya.

KONSTANTIN KLADOURAS:

ETNO represents European telecommunication network operators in 36 countries that have substantial Internet operations. ETNO has been an active participant within the IGF from the beginning of the process. The IGF is one of the most innovative U.N. processes. It provides a reliable global basis for a cooperative, pluralistic dialogue that embraces all stakeholders. Much of its success stems from its open, inclusive, multistakeholder, and nonbinding character, which allows all parties to explore difficult issues without political tensions, and to speak freely. Such an approach is essential in dealing with the challenges the Internet faces. No other mechanism or organization can achieve this or is more appropriate. ETNO believes that the IGF has broadly met its mandate. Given the nature of the Internet and the continuing need to discuss public-policy issues around Internet governance with the equal participation of all relevant stakeholders, ETNO and its members offer full support for the continuation of the IGF in its current structure, past its initial five-year mandate.

OLGA CAVALLI:

I am speaking as coordinator of the working group of Internet governance of the Latin American and Caribbean Plan of Action for the Information Society, eLAC, 2010. The following statement was produced by this group and is also supported by the IGF of Spain. The IGF has been the inspiration of national and regional processes that are building capacities. All stakeholders are able to debate on an equal footing and exchange ideas of how to make Internet move towards the principles of the Tunis Agenda of the Information Society. There must be strengthened participation by governments, civil society, and the private sector of developing countries. This has been difficult due to the lack of resources and low awareness of this process. The IGF could also propose different ways to the stakeholders in order to enhance Internet access, especially in developing countries. The eLAC working group would like to see the continuation of the IGF beyond its mandate. Like the IGF, our group wants to enhance the multistakeholder participation system in order to have a wider base for broad consensus and agreement. Thanks to the IGF Secretariat for all their hard work.

LAMBERT VAN NISTELROOIJ:

The European Parliament has supported the IGF from the beginning by participating in all the meetings, and this time we were active via our members in several panels. We are aware of the important questions about Internet governance in the future, embrace the new generation technologies, but also advocate strong governance principles. This is not a debate just for public or private actors, it should be open to everyone, including civil society from all the parts of the world. The IGF method---open, multistakeholder, nonbinding--- is a laboratory, is unique, and should be continued in its current form. We should realize that the IGF is still young, and it has grown step by step in its content and outcome. It deserves further steps, further growth. The European Parliament will participate in the IGF 5 in Vilnius, and we will stimulate broader participation from other national and regional parliaments.

LIESYL FRANZ:

I am making a statement today on behalf of the U.S.-based associations that are represented here at IGF---TechAmerica, the U.S. Council for International Business, Net Choice, and the Association for Competitive Technology. Many of our respective member companies are here and actively participating, and I am delighted to express the U.S. industry's call for continuation of the IGF. We have participated in all the IGFs and we have seen the benefits it brings. We would like to highlight three points: First, it is precisely the multistakeholder nature of the IGF that gives it its greatest value. There are no other forums where governments, civil society groups, and industry can meet and work together on equal footing on these important issues. Second, a benefit of the IGF is its ability to be dynamic and timely in addressing the pressing issues of the day which in Internet time evolve quickly. In this way the IGF is a unique venue that enables information exchange and the transfer of technical expertise and policy experiences that participants can take home to their own national, societal and corporate environments. It allows a bottom-up discussion that is fuelled by the actors with the greatest stake in a stable, resilient, and innovative Internet. And the IGF allows for open and candid discussions because it is unencumbered by negotiations over diplomatic texts. Third, the IGF has a far-reaching impact in two important ways. It enables remote participation for those that are not able to be here in person. And we have seen the emergence of national and regional IGFs that allow for active and ongoing exchanges and help people to internalize and integrate what they gain from the global IGF into their own circumstances. We suggest the invitation of statements in written form from those that do not have the chance to do so during this session today. I would also like to give my gratitude to the IGF Secretariat, Markus Kummer and Nitin Desai, for their artful and graceful hosting of this event, and our Egyptian hosts as well.

SECK MACTAR:

The Economic Commission for Africa in the U.N. has called upon countries from Africa to apply the Tunis principles in the IGF process. We have analyzed the impact of the IGF in Africa, and it has been positive. This was also made clear at a recent African Union meeting. We think that IGF could come up with key ways to allow more active participation from developing countries, specifically African countries. This could be done by organizing sub-regional and regional IGFs like an East African IGF or a West African IGF. This would allow us to prepare before going to the global IGF, and to regionally examine key issues, such as security, Internet security, protecting children online, resources, capacity building, and access to broadband infrastructures. I conclude by congratulating our colleagues in the Secretariat for the difficult work that they have complete over the last few days, and all of our partners who have supported U.N. ECA and helped developing countries and African countries, specifically our partners in ICANN, the European Union, I.F., and others.

JOHAN EKMAN:

The European Youth Forum supports the continuation of the IGF. It provides a very good opportunity to bring forward the concerns and ideas of young people from across the world. Le me also use thank the Council of Europe for bringing us on board, it is a very good example on how youth can be brought into political processes at an international level. No policy that is directed towards young people can be credible if they are not strong stakeholders in the process from the beginning to the end. I want to add that while safety and privacy issues are a concern for many youth, we should not forget that political participation and freedom of expression should also be priorities.

PETER VOSS:

This forum was established as a unique platform for nonbinding, multistakeholder dialogue at the global level. It is the only forum that allows a gathering of representatives from all geographical regions, across all stakeholder groups, to discuss all aspects of Internet governance on an equal footing. The lack of pressure to negotiate binding outcomes contributes to frank and open exchanges. It is the opinion of Germany that the IGF meetings held so far have demonstrated its value. Firstly, the number and diversity of the participants, and the impressive amount of workshops and best practice forums, show that the forum is perceived to be useful. Secondly, the IGF has triggered follow-up discussions in dynamic coalitions and has inspired debates at regional and national level. Thirdly, the IGF complements other existing structures dealing with Internet governance issues. Fourthly and above all, the IGF has provided a space to address controversial issues and discuss possible solutions.

Germany therefore believes that the IGF should be continued beyond its initial time frame of five years and that its basic characteristics should be retained. However, Germany sees room for improvement. Given that the mandate of the IGF was agreed at the level of heads of state, it would be extremely difficult to alter that mandate. But it might be possible to interpret the Tunis outcome in a manner that could open up fresh avenues to explore. We could, for instance, improve the visibility of the outcomes by creating a database of good practices identified during IGF meetings, and by promoting the use of effective remote participation.

ANUPAM AGRAWAL:

I believe that it is imperative that IGF get an extension of another five years. I attended last year in Hyderabad as a simple Internet user, and therein I picked up the theme of security. It gives me immense pleasure to announce that in the last one year we have formed the Kolkata chapter of Internet society and are working extensively on data insurance, which could be very relevant in the forthcoming year of cloud computing. However, there are certain suggestions from my chapter. One, more participation from developing countries and emerging economies should be encouraged, and mechanisms for people could be put in place. Second, best practices case studies could be compiled from the IGF participants so that others can benefit.

BERTRAND DE LA CHAPELLE:

The answer is yes, five more years. 2015 is the timeline of the WSIS Plus Ten review mandated by Article 111 of the Tunis Agenda, point one. Second, improvements, yes again. Because it has matured each year, France is confident that the IGF will continue to progressively structure its working methods. France has submitted detailed proposals for operational improvements in the online consultations and is looking forward to making additional suggestions. During the now traditional annual consultations in February in Geneva, the working methods of the IGF are fully consistent with the mandate of paragraph 72 and the multistakeholder spirit of the WSIS. We must preserve this. And let's use the self-organizing capacity of the IGF to continue to improve its functioning. Finally, France is also looking forward to a first discussion in the CSTD in May of the U.N. Secretary-General's report following this consultation, as well as to IGF 2011, hopefully in Kenya.

WILLIE CURRIE:

The Association for Progressive Communications (APC) is of the view that the IGF has fulfilled its core mandate in terms of Paragraph 72 of the Tunis Agenda to constitute a space for multistakeholder policy dialogue on Internet governance. As an international civil society network that has participated in the formation of the IGF from the beginning, APC wishes to express its firm view that the IGF should continue. We say this because we believe Internet governance is distributed across a broad number of organizations responsible for the Internet. It is a unique form of participatory governance where all stakeholders concerned with Internet governance and development gather together for open dialogue and debate. This unique hybrid is necessary to create a space where all stakeholders feel comfortable and can contribute meaningfully and openly in discussion, debate, and collaborative planning with other stakeholders. It is important that we maintain this hybrid culture, which sits somewhat in the middle of the intergovernmental and nongovernmental landscape. However, it is also important that all stakeholders understand the nature of this hybrid culture, the challenges it presents, and the negative impact and consequence of any stakeholders exploiting their access to this forum or their positional power to control participation and determine outcomes. The purpose of a multistakeholder forum is to listen to others and try and reach common understanding instead of insisting on one's own point of view.

The IGF has developed as an adaptive ecosystem in which all stakeholders can interact on a basis of equality of input. This is an important dimension which depends on the adroit and careful shepherding of the IGF performed by the IGF Secretariat under the effective and diplomatic leadership of Nitin Desai and Markus Kummer. The vital role of the IGF Secretariat in its current form to the success of the IGF should not be underestimated. We have heard a lot of corridor talk that the status of the Secretariat should be changed in some way and located more firmly in the U.N. system. We feel that the IGF should continue to operate under the auspices of the U.N., while continually aiming to enhance its multistakeholder nature. We have also heard a perspective that says that those countries who provide financial support for the IGF have more say over its annual program. We have not found this assertion to be true. The IGF Secretariat needs independence from any form of undue influence. If this is a source of concern to some stakeholders, terms of reference for donations could be put in place to protect the IGF Secretariat's independence.

Consideration should be given to extending the time for written comments in this review to three weeks, so as to enable those who have been unable to express their views today to make an input. We also feel the IGF should be allowed to evolve as a forum that can produce outputs. The exact modalities of such outputs should be a matter for the stakeholders of the IGF to determine. One way of doing this may be to hold intersessional thematic IGFs during the year that discuss key issues and feed the results of their deliberations into the annual IGF meeting. Regional and national IGFs address more localized priorities while also informing the main IGF, and we propose that consideration be given to doing something similar on a thematic basis. Overall, participation from developing countries should be improved from all stakeholder groups. One way of doing this is to shift development from a cross-cutting theme to a major theme of the IGF. The IGF works, it's evolving, and it should continue.

ANA CRISTINA AMOROSO das NEVES:

Mr. Chairman, regarding the three questions that you put for us to think about, I can give you replies. Has IGF fulfilled its mandate? No. The task, the Tunis Agenda, is so huge that definitely we need more time to change the paradigm. If it can be improved, yes, of course. The IGF Secretariat, together with the IGF host countries, have shown us how much improvement we can get from the experience gained each year. Continuation of the IGF? Yes.

The IGF has been unique in providing a conscience to the Internet community. This is essential for the development of economies and societal improvement all over the globe. It has become a network providing incredible robustness. One of the most powerful outcomes of IGF until now is the spontaneous and diversified national and regional IGFs all over the world. They are the evidence that the IGF process is a great and powerful idea, and they generate ideas that can be brought up to the global IGF. When movements are spontaneous, it's because they are powerful, and they are meaningful for societies and for their citizens, and that can change the paradigm. And the IGF set-up is a remarkable cooperation geometry involving public and private institutions and not-for-profit organizations in countries and providing a space where the individual citizen and civil society participate on an equal footing along with more powerful entities. These features are not compatible with any hierarchical formal structure. No existing structure has ever produced such deliverables, and IGF should evolve as creatively as it has in the last four years. IGF is a unique platform that must continue for our own and future generations' sake.

GIACOMO MAZZONE:

The World Broadcasting Union gathers eight unions of broadcasters all around the world and more than 600 broadcast organizations with a total average audience of more than 3 billion people a day. We participated in the WSIS in 2003 and 2005, have organized and hosted with other members of the group this year's EuroDIG meeting, have attended the IGF from the first meeting, and have cooperated closely with the IGF Secretariat since the beginning. We are committed to this process, and keen to achieve the IGF's mandate in the Tunis WSIS agenda.

Mr. Sha Zukang asked us to answer to three questions. The first question: Yes, the IGF has been very valuable, we expect it will be even more valuable in the future, and we expect a lot from the next edition in Vilnius. This edition will have to deliver a report to the Secretary-General that will be very important for all of us because it will say something about the governance of the Internet. We wish that the Secretariat of the IGF will be strengthened in the next year and for the future. The second question: Yes, we consider that the IGF has achieved a lot in a multistakeholder environment, this is part of the reason for its success, and this environment has allowed new actors like the media to participate. Links of trust and even friendship has been built around these years, and on this basis we can achieve a lot. The third answer is: yes, but... As I've heard from other voices today, we hope that the mandate for the next IGF will be enlarged and new tools will be made available. We would like that the IGF be able to provide recommendation, guidelines, and best practices. We would like that it become the place where many of the functions that ICANN and ITU cannot be responsible for could be implemented. If you remember what Mr. Pepper said in this room just a few hours ago, that video will represent 60% of the traffic over the Internet in just two years, you can understand why we are so concerned about Internet governance and why we are so committed to the positive results of this process.

WILLIAM DRAKE:

The IGF has been a real success and deserves to be continued for at least another five years, pretty much in its current form. It has encouraged national and regional IGFs. It has promoted dialogue and mutual understanding. It has clarified issues that a few years ago were very complex and confusing to many people. It has served the international community in all kinds of ways that are really irreplaceable. It is uniquely able to address a broad range of issues, including cross-cutting issues that would not fit under the mandate of any one organization. Its design and operations are very forward looking and innovative, and they've brought positive attention to the United Nations from a wide variety of circles around the world. In particular, having a small, non-bureaucratic Secretariat that is open and responsive to all stakeholders has encouraged diverse participation by many people around the world who might not otherwise participate in a more formalized structure. These kinds of dimensions should be built upon. At the same time, clearly there's a need to undertake some targeted outreach, to enhance the participation of governmental and nongovernmental actors from the developing countries, and for the resources to do that with. It would be very useful to have a transparently administered program of travel funding for participants from least developed countries in particular.

About the main sessions, I think that the existing themes have proven to be very useful in the initial phases of the IGF, but it may be time now to consider some innovation and blending in of new topics that have not received as much attention as they might have. I would suggest two possibilities in particular that have been discussed here before, including in yesterday's session on the WSIS principles. Development would be a useful focus of a main session on an ongoing basis, so that we could really begin to talk about how global Internet governance arrangements do or do not affect development and what is the real meaning of IG4D. There are a lot of complex issues that require thinking through, and this is the place that it could be done. Similarly, it would be useful to have a session on the procedural aspects of the WSIS principles, one that looks at the transparency and inclusive participation of the different institutions involved in Internet governance, shares good and best practices, and identifies concrete ways in which organizations and networks have been bringing people in and making documents available to the world. Such sessions would increase the value of the IGF to the international community. Lastly, on the format of the main sessions, it might be useful to generalize the model that we've followed in the critical Internet resources sessions. The original model of having speaker after speaker increasingly is feeling a bit worn. It could be more interesting to have a session on a general topic like development in which perhaps three main issues associated with it would be identified and the focus of a well-structured and moderated discussion. The Secretariat could even provide some paragraphs of background to contextualize the issues and lay out the different positions, or you could involve people in some task groups to prepare these questions. There are all kinds of things that could be done between meetings to make the main sessions more responsive and interesting. At the end of the day, we might even be able to get a real sense of the room, of what level of consensus exists on the issues, or at least to identify more clearly where the areas of disagreement are that merit further consideration. That could give us more sense of a takeaway and make the experience more valuable to everybody.

THOMAS SCHNEIDER:

The Swiss government believes the IGF should continue and be based on the model that's been developed during the last four years. It should not be turned into something different. We support the statement made by the European Union on why the IGF should continue. How could it be further improved? First, we would like to see more tangible outcomes like a written document, but not one that has been negotiated. At EuroDIG, the European IGF, we produced a document with "messages." Each multistakeholder team organizing a session at EuroDIG formulated in their personal capacity a few bullet points on what they perceived as were the keys issues discussed, including recommendations on which there was common ground but also stating areas where there were differences of opinions. You can have a look at this document called "Messages from Geneva" on the Web site, EuroDIG.org. The global IGF could ask the organizers of the main sessions to draft such a document. Second, we propose that the global IGF could try to have sessions and workshops with no panels at all, but rather involving the whole audience in a discussion from the very beginning. This would avoid the problem of having the same panellists talk about the issues, and would allow more opportunities for more people to speak and create more interactive discussions and maybe new ideas.

Third, we should set a maximum number of workshops, like fifty. That would mean we fix a number of workshops, perhaps five, that are related to each main session, and maybe ten that were not related to any main session. And encourage people to merge their proposals. Finally, we should continue to enhance participation of youth, parliamentarians, small businesses, and stakeholders from developing countries in general. These are concrete steps that can be discussed. We will hand in our full position paper by e-mail tonight. To conclude, Switzerland as one of the largest contributors to the IGF trust fund invites all other stakeholders to contribute into that fund for the IGF Secretariat and the participation of stakeholders from the developing world.

CHARLES MOK:

This year we are working with the dot Asia organization, which is a non-profit top level domain name organization based in Hong Kong, to bring along six university students from Hong Kong and the China mainland to join IGF for the first time under the Internet Society's Ambassador Program. We find the IGF to be the most effective place for developing capacity on Internet governance because it allows equal participation from all sectors and levels of society. The Internet Society of Hong Kong concurs with the global Internet Society that the IGF should continue in its current format beyond the original five-year mandate.

Y.J. PARK:

The IGF has done a tremendous job implementing multistakeholder principles under the leadership of ICANN and ISOC. An ICANN-like, private sector-led multistakeholder process without a decision-making role, the IGF has became a great place to transfer knowledge and policy from the ICANN community to the developing world. Most actors from developing world, including governments, become recipients and learn the lessons. But in WSIS, the issue of who controls the Internet heavily engaged many of us. The IGF was created as a compromise between those who supported the status quo under one nation's provision and those who wanted more balanced roles for governments and international supervision of the Internet. While the IGF has achieved great success in diluting such political tension, ironically it became a forum without governance. So we have to admit that it failed to deliver on another WSIS mandate, namely continuing discussion of how to design Internet governance institutions.

It has been always challenging to put institutional aspects of Internet governance on the agenda of the IGF. In turn, this practice once in a while invited accusations of the IGF being a useless forum. Some stakeholders are content with IGF's networking and knowledge transfer functions and ask for a continuation. Others think the IGF is dysfunctional because it does not discuss how to design institutions and thus ask for its discontinuation. If the 2010 IGF can deliver on the WSIS mandates in a balanced manner, both knowledge transfer and negotiations over institutions, those who have different expectations may be able to build a consensus. Otherwise, I would like to propose that the IGF community should have a different forum for the different WSIS mandates. The current IGF continues to function as a knowledge transfer vehicle of ICANN's values to other stakeholders, while those who want to negotiate on institutions should have another platform.

ZAHID JAMIL:

I speak in part on behalf of PASHA, the sole Pakistani trade association of I.T. and I.T.-enabled businesses. At Sharm El Sheikh, we find the travel funding in relation to Pakistan to be interesting. The president of our I.T. association is funded by the APC. The telecom regulator is funded by ISOC. An academic is funded by a government. And a civil liberties advocate by a business, which is the ccTLD dispute resolution provider. The discussions, dialogue, and cooperation in implementation of policies catalyzed by the IGF on the ground in Pakistan is truly unique. Our interactions in the IGF have led to change in the format and processes of discussions in Pakistan.

The IGF also influenced the introduction in Pakistan of internationally compatible cybercrime legislation in consultation with business, civil society, legislators, and law enforcement agencies. The engagement of some governments and the Council of Europe has been valuable in this regard. Just yesterday, our federal investigation agency set up a cybercrime committee in the multistakeholder spirit of the IGF. The IGF helps local stakeholders, and the direct engagement of ICC/BASIS and Oracle in the policy process resulted in data protection guidelines that are also business-friendly and enable trade in I.T. services and outsourcing for Pakistan. It led to Nominet and DENIC exchanging best practices for the creation of what is now a successful domain name dispute resolution centre, thus demonstrating that dispute resolution can be effective in Pakistan's challenging environment, even as an online service. It has given us the model of multistakeholderism that has been injected into our ccTLD. It initiated engagement by Pakistani stakeholders within ICANN, not just for dot pk, but also on policy issues related to gTLDs and IDNs. It has allowed us to sensitize international governments, businesses, donors, and civil liberties groups and initiatives about the needs of all sectors in Pakistan. Here in Sharm, frank and constructive exchanges with the Commonwealth IGF is leading to exciting projects being initiated on the ground in Pakistan and other commonwealth countries. The IGF catalyzed these and many other efforts. They likely would not have happened, or would not have been successful, but for the IGF.

Developing countries at policymaking forums can find themselves caught between extreme views and politicization because language and outcomes need to be negotiated. The IGF provides a forum for dialogue and the exchange of best practices relatively free from such politicization. As such, we strongly and even passionately request that the decision-makers work to ensure that this unique and valuable forum is continued. Please do not take this opportunity away from us. We also hope that we maintain the founding principles of this unique process. Ensure the independence of the Secretariat, which has worked hard under the effective leadership and careful diplomacy of Mr. Desai and Mr. Kummer. Keep IGF multistakeholder, giving an equal space at the table to all stakeholders. Make national and regional IGFs an imperative, but not at the cost of this global IGF being available on an annual basis. I would just add that we don't see this as a platform for the capture of CIR. It is not a CIR forum. It deals with many other issues that are important to us all. Please let us see less of these politics. It doesn't help us, the users in the developing world, and puts the priorities of citizens and businesses on a back burner.

SUE BAXTER:

The question hanging over this conference has been should the IGF continue beyond next year, but a more fitting question would be why think about stopping a process that has proved itself to be useful, popular and gaining in momentum? We have a large number of people from so many walks of life and from all over the world here to network, share ideas, and solve common problems. Their enthusiasm is testimony to the value of the forum, and if they didn't find it useful they simply wouldn't come. And they have come this year, in record numbers. The reason the IGF is growing in momentum is due to its informality, its non-decision-making format, and its open participatory structure. No time is wasted in agreeing text, and the debate is on substantive issues. How many conferences offer an opportunity for teenagers to debate with senior statesmen? How many conferences spawn regional and national models based on the same organizing principles? The answer is not ones that have run their course. The challenges that are debated at the IGF will face us in each of our countries. And as long as those challenges persist, there will be room for an IGF. So the United Kingdom fully supports continuing the IGF mandate, and it fully supports continuing with an independent Secretariat, but funded perhaps by a wider range of stakeholders.

Of course there is room for improvement. The IGF could be more inclusive, in particular of developing countries and least developed countries. The agendas of the conferences could be more streamlined around core themes and more focused on emerging applications, and we could have sharper and more accessible summaries of proceedings capturing the diversity of views expressed, but not, I stress, conclusions or recommendations. However, we have made a great start, and the significance of this conference has resonated throughout the world. It has promoted the principle that the Internet is the future and the Internet is for everyone, and those are principles which the U.K. supports.

GAO XINMIN:

We are very concerned about the progress of Internet governance. The IGF plays an active role in promoting the development of Internet, and we have learned much from, and are much inspired by, the forum. However, we think the IGF should generate more tangible and practical results and propose the following improvements. Firstly, the IGF should concentrate on the main issues which are trans-national, and needed to be solved urgently in the process of Internet development, such as issues of critical Internet resources management, trans-national network security and privacy protection etc. We should raise the priority of these issues, establish experts committees, and pose solutions based on full discussion and common understanding among multi-stakeholders. A timetable is needed for these issues to be urgently resolved. Secondly, on national or regional issues such as a country's domain name, the management of illegal content, Internet for development, etc, we should encourage each country to formulate reality-based and effective governance measures on the base of common principles. It is necessary to respect the different realities in different countries, such as differences in the Internet's penetration and application levels, and to understand the diversities of national and cultural backgrounds. The IGF should continuously play the role of a best practice exchanged platform to create more opportunities for participation from the developing countries. Finally, the IGF should cooperate with Internet-related international organization as IETF to set up a consultation-based decision-making mechanism, and IGF policy proposals should be included in related international laws or regulations.

LILLIAN SHARPLEY:

The Number Resource Organization consists of five Regional Internet Registries: AfriNIC, APNIC, ARIN, LACNIC, and the RIPE NCC, all of which are represented here today. Together, the RIRs represent thousands of organizations worldwide according to the multistakeholder model. The RIRs have participated with a high level of commitment in the IGF since its inception. The RIRs were established by individuals and organizations from the community that operates the fundamental infrastructure of the Internet. The perceptions and concerns of developed and developing areas have always been incorporated equally into RIR discussions. The NRO believes that the IGF, as a non-decision-making forum, is an important and positive environment in which all stakeholders can participate openly and equally. If the IGF moves away from these fundamental principles, it will affect the ability of various stakeholders to participate equally and openly. So the NRO firmly supports the IGF continuing in its current form. Other alternatives will not satisfy all of the requirements of the IGF as defined in the Tunis Agenda. On the assumption that the IGF will continue being an open forum where no decisions are made, the NRO is committed to engaging with and financially contributing to the IGF as we have done for the past four years. At the same time, we call on other governments and organizations to join us in contributing financially to the IGF to guarantee its continued success.

WOLFGANG BENEDICT:

I am speaking on behalf of the Internet Governance Caucus, the main civil society group in IGF with around 100 member organizations from all over the world. We have three short messages. First, the IGF has to continue because the process has been successful and still has a lot to deliver. Second, the multistakeholder approach should be deepened and enlarged as it has proven its value for open discussion and jointly seeking solutions for present and emerging problems. We would like to underline the importance of the human rights dimension, which was once again confirmed in many sessions here in Sharm El Sheikh, and which should be further mainstreamed in future meetings. And third, the IGF Secretariat should continue in its present form.

JYRKI KASVI:

The IGF is the most concrete, successful, and promising outcome of the WSIS process. Let's not stop here. We continuously face new opportunities and challenges that need to be addressed together like consumer protection in cloud computing and freedom and responsibility of expression in new social networks. The IGF in its current format, with its Secretariat in UNDESA, is well placed for such open dialogue. After every IGF meeting I return home with new thoughts and ideas and my experiences have influenced my work in parliament. I cannot stress enough how useful the IGF is from national legislatures' perspective, because national legislation is not created in isolation from international context. We should give the IGF another five-year mandate to let it grow and mature and revisit the issue as we make the overall assessment of WSIS in 2015. It is the best demonstration of enhanced cooperation since its invention as part of a compromise deal in the late hours of Tunis in 2005. The Affirmation of Commitments is another promising example of giving governments a better chance to be involved. We should move on from the political deadlock that we have created around the term "enhanced cooperation." Stop demanding the Secretary-General to initiate something on which there is no agreement, and concentrate on action and making progress happen. So let's get involved and engage.

HEATHER CREECH:

IISD values the IGF as an open space for the frank discussion of views. However, it needs to engage a broader community of stakeholders, in particular the major civil society and other organizations that are established and active in other domains. The consumer associations, the environmental NGOs like WWF and ICUN, development groups like Oxfam and Save the Children, rights and citizens' groups like Transparency International and CIVICUS to name only a few. It is true that the IGF is open and anyone can come, but the IGF needs to reach out and demonstrate its relevance to those who need the Internet and are trying to utilize it to solve the environmental and developmental challenges of the day. And as the IGF begins to explore issues of development, the environment, and so on, these other experts and actors should be here. We are not going to get climate change solutions like smart grids without addressing fibre and cable infrastructure to the last mile and the addressing required for the Internet of things. We are not going to get to a green economy without the incentives for ICT innovation. We are not going to get a more informed and engaged global citizenry without addressing the challenges of access to knowledge, privacy, and digital accountability. But the stakeholders who work in these parallel domains are underrepresented here, and the IGF does not have a presence in their forums. The absence of the IGF from the climate change negotiations in Copenhagen, for example, is the type of disconnect that the world can no longer afford. The IGF is dealing with serious issues. Its mandate should be renewed, but that mandate needs to include a directive for broader engagement with other actors beyond the founding community of the forum.

FRÉDÉRIC RIEHL:

I will express myself in French to provide a little diversity. Very briefly, I will describe the WSIS follow-up process within the UN Commission on Science and Technology for Development (CSTD), which is one of the ECOSOC commissions, as a number of you wanted clarification of this process. The Tunis declaration, in its paragraphs 104 and 105, charges the CSTD with conducting the review of progress on the implementation of the Tunis Agenda. And in its resolution 2006-46, in paragraphs 4 and 6, the UN Economic and Social Council (ECOSOC) stated that CSTD is a centre for coordination of WSIS follow-up. So as of 2007, the CSTD has regularly been informing ECOSOC and the General Assembly on the progress implementing the Tunis Agenda. In 2009, the ECOSOC asked us in its resolution 2009-7, paragraph 46, that during its thirteenth session in May 2010, CSTD organize a substantive discussion on the progress in WSIS implementation. The CSTD comprises member states but will include in its meeting the private sector, civil society, and other organizations. The meeting will deal with the issues of follow-up, including the report of the Secretary-General on the enhanced cooperation, which ECOSOC didn't address during its July session. This is in paragraph 19 of the resolution of the same ECOSOC 2009-7. Also, we will be talking about the future of the IGF on the basis of the report of the Secretary-General, which is transmitted every year to the CSTD about the WSIS implementation according to paragraph 18, of the resolution 2006-46. This is what we will be accomplishing in May 2010. And as chairman of CSTD, I listened very carefully to what's been said here in Sharm El Sheikh, and I think that this will be very useful for us when we meet in May next.

MS. CHRISTINE ARIDA:

The IGF process is unique. It has enabled discussion and the exchange of information and experience and thus provides a great opportunity for capacity building. Its flexibility and dynamic use of topics and formats allows participants to converse freely, highlight points of agreement, and identify areas that need further discussion. It helps stakeholder groups to build common understandings of problems and to explore ways forward. The government of Egypt believes that this process should continue to remain open, inclusive, and based on the WSIS principles, and should always be directed to the attainment of WSIS development goals. The IGF has had a positive impact at the national and regional levels and is promoting dialogue there and linking it to the global dialogue. The adoption of remote participation tools has had an increasing effect on broadening participation of stakeholders, yet the participation of stakeholders from developing countries is still low and needs to be further strengthened at the IGF meetings and during the preparatory meetings. There is a need for more localization of the IGF agenda, with an increased focus on developmental aspects. And there is a growing need to encourage more national and regional IGFs and to extend their institutional relationships with the global IGF. There is a need to revise the working modalities of the open consultations as well as those of the MAG, and to explore the possibility of enhancing the financial and administrative capacity of the Secretariat. The IGF should continue to play an important role in influencing decisions made within other relevant bodies by reaching out to them in various ways. In conclusion, we support the continuation of the IGF beyond its five-year mandate, while maintaining its dynamic nature and the legitimacy provided by the United Nations umbrella.

MR. SHA ZUKANG:

So we have reached the end of the list of the speakers. I really enjoyed this session and listened carefully to your open and frank exchanges of views in the spirit of the multistakeholder approach, which has now become the signature of IGF. I would like to remind you that you will be given a last chance to submit written statement to the IGF Secretariat by the end of the day, today. For those who are not present here or did not have the opportunity to speak, you may likewise submit your written statement online. I will report to the Secretary-General of United Nations. He will then make recommendations in his report to the General Assembly next year on desirability of the continuation of the IGF. Once again, I extend my thanks to all of you who participated in this consultation, both online and off-line.

Taking Stock and Looking Forward:

On the Desirability of the Continuation of the Forum--

Written Statements not Presented in the Consultation

Statements received before the 18 November deadline

Singapore, Infocomm Development Authority

Jeff Brueggeman
Vice President Public Policy, AT&T Services, Inc.

Arthur Reilly
Senior Director, Strategic Technology Policy, Cisco

Jeremy Malcolm, Project Coordinator
Consumers International-KL Office for Asia Pacific and the Middle East

Google

IT for Change

Jacquelynn Ruff
Vice President, International Public Policy and Regulatory Affairs, Verizon

Lisa Horner
On behalf of the Freedom of Expression and the Media Online Dynamic Coalition

Pranesh Prakash
Programme Manager, the Centre for Internet and Society
on behalf of the Dynamic Coalition on Open Standards

Statements received after the 18 November deadline

Government of India

The Gender Dynamic Coalition

Extracts from the Statements

Singapore, Infocomm Development Authority

Governments have an important role to play in Internet governance---not only by implementing policies that will ensure citizens have access to the Internet and ensuring a safe and secure Internet, but also in creating a conducive investment environment for service providers and operators to rollout and upgrade the Internet infrastructure. Technical and commercial aspects of the Internet architecture, however, are best left to the private sector and free market forces. Likewise, civil society organisations and individual communities have a role in creating relevant content and community services that cater to the unique needs and situation of each society. Given the multiple roles played by different stakeholders, IDA believes that a multi-stakeholder model is the most appropriate for Internet governance issues. IDA considers the IGF to be a useful and open platform for different stakeholders to discuss and exchange diverse views on issues relating to Internet governance. IDA therefore supports the continuation of the IGF's mandate.

Jeff Brueggeman, Vice President Public Policy, AT&T Services, Inc.

AT&T strongly supports the continuation of the IGF and its truly unique model of multi-stakeholder interaction, which promotes an open and non-binding exchange of ideas and information on Internet governance policy issues. We have seen firsthand the continued evolution and improvements that have taken place within the existing IGF framework, which is flexible enough to accommodate ongoing improvements without the need for fundamental changes to the model. The IGF's policy discussions have been evolving over time, so that the process now encompasses both an exchange of views on challenging issues and an exchange of best practices and consensus views on more mature issues. At the same time, the flexibility of the workshop and dynamic coalition process has allowed a diversity of issues and views to be brought into the IGF process. Moreover, the IGF is having a broader impact beyond the annual meeting. The policy dialog and exchange of ideas is now being expanded and continued throughout the year through the emergence of regional and national IGF meetings, ongoing dynamic coalition discussions and the public consultations hosted by the IGF Secretariat. These opportunities for interaction are, in themselves, facilitating new interactions and openness to working across traditional stakeholder lines. These are additional positive indicators of the culture being established by the IGF community and the desire of participants to build on their experience at the annual IGF meetings. AT&T recommends that the IGF be charted for at least an additional five years, in order to provide stability for IGF participants and stakeholders.

Arthur Reilly, Senior Director, Strategic Technology Policy Cisco

Cisco has actively participated in all four IGFs and has seen its remarkable evolution into an increasingly valuable event that is a key focal point for many national, regional and global entities. Cisco strongly supports the continuation of the Internet Governance and its founding principles beyond the IGF's initial five-year mandate. Its founding principles, which have served to implement the IGF mandate in the Tunis Agenda, have provided a unique platform that: is open and transparent; multistakeholder, with everyone participating on an equal footing; focused on sharing ideas and experiences; does not develop a negotiated text; and has a light Secretariat that is funded by voluntary contributions from the multiple stakeholder groups and assisted by a Multistakeholder Advisory Group. These principles have made the IGF flexible enough to plan a substantive program while also easily adaptable to allow emerging issues to be introduced. The IGF has matured significantly since Athens as the individual members of the stakeholder groups have worked together under the above principles. They have been able to speak candidly, but also to listen. They have not had to position their comments to create output documents as they took valuable time to debate in support of their views. Instead, they could focus on sharing and receiving practical information. The human capacity building aspects of the IGF are significant and the potential in this regard is immense.

Jeremy Malcolm, Project Coordinator, Consumers International-KL Office for Asia Pacific and the Middle East

In 2005 in Tunis, it was observed that there was a gap in the existing regime of Internet governance in that there were transnational policy issues that were not being addressed in any global forum. That gap hasn't gone away, and the IGF is yet to develop from a simple discussion forum into a body that helps to develop public policy in tangible ways. To do this we would need to effect both structural and procedural changes so as to increase the IGF's legitimacy and effectiveness. The keys would be for the IGF to overcome the democratic deficit that plagues conventional international organizations, and to develop the capacity to produce non-binding policy recommendations as the Tunis Agenda expected it would do. Although the IGF is a multi-stakeholder organization without a defined membership, it is still possible to develop policy recommendations as is done in similar organizations. If the IGF's mandate is renewed as we hope, this can be made conditional on the reforms to make it renewed, stronger, and better.

Google

The IGF was designed to deal with global and transnational issues that demand coordination across political boundaries and sectors. The IGF is an incredible platform for bringing together people who care deeply and are passionate about finding reasonable and effective solutions to organize the globally shared online sphere. This multi-stakeholder community replicates the pluralistic nature of the net, with the IGF Secretariat a lightweight but smart institutional centre, self-organized workshops, and most of the organizational and thematic intelligence with the participants. Companies such as Google benefit from engagement with and feedback from the different stakeholders on a great variety of issues. In terms of the format of the IGF: The allows for outspoken exchange of ideas and views, and discussion across a wide range of issues, with the aim of understanding the various positions of the different sectors. This is possible because the IGF forum allows every sector an equal level of access and room to be heard; civil society and academia have the same voice as governments or private sector. Rather than being focused on end reports and statements, the very aim of the forum is issue-surfacing and issue-mapping, and the analysis of potential joint actions. The IGF is best understood as an early warning system that allows stakeholders to identify issues and frame them in a way that more formal and specialized institutions can work through to develop appropriate standards, self-regulation, codes of conduct, regulations, and laws. In sum,

Google believes that the IGF should continue and evolve based on the current multistakeholder format.

IT for Change

The IGF needs to be a standing or a permanent body, or at least be around for a very long time to come. But it cannot remain a 2-3 days conference held once a year. It needs to evolve an around-the-year work plan with substantive outputs. At present the 3 times a year MAG meeting mostly grapples with procedural issues, but as institution building stabilizes, these process issues will become relatively less important. It will be important to be able to produce substantive output, and keep up a substantive dialogue. Unfortunately, many in the MAG try to limit its role to a program committee, thought it is a fact that increasingly, directly or indirectly, a good amount of substantive stuff gets done in the MAG meetings. With institutional stabilization, such a substantive role has to be more clearly articulated/formalized. The best way to do so is to formally accept a clear role for MAG to do some degree of substantive discussions and produce outcomes on Internet policy related issues, to structure itself for this purpose. MAG working groups, taking in some outside members, around specific issues may be a very useful way to do so. The structure and work of WGIG may offer some good leads for this. A WGIG like work and output mode has to be taken up because both the annual meeting of the IGF and the larger global IG community require specific inputs based on a broad-based expertise.

Jacquelynn Ruff, Vice President, International Public Policy and Regulatory Affairs, Verizon

Verizon believes that the IGF is a unique and valuable venue that has demonstrated the feasibility and benefits of multistakeholder interaction as called for in the WSIS Tunis Agenda. Verizon has participated in every stage of the WSIS process and in all previous Forums. We have also lent our financial support to the IGF Secretariat so it can assist efforts to organize the best possible conferences. It is our intention to continue our participation if the IGF is extended with its current format and structure---namely, a non-decisional, non-binding, multistakeholder approach where all stakeholders participate on an equal footing. The IGF is not only fulfilling its mandate, it has become a premier venue for discussing key elements of Internet governance. It has welcomed diverse views, permitted a deeper interaction between all stakeholders, and fostered a culture of engagement. We look forward to continuing our support and participation in this successful effort.

Lisa Horner, on behalf of the Freedom of Expression and the Media Online Dynamic Coalition

We support the continuation of the IGF as a space for multi-stakeholder dialogue and cooperation. The Internet governance terrain is highly complicated and made up of a diverse and dispersed range of actors, institutions and processes. This makes the existence of a common, participative and collaborative space all the more important for coordinating our efforts and learning from each other. The WSIS Declaration of Principles reaffirms the importance of freedom of expression which, like freedom of the media, is a crucial component of the Internet governance agenda. The Internet is helping to more fully realize freedom of expression, but is also presenting new challenges and threats like enhanced censorship and surveillance. In this context, it is important to remember that freedom of expression is an integral aspect of the development process that cannot be ignored, replaced by symbolism or appended at a later date. We therefore advocate that the Forum continue, and for the importance of freedom of expression to be reflected in its activities and in its program. We also call for efforts to be made to make multi-stakeholder collaboration more meaningful, so that civil society, business and government stakeholders have equal input into governance policy and processes. This is necessary to ensure that progress in made in fostering an Internet that embodies and supports the WSIS Principles and human rights.

Pranesh Prakash, Programme Manager, Centre for Internet and Society, on behalf of the Dynamic Coalition on Open Standards

Open standards are crucial towards the realization of many of the WSIS principles and are instrumental in guaranteeing some rights that are not explicitly stated in therein. For these to be realized through a multi-stakeholder process, we believe that it is advisable that the IGF be continued beyond its present five-year mandate. Standards, although not created by legislatures, states or courts, create regulatory structures that transcend international boundaries, affect numerous public policy issues and impact developing countries and stakeholders who do not have an equal voice in their creation, management or adoption. The IGF affords these stakeholders a voice through bodies such as our dynamic coalition. Our work has benefited greatly from the openness and discussions at IGF. In 2006 we produced a set of principles on open standards that overcome the definitional debates and focus instead on use and effects of open standards. In 2008 we managed to build agreement around procurement guidelines. This year, 2009, we are taking the opportunity to highlight all the important rights for which open standards are essential, and are thereby connecting with the work being done by many of the other dynamic coalitions. While we have made a good start, there is much that still remains to be done. We advocate that the IGF continue in order to ensure that the WSIS Declaration of Principles, specifically in the area of open standards, be realized through a multi-stakeholder process.

Government of India

For most of the under developed and developing countries, present Internet management and allocation policies do not make Internet access costs manageable. India finds that the IGF meetings have facilitated open and inclusive deliberations and the exchange of information and expertise on the Internet and its governance. We find the process to be effective and the IGF Secretariat's capabilities to be unquestionable. It is therefore desirable that the IGF continues for a further period of 5 years. India proposes that the following items be pursued in the IGF: Regulation and legislation; ICT for development; community empowerment through integrated digital inclusiveness; addressing information poverty through content inclusiveness and integrated tele-centres; technological solutions for localization/multilingualization; and the impact of convergence technologies, the mobile Internet, and next generation networks.

The Gender Dynamic Coalition

The Gender Dynamic Coalition is of the view that the IGF is a unique innovation providing new avenues for deliberative democracy, and that its mandate should be renewed. However, significant structural improvements are needed for the IGF to fulfil the mandate and the expectations set by the WSIS. Governance is caught in masculine practices and women get excluded both in the name of "expertise" and by the masculine culture of the discourse. Special efforts are needed to recognize and privilege the substantive agendas of women from the global south and that women's rights advocates have articulated on gender and global justice issues. The IGF should also adequately strengthen its capacity building role and do so particularly with respect to the interests of communities in the global south and their women representatives. Lastly, though IGF's format gives women a much better chance of having their voices heard, its "formal" openness is not enough. More efforts should be made to improve substantive participation, including with speaking slots. We appreciate the efforts made towards keeping a good gender balance in the MAG, and the attempts to improve the balance of panellists in workshops, but much more needs to be done. It is not just important to have the numbers reflect gender-based parity, but also to have the agenda of the IGF shaped in a manner that is sensitive to and inclusive of a full range of gendered concerns that make explicit women's interests.

Emerging Issues:

Impact of Social Networks

18 November 2009

Chairs:

H. E. Mr. Samuel Poghisu
Minister of Information and Communications of Kenya

Mr. Tarek el Saadani
Advisor to Minister of Communication and Information Technology for Technology Policies, Egypt

Moderator:

Mr. Simon Davies
Founder and Director of Privacy International

Panellists:

Mr. Sunil Abraham
Director of Policy, Centre for Internet and Society, Bangalore

Ms. Dorothy Atwood
Chief Privacy Officer, AT&T

Ms. Grace Bomu
Manager, Actor and Policy advocate, Kenya-Heartstrings Kenya and Fanartics Theatre Company, Kenya

Ms. Rebecca MacKinnon
OSI Fellow, Global Network Initiative co-founder, Hong Kong

Mr. Sergio Suiama
Prosecutor for the State of São Paulo, Brazil

Ms. Rachel O' Connell
Vice President of people networks and chief safety officer for Bebo

Extracts from the Transcript of Proceedings

H.E. SAMUEL POGHISIO:

This session is about social networks, including user-generated content sites, micro-blogging, collaboration tools, and so on. In Kenya, we have developed one where our ministry is allowing the exchange of ideas with everybody in the industry, called the Kenya ICT Action Network, This helps us to foster dialogue and learning. But with every new development and technology, as you know, we have challenges that might require that we look seriously at the way we've done policy, business models, and the like.

SIMON DAVIES:

If I can suggest a focus, what have we brought out of this last few days that tells us something about the way the future will go in terms of social interaction? And imagine that future. What I'd like to do first is to take a look at the darker side, if you like, of what is emerging, and some of the threats and some of the consequences of the sort of social interaction that has been happening in the Web 2.0 space.

SERGIO SIUAMA:

Nowadays, social networks are the fourth most popular online activity, ahead of personal e-mail. Almost 70% of the Internet population in the world, and 80% of the Brazilian Internet users, actively interact through social networking sites such as Facebook, MySpace, Twitter, and BEBO. In Brazil as well in India and Pakistan, the most popular social networking service is Google's Orkut. More than 30% of Brazilian users access regularly Orkut and about 25% of them are children and teenagers. The most accessed Internet services in Brazil are provided by companies which are physically located in the United States, but tailor their services with local content and local language in order to facilitate the development of their business. In 2005, Google set up a branch in São Paulo but the small structure provided by the company wasn't able to cope with predictable problems that occur in a space cohabited by 30 million people. Brazilian authorities have been receiving reports of distribution of child abuse images, exposure to racist material, drug dealing, cyber bullying, defamation, and encouragement of violence or self-harm behaviour on Orkut. In August, 2006 the federal attorney's office for the state of Sao Paulo started a lawsuit against Google Brazil because the company initially refused to comply with Brazilian judicial orders in cases of violations of users' rights on Orkut. After two years litigating, in July 2008, the parties reached a settlement according to which the company agreed, among other obligations, to comply with Brazilian legislation; store traffic data for at least six months; take down child abuse images; develop a proactive system of child abuse images detection, removal and report to law enforcement; and to establish a customer service able to quickly respond to all users' complaints. But the number of reports of child abuse images increased significantly, it's an average of almost 2,000 new cases every month.

We are investing in prevention projects developed in a multistakeholder environment. Last February we sponsored the Safer Internet Day Brazil, which included activities addressed to teachers and to the general public of the Internet. To conclude, I wish to point out some of the main governance issues that have been raised by this case. First, which criteria should be used to define the ability of a particular country to legislate over and sanction conduct committed on the Internet? Second, is it legitimate to impose rules on a company's local office regarding a service operated from the United States. The international cooperation instruments are very weak. Third, what are the basic standards that should be adopted by Internet Service Providers (ISPs) in order to cope with human rights violations on the Internet? Fourth, is national law enforcement prepared to deal with the massive number of crimes committed on social networking sites, and what if we cannot? And lastly, is it necessary to ensure minimum levels of transparency and social accountability of service networking services? We have the data of Google Orkut, but what about Facebook, MySpace, BEBO, and other social networking sites? How many cases of child abuse images and other human rights violations do they have and how many reports do they send to the National Center of Missing and Exploited Children in the United States?

Ours is the first agreement according to which a social networking company based in the United States will comply with national legislation, and we are concerned to avoid any kind of criticism regarding authoritarian measures. That's why we base our position on international treaties concerning the protection of children, discrimination, racism and so on. This sets us apart from other attempts to impose national legislation.

SUNIL ABRAHAM:

I'm going to raise nine emerging issues about social media and I categorize them into four categories: Intellectual property rights (IPR), morality laundering, the hegemony of the connected, and the hegemony of text. Issue one, under intellectual property rights, exceptions and limitations to copyright law that have traditionally protected consumers during the age of offline software are completely irrelevant in the age of online software. Examples include the right of the consumer to review, the right of the consumer to privacy, and the right of the entrepreneur or enthusiast to make interoperable, complementary, or competing products. All these rights used to be protected under the right to reverse-engineer. Issue two under IPR: On some corporate social media platforms, copyright takedown notices from one political party are acted on much more swiftly when compared to similar takedown notices from an opposing party. Issue 3, under IPR: Some rights holders, and in particular news organizations, use copyright takedown notices selectively on contents that oppose their editorial viewpoints. Issue four under IPR: The increased use of automated enforcement of copyright by rights holders is seriously undermining freedom of expression on the Internet, as in the case of the baby dancing to Prince's "Let's Go Crazy."

Issue 5: Morality laundering, like policy laundering, is trying to impose a globally homogenized morality regime. Breast-feeding pictures on a social network were deleted because they were considered obscene by a social media Web site. Issue six under morality laundering: A topic from a micro-blogging site was considered a racial slur in a northern country and was then deleted by the owners of the Web site, even though this was not considered a racial slur in the southern country where the Twitter community was using it. Issue seven under morality laundering: Photographs of public life on a beach in a country where nudism is the norm becomes child pornography in another country. Issue eight under the hegemony of the connected: The multiplicity of religious traditions is reduced to a monoculture on community-managed social media platforms that depend on editors to determine the truth. That is because upper crust and upper class populations

521

have greater access to the Internet. Issue nine on the hegemony of text: Literate communities will try to maintain their hegemony on the Internet. Community managed social media platforms that depend on textual citations often ignore the knowledge of oral communities from the south.

SIMON DAVIES:

Should the automation of enforcement be outlawed?

SUNIL ABRAHAM:

It's not possible to remove machine involvement in moderating content online, but the process has to become more transparent so that the public will know what happened and why and there is the possibility of appeal.

RACHEL O'CONNELL:

I chaired the E.U. Safer Social Networking Cross-Industry Task Force, that's 18 social networking companies that have come together and are working with the European Commission and a number of civil libertarian, child welfare, law enforcement, and parenting groups to discuss on what principles should we operate our services. We came up with seven principles that relate to education and ensuring that we have prominent and easily accessible safety messages, and to reporting abuse and providing people with the technologies and the capabilities to use the Internet safely. As an industry we are actually doing a lot of filtering at the back end and have very strong links with law enforcement. We look at the legal issues in each of the countries and the markets in which we operate and see how that ties with being a U.S.-based company. And we're also aware of the multinational legal assistance treaty, in terms of working with law enforcement and investigators.

If you Google you'll come to the E.U. page that contains the principles, and we decided that each of the now 23 signatory companies needs to self-declare how it's implemented them and each of the substantive recommendations. In addition, those self-declarations are being reviewed by expert independent researchers, and their report will be released to coincide with European Safer Internet Day, which actually has become almost a global Safer Internet Day. So very shortly, we'll have a review of the social networking sites and how they've implemented. Similarly in the U.S., the attorney generals had some concerns about how social networking sites were operating, and you will know that Facebook has an internal auditor to ensure that they are meeting the requirements outlined by the attorney generals, and similarly MySpace has an agreement with the attorney generals. So there is an incredible amount of work going on ensuring that due diligence is conducted and that there's transparency and accountability. That said, there is still a lot of work to do, as there always will be. And on child pornography, for example, AOL has been working very closely with the National Center for Missing and Exploited Children.

GRACE BOMU:

I'm here to talk about the impact of social networking tools in marketing plays in Kenya. I work for two theatre companies. Our system is not the traditional theatre system---it's actors who write the scripts, and nowadays even our friends help us. On our Facebook book, people propose lines, other people propose that they be actors, and this has really changed the way we do business. Also, the company used to do marketing for itself, now we are doing it through our friends. Our management uses a mobile phone to update our Facebook page, take the comments, and so on. People pay for plays using mobile money payment systems on their Facebook pages. And while Kenya is an oral literature kind of state where it's the older people who hold traditions, now even younger people are able to say proverbs and things that were previously reserved for the older generation.

The challenge that we're facing is fan control because people are using anonymous names to give negative criticism, and competitors are also doing this. We have also had a problem of balancing what some people call abusive language and what others think is within artistic expression. Dispute resolution where there are no laws is a hard thing, such as if somebody insists that they were defamed on our page and the other person claims it was artistic expression, or when the page manager is in a place with no network coverage so it takes hours to take down the content. And we are using Facebook and Twitter which are hosted in the United States, instead of generating local content, which is one of the things that Kenya really needs. So these tools have really helped open up the culture and expand freedom of expression. But we as a company need to come up with a code to help in balancing the competing interests.

REBECCA MacKINNON:

I have been asked not to name any member U.N. member countries, so I will speak generally. But one of the things that people have been saying throughout this IGF, both in plenary sessions and in workshops, about social networks is they are spaces where individual citizens can speak truth to power. Spaces that help to make government and other institutions more accountable to individuals. This is happening all over the world, across a range of political systems. And that governments all over the world are also responding positively and using social networks to have better dialogue with their citizens. But there are a few trends that are counteracting the potential of social networks to be a force that can truly help citizens participate in public life. And that may, perhaps, be contributing to social networks acting as more opaque extensions of incumbent power in some situations, rather than as transparent conduits between citizens and institutions.

I'll raise four basic points. One has to do with the liability that is placed by governments on social networking services. In some jurisdictions, international social networking sites end up being blocked because the government is not happy with some of the content being posted. And in some of those jurisdictions, what ends up happening is that a robust set of domestic social networking sites evolve that are held liable for all the content. And so in order to comply with government requirements and definitions of what constitutes legal speech, these sites end up having to develop large departments of people whose job it is to police content. And so in addition to child pornography and things that are universally considered bad, certain political speech is also is considered to be against the law, and companies are expected to censor that. So international social networking sites that want to operate in certain jurisdictions have to make a choice, either to be blocked to users in that country, or agree to develop a locally hosted site in the local language which would then be subject to greater local jurisdiction, and agree to police it. And certain companies have chosen to host locally and comply with government requests for political censorship.

Another point has to do with different regulations across countries on whether users are allowed to be anonymous. And there's at least one country where now anybody who uses a social networking site or Web service over a certain size has to register with their national ID number. A number of human rights groups have expressed concerns about some users who have been traced for political speech. As a result, at least one international social networking service decided to disable the local uploading of videos and comments onto their service, so people in that country have to use the international version of the service. Third, we also see situations where administrators of global social networking sites will perceive something as being against the terms of service when it's intended to be quite different from what they think. There are political activists from a range of countries who found their Facebook accounts frozen because their pattern of activity resembled spamming, and this had an impact on their ability to conduct political activities. And there have also been situations on video and photo hosting sites where political activists posted images of abuse by authorities, and these were quite graphic and deemed to be against the terms of service. The people concerned felt that if even these sites do not enable me to speak truth to power, then where can I go? So that's a sort of human rights issue.

To conclude, I am part of a new multistakeholder initiative called the Global Network Initiative (GNI) that is set up around some core principles of free expression and privacy for the ICT sector. Our approach is that a lot of these issues are very difficult to legislate for because they involve very nuanced situations that differ greatly from service to service and context to context. And yet companies do feel that there is a need to have some kind of assistance in doing the right thing. How can social networks really fulfil their potential and serve their users and be trustworthy so that people can use these services without becoming victims of oppression, or at least be able to make informed choices about what is possible on these services. And so the GNI combines companies, human rights groups, socially responsible investment funds, and academics to help companies proactively figure out how do you assess in advance what might some of the free expression issues in order to avoid problems and to make difficult choices about how to structure businesses, e.g. what markets you can go into or perhaps what markets one might not go into. There is really no jurisdiction on the planet where Internet companies do not come under some kind of pressure from governments to do things that arguably may infringe on the civil liberties of users. And so that this is really a global initiative, trying to come up with global solutions that need to be flexible and tailored to individual situations.

SIMON DAVIES:

What is best for an unnamed company in deciding whether to go into an unnamed country with restrictive conditions? Is it better to go in and help develop the infrastructure, or should it stay out?

REBECCA MACKINNON:

It's not a black-and-white answer. There are nuanced choices you can make about where are you hosting your data, how are you structuring your business processes, etc. Some companies have made decisions about going into difficult markets but managing their data in a certain way that it makes users less vulnerable. Or being very clear with users how and where their data is being hosted and with whom it will be shared so that they can make informed choices. Just to disengage is not the answer. It's more about intelligent, thoughtful engagement because pretty much all markets are difficult in one way or another and, you'd have to restrict yourself to the moon if you really wanted to avoid all difficult situations.

FROM THE FLOOR:

I was invited to contribute to this session on behalf of UNESCO as a digital literacy expert. I would like to emphasize the benefit of social media in general. They have lowered the threshold for all users to produce their own content in their language and tradition. And it is not only uploading text, video, photos, it's also tagging or labelling or rating content that is already produced by other users. It's important to focus on the responsibility of the users, who are not well equipped to take on this responsibility.

FROM THE FLOOR:

This is Pavan Duggal. I am the president of Cyber Law Asia. This morning we had a workshop on social media and legal issues and challenges. And one of the most concrete things that came out was the need to form a dynamic coalition on social media and legal issues, so we have. Everybody is aware of the various legal issues surrounding social media like data protection and privacy, jurisdiction, and the ownership, storage, retention, and transmission of user-generated content. For some of the rights discussed this morning and there are no concrete answers. For example, do we have a right to be anonymous? Do we have a right to oblivion? Can there be a right to delete in the context of social media? Is there a right of purging of children-generated content? And finally, can there be a right to forget and to forgive in the context of information? There was almost unanimity that we need to talk more. People who use social media normally perceive as a matter of trust that whatever they are putting in on any social media platform is theirs and will remain for them, with them for posterity. Now, those are premises that are going to be challenged as things go. And there is the liability and responsibility of service providers. There is no international consensus or agreement on the international response to these legal challenges, and national legislations have not yet addressed the issues. It's time for stakeholders to come together. So the dynamic coalition came up with draft objectives, including to disseminate more information and knowledge as to where things are because right now. We just began scratching the tip. An online list could be created. The relevant stakeholders could be invited. We need to make it as broad-based as we can. Certain online activities are proposed. If we can identify critical areas vis-à-vis legal issues and social media this could be part of the overall thought process and evolution of the IGF. So the coalition hopes to contribute in this small manner by contributing more awareness, by disseminating knowledge, and also by providing the relevant platform for relevant stakeholders to come, discuss, deliberate, analyze and thereafter encourage national governments.

FROM THE FLOOR:

Alejandro Pisanty, ISOC Mexico, National University of Mexico. Let us just remember social media don't kill, rape, or traffic with images of children abuse. People do.

FROM THE FLOOR:

My name is Max Senges. I am chair of the Internet Rights and Principles Coalition, and I work for Google. I co-organized a workshop with Bertrand De La on the governance of social media. It was an issue mapping exercise where we tried to get some of the vocabulary right. Is it social media and Internet governance or the governance of social media. We also experimented with a little bit new format where we spread the discussants across the room and had really short introductory statements to open up the discussion, and then tried to really interact with participants, which I think was a quite lively and interactive format. We're thinking about ethical principles online, how to prevent and punish harmful conduct. And to what degree and how must user generated content be governed by users directly. An interesting example is that Wikipedia has come up with an intense debating and governance structure. Should we have something similar for the social networks? Another issue was the data that is produced when somebody tags somebody else on a photo on a social network. We all agree what we're talking about but we don't even know how to call it, and that indicates that while the traditional definitions of human rights are still valid, we need to think about how to use them in this new context, and to develop meaningful human readable warnings that are easily understood by the users.

H.E. SAMUEL POGHISIO:

With the IGF and engaging each other we are able to meet the challenge. The examples given are very practical and in governments especially we need to be listening to what these contributions mean for legislation and for the way that we handle situations. It moderates the way governments will respond when people complain about the effects of social networks. We should encourage it and build more usages, but be ready then to deal with legislation and regulations. I believe we are moving in the right direction, and that more communication, more of the IGF, will help us.

Closing Ceremony

18 November 2009

Mr. Sha Zukang
United Nations Under-Secretary-General for Economic and Social Affairs

Ms. Anja Kovacs
Fellow, Centre for Internet and Society, Bangalore, India

Mr Raul Echeberria
CEO of LACNIC and Chair of the Board of Internet Society (ISOC)

Mr Herbert Heitmann
Chief Communications Officer, Global Communications, SAP; Chair, EBITT
Commission, ICC, Germany

Mr Aurimas Matulis
Director, Information Society Development Committee, Lithuania

H.E. Mr. Tarek Kamel
Minister of Communication and Information Technology, Egypt

Extracts from the Transcript of Proceedings

H.E. TAREK KAMEL:

I'm delighted to introduce our first speaker this evening, Mr. Sha Zukang, the
United Nations Under-Secretary-General for Economic and Social Affairs and
the co-chair of this event, to give his closing remarks.

SHA ZUKANG:

Let me begin by thanking the government of the Arab Republic of Egypt, our
most able and generous host. We are extremely grateful by the unprecedented
support given by Her Excellency Mrs. Suzanne Mubarak, the Prime Minister
Dr. Ahmed Nazif, and particularly, of course, national but not least, our
minister, Tarek Kamel. This has been a good opportunity for us to come
together and express our views on the many challenges we face in Internet
governance. With each IGF, we have seen progress as we build our shared
understanding and knowledge of Internet-related issues. The meeting here in
Sharm El Sheikh has built on the experience of the previous meetings. Athens,
in many ways, was an experiment, and Rio, as our Brazilian friends put it,
was Athens-plus, just as Hyderabad was Rio-plus. Each time, the IGF
matured and allowed for constructive discussions in a way that was not
possible before. Sharm El Sheikh is definitely Hyderabad-plus. The quantity
of participation has been impressive, and so has its quality. Delicate issues
that were once uncomfortable to address are now discussed with noticeably

greater ease and candour. I expect that there will be an equally open, honest, and enlightened exchange of ideas at the 5th meeting of the IGF in Vilnius, Lithuania, next year.

Here are some points I take away from our four days of discussion. First, as Her Excellency, Mrs. Suzanne Mubarak reminds us, children and youth are the driving force behind many of the new technologies and services that are of increasing importance to the Information Society. While I acknowledge the powerful role of young people in shaping the future Internet, we must also be aware of the threats to their well-being that the Internet can bring. Education and sharing of knowledge are useful starting points for addressing this critical issue. Second, consensus has been building that cybercrime, cybersecurity, privacy and openness is the joint responsibility of all stakeholders. The United Nations General Assembly is considering the issue of cybersecurity in its current session. I'm sure it will be very helpful for United Nations member states to know the views of IGF participants in this regard. Third, there is general agreement that the issues of access and diversity remain central to IGF. As the next billion people come online, new challenges and opportunities will emerge. The Internet offers unprecedented opportunities for countries and peoples in all corners of the world to promote economic development, social inclusion, expression of culture, and ideas in the rich array of languages. The conversion of that potential into reality requires that the Internet be managed for the benefit of humanity as a whole. Let us not leave anyone behind. The dialogue on issues of inclusion of disabled persons reminded us of the need to create an information and knowledgeable society accessible to all. Human rights are at the heart of the United Nations. It was pleasing to see the IGF raising awareness of the obligations we have towards disabled persons and for promoting tools that enable their full participation in society on an equal basis with others.

Fourth, the forum has raised questions about social media. Some participants have suggested that the real issue may not be as much in determining whether new media are either fostering or jeopardizing diplomacy or whether they are bringing down barriers. The real issue is whether the content available through social media is assuring a better informed society. We see the importance of bringing youth who are active users of social media into the discussion. Fifth, on the desirability of the continuation of the forum, we have noted the centrality of the WSIS principle of inclusiveness and the need for continued discussion on public policy issues related to Internet. In the lead-up to Sharm El Sheikh, opinions ranged from the status quo to termination of the IGF mandate to calling for improvements. We will have to spend some time to make sense of all viewpoints when reporting back to the Secretary-General. The Secretary-General will then make his recommendation to the U.N. General Assembly, taking the opinions expressed during the consultations into account.

I express my personal thanks to all staff from the United Nations including those from the United Nations headquarters, the Division for Public Administration and Development Management of DESA, the finance office, the capacity development office, the Department of Public Information, the legal office, the security staff from Geneva, the translators, and my IGF Secretariat, led by Mr. Markus Kummer who has done an excellent job as usual. My brother, Nitin Desai, has also made big contributions. They have all contributed to the success of this forum. Most of all, I thank you the participants for making this such a constructive event. We registered more participants than ever before, more than 1,800. The sessions and workshops are made possible through the hard work of the participants. The IGF was set up to promote dialogue among stakeholders, and we should be pleased that the multistakeholder collaboration the IGF embodies has been a foundation of its success. Thank you, and we shall all meet in Vilnius next year.

ANJA KOVACS:

Thank you for this opportunity to address the assembly on behalf of civil society, it is a real honour. And thank you also to the organizers and the government of Egypt for creating such an excellent environment for us to meet and hold our deliberations. I would like to celebrate with you two important achievements we have made during this IGF. The first is the progress in recognizing the importance of human rights and a people-centred, development-oriented, non-discriminatory Information Society. For example, in the main session on security, openness, and privacy, speakers across all stakeholder groups no longer couched the debate in terms of security versus privacy, but rather in terms of security and privacy. Security, it was consistently argued, while obviously deserving our attention, should not be used to justify curtailing long-standing gains in human rights. Another achievement was the attention to where we stand in promoting a people-centred, development-oriented Information Society more generally. The main session on Internet governance in the light of the WSIS principles clearly confirmed the urgent need to pay greater attention to this issue. Suggestions included devoting a main session to Internet governance for development for next year, and I hope this will be taken up.

While we have reasons to celebrate, important challenges remain. Throughout the IGF the value of the multistakeholder model has been recognized by all the stakeholder groups. But we need to further strengthen participation from underrepresented countries and groups. It is important that we do not restrict our efforts to capacity building, significant as that may be. More crucial is that the agenda consistently speaks to the concerns of actors in the developing parts of the world. The reconfirmation of the importance of a development agenda is a very important step forward. Within this agenda, it is crucial that we start to discuss some of the specific issues that require our attention like access to knowledge, which increasingly is threatened by new policies that make intellectual property regimes more stringent day by day. Starting the debate here in the IGF is certain to attract a large number of developing countries participants, including governments. I hope with all my heart that we will continue to get the opportunity to work together on important Internet governance issues with the support of an independent Secretariat that can ensure an environment generally inclusive of all stakeholders. Only when such open, inclusive conditions govern our own processes may we create a genuinely inclusive Information Society with opportunities for all.

RAUL ECHEBERRIA:

Mr. Chair, Minister Kamel, distinguished colleagues, I thank the government and the people from Egypt for their generous hospitality and congratulate our host for the magnificent organization of this meeting. From this meeting have emerged a lot of opportunities for partnerships and collaborations between stakeholders. In our case, the technical community and its organizations have held a lot of workshops working with other stakeholders on matters like IPv6, IXPs, international connections, and those experiences have been very successful. We are very happy with the results that were achieved in those activities and think that it will be the basis for future work. The ways in which stakeholders related to each other has changed in a positive way. This forum is a powerful opportunity to participate in a global and diverse community, sharing information and practices and receiving feedback. We should continue working in this way and going to different regions to get more and more people involved. We will continue working in ensuring that the IGF meets the expectations and the needs of both developing and developed regions.

Next year when we meet in Lithuania, we will appreciate the impact of the IGF in the reports the different organizations bring to that meeting. When we started we didn't expect to set up a new governance model. But this experience has impacted other environments, influencing the Internet governance models at the regional and local levels as well as other forums on other matters different from Internet governance. We weren't trying to set an example, but we have contributed very much to change in the stakeholders participate in many different settings. This is the right path. I would like to thank Nitin Desai and Markus Kummer for their excellent work in organizing the IGF and the Multistakeholder Advisory Group, which has proven to be a very good model for working with this IGF. The participation of all stakeholders in that group has been one of the reasons of the success of this IGF. And we hope that it will continue in that way.

HERBERT HEITMANN:

Minister Kamel, Under-Secretary-General Sha, I would like to second all the previous speakers in thanking the people and government of Egypt for hosting this year's event and their great hospitality. Like the IGF, BASIS and ICC's EBITT commission are no strangers to mobilizing stakeholders with varying perspectives, with the intention of finding common ground and of working towards a common goal. The last four days have provided us with a unique opportunity to undertake frank and open discussions on a wide range of issues. We have done this with interest groups that we might not otherwise have had a chance to engage with. We have exchanged best practices and considered the best policy approaches to access and diversity, online safety in Web 2.0 environments, and so on---there is nothing that cannot be discussed here. The IGF never fails to underscore how vital the Internet is as a vast resource of information, tools, knowledge, and services. Tapping into these resources can help us find solutions to many of the issues we face in today's fast-paced global economy, from climate change to health, the digital divide, education, and economic recovery.

Business has long been a supporter of the unique IGF multistakeholder format, and appreciated the range of voices that contributed to and enriched the discussions. As a major contributor to the success of the Internet, business knows that effective, Internet-related policies can bolster the Information Society and bring more benefits to more people. We also know that the most effective policies are those that are well informed. Informed policy approaches are pro-competitive and consider issues such as free flow of information, data protection, and security. We came to Sharm El Sheikh not only to have our say but, equally important to us, to listen and learn from others. Over the last four days, the forum has provided us with insight into the priorities and concerns of the others. We come away better informed about who is doing what in technical areas and other Internet-related matters. This one-of-a-kind environment of multistakeholder exchange helps us to find new understandings, common interests and opportunities.

Because our focus has been on substantive exchanges instead of negotiating texts, our time here has been put to good and practical use. This will enable us to take a more informed policy approach to Internet governance. It will move us towards collective solutions that are both coordinated and comprehensive. This is why the continuation of the IGF in its current format and based on its founding principles, is crucial. The IGF is a great success, and today we have seen overwhelming support for its continuation. If imitation is the sincerest form of flattery, then the national and regional IGFs that we have seen emerging pay testimony to the value of the IGF. Business applauds these budding initiatives that enrich bottom-up global IGF discussions. Lack of multistakeholder involvement has often led to ill-informed decision-making, resistance in society, suspicions among the different players. The Internet Governance Forum as we know it today has fortunately prevented these shortfalls so far. It has helped to make the Internet a universally applauded, appreciated and heavily utilized medium globally.

Business wants the IGF to be continued and strongly opposes changes to its founding principles. We have seen how the IGF can be extremely responsive and adaptive in its annual format. The event has evolved from cautious beginnings to balanced interactive workshops and main sessions that respond to relevant Internet policy topics of the moment. Business has witnessed this evolution and has been a proud participant. The closing of the fourth IGF gathering presents us with an opportunity to reflect on our accomplishments here and to think ahead to the things we will have to do when we return home. We have to increase participation. We want to be present at the next IGF with more business representatives from Asia and Africa, and from small and non-I.T. business. We thank Under-Secretary-General Sha, Nitin Desai, Markus Kummer, and the IGF Secretariat team as well as the members of the MAG who have made this event such a tremendous success.

MR. AURIMATIS MATULIS:

I would like to thank the United Nations and all stakeholders and speakers. It's my honour on behalf of government of Lithuania to deliver a message of appreciation of the United Nations and advisory group's cooperation and decision to host the IGF in the year 2010. Lithuania is committed to the Tunis Agenda and considers this a tool to build an Information Society which is inclusive, human-centred, and focused for development. So when we expressed our wish to host the fifth IGF we were fully aware of the huge scope and importance of that we are about to do. The IGF is the forum in which we can shape our global vision for development and growth of Internet. Lithuania is willing to contribute to shaping principles, rules, and democratic processes which will provide and facilitate access to knowledge, provide citizens with necessary skills in order to get freedom of expression and also free movement of ideas. It's our aim to extend this availability in accessibility to every human being through the detection of interconnection and multilingualism. It's an honour for me to stress that Lithuania is ready to host the IGF in year 2010. In this spirit I would like to invite all participants in this meeting as well as stakeholders around the world to come to Vilnius.

NITIN DESAI:

I do not wish to say a great deal. Maybe I can just very quickly just place this in the context of the previous IGFs and the next one in Vilnius. As many of you know, I have had this running metaphor drawn from my country where the boyfriend and the girl are brought together by the parents. We call them "arranged marriages." And I've said the Athens meeting was where the boy and the girl were brought together. They were a little suspicious of each other, but they scoped each other out and discovered that really, there's not that much that one should be suspicious about. At the next meeting in Athens, the boy and the girl really started talking with each other, including about difficulties like critical Internet resources. When we got to Hyderabad, they seemed to like each other. There was some evidence that they were occasionally holding hands, developing partnerships, and so on. Now, at this meeting, there's clear evidence that they actually like each other, and who knows, some longer term relationship may emerge out of all this. There's even a smell of romance in the air, you know? And a lot of the credit must go to the warm hospitality of our Egyptian hosts, to the enthusiastic leadership of our chairman, Mr. Kamel, and to the hard work and dedication of his collaborators. So I thank you for all that you have done to bring the IGF to maturity with this exercise. I look forward to the meeting in Vilnius, where we will hopefully carry forward this momentum and let us see where this romance leads.

MARKUS KUMMER:

This is a welcome opportunity to say thank you Mr. Minister, and your team led by Nermine and also Nashwa, Christina, Manal. We had a very intense working relationship during the past year, and it was always easy. It was pleasure working with your team. I would also like to thank the Under-Secretary-General for the cooperation extended to me by his team in New York, but above all, I would like to extend my thanks to you all, you participants. It was your energy, your enthusiasm, and your support that made this meeting a success.

H.E. TAREK KAMEL:

I would like to thank Mr. Sha Zukang, the Under-Secretary of the U.N., the chairman, Nitin Desai, and the whole U.N. team. Special thanks to the IGF

Secretariat, led by Mr. Kummer, and his assistants, as well as the interpreters, the scribes, and the local team from Egypt at the ministry of communication and information technology, the technical team, the organization team, as well as the support level. Special thanks are due to the team led by Dr. Hoda Baraka, the deputy minister, Nermine El Saadany, Christina Arida, Manal Ismail, and Nervine Tawfik and their supporters. I also want to thank the chairs of the various sessions and the sponsors of our events, the Telecommunication Regulatory authority, Telecom Egypt as well as the private sector sponsors. Special thanks are also due to the high level of participation for Egypt's First Lady Mrs. Mubarak as well as Prime Minister Nazif.

This huge participation shows the need for the IGF to continue. We had participants that exceeded 1800, more than 200 remote participants from all corners of the world, plus 27,000 viewers from 116 countries have watched the live on demand Webcast. Egypt's technical team immediately responded to the request of the forum participants and established on the spot IPv6 networking in the congress centre. And I want to give them special thanks for their support of the whole Congress.

Access should remain on the IGF discussion table, because African countries and other developing countries still have issues of affordability and major barriers to broadband connectivity. We need to come up with innovative solutions and business models for remote access in the private area. The importance of multilingualism was very much highlighted. We still need to work more together on enriching local content. We welcome the ICANN's decision starting the fast-track process, and choosing the IGF to announce this major step. We acknowledge the U.S. administration for the Affirmation of Commitments with the ICANN, but we still need further steps for more international involvement in the management of critical Internet resources by revisiting the IANA contract. I sense consensus among our participants for my call the other day to start a dialogue in 2010 on the IANA contract before its expiration in October 2011. This step would add to the improving overall spirit that has been witnessed here in Sharm El Sheikh. My thanks to all the stakeholders for the spirit of cooperation and a special thanks to the ITU for their understanding of the IGF issues and especially the opening remarks of Secretary-General Hamadoun Touré. There has been a very positive spirit from other decision-making bodies to work on implementing the outcomes of the mature discussions within the IGF process.

There is an rising need that the regional IGFs become part of the process in the future and that we out mechanisms for more funding, for stronger regional participation, especially from the developing countries. I also urge the IGF to increase youth participation. I saw a wide consensus on the need to continue the IGF process with the legitimacy provided by the U.N. umbrella, and for preserving the dynamic nature of the event. I see this well reflected in the chair's report that was just printed and distributed. And I'm pretty sure that Under-Secretary Sha will convey this message to the Secretary-General of the U.N. Lastly, I wish Lithuania, our next host, all the success in preparing their event, and you, distinguished participants, a safe trip back home. Thank you, ladies and gentlemen.

VI. Appendices

Host Country Honorary Session

Preparing the Young Generations in the Digital Age: A Shared Responsibility

18 November 2009

Introduction & Welcome:

H.E. Mr. Tarek Kamel
Minister of Communications and Information Technology, Egypt

Keynote Speech:

H.E Ms. Suzanne Mubarak
First Lady of Egypt, President and Founder of the Suzanne Mubarak Women's International Peace Movement

Acknowledgement:

Mr Sha Zukang
Under- Secretary-General for Economic and Social Affairs, United Nations

Panel Moderator:

Ms. Hoda Baraka
First Deputy to the Minister of Communications and Information Technology, Egypt

Panellists:

Ambassador David Gross
Former U.S. Coordinator for International Communications and Information Policy at the U.S. Department of State

Mr. Robert Pepper
Vice President Global Technology Policy, Cisco

Ms. Marilyn Cade
President, ICT Strategies, mCADE llc

Mr. Jovan Kurbalija
Founding Director of DiploFoundation (Malta/Geneva), Serbia

Mr. John Carr
Secretary of the Children's Charities Coalition on Internet Safety, UK

Extracts from the Transcript of Proceedings

H.E. MR. TAREK KAMEL:

I am delighted on behalf of the IGF participants and as a co-chair of the event to welcome Her Excellency Mrs. Suzanne Mubarak, First Lady of Egypt, and president and founder of the Suzanne Mubarak Women International Peace Movement. Mrs. Mubarak is honouring us today with her valuable presence as one of the very early voices worldwide to have supported the empowerment of views on the Internet and realized the associated challenges for child online safety. The Internet Governance Forum, in its fourth edition in Sharm El Sheikh, has adopted youth empowerment and child online safety as emerging issues, and we have witnessed very valuable workshops with global participation. We look forward to Mrs. Suzanne Mubarak's keynote speech this morning and to the international panel on this interesting topic.

H.E. MRS. SUZANNE MUBARAK:

Excellencies, distinguished guests, ladies and gentlemen, good morning. It is a pleasure to be here today and personally welcome you to Sharm El Sheikh on the occasion of the fourth Internet Governance Forum. We are delighted to be hosting this timely and opportune international gathering here in Egypt.

What an incredible turnout. 1,500 leaders, innovators, pioneers, youth, gathered here to explore ways of using the Internet to benefit all people. I would like to start by commending you for the insight, technical expertise, and the determination to act that you have brought here to the fora. Together, you have enriched the debate, integrating central topics and ideas such as digital citizenship, media literacy, culture creation, and youth empowerment. You have stressed the necessity of looking at the ethical dimension of the Internet through a lens of shared responsibility, and of protecting the rights, identity, and dignity of Internet users. Let me also congratulate you on the choice of the theme of this year's event: Creating Opportunities for All. And for bringing this vital social dimension of governance to the heart of our discussions and policy concerns. This essential theme shares an important interdependency with other human development goals, including health for all, education for all, and a topic that I just addressed at the Food and Agriculture Organization this week, food security for all. It raises questions pertaining to the current status of our socioeconomic development, and about our ability to achieve the Millennium Development Goals by 2015. It requires that we frame our strategies through a perspective of human rights policies and human rights practices.

It is for this reason that the Internet Governance Forum is so vital, because it gives us the power to realize these objectives. To find an appropriate balance between rules and freedoms, rights and responsibilities, aspirations and realities. To enhance the synergy and coordination of multiple stakeholders. To encourage us to shape policies that are in tune with our diverse national and cultural needs.

In Egypt, with a population of over 80 million and rising, we have struggled to bridge the divides that hinder our capacity to use the Internet to advance our human development goals. We have worked hard to reduce access and language barriers to modern technologies whilst at the same time increasing the affordability and usability of information and communication technologies (ICTs). For it is not just a matter of ensuring that people will access online information, but more importantly, how this information will serve them. How they will use it off-line. We do not want people to become passive recipients of what the Internet has to offer. We want them also to become its active users and creators.

In spite of many obstacles, our efforts have paid off and progress is being made. Over the last couple of years, we have witnessed a phenomenal expansion in the use of ICTs in Egypt across the country, driven by steady growth rates for computer penetration, Internet access, and mobile phones. I think you have heard this figure before---15 million Internet users and 55 million mobile users in Egypt---a phenomenal figure.

The recent introduction of the first Arabic domain will undoubtedly also serve to further enhance access to millions of people, giving rise to new forms of creativity and innovation, empowering citizens with new means for self-assertion and achievement. And as you can imagine, these trends continue to have a profoundly positive impacts upon the society, especially in terms of youth empowerment.

Through its dynamic infrastructure, diverse content, and interactive communities, the Internet is playing a key role in helping young people to access quality education, find employment, and enhance their participation in all fields of life. Capitalizing on this power medium for change, our Women's International Peace Movement has launched the Cyber Peace Initiative (CPI), in cooperation with many partners, many whom are here today.

I know that throughout your panel discussions, you have had the chance to become more familiar with the vision and activities of our CPI. This initiative is particularly close to my heart because it promotes young people as leaders, as equal and active partners in solving global challenges. We seek to nurture their creativity, focus their determination, and empower their efforts to create a world of peace. Or, as we always say, to foster a global culture of peace. CPI is about using Internet technology to create platforms for dialogue, and for disseminating principles of tolerance, respect, justice, and human rights across nations. It is about amplifying the Internet's ability to support positive social change, whilst minimizing its capacity to exacerbate insecurities. Accordingly, an integral part of our initiative is devoted to promoting and fostering Internet safety through education, awareness raising, multistakeholder cooperation, and active community involvement.

In Egypt, we have succeeded in reaching out and engaging parents, educators, youth, and members of government, law enforcement, the judiciary, the private sector, and the civil society in a serious dialogue on Internet safety. Taking practical steps to protect and expand children's rights within our work and activities, we formed youth and parent Internet safety focus groups. Our youth focus groups, who call themselves Net Aman, and who are here with us today, have been extremely active, travelling across the globe to disseminate safety messages, to collaborate with other young people, to find innovative ways of protecting children online, and of protecting them from exploitation and abuse. These young ambassadors have greatly enriched our agenda. They have brought to our attention the necessity of bridging the digital divide between generations, including my own. Training teachers, parents, and adults in general to understand the grammar and vocabulary of the Internet. To be good listeners, and to appreciate the spirit and the trends of the Internet generation.

As adults, we realize the need to rise up to the challenge and become lifelong learners of this new culture and its tools. In this respect, I was pleased to note that this distinguished gathering of Internet experts has allocated time to listening to youth and teens' voices, and to integrating their ideas and perspectives into their discussions. Indeed, youth empowerment and engagement is supremely relevant to the IGF themes. You cannot review the technical dimensions of the Internet---such as information leakage and regulatory models for privacy, critical Internet resources, or the ethical dimensions of the Internet, such as control of one's own data and respect for privacy---without considering the impact of policies on children and young people as the direct beneficiaries.

Our CPI parents' group has effectively contributed to our mission. It has played a significant role in attenuating the fears of many parents, the feeling that they were powerless to protect their children in this vast medium. Many of the parents who we have worked with now fully understand how they can protect their children without undermining their character or diluting their identity.

They have learned to differentiate between the positive and negative aspects of the net, the ethical and non-ethical usage of information, the values and dangers of connecting with people from different parts of the globe. I am very proud of the way that our team has been working. As a result of their accomplishments, our CPI has been leading the way regionally, sharing knowledge, developing content, and awareness-raising materials in Arabic and forming strategic partnerships. And as we have seen in this forum, there is so much more that we can do together on the international scene. It is exciting to see all these dynamic coalitions being formed. The creation of new ventures, such as World Wide Web Foundation, launched by Sir Tim Berners-Lee at the opening session of this forum, the 2CENTER Cybercrime Training Initiative and the teens' Internet safety camps. We must keep this momentum going, keep building on this progress and keep building on our partnerships. Ladies and gentlemen, the future Internet promises super fast optical core networks, hyper realistic gaming and magical virtual experiences. It vows to be quicker, cheaper, and more pervasive.

But in spite of these impressive developments, the Internet will continue to be a reflection of the global reality we live in. A vivid reminder of the interdependent challenges that bind us, from poverty to food shortages to epidemics and climate change. Moreover, as the divisions between transparency and privacy are erased, as the walls between the physical and virtual reality fade away, we will continue to feel reverberations of these challenges on the net. More discrimination, more violence, more instability. And it is for this reason that we must work harder to ensure that the focus of Internet governance becomes more people-centred, and that the Internet itself becomes a catalyst for human development. For therein lies the real promise of the Internet of tomorrow. It is being able to look at our computer or mobile screens and see a world where people are living in dignity, security, and peace. And I thank you.

MR. SHA ZUKANG:

Your Excellency, Madam Mubarak, Excellencies, ladies and gentlemen, on behalf of the United Nations and the Secretary-General, Ban Ki-moon, I thank you, Madam First Lady, for sharing such an important message. We are gathered here in the Internet Governance Forum to exchange ideas and knowledge as we strive to build the foundations of the information society. The United Nations seeks to enhance digital opportunities for all, and to find innovative ways for technologies to advance economic and social development. The future of the information society will be led by today's youth and children. Fundamentally, sustainable development is about meeting the needs of the present without compromising the ability of future generation to meet their own needs. The information society must be safe for our children. This can be achieved through education and the sharing of knowledge, and by encouraging our children and young people to grow and to achieve their potential. The First Lady has provided much food for thought for our session on new social media and collaboration tools. Many of these tools are already widely used by young people. Thank you once again for hosting this important event. We are deeply grateful for the warm hospitality of the government and the people of Egypt. Now I and Minister Mubarak, on behalf of the IGF, will present a small token gift to madam Mubarak.

MS. HODA BARAKA:

Your Excellency Mrs. Mubarak, Mr. Tarek Kamel, Mr. Sha Zukang, ladies and gentlemen, we now start our international panel. In the past couple of days, the IGF has held more than ten workshops dealing in one way or another with the issue of youth empowerment and safety on the Internet. We have examined, analyzed and discussed this subject from different angles and dimensions, because we are convinced that young people are the primary users and innovators of the Internet. The meeting has definitely set a precedent in including young people in the Internet debate---as Her Excellency has mentioned, by increasing their physical participation and by amplifying their voices throughout the different channels of the forum. We saw them in the workshops, in the exhibition, in the preconference activities, as organizers and speakers, discussants and commentators through their daily newsletter. Our panel today would like to capture and illustrate in 45 minutes the way young people were integrated into the debates on diversity, on privacy, on openness, and development and safety in the last couple of days. We will be listening to some of our key experts in the field about the most important recommendations of the last days, as well the hot issues that have emerged in these debates. That's why our distinguished panellists today includes representatives from the private sector, from NGOs, and from the industry who were deeply involved in preparing IGF 2009. By the end of this panel, we hope to reach an agenda for action by the international community in the coming year in terms of youth empowerment and safety and guiding our work and spirit of shared responsibility.

We start with Dr. Robert Pepper. Dr. Pepper, at the ICC 14th annual meeting, you were talking about the exabyte broadband worlds. Cisco actually has developed a visual networking index to reflect what is going on in the Internet, so what are the projections, requirements and trends worldwide? How do you see these affecting the whole world, and in particular developing countries vis-à-vis narrowing or increasing the digital divide, and how will video play a role in our citizens' lives?

MR. ROBERT PEPPER:

We all know about the mobile revolution. We now have over 4 billion people on earth with mobiles. Ten years ago, nobody would have even imagined that. Today we have over 1.5 billion people using the Internet through dial-up and broadband. And the Internet is on a path to 2 billion, 3 billion, 4 billion users, led by youth. And that's important globally, but especially in countries like Egypt where 50% of the population is 25 years old or younger. We also see that the Internet is moving from narrowband to broadband. One of the ways that we see this is through the project that Dr. Hoda mentioned called the visual networking index. We have been looking at trends in network usage globally, and we're seeing that the patterns are pretty much the same everywhere. This is putting huge demands on networks, because of the way people are using the Internet. So, for example, we have projected that traffic over the backbone from 2007 to 2012 will increase six fold to about 500 exabytes, which is ten to the 18th exabytes per month. It's growing at about a 46% compounded annual growth rate, driven by video. We are seeing this not just in the fixed networks, and we are seeing that video traffic will grow from about 10% of the traffic in 2007 to about 50% of the traffic by 2012. On the mobile Internet, we are projecting that from 2008 to 2013, the annual compounded global growth rate will be 131%, more than doubling each year.

By 2013, over 60% of the global mobile traffic will be video. The most recent study that we did, which we released last month, globally for the average broadband connections, consumers used 3 gigabytes of visual applications per month, including video, video -two-way video, social networking, and collaboration, equivalent to over 20 short-form videos per day, or about 1.1 hours of Internet video per day. So video really is the driver, and it creates huge opportunities overcoming some very significant barriers to Internet adoption and usage such as insufficient local language content and literacy constraints because the traditional Internet is text based. Video is natural language, it's local content, it's people talking to each other, it's people communicating. It's everybody having the opportunity to become a content producer and a creator, not just a consumer. Video fosters participation, personalization and collaboration, and it actually promotes applications that really achieve national and global goals of education, understanding, cultural cohesion, and cultural diversity. So we can all learn from each other and appreciate each other, and particularly for youth, these are important implications. Youth using video on broadband is really driving the usage, and it's allowing for creativity, like we saw here in the IGF Village with the youth going around taking videos and interviewing people. They are becoming tomorrow's producers and creators.

But even more important are the issues that Your Excellency raised about how do we train youth and help them become Internet and media literate. How do we help youth become not just good creators but good consumers, and critical consumers of broadband and the Internet? So programs like the CPI are only going to become more important, not less important. And if we want these trends to be positive forces for society, then these are the kinds of issues that we need to address, and we have been addressing them here at the IGF.

MS. HODA BARAKA:

Thank you very much, Dr. Pepper. Ambassador Gross, we were hearing many discussions in the workshop about the way youth are drivers for change in the digital age. In the workshop dedicated to listening to the voice of teens, the debate went around the opportunities that Internet is offering for our teens, and what are their roles, responsibilities, and rights, and how to find the proper balance between openness and security. Can you please tell us how we can leverage the opportunities for our younger generations?

AMB. DAVID GROSS:

As many of you know, I had the honour of leading and co-leading the U.S. delegation to both phases of the World Summit on the Information Society, and I was very much a part of the long and sometimes quite difficult negotiations about the creation of the IGF. I've also had the honour and privilege of attending all three prior IGFs, which have been excellent. But I have no doubt that thanks to the very hard work of Minister Kamel and his extraordinary team, this IGF Sharm El Sheikh has been the best one ever. Congratulations, minister.

As Dr. Pepper just highlighted, the growth of the Internet has been remarkable by any measure. Today, much of that growth is driven by our youth. They are also driving new and innovative applications that are fundamentally reshaping the world. What we are seeing, as Dr. Pepper indicated, is a fundamental sea change in what is on the Internet and in how we interact with it, and that is being led by our youth. They are leading the way towards a new paradigm of social interaction, where the Internet and all these new applications provide opportunities for connectedness never before possible in human history. They are changing the world at the speed of light, and these new opportunities pose new challenges for all of us, such as privacy and security. Parents, teachers, NGOs, industry, government, all must all play a constructive and positive role here.

In the United States, this has been the source of great discussion amongst policymakers and decision-makers. We have passed a number of pieces of new legislation that seek to address these issues over the past eight to ten years, and there's been a tremendous amount of hard work done by the U.S. government. Our Department of Commerce and its National Telecommunications and Information Administration, which has an online working group on child security, are helping to lead the way. Similarly, our independent regulator, the Federal Communications Commission, has been very active in this area. And in fact, the U.S. government has helped to establish dot kids as a result of legislation designed to create a domain area where children can go and parents can feel that they are protected. But I've been especially struck by the proactive, creative, and inclusive work being done by various other groups, such as FOSI, the GSM association and many others that seek to provide parents, children, and others with the tools to help solve these ever-changing problems.

It is extraordinarily important that tools be created, that information be exchanged, that there are a series of interchanges among parents and teachers and industry and NGOs. But the long-term way to deal with this problem is through active intervention by parents in teaching them values and what is right and what is wrong, what is and is not appropriate, and in then trusting our children, who will undoubtedly make mistakes but inevitably have the tools that they will need as they explore the Internet. The challenges are great, but the opportunities clearly are so much greater---a future where information flows freely and our personal connections truly last a lifetime. That is the legacy we are bestowing upon our children who are going to grow and prosper in ways unimaginable to each and every one of us. It is an opportunity to be seized and will be seized by our children, and we need to help facilitate that. Thank you very much.

MS. HODA BARAKA:

Thank you, Ambassador Gross. Now we'll move to Dr. Jovan Kurbalija, founding director of DiploFoundation. What is fascinating about DiploFoundation is your approach to knowledge generation and the way you have succeeded in capturing the rapid and continuous developments of the Internet in a teaching curricula that is engaging young people all around the world. How did you succeed to mobilize all these young people?

MR. JOVAN KURBALIJA:

Throughout history, people were coming here to Egypt to experience new ideas, to enrich their horizons, to learn about new developments, and Internet Governance Forum is part of this long tradition. Over the last four days, the IGF served as a bridge. A bridge between digital natives and digital migrants, between different professional cultures, between programmers, lawyers, diplomats and civil society, a bridge between old and new, traditional perceptions and new ways of looking at the world. In this room and other rooms in the Conference Center, but especially in corridors during the coffee breaks, we had a chance to discover new ideas, to connect cognitive dots between things that we already knew, to develop new insights, to meet new people, and it was like in every bazaar---by exchanging we are enriching ourselves.

The preparation for the IGF Sharm had---for the Internet---a long history. One year ago, in the coffee break during the IGF in Hyderabad, we met with a team led with Nermine El Saadany, and agreed that the success of Sharm will be based on the preparation that truly started the next day after the conclusion of Hyderabad, and there has been a lot of work and creativity that has been put in the preparation for this IGF and is the reason why the IGF is so successful. When we created this roadmap back in November, one of the highlights was to prepare youth but also other participants to experience and to use these four days in the most effective way. We started the first training for Egyptian participants in February 2010, and then our capacity-building program started in March, involving three phases and involving close to 200 participants from all over the world. From March to June, they were involved in online learning on Internet governance basics like the DNS, ICANN, privacy, social issues development, and other issues. After gaining the basic knowledge, they were engaged in policy research, applying their knowledge to the concrete issues and problems related to their communities and countries. This was the second phase, policy research. The third phase, in this process, was what we call policy immersion, and it has been happening here in Sharm. With their knowledge, insight, and skills they came here to experience firsthand how the global policy processes work, to interact with other colleagues, to participate in sessions, to get information in what is called corridor diplomacy.

It was a unique experience for most of them, and it was done in the partnership with the CPI, Net Aman, and the U.N. Secretariat, which has been very supportive of this capacity-building program since its very early days. In this way, from completely novice people, in nine months we got specialists who can fully participate in Internet governance process and represent their countries, local communities, their organizations. Most of them are youth. And the voice of youth has been significantly strengthened through this process that started in March this year, and which is ending today in Sharm El Sheikh. The next phase will be the continuation. In Sharm, youth have found different ways to send their message. Usually we try to put them in our pre-designed ways of communicating, like conference sessions and meetings. But also, they invited us to the youth corner, as digital migrants, to show how is the world of digital natives, and to explain the future Internet governance will have. They were also interactive in what they called Twitter diplomacy, with short messages, short interviews in corridors, asking us direct questions, cutting the long explanations, and it was their way, their modus operandi to participate in the new diplomacy.

What we have learned from this process is first, that the talents of youth of young people are rich and diverse. We are teachers, we are guides and we have to create context for them to learn. We shouldn't be sages on the stage; we should be guides on the sides. We have to incorporate their experience into the new mosaic of understanding. Second, we are sometimes asked at Diplo if online learning is appropriate for developing countries, because a stereotype is the developing countries do not have sufficient infrastructure. Our experience is extremely encouraging. When there is a will, there is a way. Usually our students from all over the world find a way to participate in online learning, because sometimes it is the only way to build capacity, to get new insights, and to learn new things. Third, by strengthening the voices of youth and others who are marginalized in global governance, we are helping all of us. If they're not involved in global policymaking, they will find other ways to express their opinion. Inclusive governance is not just an ethical slogan, it is practical necessity for an increasingly interdependent world.

MS. HODA BARAKA:

Thank you very much, Jovan. Ms. Cade, can you please tell us how we can move one step further from online safety, which is something we are all concerned about, to what we are learning about, which is digital citizenship and using technology appropriately, and how we can reconcile the requirements of accessibility and infrastructure with the dissemination of the Internet culture and new concepts of digital citizenship?

MS. MARILYN CADE:

Thank you, Dr. Hoda. One of the things that I have seen, as we have been working in the four years in the IGF, is the evolution of a culture. And using that term here in Egypt, which is so rich in the contributions that it has made throughout history to education, science, and medicine, is sort of a rare opportunity for us to say, "What are we doing now to bridge together a world Jovan described as a world which has the digital citizens and the digital migrants?" It is very important we think about this as a journey, not a destination, and that we think about how we are all involved in preparing for that journey and how we can build together a culture of shared responsibility. And that means that every individual, whether they are a parent or a schoolteacher, a policymaker, a judge, a labourer, or are working in an office, every one of us has to think about how are we acting as digital citizens. When we think about our own role and responsibility in the physical world, we often have assumptions about ethics and ethical behaviour, but we're now in an environment where we have to be not only translating that into the online world, but thinking about how our children and our youth actually have a different experience than we do, because they're immersed in this world. They don't think of this as the offline world and the online world. They're integrating technology into how they communicate and adapting how they communicate in ways that technology can support. I've been thinking a lot about how different the IGF here in Sharm El Sheikh has been because youth have been integrated into the workshops and the forums and even the planning, and inspired by what we knew we would experience in Sharm, those of us who worked to organize the IGF USA felt we had to have one panel of youth. And we learned things from them that have led us to plan on a lot more youth as we go forward in examining policies and determining questions that are about them.

The roles of young people are reversed in our digital world. And we have to learn to listen to our young people in ways we have not before. So now I'm just going to say something about my experience in looking around the world at the approaches that are being taken, and to note that the CPI is a very unique model that integrates, in ways that I have not seen in other countries, the concerns about digital literacy, digital empowerment, capacity-building, the involvement of parents and other caregivers and policymakers and lawyers and judges, and the youth themselves. So I'm particularly interested to go back to thinking about how we develop this and evolve this culture of responsibility for an online world. The unique and important contribution of the IGF here in Sharm El Sheikh has been imbued with the spirit and vision of Egypt's view of how the Internet can empower. So on the journey that I see ahead of all of us in creating and enhancing a culture, I see a role for us to remember that we have had all these experiences here, but the beauty of the IGF is that we take back with us an ongoing interaction that will bring us together again in only a year, and to examine the enhancements we've made and that youth will make with us in that culture that we need.

MS. HODA BARAKA:

Thank you very much. In 2006, Mr. John Carr was named by the *New Statesmen* as one of the 50 modern heroes for his work making the Internet safer for children. Recently, John has produced an additional manifesto and he was also a supporter of the new ITU resolution establishing a working group on Internet safety. John, can you please tell us what happened in the last four days concerning especially the issues of Internet safety.

MR. JOHN CARR:

Like Ambassador Gross, this is also my third consecutive IGF, and in Brazil I couldn't find a workshop that was specifically addressing the issues around children and young people's use of the Internet. There was certainly more in Hyderabad, but at this IGF there has been a proliferation to well over a dozen different workshops addressing issues of children and young people's use of the Internet involving hundreds of people and involving young people speaking for themselves and giving us their qualitative insights into some of the issues that we older folks think we know well enough.

There are questions of legal rights here. The U.N. convention on the rights of the child, a very important international treaty which I think almost every single country represented in this room is a signatory to, including its optional protocol on child prostitution, child pornography and trafficking, enshrines a number of legal rights. Under the convention, which incidentally has its 20th birthday this Friday, children have a legal right to be protected by the state, by the authorities in a given country, so it's not simply that we want to be nice. There are also other excellent legal instruments that many countries have signed up to like the Council of Europe's Convention of Cyber crime. And more recently I have been engaged with the ITU on their child online protection initiative, a fantastic development. Here was a major global player, a major global institution not just talking about the issue of child protection but actually developing concrete resources that it has published and is making available to governments and to industry across the world. And it also conducted a survey amongst 191 member states within the ITU asking individual governments what their perceptions were about the priority issues in the field of child protection and child safety on the Internet. Over 80% of the governments that replied to the survey agreed that exposure to illegal and harmful content and bullying were the number one issues. Over half of the countries that replied did have programs that worked in schools to try and teach children about cyber citizenship. But the point about that, over half did, but nearly half didn't. And again, the survey asked what programs and materials were available specifically directed at parents and at teachers, and around half of all of the countries that replied said they were not aware of any resources of that kind in their countries that could be used in their school. But they all agreed there was a great thirst for help, knowledge, information that they could use locally to help develop this digital citizenship.

Dr. Baraka intimated in her introduction that I am often the person who says the things that people don't like hearing. I am not going to disappoint you on this occasion, because you do get a sense sometimes, when you go to these events, that we're all congratulating ourselves on how wonderfully well we are doing and isn't the world a better place for the fact that we are here and talking like this. Actually, when you look at the Internet, not enough progress has been made fast enough. And I am going to just take one example because it's one that we care about very deeply. Child abuse images. Some countries refer to it as child pornography. Some countries have taken great steps forward in blocking access to known illegal Web sites. In other words, we're not talking about trying to find this stuff. We're talking about places where we know that illegal images already exist. But if you were to add up the number of countries that were doing it, I doubt it would come to more than twenty.

And yet it is open to the Internet industry to deploy these types of technical measures to block access to these sites. Why aren't they doing it? Why aren't more ISPs, why aren't more electronic service providers using now tried and tested methods to block access to the most horrible images that abuse the children and pose a threat to other children? I work with organizations that provide psychotherapeutic support to children who have been raped and who have been sexually abused and whose images have appeared on the Internet. One of the things that the children say in the course of their therapy is the thing that they now worry about most is the thought that those images are being seen time and time again. Every time that image is republished and reappears on the Internet, it's a way of re-abusing that child. They cannot know, they do not know who might have seen those images. It could be their next-door neighbour, it could be their teacher, it could be their future employer. So it's not just that we want to be nice. This is a genuine need that children who have been abused articulate to their therapist, to their social workers. And what's important to understand about that is that we have the technical means at our disposal to deal with it very substantially, at least insofar as the Web is concerned. There are issues around encryption, there are issues about peer-to-peer, there are issues around other new technologies which are emerging, but in relation to the Web, we know how to deal with this problem. We can do it and the industry is not doing it. So talking about developing a sense of digital citizenship is all very well, but that must include the industry as well. It isn't all down to parents. It isn't all down to teachers to take the necessary steps to make the Internet better for children. Industry has to step up to the plate as well.

MS. HODA BARAKA:

Thank you very much, distinguished panellists. Your Excellency, Mrs. Mubarak, ladies and gentlemen, the Cyber Peace Initiative of the Suzanne Mubarak Women's International Peace Movement was, since its inception, a model for public-private-social partnership. We have a firm belief that youth empowerment, innovation and safety can be achieved only in cooperation with other organizations, and in a true spirit of shared responsibility. Today, we are proud to be signing in the presence of Your Excellency and at the IGF 2009 four new partnership agreements with a number of key organizations and multinational corporations. The first agreement is with the Family Online Safety Institute and the agreement will actually commit us to work together to promote digital citizenship in Egypt, the Arab world, and wider international community. Our second partnership agreement today is with a major multinational corporation, IBM. Our third agreement today is with a founding partner of the CPI, Microsoft. Today we explore together a new area of cooperation, the establishment of a national centre for online safety in the framework of the 2 CENTER project, the cybercrime centres of excellence network for training research and education. Last but not least, we are happy to have Oracle joining the CPI through the joint development of an online learning project on the subject of global citizenship.

Your Excellency, ladies and gentlemen, the final part of our honorary session today, we celebrate the efforts of young people who have excelled in the service of their peers and the international community using ICT and the Internet. Her Excellency Mrs. Suzanne Mubarak will be presenting a certificate of recognition. The first certificate of recognition will go to the youth Internet safety focus group, the Net Aman founders, in recognition of their role in disseminating the safety message throughout Egypt. The second certificate will go to an organization well-known for its distinctive role in knowledge generation and special teaching methodology on Internet issues for young people, the Diplo Foundation. The third recognition will go to the U.N. GAID committee of e-leaders for ICT and youth in recognition of its special efforts in engaging the young talents in the field of ICT for development.

Ladies and gentlemen, please join me in thanking her Excellency Mrs. Suzanne Mubarak. This concludes our honorary session.

Postscript:

Open Consultation (Assessment of the Meeting)

9 February 2010

Extracts from the Transcript

CHAIR DESAI:

We can all be quite satisfied with the way that meeting shaped up, the level of participation, the number of people who came, and the quality of the discussions. One of the characteristics of this whole process has been its capacity to learn from the past. We have never tried to do things a certain way because we have always done them that way.

There is a paper on the net based on the inputs that have been received from different participants. I hope some of you have had a chance to look at it. I wonder whether Markus would wish to walk us through that.

SECRETARY KUMMER:

On the whole, the feedback we received was very positive. However, there were some aspects where the contributors felt there was room for improvements. In particular, many commentators said there were too many speakers in some of the meetings. Other commentators argued that there were too many workshops and that too many workshops had overlapping or duplicated topics. On the number of workshops, this is also related to the number of participants. I was told as a rule of thumb, you can expect three times as many participants as you have speakers. We had roughly 100-plus workshops. That means 600 speakers in these workshops, and that corresponds fairly accurately to the number of participants, 1800. So by limiting the number, you could also automatically limit the number of participants. With 1800 we had reached the limits of our capacity.

We had substantive comments on the existing themes. It was noted that there was some consensus reached on access and diversity and that there was an opportunity to showcase and to share innovative practices by operators and regulators that had successfully advanced people's access to the Internet. On security, openness and privacy, participants agreed that privacy and security could not be traded off against one another, or seen as opposing priorities that needed to balance. Both were seen as equally important. In this context, a proposal was made to discuss the Madrid Privacy Declaration which was adopted last. The most critical comment was on whether the theme "Internet governance in the light of WSIS principles" should be repeated as a main theme. On new themes it was proposed that Internet rights and principles should be a major theme for the 2010 IGF. Also, the importance of climate change was again highlighted. Some said it was a key factor in any and all policies and frameworks that will shape the future growth of the Internet.

And it was also suggested that Internet governance approaches should meet innovation challenges to help CO emissions.

Child protection has been an ongoing priority issue, and the proposal was made that in addition to discussing child abuse and pornography in relation to the Internet, the IGF should also discuss the positive effects the Internet has in terms of access to information, knowledge, freedom of expression, and openness. Privacy issues of cloud computing were proposed as a possible theme, and a more organizational suggestion was to introduce technical or introductory sessions to cover specialized topics such as cloud computing, DNS redirections, or net neutrality for the non-technical participants. And there are many more detailed topics suggested as candidates for workshops and main sessions.

On the program logistics, I think the general thread was that the number of workshops should be reduced or limited. One specific suggestion was that no more than a predetermined, fixed number -- for example, 50 -- workshops should be allowed, with some assigned to each of the main sessions, and then to have some more general workshops. Another suggestion was that the experience of previous years could be reviewed for those themes that had generated significant interest with the MAG then putting out the call for one or two workshops on these themes, as well as an open call on new themes. Also, on the moderators, generally the format we had for the main session on critical Internet resources was well received, and there was support for continuing with that format with two moderators, and there were also suggestions to use a similar format also for other sessions.

Then there were calls for more tangible outcomes. Several of them said we should consider issuing messages from the IGF. Building on the experience in the European IGF, the EuroDIG, messages could come out of each session. Rapporteurs could be appointed to publish these in their own names, and they could then be put online for other participants to comment on.

Some comments suggested a different balance between main sessions and workshops. For instance, the point was made that all main sessions did not need to be three hours in length. Or every time slot should not necessarily have a main session. And one idea was to reduce the emphasis on main sessions in favour of workshops. Or again, a possibility mentioned was that workshops could be held in the morning without any conflicting main sessions. Now, here we run into some difficulties. The U.N. has fairly fixed rules that are set by the member state and supervised by various committees for budget and utilization of resources. And U.N. slots are two times three hours, and that is mainly because the interpreters work in three-hour slots. We cannot change that, and we are required to make maximum use of these resources. So whether or not we call it a main session in the morning or they are workshops, we are obviously going to use the interpreters that are there in a three-hour slot. The only flexibility we have is to split the three-hour slots into two sessions of one and a half hours each.

More on the substantive issues. It was recommended that on some of the more mature themes, we could allow for longer workshops, two hours instead of 90 minutes. Again, roundtable discussions were floated as a

549

possibility last year, and we did this in Sharm El Sheikh in some of the workshops. It was recommended that it should be revisited as a possible format also for main sessions. And again, it was proposed that organizers of workshops should produce background documents and issue papers prior to the meeting. And reports from the workshops held at Sharm El Sheikh should be consulted in developing the agenda for the main session in Vilnius.

That brings me to workshop reports. We have set various deadlines and extended the deadlines. I think we have been more successful than in previous years, but nevertheless, we have not received reports on many of the workshops. We said it's a precondition for being allocated a slot for this year's meeting, but it is also good to have the documentation on the workshop, both on our Web site and then again in the book we are planning to produce that will document the Sharm El Sheikh meeting.

Then we received concrete suggestions on the organization of the physical meeting. Most of them are sensible and are also part of our objectives, such as registration should be quick and efficient. However, there are also limitations when you have to handle such huge quantities of people queuing up. Other suggestions are maybe more difficult to implement. One of the suggestions was venue hotel should be close to the venue and close together to facilitate network among participants and to minimize travel time. Of course, this would be nice to have, but we cannot rebuild cities to fit our purposes. And in Vilnius, I am afraid the conference centre will not be close to hotels. It is slightly on the outskirts of the city. It is an excellent facility and all the hotels are in the historic centre of the city. So participants will be close to each other. They will be able to network; however, they will have the slight inconvenience that they will have to be bussed to the conference centre.

Then there were some general comments on the functioning of the IGF. In particular, the role of dynamic coalitions should be clarified with regard to structure, multistakeholder representation and their ability to do intersessional work. And this will be on our agenda, as is the relationship between national and regional IGFs and the global IGF meeting.

Then some comments were also on the multistakeholder advisory group, such as there should be more youth representation. Also the question of balance in the MAG, the openness of MAG meetings, and how the MAG should operate in 2010. Again, these are part of our agenda. Also, suggestions were made that more outreach should be made to communities that are not yet participating. Suggested were the elderly, youth in general, people with disabilities, again representatives from developing countries. One suggestion was to appoint representatives whose participation is supported and who are responsible for aiding in the outreach. My answer is, that's basically what we have the MAG for. We have MAG members from developing countries, and we fund their participation and we expect them also to engage in outreach to their colleagues in developing country. And also, another group was mentioned, non-specialist lay people whom we should outreach to a bit more.

[COMMENTS AND DISCUSSION FROM THE FLOOR]

CHAIR DESAI:

The lessons which I would draw is that we need to look at the way in which we manage the workshops. I can't say that there is general agreement about numbers. Let me point out one thing, that there is a natural limit provided by the physical space available. It so happened that in Sharm El Sheikh, there were many rooms available, so we could have over a hundred of these. But I'm not sure that at every event the location will be able to accommodate so many. So there's a natural limit. We cannot have more workshops than what have physically space for.

The second lesson I would describe as---I will use the word "quality," a performance review. We've had four years now. And there are people who have been doing these workshops again and again. And we have some assessment possible of how well they have performed in terms of the variety of participants they have been able to bring to the table, the panellists, whether they have submitted reports or not. And my suggestion is that we take that into account when somebody submits a proposal for a workshop.

The other thing that struck me was the idea that we need to pay more attention to the link with development. And somebody else mentioned the fact that we have to connect with other policy areas. There are those who have something useful to say, for instance, on privacy and security issues, who are involved in other areas of work, not necessarily in the Internet. How do we get them? It may be easier to do that through a workshop. If there is a workshop proposal on financial services that touches on issues of privacy and which could bring people from the financial services industry, we should keep that in mind.

A further theme that has come up frequently is the connection between the workshops and the plenary. Several people referred to the procedure that we had in Rio, where people reported in. The fact is that usually at these sessions, other than me and the person making the presentations, nobody else was there to listen. And it was rather tedious to have one person after another come up and speak for five minutes with hardly anybody listening. I would ask the MAG to look into this. Maybe instead giving everybody five minutes to give a summary, we could have a structured set of questions as the starting point for a particular main session and ask the people who have been involved in the workshops to sit on a moderated panel where they're asked these questions, and okay, what did your workshop have to say on this?

And remember this, that as a forum, a lot of people who come to our meetings have to mobilize resources to come to the meeting. They will not get a travel grant to attend the main session. But they may get a travel grant if they are part of a workshop process which somebody is funding. So don't be too hasty in throwing this out, because you may end up then cutting off an important source of support for the IGF.

Remote participation is something which was certainly much better in Egypt than ever before. The main thing that we should probably start looking at now is to see how we can structure it so that it's integrated better into the main process. One thought that has come up is to insist on moderators at the remote end so there is a more structured way of people to get through. I am concerned about the point which Madame Diop raised about the difficulty for people in developing countries in getting remote participation organized. I would ask the MAG again to see how we can integrate remote participation more fully.

There were many questions raised about participation. This is largely a matter of mobilizing resources. But it's also a matter of finding spaces for people from developing countries, for young people, to play a fuller role in the work of the IGF. You cannot expect them to come there simply as audience members. You have to create a space in which they can connect more completely into the work.

Is it possible that we have given too much emphasis on "experts" as far as panellists are concerned? Maybe we should be worrying about getting people who can speak for a user community, who are not necessarily experts in a particular area. I would like the MAG to look into this, but not just in terms of a general statement saying, "let's bring more people," but also how, what for.

A final thought, we have had people from the Internet community participating in our work, particularly from the business sector. I sometimes have felt that we need more organized participation from the Internet Service Providers and network managers in university or government departments. The people who are managing this network of thousands of computers and are setting the standards, deciding controls and everything---we don't have enough of them participating. There are many other questions that have arisen but most do not have a strong relation to the question of themes. So I would suggest the above as sort of broad guidelines for the MAG to look at over the next couple of days.

About the Book

Editor's Biography

William J. Drake is a Senior Associate of the Centre for International Governance at the Graduate Institute of International and Development Studies in Geneva, Switzerland. In addition, he is co-editor of the MIT Press book series, *The Information Revolution and Global Politics*, and a consultant on global information and communication technology governance issues. Previously he has been the President of Computer Professionals for Social Responsibility and a Senior Associate and Director of the Project on the Information Revolution and World Politics at the Carnegie Endowment for International Peace, and has taught at Georgetown University and the University of California, San Diego. He received his Ph.D. in Political Science from Columbia University. Among his recent publications are, *Governing Global Electronic Networks: International Perspectives on Policy and Power*, MIT Press, 2008 (co-editor); and, *Reforming Internet Governance: Perspectives from the UN Working Group on Internet Governance*, UNICT Task Force, 2005 (editor).

Authors of Introductory Materials

Sha Zukang
Under-Secretary General, United Nations Department of Economic and Social Affairs (UNDESA)

Markus Kummer
Executive Coordinator, IGF Secretariat

Nitin Desai
Chairman, Multistakeholder Advisory Group for the IGF; Special Advisor to the United Nations Secretary-General for Internet Governance

Authors of Background Papers

Olga Cavalli
Advisor, Professor, Universidad de Buenos Aires; Director, South School on Internet Governance; Argentina

Bertrand de La Chapelle
Special Envoy for the Information Society, Ministry of Foreign and European Affairs; France

Willie Currie
Manager, Communications and Information Policy Program, Association for Progressive Communications; South Africa

Anriette Esterhuysen
Executive Director, Association for Progressive Communications; South Africa

Jeanette Hofmann
Senior Researcher, London School of Economics and Political Science; and the
Social Science Research Centre Berlin; United Kingdom and Germany

Wolfgang Kleinwächter
Professor of Internet Policy and Regulation, Department for Media and
Information Studies, University of Aarhus; Germany

Alejandro Pisanty
Professor at Facultad de Quimica, National University of Mexico; Mexico

Hong Xue
Professor of Law and Director of Institute for the Internet Policy & Law,
Beijing Normal University; China